THE
HUMAN CAREER

THE

HUMAN CAREER

Human Biological and Cultural Origins

Richard G. Klein

The University of Chicago Press • Chicago and London

The University of Chicago Press, Chicago 60637
The University of Chicago Press, Ltd., London
© 1989 by The University of Chicago
All rights reserved. Published 1989
Printed in the United States of America

98 97 96 95 94 93 92   54

Library of Congress in Publication Data

Klein, Richard G.
  The human career.

  Bibliography: p.
  Includes index.
  1. Man—Origin.   2. Fossil man.   3. Human evolution.
I. Title.
GN281.K55   1989   573.2   88–36259
ISBN 0–226–43962–3

CONTENTS

ILLUSTRATIONS

PREFACE

Superficially, the study of human evolution seems remarkably abstruse and impractical. Yet, each year the popular press covers major finds, large prime-time audiences watch televised documentaries, and thousands of students enroll in pertinent university courses. *Australopithecus* and Olduvai Gorge feature in nationally syndicated cartoons, and some discoverers of important fossils are better known than their counterparts in more practical fields such as physics and medicine. Clearly, in spite of its apparent irrelevance to everyday affairs, the origin of the human species is intensely interesting to most modern humans, who are fascinated by the growing number of fossils, artifacts, and related facts that scientists have amassed. They want to know what these data tell us about the appearance and behavior of our remote ancestors. This book is a summary of what I think the data say.

There are many perspectives on how the data should be interpreted, and this book, of necessity, reflects just one. In writing it, I have tried to steer a middle course between what I see as two extreme approaches—one in which the data are simply a springboard for stimulating speculation about what might have happened in the past and another in which they are meaningless except to test and eliminate all but one competing explanation of what really happened. The difficulty with the first perspective is that it emphasizes imagination over validity. The difficulty with the second, whose roots lie in a perception of how the physical sciences have advanced, is that it assumes an unrealistic degree of control over data quantity and quality. In fact, substantial control is unusual in human evolutionary studies, where carefully planned experiments are rare and most data are obtained through excavations and field surveys whose success often depends more on chance than on design. Under these circumstances, I think that the physical sciences provide a less suitable role model than the judicial system, in which often limited evidence is weighed to deter-

mine which of two or more competing explanations or interpretations seems most reasonable. In most instances, the
possible alternatives are not pared unequivocally to one, but
one is selected because it seems more justifiable, given the
evidence on hand.

Of course, in human evolutionary studies, as in the
judicial system, both lay people and specialists may disagree
about what is reasonable or justifiable and also about the
soundness of the supporting evidence. All too often, the
evidence is incomplete, ambiguous, or even contradictory, and
it cannot be used to bolster any particular theory or explanation very strongly. In this book, I have tried hard to present the
major competing opinions on prominent unresolved issues,
and, whenever possible, I have explained why I think one view
is more reasonable than others. More often than I would like,
I have had to say that a firmer choice will require more data. I
know that not everyone will agree with the positions I have
taken or even with my decision to abstain on some matters.
However, I think that such differences of opinion are unavoidable, given the imperfect nature of the evidence; and the point
is that this book is inevitably just one of many possible
summaries of what we know about human evolution. Its
success will depend on the extent to which the readers, experts
and lay people alike, think that the presentation and argumen-
tation are sensible.

Philosophical approaches aside, there are several possible
ways to organize the evidence for human evolution. The way I
have chosen is perhaps the most conventional, focusing on a
series of chronologically successive stages—beginning with
the earliest Primates, dating from perhaps 80 million years ago,
and ending with the emergence of anatomically modern people, within the past 200,000 years. The presentation does
depart from the norm, however, in that I have given roughly
equal weight to the fossil record and to the accompanying
archeological evidence over the 2.5-million-year interval for
which this is available. Most summaries focus largely on the
fossils or on the archeology, thereby forgoing one of the major
points that I have sought to make, namely, that the human
form and human behavior have evolved together and that
neither can be fully understood or appreciated without a full
understanding of the other. At the same time, however, it
remains true that the fossils are far easier to arrange into a set
of chronologically successive, interrelatable units; and, since
the fossil record is also far longer than the archeological one, I
have relied on the fossils to define the chronologically succes-

sive stages that structure the text. This is not to say that there
are no problems in defining the fossil units, but these pale
beside the difficulties in defining and interrelating corresponding archeological categories. The difference stems from our
much weaker understanding of the mechanisms underlying
artifactual (cultural) change and differentiation.

A second way in which this survey differs from many
others is that it includes more information on specific sites,
fossils, artifacts, etc.—in short, it is more detailed, with more
concern for the factual evidence that underlies our understanding of human origins. It is a formal rendering of the lectures I
give in an upper-level undergraduate course at the University
of Chicago, and it has been written with upper-level under-
graduates, graduate students, and professionals in mind. In my
experience, the audience for whom it is primarily intended will
already have a basic understanding of how evolution occurs
(through natural selection, mutation, gene flow, and gene drift),
and therefore this latter topic is not explicitly addressed.
However, at least some members of the audience will lack
essential background information on skeletal anatomy, zoological classification and nomenclature, stone-tool typology and
technology, and, especially, the geologic time frame for human
evolution; and these subjects therefore are covered. In general,
I think the book is too detailed to be a central text in
lower-level courses, especially ones that also deal with modern
human variation, genetics, and the like; but I hope it will find
use there as one of the sources the instructor consults or
recommends to those students who are especially curious
about the fossil and archeological records.

In keeping with the comparatively technical orientation
of the book, I have employed an in-text citation system that is
common in professional scientific publications. I rejected the
usual textbook system of grouping sources at the end of each
major section or chapter because I felt the target audience for
the book would prefer to know precisely where to look for
further information on a particular topic. I also wanted to give
credit directly where it was due. I rejected a system of linking
references to numbers because I thought the risk of serious
error would be too great when so many references are involved.
The large number of references was unavoidable, given the
broad theme, but I have tried to keep the list manageable by
stressing recent sources that can serve as guides to older ones,
and I have also excluded many non-English primary sources in
favor of secondary English ones with their own extensive
bibliographies of important non-English publications.

No synthesis of human evolution would be successful without good illustrations, but these can be very expensive and time-consuming to produce. As a result, even many commercially produced texts are underillustrated. I have attempted to compensate for the limitations of time and expense that were important here by adapting many illustrations from published sources, which are gratefully acknowledged. Thanks mainly to the efforts of Kathryn Cruz-Uribe, most of the illustrations have been substantially modified to support pertinent points in the text and to provide stylistic consistency. In addition, whenever possible, I have labeled important features directly on fossils, artifacts, site plans, and so forth, and I have attempted to make the captions freestanding supplements to the text, to emulate the useful sidebars that are common in commercially produced texts. My goal was to make the illustrations especially helpful to those with little or no prior knowledge of skeletal anatomy, stone artifacts, stratigraphies, etc.

It was not easy to choose a title for the book, because the most obvious ones, such as "Human Origins" and "Human Evolution," have been used many times before. The final choice—*The Human Career*—is the name of a graduate course I took at the University of Chicago in 1962, in which F. Clark Howell introduced me to the concept of human evolutionary studies as an amalgam of human paleontology and paleolithic archeology. Howell's alternative name for the subject matter, "paleoanthropology," would do equally well—though it too has been used before and has often been applied to human paleontology alone rather than to the broader paleontological/archeological field that Howell had in mind. In both the title and the text, I intend the vernacular term *human* (and its complement, *people*) to refer to all members of the zoological family Hominidae, as conventionally defined, and not simply to living humans.

My own research on human evolution has focused mostly on behavioral (archeological) evidence from middle- and late-Quaternary sites in southern Africa and parts of Europe, and my acquaintance with the remainder of the record comes mainly from published sources. In synthesizing these, I have tried hard to make the text as accurate, comprehensive, and up-to-date as possible, and I have been greatly helped by comments and criticisms from Peter Andrews, Kathryn Cruz-Uribe, Janette Deacon, Leslie Freeman, Fred Grine, Clark Howell, Philip Rightmire, Chris Stringer, Russell Tuttle, and Tom Volman. I hope they find that I have employed their suggestions productively and that I have not introduced any new errors in the process. Inevitably, however, some defects remain, and I would be grateful to hear from anyone who finds a specific problem or who has suggestions on how the interpretations or overall organization can be improved.

Richard G. Klein
Chicago, Illinois
July, 1988

THE GEOLOGIC TIME FRAME

1

Among all the variables behind human evolution, none is more crucial than time, and a discussion of the geologic time frame must precede any consideration of fossils and artifacts. In the best of all possible worlds, the ages of all ancient sites or fossils would be known in calendar years, and a discussion of time could focus entirely on how calendric or "absolute" ages are obtained. In fact, methods for determining absolute ages are treated here—but not exclusively, because they have not or cannot be applied to many sites. The most important and widely useful methods were developed only in the late 1940s and 1950s, nearly a century after the first real scientific inquiry into human origins. In the early decades of serious study, dating was almost entirely "relative," based mainly on the obvious or inferred stratigraphic position of one site with respect to others. Even today, many sites can be dated only this way, either by their stratigraphic location in a sedimentary sequence or, more often, by the stratigraphic implications of their fossil or artifactual contents. Additionally, even at those sites where absolute dating is possible, stratigraphic context furnishes a vital cross-check on the results. Finally, there is a genuine sense in which absolute dates are only unusually precise indicators of stratigraphic position. In sum, the concept of stratigraphy remains fundamental to research on human evolution.

Stratigraphic Units and the Geologic Time Scale

In general, any geological objects that can be arranged in a sequence from younger to older can be used to construct a stratigraphy. The most obvious and most basic items are successive layers of rock whose distinctive qualities can be used to define *rock-stratigraphic* (= lithostratigraphic) *units*. Fossils extracted from rock layers provide the basis for *bio-stratigraphic units*, which can be subdivided into faunal and floral stratigraphic units or into particular kinds of faunal or floral units. Thus, as illustrated below, biostratigraphies can be founded on fossils of rodents, pigs, horses, elephants or on some combination of the fossils of these creatures and others. Even human (or prehuman) fossils and artifacts can serve, though entities based on artifacts or other behavioral debris are probably best placed in a separate class of *culture-stratigraphic units*.

Although stratigraphic units are always based on objects found in rock layers, different kinds of units need not correlate on a one-to-one basis, and a single biostratigraphic unit, for example, may incorporate several rock units. Units that are correlated are assumed to have formed or existed during the same time interval, and the successive time intervals that correspond to particular rock units, biostratigraphic units, and so forth are generally called *time-stratigraphic* or *chronostratigraphic units*. While units defined by rock type (lithology), fauna, flora, or other properties tend to be geographically localized, chronostratigraphic units have no spatial bounds, and different rock or biostratigraphic units from many different areas can correspond to a single chronostratigraphic unit. Chronostratigraphic units in turn correspond to intervals of real geologic time, which are at once the most abstract and most concrete components of the system. They are not themselves stratigraphic units but simply are named time spans to which geologists ascribe particular chronostratigraphic units.

In both theory and practice, the various kinds of stratigraphic unit can usually be recognized at different scales, for which sets of hierarchical terms are available (Hedberg 1976). Thus, with respect to rock-stratigraphic units, the smallest definable ("mappable") unit is generally a *bed*, spatially and lithologically related beds are grouped into *members*, and related members are grouped into *formations*. The australopithecine site descriptions in Chapter 3 illustrate the principle. The hierarchy of words for biostratigraphic units is less formalized, but many specialists use terms such as *faunal complex, stage, zone* or *biozone*, sometimes prefixed to indicate hierarchical rank or status. With regard to chronostratigraphic units, the smallest one in common usage is the *stage*. A related group of successive stages constitute a *series*, related series constitute a *system*, and related systems constitute an *erathem*. The corresponding time terms (from least to most comprehensive) are *age, epoch, period*, and *era*. Table 1.1 presents a list of named eras and a partial list of included periods and epochs, spanning the entire history of the earth, from roughly 4.6 billion years ago to the present. The scheme is rooted mainly in biostratigraphy, while the boundary dates

Table 1.1. Geologic Time Scale

Era	Period	Epoch	mya
			0
Cenozoic	Quaternary	Holocene or Recent	
			0.01
		Pleistocene	
			1.7
	Tertiary	Pliocene	
			5.5
		Miocene	
			23
		Oligocene	
			38
		Eocene	
			54
		Paleocene	
			65
Mesozoic	Cretaceous		
			144
	Jurassic		
			213
	Triassic		
			248
Paleozoic	Permian		
			286
	Pennsylvanian		
			320
	Mississippian		
			345
	Devonian		
			408
	Silurian		
			438
	Ordovician		
			505
	Cambrian		
			590
Precambrian or Proterozoic			
			4,600

Source: Modified after Harland et al. 1982.

have been estimated mainly by the absolute dating methods discussed below. The table is relatively undetailed for eras before the Cenozoic because they are largely irrelevant to this book, which focuses on the evolution of the Primates, which began, at the earliest, late in the very-late-Mesozoic era.

Into the 1970s, treatments of primate evolution accentuated the Quaternary (or last) period of the geologic time scale, partly because it seemed to coincide with the appearance and evolution of people and partly because it was considered climatically or faunally unique. However, it is now clear that the base of the Quaternary, formally defined by local changes in marine fossils in Italy, dates to, at most, 2.1 million years ago (mya) (Kukla 1987) and perhaps to only 1.7–1.6 mya (which is tentatively accepted here) (Tauxe et al. 1983), while, as shown below, human evolution began more than 4 mya. In addition, there is no sharp faunal or climatic break between the Quaternary, formally defined, and the immediately preceding Pliocene. The Quaternary will therefore not be treated separately here, except to note that it is now commonly subdivided into three parts: (1) the early Quaternary, between 1.7 mya and the beginning of the Brunhes Normal Polarity Chron, roughly 730,000 years ago; (2) the middle Quaternary, between roughly 730,000 years ago and the beginning of the Last Interglaciation about 130,000 years ago; and (3) the late Quaternary, spanning the past 130,000 years. The Brunhes Normal Chron and the Last Interglaciation are discussed below.

Relative Dating Methods

As indicated previously, the techniques for placing sites, fossils, artifacts, and other objects in geologic time may be divided into absolute methods that determine ages *in years* and relative methods that say only whether one item is older than another. Relative methods were developed first and are more widely applicable. In addition, all absolute methods are obviously also relative ones, and their credibility depends in part on their consistency with other, standard relative methods. In short, relative methods remain basic to all historical geological studies, including research on human evolution.

Among relative methods narrowly defined, the most fundamental is unquestionably the principle of stratigraphic superposition. This underlies the concept of stratigraphic units introduced in the previous section and states, in essence, that, all other things being equal, objects found in higher rock layers postdate ones found in deeper layers. The qualification "all other things being equal" is necessary because burrowing animals, invading roots, and the like can displace objects into lower or higher layers, while crustal movements, landslides, and other geomorphic events can even reverse a stratigraphic sequence, placing older layers on top of younger ones. However, where such disturbances occur, their effects are often minor, detectable, or both, and the principle of superposition has been fruitfully applied at countless archeological and fossil sites. Its main limitation is that, in the most literal sense, it cannot be used to date objects in layers that do not physically overlap, that is, ones that occur at physically separate sites.

In situations where physical overlap does not occur, stratigraphic dating depends on perceived similarities or differences in the properties of two (or more) layers. The properties can be lithological, physical, chemical, or fossil, taken separately or in combination. In a sense, absolute dating methods simply illustrate the stratigraphic principle applied to the physicochemical composition of rock layers. Absolute methods are special not only because they indicate stratigraphic ages in years but also because they usually do not require a special knowledge of local geological history and can be applied in the same way anywhere in the world. In contrast, relative dating methods require detailed local information, which restricts their application to limited geographic areas. The size of the area can vary from the immediate neighborhood of a site to a large region or even a continent. As illustrated below, relative methods that employ physicochemical analysis tend to be most tightly restricted, while ones that rely on fossils tend to have the broadest geographic application.

Relative Dating by Chemical Content: The Fluorine Method

Among relative dating methods that depend on chemical analysis, the most influential in human evolutionary studies has certainly been the fluorine method (Oakley 1969). It is based on the observation that buried bones adsorb fluorine from groundwater. Bones that were buried in the same site at the same time should contain the same amount of fluorine, and gross differences in fluorine content thus suggest noncontemporaneity. The fluorine method was instrumental in unraveling the notorious Piltdown hoax, named for a site in Sussex, southern England, where a seemingly ancient skull and mandible were found in 1911–12. The skull was thickwalled but otherwise remarkably modern in appearance, while the jaw was very apelike in basic structure, including a bony (simian) shelf behind the mandibular symphysis (chin region). The combination became increasingly incongruous as new fossil finds from elsewhere failed to replicate it, and in 1953 it was shown to be a forgery (Weiner et al. 1953; Weiner 1955). A major part of the evidence was that the skull and mandible contained different concentrations of fluorine and that both contained much less of it than most of the associated animal bones that were the main evidence for great antiquity. It is now known that the skull came from a relatively recent human, while the mandible came from an orangutan (Lowenstein et al. 1982).

In the Piltdown case, and in others where the fluorine method has been used to check the contemporaneity of bones from the same site, the value of this method is plain; but it cannot be used to determine the relative ages of bones from different sites. This is because there is great geographic variation both in the amount of groundwater and in the amount of fluorine it contains. The same limitation affects virtually all other relative dating methods based on the accretion or deletion of chemicals (for example, nitrogen or uranium) in buried objects.

Biostratigraphic Dating

In most instances, sites that do not physically overlap in some way and that are not amenable to absolute dating can be dated relative to one another only by their contents. There is an obvious danger of circularity here, if dating is based on objects whose relative age has not been independently determined. Thus, it would be unwise to conclude that one site is older than another simply because it contains simpler artifacts, because this assumes a directionality of artifact change that may be invalid, as has been shown by irrefutable examples. Artifacts can be used for dating only when the cultural stratigraphy of a region has been established on independent empirical grounds. Likewise, fossils can be used only when the basic biostratigraphy of a region has been worked out in advance; but fossils have at least two clear advantages over artifacts. First, of course, they can be used to date sites where artifacts do not occur or that formed before artifacts were made. Second, at least with regard to the earlier stages of human evolution, they often define stratigraphic units that cover larger areas and shorter time intervals than do units defined by artifacts.

For biostratigraphic purposes, the most useful fossils come either from taxa (species, genera, etc.) that spread very quickly and very widely, from taxa that appear to have died out over large areas at about the same time, or from taxa that were evolving rapidly, so that their stage of evolutionary development is itself a clue to their relative age. The aim is to define biostratigraphic units that are as fine as possible and that transgress time as little as possible (that is, that correspond to the same time interval in different regions). Some time transgression is inevitable, since no species can appear or disappear everywhere simultaneously and since evolutionary changes cannot occur at exactly the same time in all populations of a widespread species. However, both theory and empirical research suggest that some taxa provide a basis for defining units whose time transgressiveness is negligible, at least compared with the antiquity of the human fossils or artifacts they can be used to date. In this context, in Eurasia the most productive biostratigraphy developed so far involves the microtine rodents, while in Africa the biostratigraphy of elephants, pigs, and horses has proved most useful.

Microtine Biostratigraphy in Europe. The microtine rodents, including the voles, lemmings, and their relatives, are a branch of the cricetids (hamsters) characterized by hypsodont (high-crowned) molars whose occlusal surfaces comprise a series of alternating, triangularly prismatic cusps (Fig. 1.1). The heartland of microtine evolution has been in northern Asia, and over the past 5 million years, at times when climatic conditions were right, various microtine species have spread both eastward to North America and westward to Europe (Repenning 1980). They are currently the most successful rodent group in the Northern Hemisphere, and their past success is reflected in numerous fossil occurrences, particularly ones where bones were accumulated partly or wholly by owls or other birds of prey.

The biostratigraphy of the microtines has been studied most thoroughly in Europe, especially in central Europe (W. von Koenigswald 1973; Jánossy 1975; Fejfar 1976a; Heinrich 1982, 1987), France (Chaline 1976; Chaline and Laurin 1986); and Britain (Stuart 1982). In each place, microtine biostratigraphic units can be defined by first appearances, by evolutionary changes within established lineages, or by both. Important first appearances include the immigration (from northern Asia) of the Norway lemming, *Lemmus*, in the mid-Pliocene, perhaps 3.5 mya, and of the collared lemming, *Dicrostonyx*, at or shortly after the beginning of the Pleistocene, 1.7–1.6 mya. (This date and others presented below depend mainly on correlations between microtine evolutionary events and the

Figure 1.1. Stages in the evolution of the voles *Mimomys, Arvicola,* and *Microtus,* on the basis of morphological changes in the lower first molar (modified after Heinrich 1987: 402). The horizontal arrows indicate approximate times of first appearance for species in the *Mimomys-Arvicola* lineage. Broken lines indicate two major transitions in this lineage, the first approximately 3.2–3.3 mya, when cementum first appeared between molar prisms, and the second between about 800,000 and 600,000 years ago, when ever-growing, rootless molars evolved.

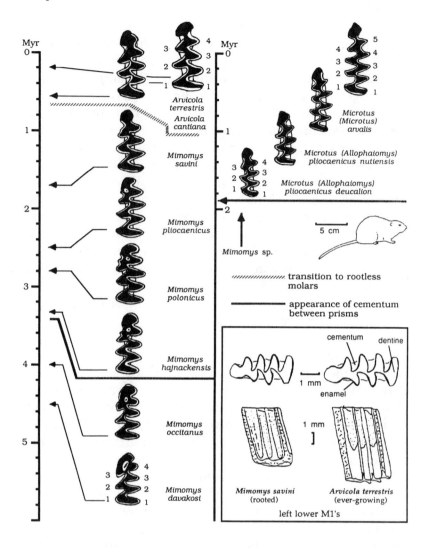

global paleomagnetic stratigraphy outlined later in this chapter.) On the basis of their historic distribution and climatic preferences, *Lemmus* and *Dicrostonyx* probably both migrated to Europe during periods of very cold climate. Their episodic expansion counts among the clearest biological evidence for repeated climatic deterioration (glaciation) later on, as discussed in the final section of this chapter.

In nearly all microtine lineages, evolutionary change involved the development of increasingly high-crowned molars. In some, this was accompanied by a tendency for cementum to pack between the triangular prisms of the molar crowns. Separately and together, these trends permitted increasingly efficient feeding on grasses, which are an important but highly abrasive component of most microtine diets. Increases in crown height and cementum packing are particularly useful for characterizing successive stages in the evolution of the modern water vole, *Arvicola*, from its immediate ancestor, *Mimomys*. On the basis of changes in the first lower molar (M_1), Figure 1.1 illustrates the major stages and shows two especially striking transitions, one about 3.25 mya, when cementum first appeared between prisms, and a second roughly 800,000–600,000 years ago, when the molars became ever-growing and ceased to develop roots, even in elderly individuals. As the figure suggests, the evolution of rootless molars is used to define the appearance of *Arvicola*. Subsequent stages in the evolution of *Arvicola* can be defined especially by a tendency for the enamel to become thinner on the rear (convex) and thicker on the fore (concave) surfaces of the molar prisms (Heinrich 1982, 1987; Stuart 1982).

Figure 1.1 also illustrates stages in the evolution of the common (or field) vole, *Microtus*, an inference founded mainly on an evolutionary increase in the length of the first molars and on an accompanying increase in the number of triangular prisms or angles. *Microtus* perhaps evolved in Asia from a species of *Mimomys* and then migrated to Europe roughly

Time Units		Regional Climatic Stratigraphy	Central European Biostratigraphy (Arvicolidae)		Important fossil sites, with values for an index of molar enamel thickness in *Arvicola* and *Mimomys*
Quaternary	Holocene	Holocene	*Arvicola-Microtus* Stage (Toringian)	*Arvicola terrestris* Zone	Central Europe — Southeastern Europe (Pannonian Basin) *Arvicola* Euerwanger Buhl H: 83.03 — Pilisszántó : 84.48 Krockstein/Rübeld : 89.08 — Peskö : 89.31 Kremathenhöhle : 89.23 — **Istállóskö** : 89.54 Dzerová Skala : 92.04 Roter Berg/Saalfeld: 97.25 — **Subalyuk:** (96.43) Burgtonna 2 : 98.44
	Pleistocene	Weichsel Glaciation			
		Eem Interglaciation			Untertürkheim: 100.81 — **Tata:** 99.22 Adlerberg/Nördlingen: 100.83 Taubach: 105.15 Schönfeld : 106.02
		Saale Complex		*Arvicola cantiana* Zone	Hórvölgy: 101.91 **Weimar-Ehringsdorf** — Solymár: 108.32 (lower travertine) : 112.30 Budapest-Várbarlang 2: (116.83)
		Holstein Complex			Dobrkovice 2: (123.21) — Budapest-Várbarlang 1: **Bilzingsleben:** (132:52) — 123.08 Mosbach: (133.54) — Tarkö 4: (129.00) Hundsheim: 135.15 — **Vértesszöllös:** (136.14)
		Elster & Cromer Complex	*Microtus-Mimomys* Stage (Biharian)	*Mimomys savini* Zone	*Mimomys* **Prezletice:** 132.98 Voigtstedt: 139.09 Koneprusy C 718: 141.69

Figure 1.2. Middle- and late-Pleistocene biostratigraphy of central and southeastern Europe, on the basis of the voles *Mimomys, Arvicola,* and *Microtus* (modified after Heinrich 1987: 395). The rightmost column lists key sites with vole fossils, followed by average values for a biostratigraphically significant index of first-lower-molar enamel thickness ([thickness on the concave margin of the molar prisms/thickness on the convex margin] × 100). Sites shown in boldface type are those with important human fossils or artifacts.

1.7–1.6 mya. Like *Arvicola,* it was initially distinguished from *Mimomys* by the development of ever-growing, rootless molars. Together, *Mimomys, Arvicola,* and *Microtus* can be used to construct biostratigraphies that are plainly relevant to human evolution and prehistory. Figure 1.2 shows one that has wide application in central and southeastern Europe over the entire (middle-Pleistocene-to-Holocene) time span that people have occupied the area. Sites providing crucial microtine fossils are listed in the rightmost column together with average values for a biostratigraphically significant enamel-thickness index ([rear-band thickness/fore-band thickness] × 100) that

Figure 1.3. Time ranges of the Elephantinae in Africa (redrawn after Cooke 1984: Fig. 2). The successive stages of *Elephas recki* are particularly useful for establishing the chronological relationships among otherwise undatable early- and middle-Pleistocene sites.

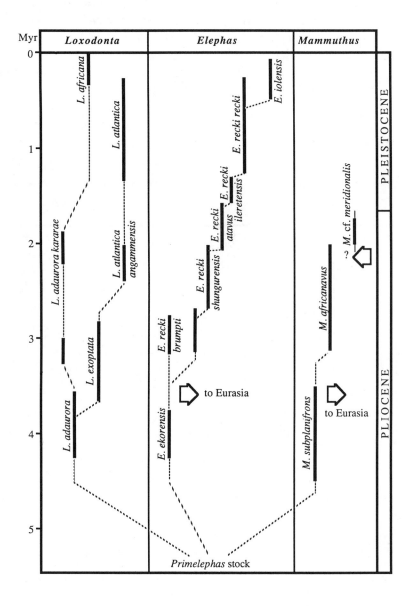

decreases with time. At sites shown in boldface type, the microtine bones are associated with important human fossils or artifacts.

The Biostratigraphy of Elephants, Pigs, and Horses in Africa.
Since the microtines are restricted to Eurasia and North America, they can play no role in African biostratigraphy. However, many African groups can be used, of which, from a paleoanthropological perspective, the most noteworthy are clearly the elephants, pigs, and horses (Cooke 1984, with references). During the time span of human evolution, all three groups were characterized by important first and last appearances and also by lineages for which directional evolutionary trends have been established. Fossil elephants, pigs, and horses provide the main basis not only for dating many important African sites relative to each other but also for cross-checking the validity of absolute dates, when these are available.

Figure 1.3 summarizes the biostratigraphic aspects of the elephants. Until the late Quaternary, the most common genus in Africa was *Elephas*, which appeared shortly before 4 mya. An early species, *Elephas ekorensis*, was ancestral to the especially common *Elephas recki*, which evolved somewhat before 3 mya and then underwent progressive change through time. This change is particularly obvious in the molars, which became increasingly high crowned while the enamel surrounding individual molar plates became thinner and more tightly folded (Maglio 1973; Beden 1979). From molar change, several stages of *Elephas recki* have been defined, and where appropriate fossils occur, these can be used to bracket sites within an average range of about 500,000 years.

The pigs and horses provide a broadly comparable picture (Figs. 1.4, 1.5). With respect to the pigs, there is minor disagreement on details (Cooke and Wilkinson 1978; J. M. Harris and White 1979), but both first appearances and directional changes in molar dimensions and morphology can be used for biostratigraphy. The horses are most useful with regard to first appearances, especially since most major events in horse evolution took place outside Africa and since immigrant taxa then dispersed rapidly through much of the continent. Both the spread of the three-toed horse, *Hipparion*, and that of the modern one-toed form, *Equus*, are key time markers for relative dating. From a north African entry, three-toed horses spread between 12 mya and 10.5 mya, perhaps mostly (if not entirely) around 10.5 mya. One-toed horses dispersed shortly before 2 mya. For perhaps 1.5 million years, they

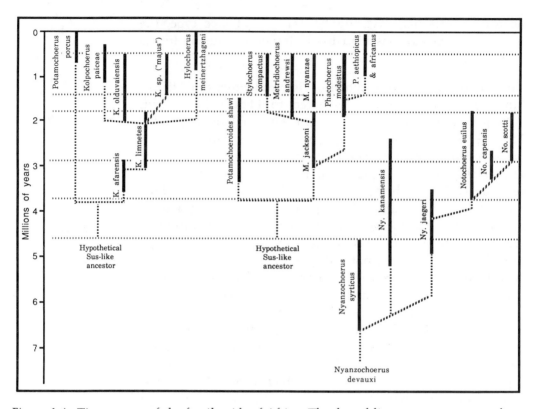

Figure 1.4. Time ranges of the fossil suids of Africa. The dotted lines separate proposed biostratigraphic zones or stages (redrawn after Cooke 1984: Fig. 3). The chart shows that the suids burgeoned between roughly 5 mya and 1.5 mya but then suffered severe losses (extinctions), probably mainly between 1 mya and 400,000 years ago. The reason(s) for the losses remain conjectural, but the ongoing, parallel success of the bovids was probably at least partly responsible.

overlapped with three-toed species, which became extinct about 500,000 years ago. Together with pig taxa, the one-toed horse was especially crucial in demonstrating a large absolute (radiopotassium) dating discrepancy between the Koobi Fora and the Lower Omo sites in east Africa. At first, it seemed that a fauna including one-toed horse had appeared some 600,000 years earlier at Koobi Fora than in the Lower Omo, only 100 km north. As discussed in Chapter 3, this led to further checking of the absolute dates, and it was ultimately shown that the original Koobi Fora estimates were in fact roughly 700,000–600,000 years "too old."

Absolute Dating Methods

Although biostratigraphy and other relative dating methods remain basic to human evolutionary studies, the impact of absolute dating methods cannot be overstated. This is especially true of so-called radiometric methods, which have revolutionized thinking since their initial development in the 1940s and 1950s. Until 1960, the best guesstimate for the time span of human evolution was perhaps the past 1 million years or so. This notion changed radically in the early 1960s, when the publication of radiopotassium dates from Olduvai Gorge, Tanzania showed that people in the broad sense (hominids) already existed at least 1.75–1.85 mya (L. S. B. Leakey et al. 1961; Evernden and Curtis 1965). More recently, as detailed in Chapter 3, the radiopotassium method has been applied at

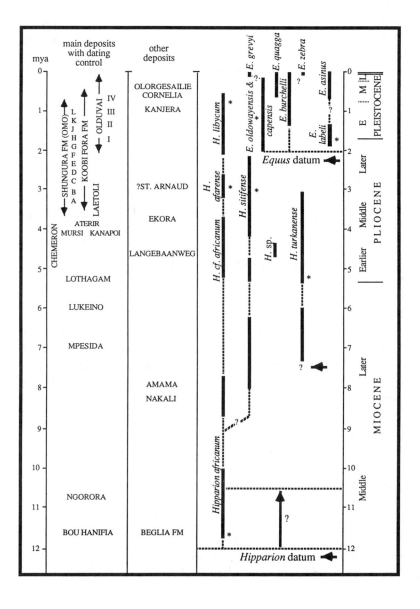

Figure 1.5. Time ranges of the later Miocene-to-Holocene equids of Africa, with some important sites in which equid fossils occur (modified after Cooke 1984: Fig. 1). From a biostratigraphic point-of-view, the two most important events were the arrival and dispersal of three-toed horses (*Hipparion*) sometime between 12 mya and 10.5 mya and of one-toed horses (*Equus*) shortly before 2 mya.

many other east African sites, where, in conjunction with relevant evidence from biostratigraphy and other sources, it shows that human evolution began substantially earlier, certainly before 4 mya. The radiocarbon method has had a comparable impact at the recent end of the time scale, where, for example, it has helped show that fully modern people did not appear everywhere at the same time. The implications of this are considered in Chapters 6 and 7.

The main purpose of this section is to summarize the principles behind radiopotassium dating, the radiocarbon technique, and other radiometric methods that have become so vital to human evolutionary studies. It also touches briefly on nonradiometric absolute methods, of which the most important are clearly paleomagnetism (paleomagnetic stratigraphy) and the "biomolecular clock." Inevitably, it also points up some important limitations of absolute dating, above all the nagging difficulty of obtaining reliable dates in the interval between the practical upper limit of the radiopotassium method, at perhaps 500,000–300,000 years ago, and the lower limit of conventional radiocarbon dating, at 40,000–30,000 years ago.

Some General Features of Radiometric Dating

All radiometric dating methods rely on the decay of naturally occurring radioactive elements or isotopes (varieties of elements). In the process of decay, radioactive atoms are literally transformed from one isotope into another (not necessarily of the same element). For example, the justly famous radioactive isotope of carbon, carbon-14 (^{14}C), decays to nitrogen-14 (^{14}N). For each isotope, the rate of decay is a constant, unaffected by ordinary environmental variables such as temperature and humidity or by the chemical compound in which the isotope occurs. Each isotope's decay rate is ordinarily expressed as its half-life, the average amount of time necessary for half the radioactive atoms in a sample to decay. Table 1.2 presents the half-lives of several radioactive isotopes that are important in radiometric dating.

As an example, the table lists the half-life of ^{14}C as 5,730 years, which means that roughly half the ^{14}C atoms in a sample will disintegrate within 5,730 years, half of the remainder at the end of 11,460 ($5,730 \times 2$) years, half of what is then left at the end of 17,190 ($5,730 \times 3$) years, and so forth. Technically, some ^{14}C will always remain in a sample, though, with conventional technology, it will be very difficult to measure the amount after a lapse of 25,000–30,000 years.

Table 1.2. Some Basic Parameters of Isotopes Used in Radiometric Dating

Isotope	Material Dated	Potential Range (years)	Half-life (years)
Carbon-14	wood, charcoal, shell	40,000, using conventional technology; 100,000, using linear accelerators	5,730
Protactinium-231	deep-sea sediment, shell, coral, travertine	150,000	34,300
Thorium-230	deep-sea sediment, shell, coral, travertine	350,000	75,200
Uranium-234	coral	1 million	250,000
Chlorine-36	groundwater	500,000	310,000
Beryllium-10	deep-sea sediment, polar ice	1,600,000	8 million
		. . .	1,600,00
Potassium-40	volcanic ash, lava	. . .	1.3 billion
Rubidium-87	igneous and metamorphic rocks	. . .	48.8 billion

To obtain a radiometric date, several conditions must be met. First, of course, the object to be dated must contain a radioactive isotope with a known half-life. Second, at the time of formation, the object should have contained only the radioactive "parent" and none of the "daughter" into which it decays. In mathematical terms, at time of formation, the daughter/parent ratio should have been 0/1 (= 0). Finally, there must be some means for measuring the amount of parent and daughter in the object today, that is, for establishing the modern daughter/parent ratio. Then, it is possible to use the half-life of the parent (= the known rate at which it decays to the daughter), to calculate the time that has elapsed since the daughter/parent ratio was 0, that is, since the object formed. In practice, the condition that there be no initial daughter (that the daughter/parent ratio be zero) is frequently violated, but fortunately it is often possible to separate original daughter from "radiogenic" daughter.

From a paleoanthropological perspective, the most important radiometric dating techniques are the radiopotassium method, the fission-track method, the uranium-series method(s), the radiocarbon method, and the thermoluminescence method.

Radiopotassium (= Potassium/Argon) Dating

This method relies on radiopotassium (^{40}K), which comprises about 0.01% of all naturally occurring potassium (K). Potassium-40 decays to argon-40 (^{40}Ar) and calcium-40 (^{40}Ca) in a known ratio, and theoretically either the $^{40}Ca/^{40}K$ or the $^{40}Ar/^{40}K$ ratio could be used for dating a geological sample.

However, in practice the $^{40}Ca/^{40}K$ ratio is not useful because radiogenic ^{40}Ca cannot be distinguished from original ^{40}Ca, which is very abundant in nature.

In contrast, the $^{40}Ar/^{40}K$ ratio is very useful. This is because rocks heated to a very high temperature (generally, above 300°C) tend to lose any original argon (an inert gas) they contain. When they cool, radiogenic argon begins to accumulate again. Since the rate of accumulation is known (it is the rate at which ^{40}K decays into ^{40}Ar), the $^{40}Ar/^{40}K$ ratio in a rock is a direct function of the time elapsed since the rock cooled.

As outlined by Dalrymple and Lanphere (1969), Gentner and Lippolt (1969), and Hall and York (1984), radiopotassium dating is more complicated in practice than in principle. It works best on rocks—or, more precisely, on minerals within rocks—that are rich in potassium. Some minerals tend to lose their argon under physical or chemical stress, independent of heating, and secondary heating may cause some but not all radiogenic argon to escape. A date on a rock that has been secondarily heated may thus reflect a mixture of two (or more) heating events.

Because radiopotassium dating generally requires high temperatures to set the clock (daughter/parent ratio) to 0, its use is restricted mainly to volcanic extrusives, such as lavas and ash falls. Meteorites that were heated during passage through the atmosphere may also be dated, but they are much rarer than volcanic rocks. The very long half-life of ^{40}K means that the radiopotassium method has no practical lower limit (it can be used to estimate the age of the earth) but that, in most cases, it cannot be used to date rocks younger than a few hundred thousand years old. This is because they contain too little ^{40}Ar for accurate measurement and because the statistical error associated with the age estimate therefore may be as large as the estimate itself.

The radiopotassium method has been extensively applied in east Africa, where vulcanism has been nearly continuous since the early Miocene. Dates on volcanic extrusives, such as ash layers, that lie stratigraphically above or below a fossil or archeological site can be used to estimate the latter's age, as, for example, at Olduvai Gorge, where a series of dates indicate that the oldest deposits, with their artifacts and bones, accumulated about 1.8 mya. Another paleoanthropologically important application of the radiopotassium method is the dating of paleomagnetic reversals recorded in volcanic extrusives (see below). Since paleomagnetism is also recorded in nonvolcanic sediments, it can often be used in turn to provide rough dates at fossil or archeological sites where direct radiopotassium dating is impossible.

Fission-Track Dating

This method utilizes the "tracks" that particles emitted by uranium 238 (^{238}U) create in naturally occurring glasses and minerals (Fleischer et al. 1969; Green 1979; Naeser and Naeser 1984). The tracks are annealed (erased) when a substance is heated to a high temperature, and they reform when it cools. Since the rate of track formation is directly proportional to the half-life of ^{238}U, the last time a sample cooled can be determined from the density of tracks relative to the amount of ^{238}U in a sample. The tracks, usually enlarged by acid etching in the laboratory, are counted under high magnification. A potential complication is that, depending on the substance, some annealing (track loss) can occur at low temperatures. This is particularly likely in glasses, which therefore tend to produce ages that are "too young." Like the radiopotassium technique, fission-track dating is applicable mainly to volcanic extrusives. It requires minerals that are moderately rich in ^{238}U (if there is too much, the tracks are too packed for counting). It has been used much less often than radiopotassium, largely because it is more tedious. From a paleoanthropological perspective, its main importance has been to check radiopotassium dates at the important east African sites of Olduvai Gorge (Fleischer et al. 1965) and Koobi Fora (Hurford et al. 1976; Gleadow 1980).

Uranium-Series (U-S) Dating

Uranium-Series (U-S) dating is actually a set of methods based on the parent isotopes ^{238}U, ^{235}U, and thorium-232 (^{232}Th) (Ku 1976; Schwarcz 1980; Schwarcz and Gascoyne 1984). All three decay, through a series of intermediate radioactive isotopes, to stable isotopes of lead. Some of the intermediate products decay too rapidly to be useful for dating geologic events, while those with longer half-lives tend to decay at rates about equal to the rates at which they are produced. This means they can only be used for dating when they are transferred from the system in which they were produced to another, where their removal or introduction sets the clock to zero.

In general, U-S dating depends on the high solubility of uranium in water, while its decay products, such as ^{230}Th (from ^{238}U via ^{234}U) and protactinium-231 (^{231}Pa) (from ^{235}U)

tend to precipitate out as they form. Uranium in sea-water or lake water thus tends to remain in solution, while ^{230}Th and ^{231}Pa tend to become incorporated in salts that accumulate on the floor below. If it is assumed that the ^{230}Th and ^{231}Pa content was always the same as it is at the sediment surface today, the quantity of ^{230}Th or ^{231}Pa in a buried level can be used to calculate its age. This method is obviously applicable only to sea- or lake-bottom sediments, where it can, however, date climatic events that may bear on human evolution. There are several sources of potential error, including the possibility that the ^{230}Th and ^{231}Pa in ancient sediments came partly from uranium in detrital particles washed in from a terrestrial source. In addition, the sedimentation rate (= the rate at which ^{230}Th and ^{231}Pa settle out) is not necessarily constant over time.

In theory, the principles behind U-S dating of sea- or lake-floor deposits should also permit U-S dating of aquatic shells. These are usually built of carbonates that have been dissolved in the surrounding water. With the carbonates, there is also some dissolved uranium—but virtually no (insoluble) ^{230}Th or ^{231}Pa. The ^{230}Th/^{234}U and ^{231}Pa/^{235}U ratios in a shell should therefore reflect the time elapsed since the shell formed. U-S analysis of shells has dated ancient (raised) beaches in the Mediterranean that are stratigraphically related to archeological or fossil sites (Stearns and Thurber 1965), but, in general, shell dates are problematic because shells tend to adsorb uranium from their burial environment. This is also commonly the case with bones; fossil bones typically contain 10–1,000 ppm (parts per million) of uranium, compared with only 0.1 ppm in fresh bone (Cook et al. 1982).

Among carbonates of organic origin, the most reliable ones for U-S dating are corals, partly because they tend to be relatively rich in uranium to begin with and partly because uranium intake after death is rarer and relatively easy to detect. Fossil corals from various parts of the world have provided concordant dates of 125,000 ± 10,000 years ago for a high sea level generally correlated with the Last Interglaciation (discussed in the section on Cenozoic climates below) (Harmon et al. 1981; Stearns 1984).

Finally, the ^{230}Th/^{234}U and ^{231}Pa/^{235}U ratios can be used to date inorganic carbonates—limestones, speleothems (stalagmites and stalactites), travertines, etc.—that precipitate out of solution in cave, spring, or lake deposits. Since thorium and protactinium are relatively insoluble, they tend to be absent from recently precipitated carbonates, which will, however, contain tiny amounts of coprecipitated uranium. After precipitation, ^{230}Th and ^{231}Pa accumulate in the carbonate as a result of uranium decay. Either the ^{230}Th/^{234}U ratio or the ^{231}Pa/^{235}U ratio can then be used to estimate the age of the carbonate.

From a paleoanthropological perspective, U-S dating of inorganic carbonates is certainly its most important application, because these materials occur in many archeological sites and because U-S dating covers a time range that is not well covered by other methods. The ^{232}Pa/^{235}U and ^{230}Th/^{234}U ratios permit dates back to about 150,000 and 350,000 years ago, respectively, well beyond the lower limit of radiocarbon and near the practical upper limit of radiopotassium. Cave dripstones (speleothems) and spring limestones (travertines) form mainly under humid conditions, and the extensive application of U-S dating to these deposits has confirmed inferences from other sources that global climate was much moister during the Last Interglaciation, between roughly 130,000 and 90,000 years ago, than it was during the Last Glaciation, between about 90,000–80,000 and 15,000–10,000 years ago (G. J. Hennig et al. 1983). The method has also provided interesting ages for some important fossil hominid sites, especially in Europe (Cook et al. 1982, and Chapters 4 and 5 below), but these remain controversial, partly because they are not always internally consistent and partly because they often seem to contradict dates implied by biostratigraphy or other methods. Sources of error include the possibility that the dated carbonate was contaminated by "detrital" uranium (in particles introduced by wind or flowing water) and the possibility that uranium or its daughter products were leached from the carbonate after precipitation.

Radiocarbon (Carbon-14) Dating

The radiocarbon or carbon-14 (^{14}C) method is the most celebrated of all radiometric techniques because of its widespread application in archeology. It relies on four major assumptions: (1) that the amount of ^{14}C, which results from a reaction between cosmic radiation and ^{14}N in the atmosphere, has remained constant in the atmosphere over the time interval covered by the method; (2) that ^{14}C is as likely to be oxidized to carbon dioxide as is nonradioactive carbon (mainly ^{12}C); (3) that carbon dioxide mixing in the atmosphere is relatively rapid, so that the atmospheric ratio of radioactive and nonradioactive carbon is about the same everywhere; and (4) that most organisms do not discriminate between radioactive and nonradioactive carbon when they build their tissues. Since most plants obtain all their carbon from atmospheric carbon dioxide, and since most animals obtain their carbon directly or indirectly from plants, the $^{14}C/^{12}C$ ratio in plants and animals will closely reflect the ratio in the atmosphere. However, after an organism dies and carbon assimilation ceases, the amount of ^{14}C in its tissues decreases by half approximately every 5,730 years (= the half-life of ^{14}C.) The ^{14}C decays back to ^{14}N, but dating depends on the $^{14}C/^{12}C$ ratio in a sample, which is compared with the $^{14}C/^{12}C$ ratio in the atmosphere. The difference is a function of the time elapsed since the death of the organism providing the sample (Libby 1955; Gribbin 1979; Terasmae 1984).

Some of the assumptions behind ^{14}C dating are clearly problematic. First, the $^{14}C/^{12}C$ ratio in the atmosphere has plainly varied through time. The combustion of huge amounts of fossil fuel (coal, oil, and gas) following the Industrial Revolution in the nineteenth century has released large quantities of "old" carbon (with essentially no ^{14}C) into the atmosphere, while nuclear explosions since 1945 have produced an opposite bias, increasing the proportion of ^{14}C. Fortunately, these factors can be circumvented by relying on the $^{14}C/^{12}C$ ratio in calendrically dated objects from before the Industrial Revolution, and they do not materially affect dates obtained since 1955, when a standard ratio was widely adopted.

More difficult to accommodate are much earlier fluctuations in the atmospheric $^{14}C/^{12}C$ ratio that are indicated by repeated discrepancies either between ^{14}C dates and calendrically dated artifacts or between ^{14}C dates and dates from more secure methods, such as tree-ring dating (dendrochronology) (Seuss 1986). Such fluctuations were probably caused mainly by significant variation in solar activity (the main source of cosmic radiation), supplemented by changes in the strength of the earth's magnetic field which acts as a shield against cosmic radiation, and perhaps also by long-term changes in the amount of carbon dioxide dissolved in the world ocean. The ^{14}C analysis of tree rings whose age is known implies that ^{14}C dates for the past 7,000–7,500 years often differ from true ages by between 1% and 10%. Over the 7,500-year interval for which paired ^{14}C determinations and tree-ring dates exist, the tree rings can be used to correct (or "calibrate") the ^{14}C chronology, but the possibility of a 10% (or perhaps greater) error in older dates means that they should be read in "radiocarbon years" rather than in calendar (solar) years. From this perspective, it might be said that ^{14}C is an excellent relative dating method of worldwide application but one that is less useful for absolute dating.

Another problematic assumption is that all the carbon in a sample originated from the atmosphere. Some living creatures (particularly some mollusks and water plants) are known to assimilate carbon from old rocks. They will thus contain more ^{12}C than they "should," and if they are dated, they will seem to be "too old." An even more serious problem occurs when carbon enters the remains of a creature after its death. Most common and most serious is contamination by "young" carbon, for example, from humic acids penetrating a buried archeological level. If the young carbon is not detected and eliminated, the ^{14}C age will be "too young."

There are sample preparation procedures to detect and eliminate contaminants, but they are not foolproof, and the best course remains careful sample selection in the field. Some materials are also easier to cleanse or are less likely to be contaminated to begin with. Charcoal (charred wood) is probably best in this regard. The inorganic components of shell and bone are generally not useful, because they tend to exchange carbon with their burial environment. The organic (protein) component of shell or bone is suitable but is rarely present in its original form; more commonly, all that remain are some amino-acid constituents of protein, which might come from the burial environment, rather than from the shell or bone itself. Among the constituents of bone protein, one—hydroxyproline—is rare elsewhere in nature and is thus specially sought for ^{14}C dating (R. Gillespie et al. 1984). Unfortunately, it is highly soluble and is therefore often leached from bones in the ground.

Carbon-14 (and other radiometric) dates are properly stated with a plus-or-minus figure, for example, 14,000 ± 120 years ago. This figure is a measure of the statistical uncertainty associated with a particular age determination. It is necessary mainly because the decay rate of ^{14}C is constant only over a very long period of time; over the very short interval when a sample is being processed in a laboratory, the rate may vary slightly from its long-term value. The plus-or-minus figure is computed so that the chances are about 67% that the actual radiocarbon age of the sample has been bracketed. In the case of a date given as 14,000 ± 120 years ago, the bracketing interval would be 13,880–14,120 years ago. The figure will be larger for a sample that contains relatively little carbon or that was "dated" only briefly. If the figure is doubled, the probability that the actual age of the sample has been bracketed increases to 96%. If the figure is tripled, there is no practical chance that the age of the sample lies outside the bracketing interval.

The time range covered by the ^{14}C method is limited by the short half-life of ^{14}C. Samples that are older than 30,000–40,000 years contain too little ^{14}C for accurate measurement by conventional technology. This technology counts only radioactive emissions (decaying ^{14}C atoms), not all ^{14}C atoms in a sample. Linear accelerators functioning as sensitive mass spectrometers now allow direct counting of ^{14}C atoms before they decay, and since the overwhelming majority in a sample do not decay during the brief interval when a sample is analyzed, the ^{14}C content of old samples can be measured much more accurately (Berger 1979; Hedges 1981; Rucklidge 1984; Taylor et al. 1984). In theory, accelerator dating could provide reliable ages up to 100,000 years ago or even beyond. It also allows very small samples to be dated, and so far this has been its main application (Hester 1987). One reason is the problem of obtaining truly suitable samples for very old dates. Only a tiny amount of contaminant is necessary to make a sample that is more than 40,000 years old seem much younger. For example, a 1% increment of modern carbon in a sample whose true age is 67,000 years will produce a ^{14}C age of 37,000 years. This leads to the important point that, in general, a date of more than 40,000 years should be regarded as only a minimum age. The true age of a sample may be significantly greater.

Thermoluminescence (TL)

Thermoluminescence (TL) dating depends on the fact that electrons become trapped in the crystal structure of substances irradiated by naturally occurring uranium, thorium, and radio-potassium. When the substance is heated, the electrons are released along with a quantity of light that is directly proportional to the number of electrons that were trapped. This light is known as TL. If the rate of electron accumulation (= the annual radiation dose) can be established, the amount of TL can be used to estimate the time elapsed since an object was last heated (Wintle 1980; Wintle and Huntley 1982; Aitken 1985). The quantity of trapped electrons can also be measured directly by a method known as electron spin resonance (ESR) (G. J. Hennig and Grün 1983).

TL dating has been applied mainly to pottery, but it can also be used to date burnt-flint artifacts or other materials from which trapped electrons were freed by heating in the past. The

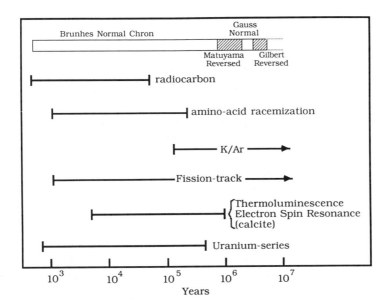

Figure 1.6. Time ranges covered by the absolute dating methods discussed in this chapter (adapted from Schwarcz and Gascoyne 1984: 84). Note that the horizontal scale (years) is logarithmic. In practice, dates near the limits of each method may be difficult to obtain and their reliability may be especially questionable. This is perhaps particularly true of very "old" dates from the ^{14}C method and of very young ones from the [40]K/[40]Ar method.

particles in wind-deposited dust (loess) and some other sediments are potentially datable, since they give up trapped electrons on exposure to sunlight (Lamothe et al. 1984). One potential complication affecting all materials is that trapped electrons may escape naturally, independent of further heating. Ages may also be miscalculated if the annual dose rate is misestimated. The annual dose rate is a composite of the internal dose rate, produced by radioisotopes inside the dated object, and the external or environmental dose rate, produced by radioisotopes in the surrounding soil. The internal dose rate can be measured in the laboratory. The external rate must be measured on site and is more problematic, since it may have changed through time, depending especially on changes in the water content of the soil.

Like U-S dating, TL dating is appealing because it partly covers the gap between the radiocarbon and radiopotassium methods (Fig. 1.6) and because it is applicable to a different range of materials. As discussed in Chapters 6 and 7, some extremely interesting TL dates are now available for European and Near Eastern sites that are beyond the 40,000–30,000-years-ago range of conventional radiocarbon dating. These dates are based on burnt flints, and their reliability is supported by reasonably close agreement between TL dates on flints and radiocarbon dates at much younger sites (Aitken et al. 1986; Valladas and Valladas 1987). More than any other available method, TL dating promises to resolve some vexing chronological issues bearing on the relationship between modern and nonmodern human populations in the interval from 200,000 to 40,000 years ago.

Nonradiometric Absolute Dating Methods

The most important nonradiometric absolute dating methods are tree-ring dating (dendrochronology) and varve dating. They are highly accurate but can be applied only in certain restricted geographic regions, and they cover only the past 8,000–10,000 years. Only varve dating will be summarized here, but tree-ring dating follows broadly similar principles. An additional absolute dating method—amino-acid racemization—also deserves brief mention, because it was briefly fashionable in the 1970s.

Varve Analysis

A varve is a distinctive band of sediment, often made up of two subbands, that is laid down each year on the floor of a lake or other relatively calm water body. For dating purposes, the most useful varves are ones that form in quiet glacier-fed lakes. Each year, after the spring thaw, material washed into such a lake consists of both coarse and fine particles. The coarse ones settle out first, forming the lower subband of a varve. The finer particles settle out later, forming the upper subband. The overall characteristics of a varve, particularly its thickness, are determined by annually variable events, especially the intensity of the thaw.

In an area with several glacier-fed lakes, each year will produce its own distinctive varve, alike from lake to lake. In some regions, above all Fennoscandinavia, there are varved sediments that formed under lakes whose times of existence overlapped. The bottommost varves in one set thus correspond to the uppermost varves in another. In Fennoscandinavia, it has thus been possible, when starting with varves of known age, to establish a reliable varve sequence covering the past 10,000–12,000 years (Tauber 1970). The varves can be used to date any materials they contain and to trace the retreat of the Last Glacial ice sheet in its waning phases. Varves of known age have also been used to calibrate the ^{14}C method, though they are less useful for this purpose than are tree rings.

Amino-Acid Racemization

The amino acids that make up proteins can exist in two molecular forms, L–amino acids and D–amino acids. Only L–amino acids occur in the tissues of living animals, but they are converted after death to D–amino acids at a rate that is dependent on temperature, moisture, and pH and that differs for each amino acid. The reaction that produces the conversion is known as racemization. Fossil shells and bones often still contain some amino acids, and if the postmortem temperature and moisture history of a specimen is known, the D-form/L-form ratio for a particular amino acid is a measure of the time since death.

The method has been applied fruitfully to shells, but its principal application in paleoanthropology has been to bones (Bada 1985). Like U-S or TL dating, the amino-acid method can provide dates in the interval between 40,000 and 100,000 or more years that is not well covered by either radiopotassium dating or radiocarbon dating. Several interesting racemization dates on fossil human bones or on animal bones accompanying human bones were widely cited in the 1970s, but they fell from favor later, partly because they were inconsistent with other dating evidence and partly because they depend on postmortem temperature and moisture (Hare 1980). In most cases, these variables are difficult or impossible to estimate accurately, and few paleoanthropologists today accept racemization dates at face value, though the method can provide useful relative dates and perhaps, in some instances, paleotemperature estimates.

Paleomagnetism (Paleomagnetic Stratigraphy)

Paleomagnetic (or geomagnetic) dates are generally much less precise than those of other absolute dating methods, and paleomagnetism is perhaps best described as a cross between absolute and relative dating. In essence, it provides the basis for a special kind of stratigraphy, with broadly the same kind of dating implications as are seen in biostratigraphy. At its root are past fluctuations in the intensity and direction of the earth's magnetic field. From a paleoanthropological perspective, the most important changes are in polarity, from times when a compass would point north to times when it would point south and vice versa. Almost certainly, the cause of such shifts are reversals in currents within the earth's fluid core, though these currents are poorly understood and the timing of shifts appears irregular (Cox 1969, 1972; Harland et al. 1982). Shifts do, however, clearly occur on two scales: very long intervals characterized by essentially the same polarity are punctuated by much shorter ones of opposite polarity. The long intervals, lasting hundreds of thousands or even millions of years, are called *polarity chrons* (formerly *epochs*). The shorter ones, lasting no more than a few tens of thousands of years, are known as *polarity subchrons* (formerly *events*).

Ancient polarity can be detected most readily in volcanic rocks and in sediments made up of fine-grained particles that settled into place relatively slowly, for example, on the ocean floor. The alignment of ferromagnetic particles in a volcanic rock reflects the direction of the field when it cooled, while the alignment of particles in fine-grained sediments reflects the direction at settling time. Subsequent compaction of the sediments prevents realignment.

The sequence of polarity changes is especially well known for the past 5 million years. It comprises four polarity chrons and seven or more polarity subchrons (Fig. 1.7). Dating is based on volcanic rocks, by means of paired radiopotassium and paleomagnetic determinations. The boundary dates between chrons are averages that are subject to both empirical and statistical revision, but they are reasonably well fixed. The dates for subchrons are less secure because of their short duration, which may be less than the statistical uncertainty associated with radiopotassium dates. Even the existence of some subchrons remains controversial.

Accurate measurement of remanent magnetism in ancient rocks or sediments requires not only proper instrumentation but also care in field removal. Complications can be introduced by secondary heating of a volcanic rock and by postdepositional chemical processes that alter the behavior of ferromagnetic particles.

Unlike either the first appearance of a biological taxon (a species, genus, etc.), which may be time transgressive and regionally restricted, or global climatic change, whose impact may be harder to detect in some places than in others, a change in polarity affects the entire world simultaneously, and, given appropriate deposits, should be detectable everywhere. This makes the geomagnetic stratigraphy attractive for defining boundaries between time intervals, including, for example, (a) that between the Pliocene and the Pleistocene, now sometimes fixed at the top of the Olduvai Subchron, roughly 1.7–1.6 mya, and (b) that between the early Quaternary and the middle Quaternary, now commonly equated with the boundary between the Matuyama Reversed Chron and the Brunhes Normal Chron, about 730,000 years ago.

The geomagnetic stratigraphy is also very useful for bracketing sites in time that cannot be dated more directly. An example is the famous Peking-man site of Zhoukoudian, north China, where there is no material ideally suited for radiometric age determination. Paleomagnetic determinations from fine-grained parts of the fill, however, have isolated the Brunhes /Matuyama boundary at a level below that containing the

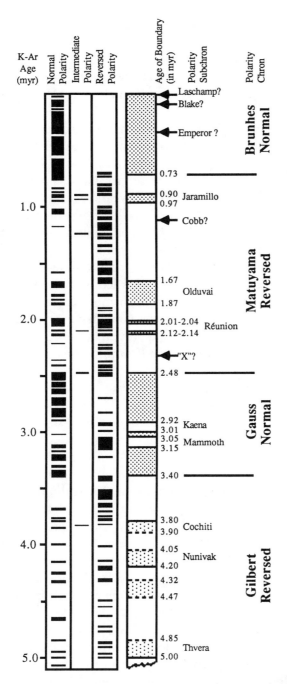

Figure 1.7. Global paleomagnetic stratigraphy for the past 5 million years, as determined from dated individual polarity measurements (left three columns). Normal polarity is indicated by dotting, reversed polarity by blank space (modified after Mankinen and Dalrymple 1979).

earliest Peking-man fossils and artifacts (Liu 1985). In combination with paleoclimatic evidence allowing broad correlation with the global marine record, the Zhoukoudian paleomagnetic data suggest that the deposits with human fossils and artifacts span the interval between about 500,000 and 230,000 years ago.

Paleomagnetic determinations can also serve as an important cross-check on dating by other methods. the Lower-Paleolithic site of Isernia La Pineta in central Italy provides a case in point. Radiopotassium determinations indicate that the site dates from about 730,000 years ago, while the fauna suggests a significantly younger age within the middle Quaternary (Coltorti et al. 1982). The available paleomagnetic determinations indicate the polarity was probably reversed at the time the artifacts and bones accumulated (?end of the Matuyama Reversed Chron). This lends support to the radiopotassium determinations, though more dates and paleomagnetic readings are needed for a conclusive case. Should such additional data continue to support an age of 730,000 years, the chronology of European faunal stratigraphy will have to be partly revised.

The Biomolecular Clock

The biomolecular clock is the last absolute dating method to be presented here. It differs radically from all the others in that it is applied not to ancient objects but to living creatures. In essence, it assumes that protein or DNA differences between taxa accumulate at a more or less constant (linear) rate, that the rate can be established from the degree of difference between taxa whose time of divergence is known from the fossil record, and that the rate can then be used to determine the time when other taxa diverged from one another, that is, when they last shared a common ancestor (Andrews 1985b).

Thus, if a fossil (geological) date of 25 mya for the divergence of Old World monkeys from apes is assumed, recently developed DNA hybridization data imply that the human and chimpanzee lines split about 5.5 mya and that the gorilla lineage became distinct about 7.7 mya, the gibbon lineage about 16.4 mya, the orangutan lineage about 12.2 mya, and (by definition) the line leading to Old World monkeys about 25 mya (Sibley and Ahlquist 1987). These age estimates agree closely with ones developed from an earlier set of the same data by using a fossil date of 12 mya for the emergence of the orangutan line (Pilbeam 1986). If it is assumed that the orangutan line actually diverged about 17 mya, the full data set places the separation of humans and chimpanzees at 7.7 mya, and the emergence of the gorilla, orangutan, gibbon, and Old World monkey lines at 11.0 mya, 17.0 mya, 23.0 mya, and 34.0 mya, respectively. As discussed in Chapter 7, essentially the same methodology can be applied to the origins of anatomically modern humans, where it suggests that fully modern people emerged in Africa within the past 200,000 years.

The biomolecular clock has been controversial since it was first applied to human evolution (by Sarich and Wilson [1967] and by Sarich [1971, 1983]), mainly because it often contravenes dates that fossil evidence appears to support. Critics have often argued that the rate of protein or DNA divergence need not be and is not constant and that it cannot be reliably established from the fossil record, where few if any times of evolutionary splitting are well fixed (Gingerich 1984c, 1986c; Lewin 1988). There is also the possibility that viral infections may occasionally transfer genetic material between closely related species, with the result that they would appear to share a much more recent common ancestor than they really do (Syvanen 1987). Nonetheless, biomolecular dates were instrumental in provoking a reevaluation of the claim, fashionable in the 1960s and 1970s, that, on the basis of fossils from the Indian subcontinent, people have been distinct from apes for at least 12–14 million years. In the wake of this reevaluation, conducted partly with new fossils, most paleontologists would probably now favor a human-ape split in the 5–8-mya range suggested by the molecular clock, and there is broad agreement between other molecular and fossil dates, as discussed in Chapter 2.

Cenozoic Climates

Beyond furnishing the chronological framework for human evolution, geologic studies can also illuminate the natural selective forces that drove it. Among these, none is potentially more important than climate—or, more precisely, climatic change. For example, as discussed in the next chapter, the development of drier, more seasonal climates between 10 mya and 5 mya (in the late Miocene) could at least partly account for the broadly contemporaneous emergence of the human family (Hominidae). The purpose of the final section of this chapter is to summarize Cenozoic climatic change as it may bear on human evolution, with particular reference to the later-Cenozoic ice age, which, in one of its milder phases, still grips the planet. The evidence for Cenozoic climatic change is incomplete and sometimes ambiguous or even contradictory

Figure 1.8. Composite ∂ oxygen–18 (^{18}O) record for Atlantic and Pacific Cenozoic localities. The vertical scale is time in millions of years before the present. The horizontal scale tracks relative change in the concentration of ^{18}O in deep-water (benthic) foraminifera. The larger the value (to the left), the greater the chance that a substantial amount of water was locked in continental ice. Values to the left of the vertical line indicate the presence of the Antarctic and possibly other ice sheets. Values to the right of the line indicate the possible or probable absence of large continental ice sheets. The figure shows that the first indisputable oxygen-isotope evidence for the Antarctic ice sheet comes from later-Miocene deposits, dating to roughly 14 mya (modified after Miller and Fairbanks 1985: 248).

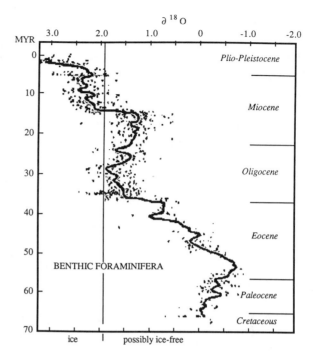

(Mercer 1983; Brain 1984, with references), and the following account should be regarded as only tentative, particularly with regard to the timing of climatically significant events in Antarctica.

In the early Cenozoic, global climates were relatively warm and equable, with relatively little difference in temperature between the equator and the poles. World temperatures rose slightly during the Paleocene to a peak in the early Eocene, before beginning a long decline. A sharp drop occurred in the very early Oligocene, about 36 mya, perhaps associated with transient glaciation in Antarctica (Fig. 1.8) (Shackleton and Kennett 1975; Miller and Fairbanks 1985; Shackleton 1986). This and later drops were probably caused mainly by changes in atmospheric and oceanic circulation patterns brought about by changes in the configuration and topography of the continents (Laporte and Zihlman 1983). Throughout the Oligocene and earlier Miocene, global temperatures were generally lower than in the earlier Cenozoic, but they were relatively stable. Two later-Oligocene temperature minima, at approximately 31 mya and 24 mya, may also have been associated with temporary glaciation in Antarctica. A sharp temperature plunge in the late Miocene, between 16 mya and 13 mya, probably coincides with the formation of a permanent East Antarctic Ice Sheet, which has retained roughly its present dimensions ever since.

An acute cold episode near the end of the Miocene, between roughly 6.5 mya and 5 mya, perhaps added a permanent West Antarctic Ice Sheet to its East Antarctic neighbor. The growth of glaciers during this interval sucked so much water from the oceans that the connection between the Atlantic and the Mediterranean was broken, and the Mediterranean completely dried up, leaving behind vast salt deposits. In the interval immediately following 5 mya, global temperatures partly recovered, and the Mediterranean refilled (and has remained full since). Then, in the mid-Pliocene, roughly 3.2 mya, temperatures fell again, initiating the formation of glaciers on the northern continents; and a pattern of cyclic climatic oscillation between long cold intervals and shorter, warmer ones began (Shackleton and Opdyke 1977). The cold intervals apparently intensified about 2.5 mya and again about 800,000–900,000 years ago (Prell et al. 1982; Roberts 1984; Shackleton et al. 1984).

This late-Cenozoic cold-warm oscillation was probably caused mainly by minor, cyclic variation in the amount of solar heat the earth receives, reflecting regular, cyclic changes in the shape of its orbit and in the tilt and wobble of its spin axis (Hays et al. 1976; Imbrie and Imbrie 1979; Imbrie et al. 1984). Calculations based on the known periodicity of these variables indicate that heat reception varies in three main cycles lasting roughly 21,000, 40,000, and 100,000 years, respectively. The beginning and end dates of the predicted 100,000-year cycles closely match the dating of the late-Cenozoic cold intervals observed in the geologic record.

The cold intervals, with their greatly enlarged ice sheets, are commonly called *glaciations* or *glacials*, and the intervening milder intervals, with their reduced ice sheets, are commonly called *interglaciations* or *interglacials*. The Holocene of Table 1.1 is simply the most recent interglaciation and might better be known as the Present Interglaciation. From a climatic perspective, it is not truly separate from the preceding Pleistocene, and some specialists prefer to extend the Pleistocene to the present, equating it with the Quaternary (Lowe and Walker 1984).

The existence of glaciers far beyond their present limits was documented first in Norwegian and Swiss mountain ranges in the early 1800s (Lowe and Walker 1984). Evidence for greatly expanded continental ice sheets was developed somewhat later in the nineteenth century, initially by the great Swiss zoologist Louis Agassiz. As land-based evidence for ancient glaciations accumulated in both North America and Europe, it seemed to indicate four major late-Cenozoic glaciations, separated by three main interglaciations (excluding the last or present one). The names of the four main glaciations—(from older to younger) Günz, Mindel, Riss, and Würm—identified in a classic study by Penck and Bruckner (1909) in a small Alpine region south of Munich in Germany were widely extended to incorporate supposedly like-aged glacial phenomena elsewhere, and sites, fossils, artifacts, etc. were commonly dated by reference to the time intervals these four glaciations or the intervening interglaciations were supposed to occupy. Beginning in the mid-1950s, however, studies of sediments from the deep-sea floor have shown that the number of major glaciations was far greater. There were eight during the past 730,000 years, seventeen in the past 1.7 million years, and at least twenty-one during the past 2.5 million years (van Donk 1976). Although the four-glaciation Alpine scheme survives in some textbooks, it should be totally abandoned.

The reason that climatic inferences drawn from the deep-sea floor are more reliable is because deposition on the sea-floor tends to be more continuous. Major interruptions or discontinuities are more common in land-based sequences, especially in areas that were glaciated, since each succeeding glaciation tended to remove the evidence of its predecessors. In fact the only land-based records that approach the deep-sea floor for continuity over long intervals come from areas beyond the reach of the glaciers, such as central Europe and central China, with their deep covers of wind-blown dust (loess) (Kukla 1975, 1987), and the lake bottoms of Bogotá in the Colombian Andes (van der Hammen 1974), Grand Pile in northwestern France (Woillard 1978; Woillard and Mook 1982), Lake Biwa in Japan (Kashiwaya et al. 1988), and especially Lake Phillipi in northern Greece (van der Hammen et al. 1971; Wijmstra and van der Hammen 1974). For the intervals these unusually long land-based records cover, they corroborate and fill out the basic history of late-Cenozoic climatic change now standardized on the basis of data from the deep-sea floor.

The deep-sea record for late-Cenozoic climatic change has been established in sediment cores removed from the seafloor by sophisticated equipment that barely disturbs the sediment structure. Climatic change is inferred from the species of foraminifera and other sea-dwelling microorganisms represented in different parts of a core and also from the changing chemical composition of their tests (shells). Variation in the content of oxygen-16 (^{16}O) and oxygen-18 (^{18}O) is particularly informative. These are naturally occurring, stable (nonradioactive) varieties (isotopes) of oxygen, which foraminifera and other marine organisms extract from seawater and build into their tests. Because ^{18}O is heavier, water molecules

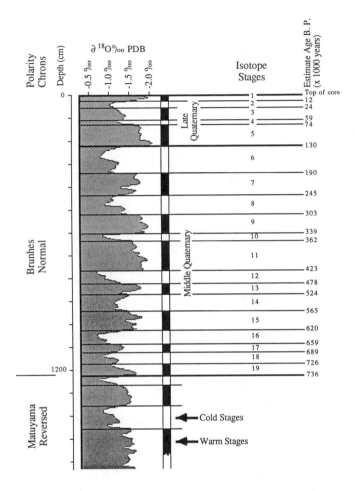

Figure 1.9. Oxygen-isotope and paleomagnetic stratigraphy of equatorial Pacific deep-sea core V28-238 (formatted after Champion et al. [1984: Fig. 2.3] from data in Shackleton and Opdyke [1973]). Odd-numbered isotope stages indicate relatively warm intervals, while even-numbered stages indicate colder ones. The estimated boundary dates between stages are from Imbrie et al. (1984) and Martinson et al. (1987).

that contain it evaporate less readily than do those containing ^{16}O, and during glacial intervals, when large amounts of water from the oceans became locked in ice sheets, seawater became richer in ^{18}O. The $^{18}O/^{16}O$ ratio in seawater is thus a measure of global ice volume. Although the ratio in microorganismal tests partly depends on the temperature and salinity of the water in which the microorganisms lived, it mainly reflects the original ratio in the water, and changes in the oxygen composition of tests from deep-sea cores therefore track the cyclic growth and decline of the ice sheets (Shackleton 1967, 1975, 1987).

The climatic stages detected from oxygen-isotope analysis are designated by arabic numerals, with odd numbers for the interglacial stages and even numbers for the glacial ones (Emiliani 1955, 1969; Shackleton and Opdyke 1973, 1976) (Fig. 1.9). Thus, the Holocene or Present Interglaciation is known as isotope-stage 1. There is the complication, however, that a long, milder interval, generally agreed to fall within the Last

Glaciation, has been designated as stage 3 and that the Last Glaciation thus includes stages 4 through 2. Stage 5 corresponds to the Last Interglaciation, though only its earliest substage, known as 5e, was comparable to stage 1 in terms of ice-sheet reduction and global warmth. The later substages, 5d through 5a, reflect varying but generally cooler climate, and some authorities would prefer to place them in the early part of the Last Glaciation. Almost certainly, they correspond to some land-based deposits that have long been assigned to the early part of the Last Glaciation—for example, to the Würm I in France (Butzer 1986).

The oxygen-isotope stages have been dated by a variety of methods, including ^{14}C, used near the top, and a combination of paleomagnetism and extrapolated sedimentation rates, used further down. One important conclusion from the dating is that, within the past 800,000–900,000 years, intervals as warm as stage 1 or substage 5e—that is, interglaciations in the narrowest sense—have probably lasted only about 10,000 years each, while the intervening cold intervals have lasted far longer, about 100,000 years each. This means that during the later phases of human history—or, more precisely, prehistory—people lived mainly under glacial conditions.

The most obvious aspect of glaciations was the mushrooming of ice on the continents, and at their maximum the ice sheets covered nearly a third of the earth's surface (Fig. 1.10). However, in partial compensation, as the ice sheets grew and less water flowed back to the sea, sea level dropped by 130–160 m and new land was exposed on the continental shelves. The emergent shelves not only became available for occupation but, in some cases, connected previously isolated landmasses, allowing people and other animals to inhabit new areas. For example, it was the lowering of sea level during a late-early- or early-middle-Quaternary glaciation that allowed early people to occupy Java, and the broad land bridge that connected Siberia and Alaska during the Last Glaciation permitted or at least facilitated the initial human colonization of the Americas.

The impact of glacial climate was worldwide (Street 1980). From a human point of view, one of the most important effects was a large-scale redistribution of plants and animals. Tundra and steppe replaced forest in midlatitude Eurasia, and arctic animals such as reindeer penetrated far south of their interglacial range. Mean annual temperatures declined everywhere, by as much as 16°C in higher latitudes and perhaps by as much as 3°C near the equator. In most places, precipitation also declined, probably mostly because of reduced evaporation

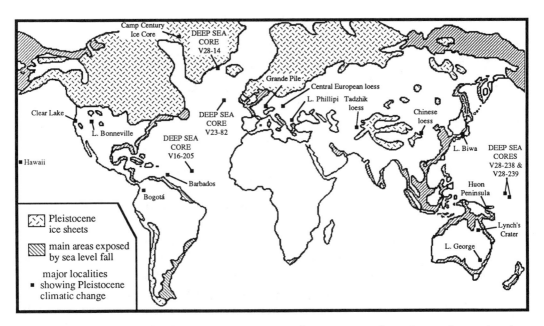

Figure 1.10. Map showing the maximum extent of Quaternary glaciation and associated sea-level change (redrawn after N. Roberts 1984: Fig. 2.1).

from colder oceans. The effects of reduced precipitation are particularly obvious at lower latitudes (between roughly 30°S and 30°N), where large areas that are presently rain forest became grassland or savanna, while grassland and savanna regions turned to desert. The broad correlation between glacial climate and significantly greater aridity contradicts an ill-founded earlier idea that wetter conditions (pluvials) characterized lower latitudes while glaciations affected higher ones. In fact, pluvial conditions were mainly an aspect of interglaciations (Butzer 1978), though lakes did grow during glaciations in some midlatitude areas because of altered atmospheric circulation, lowered evaporation, or both. The recurrent and persistent aridity of the tropics during glaciations probably impacted human populations as much as or more than increased cold in higher latitudes, and the selection pressures that aridity exerted may explain some of the important evolutionary events discussed in later chapters. The most important of these was perhaps the emergence of anatomically modern people in Africa, considered in Chapters 6 and 7.

2 PRIMATE EVOLUTION: LATE CRETACEOUS TO LATE MIOCENE

The Primates are the great zoological order to which hominids (people in the broad sense) and their closest living relatives among the mammals all belong. This chapter outlines the main features of primate evolution prior to the emergence of hominids in the late Miocene. The presentation is relatively detailed, but the emphasis is on basic stages in primate history rather than on specific ancestor-descendant relationships. This reflects the growing realization among specialists that such relationships have often been wrongly inferred because the potentially ambiguous meaning of similarities among species has not been adequately appreciated. The crucial similarities are ones that indicate a shared common ancestor, but, to begin with, these can be very difficult to distinguish from similarities that reflect only adaptation to shared circumstances (analogy) or parallel evolution (homoplasy) in distantly related lines.

Equally important, it is increasingly clear that similarities due to common descent must be divided between "primitive" ones that developed early in the history of a species or species group and "advanced" or "derived" ones that developed much later. Only shared derived features indicate a closely shared origin or a possibly close ancestor-descendant relationship between time-successive species, yet, as discussed in this and later chapters, shared derived characters are often hard to separate from shared primitive ones or even from shared characters developed independently in two species as a result of adaptation to similar natural conditions. Under the circumstances, compelling ancestor-descendant relationships are far harder to establish than to disprove. (In general, for disproof, it is necessary only to show that the supposed descendant lacks derived or advanced features found in its putative ancestor.) The key issue outlined here is addressed again below and is discussed further in Appendix 1, which also summarizes some basic principles of zoological classification and nomenclature that are integral to this and subsequent chapters.

The remainder of this chapter consists of three parts—a brief introduction to the skeleton, mainly to define basic anatomical terms relevant here and in later chapters; a longer discussion of the living primates, emphasizing those aspects that are essential for understanding primate (including human) evolution; and, finally, the central focus, a summary of the nonhuman primate fossil record organized by time interval, from the Cretaceous through the Miocene.

The Skeleton

For descriptive purposes, the skeleton is conventionally divided into two main parts—the cranium (skull) and the postcranium (trunk and limbs). The cranium itself is often divided into three principal sections—the braincase (= the vault or neurocranium); the face (including the upper jaw or maxilla), which is attached to the braincase by bone; and the lower jaw or mandible, which is attached to the braincase and face only by soft tissue. The braincase and face are formed of several bones that grow separately and that fuse together only in adults, if at all. Figure 2.1 illustrates a hominid cranium with the conventional names for the principal parts.

Teeth are especially prominent in fossil studies, because they are the most durable skeletal parts and thus dominate most fossil samples. Their specific morphology usually also reflects the dietary adaptation of a species, and, since much evolution has involved dietary specialization and divergence, teeth play a key role in reconstructing evolutionary trends and relationships. Like other mammals, primates have four basic

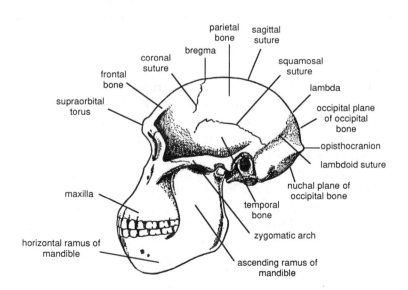

Figure 2.1. Reconstructed skull of *Australopithecus africanus* ("Mrs. Ples"), showing the principal anatomical parts or regions (redrawn after Le Gros Clark 1964: 130).

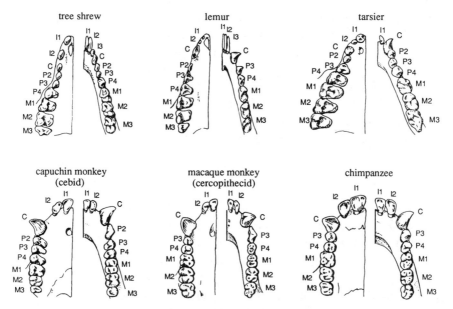

Figure 2.2. Right upper and lower dentitions of various primates (in each case, the upper is to the left and the lower is to the right) (redrawn after Schultz 1969: 102). The primitive mammalian dentition is thought to have comprised, on each side of each jaw, three incisors, one canine, four premolars, and three molars. In the course of evolution, all living primates have lost the first premolar (P1), while all catarrhine primates have also lost the second (P2). Both catarrhines and platyrrhines have lost the third incisor (I3), and the platyrrhines have either lost the third molar (M3) or retain it in reduced form, as in the capuchin monkey whose dentition is illustrated here.

types of permanent teeth—known, from front to back, as incisors, canines, premolars, and molars (abbreviated as I, C, P, and M, respectively). The juvenile or deciduous dentition contains only incisors, canines, and premolars (abbreviated as dI, dC, and dP, respectively).

On each side of each jaw, the earliest mammals had three permanent incisors, one canine, four premolars, and three molars. By convention, the incisors are called (from front to back) I1, I2, and I3; the premolars P1, P2, P3, P4; and the molars M1, M2, and M3. Most living mammals have lost teeth in the course of evolution, but the ones they retain are designated by the numbers of their primitive mammalian antecedents or homologues. Thus, humans and their closest living relatives within the Primates have lost the first two premolars of their remote ancestors, and the two premolars still found on each side of an adult human jaw are called P3 and P4. Figure 2.2 illustrates the adult dentitions of some representative primates, with the numeric designations of their teeth.

The description of teeth often requires an indication of their separate sections or orientation, and for this purpose four terms are in common use: *buccal*, to indicate the portion of a tooth nearer the cheek (it is replaced by *labial* for teeth that abut the lips); *lingual*, for the portion nearer the tongue; *mesial*, for the portion nearer the front of the mouth (or nearer the midline, depending on circumstances); and *distal* for the portion nearer the rear of the mouth (or further from the midline).

At fossil sites, postcranial bones are usually less common than teeth, because they tend to be softer and more fragile. They are often at least equally informative, however, revealing

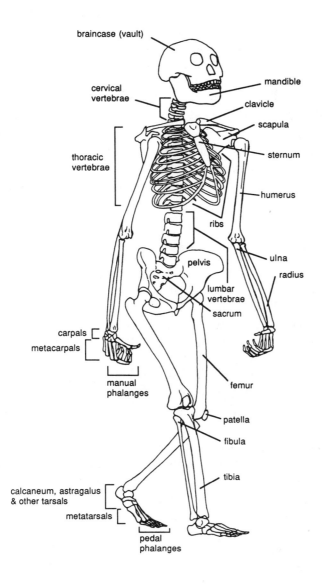

Figure 2.3. Reconstructed skeleton of *Australopithecus afarensis*, showing the names of the main skeletal parts.

behavioral aspects, such as locomotor pattern, that are much harder to detect from teeth or skulls. Since much evolution has involved specialization and divergence in locomotor modes and other postcranial behaviors, postcranial bones supplement and complement teeth and skulls for the reconstruction of broad evolutionary patterns and relationships. All mammals have fundamentally similar postcranial skeletons, inherited from their common ancestor, and primates are distinguished mainly by a tendency to retain specific parts that many other mammals have lost during their evolution. Figure 2.3 illustrates a hominid skeleton, with the names of the main postcranial bones attached.

Like teeth, individual postcranial bones can be described with respect to their orientation in a complete skeleton. The common terms are: *proximal,* for the portion of a bone closer to the skull; *distal,* for the portion further from the skull; *medial,* for the portion closer to the midline of the body; *lateral,* for the portion further from the midline; *anterior,* for the portion closer to the front of the body; and *posterior,* for the portion closer to the back. These terms can be combined, as, for example, in "anterior distal humerus" to mean the elbow end of the humerus when viewed from the front.

Where context requires, other anatomical parts and terms are introduced below, with illustrations to the extent this is practical.

Definition of the Primates

The order Primates was first defined by the eighteenth-century inventor of modern biological classification, Carolus Linnaeus, who wanted the name to indicate a natural primacy for the order, since it included people. Linnaeus's original definition has long since been discarded, but no universally accepted replacement has emerged. The problem is that, compared with the Cetacea (whales and dolphins), Rodentia (rodents), Carnivora (carnivores), Artiodactyla (even-toed ungulates), Perissodactyla (odd-toed ungulates), Proboscidea (elephants), and most of the other eighteen living orders of mammals, the Primates are difficult to characterize on the basis of unique traits they all share (Simpson 1955; Wible and Covert 1987). However, in distinction from other mammals, the living primates generally possess the following features (Le Gros Clark 1960; Cartmill 1975; R. D. Martin 1986):

1. A body structure preserving the clavicle (collarbone), pentadactyly (five digits on the end of each limb), and other

primitive characters that have commonly been lost or modified in other mammalian orders

2. Grasping extremities (hands and feet) with highly mobile digits, including a divergent hallux (big toe) and usually also an opposable pollex (thumb)

3. Flattened nails replacing primitive mammalian, sharp, bi-laterally compressed claws on the hallux and usually on other digits, associated with highly sensitive tactile pads on the tips of the digits opposite the nails. Besides enhancing the sense of touch, the pads bear friction ridges (dermato-glyphs) that facilitate grasping.

4. Orbits (eye sockets) that tend to be convergent, that is, closely spaced and facing in the same direction, producing substantial overlap between the fields of vision and thus a high degree of stereoscopic, three-dimensional vision (depth perception). Also, in primates, unlike the case in many other mammals, the orbits are completely surrounded by a bony ring (the post- or circumorbital bar), supplemented in higher primates by a bony wall (the postorbital plate or septum) separating the orbits from the skull behind. The high degree of stereoscopic vision reflected in the orbits is associated with a unique neural apparatus for processing visual signals and with enlargement of the visual centers in the occipital and temporal lobes of the brain.

5. A shortened muzzle or snout compared with that in most other mammals, generally associated with a more limited olfactory sense (sense of smell) and with a tendency for the olfactory bulbs in the brain to be relatively small

6. Reduction in the number of incisors and premolars compared with those in the earliest mammals and many living ones, combined with a relatively simple and primitive cusp pattern on the molars

7. A unique sulcal (fissure) pattern on the surface of the cerebral cortex of the brain. Also, relative to body size, primates tend to have larger brains than other mammals.

Classification of the Primates

Modern biological classification is hierarchical, closely following the scheme devised by Linnaeus in the mid-eighteenth century. The species is the most basic unit and is usually defined today as a group of organisms that look more or less alike and that can interbreed to produce fertile offspring. Groups of related species are combined into genera (singular genus), genera into families, families into superfamilies, super-families into infraorders, infraorders into suborders, suborders into orders, and so forth. A species or group of related species at any level in the hierarchy is known as a *taxon* plural *taxa*). Individual species and genera—for example, the species *Homo sapiens* and the genus *Homo*—are known as lower taxa. Groups of related species above the genus level—for example, the family Hominidae, the superfamily Hominoidea, the infraorder Catarrhini, or the suborder Anthropoidea—are known as higher taxa. Appendix 1 provides additional background for those unfamiliar with the basic system, together with information on how taxa are named.

In modern biological classification, the arrangement of species within genera and higher taxa is supposed to reflect their evolutionary relationships, such that species placed in the same higher-level taxon share a closer (more recent) common ancestor than ones placed in other taxa at the same level. Thus, the inclusion of modern people, *Homo sapiens*, and the (extinct) "robust" australopithecine, *Australopithecus robustus*, in the family Hominidae reflects the belief that they share a more recent common ancestor than either does with the orangutan, *Pongo pygmaeus*, which is placed in a separate family, the Pongidae. In turn, modern humans, the robust australopithecine, and the orangutan are placed in a common superfamily, the Hominoidea, on the basis of evidence that they are more closely related to each other than any are to the Old World (African and Eurasian) monkeys, which are placed in a separate superfamily, the Cercopithecoidea.

Until recently, zoological classification in general and primate classification in particular depended mainly on gross morphological similarities and differences among living species, on the assumption that detailed anatomical similarity implies close evolutionary relationship. However, especially since the 1960s, the results of gross anatomical studies have been significantly supplemented and altered by information on biomolecular differences and similarities. At the same time, new discoveries have shown that many fossil species cannot be readily accommodated in the same higher taxa as can living ones.

As a result of fresh biomolecular and fossil research, the long-standing, traditional classification of the Primates has been abandoned. No new consensus is in sight, but, at least for heuristic purposes, most authorities would probably accept the breakdown into suborders, infraorders, and superfamilies presented in Table 2.1. A major problem concerns the proper classification of the Tarsiiformes (tarsiers). They have been included here in the suborder Prosimii (lower primates), though many specialists believe they are more closely related

Table 2.1 Traditional Classification of the Primates,[a] Modified to Separate the Tarsioidea from the Omomyoidea and the Propliopithecoidea and Parapithecoidea from the Cercopithecoidea/Hominoidea and to Correct the Date for the Earliest Ceboidea

Classification	Known Temporal Distribution	Geographic Range
Order Primates		
Suborder Anthropoidea (or Simii)		
Infraorder Catarrhini		
Superfamily *Propliopithecoidea	Oligocene	Africa
Superfamily Hominoidea	Miocene to Recent	Africa, Europe, Asia (worldwide today)
Superfamily *Parapithecoidea	Oligocene	Africa
Superfamily Cercopithecoidea	Early Miocene to Recent	Africa, Europe, Asia
Infraorder Platyrrhini		
Superfamily Ceboidea	Late Oligocene to Recent	South America
Suborder Prosimii		
Infraorder Tarsiiformes		
Superfamily Tarsioidea	Recent	Asia
Superfamily *Omomyoidea	Eocene to Oligocene	Europe, North America
Infraorder Lemuriformes		
Superfamily *Adapoidea	Early Eocene to late Miocene	Africa, Europe, Asia, North America
Superfamily Lorisoidea	Early Miocene to Recent	Africa, Asia
Superfamily Lemuroidea	Pleistocene to Recent	Madagascar
Suborder Praesimii		
Infraorder Tupaiiformes		
Superfamily Tupaioidea	Late Miocene to Recent	Asia
Infraorder *Plesiadapiformes		
Superfamily *Plesiadapoidea	Middle Paleocene to late Eocene	North America, Europe
Superfamily *Microsyopoidea	Early Paleocene to late Eocene	North America, Europe

[a]After Gingerich 1984c, p. 60.
Note: Asterisks designate extinct taxa.

to creatures in the suborder Anthropoidea (higher primates). In the latter view, which is perhaps gaining momentum, the names Prosimii and Anthropoidea are commonly abandoned in favor of Strepsirhini (the Prosimii without the Tarsiiformes) and Haplorhini (the Anthropoidea with the Tarsiiformes). The issue involved here is addressed again below, where some of the evidence on both sides is introduced.

Another problem, which is more central to this book, concerns families, above all those within the Hominoidea. Traditionally, specialists have recognized three—the Hominidae, for people; the Pongidae, for the "great apes"; and the Hylobatidae, for the "lesser apes" (gibbons and siamangs). However, it is increasingly clear that most fossil apes cannot be comfortably included in the Pongidae or Hylobatidae and thus will have to be placed in their own extinct families. Perhaps

Figure 2.4.
Geographic distri-
bution of the liv-
ing nonhuman
primates (modi-
fied after Schultz
1969: 39, 41). The
distributions of
the Callithricidae
and Colobinae
completely over-
lap those of the
Cebidae and Cer-
copithecinae,
respectively, and
so have not been
shown indepen-
dently.

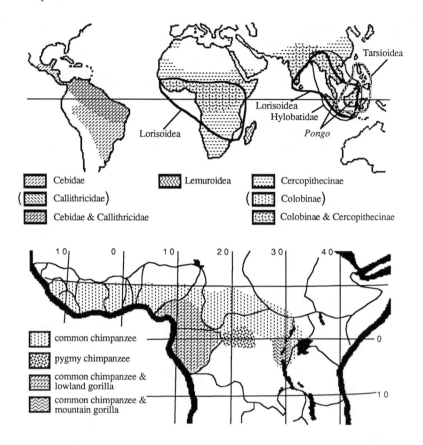

even more important, biomolecular studies show that the
living African pongids—the gorilla and the chimpanzee—are
actually more closely related to people than either is to the
living Asian pongid—the orangutan. Technically, this means
that the African apes should be lumped with people into the
Hominidae, leaving the orangutan as the sole living member of
the Pongidae. However, the use of the term Hominidae and its
anglicized form, hominid, to refer exclusively to people is so
entrenched that a change might seriously impede scientific
communication, and Hominidae continues to be used in its
traditional, restricted sense. It will be used this way here, to
refer only to people, living and extinct.

Fossil primates and thus primate (including human) evolution can be understood only by reference to the living
primates, and any overview of fossil forms must include a
survey of living ones. The following brief survey is designed
only to provide essential background information. It begins
with those taxa that are most closely related to people and
proceeds downward through Table 2.1 to progressively more
distant relatives, which it treats in progressively less detail. It

is based mainly on information in recent monographic summaries by Napier and Napier (1967), Schultz (1969), Richard (1985), and Tuttle (1986). It should be read in conjunction with Figure 2.4, which summarizes the geographic distribution of various living nonhuman primates and shows that they are all basically tropical or subtropical animals.

The Living Primates

The Anthropoidea

The living Anthropoidea or higher primates belong to three superfamilies—the Hominoidea, including people and apes; the Cercopithecoidea, including the African and Eurasian or Old World monkeys; and the Ceboidea, including the South and Central American or New World monkeys. Although the Old World monkeys superficially resemble the New World monkeys more than they resemble apes and people, numerous anatomical and biomolecular studies show that they are actually more closely related to apes and people. Among features that Old World monkeys, apes, and people share are a common dental formula, comprising, on each side of each jaw, two incisors, one canine, two premolars, and three molars; an external auditory meatus (bony tube) projecting outward from the middle ear; and complete closure of the bony wall behind the orbit. In New World monkeys, the dental formula involves the same number of incisors and canines, but there are three premolars on each side of each jaw and, in some species, only two molars. New World monkeys also lack the external auditory meatus, and their postorbital closure is less complete.

There are many other differences, among which the most commonly cited is perhaps the orientation of the nostrils (Fig. 2.5). In general, in the New World monkeys the nostrils tend to be widely spaced and to face sideways, while in the Old World monkeys and Hominoidea they tend to be closer together and to face more forward or downward. This has led to the use of the terms *platyrrhine* ("flat nosed") and *catarrhine* ("downward nosed") to distinguish the two groups. More formally, the Old World higher primates, living and extinct, are commonly placed in the infraorder Catarrhini, while the New World forms are assigned to the infraorder Platyrrhini.

Within the catarrhines, the apes are clearly closest to people. In distinction from catarrhine monkeys, apes and people share numerous gross anatomical features, such as a short, flat, broad trunk, a shoulder structure that permits free rotation of the arms around the shoulder joint, and the absence

New World Monkey
Cebus

Old World Monkey
Macaca

Figure 2.5. Representative New World and Old World monkeys, illustrating the sideways orientation of the nostrils typical in the New World monkeys and the downward or forward orientation typical in the Old World monkeys (redrawn after Schultz 1969: 22).

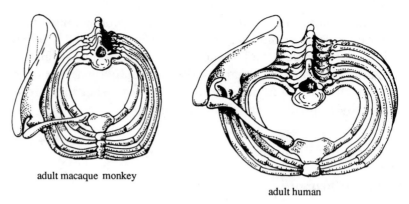

adult macaque monkey

adult human

Figure 2.6. Cephalic (= top-down) views of the rib cage and right shoulder girdle of an adult macaque monkey and of an adult human, showing the deeper, narrower chest of the monkey and the different arrangement of the scapula and clavicle, which limits the monkey's ability to rotate its arm around the shoulder (redrawn after Schultz 1969: 81).

of an external tail. The apes and people inherited their shared trunk form and shoulder structure from a common ancestor in which it was an adaptation for underbranch suspension and for forelimb-based tree climbing with the body in an orthograde (upright) position. Some apes use it in exactly this way today, while, for various reasons, other apes and people have largely abandoned living in the trees. In contrast to apes and people, but like most other land mammals, the catarrhine monkeys have long, narrow, deep trunks and a shoulder structure that restricts arm movement largely to a plane paralleling the body (Fig. 2.6). This reflects the retention in monkeys and most other mammals of primitive quadrupedalism. Unlike apes (and people), the monkeys are quadrupedal even in the trees, where they walk along the tops of branches. They commonly use their tails as balance organs to keep their center of gravity over a branch, and it is possible that the common ancestor of the living hominoids lost its tail when it evolved an under- (vs. over-) branch posture or locomotor mode.

As already noted, the apes have been traditionally divided between two families—the Pongidae and the Hylobatidae—both of which are readily distinguished from people (Hominidae) in numerous characters. Of these characters, perhaps the most notable are a relatively smaller brain, lower limbs that are not constructed for efficient bipedalism, and a dentition in which the anterior teeth (incisors and canines) are large relative to the posterior ones (premolars and molars). The canines are especially large and, unlike human ones, tend to wear along their mesial and distal (fore and rear) surfaces rather than from their tips. Associated with this, the lower third premolar (P$_3$) just behind the lower canine is sectorial (elongated mesiodistally and essentially unicuspid). When the mouth is shut, the mesial surface of the upper canine shears between the distal surface of the lower canine and the mesial edge of the sectorial premolar (Fig. 2.7). The lower canine fits in a gap (diastema) between the upper canine and the upper lateral incisor (I^2). In the Pongidae, the canines are not only large overall, but, in further distinction from people, males have much larger ones than females.

Both gross anatomical and biomolecular studies show that the Pongidae resemble people far more than the Hylobatidae do. There are three extant pongid genera—*Pan*, the chimpanzee; *Gorilla*, the gorilla; and *Pongo*, the orangutan. As indicated above, on biomolecular grounds the chimpanzee and the gorilla are more closely related to people than either is to the orangutan. Arguably, biomolecular similarities also imply that the chimpanzee is closer to people than it is to the gorilla (Sibley and Ahlquist 1984, 1987; M. J. Bishop and Friday 1986; Andrews and Martin 1987a). However, detailed anatomical similarities linked to a shared mode of locomotion ("knuckle walking," described below) and impressive similarities in dental enamel development and structure suggest that chimpanzees and gorillas may be more closely related to each other (Andrews 1986a, 1986b); if not, they have undergone a remarkable degree of parallel evolution.

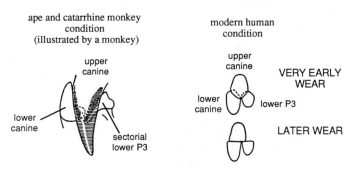

Figure 2.7. Occlusal relationship between the upper canine, lower canine, and lower third premolar (P$_3$) in a nonhuman catarrhine primate (*left*) and a human being (*right*) (early wear above, later wear below) (redrawn after Le Gros Clark 1964: 182). In catarrhine monkeys and apes, the upper canine is part of a shearing complex involving the lower canine and the elongated, unicuspid (sectorial or "cutting") lower third premolar. When the jaws close, the canines interlock and wear occurs mainly on their fore and rear surfaces. In people, the canines do not interlock and wear occurs primarily at the tips. In addition, in people, the lower third premolar is bicuspid and more rounded in outline.

The chimpanzee is a roughly human-sized ape in which adult males average approximately 50 kg and females about 40 kg. It is found in suitable forest and woodland habitats across equatorial Africa, from Gambia on the west to the shores of Lake Victoria and Lake Tanganyika on the east. A small variety—the pygmy chimpanzee or bonobo—lives in the forests of central Zaire and is usually regarded as a distinct species (*Pan paniscus*—vs. *P. troglodytes* for its larger, more common relative).

Chimpanzees feed mainly on ripe fruits, which they climb trees to obtain. They travel between trees mainly on the ground, where they assume a quadrupedal posture, with the feet flat and the hands curled, so that the weight of the forequarters rests on the knuckles (Fig. 2.8). They have a relatively fluid social organization in which each female tends to forage by herself through a relatively small territory and in which groups of related males patrol the territories of several females, fending off neighboring males. Beginning with Jane Goodall in Gombe National Park, western Tanzania, observers have now repeatedly documented two unexpected, humanlike aspects of chimpanzee behavior that do not characterize other free-ranging

Figure 2.8. Quadrupedal postures in (clockwise) an Old World monkey, a human, a chimpanzee, and a gorilla (redrawn after Schultz 1969: 55). Note that the monkey and human are standing with their palms flat, while the chimpanzee and gorilla are standing with their knuckles curled. Note also that the chimpanzee and gorilla have much longer arms relative to their legs.

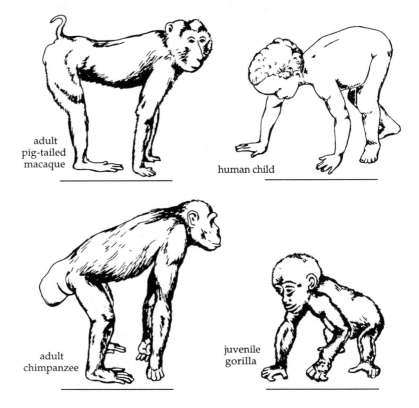

adult pig-tailed macaque

human child

adult chimpanzee

juvenile gorilla

apes: chimpanzees periodically kill and eat other animals, such as monkeys or small antelope with whom they share their range, and they make and use tools, including stones to crack nuts and branches modified to probe termite nests (the termites that cling to the invading probes are eaten). The implication may be that propensities to meat eating and tool use were already present in the apelike common ancestor of chimpanzees and people.

The gorilla is the largest living ape, with wild adult males averaging around 180 kg and females averaging perhaps 90 kg. Their distribution overlaps that of chimpanzees, but they are far less widespread and abundant, being concentrated in two distinct enclaves—a larger one in the lowland forests around the Gulf of Guinea in west Africa and a smaller one in the mountainous areas of eastern Zaire, western Uganda, and western Rwanda in east-central Africa. The two populations are known, respectively, as the lowland and mountain gorillas and are usually regarded as subspecies of a single species, *Gorilla gorilla*. Some authorities further divide the lowland gorilla into two subspecies (Groves 1986).

Adult gorillas rarely enter trees, except occasionally to sleep and, like chimpanzees, are quadrupedal knuckle walkers on the ground. They feed mostly on leaves which they find at ground level. Their social groups usually comprise a single dominant mature male, some subadult males, and several unrelated females with immature young. Males compete fiercely for females, but, by comparison with chimpanzees, gorillas enjoy more stable and coherent social groups, perhaps because the leaves that they eat are more evenly distributed than the ripe fruits that chimpanzees prefer.

The orangutan is slightly larger than the chimpanzee and is much more sexually dimorphic. Free-ranging adult males probably average around 65 kg, and females average perhaps 37 kg. There is only one living species, *Pongo pygmaeus*, narrowly restricted in historic times to the Southeast Asian islands of Borneo and Sumatra. Fossils show, however, that it was much more widespread in the Pleistocene, through mainland Southeast Asia to southern China. Unlike chimpanzees and gorillas, orangutans are almost exclusively arboreal, coming to the ground relatively rarely. They feed mainly on fruits, supplemented to some extent with insects. Unlike other apes, they have relatively thick dental enamel, perhaps because they eat a high proportion of hard-coated fruits. They are essentially solitary (nongregarious), and the only coherent social unit is a female and her dependent young.

As their vernacular name implies, the Hylobatidae or lesser apes are far smaller than the great apes, with adult body weights between 4 and 13 kg. Also unlike the great apes, they exhibit relatively little sexual dimorphism, and at a distance males and females can be difficult to distinguish. Historically, they were distributed from southern China through the forests of Southeast Asia, including the offshore islands of the Indonesian Archipelago where they overlapped the orangutan. As many as eight species are recognized, divided between two subgenera of the genus *Hylobates.* The single species placed in the subgenus *H. (Symphalangus)* comprises the largest of the lesser apes, often known as the siamangs. The several species placed in the subgenus *H. (Hylobates)* include a variety of smaller apes commonly known as the gibbons. However, like the term *lesser apes*, the term *gibbons* is often used to include both the gibbons and siamangs.

Gibbons and siamangs rarely leave the trees, where they use their powerful, elongated arms to propel (brachiate or "arm swing") themselves from branch to branch. The gibbons proper eat mainly ripe fruits, supplemented with insects and birds' eggs, while the siamangs concentrate more on fresh leaves and shoots, supplemented with fruits and insects. Unlike other apes, both gibbons and siamangs have a social organization involving male-female pairs mated for life. Each pair and its immature offspring inhabit a territory that it defends against neighboring paris. Adult males do not regularly compete for females, which perhaps explains the limited amount of sexual dimorphism.

The cercopithecoid or Old World monkeys are far more widespread and diverse than the apes, though this is a relatively recent development, and the fossil record shows that apes were once much more diverse than monkeys. Historically, cercopithecoid monkeys were found more or less throughout Africa and southern Asia, except in extreme deserts. During parts of the Pleistocene, they also occurred in Europe, and an isolated population persists today on the Rock of Gibraltar.

The taxonomy of the cercopithecoids is disputed, but there are perhaps seventy-five living species in seven genera usually divided into two subfamilies—the Cercopithecinae and the Colobinae—within a single family, the Cercopithecidae. The cercopithecines are the common monkeys of sub-Saharan Africa (*Papio, Theropithecus, Cercocebus, Erythrocebus,* and *Cercopithecus*), with only a single genus (*Macaca*) in north Africa and Eurasia. In contrast, the colobines are more abundant in Asia (*Nasalis, Presbytis, Pygathrix,* and *Rhino-*

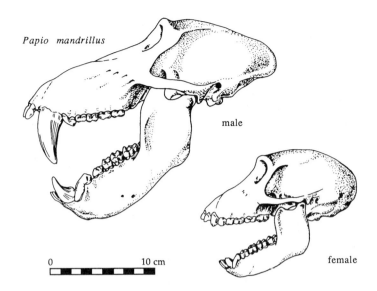

Papio mandrillus

male

female

0   10 cm

Figure 2.9. Skulls of male and female adult mandrills (*Papio mandrillus*), illustrating the extraordinary degree of sexual dimorphism, in both overall size and canine development, that characterizes many cercopithecoid monkeys (redrawn after Schultz 1969: 202).

pithecus), though one genus (*Colobus*) is restricted to Africa, where it is locally common.

The difference between cercopithecines and colobines is primarily dietary—whereas cercopithecines tend to focus on fruits (both ripe ones and ones not ripe enough for ape consumption), colobines emphasize leaves. To subsist on leaves, which are relatively high in nonnutritive bulk (fiber), colobines have evolved elaborate, sacculated stomachs. They also have relatively long, sharp crests on their molars, which are thus well suited for shearing leaves—unlike the shorter, blunter crests on cercopithecine molars, which are better suited for crushing fruits.

All cercopithecoids are almost exclusively quadrupedal in their movements and habitual postures, and none exhibit the suspensory capabilities or postures of the apes. Most species are primarily arboreal, but some appear equally at home on the ground, and a few cercopithecines are largely or wholly terrestrial. Both in the trees and on the ground, all species tend to move or rest on their palms; knuckle walking is unknown. Terrestrial species tend to be larger than arboreal ones, and body size varies from the highly arboreal, 1–2-kg talapoin monkey (*Cercopithecus talapoin*) to the largely or wholly terrestrial baboons (*Papio* and *Theropithecus*), in which adult males reach 40 kg. Most species are organized in mixed-sex troops, numerically dominated by females. Adult males compete vigorously for females, which perhaps explains why they usually have much larger bodies and canines (Fig. 2.9).

The ceboid or New World monkeys are commonly divided into two families—(1) the Callithricidae or marmosets and tamarins and (2) the Cebidae or New World monkeys in the narrow sense. The Cebidae are more diverse, with a minimum of eight genera (*Saimiri, Cebus, Aotus, Callicebus, Pithecia, Alouatta, Lagothrix,* and *Ateles*), versus five (*Callimico, Callithrix, Cebuella, Leontopithecus,* and *Saguinus*) for the marmosets and tamarins. On average, the marmosets and tamarins are much smaller than the cebids, and, in size and some morphological attributes, they are reminiscent of lower primates. Also, like many lower primates, they include species that feed primarily on insects or gum, versus the fruits or leaves favored by all other higher primates. Most cebids concentrate on fruits, variably supplemented with leaves and insects.

The ceboids are all strictly arboreal and basically quadrupedal, but, unlike any cercopithecoids, some cebid species have shoulder and arm specializations that allow them to hang from branches as do gibbons and siamangs. The same cebids also have a prehensile tail that functions as a fifth limb in under-branch suspension. Like the gibbons and siamangs, they occupy forests where they can feed near the ends of slender branches that could not be reached by strictly quadrupedal forms.

The Prosimii

The living prosimians or lower primates include three super-families in two infraorders—the Tarsioidea in the Tarsiiformes and the Lemuroidea and Lorisoidea in the Lemuriformes. A fourth superfamily—the Tupaioidea—is sometimes placed in the Lemuriformes, when it is included in the Primates at all. In accordance with the classification of Gingerich (1984c), it has been subsumed here in its own infraorder—the Tupaiiformes—within a third primate suborder, the Praesimii.

The Tarsioidea or tarsiers are tiny (100–200-g) animals represented by a single genus (*Tarsius*) with three or four species. They are restricted to Sumatra, the southern Philippines, and the Celebes Islands off Southeast Asia, where they inhabit bush and forest. In their activity pattern, they are almost totally nocturnal, and they have enormous eyes, for night vision. They feed primarily on insects, supplemented with small vertebrates and perhaps with vegetal material. They take their name from their highly elongated tarsus (ankle), which they use to propel themselves in long leaps between near-vertical branches to which they cling in an upright position. This distinctive mode of locomotion has been called "vertical clinging and leaping" and is aided by a long nonprehensile tail which can be shifted in midair to ensure an upright landing.

As already indicated, the taxonomic and phylogenetic status of the tarsiers has been a matter of intense disagreement (Aiello 1986; Schwartz and Tattersall 1987), because, unlike other so-called lower primates, they share some important features with the higher primates. Thus, like higher primates, they lack both a naked rhinarium (spot of hairless, glandular, and moist skin) around the nose and an accompanying cleft in the upper lip, while they have an advanced hemochorial type of placenta. Many authorities, such as Szalay and Delson (1979), believe that the features tarsiers share with higher primates, together with the arguable results of biomolecular studies (Baba et al. 1980; Sarich and Cronin 1980), indicate that tarsiers should be classified with the higher primates in a shared primate suborder, the Haplorhini, as distinct from the suborder Strepsirhini for the Lemuriformes.

The Lemuroidea or lemurs are a diverse group of monkey-size animals confined entirely to Madagascar and the nearby Comoro Islands. In keeping with their limited geographic distribution, they are often known as the Malagasy lemurs. The Lorisoidea or lorises are broadly similar creatures that live in Africa and southern Asia. In contrast to higher primates, both lemurs and lorises tend to have faces like those of other ("lower") mammals, with a relatively long snout, a rhinarium, a cleft upper lip bound down to the gum, relatively large and free-moving ears, and an immobile facial expression. Like the tarsiers, they are also distinguished from higher primates by the absence of a postorbital plate; more laterally placed incisors; relatively sharp, unmolarized premolars; and, in most species, by a mandible in which the two halves remain unfused at the symphysis (midline) (Fig. 2.10). Further like the tarsiers, they exhibit much less sexual dimorphism than do most higher primates. Among external features, those that link them most clearly to the higher primates are their hands and feet. These are functionally adapted for grasping, with mobile digits tipped by flattened nails, except for the second toe, which bears a claw used in grooming.

The lorises comprise two major types—the Lorisidae or lorises in the narrow sense and the Galagidae or galagos. The lorises are mainly Asian (nine species in four genera), but some occur in equatorial Africa (two species in two genera). The galagos (or "bush babies") (four to six species in one genus) live exclusively in Africa, where they have a broader distribution than the lorises, extending far to the south in savanna and bush. In sharp distinction from the exclusively diurnal catarrhine monkeys and apes with whom they share their range, the lorises and galagos are all nocturnal. The lorises proper tend to be slow-moving arboreal climbers, while the galagos are vertical clingers and leapers like the tarsiers. In both groups, some

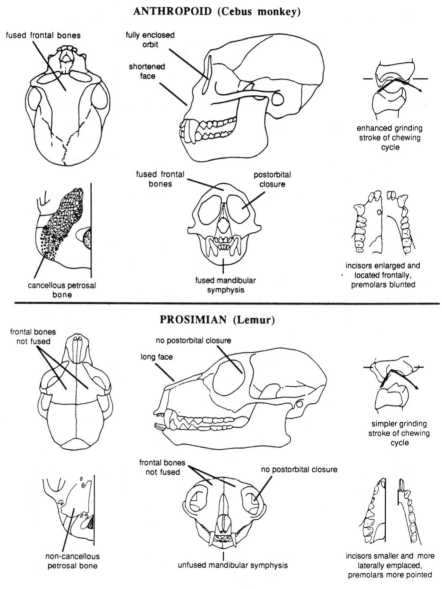

Figure 2.10. Comparison between the skulls of a Malagasy lemur (*Lemur*) and a New World monkey (*Cebus*) to illustrate some of the features that commonly distinguish prosimians from anthropoids (redrawn after Rosenberger (1986: Fig. 4.1).

species feed primarily on insects, while others focus more on gum or fruits.

The lemurs are a much more diverse group of animals; this is in keeping with their evolution in isolation from monkeys and apes, which never reached Madagascar. Presently, there are twenty-two lemur species in perhaps ten genera, and at least fourteen additional species and seven genera probably became extinct only within the past 1,500 years, following the initial human colonization of Madagascar (Dewar 1984; Burney and MacPhee 1988). Most lemurs are arboreal, but some are more terrestrial, and to judge from their morphology and large size, some recently extinct forms may have been totally terrestrial. In feeding, some species focus on insects or gum, while others emphasize fruit or leaves. They also vary greatly in locomotor pattern, preference for nighttime versus daytime activity, social behavior, and other features, and while many species recall lorises in their overall level of organization, others are more reminiscent of monkeys. The monkeys and monkeylike lemurs are an oft-cited example of parallel evolution, whereby creatures with similar genetic backgrounds exposed to similar environmental conditions have evolved in similar or parallel fashion.

The Praesimii

The only extant superfamily of Praesimii is the Tupaioidea or tree shrews, widely distributed throughout southern and Southeastern Asia, including the offshore islands. In total, there are perhaps five genera, all of which resemble true shrews (order Insectivora) or tropical squirrels (order Rodentia) in overall appearance. All are highly active diurnal inhabitants of forest undergrowth, where they feed mainly on insects, supplemented with vegetal material and small vertebrates.

Like the undoubted primates already discussed, tree shrews have a complete post- or circumorbital bar, and they possess a few minor features of the teeth, eye, brain, and limbs that suggest some relationship to lemurs. However, they lack the bony ear structure (petrosal bulla, discussed below) that all other primates share, their orbits are not notably convergent, they have claws on all the digits, and their hands and feet are not especially well adapted for grasping. These and other nonprimate features may be used to exclude them from the Primates; but even if they are not primates, they are clearly very close relatives, and it is from creatures perhaps broadly like them that the Primates first emerged. They are thus commonly included in discussions of primate evolution.

The Ancestors of the Primates

The great zoological class Mammalia, to which the Primates belong, evolved from mammal-like (therapsid) reptiles during the Triassic Period of the Mesozoic Era, roughly 200 million years ago (mya). The early mammals soon diversified into several different stocks, including one leading to the therians, a branch or subclass of the mammals that includes the marsupials, placentals (= eutherians), and some other, extinct infraclasses. The marsupial and placental lineages were distinct by the early Cretaceous period, about 120 mya. The earliest placentals were diverse but were all variously similar to shrews, moles, tenrecs, or other living creatures that have traditionally been lumped into the order Insectivora.

It is from Cretaceous insectivorelike creatures that all later placental orders sprung. A tiny (1.85-mm-long) lower molar from late-Cretaceous (70–80 million-year-old) deposits in eastern Montana suggests that the Primates were among the first to differentiate. The tooth has been assigned to the genus *Purgatorius*, which is better known from succeeding early-Paleocene deposits in the same region (Van Valen and Sloan 1965; Szalay and Delson 1979). The higher taxonomic assignment of *Purgatorius* is debatable, but, even if it represents only an insectivore in the narrow sense, a Cretaceous genesis for Primates is still suggested by their diversity and abundance in the middle and late Paleocene. Some background on the Cretaceous world is thus pertinent to an understanding of primate origins.

Cretaceous geography was very strange by modern standards (Fig. 2.11). In the very early Cretaceous, South America was still joined to Africa, but the two continents began to drift apart roughly 125 mya, and by 70–80 mya, when the Primates perhaps emerged, the two continents were separated by a narrow but expanding South Atlantic. South America and North America were separated throughout the Cretaceous, but North America was connected to Europe via Greenland. Also, more or less throughout, global climate was remarkably mild, and there was relatively little temperature difference between the equator and the poles. In both the Southern and Northern Hemispheres, temperate forests thrived at high latitudes.

Biologically, the Cretaceous is often known as the "age of dinosaurs," because they were its most conspicuous, if not its most numerous, vertebrates. However, it also witnessed important evolutionary developments and diversification in other kinds of reptiles, in birds, in early mammals, and, not least, in

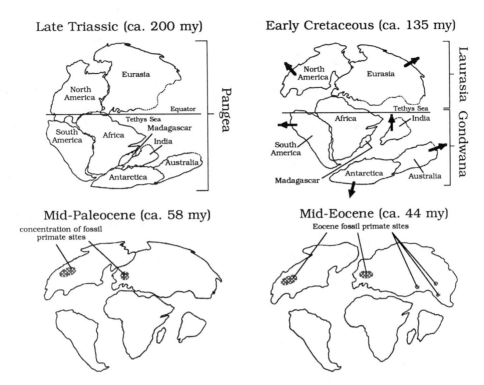

Figure 2.11. Changing positions of the continents from the late Triassic, roughly 200 mya, to the middle Eocene, roughly 44 mya (modeled after Zihlman 1982). In the late Triassic, the modern continents were essentially joined in a single supercontinent known to geophysicists as Pangaea. Subsequent fragmentation (drift) divided Pangaea into a northern-hemisphere landmass known as Laurasia and a southern-hemisphere mass known as Gondwana. Yet further fragmentation divided Laurasia and Gondwana into separate parts, foreshadowing the modern continents. The conjunction of North America and Eurasia in the Paleocene and early Eocene accounts for the close similarity of their early primate faunas, as discussed in the text.

plants. Prior to the Cretaceous, the principal plants were gymnosperms (nonflowering plants such as conifers, palms, and cycads). In the course of the Cretaceous, the angiosperms (flowering plants, including trees, grasses, herbs, etc.) underwent a major adaptive radiation and became the dominant plant forms. This opened up niches for creatures that could feed on the nectar, nuts, berries, or fruits that flowering plants produce. One result was an explosion in insects, particularly ones that promote plant pollination. Birds and mammals diversified to exploit the increase in both edible plant parts and insects. Virtually all Cretaceous mammals had sharp cutting ridges on their molar teeth that were well suited for slicing through insect tissue. The earliest primates probably continued to eat insects, but their molars had lower and less pointy cusps, blunter ridges, and other distinctive features that suggest they took more fruits, seeds, and other vegetal matter than did their more insectivorelike ancestors (Szalay 1972; K. D. Rose and Fleagle 1981).

In order to specialize dietarily on insects or fruit, early primates were probably at least partly arboreal, and it has long been assumed that a primeval adaptation to life in the trees accounts for such characteristic primate features as grasping extremities (hands and feet), relatively sophisticated vision, and a diminished sense of smell. Grasping extremities facili-

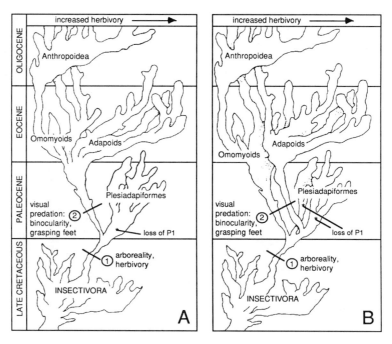

Figure 2.12. Two interpretations of early primate phylogeny (adapted from Cartmill 1975: Fig. 8). In both, the earliest primates diverged from their insectivore (or insectivorelike) ancestors by a greater emphasis on arboreality and herbivory. In both, the evolution of the omomyoids and adapoids (Eocene prosimians) involved a subsequent shift back toward insectivory, based now on binocular vision and grasping extremities. Finally in both, increasing emphasis on herbivory is a crucial element in the evolution of the anthropoids. The main difference between the two interpretations is that in A (*left*), the omomyoids and adapoids share a single Paleocene ancestor, while in B (*right*) they have separate ones in which binocular vision and grasping extremities evolved independently. On present evidence, A is more likely. Both interpretations suggest that the omomyoids and not the adapoids were ancestral to the anthropoids, but this issue remains debatable. The asterisks mark the loss of the first premolar (P1) in the plesiadapiforms. This is one of the specializations that makes them unlikely ancestors for Eocene prosimians.

tate movement over branches, and vision is more useful than smell for locating food or for moving safely and rapidly in a three-dimensional, arboreal habitat. However, squirrels provide abundant proof that typical primate grasping extremities and vision are not essential for active arboreal life, and the Cretaceous ancestors of the Primates probably had extremities and vision more like those of squirrels than like those of later primates. It is thus necessary to find a more specific explanation for the development of primate extremities and vision. Perhaps the most plausible alternative is that they facilitated visual predation on insects among slender branches in forest undergrowth (Cartmill 1974, 1975). This view is incorporated in Figure 2.12, which illustrates two similar but competing views of early primate evolution linked to major dietary shifts.

Paleocene Primates

After dominating the earth's fauna for 150 million years, the dinosaurs became extinct at the end of the Cretaceous. The reasons are hotly debated, but the resulting environmental opportunities help explain why mammals burgeoned in the Paleocene. Among the mammals that profited were the early Primates.

Geographically, the Paleocene differed little from the late Cretaceous: North and South America were separated by ocean, while North America and Europe were still connected (Fig. 2.11). Climate was generally very mild, and tropical or subtropical forests flourished in middle latitudes.

So far, Paleocene primate fossils are best known from western North America and western Europe, which were connected by a broad, forested land bridge stretching over what is now the subpolar ocean and islands in between. Environmental conditions were apparently very uniform across the land bridge, and the primate faunas on both sides were very similar (Gingerich 1973). They shared at least two genera, *Chiromyoides* and the better known *Plesiadapis*, which, with two or three Eocene genera and *Homo*, were the only primate genera to become naturally distributed in both the Old World and the New World. From the distributional evidence, it has been suggested that Primates originated in North America or perhaps on the combined North American/European landmass. However, among other continents, only South America can be reasonably ruled out, since its relatively well-known late-Cretaceous-to-Eocene fossil record contains no early Primates or likely primate ancestors. Asia has never been seriously suggested, but it has provided Paleocene Primates, albeit rare and only recently recognized (Szalay and Li 1986). No Paleocene primates have been reported from Africa, but appropriate terrestrial, fossiliferous localities are virtually unknown there (Cooke 1978; Savage and Russell 1983), and in their absence Africa's possible candidacy as the primate birthplace cannot be dismissed (Hoffstetter 1974; R. D. Martin 1986).

At most Euroamerican sites where Paleocene primates occur, they are very abundant and very diverse (Szalay 1972; Simons 1972; Szalay and Delson 1979; K. D. Rose and Fleagle 1981; Covert 1986), suggesting they were highly successful. There is incomplete agreement on which taxa are truly Primates, but many specialists would accept at least sixteen genera in four families: Paromomyidae, Picrodontidae, Carpolestidae, and Plesiadapidae. Sometimes, the Paleocene Microsyopidae and, less often, the Apatemyidae are also regarded as primates (Gingerich 1986b). Unfortunately, however, in spite of their abundance, most Paleocene primate fossils are

Figure 2.13. *Below:* Skulls of Paleocene and Eocene plesiadapiform primates, illustrating their large procumbent incisors, long snouts, and laterally placed (nonconvergent) orbits that were open to the sides. *Above left:* Skulls of Eocene and Oligocene prosimians, showing their smaller, less specialized incisor teeth, reduced snouts, and more convergent orbits that were totally surrounded by a post- or circumorbital bar. *Above right:* Artist's reconstruction of an Eocene lemuriform prosimian (the adapid *Notharctus*) (redrawn after K. D. Rose and Fleagle 1981).

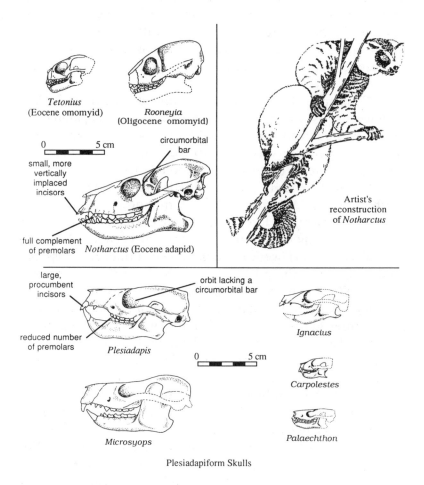

Plesiadapiform Skulls

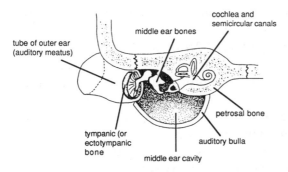

Figure 2.14. Diagrammatic section through the right ear region of a therian mammal, seen from the front (redrawn after Cartmill 1975: Fig. 3). In most nonprimates, the auditory bulla is either cartilaginous or formed by a separate entotympanic bone. In primates, it is formed by an extension of the petrosal. The primate character of the bulla has been used to assign the plesiadapiforms to the Primates. However, it is conceivable that the floor of the plesiadapiform bulla was formed by an entotympanic that fused seamlessly with the petrosal. This occurs in some nonprimates today. The true character of the plesiadapiform bulla could be determined only from fetuses, which are lacking in the fossil record.

fragmentary jaws and isolated teeth. Limb bones and skulls are much rarer, and the available skulls tend to be badly damaged.

The known Paleocene primates were all relatively small, from shrew size (100 g or less) to house-cat size (roughly 5,000 g). All were perhaps omnivorous to a degree, but differences in body size, dental morphology, or both suggest that dietarily some concentrated more on insects, others more on seeds or fruits (Covert 1986). Insofar as their skulls are known, mainly for *Plesiadapis*, they were very primitive, with large snouts and laterally placed (nonconvergent) orbits that indicate a well-developed sense of smell and limited overlap between the fields of vision (Fig. 2.13). The orbits were open to the sides, as in primitive mammals generally, rather than surrounded by a post) or circumorbital bar, as in later Primates. The postcranium was equally primitive, at least as deduced from *Plesiadapis* fossils. The elbows and ankles were relatively mobile and probably facilitated climbing (Szalay et al. 1975), but the digits retained sharp, compressed claws (vs. flattened nails) (Gingerich 1986b), and there is no evidence for the grasping hands and feet of later Primates.

In overall form, most Paleocene primates probably resembled modern tropical squirrels, and it may reasonably be asked why they should be classified as primates. The answer is in fact equivocal. Perhaps most important, their cheek teeth closely resembled those of later, undoubted primates. They may also have possessed a uniquely primate structure of the middle ear or auditory bulla (Fig. 2.14). In the earliest mammals, the floor of the bulla was cartilaginous, but in most later mammals, including Paleocene primates, it is usually formed from the union of two bones. One of these is the tympanic ring or ectotympanic bone across which the eardrum is stretched. In most mammals, the other is a special, separate entotympanic bone. In primates, however, the entotympanic bone is absent, and its place is taken by an extension of the petrosal bone that encloses the inner ear. The middle ear is floored either by the petrosal extension and the tympanic ring or by the petrosal alone, completely enclosing the tympanic ring.

In those Paleocene primates for which the middle ear is known, the floor has been diagnosed as petrosal (Szalay and Delson 1979), but it could in fact be made of an entotympanic bone that fused imperceptibly with the petrosal (MacPhee et al. 1983). Seamless fusion of the entotympanic and petrosal occurs in some extant nonprimates, and in these cases only fetal individuals show that the bulla is not truly petrosal. Since fetuses of Paleocene primates are unknown and unlikely to be found, the true character of the bulla is indeterminate, and this feature does not clearly link any Paleocene primates to later ones. Their primate status thus depends primarily on their cheek teeth and on the assumption that primates existed in the Paleocene and must be represented by those Paleocene mammals that are most like later, undoubted primates.

Curiously, in spite of their abundance and diversity, the presumed Euroamerican Paleocene primates provide few clues to the origins of later, Eocene-to-Recent forms. They are unlikely ancestors themselves, because they evolved dental specializations that later forms lack (Simons 1972; Cartmill 1974, 1975; K. D. Rose and Fleagle 1981). These specializations include large, procumbent central incisors, perhaps used to grasp food, and a reduced number of lateral incisors, anterior premolars, or both. Except for some basically Paleocene taxa that survived into the early Eocene before becoming extinct, Eocene primates tended to have smaller, more generalized incisors, and they commonly retained incisors or premolars lost in the Paleocene forms (Fig. 2.13). Among known Paleocene taxa, only the earliest, *Purgatorius*, was sufficiently generalized to be ancestral to Eocene-to-Recent forms, but there is no reason to suppose it evolved in their direction. More likely, it gave rise to later, more specialized Paleocene primates.

Because the Euroamerican Paleocene primates combined very primitive features with specializations lacking in all later primates, they are now commonly placed in their own infraorder, the Plesiadapiformes, named for *Plesiadapis*, the best-known genus (Simons 1972). None of the known Plesiadapiformes survived the Eocene, and their extinction was probably at least in part a result of unsuccessful competition with evolving rodents and more advanced primates. The origins of more advanced primates remain obscure, but sparse fossils of mid-Paleocene age from southern China suggest a possible Asian ancestry (Szalay and Li 1986). The geographic distribution of Oligocene-to-Recent prosimians makes an African origin at least equally plausible (Gingerich 1986a, 1986b), but Paleocene and Eocene fossils to support it are still lacking.

Eocene Primates

Climatically, the Eocene was mainly similar to the Paleocene. Subtropical forests covered much of the western United States and also western Europe, as far north as the modern English channel. As in the Paleocene, North and South America were separated by ocean, but in the early Eocene, perhaps about 50 mya, the previous land connection between North America and Europe was broken (Fig. 2.11).

Like Paleocene primate fossils, Eocene ones come mainly from western North America and western Europe. Some are also known from southern and eastern Asia (D. E. Russell and Gingerich 1987). They have yet to be found in Africa or South America, although it is possible that Primates had reached South America by the late Eocene, and they probably existed in Africa more or less throughout the Eocene. The problem in Africa is the rarity or absence of continental (vs. coastal or marine) fossil localities (Cooke, 1978; Savage and Russell 1983).

Aside from some specialized plesiadapiforms that survived into the Eocene before becoming extinct, most Eocene primates were broadly similar to living prosimians. On present knowledge, they were in fact "the first primates of modern aspect" (Simons 1972), and, if they were alive today, they would undoubtedly be called lemurs and tarsiers. Technically, they can be readily accommodated in the extant infraorders Lemuriformes and Tarsiiformes within the suborder Prosimii. Arguably, some may even be placed in extant prosimian superfamilies or families.

In the very early Eocene, the primitive lemuriform *Can-*

tius and tarsiiform *Teilhardina* appeared on both sides of the Euroamerican land bridge (Gingerich 1984b, 1984c). Their dental resemblances suggest a recently shared (?late-Paleocene) ancestry, perhaps in Asia (Szalay and Li 1986) or in Africa (Gingerich 1984c, 1986a). Whatever their origin, they became stem forms for separate Eocene prosimian radiations in Europe and North America when the land bridge linking these continents was severed. Specialists disagree on the precise taxonomy of later-Eocene prosimians, but minimally there were perhaps forty genera in two families (Simons 1972; Szalay and Delson 1979; Rose and Fleagle 1981; Covert 1986), and, like the plesiadapiforms before them, the Eocene prosimians tend to be very abundant at sites where they occur. Also like the plesiadapiforms, they are represented mainly by jaws and teeth, but there are more skulls and limb bones and even some nearly complete skeletons.

Differences in orbit size indicate that some Eocene prosimians were diurnal, while others were nocturnal like the living tarsier or the African galago. The Eocene lemuriforms tended to be larger than their tarsiiform contemporaries, and in overall body size some approached the larger historic Malagasy lemurs. Their relatively large size, combined with the morphology of their cheek teeth and jaws, suggests that most species fed mainly on fruits or leaves (Covert 1986). In contrast, the smaller size of the Eocene tarsiiforms, together with their tooth and jaw morphology, implies that they focused more on insects.

Unlike *Plesiadapis* and probably other plesiadapiforms, those Eocene prosimians for which appropriate postcranial bones are known had hands and feet that were well adapted for grasping. The digits were long and mobile, with nails instead of claws on most, if not all, digits. The postcranial bones of the Eocene lemuriforms indicate they were arboreal quadrupeds remarkably similar, in body form and function, to living lemurs and lorises (Fig. 2.13) (K. D. Rose and Walker 1985; Covert 1986; Rasmussen 1986). In contrast, the Eocene tarsiiforms had elongated tarsal bones that probably facilitated tarsierlike vertical clinging and leaping (Gingerich 1984a; Covert 1986).

The relatively numerous Eocene prosimian skulls suggest evolutionary advances comparable to those in the hands and feet. In contrast to the plesiadapiforms, in Eocene prosimians the orbits were completely surrounded by a post- or circumorbital bar, as in later Primates (Fig. 2.13). Probably even more significant, by comparison with plesiadapiform skulls, Eocene prosimian ones indicate less reliance on the sense of smell and more on vision. The snout was reduced, and the orbits faced more forward and less laterally, so that there was greater overlap between the fields of vision. Endocasts show that Eocene prosimians had correspondingly smaller olfactory bulbs and an expanded visual cortex (larger occipital and temporal lobes) (Radinsky 1975). More generally, after correction is made for body size, they had much larger brains than the plesiadapiforms did, though, by the same measure, most probably had smaller brains than modern prosimians do (Radinsky 1977).

The known Eocene tarsiiforms and lemuriforms may not include, respectively, the ancestors of the living tarsier and living Malagasy lemurs, but they were certainly close to them. With living lemurs, the Eocene ones share a unique, derived ear structure—the tympanic ring is entirely enclosed within the bulla, instead of framing the opening to the outer ear as it does in other primates. Also, at least some Eocene lemurs closely resembled living lemurs and lorises in derived features of the wrist and ankle (Beard et al. 1988; R. D. Martin 1988). The overall degree of similarity has even led some authorities to place the Eocene lemurs in the extant superfamily Lemuroidea. However, the known Eocene lemurs were more primitive than living ones in several important characters, such as the retention of four premolars on each side of each jaw (vs. three in living lemurs) and the possession of generalized lower incisors and canines (vs. the protruding, elongated ones that form a specialized dental comb in living forms). Thus, the Eocene lemurs are probably best assigned to a separate (extinct) superfamily, the Adapoidea (Hoffstetter 1974; Gingerich and Schoeninger 1977). However, it is possible that a so far unknown African adapoid, transported to Madagascar accidentally on a natural raft of vegetation sometime in the Eocene, was the direct ancestor of the Malagasy lemurs. The same or a similar adapoid may also have been ancestral to the modern African and Asian lorises (Gingerich and Schoeninger 1977).

Further, an adapoid may be ancestral to the higher primates (Gingerich 1980), though this role is more commonly assigned to one of the Eocene tarsiiforms in the superfamily Omomyoidea (Hoffstetter 1974; Szalay and Delson 1979; Delson and Rosenberger 1980; McKenna 1980; Rosenberger and Szalay 1980) (Figs. 2.12B). Omomyoid teeth and skulls are generally similar to anthropoid ones in some important respects, and biochemical and morphological similarities suggesting a link between living tarsiers and anthropoids have been noted above. However, not all biochemical studies agree that anthropoids are closer to tarsiers than to lemurs (Sarich

and Cronin 1980), and the morphological resemblances between the tarsier and anthropoids could be parallelisms (analogies). The teeth of some adapoids also generally resemble
those of anthropoids, so much so that specialists disagree about
the anthropoid—versus advanced-adapoid—identification of
some late-Eocene and early-Oligocene dentitions from Asia and
Africa.

In addition, adapoids share with early anthropoids several
features that neither taxon shares with omomyoids (Gingerich
and Schoeninger 1977; Gingerich 1980; Rasmussen 1986).
These features include a relatively long snout with near-
parallel tooth rows (vs. a short snout and more divergent teeth
rows in omomyoids); symphyseal fusion of the two halves of
the mandible in several adapoids and all anthropoids but in no
omomyoids; short, vertically placed, spatulate incisors in
adapoids and anthropoids (vs. more procumbent, more sharply
pointed ones in omomyoids); large, interlocking, sexually
dimorphic canines in some adapoids and in anthropoids (vs.
small, nondimorphic, premolarlike canines in omomyoids);
and the lack of an external auditory meatus (tubular ectotympanic) in adapoids and early anthropoids (vs. its presence in omomyoids).

The controversy concerning an omomyoid—versus
adapoid —ancestry for the anthropoids illustrates a common
problem in the construction of phylogenetic (evolutionary)
trees—disagreement as to which similarities and differences
among taxa are truly relevant to the latters' evolutionary
relationships and, especially, uncertainty among specialists as
to whether shared specializations genuinely reflect close relationship (recent common descent). As indicated above the
alternative possibility is that the specializations evolved independently (in parallel or convergently) in distantly related
lineages that were adapting to similar conditions. Often, there
is the additional problem of deciding whether shared similarities are actually unique specializations inherited from a recent
common ancestor or primitive retentions from a much more
distant one. Like other phylogenetic controversies, the one
surrounding omomyoids versus adapoids can be resolved only
by a denser, more complete fossil record.

Whatever the outcome, a late-Eocene origin for the anthropoids is suggested by their abundance and diversity in the
succeeding Oligocene and, more directly, by some fragmentary
jaws from central Burma, associated with a fauna that is
probably about 44–40 million years old (late Eocene) (Ba Maw
et al. 1979; Ciochon 1985; Ciochon et al. 1985). At least two
possible anthropoid species are represented—*Amphipithecus*

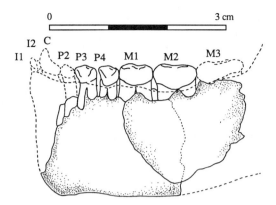

Figure 2.15. Partially reconstructed mandible of *Amphipithecus mogaungensis* (redrawn after Ciochon 1985: 30). Dated to about 40 mya, it is arguably the oldest higher-primate fossil yet found. A higher-(vs. lower-)primate assignment is suggested by several features, including the great depth of the jaw relative to the molar crown height and the near equal depth of the jaw from back to front. Typically, in lower primates, the mandible is shallower overall, and it becomes especially shallow toward the front.

mogaungensis and *Pondaungia cotteri*. *A. mogaungensis*, which was apparently about gibbon size, is somewhat better known. It differed from prosimians and resembled anthropoids in several ways (Ciochon et al. 1985):

1. Its mandible was deep compared with its molar crown height, and the depth remained nearly the same all along the jaw (Fig. 2.15). In prosimians, the mandible is shallower overall, and it becomes especially shallow toward the front.
2. The second molar was parallel sided, as in anthropoids, and did not narrow toward the front, as in prosimians.
3. The two halves of its mandible were fused at the symphysis, as in all known anthropoids, and the symphysis was reinforced internally by two distinct horizontal shelves, the inferior and superior transverse tori. Those prosimians that have fused symphyses (some adapoids and Malagasy lemurs) have only an inferior transverse torus.

In addition, the molar crowns of *Amphipithecus mogaungensis* were relatively flat, with low, blunt cusps, suggesting that it fed less on insects and more on leaves and fruit than prosimians commonly do. In this respect also, it may have been more like known anthropoids.

Additional, more complete fossils may show that *Amphipithecus mogaungensis* and *Pondaugia cotteri* were advanced adapoids rather than primitive anthropoids (Gingerich 1980).

Even in this case, however, they could still be close to the ancestry of later anthropoids, and, on present evidence, at least *A. mogaungensis* was generalized enough to be ancestral to both New World anthropoids (with which it shared three premolars on each side of the mandible) and Old World ones (which retain only two).

Oligocene Primates

In the very late Eocene or early Oligocene, prosimians disappeared from Europe, and by the very late Oligocene or early Miocene, they were also gone from North America. The Oligocene prosimians of North America were all omomyoids, and to judge by their limited numbers and diversity, they were much less successful than their Eocene forbears. Adapoids survived to the late Miocene (until approximately 9 mya) in southern Asia (Gingerich and Sahni 1984), and evolution toward living prosimians obviously continued during and after the Oligocene in Africa, Asia, or both. However, except in Madagascar, beginning with the Oligocene the numbers and diversity of prosimians were greatly reduced, and they became largely confined to nocturnal niches.

In both Europe and North America, the Oligocene extinction of the prosimians coincides broadly with a trend toward cooler, drier climatic conditions, which eventually eliminated suitable prosimian habitat (subtropical forest) from middle latitudes. Suitable habitat persisted in Africa and Asia, but here the prosimians suffered from the emergence and subsequent success of anthropoids (higher primates) in diurnal forest niches. Fossiliferous deposits in the Fayum depression of Egypt, about 100 km southwest of Cairo, indicate that the catarrhines had already radiated extensively by the early Oligocene, roughly 35 mya. By the late Oligocene, roughly 25 mya, the platyrrhines were also established in South America.

African Oligocene Anthropoids

The Fayum primates come from various levels of the Jebel Qatrani Formation, which is bracketed between about 35 mya and 31 mya by radiopotassium dates on an overlying basalt, by estimated sedimentation rates, and by faunal correlations with Eurasia (Simons 1967, 1984; Fleagle et al. 1986a, 1986b). Plant and animal fossils, together with sedimentologic/geomorphologic analyses, indicate that the Jebel Qatrani sediments accumulated under warm, moist, relatively nonseasonal climatic conditions on a heavily vegetated, swampy plain crossed by large, meandering streams (Bown et al. 1982; Olson and Rasmussen 1986). The streams were flanked by large trees, whose silicified trunks are preserved in the deposits.

The Fayum is the only published source of Oligocene primates in the entire Old World. Fortunately, however, it is very rich, and it demonstrates not only the early diversification of the anthropoids but also the corresponding decline of the prosimians. These are represented by only four fossils versus about one thousand for the anthropoids and also by a smaller number of taxa, comprising two tarsiiforms and a possible adapoid or lorisoid (Fleagle 1986b; Fleagle et al. 1986b; Simons et al. 1986, 1987).

As currently described (Fleagle and Kay 1985; Fleagle 1986b; Fleagle et al. 1986b; Simons et al. 1987), the Fayum anthropoids comprise seven genera: *Qatrania, Apidium, Parapithecus, Simonsius* (= *Parapithecus grangeri*), *Propliopithecus* (including "*Moeripithecus*" and "*Aeolopithecus*"), *Aegyptopithecus,* and *Oligopithecus. Propliopithecus* is represented by four species, *Apidium* by two, and the remaining genera by one each, for a total of eleven species. Not all were coeval, and some may have evolved from others. Probably most important, an early species of *Propliopithecus* could have been ancestral both to later species of *Propliopithecus* and to *Aegyptopithecus.*

Fossil teeth and jaws predominate for all taxa, but there are postcranial bones for *Apidium, Simonsius, Propliopithecus,* and *Aegyptopithecus,* while *Apidium, Simonsius,* and above all, *Aegytopithecus* are represented by partial skulls, the oldest known for any anthropoids. By analogy with living primates, the teeth of the Fayum species can be used to infer their body size and ecology (Fleagle 1978; Kay and Simons 1980; Fleagle and Kay 1985). The Fayum taxa were all at or below the low end of the modern anthropoid range, varying from mouse size (300 g) (*Qatrania*) to very small monkey size (900–1,700 g) (*Apidium, Parapithecus,* and *Oligopithecus*) to medium monkey size (3,000–4,000 g) (*Simonsius* and *Propliopithecus*) to perhaps gibbon size (5,900 g) (*Aegyptopithecus*). However, except for *Qatrania,* they were all larger than living (mainly prosimian) primates that are primarily insectivorous, and they fit comfortably within the range of those that are mainly fruit eaters (frugivores) or leaf eaters (folivores). To judge by their relatively short molar shearing crests (shorter than those of living folivores but comparable to those of living frugivores), most of the Fayum taxa, including *Qatrania,* were probably frugivorous. Frugivory in *Aegyptopithecus* is further implied by its relatively large incisors. Only *Simonsius* possessed sufficient molar shearing to suggest some folivory.

By analogy with living primates of similar size, most, if not all, the Fayum species were probably arboreal. The morphology of the available limb bones implies they were either arboreal quadrupeds/climbers (*Propliopithecus* and *Aegyptopithecus*) or arboreal quadrupeds/leapers (*Apidium*) (Gebo and Simons 1987). There is no evidence for the suspensory abilities of the living apes. The available faces (from *Apidium*, *Simonsius*, and *Aegyptopithecus*) all have small orbits, indicating an essentially diurnal activity pattern, as in all known later Old World anthropoids (Fleagle and Kay 1985).

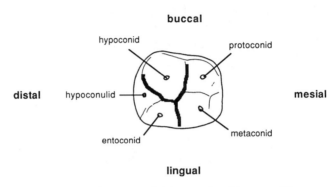

The Y-5 pattern on a left lower molar of *Aegyptopithecus*.

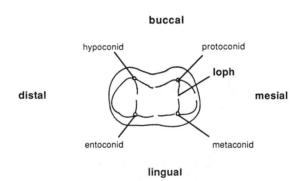

Bilophodont pattern on a left lower molar of *Colobus*.

Figure 2.16. Lower molars of the early-Oligocene catarrhine, *Aegyptopithecus*, and of the extant leaf-eating monkey, *Colobus* (adapted from Butler 1986: Figs. 2, 8). The monkey molar exhibits the typical bilophodonty of all cercopithecoids, with two pairs of cusps linked by shearing crests (lophs). The *Aegyptopithecus* molar shows a pattern of five distinct cusps separated by a Y-shaped fissure system that is broadly characteristic of all Miocene-to-Recent hominoids. The Y-5 pattern is believed to be primitive in catarrhines, and the bilophodont condition probably evolved from it.

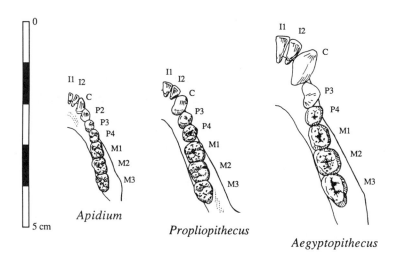

Figure 2.17. Mandibles of *Apidium*, *Propliopithecus*, and *Aegyptopithecus* (partially restored) (based mainly on photos in Szalay and Delson 1979: Fig. 156; Fleagle and Kay 1983: Figs. 4, 9, 10). Note the presence of three premolars on each side of the jaw in *Apidium*, versus two in *Propliopithecus* and *Aegyptopithecus*. The mandibles and teeth of *Propliopithecus* and *Aegyptopithecus* are strikingly apelike in overall form and differ from each other only in size and some basic proportions, particularly in the relatively larger size of M_1 in *Propliopithecus*. On mandibular and dental morphology, either *Aegyptopithecus* or *Propliopithecus* could be ancestral to all later catarrhines.

In earlier descriptions of the Fayum taxa, they were divided into probable or certain early hominoids (*Oligopithecus*, *Propliopithecus*, and *Aegyptopithecus*) and possible early cercopithecoids (*Apidium* and *Parapithecus*) (Simons 1967, 1972). This interpretation is still arguable (Gebo and Simons 1987; Simons 1987), but a more recent, more conservative view is that they are all simply early anthropoids, antedating the divergence between hominoids and cercopithecoids (Kay et al. 1981; Fleagle and Kay 1983; Simons 1984; Andrews 1985a; Fleagle 1986b; Fleagle et al. 1986b; Harrison 1987).

The question of their phylogenetic relationships to hominoids and cercopithecoids hinges largely on their teeth. The molars of undoubted cercopithecoids are uniquely derived in form, with two pairs of relatively high cusps, each pair linked buccolingually by a crest or loph (Fig. 2.16). The full pattern is usually called bilophodont, and *Apidium*, *Parapithecus*, and especially *Simonsius* show a configuration that might anticipate it. However, other dental features suggest they were only distantly related to cercopithecoids or to any other catarrhines. All three genera retained three premolars on each side of each jaw, versus two in cercopithecoids and all known hominoids, including *Propliopithecus* and *Aegyptopithecus*. If they stand near the cercopithecoid stem, it follows that the reduced number of premolars that cercopithecoids and hominoids share (two on each side of each jaw) is a result of convergence (parallel evolution) rather than of shared (common) descent. This seems unlikely. Furthermore, *Parapithecus* and *Simonsius* are clearly excluded from cercopithecoid origins by the loss of permanent lower incisors, which were reduced to one on each side of the jaw in *Parapithecus* and to none in *Simonsius* (the canines met at the midline of the symphysis in a derived condition unique among the anthropoids) (Kay and Simons 1983; Simons 1986). Only *Apidium* retained the right number of incisors (two in each quadrant; Fig. 2.17) to be near the ancestry of the cercopithecoids.

The relatively well-known dentitions of *Propliopithecus* and *Aegyptopithecus* exhibit no uniquely derived cercopithecoid features, and in virtually all important respects they recall hominoid teeth far more than they do cercopithecoid ones. Especially notable are the crowns of the lower molars which resemble those of all Miocene-to-Recent hominoids, with three rounded cusps on the lingual side and two slightly larger, shorter ones on the buccal side, separated by a Y-shaped groove or fissure (Fig. 2.16). It is conceivable, however, that this represents the primitive catarrhine condition and that cercopithecoid bilophodonty evolved from it. The earliest known, unquestionable cercopithecoid molars, from the early Miocene of eastern and northern Africa, exhibit a morphology, including a fifth cusp and incomplete lophs, that is plausibly derived from the molar morphology of *Propliopithecus* and *Aegytopithecus* (Delson 1979). By comparison with the round-cusped early-catarrhine/hominoid type of molar which is well suited for crushing fruits, bilophodont molars are better suited for shearing leaves, and the development of bilophodonty may signal a dietary shift from frugivory toward folivory among the earliest cercopithecoids (Andrews 1981c; Temerin and Cant 1983).

Much new fossil evidence will probably be necessary to resolve the relationships of the Fayum catarrhines to later ones, but for the moment *Qatrania*, *Apidium*, *Parapithecus*, and *Simonsius* are probably best placed in their own extinct superfamily, the Parapithecoidea. A parapithecoid may have been ancestral to the cercopithecoids, but at present it seems more likely that the parapithecoids were a specialized group of early anthropoids with no special link to any later catarrhines (Harrison 1987). Conceivably, they represent a totally separate, extinct anthropoid branch, parallel to the catarrhines and platyrrhines (Fleagle and Kay 1987).

Propliopithecus and *Aegyptopithecus* may also be placed in an extinct superfamily, the Propliopithecoidea, which perhaps includes the ancestors of both hominoids and cercopithecoids. Taxonomically, *Oligopithecus* remains the most problematic genus, partly because it is known from only a single mandible fragment and an isolated lower molar and partly because it exhibits a unique combination of features. It had only two premolars, like *Aegyptopithecus*, *Propliopithecus*, and all other known Miocene-to-Recent catarrhines, but it retained a more primitive molar occlusal morphology. It could represent a distinctive early anthropoid group, perhaps ancestral to all others in the Fayum (Kay et al. 1981). Alternatively, it could even be an advanced adapoid (Gingerich 1977, 1980).

Taxonomic and phylogenetic considerations aside, the relatively abundant jaws, limb bones, and partial skulls of *Aegyptopithecus* exhibit a remarkable mix of advanced and primitive features that could never have been predicted beforehand (Kay et al. 1981; Simons 1987). The most obvious advanced features are in the teeth, which were strikingly apelike, even including substantial sexual dimorphism in the size of the canines and lower anterior premolars. Other significant, typically anthropoid, derived features include fusion of the two halves of the mandible at the symphysis, which was buttressed internally by both inferior and superior transverse tori; olfactory bulbs that were significantly smaller and a visual cortex that was significantly larger than those in most prosimians (Radinsky 1977); and cuplike orbits that, unlike prosimian ones, were closed off from the skull behind by a postorbital plate or septum. This was somewhat less complete than in extant catarrhines, resembling the more primitive condition retained in platyrrhines. Arguably, it developed as a structural response to static stresses created in the skull when the anterior teeth were used to open hard-coated fruits or large nuts (Rosenberger 1986). The same or similar stresses could explain the fusion and internal buttressing of the mandibular symphysis.

Among strikingly primitive skull characters, *Aegyptopithecus* had a snout that was somewhat variable in size but that was always longer and more protruding than in later anthropoids (Fig. 2.18); a brain that was bigger for body size than that in prosimians but that was still below the lower limit for other anthropoids; more extensive postorbital constriction than in any other known anthropoid, recalling the condition in some Eocene adapoids; orbits that faced more laterally than in other known anthropoids; and a bony ear that lacked an external auditory meatus (tubular extension of the ectotympanic bone).

The best-known postcranial bone of *Aegyptopithecus*, the humerus, also exhibits manifestly primitive features, including an entepicondylar foramen at the distal end (Fig. 2.19). This occurs in prosimians and some platyrrhine monkeys but not in extant cercopithecoids or hominoids. The known postcranial bones show no specializations for suspensory postures or locomotion but instead suggest that *Aegyptopithecus* was a

Figure 2.18. *Top:* Facial and lateral views of an *Aegyptopithecus* skull (drawing from photos in Simons [1967]). The mandible has been partially reconstructed from pieces that were not directly associated with the skull. *Bottom:* Lateral view of the same skull, compared with those of extant catarrhines of roughly similar size (redrawn after Bown et al. 1982: Fig. 2). Note that *Aegyptopithecus* had a significantly longer snout, more laterally placed orbits, and a braincase that was absolutely and relatively smaller than that in the other catarrhines.

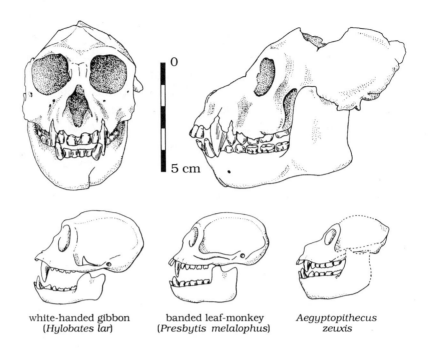

0

5 cm

white-handed gibbon
(*Hylobates lar*)

banded leaf-monkey
(*Presbytis melalophus*)

*Aegyptopithecus
zeuxis*

slow-moving, arboreal quadruped broadly similar to many living monkeys (Fleagle, in Bown et al. 1982; Fleagle 1983). Also like them, it may have had a tail. On present evidence, in the postcranium as in the skull, *Aegyptopithecus* was sufficiently primitive to be near the ancestry of both monkeys and apes.

The postcranium of *Propliopithecus* is more poorly known, but the only obvious difference from *Aegyptopithecus* is smaller size. *Propliopithecus* also had primitively apelike teeth and jaws, which differed from those of *Aegyptopithecus* mainly in the proportions of the molars (Kay et al. 1981). In *Propliopithecus* the first molar, M_1, and the second molar, M_2, were about the same size, while in *Aegyptopithecus* M_1 was much smaller than M_2 (Fig. 2.17). In this important respect and some others (Simons 1985), *Aegyptopithecus* was more like Miocene-to-Recent hominoids, for which it is therefore a more likely ancestor than is *Propliopithecus*.

If *Aegyptopithecus* and *Propliopithecus* had been represented only by postcranial bones or skulls without teeth, they might have been identified as monkeys (cercopithecoids). When their postcranial bones, skulls, and teeth are considered together, the conclusion is more complex. Whether *Aegyptopithecus* and *Propliopithecus* antedate or postdate the hominoid-cercopithecoid split, together with early-Miocene fossils discussed below they suggest the split resulted from divergent dietary adaptations (Andrews 1981a; Temerin and

Cant 1983)—not from locomotor ones, as the contrasts between living monkeys and apes might imply.

South American Oligocene Anthropoids

The oldest known anthropoid fossils from South America are two maxillary and two mandibular fragments, possibly from a single individual, assigned to the species *Branisella boliviana* (Hoffstetter 1969, 1974; Wolff 1984). They come from the Salla Beds of northern Bolivia, which were originally thought to date from the early Oligocene, that is, broadly the same time as the Jebel Qatrani Formation. However, a radiopotassium date on an

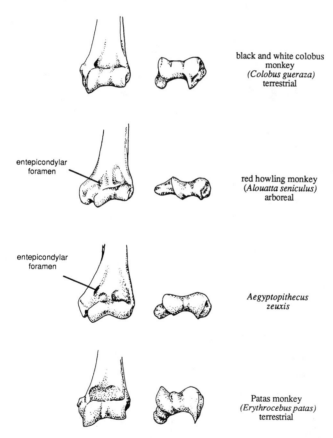

Figure 2.19. Anterior and distal views of the distal left humerus in a black-and-white colobus monkey, a red howling monkey, the primitive Fayum catarrhine *Aegyptopithecus*, and a patas monkey (redrawn after Bown et al. 1982: Fig. 3). Note that like all extant catarrhines, the colobus and patas monkeys lack an entepicondylar foramen, which does occur in some platyrrhines and in *Aegyptopithecus*. Note also that in basic distal humerus structure *Aegyptopithecus* was more like the colobus and howling monkeys, which are arboreal, than like the patas monkey, which is terrestrial.

underlying basalt now shows that the Salla Beds postdate 26 mya, and the age of *Branisella* is now estimated to be about 25 mya, corresponding to the very late Oligocene (MacFadden 1985; MacFadden et al. 1985). In its greatly reduced M^3 and other dental features, *Branisella* clearly anticipates extant platyrrhine (ceboid) monkeys, and more abundant fossils from localities in Argentina and Colombia show that platyrrhine monkeys remarkably similar to extant genera were already established by the early-to-middle Miocene, roughly 19–16 mya (Gingerich 1980; Hoffstetter 1980; Fleagle 1986a; Kay et al. 1987).

Since the early-Tertiary mammals of South America included no primates or likely primate ancestors (McKenna 1980), the ancestors of the platyrrhine monkeys almost certainly evolved on another continent and migrated to South America, probably sometime between the late Eocene and the late Oligocene. As the home continent, some authorities have favored North America or Africa or Asia via North America (Gingerich and Schoeninger 1977; Ciochon 1985; Rosenberger 1986), while others have preferred Asia via Africa or Africa directly (Ciochon and Chiarelli 1980; Hoffstetter 1974, 1980). Since South America was certainly an island continent from the middle Cretaceous to the Pliocene (Fig. 2.11), the dispute depends partly on whether it was more accessible from North America or from Africa. A second vital question concerns the nature of the relationships between platyrrhines and other primates.

Wherever the platyrrhines originated, their crossing to South America was certainly accidental, probably being due to animals stranded on rafts of vegetation washed out to sea. The channels that separated South America from North America and Africa were both hundreds of kilometers wide, but both probably contained intervening islands to serve as stepping-stones in animal dispersal (Hoffstetter 1974; Gingerich and Schoeninger 1977; McKenna 1980). The plausibility of a crossing from Africa to South America is enhanced by increasing evidence that African hystricomorph rodents reached South America in the Oligocene (Fleagle 1986a). However, for the moment, strictly on the basis of the paleogeographic evidence, the early platyrrhines could have migrated from either North America or Africa.

The available phylogenetic and fossil evidence is less ambiguous. At least some early platyrrhines exhibit striking dental similarities to some Fayum Oligocene catarrhines (Fleagle 1986a), supporting biochemical studies that link platyrrhines more closely to catarrhines than to any extant prosimians (Baba et al. 1980; Sarich and Cronin 1980). The implication is clear that platyrrhines and catarrhines are descended from a common anthropoid ancestor rather than from separate prosimian ones. The upwardly revised dating of *Branisella* suggests that the earliest platyrrhines may postdate the earliest African anthropoids (from the Fayum) by as much as 10 million years. It thus seems increasingly possible that the platyrrhines evolved from early-Oligocene African anthropoids, perhaps broadly similar to the Fayum parapithecoids. A firm test of this hypothesis will require so far unknown late-Oligocene (30–25-million-year-old) anthropoid fossils from Africa, South America, or both.

Miocene Primates

During the Miocene, the continents came to occupy basically the same positions they do today (Fig. 2.20). In the early mid-Miocene, about 17–18 mya, the northward drift of the African plate brought it into broad contact with Europe and western Asia, reducing both the lateral extent of the intervening Tethys Sea and its climatic influence on the adjacent continents. As a result, southern Eurasia became generally cooler and drier, and the trend was accelerated by broadly simultaneous mountain building in the Mediterranean and Himalayan regions (Laporte and Zihlman 1983). Equally im-

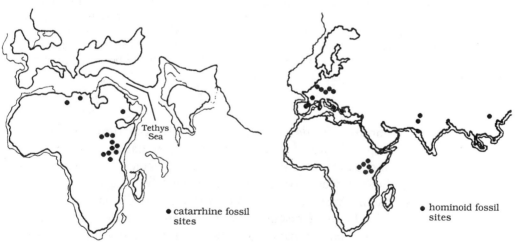

Early Miocene (ca. 22 - 17 my)   Middle Miocene (ca. 16 - 10 my)

Figure 2.20. Relative positions of Africa and Eurasia in the early and middle Miocene (modified after Laporte and Zihlman 1983: Figs. 3, 4). The middle-Miocene higher primates of Eurasia probably evolved from African forms which dispersed to Eurasia when the northward drift of the African plate facilitated faunal interchange roughly 17–16 mya.

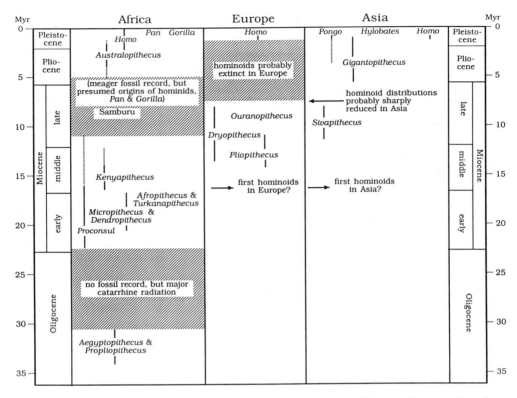

Figure 2.21. Temporal distribution of some important hominoid genera discussed in the text. Note the unfortunate gaps in the African fossil record between roughly 31 mya and 22 mya and between roughly 12 mya and 5 mya. The first gap was almost certainly a time of major catarrhine evolution when the hominoids differentiated from the cercopithecoids, while the second gap includes the time when the line leading to hominids diverged from the lines leading to the chimpanzee and the gorilla. Hominoids are unknown in Eurasia before the mid-Miocene, probably because they evolved in Africa and were unable to reach Eurasia until the contact between Africa and Eurasia was significantly broadened about 17–16 mya. In the late Miocene, about 8 mya, hominoids became extinct in Europe and their numbers and distribution were greatly reduced in Asia, probably because climatic change eliminated suitable habitat in middle latitudes.

portant, the newly developed land connections promoted an unprecedented degree of faunal interchange between Africa and Eurasia. Among the African species that migrated to Eurasia were hominoids, which rapidly radiated through Eurasian forests, from Spain on the west to China on the east.

In most discussions of primate evolution, the acceleration of faunal exchange between Africa and Eurasia is used to divide the Miocene between an early part, before 17–16 mya, when hominoids are known only from Africa, and a later part, after 16 mya, when they are actually better known from Eurasia. Although the early-Miocene hominoids are plausibly derived from Oligocene ones, they are actually separated from them by a 9–10-million-year gap in the record (Fig. 2.21),

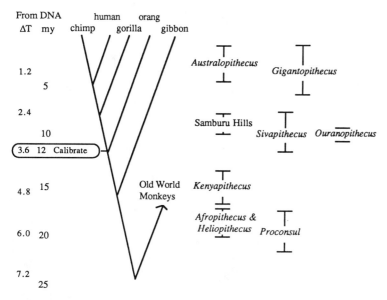

Figure 2.22. Framework of catarrhine evolution as deduced from DNA hybridization data (modified after Pilbeam 1986: Fig. 8). The branching times are based on the assumption that DNA differences accumulate at a linear rate, which can be calculated from the branching time of the orangutan "clade," estimated here from the appearance of *Sivapithecus* roughly 12 mya. The known or probable time ranges of some important fossil hominoids are shown to the right.

between roughly 31 mya (the upper age limit for the early-Oligocene deposits of the Fayum) and 22 mya (the lower age limit for fossiliferous Miocene sites in eastern Africa). The most recent estimate for the rate at which DNA differences accumulate suggests that cercopithecoids separated from hominoids during this gap, about 24–25 mya (Fig. 2.22). (Pilbeam 1986; Sibley and Ahlquist 1987), and this is broadly supported by the discovery of primitive but undoubtedly cercopithecoid teeth in 19–17-million-year-old deposits in eastern Africa. As indicated previously, the New World (ceboid) monkeys were also firmly established by this time (early Miocene), but their further evolution will not be discussed here, because it does not bear on human origins.

The Early Miocene

So far, early-Miocene primates are known principally from western Kenya and neighboring Uganda, mainly from sites in shallow sedimentary basins near modern Lake Victoria (Fig. 2.23). The fossiliferous layers are interstratified with alkaline volcanic ashes and lavas that helped to preserve the bones from acid dissolution and that also permit radiopotassium dates

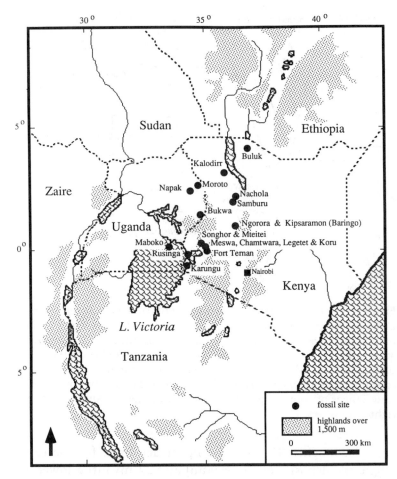

Figure 2.23. Approximate locations of the main Miocene hominoid fossil sites in eastern Africa.

confirming an early-Miocene age (W. W. Bishop 1971; Van Couvering and Van Couvering 1976; Pickford 1986a).

Associated plant and animal fossils indicate that early-Miocene primates in eastern Africa inhabited tropical forest and woodland. Forest dominated and stretched along the equator right across the continent into areas that became woodland, bushland, or savanna in the succeeding mid-Miocene-to-Pleistocene interval (Andrews and Van Couvering 1975; Andrews 1981a, 1981b; Pickford 1983). Hominoids dominate the primate samples, but prosimians similar to modern lorises and galagos also occur (Walker 1978), and there are infrequent, primitive cercopithecoid-monkey jaws and teeth, assigned to the genus *Prohylobates* (Harrison 1987; Strasser and Delson 1987). The rarity of cercopithecoids and the abundance of hominoids, which, as noted below, had a primitive, monkey-

like postcranium, suggests that in the early Miocene hominoids were occupying many niches later occupied by monkeys.
At least early on, cercopithecoids may have been more at home
in less forested environments, such as those that existed in the
early Miocene of northern Africa, where cercopithecoids occur
without hominoids (Delson 1979). The major cercopithecoid
adaptive radiation probably occurred only much later, in the
late Miocene and early Pliocene, at a time when hominoid
fortunes were in decline, owing, at least in part, to progressively cooler, drier global climate and the accompanying
growth of savannas at the expense of forests and woodlands.

Despite a growing fossil sample and more detailed, more
sophisticated analyses, the taxonomy of the Miocene hominoids has undergone numerous revisions, and no final consensus is in sight (compare, for example, Andrews 1985b; Kelley
and Pilbeam 1986; and Harrison 1987; for an overview of disagreements, see Ciochon 1983). Some disagreement is inevitable, since taxonomic judgments must often be based on small
samples, dominated by partial jaws and isolated teeth. Skulls
and postcranial bones are much rarer, and it is usually difficult
to ascertain which postcranial bones belong with which teeth.
Under these circumstances, the number of characters available
for comparison tends to be small, and it can be very hard to
separate *inter*specific variability from *intra*specific variability,
particularly intraspecific variability due to sexual dimorphism.
The problem is exacerbated by the possibility that many fossil
hominoid species were much more dimorphic than their living
counterparts, which are thus misleading guides (Kelley and
Pilbeam 1986). Finally, there is the perennial problem of determining whether some of the similarities observed among fossil
taxa reflect close common descent (homology), versus common
adaptation (analogy) or evolutionary parallelism.

However, with these difficulties in mind, specialists generally agree that most early-Miocene hominoid fossils can be
assigned to a single genus, *Proconsul*. This comprised two subgenera, *P. (Proconsul)* with two or three species and *P. (Rangwapithecus)* with one or two. The included species ranged from
siamang size to chimpanzee size, but some of the size differences that have been used to separate species may actually
reflect sexual dimorphism within species, especially in *P. (Proconsul)* (Kelley 1986; Pilbeam 1986). This is one reason why the
number of *Proconsul* species is debatable.

Proconsul is known from numerous dentitions and teeth
and from less abundant limb bones and partial skulls. The
siamang-size species, *P. africanus*, has provided the largest
number of fossils, including a nearly complete skeleton from

site R114 on Rusinga Island, Kenya (Fig. 2.24, upper) (Walker and Pickford 1983; Walker et al. 1986b). In the skull (Fig. 2.24, lower), *Proconsul* was far advanced over *Aegyptopithecus* and resembled the living apes, with orbits rotated fully forward, limited postorbital constriction, a snout that was small relative to the braincase, and a large brain, both absolutely and relative to body size (Walker et al. 1983). It was arguably less advanced over *Aegyptopithecus* in the external morphology of the cerebral cortex (Radinsky 1975; Falk 1983b). Dentally, *Proconsul* resembled both *Aegyptopithecus* and the living apes, and in both cranial and dental features it is a plausible Miocene link between them. It lacked the secondarily enlarged incisors (for peeling fruit) of the chimpanzee and orangutan and the especially high-cusped molars (for masticating leaves)

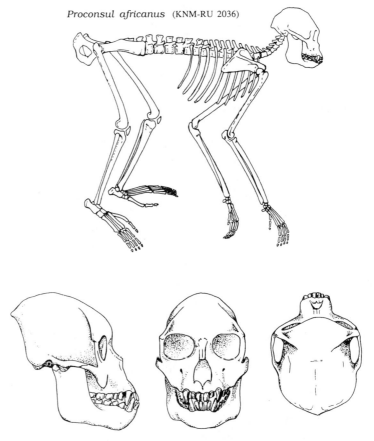

Figure 2.24. *Above:* Reconstruction of *Proconsul africanus* (Rusinga Island specimen no. 2036 in the collections of the National Museums of Kenya) (redrawn after Walker and Pickford 1983). *Below:* Reconstructed skull of female *Proconsul africanus* (redrawn after Walker et al. 1983).

of the gorilla and was thus generalized enough to be near the ancestry of all three. Its primitive, low-cusped, thin-enameled molars suggest a basically frugivorous diet (Fleagle and Kay 1985).

Postcranially, *Proconsul* was more complex. Limb proportions are known for *P. africanus* (Walker and Pickford 1983), which lacked the especially long arms (relative to legs) that characterize the living apes (Fig. 2.24, upper). The wrist was designed to bear the weight of the forequarters, probably on the palms rather than on the knuckles (McHenry and Corruccini 1983). Insofar as can be determined, in overall morphology *Proconsul* appears to have been a generalized arboreal quadruped (Fleagle 1983; M. D. Rose 1983; Walker and Pickford 1983), yet it had elbow and shoulder structures that probably facilitated underbranch suspension, and it probably lacked a tail. In its movements and positional behavior, it was probably more like a monkey than like an ape, but it was not identical to either. The nearest living analogues may be those New World monkeys that combine arboreal quadrupedalism with greater suspensory capabilities than is the case in their Old World counterparts. As in the case of the skull and dentition, the postcranium exhibits no specializations that exclude *Proconsul* from the ancestry of the living apes.

Besides *Proconsul*, several other hominoids are known from early-Miocene deposits in eastern Africa. Their taxonomy and phylogenetic relationships are imperfectly established, but at a minimum there were four genera. Two—*Dendropithecus* (including "*Limnopithecus*" in part) and *Micropithecus*—come from the same area of western Kenya that has provided abundant fossils of Proconsul, while two others—*Afropithecus* and *Turkanapithecus*—come from early-Miocene sites in northern Kenya where *Proconsul* is unknown. One of the north-Kenyan sites has also provided fossils of a third hominoid genus, *Simiolus* (R. E. F. Leakey and Leakey 1987), which is broadly similar to *Dendropithecus* as described immediately below.

Dendropithecus was a genus of roughly gibbon-size apes that is known from dentitions and a small number of postcranial bones. In its relatively elongated, slender limb bones, daggerlike canines, highly sectorial lower third premolars, and relatively simple lower molars, it resembled the gibbons and siamangs. However, the shared similarities may all be primitive catarrhine characters that the gibbons have simply retained (Andrews 1980; Fleagle 1984), and *Dendropithecus* possesses no clearly derived features that link it uniquely to the gibbons or to any other later hominoids. It need not be specially related to the gibbons and could have been on or near the line leading to all living hominoids.

Micropithecus was an extremely small, sub-gibbon-sized ape that is represented by jaws and teeth and a partial face (Fleagle and Simons 1978; Fleagle 1984). Like the gibbons and siamangs, it had a short, broad face, narrow molars, and relatively large, high-crowned incisors and canines, but in other dental features it is either unique or resembles *Dendropithecus* (Andrews 1980). As in the case of *Dendropithecus*, its small size can be used to postulate a special ancestral relationship to gibbons and siamangs, but the morphological case is not compelling.

Afropithecus was a female-gorilla-sized ape that is known from a partial cranium, fragmentary jaws, isolated teeth, and a few postcranial bones (R. E. F. Leakey and Leakey 1986a). It is readily differentiated from most early-Miocene apes by its large size and from *Proconsul* by a series of cranial and dental features, including a longer, narrower snout that merges almost imperceptibly into a steeply inclined frontal bone, a mandible that is very deep and robust, upper cheek teeth that flare outward at the base so that the occlusal surfaces seem small by comparison, upper premolars that are enlarged relative to the molars, and thicker cheek-tooth enamel. When only some jaw fragments were known, their thick enamel and some other features suggested they came from *Sivapithecus*, best known from late-Miocene (12–8-million-year-old) deposits in India and Pakistan (R. E. F. Leakey and Walker 1983). However, this assignment was contested (Delson 1985; Pilbeam 1986), and the fuller sample now on hand implies a distinct genus, possibly on the lineage that ultimately produced *Sivapithecus*.

Afropithecus may also be represented by a maxilla and four isolated teeth from the Ad Dabtiyah early-Miocene (ca. 17-million-year-old) site in Saudi Arabia, though, pending further discoveries, this material has been referred to the separate genus *Heliopithecus* (Andrews and Martin 1987a, 1987b; Andrews et al. 1987). In their enlarged premolars, thickened enamel, and some other features, *Afropithecus* + *Heliopithecus* are advanced in the direction of the later great apes and people. Since living gibbons maintain the primitive condition for these features (relatively small upper premolars, thin enamel, a relatively slender, shallow mandible, etc.), even in the absence of fossils with derived gibbon features, *Afropithecus* + *Heliopithecus* can be used to argue that the great apes and gibbons must have diverged before 17–18 mya (Andrews and Martin 1987a). This is broadly consistent with a divergence estimate of 22–18 mya based on one molecular system and calibration date (Sibley and Ahlquist 1984, 1987) but not with others of 16 mya (Pilbeam 1986; Sibley and Ahlquist 1987) and 15–12 mya (Cronin et al. 1984) based on other systems or calibration points.

Turkanapithecus was a gibbon-sized ape represented by a partial cranium, mandible, and some possibly associated post-cranial bones (R. E. F. Leakey and Leakey 1986b). It is easily distinguished from *Afropithecus* by its much smaller size and by its shorter, less protruding snout, which was nonetheless more conspicuous than in *Proconsul*. It is differentiated from all other known hominoids by the presence of small accessory cusps (cuspules) on the upper molars and fourth premolars. It has no obvious affinities to any contemporaneous or later hominoids, and, together with *Afropithecus*, it is significant mainly because it shows that early-Miocene hominoids were probably much more diverse than discoveries in western Kenya and neighboring Uganda had previously implied. There is no reason to suppose that the discovery of *Afropithecus* and *Turkanapithecus* exhaust the actual diversity, and it is increasingly clear that the apes (broadly understood) were far more successful early on than they were historically.

Middle and Late Miocene

During the middle and later Miocene, global climatic change produced generally cooler conditions in middle and upper latitudes and drier ones in lower latitudes, at least seasonally. In eastern Africa, drier and probably more seasonal climate combined with large-scale crustal movement (rifting) to reduce the extent of tropical forest, which was largely replaced by more open tropical woodland in the middle and later Miocene (Andrews 1981a; Laporte and Zihlman 1983; Pickford 1983). In eastern Africa, middle- and especially later-Miocene fossils are less abundant than early-Miocene ones, but they show that *Proconsul* or a descendant persisted until at least 14 mya and perhaps until 8 mya or 9 mya (Hill et al. 1985). A second hominoid, *Kenyapithecus*, occurs at several Kenyan sites dated between roughly 16 mya and 14 mya or possibly somewhat later (Pickford 1985, 1986b). Even more than *Afropithecus* + *Heliopithecus*, it was distinguished from *Proconsul* by a robust mandible, enlarged upper premolars, thick enamel, and other advanced features that ally it with later great apes and people (Andrews and Martin 1987a). A supposed ancestor-descendant relationship between an older (16–15 mya) species, *K. africanus,* and a younger (ca. 14 mya or later) species, *K. wickeri,* is not firmly established, mainly because *K. wickeri* is represented by only a small number of highly fragmentary fossils. The better-known *K. africanus* is a plausible though not compelling ancestor both for several later-Miocene hominoids in Eurasia (*Ouranopithecus, Sivapithecus,* and *Gigantopithecus*) and for the living African hominoids (Pickford 1985, 1986b).

As drier, more seasonal woodlands spread in eastern Africa during the mid-Miocene, the distribution of fruits probably became patchier and more seasonal, and leaves became more attractive as a dietary staple. Probably in keeping with this, mid-Miocene (ca. 15-million-year-old) deposits contain more monkey fossils (Harrison 1987), and the molars are clearly advanced over early-Miocene ones, with complete bilophodonty. So far, only one genus, *Victoriapithecus,* has been identified. It was formerly thought to comprise two species (Delson and Andrews 1975; Delson 1979), but only one is recognized at present (Benefit and Pickford 1986; Strasser and Delson 1987). Morphologically, it shares no indisputably derived features with either cercopithecines or colobines and may antedate their split. So far, some undoubted (derived) colobine fossils from later-Miocene (ca. 10.5–8.5-million-year-old) sites in east Africa constitute the oldest evidence for the colobine-cercopithecine divergence (Benefit and Pickford 1986).

As already indicated, the broadened land connections between Africa and Eurasia beginning about 17–18 mya facilitated the spread of hominoids to Eurasia. Here, they flourished in a wide band of broad-leaved sclerophyllous woodland that stretched from southern Europe to southwestern China (Andrews 1981a). Thanks to the vagaries of preservation and discovery, Eurasian middle- and late-Miocene hominoids are actually better known than their African contemporaries. Their taxonomy and relationships are controversial, but at a minimum there were probably six genera—*Dryopithecus, Pliopithecus, Ouranopithecus, Sivapithecus, Gigantopithecus,* and *Oreopithecus*—considered separately below. Late-Miocene deposits in southern Europe have also provided an undoubted (derived) colobine monkey, *Mesopithecus.* Together with colobine fossils from late-Miocene sites in southern Asia (Heinz et al. 1981; Barry et al. 1982), this reconfirms African evidence for the late-Miocene divergence of colobines and cercopithecines. By the very late Miocene or early Pliocene,

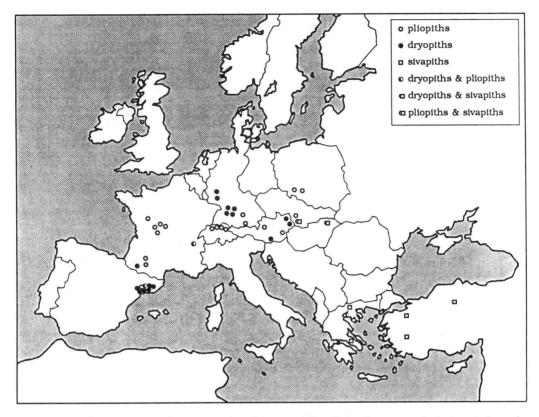

Figure 2.25. Distribution of Miocene fossil hominoid sites in Europe and Turkey (adapted from Nagatoshi 1987: 147). For heuristic purposes, the hominoids have been broadly divided into pliopithecines, dryopithecines, and sivapithecines. Note that the pliopithecines and dryopithecines are essentially limited to western and central Europe, while sivapithecines occur only in southeastern Europe and Turkey. Note also that pliopithecines and dryopithecines rarely occur at the same site.

both the colobines and cercopithecines had undergone extensive radiations (Delson and Andrews 1975), perhaps in response to the same general environmental change that reduced overall hominoid diversity and sparked hominid origins.

Dryopithecus includes two to four species of chimpanzee-sized apes represented by dentitions and a few limb bones at central and west European sites dated to between roughly 14 mya and 8 mya (Fig. 2.25). Its extinction at or shortly after 8 mya was probably due to adverse climatic change that eliminated its preferred forest habitat. Dentally and postcranially, it was broadly similar to *Proconsul*, from which it may have evolved. It differed from *Proconsul* mainly in the loss of some decidedly primitive features, including a pronounced cingulum or collar of enamel at the base of the molar crowns (Kelley and Pilbeam 1986). With *Proconsul* and most other hominoids, it shared projecting, sexually dimorphic canines and the Y-5 cusp and fissure pattern on the lower molars. It was in *Dryopithecus* that this pattern was first recognized, and it is thus often known as the dryopithecine Y-5 pattern. The postcranial bones of *Dryopithecus* suggest it was a relatively unspecialized arboreal quadruped, perhaps having more aptitude for underbranch suspension than did *Proconsul* (M. D. Rose 1983).

Pliopithecus includes several species of siamang-sized apes found at western and south-central European sites dated between roughly 16 mya and 11 mya (Fig. 2.25) (Ginsburg 1986). It appeared in Europe before *Dryopithecus* and to judge by the associated fauna, was generally tied to moister, more heavily wooded areas (Nagatoshi 1987). It rarely occurs in the same sites as *Dryopithecus* and became extinct earlier, probably because the mid-Miocene trend to cooler, drier climate eliminated its habitat first. Its taxonomy is controversial, and some of the included species may be distinct enough to warrant separate generic status (Ginsburg 1986; Harrison 1987). By far the best known is *P. vindobonensis* from mid-Miocene deposits in Czechoslovakia (Fig. 2.26). With the gibbons and siamangs it shared some cranial and dental features, such as a short, broad face, projecting orbital margins, a gracile mandible that deepened toward the front, relatively narrow incisors, canines that were sexually dimorphic but large in both sexes, and some degree of intercusp cresting (Delson and Andrews 1975). However, unlike gibbons and siamangs, it had third molars that were both relatively and absolutely long, orbits that were backed by bone only to the extent seen in *Aegyptopithecus* and the platyrrhine monkeys, and an external auditory meatus that was incompletely ossified. Like gibbons and siamangs, it had a gracile postcranial skeleton with relatively indistinct muscle markings, but it lacked their forelimb specializations for brachiation. Its limb proportions resembled those of quadrupedal monkeys, and its overall postcranial morphology suggests it was an arboreal quadruped with some suspensory capabilities (Fleagle 1983). Like *Aegyptopithecus*, it maintained an entepicondylar foramen on the distal humerus, and it may have had a tail.

In retaining such primitive features as an entepicondylar foramen and an incompletely ossified auditory meatus, *Pliopithecus* recalls *Aegyptopithecus* and differs from all other known Miocene-to-Recent hominoids. It could be ancestral to gibbons and siamangs only if they independently developed many of the derived features they share with the great apes. These include not only a completely ossified meatus and

complete postorbital closure but also numerous detailed similarities in the structure of the shoulder, elbow, and trunk. It is
more likely that the similarities between *Pliopithecus* and the
gibbons and siamangs reflect a combination of shared, retained
primitive features and of convergence, relating, for example, to
a shared gracile postcranium. Most probably, then, *Pliopithecus* had nothing to do with gibbon origins and was simply a
unique Miocene catarrhine that became extinct without issue.
Its peculiar mix of primitive and advanced features suggest it
should be placed in its own family, the Pliopithecidae, within
the Hominoidea—or perhaps within the Propliopithecoidea,

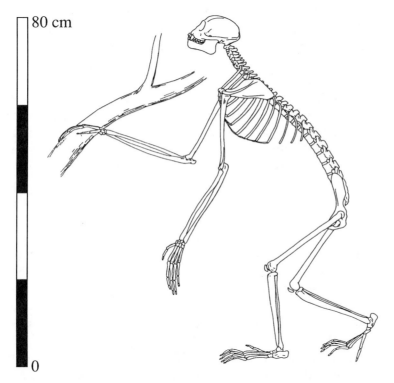

Figure 2.26. Reconstructed skeleton of *Pliopithecus vindobonensis*
from mid-Miocene (ca. 15-million-year-old) deposits in Czechoslovakia (redrawn after Zapfe 1960: Fig. 106). In its short, broad face,
slender postcranial bones, and other features, *P. vindobonensis*
resembled the living gibbons and siamangs, but it lacked their
extraordinarily long arms and other morphological specializations
for brachiation. It also retained some remarkably primitive features,
such as an incompletely ossified external auditory meatus and an
epicondylar foramen on the distal humerus. Most authorities now
regard it as one of a group of closely related small hominoids that
inhabited western and central European forests between roughly 16
mya and 11 mya and that bear no relationship to any later hominoids.

separate from the Hominoidea. Placement within the Propliopithecoidea would imply descent from Oligocene creatures such as *Aegyptopithecus* and *Propliopithecus* through an as yet unknown early-Miocene form.

The removal of *Pliopithecus* from possible gibbon and siamang ancestry, and the failed case for a special relationship between the gibbons and siamangs on the one hand and early-Miocene *Dendropithecus* and *Micropithecus* on the other, leaves the gibbons and siamangs with no fossil record until they appear in modern form in Pleistocene and Holocene deposits in their historic Southeast Asian range (Fleagle 1984). By geographic location, estimated 16-mya (mid-Miocene) date, and observed morphology, a poorly known Chinese genus, *Dionysopithecus*, and an even more poorly known, like aged, possibly congeneric form from Pakistan could represent early members of the gibbon-siamang lineage (Fleagle 1984; Barry et al. 1986); but the fossils are insufficient for a binding judgment.

Ouranopithecus was a chimpanzee-sized ape known from jaws, teeth, and a partial face from late-Miocene (ca. 9–11-million-year-old) deposits in Greece (de Bonis and Melentis 1984; de Bonis et al. 1986). It is readily distinguished from most early-Miocene hominoids and from *Dryopithecus* and *Pliopithecus* by its thick molar enamel, a feature it shared with *Sivapithecus*, *Gigantopithecus*, and *Kenyapithecus*. The taxa associated with *Ouranopithecus* and the other thick-enameled hominoids indicate woodland environments in which nuts, seeds, subterranean tubers, and other hard or grit-encrusted foods probably outnumbered fruits. Thick enamel was probably essential for extensive reliance on such foods (Kay 1981), and its various mid-to-late-Miocene hominoid proprietors may all share a common east African ancestor who developed it as woodland replaced forest in the early mid-Miocene (Andrews 1981a; 1983a).

Like modern woodlands, mid-to-late-Miocene ones probably provided an incomplete tree canopy, and many nuts and other hard foods undoubtedly occurred at ground level. They were probably also distributed in patches that could only be reached by movement on the ground, and *Ouranopithecus* and other thick-enameled hominoids may thus have been more terrestrial than their thin-enameled relatives. The special interest of this is that thick enamel and some degree of terrestriality were almost certainly features of the line leading to *Australopithecus*, the earliest known hominid. Besides thick enamel, *Ouranopithecus* and *Australopithecus* also shared round, swollen molar cusps, the absence of a honing facet (from

contact with the upper canine) on the mesial (anterior) face of
the lower third premolar (P_3), and substantial sexual dimorphism in cheek-tooth size (especially notable in the oldest *Australopithecus*). If *Ouranopithecus* occurred in Africa, it would
even be a plausible ancestor for *Australopithecus*. On combined
geographic/morphologic grounds, however, *Kenyapithecus* or
its immediate descendant is a better candidate.

Sivapithecus comprised several siamang-to-orangutan-
sized species represented in later-mid-Miocene (ca. 12–8-
million-year-old) deposits in the Siwalik Hills on the India-
Pakistan border and in Turkey. Arguably, it also occurs in
late-middle-Miocene sites in Europe (Neudorf an der March,
Czechoslovakia), China (Lufeng), and western Kenya (*Kenyapithecus wickeri* of Fort Ternan) (Kelley and Pilbeam 1986;
Pilbeam 1986). Whether or not the European, Chinese, and
African specimens are included, *Sivapithecus* is still best
known from the Siwaliks, which have provided numerous
dentitions, some limb bones, and a partial skull.

Sivapithecus can be distinguished from *Ouranopithecus*
by several features, including a much more robust mandible;
larger incisors and canines relative to the cheek teeth; a
narrower, higher-crowned, and more sectorial lower third premolar; and a distinctly derived nasal and subnasal morphology
resembling that of the orangutan (see below) (Andrews and
Tekkaya 1980; Simons 1981; Kelley and Pilbeam 1986). However, in other respects, especially in the thickness of the molar
enamel, the two taxa were very similar, and, like *Ouranopithecus*, *Sivapithecus* apparently exhibited considerable sexual
dimorphism. It now appears that specimens formerly assigned
to a separate genus, *Ramapithecus*, may simply represent a
small species of *Sivapithecus*; and many specialists now regard
Ramapithecus as a "junior" synonym of *Sivapithecus*.

As already noted, *Sivapithecus* inhabited relatively open
woodland where it could have used its thick enamel to exploit
hard or abrasive subterranean plant foods that were probably
more abundant and more reliable than soft-coated fruits.
Circumstantially, then, it has been suggested that *Sivapithecus*
was at least partly a hard-object feeder, rather than strictly
frugivorous (Andrews 1983a). This remains a reasonable hypothesis, though preliminary studies show that, in dental
microwear, *Sivapithecus* was more like the chimpanzee, a
known soft-fruit eater, than it was like other primates that are
known hard-object feeders (Teaford and Walker, 1984).

The postcranium of *Sivapithecus* is not well known, but
it appears to have been predominantly a non-knuckle-walking

quadruped, with wrist, ankle, and hand well suited for arboreal climbing and with an elbow structure that may reflect greater suspensory ability than that in early-Miocene hominoids (Morbeck 1983; Raza et al. 1983; M. D. Rose 1983, 1984, 1986). It exhibited no postcranial specializations that either link it to or exclude it from the ancestry of any later hominoids.

In those dental features it shares with *Ouranopithecus, Sivapithecus* also resembles *Australopithecus,* with which it further shared *(a)* molars that were large relative to the front teeth (and to estimated body size) and *(b)* relatively short, stubby canines that tended to wear from the tips as well as from the mesial and distal surfaces. Because of obvious dental resemblances to *Australopithecus,* fossils assigned to *Ramapithecus (= Sivapithecus)* were once thought to represent the earliest known hominid. However, in its face, known from both Pakistan and Turkey (Andrews and Tekkaya 1980; Pilbeam 1983; Ward and Pilbeam 1983), *Sivapithecus* shares several derived features with the orangutan. These include a narrow interorbital region, high narrow orbits, a subnasal plane that is continuous with the floor of the nasal cavity (not stepped), and upper central incisors that are much larger than the lateral ones (Fig. 2.27) (Andrews and Cronin 1982; L. Martin and Andrews 1982; Ward and Brown 1986). The orangutan also has thick enamel on its molars, and there is now wide agreement that *Sivapithecus* was on or near the line leading to the orangutan.

It might be argued from enamel thickness that *Sivapithecus* (including *Ramapithecus*) was near the ancestry of both the orangutan and hominids, but this hypothesis is highly problematic. The biggest objection is that biomolecular evidence shows that hominids are much more closely related to the chimpanzee and the gorilla than to the orangutan (Andrews and Cronin 1982), yet, unlike hominids and the orangutan, the chimpanzee and the gorilla have thin enamel. The implication is that enamel thickness by itself may not be taxonomically relevant. In fact, scanning electron microscopy indicates that hominid, chimpanzee, and gorilla enamel are basically similar in ultrastructure and development and that the thin enamel of the chimpanzee and gorilla is secondarily derived from thick enamel (L. Martin 1985). The chimpanzee, the gorilla, and hominids could thus share a thick-enameled ancestor, perhaps *Kenyapithecus* or its immediate descendant in Africa.

In this light, *Sivapithecus* is significant not because it was ancestral to hominids but because it shows that the line leading to the orangutan had probably split from the line

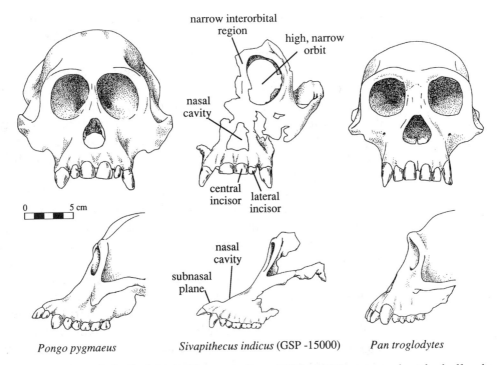

Figure 2.27. Partial skull of *Sivapithecus indicus* (GSP-15000) compared with skulls of an orangutan, *Pongo pygmaeus*, and of a chimpanzee, *Pan troglodytes* (drawings by K. Cruz-Uribe, from photographs and casts). In its high, narrow orbits, narrow interorbital region, (nonstepped) continuity between the floor of the nasal cavity and the subnasal plane, and large size of the central incisors compared with the lateral ones, the *Sivapithecus* skull closely resembles that of the orangutan and differs from those of the African great apes. The implication is that *Sivapithecus* is near the ancestry of the orangutan.

leading to the African apes and hominids by 12 mya (Fig. 2.22). Unfortunately, the fossil record sheds very little light on the probable common ancestor of chimps, gorillas, and people or on the actual history of chimps and gorillas. The main problem is the extreme rarity of hominoid fossils from African late-Miocene deposits (between 14 mya and 5.5 mya). The most significant specimen is a fragmentary maxilla from the Namu-rungule Formation in the Samburu Hills (Baragoi region) of north-central Kenya (Ishida et al. 1984). Fission-track and radiopotassium datings, together with the associated fauna, indicate an age between 10.5 mya and 6.7 mya (Matsuda et al. 1986). With gorillalike molars and very thick enamel, the maxilla could represent the ancestor of the gorilla or even the common ancestor of the gorilla, chimpanzee, and people, but additional, more complete finds are necessary for confirmation (Andrews 1986b; Pilbeam 1986; Andrews and Martin 1987a). Tracing the full history of the gorilla and chimpanzee may also require the discovery of so far unknown Miocene and Pliocene localities in parts of west and central Africa where these creatures were abundant historically.

Gigantopithecus, as the name suggests, was a very large hominoid, somewhat larger than the gorilla and perhaps the largest primate that ever lived. It has been found in Siwalik deposits dated to approximately 6.3 mya (Barry 1986) and may have survived in south China until 500,000 years ago, overlapping there with *Homo erectus* (references in Chapter 4). It is known only from mandibles and isolated teeth. In its dentition, *Gigantopithecus* dwarfed *Sivapithecus* but was otherwise generally similar: the cheek teeth were very large relative to the front teeth, the molars had thick enamel, and the canines were robust but low crowned, wearing from the tips (Delson and Andrews 1975). The dental similarities suggest a broadly similar diet, if not a closely shared ancestor. Since postcranial bones have not been found, the precise positional behavior of *Gigantopithecus* remains speculative, but, given its size, it was probably completely terrestrial. Its origins remain unclear, but together with *Ouranopithecus* and *Sivapithecus* it may ultimately derive from *Kenyapithecus*.

Finally, *Oreopithecus* was a siamang-sized anthropoid that inhabited swampy, late-Miocene (ca. 9–8 mya) forests in Italy (Azzaroli 1985; Azzaroli et al. 1986). Its relatively flat face, vertically implanted incisors, low-crowned canines, and bicuspid lower third premolars, together with features of its pelvis, once suggested it might be on the line leading to humans. However, its relatively long slender arms, short hind limbs, curved phalanges, and extremely mobile limb joints imply it was primarily arboreal and suspensory in its habits (Fleagle and Kay 1985). Its lower molars possessed six major cusps, in distinction from all other known hominoids, and the cusps on both the upper and lower molars were partly linked by crests, similar to those in cercopithecoids (Delson and Andrews 1975). Its affinities are highly controversial, and it is commonly placed in its own extinct family, the Oreopithecidae. It could be either an aberrant hominoid, to judge from significant postcranial specializations it shares with established hominoids (Harrison 1986b), or a strange cercopithecoid, to judge from its dentition (Szalay and Delson 1979; Rosenberger and Delson 1985). From limited dental similarities, it has been suggested that it evolved from Oligocene *Apidium* of the Fayum (Simons 1972), but its most secure phyletic link is to *Nyanzapithecus*, an early-mid-Miocene (19–16 mya) catarrhine from western Kenya (Harrison 1986a, 1986b). Dentally,

Nyanzapithecus (including specimens formerly assigned to *Proconsul (Rangwapithecus) vancouveringi*) is nicely intermediate between more generalized, early-Miocene, east African anthropoids and *Oreopithecus*. It possessed some dental specializations that eliminate it from the direct ancestry of *Oreopithecus*, but it still implies an east African origin for the Oreopithecidae, and *Oreopithecus* itself may be represented in the later-mid-Miocene (ca. 14-million-year-old) deposits of Fort Ternan and a neighboring site in western Kenya (Harrison 1986a, 1986b).

Summary and Conclusion

From the preceding account, it is clear that the primate fossil record is flawed by major temporal and geographic gaps and that even where fossils occur they are mainly fragmentary jaws and isolated teeth. The spotty record with its incomplete fossils is the main reason that informed specialists often disagree about the probable behavior and ecology of fossil species and especially about their evolutionary relationships. Some disagreement also stems from different a priori expectations or theoretical perspectives, which themselves are partly determined by the state of the record (Cartmill 1982; Fleagle and Jungers 1982).

Much research on fossil primates has understandably been motivated by a desire to trace the origins of living ones, but as the fossil record has improved, especially since the 1960s, tracing the descent of living Primates has become more problematic, not less. This is because the fuller record shows that few known fossil primates possessed derived features or specializations that link them clearly and uniquely to any living form. Many fossil species, in fact, had their own unique specializations that effectively eliminate them from the ancestry of later species and that suggest they became extinct without issue. To the extent that fossil forms resemble living ones, the shared features are often primitive characters which the fossil and living species could have inherited from a common ancestor and which therefore do not demonstrate ancestor-descendant relationships. In this regard, the fossil record actually presents more potential ancestors than the living Primates require, which further implies that many fossil forms have no living descendants.

However, even if it is not possible to draw a full and compelling family tree linking successively younger fossil primates to living species, it is possible to outline it, along with the probable times when major primate groups diverged from each other (Fig. 2.28). Equally important, fresh discoveries and increasingly sophisticated analyses have revealed the main stages of primate evolution, which can be conceptualized as a series of adaptive radiations preceding the emergence of hominids:

1. An initial radiation beginning in the Paleocene or perhaps the late Cretaceous, leading to the Plesiadapiformes. These were distinguished from their insectivore (or insectivore-like) ancestors primarily by the morphology of their cheek teeth and perhaps by their ear structure. They hardly differed from insectivores in their brains, special senses, or locomotion, and their main behavioral distinction was perhaps the significant addition of seeds, fruits, or other vegetal matter to a basically insectivorous diet.

2. A second radiation beginning in the late Paleocene or earliest Eocene, producing a wide variety of much more advanced, lemurlike and tarsierlike forms. These were distinguished from their Paleocene predecessors by the development of typically primate grasping hands and feet with nails instead of claws and by a reorganization of the brain and face to emphasize vision relative to olfaction. The selective advantage of these morphological advances was perhaps an enhanced ability to hunt insects among slender branches in forest undergrowth.

3. A third radiation beginning in the late Eocene or early Oligocene, producing a variety of primitive higher primates. In their body form and basically quadrupedal, arboreal habits, they probably differed little from their lemurlike or tarsierlike ancestors, but they had larger brains in which vision was even more important versus olfaction. Perhaps most significant, their molar morphology indicates they were mainly frugivorous, and it was this dietary specialization that probably set them off most strongly from their prosimian predecessors and contemporaries.

4. A fourth radiation or set of radiations during the late Oligocene or early Miocene, in which higher primates differentiated into forms clearly anticipating extant apes and monkeys. To begin with, the main difference between apes and monkeys was dental, and this suggests that the earliest monkeys differed from their apelike contemporaries mainly in their greater propensity to eat leaves. The early apes and monkeys were probably very similar in their palm-flat, quadrupedal, nonsuspensory habitual postures

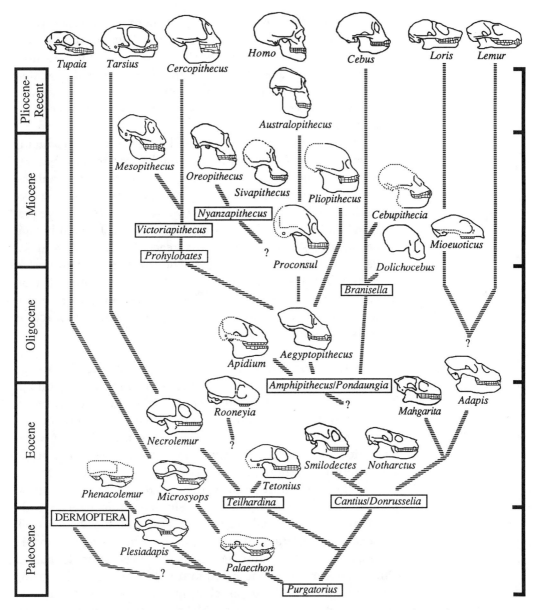

Figure 2.28. Skulls of representative living and fossil primates arranged in relative stratigraphic order (modified after Gingerich 1984c: Fig. 2). Dashed lines show the proposed pattern of phenetic linking in a very general way. The skulls aligned along the top are meant
only to symbolize the seven extant primate superfamilies (from left to right): Tupaioidea,
Tarsioidea, Cercopithecoidea, Hominoidea, Ceboidea, Lorisoidea, and Lemuroidea. The
linkages among fossil and living forms are highly conjectural, the times of divergence
among major groups less so.

and locomotion. Almost certainly, both were basically arboreal, though the early monkeys may have been relatively more terrestrial. To begin with, the apes were much more abundant and diverse than the monkeys, probably because forested, fruit-rich settings dominated the tropical and subtropical portion of Africa where monkeys and apes first diverged.

5. A fifth radiation in the middle and later Miocene, producing a variety of apes with thick enamel, large molar chewing surfaces, and relatively small, noninterlocking canines. This radiation was probably sparked by a progressive middle-to-late-Miocene trend toward cooler, drier, more seasonal continental climates, which in tropical and subtropical latitudes encouraged the spread of woodland and savanna at the expense of forest. The thick enamel and other dental features that mark this radiation were probably an adaptation for masticating hard or grit-encrusted plant foods that became an increasingly important resource as woodlands and savannas grew.

In their forelimbs, at least some of the thick-enameled apes were probably better adapted for tree climbing and under-branch suspension than were their early-Miocene predecessors, but to find their food or to move between food sources some probably also became more terrestrial. In the very-late-Miocene, between 10 mya and 5 mya, in response to an ever more open, nonwooded environment in eastern Africa, one of the more terrestrial forms began to alter its habitual pattern of ground locomotion to emphasize an energetically efficient form of bipedalism, and the hominid lineage emerged. More or less simultaneously, the monkeys burgeoned, probably in response to the same late-Miocene vegetational change. Under pressure from the protohominids and the proliferating monkeys, many thick-enameled apes became extinct in the late Miocene, but some probably readapted to more forested conditions. Such readaptation could explain the secondary dental and locomotor specializations that the chimpanzee and gorilla exhibit today.

As the protohominids became more bipedal, they doubtless became even more terrestrial, and there was further canine reduction and molar enlargement to permit even more effective processing of hard, tough foods. Like living chimpanzees, the protohominids probably occasionally used tools and ate meat, but as they developed their distinctive hominid locomotor and dental anatomy, their savanna habitat probably selected for much greater reliance on both tools and meat. At least one early hominid lineage responded strongly to these selective pressures, and in this lineage, ground living, tool use, and meat eating interacted to favor a dramatic increase in brain size. This interpretation is developed further in the next chapter, devoted specifically to the anatomy and behavior of the earliest known hominids.

3 THE AUSTRALOPITHECINES AND *HOMO HABILIS*

In 1939, Gregory and Hellman (1939) proposed that a group of very early hominid fossils from South Africa should be placed in the subfamily Australopithecinae, to be distinguished from a second subfamily, the Homininae, containing later (more advanced) hominids. The formal term *Australopithecinae* has found little favor, but its informal, anglicized derivative is now widely used to designate not only the original South African fossils but also a growing number of similar fossils from east Africa.

The australopithecines are the oldest known hominids, with a fossil record beginning before 4 million years ago (mya) and extending to sometime between 1.2 mya and perhaps 700,000 years ago. Their evolutionary origins remain vague, because of a sparse African fossil record between 8 mya and 4 mya, and their relationships to each other and to the earliest widely recognized species of *Homo*, *H. habilis*, remain controversial. However, continuing discoveries in Africa have narrowed the phylogenetic possibilities, and they have also revealed the basic morphological and behavioral course of early human evolution. It is the known pattern on which this chapter focuses.

History of Discovery: South Africa

The first australopithecine fossil was discovered by Raymond Dart, a British-trained anatomist, who, in 1922, was appointed professor of anatomy at the University of Witwatersrand in Johannesburg, South Africa. There are minor discrepancies between the discovery as recounted by Dart (Dart and Craig 1959) and as reconstructed by Tobias (1984, 1985). Dart's account is summarized here.

Dart encouraged his students to collect fossils during their vacations in order to help him stock a museum he planned to create in his department. In 1924, a student brought him a fossil baboon skull from the Buxton lime quarry at Taung in the northern Cape Province of South Africa, about 320 km southwest of Johannesburg (Fig. 3.1). Through a geologist colleague, Dart contacted the quarry manager, who then sent him two crates of fossiliferous breccia—rock-hard blocks of sandy sediment and fossils cemented together by limey glue—from a small cave exposed in the quarry. The fossils in the crates were mainly uninteresting, but one crate contained a natural endocast (mold of the inside of a skull) that Dart immediately realized came from a hominoid primate. Among the breccia blocks in the crates, Dart found one with a depression into which the endocast fitted. Inside the block, he saw traces of bone which he hoped was the front of the skull that belonged with the endocast.

The front was present (Fig. 3.2), but it took Dart many weeks to expose it with hammer, chisels, and a sharpened knitting needle. From the dentition, he determined that the skull came from a juvenile whose first molars were just erupting, and from various other features he concluded that the creature was intermediate in important respects between apes and people. For example, it was obviously apelike in the small size of its brain—or, more precisely, in its endocranial (= internal skull) volume, which Dart estimated would have reached 525 cc at adulthood. Recent reestimates have reduced this to between 404 and 440 cc (Holloway 1970; Falk 1987), but even Dart's figure was much closer to the average for common chimpanzees (ca. 400 cc) and gorillas (ca. 500 cc) than to the average for living people (ca. 1,350 cc). At the same time, the deciduous canines were much smaller and less projecting than those in apes, and the foramen magnum ("large hole"), through which connections passed from the spinal column to the brain, was much farther forward on the base of the skull. This suggested that the skull was balanced on top of the spinal column, as in people, where this position is a natural concomitant of upright, bipedal locomotion (Fig. 3.3). In short, the position of the foramen magnum implied that the Taung individual was bipedal like people rather than quadrupedal like apes.

Dart published a description of the skull in the February 7, 1925, issue of *Nature* and concluded that it came from a previously unknown species "intermediate between living anthropoids and man" (Dart 1925). He named the species *Australopithecus africanus* ("African southern ape") and stressed both the skull's intermediate or transitional morphology and its discovery far outside the geographical ranges of the living apes. Taung lies in a nonforested region where living

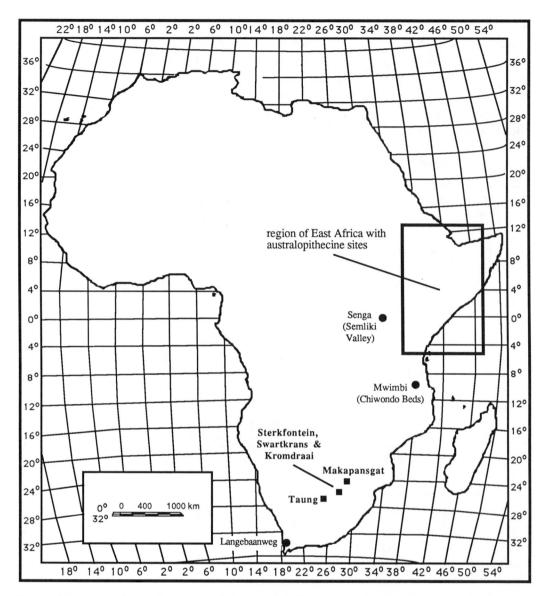

Figure 3.1. Approximate locations of the South African australopithecine sites, the Lange-baanweg Pliocene fossil site, the Senga and Mwimbi Plio-Pleistocene (Oldowan) artifact sites, and the region of east Africa where australopithecine sites occur.

apes could not survive, and from geological studies, Dart argued that the regional environment was probably similar when the fossils accumulated. The ancient vegetation was thus inappropriate for an ape in the narrow sense. It was, however, clearly suitable for an ape that was developing human traits, especially bipedal locomotion.

In the following issue of *Nature*, Dart's assessment was severely criticized by several anthropologists. A consensus soon developed that *Australopithecus* was simply a fossil ape, with no special relevance to human evolution. According to Le Gros Clark (1967), who chronicled the debate as an active witness, the reasons for doubting Dart included nonscientific considerations, such as Dart's flowery, rhetorical writing style, his reputation for coming to hasty conclusions, and his unbelievably good luck in finding such a spectacular fossil just 2 years after arriving in Africa.

However, there were fundamental scientific concerns as well. There was very little from which to estimate the antiquity of the Taung skull, but some authorities felt that the associated baboon fossils implied it was too recent to be a human ancestor. In addition, the discovery of primitive human fossils ("*Pithecanthropus*") in Java in 1891 had convinced many specialists that Asia, not Africa, was the cradle of humanity. Finally, the skull did not fit either of the current theories of human evolution (Washburn 1985). The first held that human ancestors should be equally primitive in all traits, while Dart's find showed a mix of advanced and primitive features. The second theory, supported by the famous Piltdown skull (later exposed as an elaborate fake), proposed that the peculiarly human brain had evolved before other uniquely human traits. The Taung skull, as interpreted by Dart, suggested just the reverse—that the uniquely human mode of bipedal locomotion had evolved before the brain.

Beyond these theoretical obstacles, some specialists disputed a claim by Dart that the endocranial cast indicated a

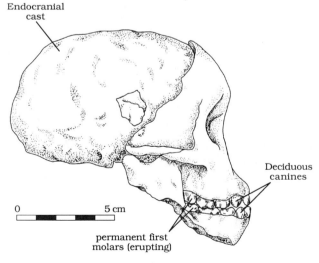

Figure 3.2. Facial skeleton and endocast of *Australopithecus africanus* from Taung, viewed from the right side (drawing by K. Cruz-Uribe from photos and casts).

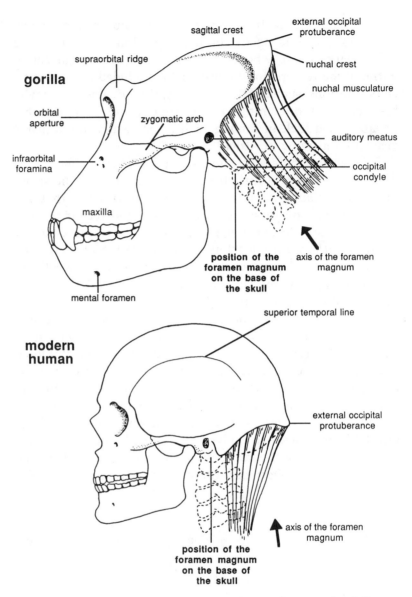

Figure 3.3. Gorilla and modern human skulls, showing the differences in the position of the skull with respect to the spinal column (adapted from Le Gros Clark 1967: 67). In people, the skull is balanced on top of the spinal column, and the foramen magnum consequently lies much farther forward on the base of the skull. The orientation of its axis is also more vertical. The more posterior position of the foramen magnum in the gorilla, together with its larger, more protruding face, also requires larger, more powerful nuchal (neck) muscles to stabilize the head.

humanlike (vs. apelike) brain. This point remains controversial
(Holloway 1983b). Even more problematic was the very young
age of the Taung individual at time of death, which was at 5–7
years, if one applies the same maturation rate and dental
eruption schedule as is seen in living people. The actual age
may have been only 3–4 years (Conroy and Vannier 1987), since
growth increments in australopithecine enamel (Bromage and
Dean 1985; Beynon and Wood 1987; Bromage 1987), together
with the relative timing of crown and root development in
various teeth (B. H. Smith 1986), suggest that the australopithecines matured at about the same rate as modern apes, perhaps
30% to 50% faster than modern people. The crucial point is
that very young apes resemble very young humans much more
than adult apes resemble adult humans; and some of Dart's
critics suggested that as an adult, the Taung individual would
have been much more apelike in all features, including the
relative position of the foramen magnum. Finally, there was
the problem that Dart was inferring bipedal locomotion from a
portion of the anatomy not directly involved in locomotion.
Without actual bones from the locomotor skeleton—especially
from the pelvis or leg—it could be argued that *Australopithecus* may not have been bipedal.

Unfortunately, Dart did not visit the Taung site to seek
additional fossils, especially adult skulls or postcranial bones
that could have won his case, and by the time qualified
specialists did go, the cave that had contained the juvenile
skull had been quarried away. However, Dart continued to
remove breccia from the skull, and in 1929 he succeeded in
separating the upper and lower jaws to permit a more complete
assessment of the dentition. He distributed casts of the dentition to many specialists, and W. K. Gregory, an eminent
American authority on mammalian teeth, concluded that it
came from a hominid rather than from an ape.

Gregory's support aside, however, additional specimens
were obviously necessary to convince many other authorities,
and Dart was not personally prepared to make the search. This
task fell to Robert Broom, a Scottish-born physician and
authority on fossil reptiles who had settled in South Africa. He
visited Dart's laboratory 2 weeks after the formal announce-
ment of the Taung find in *Nature* and was an early convert to
Dart's conclusions. He had other work to complete, however,
and it was not until the 1930s that he was able to initiate
research on *Australopithecus*. In 1936, working from his base
at the Transvaal Museum in Pretoria, about 90 km north of
Johannesburg, Broom had his attention called to the fossilifer-

ous breccia in a cave on the farm Sterkfontein, near the town of
Krugersdorp, roughly 25 km northwest of Johannesburg (Fig.
3.1). Upon visiting the site, he almost immediately recovered a
partial adult australopithecine skull.

In 1938, during one of his periodic visits to Sterkfontein,
Broom heard of another promising cave at Kromdraai, approximately 3 km to the east. Again, he was quickly rewarded with
an adult skull, which, however, differed in important respects
from the earlier Sterkfontein skull. He concluded that it
represented a different kind of australopithecine, a view that is
still widely accepted.

Having found adult skulls, by 1939 Broom could show that
adult australopithecines were no more more apelike than the
Taung child. Equally important, at Sterkfontein he had recovered a distal femur and at Kromdraai an astragalus (= talus) that
showed the australopithecines probably were bipedal, as Dart
had argued.

Partly for economic reasons and partly because of World
War II, research in the Sterkfontein region largely ceased
between 1939 and 1945. In collaboration with G. H. R. Schepers, Broom spent the war years preparing a monograph on the
Sterkfontein and Kromdraai finds. This appeared in 1946
(Broom and Schepers 1946) and was widely read and acclaimed.
As a result, most authorities came to accept the australopithecines as hominids, though some were disturbed by Broom's
tendency to divide the known fossils into more taxa than
seemed warranted: he placed the Sterkfontein and Kromdraai
finds in their own genera—*Plesianthropus* and *Paranthropus*,
respectively—distinct from Dart's original *Australopithecus*.
Most specialists today place all the fossils in the single genus
Australopithecus, divisible into two species—*A. africanus*
(Taung and Sterkfontein) and *A. robustus* (Kromdraai). However, a growing number have resurrected the category *Paranthropus* as originally defined by Broom. In the vernacular, *A.
africanus* is often called the "gracile (slender) australopithecine" and *A.* (or *Paranthropus*) *robustus* is the "robust australopithecine," although they differed less in body mass and
other features than the names imply.

In 1947–48, assisted by John T. Robinson, Broom renewed
work at Sterkfontein, with spectacular success. Among the
crucial specimens they recovered was a partial australopithecine skeleton, including a pelvis that demonstrated beyond all
doubt that the owner was bipedal. They also found a nearly
complete adult skull that is probably the most famous South
African australopithecine find after the original Taung find. It

was regarded as a female *Plesianthropus* and became popularly known as "Mrs. Ples." (It is shown reconstructed in Fig. 2.1.)

In 1947, James Kitching, participating in an expedition organized by Dart, found an australopithecine fossil at the Makapansgat Limeworks Cave in the northern Transvaal, approximately 300 km north of Johannesburg, and, in 1948, Broom and Robinson made the first discoveries in a cave on the farm Swartkrans, less than 2 km from Sterkfontein. The late-1940's research at Sterkfontein, Makapansgat, and Swartkrans greatly enlarged the available australopithecine sample, producing many skulls or partial skulls, dentitions, isolated teeth, and a small but diagnostic sample of postcranial bones that pointed consistently to bipedalism. By 1950, the mounting evidence had convinced nearly all skeptics that the australopithecines were early members of the human family. However, debate continued regarding their relationship to later people, and the issue is still not settled.

Taung, Sterkfontein, Kromdraai, Makapansgat, and Swartkrans remain the only known australopithecine sites in southern Africa, though other sites probably exist, particularly in the dolomitic limestone areas of the Transvaal. Sterkfontein, Kromdraai, Makapansgat, and Swartkrans still contain fossiliferous breccia and either are still being investigated or have been investigated recently. Together, they have provided a very large sample of australopithecine bones, comprising approximately thirty-two skulls or partial skulls, roughly one hundred jaws or partial jaws, hundreds of isolated teeth, and more than thirty postcranial bones (Howell 1978a; Day 1986). However, since 1959, the southern African sites have been largely eclipsed by spectacular australopithecine discoveries in east Africa.

History of Discovery: East Africa

The east African sites now occupy the limelight for two clear reasons. First, in east Africa, the fossils often occur in relatively friable ancient stream- or lake-edge deposits rather than in rock-hard cave fills. At some sites, such as Olduvai Gorge, australopithecine fossils can even be excavated using dental picks and brushes in the accepted archeological manner. At the southern African sites, dental picks and brushes have been second to dynamite, pneumatic drills, hammers, and chisels. Second, and at least equally important, many of the east African sites are stratigraphically related to volcanic extrusives (mainly ancient volcanic ash layers or tephra) that can be dated

Table 3.1. East African Sites That Have Provided Australopithecine Fossils

Sites	Expedition Leaders	Expedition Dates
Tanzania		
*Laetoli	M. D. Leakey	1974–79
*Olduvai Gorge	L. S. B. and M. D. Leakey	1959–72
	D. C. Johanson, T. D. White, and G. Eck	1986–present
Peninj	R. E. Leakey and G. Ll. Isaac	1964
Kenya		
Chemeron	J. E. Martyn	1965
	M. Pickford	1973
	A. Hill	1984–present
Chesowanja	J. Carney	1970
(Chemoigut)	M. Pickford	1973
	J. Gowlett	1978
Kanapoi	B. Patterson	1965
Lothagam	B. Patterson	1967
*Koobi Fora	R. E. Leakey and G. Ll. Isaac	1968–76
(east Turkana = east Rudolf)	R. E. Leakey	1976–present
West Turkana	R. E. Leakey and A. Walker	1984–present
Ethiopia		
*Lower Omo	F. C. Howell and Y. Coppens	1966–74
Middle Awash	J. D. Clark and T. D. White	1981
*Hadar	M. Taieb and D. C. Johanson	1973–76

Note: Asterisks mark the most prolific sites so far. The middle Awash sites perhaps have the greatest future potential

in years, especially by the radiopotassium method. So far, no reliable material for absolute dating has been found in the southern African sites, which have been dated mainly by comparing their animal fossils with fossils from dated layers in east Africa.

Although a partial australopithecine maxilla was found at Laetoli (Garusi) near Olduvai Gorge, northern Tanzania, in 1939, its significance was obscured by its singularity and by the onset of World War II. The first east African australopithecine to be widely recognized for what it was was a skull discovered by Louis and Mary Leakey at Olduvai Gorge in 1959. The skull was important not only because it extended the known range of the australopithecines but also because it occurred in deposits that were soon dated to about 1.75 mya by the newly developed radiopotassium method (L. S. B. Leakey et al. 1961). The 1.75 mya estimate was the first indication of the true antiquity of the australopithecines, and it nearly doubled the total time span that most specialists had allowed for human evolution.

Following their 1959 discovery, the Leakeys obtained funds for much more extensive research at Olduvai Gorge, leading to the recovery of many new early-hominid fossils, including the first remains of *Homo habilis*, the oldest known species of *Homo* (L. S. B. Leakey et al. 1964). Equally important, the Olduvai finds stimulated successful searches for australopithecines and very early *Homo* elsewhere in east Africa (Table 3.1, Fig. 3.4). So far, east Africa has provided only about half as many australopithecine fossils as southern Af-

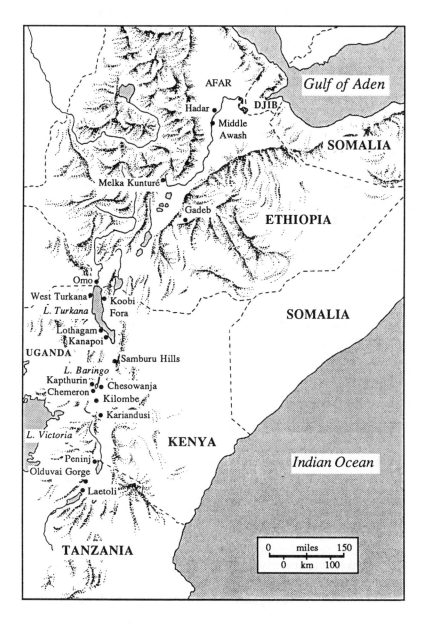

Figure 3.4. Approximate locations of the main Plio-Pleistocene sites of east Africa (adapted from J. W. K. Harris 1983: Fig. 2).

rica, but many of the east African specimens are remarkably complete, and the associated data, especially the absolute dates, have no parallel in southern Africa.

Geology of the Southern African Australopithecine Sites

The southern African australopithecine sites are all caves containing jumbles or breccias of stones (sometimes including artifacts) and fossils in a sandy-silty matrix, the whole commonly cemented together by calcareous glue precipitated from groundwater. Because the deposits tend to be very hard, excavation has involved explosives and pneumatic drills more than the trowels, brushes, and dental picks that archeologists and paleontologists prefer. The fossils, including those of the australopithecines, were brought to the caves mainly by carnivores, and they therefore provide little or no evidence for australopithecine behavior. In addition, nothing in the cave fills can be directly dated radiometrically, and their antiquity has been estimated mainly by their faunal contents (compared with faunal assemblages from radiometrically dated sites in east Africa). The essential features of the following site-by-site presentation are summarized in Figures 3.5 and 3.6 and in the following section on the geologic antiquity and geographic range of the earliest hominids. The site descriptions refer to artifact assemblages by using the terms Oldowan and Acheulean, which are only defined fully in the following sections. Readers who do not need or want a detailed introduction to the sites may wish to simply skim the individual sketches.

Taung

The child's skull assigned to *Australopithecus africanus* by Dart remains the only australopithecine fossil ever found at Taung. The cave in which it lay was largely quarried away before it could be studied by interested geologists, but it was probably part of an extensive system formed within the oldest of four limestone aprons (tufas) mantling the Gaap Escarpment near Taung (Peabody 1954; Butzer 1974, 1980; Partridge 1982a, 1985; Tobias 1985). Reddish sands, silts, and occasional bones entered the cave through fissures from the surface. The materials were subsequently cemented together by calcite (crystallized calcium carbonate) precipitated from water that periodically permeated the deposits. The origins of the bones remain

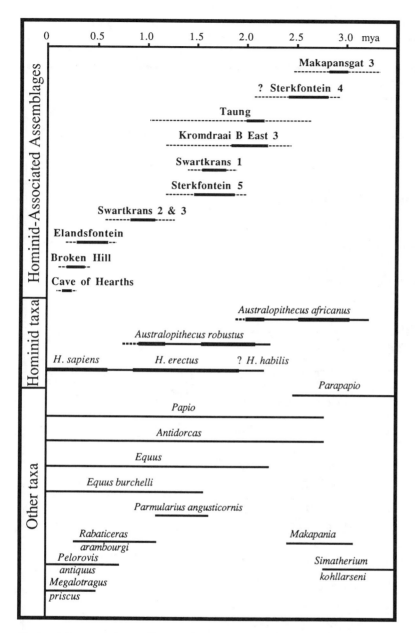

Figure 3.5. Ages (in millions of years ago) of some important south African fossil hominid sites, on the basis of their faunal contents (modified after Vrba 1982: 741). The numbers following site names are stratigraphic units (members). Also shown are the known time ranges of some important mammalian taxa used in the dating, as well as the inferred time ranges for fossil hominid species. (*Parapapio* and *Papio* are baboons, *Equus* and *Equus burchelli* are zebras, and the remaining species are buffalo or antelopes.)

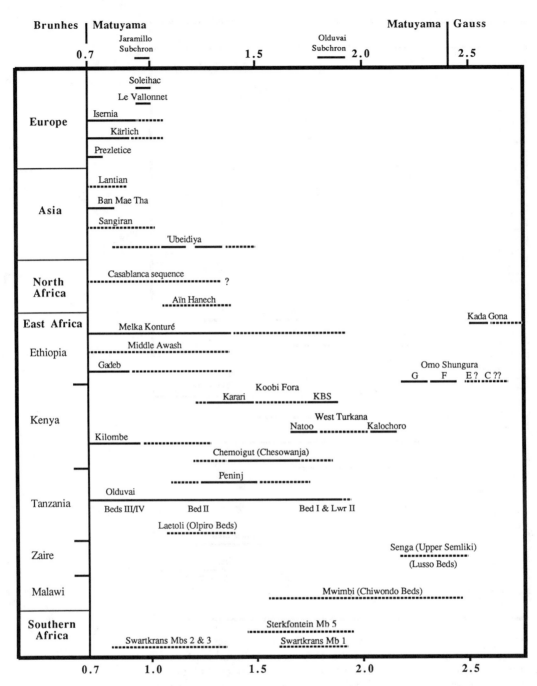

Figure 3.6. Dating of the earliest artifact industries in Africa and Eurasia (in a format suggested by Isaac 1986: Fig. 13.2). Dotted lines indicate possible or probable dates based mainly on geologic inference or faunal correlations. The best evidence for people in Eurasia before 1 mya comes from 'Ubeidiya in Israel, only marginally outside Africa. On the known record, people colonized the further reaches of Asia and Europe only after 1 mya.

obscure, but the smaller ones (from insectivores and small rodents) may have been introduced by owls roosting in or above the fissures. The larger ones, including especially those from baboons and the Taung child, may have been brought in by leopards or other large cats who used the cave as a lair. In 1949, fossil baboon skulls and limb bones damaged by carnivores were found in a nearby cave that may have been part of the Taung system (Brain 1985b).

The geologic age of the Taung skull is difficult to establish, in part because its geologic provenience is so poorly documented. An age of 1 mya or less has been suggested by calculating the time when geomorphic change first opened the cave (Partridge 1973, 1982a) and by uranium-series dates of 942,000 years on the limestone apron in which the cave occurred and of 764,000 years on the next youngest apron (Vogel and Partridge 1984). However, the assumptions behind the geomorphic dating are highly questionable, and uranium could have entered the aprons after they formed (Vogel 1985). In this case, the dates would underestimate the true age, perhaps by a substantial amount. The Taung fauna is sparse and its stratigraphic association with the skull is unclear, but it contains baboon fossils that compare closely with east African ones that slightly antedate 2 mya (Delson 1984). The Taung skull itself has figured in the dating controversy, since, at an age of 1 million years or less, it would be the latest known *Australopithecus africanus*, perhaps by more than 1 million years. This raises the possibility that it actually derives from the robust-australopithecine species, *A. robustus*, which, on evidence from Swartkrans (presented below), may have survived to 1 mya or later. However, a detailed analysis of the Taung dentition (Grine 1985a) unequivocally allies it with Sterkfontein and Makapansgat fossils of *A. africanus* that probably antedate 2 mya. On this basis, a date for Taung of 2 mya or more may seem most reasonable, but the argument is obviously circular and the true age remains uncertain.

Sterkfontein

At Sterkfontein, silts, sands, and other materials fell or were washed through a shaft descending from the surface into a solution cavern within the local dolomitic limestone. Once inside, the foreign debris, together with fragments of the cavern roof and walls, were cemented to a rock-hard breccia by calcite, which also occurs as pure interbeds and lenses within the breccia. Subsequently, erosion removed most of the cavern roof, exposing the breccia at the surface.

In accordance with the detailed study by Partridge (1978), the Sterkfontein cave fill (or Formation) is now commonly divided into six members, numbered 1–6 from bottom to top. Older deposits, so far unexplored, probably underlie these (Wilkinson 1983). Members 2–4 are generally characterized by normal magnetic polarity, which suggests they date from the Gauss Normal Polarity Chron, before 2.48 mya (D. Jones et al. 1986). This is consistent with dating based on resemblances between the Sterkfontein faunal assemblages and dated ones in east Africa.

Almost all the available Sterkfontein fossils come from Members 4–6. Unfortunately, many of the fossils were collected before the members were clearly defined, and their original stratigraphic provenience is now uncertain. This complication aside, however, faunal dating suggests that Member 4 probably accumulated sometime between 2.8 mya and 2.3 mya, perhaps mainly around 2.5 mya; Member 5 (= "the Extension Site") sometime between 1.8 mya and 1.3 mya, perhaps mainly around 1.5 mya; and Member 6 probably much later, after 200,000 years (Fig. 3.5) (Partridge 1982a, 1986; Vrba 1982).

So far, australopithecine fossils (assigned to *Australopithecus africanus*) have been found only in Member 4, while Member 5 has produced remains of early *Homo* and the oldest Sterkfontein stone artifacts (Tobias 1978; Stiles and Partridge 1979; Brain 1981; Clarke 1988). Member 6 has provided neither hominid fossils nor artifacts. From his detailed analysis of the Sterkfontein hominid and animal bones, Brain (1981) concluded that leopards or other large cats, denning in the cavern, probably accumulated the macrovertebrate bones in Member 4, while early people, sheltering near the cavern entrance, accumulated most of the bones in Members 5 and 6. He suggests that roosting owls introduced the microvertebrate bones found throughout the sequence.

Swartkrans

The geology of Swartkrans is better understood than that of any other southern African australopithecine site, thanks to the long-term efforts of C. K. Brain (1976, 1981, 1982, 1985a; also Butzer 1976a). Like nearby Sterkfontein, Swartkrans began as a subterranean dolomite cavern into which sediments fell or were washed through a shaft descending from the surface. The accumulating fill or breccia was cemented by calcite and later was exposed at the surface when erosion removed most of the cavern roof (Fig. 3.7). The stratigraphy is complex, because

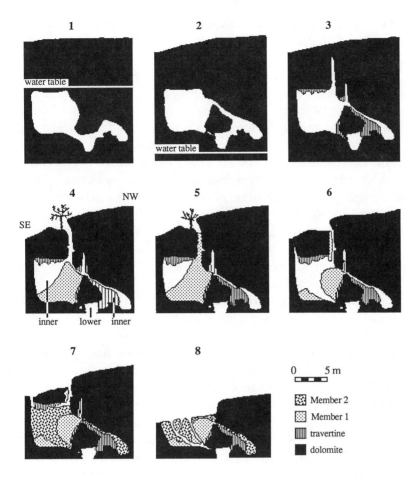

Figure 3.7. Evolution of the Swartkrans australopithecine cave, with a representation of its formation by solution inside the surrounding dolomitic limestone (Stage 1), its eventual opening to the surface (Stage 4), and the final exposure of its fill on the modern hillside (Stage 8) (adapted from Brain 1981: Fig. 185). Only the two main fossiliferous units (Members 1 and 2) are schematically depicted, along with expanses of nonfossiliferous dripstone (travertine).

later materials sometimes filled erosion or solution hollows within earlier breccia, and thus objects in close lateral proximity may differ greatly in age.

Brain (1988) now recognizes five members—numbered 1–5 from bottom to top—within the Swartkrans cave fill (or Formation). Member 2 occurs not only above Member 1 but also below a part of it that was left hanging from the roof when the middle part was eroded away. On the basis of faunal comparisons with east Africa (Vrba 1982), Member 1 probably accumulated sometime between 1.8 mya and 1.5 mya (Fig. 3.5). Member 2 is more difficult to date, because the available fauna almost certainly contains many elements inadvertently mixed in from overlying Member 3. It may span a considerable period of time, from perhaps 1 mya to 700,000–500,000 years ago. Member 3 may be only slightly younger, since thermoluminescence determinations on quartz grains tentatively suggest it is only about half as old as Member 1 (Vogel 1985), that is, between 900,000 and 600,000 years old. Member 4 is probably much younger, almost certainly postdating 200,000 years. Bones from Member 5 have been radiocarbon dated to about 11,000 years ago.

Fossils of the robust australopithecine, *Australopithecus robustus,* have been found in Members 1–3 and are especially abundant in Member 1. Some pieces in Members 2 and 3 may have been reworked by erosion from Member 1, but most are probably in place, and, if Members 2 and 3 truly postdate 1 mya, their remains of robust australopithecines may be the youngest known. Members 1–3 also contain occasional bones of *Homo erectus,* including Member 2 fragments originally assigned to *"Telanthropus capensis."*

Several stone artifacts have been recovered from Member 1, as have at least eleven bone fragments with polished tips that Brain believes were digging tools. The stone artifacts can be assigned to a local variant of the Acheulean Industrial Complex. Generally similar stone and bone artifacts also occur sporadically in the overlying Members 2 and 3. Member 4 contains Middle Stone Age artifacts, while Member 5 is artifactually sterile. Occasional burnt bones first appear in Member 3, perhaps indicating incipient human control over fire. The burnt bones are not locally concentrated, however, and there is no evidence for hearths.

From his detailed analysis of the Swartkrans animal and hominid bones, Brain (1981) suggested that leopards or other large cats accumulated the macrofaunal bones in Member 1. Leopards, brown hyenas, and Stone Age people probably jointly produced the assemblages in Member 2, and people alone were probably mainly responsible for the bones in Members 3 and 4. Hyenas again may have accumulated the bones in Member 5. Owls probably introduced the microfaunal bones found throughout.

Kromdraai

Kromdraai consists of two adjacent fossil caves, Kromdraai B, the "ape-man site," which has provided both australopithecine and animal bones, and Kromdraai A, the "faunal site," which has provided only animal bones. A and B may have been part of a single cavern system into which sediments fell or were washed through shafts descending from the surface, as at Sterkfontein and Swartkrans. Subsequent cementation of the cavern fills by calcite and removal of the roof(s) by erosion exposed the hardened cave fills (breccias) at the surface. The geology of Kromdraai B is better known, thanks to a study by

Partridge (1982a, 1982b) in connection with excavations super-
vised by Vrba (1981, 1982) between 1977 and 1980.

Partridge has described two spatially distinct areas at
Kromdraai B, called East and West. To date, hominid fossils,
assigned to a single species *(Australopithecus robustus)*, have
been found only at Kromdraai B East, where they occur in
Member 3 within a sequence of five members comprising the
Kromdraai B East cave fill (or Formation). So far, Member 3 has
provided no artifacts, though these are present in one or both of
the overlying members (4 and 5). The fauna is not especially
useful in dating, but, on the basis of the morphology of the
hominid fossils (Grine 1982), Vrba (1982) suggests that Member
3 accumulated around 2 mya (Fig. 3.5), after Sterkfontein
Member 4 and perhaps slightly before Swartkrans Member 1. A
2-million-year age is consistent with the mainly reversed
polarity of Kromdraai B sediments, which places them within
the Matuyama Reversed Chron, between 2.48 mya and 730,000
years ago (D. Jones et al. 1986).

From an analysis of the bone assemblages obtained before
Vrba's work, Brain (1981) concluded that large cats, hyenas, or
both were primarily responsible for the macrovertebrate bones
at both Kromdraai A and Kromdraai B and that owls introduced
the microfaunal bones. However, from her excavations, Vrba
(1981; also Vrba and Panagos 1982) suggests that many of the
macrovertebrate bones represent animals that fell into the cave
and were then unable to leave.

Makapansgat

Whereas the Krugersdorp australopithecine caves (Sterkfontein, Swartkrans, and Kromdraai) were probably subterranean
receptacles linked to a gently undulating surface by strongly
sloping or even near vertical shafts, the Makapansgat Limeworks cave was probably a tunnel-like cavern with a nearly
horizontal entrance from the flank of a steep-sided valley
(Maguire 1985). Relative to gravity, water flow probably played
a greater depositional role at Makapansgat than at the Krugersdorp sites, and some of the older deposits probably accumulated under standing water. It is also possible that animals,
especially hyenas, regularly penetrated deeper into Makapansgat than into the Krugersdorp Caves. As in the Krugersdorp
sites, however, after deposition the sediments at Makapansgat
were indurated, mainly by calcium carbonate precipitated
from water penetrating the deposit.

Partridge (1979, 1982a) has divided the Makapansgat cave

fill (or Formation) among five members, numbered 1–5 from bottom to top. So far, hominid fossils, generally assigned to *Australopithecus africanus*, have been found almost entirely in Member 3 (the "grey breccia"), with a single piece also in Member 4. No definite stone artifacts have been uncovered, but Dart (1957) has suggested that the animal bones in Member 3 were used as tools.

From comparison with dated east African faunas, the fauna of Member 3 suggests an age of about 3 million years, and Member 4 is probably only slightly younger (Fig. 3.5) (Partridge 1982a; Vrba 1982; Maguire 1985). Among the southern African australopithecine sites, Makapansgat is the most amenable to paleomagnetic dating. This is because the lower members were laid down partly under water, so that postdepositional disturbance of the sedimentary particles was very limited. The available paleomagnetic readings reinforce an age estimate of about 3 million years for Member 3 (Brock et al. 1977; McFadden 1980; McFadden and Brock 1984; Partridge 1986). However, Maguire (1985) cautions that the five-member scheme may seriously oversimplify much greater stratigraphic complexity and that supposedly successive members may consist in part of broadly contemporaneous depositional variants or facies. One implication is that the paleomagnetic dating may not be valid.

On the basis of the bones and their context, Maguire (1985; also Maguire et al. 1980) suggests that striped hyenas accumulated the bone assemblage in Member 3 and that leopards living near the entrance and hyenas penetrating into the depths probably contributed most of the bones in Member 4.

Geology of the East African Australopithecine Sites

Unlike the southern African australopithecine sites, the east African ones are all open-air localities, mainly in deposits that formed near ancient lakes or streams. Although many of the east African hominid fossils were probably displaced from their original resting places by flowing water, and although most had eroded from the enclosing deposits before discovery, some occur or occurred in what may be ancient "living sites." This is especially true at Olduvai Gorge and Koobi Fora. In general, then, compared with southern Africa, east Africa is potentially more informative about australopithecine behavior. Equally important, at the majority of east African sites, the layers that contain fossils and sometimes also stone artifacts are interstratified with volcanic extrusives, particularly volcanic ash layers (tuffs). The volcanic material can often be dated

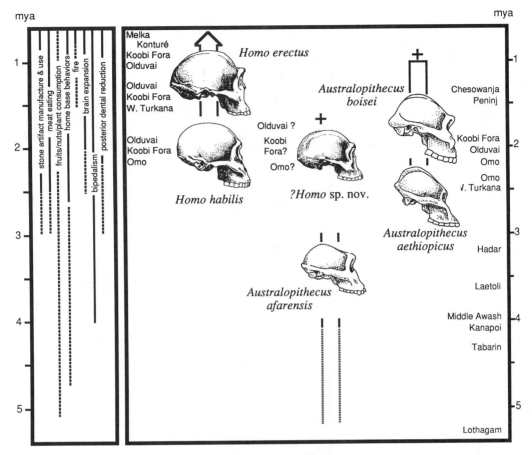

Figure 3.8. Dating of important east African Plio-Pleistocene sites, the fossil hominid species they contain, and some key behavioral and anatomical traits detectable in the fossil record (dotted lines indicate the probable durations of traits not yet demonstrated from the fossil record) (adapted from J. W. K. Harris 1983: Fig. 1).

by absolute methods (especially radiopotassium), with the result that the absolute ages of the east African sites are reasonably well fixed. As in the case of the previous section on southern African sites, a reader who does not need or want detailed information on specific east African sites may prefer to skim the individual sketches, attending mostly to the accompanying figures. The principal conclusions are summarized in Figures 3.6 and 3.8, as well as in the text sections that follow this one.

Olduvai Gorge

Olduvai Gorge is a canyon as much as 100 m deep and roughly 50 km long that is cut into volcanic, lacustrine, fluvial, and eolian deposits filling a shallow basin within the Serengeti

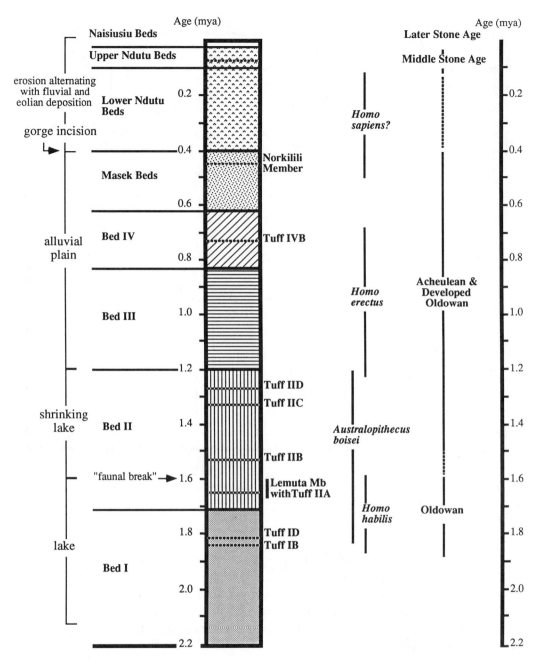

Figure 3.9. Schematic stratigraphy of Olduvai Gorge, showing the principal beds, their depositional environment, their probable age (in millions of years ago), the most important volcanic tuffs used as stratigraphic markers, and the inferred temporal extent of hominid taxa and of artifact industries represented in the deposits (modified after M. D. Leakey and Hay 1982: Fig. 2).

Plain of northern Tanzania. The exposed deposits have been divided among seven successive mappable units or formations, which accumulated between about 2.1 mya and 15,000 years ago (Hay 1976; M. D. Leakey 1978, 1980; M. D. Leakey and Hay 1982). From bottom to top, the units are: Bed I, Bed II, Bed III, Bed IV, the Masek Beds, the Ndutu Beds, and the Naisiusiu Beds (Fig. 3.9). Distinctive tuffs at various levels within the sequence aid in horizontal correlation and mapping, which has been complicated by extensive faulting of the deposits.

During the accumulation of Bed I, the Olduvai Basin contained a broad, shallow, saline, and alkaline lake, whose level and size fluctuated considerably. Most archeological and paleontological sites occur along the southeastern lakeshore where freshwater streams drained into the lake from nearby volcanic uplands. Radiopotassium dates indicate that lavas at the base of Bed I formed about 2.1 mya but that most of the sedimentary deposits, including all the fossiliferous sites, accumulated between 1.85 mya and 1.70 mya.

The lake persisted during the deposition of Lower Bed II, roughly until the accumulation of a sequence of eolian tuffs known as the Lemuta Member. A major disconformity above the Lemuta Member marks the beginning of widespread faulting and folding in the central part of the basin, as a result of which the lake progressively shrank, disappearing entirely shortly before the end of Bed II deposition. The disconformity also marks an abrupt faunal change at Olduvai, after which some archaic large mammals represented in Bed I and Lower Bed II no longer occur and several new species make their first appearance. Another disconformity separates Bed II from overlying Bed III and is believed to reflect a major phase of Rift Valley faulting that has been radiopotassium dated elsewhere to 1.20–1.15 mya. Thus, Bed II is believed to have formed between about 1.70 mya and 1.20 mya. The disconformity above the Lemuta Member, separating Lower Bed II from Upper (or Middle and Upper) Bed II, is thought to be about 1.6 million years old, on the basis of a radiopotassium date of 1.65 mya on Tuff IIA within the Lemuta Member, which also contains the top of the Olduvai Normal Subchron (ca. 1.67 mya) at or near its base.

The widespread faulting that produced the disconformity between Bed II and Bed III led to substantial erosion of Bed II. The Olduvai Basin was transformed into an alluvial plain, and Beds III and IV were primarily stream laid. The boundary between the Matuyama Reversed Chron and the Brunhes Normal Chron (ca. 730,000 years ago) lies just below Tuff IVB near the middle of Bed IV. If an age of 1.2 mya for the base of

Bed III and a relatively constant sedimentation rate for Beds III and IV are assumed, Bed IV appears to have formed between roughly 830,000 and 620,000 years ago.

The Masek Beds are mainly fluvial deposits similar to those of Beds III and IV and were the last sediments to accumulate prior to major incision of the gorge. They contain tuffs from a volcano whose activity ceased about 400,000 years ago. They are thus estimated to span the interval 600,000–400,000 years ago, which is consistent with their thickness, if one assumes the same average sedimentation rate as is assumed for Beds III and IV.

The Ndutu Beds are fluvial and eolian deposits that accumulated over a lengthy period of intermittent faulting, erosion, and partial filling of the gorge. The upper unit of the Ndutu Beds contains eolian tuffs that are mineralogically similar to but much more weathered than tuffs in the Naisiusiu Beds, whose age has been established by the radiocarbon method. If a constant weathering rate is assumed, the upper unit of the Ndutu Beds would then seem to have a mean age of 75,000 years, from which it has been suggested that the Lower Ndutu Beds accumulated between roughly 400,000 years ago (the top of the Masek Beds) and 75,000 years ago.

Finally, the Naisiusiu Beds are mainly eolian tuffs deposited after the Upper Ndutu Beds had been severely eroded and after the gorge had been cut to its present level. Radiocarbon datings bracket the Naisiusiu Beds between about 22,000 and 15,000 years ago.

Fossils of a robust australopithecine *(Australopithecus boisei)* have been found in Bed I, Lower Bed II, and Upper Bed II, while fossils assigned to *Homo habilis* occur in Bed I and Lower Bed II. Fossils of certain or probable *H. erectus* have been found in Upper Bed II, Bed III, and Bed IV, while very fragmentary fossils that may derive from early *H. sapiens* are known from the Masek and Lower Ndutu Beds. A skull of early *H. sapiens* from Lake Ndutu, at the headwaters of Olduvai Gorge, came from deposits that are probably coeval with the upper (Norkilili) Member of the Masek Beds (M. D. Leakey and Hay 1982). Stone artifacts occur throughout the Olduvai sequence: Oldowan in Bed I and Lower Bed II, Developed Oldowan and Acheulean in Upper Bed II to Bed IV, Acheulean in the Masek Beds, Middle Stone Age near the top of the Lower Ndutu Beds and in the Upper Ndutu Beds, and Later Stone Age in the Naisiusiu Beds. The Lake Ndutu skull, from deposits that are probably correlative with the Upper Masek Beds, was associated with Acheulean artifacts.

Laetoli

The Laetoli locality is approximately 45 km south of Olduvai Gorge in northern Tanzania. Technically, it was the first site in east Africa to provide australopithecine fossils. These were a lower canine found in 1935 and a small right-maxillary fragment, with premolars and an isolated third molar, found in 1939. However, initially the canine was misidentified as cercopithecoid (T. D. White 1981), and the significance of the maxillary fragment and molar was only appreciated much later, following more tightly controlled and abundant discoveries at the site between 1974 and 1979 (M. D. Leakey 1987a). These comprised teeth, jaws, and a very fragmentary immature skeleton from a maximum of twenty-three australopithecine individuals (M. D. Leakey 1987c). Most were found on the surface, but they clearly derive from the upper part of the Laetolil Beds (also known as the Garusi or Vogel River Series), which consist mainly of eolian and air-fall volcanic tuffs covering an area of about 70 square km in the Laetoli region (M. D. Leakey et al. 1976; M. D. Leakey 1980; M. D. Leakey and Hay 1982; J. M. Harris 1985; Hay 1987).

On the basis of their find spots, the individual Laetoli australopithecine fossils can be at least broadly related to eight widespread marker tuffs, numbered 1–8 from bottom to top. Most of the specimens came from between Tuff 3 and Tuff 8, and in age they are bracketed between the radiopotassium estimates of 3.76 mya, from below Tuff 1, and 3.46 mya for Tuff 8 (Fig. 3.10) (Drake and Curtis 1987). One specimen (a mandible designated Laetoli Hominid 4) is the holotype (type fossil) for *Australopithecus afarensis* (Johanson et al. 1978), to which the remaining fossils have also been assigned. *A. afarensis* was probably responsible for some spectacular human footprints preserved on a paleosurface within Tuff 7 (= the "Footprint Tuff") (M. D. Leakey and Hay 1979; Hay and Leakey 1982; M. D. Leakey 1987b). Surfaces within the tuff also preserve abundant prints from a wide variety of animals.

In addition to australopithecine fossils, the Laetoli locality has provided an archaic *Homo sapiens* skull (Laetoli Hominid 18) and a massive, heavily rolled mandible (LH 29) tentatively assigned to *H. erectus* (M. D. Leakey 1987c). The skull came from the Upper Ngaloba Beds, which cap the local stratigraphic sequence, while the mandible probably came from the somewhat older Lower Ngaloba Beds. A giraffe vertebra from the same level as the skull has been dated by thorium-230 and proctactinium-231 to 129,000 ± 4,000 years

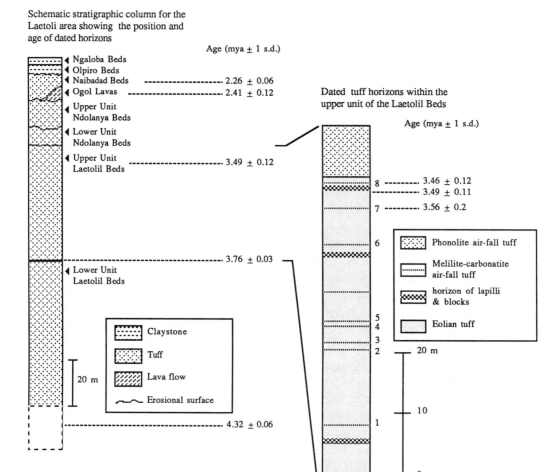

Figure 3.10. *Left:* Schematic stratigraphic column for the Laetoli area, showing the position and age of dated horizons. *Right:* Dated tuff horizons within the upper unit of the Laetolil Beds (redrawn after Drake and Curtis 1987: Figs. 2.10, 2.11).

ago and 108,000 ± 30,000 years ago, respectively (Hay 1987). These dates are tentative, but they support a previous age estimate for the skull, an estimate based on the skull's position just above a tuff that is mineralogically very similar to one near the top of the Lower Ndutu Beds at Olduvai. On the basis of both its stratigraphic position and the extrapolated sedimentation rates at Olduvai, the correlated Ndutu tuff appears to have an age of 120,000 ± 30,000 years.

No stone artifacts have been found in the Laetolil Beds. However, Acheulean or Developed Oldowan bifaces and other artifacts occur in the Olpiro Beds, which in places unconformably overlie the Laetolil Beds and are clearly much younger, perhaps being broadly coeval with Olduvai Bed II (J. W. K. Harris and Harris 1981). The Ngaloba Beds, unconformably overlying the Olpiro Beds, contain Middle Stone Age artifacts including ones that were directly associated with the Ngaloba skull.

Peninj

The Peninj site is located west of Lake Natron, approximately 80 km northeast of Olduvai Gorge in northern Tanzania. The fossiliferous sediments at Peninj accumulated mostly in and around a lake within a broad, relatively shallow basin (Isaac 1967). The deposits have been divided into two major units— the Humbu Formation (older) and the Moinik Formation (younger). Paleomagnetic readings and radiopotassium dates on a basalt near the base of the Moinik Formation and on a basalt within the Humbu Formation suggest that the Humbu Formation probably dates from between 1.6 mya and 1.0 mya (Isaac and Curtis 1974). This age is consistent with the Humbu Formation fauna, which resembles that from Upper Bed II Olduvai.

The mandible of a robust australopithecine was found in Humbu Formation deposits that are probably just older than 1.6 million years, while Acheulean artifacts occur in deposits that are probably only slightly younger.

Chemeron and Chemoigut (Chesowanja)

The Chemeron and Chemoigut Formations are two among a series of twelve successive fossiliferous formations (Fig. 3.11), spanning the interval between roughly 14 mya (mid-Miocene) and the near present (Holocene), in the Tugen Hills near Lake Baringo, central Kenya (W. W. Bishop 1971, 1978; W. W. Bishop et al. 1971; Hill et al. 1985). More than 3,000 m thick, the depositional sequence comprises fluviatile and lacustrine sediments with numerous interbedded lavas and tuffs from which radiopotassium dates have been obtained.

The Chemeron Formation consists of fluvio-lacustrine deposits divided into five members, numbered 1–5 from older to younger. Member 1 or correlative deposits have provided a hominoid proximal humerus, possibly from an australopithecine, and a fragmentary mandible, resembling smaller mandibles of *Australopithecus afarensis* (Hill 1985; Ward and Hill 1987). Deposits probably belonging to Member 4 have provided a hominoid (?australopithecine) temporal fragment. Both radiopotassium dates and faunal remains imply the Chemeron

Figure 3.11. Schematic representation of the stratigraphic sequence near Lake Baringo, central Kenya, in relation to some other important east African sites, and a postulated phylogeny of the Hominoidea (partly after Hill et al. 1985: Fig. 1, and partly courtesy of A. Hill, unpublished). Circled Hs designate the stratigraphic positions of hominoid fossils from the Baringo basin.

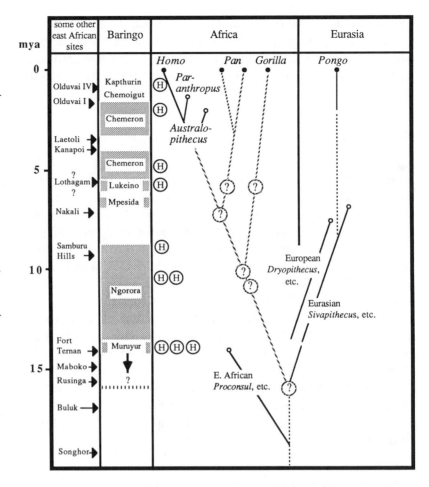

Formation spans a very long interval, from before 5 mya to after 2 mya. However, at the Tabarin locality where the mandible fragment was found, a combination of radiopotassium dates and faunal correlations implies an age between 5.25 mya and 4.15 mya (Hill 1985; Hill et al. 1985; Ward and Hill 1987). A similar age has been suggested for the proximal humerus (Pickford et al. 1983), but it is only tentative pending further stratigraphic work (Hill et al. 1985). The temporal fragment was probably associated with a much younger fauna, suggesting an age between 2.5 mya and 1.5 mya.

The Chemoigut Formation, postdating the Chemeron Formation, has provided two fragmentary skulls and some fragmentary teeth attributed to a robust australopithecine (*Australopithecus boisei*) (Carney et al. 1971; W. W. Bishop et al. 1975, 1978; Gowlett et al. 1981). On the basis of its faunal contents, the Chemoigut Formation appears to be between 2.0 million and 1.5 million years old, in keeping with a radiopotassium date of approximately 1.42 mya for the Chesowanja Basalt that immediately overlies it (Hooker and Miller 1979). Artifacts from several localities within the Chemoigut Formation have been assigned to the Chemoigut Industry, which is closely similar to the Oldowan of Bed I and Lower Bed II, Olduvai (Gowlett et al. 1981). At one site, artifacts were associated with a concentration of baked-clay fragments that may represent the oldest traces of humanly controlled or produced fire (J. D. Clark and Harris 1985). However, natural baking—for example, below a smoldering tree stump—cannot be ruled out.

The Chesowanja Formation, which unconformably overlies the Chemoigut Formation, has provided no hominid remains, but it does contain numerous stone artifacts. These have been assigned to the Losokweta Industry, which may be regarded as a variant of the Developed Oldowan or of the Acheulean, though it lacks bifaces (Gowlett et al. 1981; J. W. K. Harris et al., in press-a). Bifaces that occur on the surface of the Chesowanja deposits apparently represent a post-Chesowanja Acheulean industry.

Besides the Chemeron and Chemoigut Formations, two others in the Baringo succession have provided probable or certain hominid fossils. These are the Lukeino Formation (a lower molar), radiopotassium dated to between 6.3 mya and 5.1 may (Hill et al. 1985), and the Kapthurin Formation (two partial mandibles and four postcranial bones), dating from the mid-Quaternary, certainly after 700,000 and before 230,000 years ago (Tallon 1978; Wood and van Noten 1986). The Kapthurin fossils derive from early *Homo sapiens* or possibly from *H. erectus*. In addition, the Muruyur Beds, dated to about 13–14 mya, have furnished a calcaneum possibly from the fossil ape *Proconsul*, and the Ngorora Formation, bracketed between roughly 13 mya and 9 mya, has delivered two hominoid teeth (Hill et al. 1985). The first one found, an upper molar, is relatively undiagnostic, but the second, a lower premolar, has been tentatively assigned to *Proconsul*. If the assignment is valid, the occurrence is the latest known for *Proconsul*.

Lothagam and Kanapoi

Lothagam and Kanapoi are located approximately 75 km apart, in the drainage of the Kerio River southwest of Lake Turkana in northern Kenya (Fig. 3.12) (Behrensmeyer 1976). At Lothagam, fluvial deposits supplied a fragmentary hominoid

Figure 3.12.
Distribution of
Omo Group Plio-
Pleistocene and
Mio-Pliocene
deposits in the
Lake Turkana
Basin (courtesy of
F. H. Brown,
unpublished).

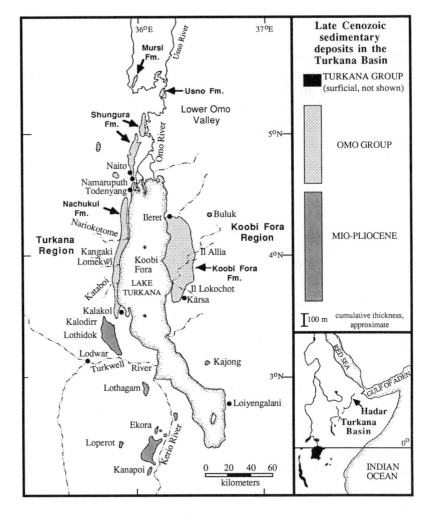

mandible associated with a fauna estimated to be 5–6 million years old. This date is consistent with radiometric dates of about 8.3 mya and 3.7 mya that bracket the sediments from which the fauna came. The specimen is too incomplete for taxonomic assignment and could represent a hominid or an ape (T. D. White 1986a).

At Kanapoi, similar sediments, overlain by a basalt that dates between 2.5 mya and 4 mya, have provided a hominid distal humerus accompanied by a fauna suggesting an age of 4–5 mya. If it is assumed that the provenience of the Kanapoi specimen has been accurately assessed, then, along with the mandible fragment and humerus from the Chemeron Formation and a cranial fragment from Belohdelie in the Middle Awash, it is among the oldest hominid fossils known.

Koobi Fora (= East Turkana = East Rudolf)

The localities collectively called Koobi Fora are located on the east side of Lake Turkana (formerly Lake Rudolf) in northern Kenya (Fig. 3.12). The fossiliferous sediments at Koobi Fora were laid down mainly by streams flowing into Lake Turkana from uplands to the east, but at least three major expansions (transgressions) of the lake are also recorded (Vondra and Bowen 1976). Tuff layers interspersed throuughout the sequence provide material for radiopotassium dating and also serve as markers for stratigraphic correlations not only within the Koobi Fora region but also between Koobi Fora and other areas, including the lower Omo River Basin to the north, the West Turkana region to the west, the Kerio Valley southwest of Lake Turkana, the Hadar region of cast-ccntral Ethiopia, and even deep-sea cores from the Gulf of Aden (F. H. Brown et al. 1985b).

All the Plio-Pleistocene deposits and interbedded tuffs at Koobi Fora are now subsumed in the Koobi Fora Formation, divided into eight successive members, each named for a tuff at its base (F. H. Brown and Feibel 1986) (Figs. 3.13, 3.14). A

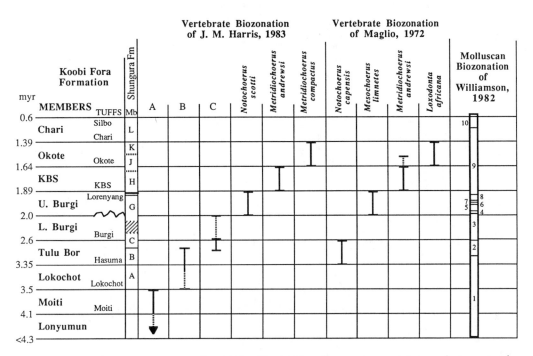

Figure 3.13. Schematic stratigraphy of the Koobi Fora Formation, with correlations to the Shungura Formation of the lower Omo River Valley and to biostratigraphies suggested by Harris, Maglio, and Williamson (redrawn after F. H. Brown and Feibel 1986: Fig. 9). *Notochoerus* and *Metridiochoerus* are genera of extinct pigs. *Loxodonta africana* is the living African elephant.

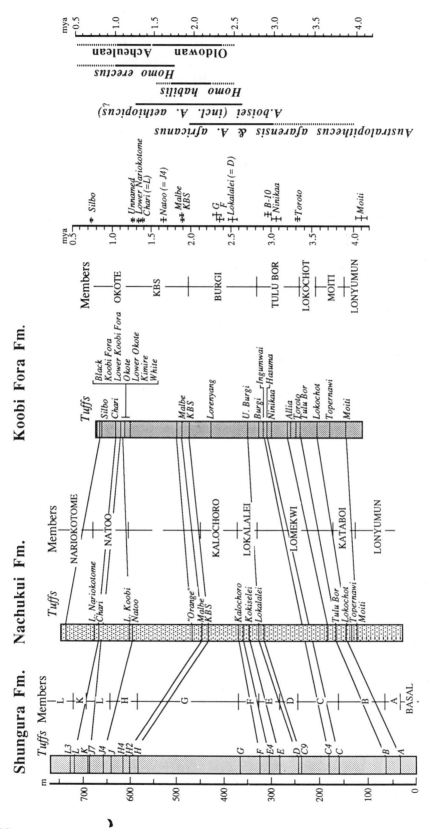

Figure 3.14. Correlation of the Plio-Pleistocene successions in the lower Omo River Valley (Shungura Fm.), (West) Turkana Region (Nachukui Fm.), and Koobi Fora Region (Koobi Fora Fm.) (courtesy of F. H. Brown, unpublished). The formations and their constituent members are scaled according to thickness, not according to age. Age has been determined by radiometric dates on various tuffs, as indicated on the time scale to the right of the Koobi Fora Fm.

combination of radiopotassium dates, paleomagnetic readings, and faunal correlations indicates that the deposits accumulated between about 4.3 mya and 600,000 years ago. In historical perspective, the Koobi Fora Formation provides a highly instructive example of how radiometric dates may be checked by faunal remains. Initially, dates of approximately 2.6 mya for the KBS Tuff implied that various mammal taxa (*Equus*, for example) had appeared at Koobi Fora at least 600,000 years before they first appeared in the lower Omo River Basin (Shungura Formation) at the north end of Lake Turkana (F. H. Brown et al. 1978). This seemed unlikely and prompted redating, which eventually showed that the original 2.6 mya estimate was about 700,000 years too old.

The majority of hominid fossils at Koobi Fora come from deposits overlying the KBS Tuff (in what was formerly known as the Upper Member of the Koobi Fora Formation = the Ileret Member at the Ileret Locality) (Walker and Leakey 1978; Walker 1981b). The KBS Tuff is now dated at about 1.89 mya. Fossils clearly representing a robust australopithecine *(Australopithecus boisei)* have been found mainly in the KBS Member, but they also occur below it and above it, especially in the overlying Okote Member. In sum, they have been found in deposits spanning the interval from somewhat before 2.0 mya to perhaps 1.4 mya. Fossils commonly attributed to *Homo habilis* or simply to early *Homo* (and including the famous KNM-ER 1470 skull) have been recovered in the Upper Burgi Member just below the KBS Tuff, where they probably date to about 2 mya. Fossils clearly representing *H. erectus* have been found in the KBS Member just below and also above the Okote Tuff, where they probably range from slightly before 1.7 mya to perhaps 1.3 mya. Finally, fossils representing yet another taxon (*A. africanus* or a new, small-brained species of *Homo*) have been found both in and below the KBS Member, where they probably date from before 2.0 mya to perhaps 1.7 mya.

The oldest stone artifacts so far found at Koobi Fora occur just below and within the KBS Tuff, where they are dated to about 2–1.8 mya. They have been assigned to the KBS Industry and resemble broadly contemporaneous Oldowan artifacts from Bed I at Olduvai Gorge (J. W. K. Harris and Isaac 1976; Isaac and Harris 1978). Somewhat younger artifacts from the Okote Member, dated to roughly 1.4 mya, have been assigned to the Karari Industry, which is broadly similar to the Developed Oldowan at Olduvai. An early-Acheulean site has been excavated in deposits that probably correlate with the Chari Member, slightly postdating 1.4 mya.

The Lower Omo River Basin

The localities collectively referred to as Lower Omo occur in the lower valley of the Omo River, just north of where it enters Lake Turkana in southwestern Ethiopia (Fig. 3.12). The Lower Omo preserves more than 1,000 m of Plio-Pleistocene sediments, deposited in a subsiding basin mainly by the meandering ancestral Omo River (Howell 1978b; Chavaillon 1982). The sequence also records four or five episodes of mainly lacustrine sedimentation under a greatly expanded ancient Lake Turkana. As at Koobi Fora, numerous interbedded tuffs provide material for radiometric dating and also serve as markers for stratigraphic correlations, not only within the Lower Omo region but also between the Lower Omo and other regions, especially Koobi Fora and West Turkana (Figs. 3.13, 3.14) (F. H. Brown et al. 1985b; J. M. Harris et al. 1988). As a result of extensive paleontological collecting, following extremely careful and thorough geologic mapping and dating, the Lower Omo has provided the standard Plio-Pleistocene biostratigraphic sequence with which other east African records are routinely compared.

Radiometric dates and complementary paleomagnetic readings show that the Plio-Pleistocene deposits of the Lower Omo span the interval between roughly 4.1 mya and 800,000 years ago. The sequence includes four main, spatially discrete geologic formations: the Mursi Formation, dated to about 4.1 mya; the Nkalabong Formation, dated to about 3.95 mya; the Usno Formation, bracketed between 4.1 mya and 2.97 mya; and the Shungura Formation (= the classic "Omo Beds"), with exposures spanning the interval from approximately 3.3 mya to 800,000 years ago. These formations are now lumped with the Koobi Fora Formation and other correlative deposits in the Lake Turkana Basin into the Omo Group. Paleontologically, the Shungura Formation is by far the most productive and is the principal source of information on dated Plio-Pleistocene faunal change in east Africa. It comprises twelve members, labeled (from bottom to top), the Basal Member and Members A–L (excluding I, which was skipped). Except for the Basal Member, each member includes at its base a tuff with the same letter designation.

At most localities, Omo Group sediments have been deformed by tilting and subsequent faulting, so that their bedding planes intersect the surface at a distinct angle. They are overlain by much younger (late-mid-Pleistocene-to-mid-Holocene) horizontal sediments assigned to the Kibish (or "Omo-Kibish") Formation (Butzer 1976b).

Most of the hominid fossils from the Lower Omo have been found in the Shungura Formation, but some are also known from the Usno Formation. Because most of the fossils accumulated in relatively high-energy (fluvial) environments, they tend to be very fragmentary, which hinders both sorting and diagnosis. However, at least four taxa have been recognized: (1) a gracile australopithecine (*Australopithecus afarensis* and/or possibly *A. africanus*) from the Usno Formation and from Members B–D of the Shungura Formation, spanning the interval from about 3 mya to perhaps 2.6 mya; (2) robust australopithecines (*A. boisei* or its immediate ancestor) from Shungura Members C–G and perhaps L, between 2.5 mya and perhaps 1.2 mya; (3) *Homo* cf. *habilis* or simply *Homo* sp. on the basis of a relatively small number of fragmentary specimens from Shungura Members E–H and perhaps L, that is, between roughly 2.3 mya and perhaps 1.3 mya; and (4) *H. erectus* in Shungura Member K, that is, about 1.4 mya.

The oldest well-dated artifacts in the Lower Omo succession come from Shungura Members F and G and are therefore probably 2.4–2.3 million years old (Howell et al. 1987). Potentially older (2.5–2.4 million-year-old) artifacts may occur in Member E or even in Member C, but this has yet to be confirmed by excavation. All the artifacts fit within the Oldowan Industrial Complex, as originally defined at Olduvai Gorge.

In addition to fossils of australopithecines and early *Homo*, the Lower Omo has provided fossils of near-modern or modern *Homo sapiens*. These come from Member 1 of the Kibish Formation, which disconformably overlies the Omo Group Formations and is believed to date from the early part of the late Quaternary.

West Turkana

West Turkana is the name informally applied to an area west of Lake Turkana (northern Kenya) (Fig. 3.12) where there are exposures of fossiliferous Plio-Pleistocene deposits broadly similar to those at Koobi Fora and in the lower Omo River Valley. Designated as the Nachukui Formation, these deposits comprise eight successive members that can be directly correlated with members of the Koobi Fora and Shungura Formations on the basis of shared volcanic tuffs (Fig. 3.14) (F. H. Brown et al. 1985b; J. M. Harris et al. 1988). The correlations and direct dating show that the Nachukui Formation accumulated between about 4.3 mya and 700,000 years ago.

The rich mammalian fauna from the Nachukui Formation (more than one thousand mammalian fossils from ninety-three species) corroborates and supplements the basic biostratigraphy previously established in the lower Omo River Valley and at Koobi Fora (J. M. Harris et al. 1988). The Nachukui sequence is particularly notable for fossil assemblages dated between roughly 3 mya and 2 mya, a time interval that elsewhere in Africa is well controlled only in the lower Omo River Valley. Hominid fossils have been recovered from several horizons. A taxon (or taxa) so far undesignated occurs in the lower part of the Lomekwi Member with a probable age of around 3.3–3.2 million years. Robust australopithecines are represented in the Upper Lomekwi Member and in the Lokalalei and Kaitio Members, where they are bracketed between about 2.5 mya and 1.6 mya. A cranial fragment attributed to *Homo habilis* has been found in the Kalochoro Member, which is probably slightly more than 2 million years old. Finally, very important specimens of *H. erectus* (discussed in Chapter 4) have been found in the Natoo Member at a level dated to about 1.6 mya (F. H. Brown et al. 1985a). Stone artifacts (undescribed as of this writing) are known from both the Kalochoro and Natoo Members.

Preliminarily, all the robust australopithecine fossils have been tentatively assigned to *Australopithecus boisei,* but those from the Upper Lomekwi Member are the oldest undeniable robust australopithecines yet found, and, as discussed below, they differ in important respects from later *A. boisei* and *A. robustus.* They may represent a distinct species ancestral to *A. boisei* or to both *A. boisei* and *A. robustus.* The same species is perhaps also represented by much less diagnostic specimens in broadly coeval (ca. 2.5–2.3 million-year-old) deposits in the lower Omo River Valley (Walker et al. 1986a; R. E. F. Leakey and Walker 1988).

Hadar

The Hadar site is located in the Awash River Valley within the Afar Depression, about 300 km northeast of Addis Ababa, Ethiopia. The fossiliferous sediments at Hadar have been grouped into the Hadar Formation, which has four members (from bottom to top); the Basal Member, the Sidi Hakoma Member, the Denen Dora Member, and the Kada Hadar Member. The Hadar Formation sediments were accumulated mainly by streams, in a basin that was also periodically inundated by a large lake (Chavaillon 1982; Johanson et al. 1982). Interbedded volcanic tuffs and a basalt provide materials for radiometric dating, while the tuffs may be used for regional and interregional correlations.

Repeated radiopotassium and fission-track analyses have provided discordant dates for the same horizons at Hadar (Walter and Aronson 1982; Hall et al. 1985). Thus, a tuff near the top of the Kada Hadar Member was originally dated to about 2.6 mya but most recently to about 3.1 mya. A basalt near the top of the Sidi Hakoma Member was first dated to about 3.0 mya and later to about 3.6 mya. The new, earlier dates are broadly consistent with the faunal evidence (T. D. White et al. 1984), but the original, later dates may still be correct, if the Sidi Hakoma Tuff near the base of the Sidi Hakoma Member represents the same eruptive event as the β-Tulu Bor Tuff in the Lake Turkana Basin, now known to be 3.3–3.4 million years old (Sarna-Wojcicki et al. 1985). The correlation is strongly implied by similarities in chemical composition. The later dates are also broadly consistent with the Hadar magnetostratigraphy (Schmitt and Nairn 1984).

All the Hadar hominid fossils are now commonly assigned to a single australopithecine species, *Australopithecus afarensis*, also found at Laetoli. Most of the Hadar specimens, including the remarkable concentration (site AL 333) called the "first family," come from the Denen Dora Member. A much smaller number are known from the underlying Sidi Hakoma Member, and only one, the famous "Lucy" skeleton (AL 288-1), comes from the overlying Kada Hadar Member, near its base. The available radiometric dates indicate that the hominids date from sometime between 3.6 mya and 2.6 mya. Depending on final resolution of the dating contradictions, the fossils may be from between 3.6 mya and 3.1 mya or from between 3.1 mya and 2.6 mya.

The oldest artifacts from Hadar occur near the top of the Kada Hadar Member along the Gona River, where a combination of radiopotassium dates and stratigraphic position suggest an age of 2.5–2.4 mya (J. W. K. Harris 1983; J. W. K Harris et al., in press-b). They are thus as old as or older than the oldest known artifacts at sites in the Turkana Basin and at Olduvai Gorge, which they nonetheless broadly resemble. They can be assigned to the same Oldowan Industrial Complex. The next youngest artifacts reported from the Hadar area are Acheulean bifaces and associated pieces found in fluvial deposits that unconformably overlie the Hadar Formation and that are clearly much younger (early or middle Pleistocene) (Corvinus 1975, 1976).

Middle Awash

The Middle Awash region includes a series of sites located along the Awash River, just south of Hadar. These have been investigated by two separate teams, one working between 1975 and 1978 (Kalb et al. 1982b) and the other in 1981 (J. D. Clark et al. 1984). Both teams recorded a thick series of fluvio-lacustrine deposits with interbedded volcanic tuffs. The first team has proposed a formal subdivision of the deposits, a scheme that the second team regards as only provisional pending further fieldwork.

As elsewhere in east Africa, the tuff horizons in the Middle Awash provide material for radiometric dating and serve as markers for regional stratigraphic correlation. One tuff, known informally as the Cindery Tuff, has produced concordant radiopotassium and fission-track datings indicating it is about 4 million years old. This date, in combination with faunal determinations, implies that the Middle Awash sequence spans the interval between the late Miocene (ca. 6 mya) and the middle Quaternary (less than 700,000 years ago).

Two australopithecine fossils, possibly from *Australopithecus afarensis*, were found in Pliocene deposits by the 1981 team (T. D. White 1984). The first, a proximal femur, came from the Maka locality, where it occurred in deposits above the Cindery Tuff. It was associated with a fauna suggesting an age of 4–3.5 mya. The second, a fragment of frontal from the Belohdelie locality (Asfaw 1987), came from below the Cindery Tuff and is thus more than 4 million years old. Except for the Chemeron (Tabarin, Baringo) mandible fragment, it may in fact be the oldest indisputable hominid specimen so far discovered.

The Middle Awash sediments contain numerous archeological sites, ranging from Oldowan through Acheulean to Middle and Later Stone Age (Kalb et al. 1982a; J. D. Clark et al. 1984). So far, the oldest Oldowan occurrences are associated with faunal elements implying an age of 1.5–1.3 mya. Several Acheulean or Developed Oldowan occurrences are known in younger (early- and middle-Quaternary) deposits. At one mid-Quaternary locality in the Bodo area, Acheulean artifacts are associated with a partial skull and a parietal fragment (from a second individual) representing very early *Homo sapiens* or possibly *H. erectus* (Conroy et al. 1978; J. D. Clark et al. 1984).

Geological Antiquity and Geographic Range of the Earliest Hominids

From the site summaries that have been presented, it is clear that the australopithecines existed from before 4 mya until at least 1.4–1.2 mya. The gracile australopithecines probably became extinct before 2 mya, either through evolution into *Homo* or through physical replacement by *Homo*. The oldest commonly accepted species of *Homo*, *H. habilis*, is known from roughly 2.3–2.2 mya until perhaps 1.8–1.7 mya, when it (or one of the constituents that may comprise it) was replaced by or evolved into *H. erectus*. The robust australopithecines became extinct sometime between 1.2 mya and 700,000 years ago. A more precise determination is currently impossible because the fossiliferous portions of the long Plio-Pleistocene sequences in the Lake Turkana Basin essentially top out at 1.4–1.2 mya, while most sites that probably monitor the immediately succeeding interval (Olduvai Gorge and perhaps Melka Kunturé and the Middle Awash) have not yet provided large fossil samples. The 700,000-year upper limit is based on the invariable absence of robust australopithecines in middle-Quaternary fossil assemblages.

So far, the australopithecines and earliest *Homo* have been found only in Africa, between roughly 27°S (Taung) and 11°N (Hadar). More than 100 years ago, Thomas Huxley (1863) and later Darwin (1871) postulated that people originated in Africa, since it was the home of their closest living relatives, the chimpanzee and the gorilla. The accumulated data amply confirm Huxley's and Darwin's prescience.

The known fossil sites are concentrated in two areas—the northern Cape and Transvaal Provinces of South Africa and along the east African Rift Valley, from northern Tanzania in the south to east-central Ethiopia in the north (Fig. 3.1). The site concentrations and specific site locations reflect the occurrence of sedimentary traps with good conditions for bone preservation, and both the australopithecines and early *Homo* surely ranged far more widely within tropical and subtropical Africa, into areas where fossil sites have not been found or may not exist.

It may never be possible to pinpoint the geographic range of the australopithecines precisely, but at this stage it seems increasingly likely that they were limited to lower latitudes within Africa, especially early on. Beyond direct evidence for this at sites where australopithecine fossils occur, there is also evidence from sites where they are absent. Almost certainly the most significant of these nonaustralopithecine sites is Langebaanweg, located at 33°S in the southwestern Cape Province of South Africa (Fig. 3.1) (Hendey 1981, 1984). Langebaanweg has delivered hundreds of thousands of vertebrate fossils from taxa that indicate a geologic age of about 5 mya (early Pliocene), when the australopithecines or their immediate hominid forebears had almost certainly emerged further north. The Langebaanweg fauna is the largest, most diverse Pliocene fauna yet found in Africa, and among the extant orders of African mammals, only one (the Sirenia = dugongs) is missing. At least fifty-six species of large mammals are present, yet, in spite of careful searches, not a single hominid fossil has been recovered. Almost certainly, this is because Langebaanweg lies outside the area where the early hominids evolved, in a temperate region that was not colonized until 1.5–1 mya, probably by *Homo erectus.*

If, as seems likely, the earliest hominids were also unable to penetrate low middle latitudes in northern Africa, their absence from Eurasia is easily understandable, since they could not leave Africa before they reached its northeast corner.

Morphology of the Australopithecines

Most authorities today recognize four species of australopithecines, all assigned to the genus *Australopithecus.* This position is accepted here, although a growing number of experts assign the so-called robust australopithecines to a separate genus, *Paranthropus,* originally proposed by Broom for robust fossils from Kromdraai and Swartkrans. This usage reflects growing evidence that the robust australopithecines represent a unique and highly specialized development within the hominid family. The four commonly recognized australopithecine species (with their known sites and probable time ranges given in parentheses) are:

1. *Australopithecus afarensis* (Hadar, Laetoli, and possibly also Chemeron [Tabarin], Kanapoi, Lothagam, Omo [Usno Formation and Shungura Formation Member B], Koobi Fora [Tulu Bor Member], West Turkana [Lower Lomekwi Member] and Middle Awash; from 3.75 mya or before until roughly 3 mya)
2. *Australopithecus africanus* (Taung, Sterkfontein, Makapansgat, and possibly also Omo [Shungura Formation Members C and D], Olduvai, and Koobi Fora; from 3 mya to 2 mya or shortly after)

3. *Australopithecus* (or *Paranthropus*) *robustus* (Kromdraai and Swartkrans; from roughly 2 mya until perhaps 1 mya or somewhat later)
4. *Australopithecus* (or *Paranthropus*) *boisei* (Olduvai, Peninj, Chesowanja, West Turkana, Koobi Fora, and Omo; from 2.5 mya until sometime between 1.2 mya and 700,000 years ago). As discussed below, an early form dated to about 2.5–2.4 mya at both West Turkana and Omo may deserve separation as *A. aethiopicus*.

All four species were clearly bipedal, and it is this more than any other feature that guarantees their hominid status. As a group, they are distinguished from *Homo* by small cranial

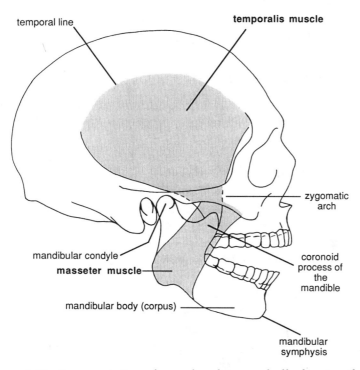

Figure 3.15. Representation of a modern human skull, showing the insertion of the masseter and temporalis muscles involved in mastication (adapted from Campbell 1966: 177). In the evolution of the later australopithecines from *Australopithecus afarensis*, the anterior (fore) part of the temporalis muscle became increasingly important relative to the posterior (rear) part. This change was accompanied by a forward shift in the root of the zygomatic arch to which the masseter muscle attaches. The result was an increase in the grinding power of the cheek teeth, also reflected in the teeth themselves.

capacity (roughly 400–550 cc); relatively large, prognathic (= projecting) faces with apelike rather than typically human external noses; and large posterior teeth (premolars and molars) with especially thick enamel. They also differed from each other in important respects, which makes it necessary to consider their morphology species by species. The descriptions below rely heavily on Le Gros Clark (1964, 1967), Howell (1978a), T. D. White et al. (1981), T. D. White (1982), Kimbel et al. (1984), and Bilsborough (1986). The most important features are illustrated in Figures 3.15–3.28. At the outset, particular attention should be paid to Figure 3.15, which shows the location and attachment of the masseter and temporalis muscles involved in mastication (chewing). Many of the key cranial differences among the earliest hominids reflect a shift in the arrangement of these muscles and an associated shift in the nature of mastication, emphasizing grinding with the cheek teeth (premolars and molars).

Australopithecus afarensis

The cranium of *Australopithecus afarensis* displays numerous primitive, apelike features, including very small endocranial capacity (range perhaps 380–450 cc, with a mean of perhaps 415 cc); mastoid processes and other lateral structures of the cranial base heavily pneumatized (that is, filled with air cavities) (Figs. 3.16, 3.19); cranial base only weakly flexed; tendency for the development of compound temporal/nuchal crests, reflecting relatively expanded posterior temporalis muscles; steeply inclined (vs. more horizontal) nuchal plane on the occipital bone; forward projection (prognathism) of the face, especially below the nose, greater than in any other known hominid; prominent canine juga (bony bulges) over the canine roots, forming lateral pillars that do not reach the nasal aperture; a lightly built, relatively short zygomatic bone, arising relatively far back on the maxilla and separated from the canine juga by a deep depression (canine fossa); no distinct articular eminence (mound of bone) anterior to the mandibular fossa (= the hollow on the base of the temporal bone for articulation with the mandibular condyle) (Figs. 3.16, 3.20); narrow, flat, and shallow palate, with limited premaxillary shelving; maxillary tooth rows converging posteriorly (Fig. 3.21); frequent diastema (gap) between the second upper incisor and the upper canine; upper incisors relatively large and procumbent; upper central incisors notably broader than lateral ones; upper canine generally asymmetric and projecting,

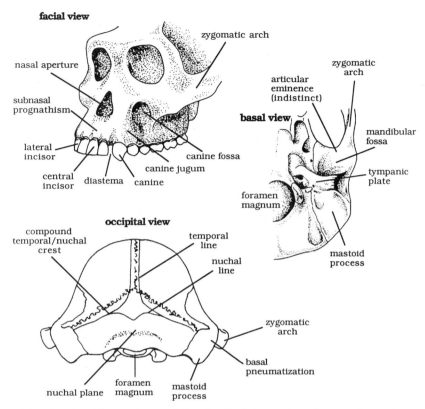

facial view

zygomatic arch

nasal aperture

zygomatic arch

articular eminence (indistinct)

subnasal prognathism

basal view

mandibular fossa

lateral incisor

canine fossa

canine jugum

tympanic plate

central incisor   diastema   canine

foramen magnum

occipital view

compound temporal/nuchal crest

temporal line

nuchal line

mastoid process

zygomatic arch

basal pneumatization

nuchal plane   foramen magnum   mastoid process

Figure 3.16. Three views of the skull of *Australopithecus afarensis*, showing important features mentioned in the text (redrawn after T. D. White et al. 1981: Figs. 8, 10, 11). *A. afarensis* exhibits many primitive, apelike features, including extensive pneumatization of the cranial base, the presence of a compound temporal/nuchal crest, pronounced subnasal prognathism, the absence of a distinct articular eminence, and a diastema or gap in the upper tooth row between the lateral incisor and the canine.

frequently with a contact facet from the lower canine on the fore (mesial) edge and one from P_3 on the rear (distal) edge (Fig. 3.22); canines much larger in males than in females; marked hollowing of the buccal wall of the mandibular corpus (Fig. 3.23), with a mental foramen that opens anteroposteriorly (rather than directly outward); frequent presence of a diastema between the lower canine and P_3; lower canine projecting, often with a wear facet from contact with the upper canine on the rear (distal) edge; and P_3 relatively long and narrow, oval in outline, with a very small lingual cusp or none at all (Fig. 3.24).

In general, the morphology of the *Australopithecus afarensis* braincase reflects small brain size, combined with a powerful masticatory apparatus and extensive pneumatiza-

Figure 3.17. *Top:* Lateral view of a mandible from Swartkrans articulated with a reconstructed *Australopithecus boisei* skull from Olduvai Gorge. *Bottom:* Occlusal view of the mandible (redrawn after Campbell 1966: Fig. 7.8). The occlusal outline has been slightly distorted by pressure in the ground, which compressed the horizontal branches inward. Note such characteristic robust-australopithecine characters as the anteriorly placed sagittal crest; dish-shaped face; thick, deep mandibular body; and molarized premolars.

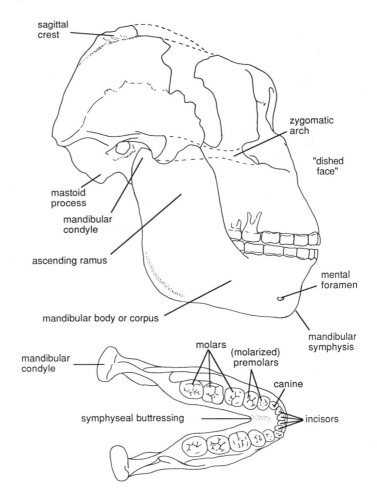

tion. The morphology of the face reflects the large size of the anterior teeth, with their very robust, curved roots. In both braincase and face, *A. afarensis* broadly recalls Miocene-to-Recent apes and demonstrates beyond all doubt the essentially ape ancestry of the hominids. In the skull, its most significant departure from the ape condition may have been in the organization of the brain. The endocast morphology of one Hadar specimen suggests enlargement of the association areas in the parietal cerebral cortex (Holloway 1983a; Holloway and Kimbel 1986). This is a distinctly human feature, though its expression on the Hadar endocast has been challenged (Falk 1985, 1986a, 1987).

Postcranially, *Australopithecus afarensis* also possessed some remarkably apelike features, including the longest arms relative to legs of any known hominid, the patently cranial orientation of the glenoid cavity on the scapula, curved (vs. relatively straight) foot and hand phalanges, and relatively long toes. The implication is that *A. afarensis* was adept at climbing trees, perhaps to obtain food or to avoid predators (Stern and Susman 1983; Susman et al. 1985). It was also, however, a proficient biped (Latimer et al. 1987), as indicated by characters such as the forwardly placed, downwardly directed foramen magnum; the structure of the foot with its basically human arch and nonopposable big toe; the distinct angle between the distal femur and the proximal tibia (Fig. 3.26) (= the valgus knee, which helps to center the body over one leg while the other is in motion); the orientation of the distal tibia articular surface nearly perpendicular to the long axis of the tibia shaft (a correlative of the valgus knee with broadly the same significance); and, above all, the pelvis, with its short, broad, backwardly extended iliac blade

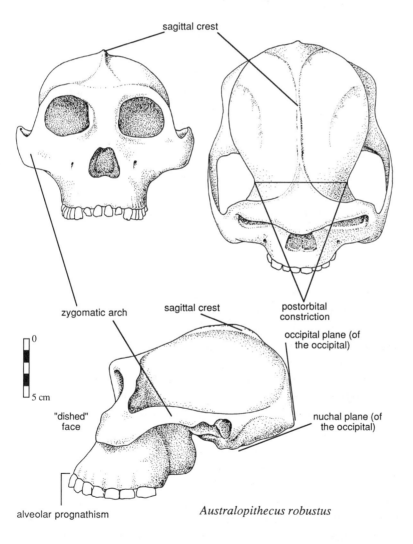

Figure 3.18. Front, top, and side views of a reconstructed *Australopithecus robustus* skull (redrawn after Howell 1978a: Fig. 10.7). Note the anteriorly placed sagittal crest, the powerfully built, widely flaring zygomatic arches, pronounced postorbital constriction, dishshaped face, and sharply angled occipital bone, which singly and together characterize the robustaustralopithecine skull.

Australopithecus robustus

Figure 3.19. Facial and occipital views of *Pan troglodytes* (chimpanzee), *Australopithecus afarensis*, *A. africanus*, *A. robustus*, *A. boisei*, and *Homo habilis* (redrawn after T. D. White et al. 1981: Figs. 9, 10). Note the pronounced subnasal prognathism, the relatively large anterior teeth, the diastema between the lateral incisor and the canine, the confluence of the temporal and nuchal lines, the great breadth of the cranial base, and other features shared by the chimpanzee and *A. afarensis*, as well as the contrast in these features between *A. afarensis* and the other hominids. (AL = Hadar; STS = Sterkfontein; SK = Swartkrans; KNM-ER = Kenya National Museum East Rudolf.)

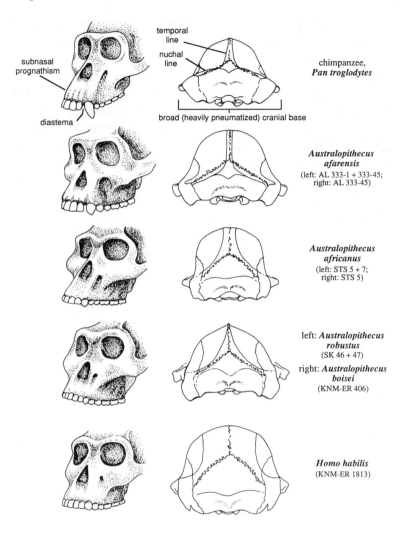

(which centers the trunk over the hip joints, reducing fatigue during upright, bipedal locomotion.) (Fig. 3.27 illustrates the very similar pelvis of *A. africanus*.) In these latter respects, *A. afarensis* was very similar to modern people, and the interpretation is relatively unambiguous.

More problematic are features such as the more posterior orientation of the anterior portion of the iliac blade (vs. the more lateral orientation in modern humans); the relatively limited difference in size between the femoral condyles (in modern people, the lateral condyle is distinctly larger than the medial one); the shape and depth of the notch for the patella (kneecap) between the femoral condyles (intermediate in shape between the shallow notch of apes and the deeper one of people); and the shape of the lateral condyles (less oval than in *Homo*) (Stern and Susman 1983). Depending upon how these features are interpreted, *Australopithecus afarensis* may have had a slightly bent-hip, bent-kneed gait, something like that of a chimpanzee on two legs (Stern and Susman 1983), or a striding gait, essentially indistinguishable from that of modern people (Lovejoy 1979). Arguably, the heel strike, nondivergent big toe, distinct arch, and other unmistakably human features of the Laetoli footprints imply the modern striding gait (T. D. White 1980; Day 1985; Tuttle 1987), while obstetrical considerations—rather than locomotion—may explain some of the pelvic differences between *A. afarensis* and modern humans (Tague and Lovejoy 1986). This is particularly likely, since significant brain expansion requiring an enlarged birth canal occurred only beginning about 2 mya, in the evolution of the genus *Homo*.

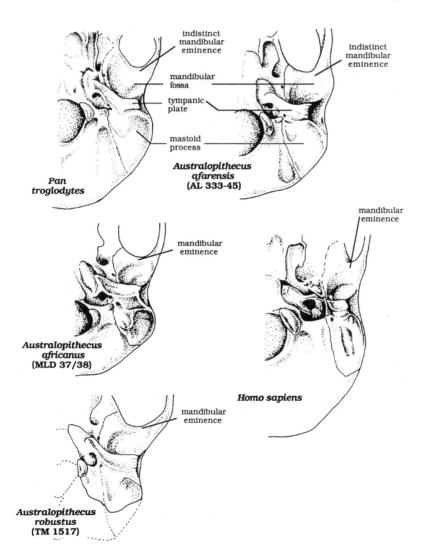

Figure 3.20. Left basal views of the skull of a chimpanzee (*Pan troglodytes*), *Australopithecus afarensis* (AL 333-45), *A. africanus* (MLD 37/38), *A. robustus* (TM 1517), and modern *Homo sapiens* (redrawn after T. D. White et al. 1981: Fig. 11). Note that in tympanic and mastoid morphology, *A. afarensis* resembled the chimpanzee more closely than it did the other hominids. (AL = Hadar; MLD = Makapansgat; TM = Transvaal Museum).

Figure 3.21. Palates of a chimpanzee, various australopithecines, and a modern human (top row redrawn after Johanson and Edey 1981: 367; bottom row redrawn after T. D. White et al. 1981: Fig. 9). Note the presence of a diastema between the lateral incisor and the canine in both the chimpanzee and *Australopithecus afarensis* and note the enlargement of the premolars versus the other teeth in *A. africanus* and especially in *A. robustus*. (AL = Hadar; STS = Sterkfontein; SK = Swartkrans.)

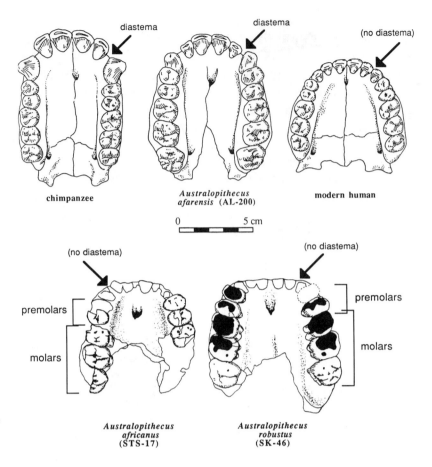

The muscular and tendinous insertions on postcranial bones indicate that *Australopithecus afarensis* individuals were heavily muscled. However, they varied considerably in body size (McHenry 1982, 1988; Jungers 1988), from a weight of perhaps 33 kg (73 lbs) and a height of 1 m (3′ 3″) to a weight of perhaps 68 kg (150 lbs) and a height of 1.7 m (5′ 7″). This size variation has been attributed to extraordinary sexual dimorphism (Johanson and White 1979; McHenry 1986b). However, it equals or exceeds the known degree of dimorphism in other hominoids and raises the possibility that *A. afarensis* actually consists of two (or more) species (Zihlman 1985). The morphology of the basicranium, nose, jaws, and teeth has also been used to divide *A. afarensis* into two species—an early robust australopithecine and an early species of *Homo* (including *A. africanus* of other authors) (Olson 1981, 1985). The robust australopithecine would be the larger species, which is more abundant in the fossil samples. Two species may also be indicated by morphological variability within postcranial categories, especially among femora (Senut and Tardieu 1985), and it is questionable whether feet with long, curved toes such as those of Hadar *A. afarensis* could have made the totally human footprints found at Laetoli (Site G) (Tuttle 1981, 1985). However, the cranial arguments for two species have been systematically

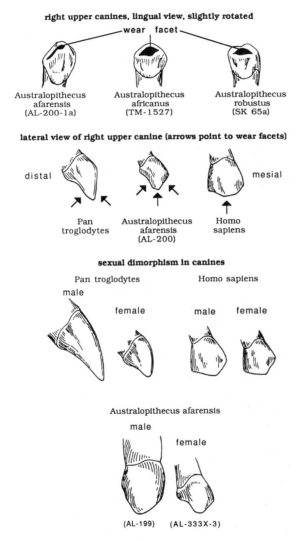

Figure 3.22. Upper-canine morphology of various australopithecines, the chimpanzee, and modern humans (top redrawn after T. D. White et al. 1981: Fig. 14; middle and bottom redrawn after Johanson and Edey 1981: 268). In *Australopithecus afarensis* the canine wore not only at the tip, as in later hominids, but also on the fore and rear (mesial and distal) surfaces, as it does in chimpanzees. *A. afarensis* was also more apelike in the degree of canine size difference between the sexes. (AL = Hadar; TM = Transvaal Museum; SK = Swartkrans.)

Figure 3.23. Cross sections of the mandibular body below P$_4$ in various australopithecines and in *Homo habilis* (redrawn after T. D. White et al. 1981: Fig. 13). Note the buccal inflation (thickening) of the mandibular body in *Australopithecus africanus* and *A. boisei*.

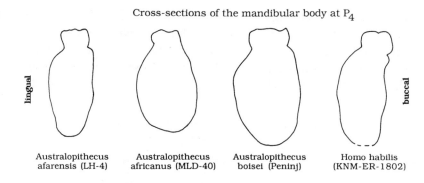

Cross-sections of the mandibular body at P$_4$

lingual

buccal

| Australopithecus afarensis (LH-4) | Australopithecus africanus (MLD-40) | Australopithecus boisei (Peninj) | Homo habilis (KNM-ER-1802) |

and vigorously refuted (Kimbel et al. 1985), and the postcranial variability could reflect sexual dimorphism, if *A. afarensis* males, being much larger than females, were also significantly more terrestrial (Stern and Susman 1983). A larger sample of more complete fossils may be necessary to reveal the full meaning of variability within *A. afarensis*, but on present evidence it need not mean that two species have been compounded.

Australopithecus africanus

In cranial features, *Australopithecus africanus* was clearly advanced over *A. afarensis*, though it was still very primitive by modern standards. Endocranial capacity (430–520 cc, with an average around 440 cc [Holloway 1975, 1983b]) was perhaps only 10% greater than in *A. afarensis*. The cranial base was not significantly more flexed (Fig. 3.25). However, the lateral portions of the base were much less heavily pneumatized, and the temporal and nuchal lines did not meet to form a compound crest at the rear of the skull (Fig. 3.19). The configuration of the temporal lines indicates a greater emphasis on the anterior (vs. posterior) fibers of the temporalis muscle. In some individuals, the anterior parts of the left and right temporalis muscles may have met at the top of the skull, promoting the development of a sagittal crest (bony ridge) along the midline. (This feature is illustrated [Fig. 3.17, 3.18, 3.28] on skulls of robust australopithecines, most of which possessed it. The possible exceptions were probably all small females.) The nuchal plane was more horizontally oriented, and there was a distinct articular eminence in front of the mandibular fossa (Fig. 3.20).

The face was notably shorter than in *Australopithecus afarensis*, with less subnasal prognathism, linked to a reduction in the size of the anterior dentition. Shortening of the premaxilla was accompanied by upward extension of the canine juga to flank the sides of the nasal aperture. The zygomatic arch was long and strongly built, and it arose vertically on the maxilla, to provide an attachment for the masseter muscles that was more anterior than that in *A. afarensis.* The palate was relatively deep, with clear premaxillary shelving.

The upper medial and lateral incisors were subequal in size, and the canines were relatively short, wearing mainly at the tips and not on the mesial and distal edges (Fig. 3.22). There was apparently little or no sexual dimorphism in canine size. Upper-second-incisor/canine and lower-canine/third-premolar

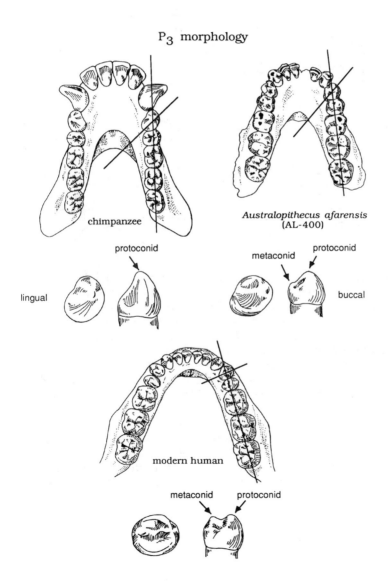

Figure 3.24. Lower-third- premolar (P_3) morphology of the chimpanzee, *Australopithecus afarensis*, and modern humans (redrawn after Johanson and Edey 1981: 269). Note that in its P_3, *A. afarensis* was intermediate between the chimpanzee and modern people. Thus, it maintained roughly the same angle between the P_3 axis and the rest of the tooth row as is seen in the chimpanzee; but the P_3 itself was somewhat rounder and sometimes had a small inner or lingual cusp (metaconid), anticipating that of later people.

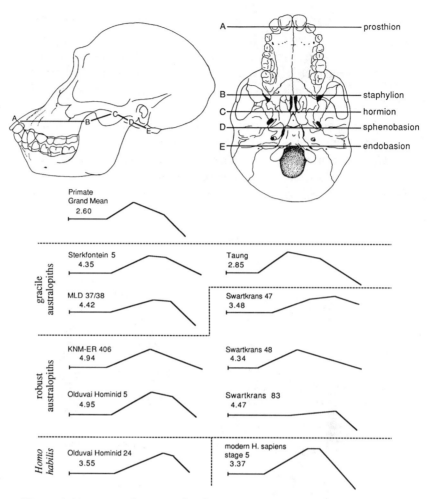

Figure 3.25. Lines showing the degree of basicranial flexion in gracile australopithecines (Sterkfontein 5, MLD [= Makapansgat] 37/38, and Taung), robust australopithecines (KNM-ER 406, Olduvai Hominid 5, and Swartkrans 47, 48, and 83), *Homo habilis* (Olduvai Hominid 24), and modern *H. sapiens* full adults (Stage 5) (redrawn after Laitman and Heimbuch 1982: Figs. 1, 2, 4). The anatomical points that define each line are shown on a chimpanzee skull. The greater the angularity between the segments of a line, the greater the degree of basicranial flexion. The lines show that the australopithecine cranial base was generally much less flexed than that of *H. sapiens*. Since the degree of flexion shapes the roof of the voice box, the less flexed cranial base of the australopithecines may imply they could not make the full range of sounds that modern people can (Laitman and Heimbuch 1982). This in turn may mean they were more limited in their ability to communicate orally.

150

diastemata were rare. The cheek teeth were enlarged, with some tendency for molarization of the premolars (Fig. 3.21). The mandibular body was significantly more robust than in *Australopithecus afarensis*, with a more heavily reinforced symphysis. The ascending ramus was broader and taller than in *A. afarensis* and arose lower and more to the side on the mandibular body.

Most of the cranial and dental differences between *Australopithecus africanus* and *A. afarensis* can be explained by a

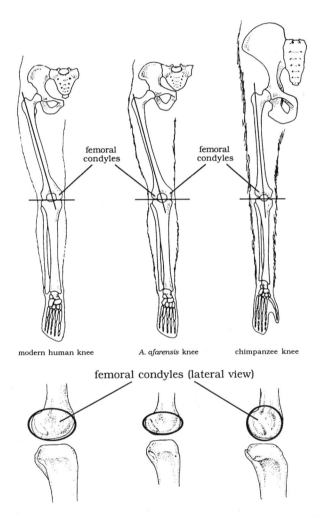

modern human knee   *A. afarensis* knee   chimpanzee knee

femoral condyles (lateral view)

Figure 3.26. *Above:* Lower limbs of a modern human, *Australopithecus afarensis*, and a chimpanzee, with emphasis on the knee joint (redrawn after Johanson and Edey 1981: 157). *Below:* Lateral views of the knee joint (distal femur and proximal tibia) in the same three species. The distinct angle between the distal femur and proximal tibia, as well as the oval femoral condyles shared by modern people and *A. afarensis* are adaptations to habitual bipedal locomotion.

Figure 3.27. Left-lateral and full-frontal views of the pelvises of a chimpanzee, *Australopithecus africanus*, and a small modern human (redrawn after Le Gros Clark 1964: 160, 161). Note the basic similarity between the australopithecine and modern human pelvises, reflecting a shared adaptation to bipedalism.

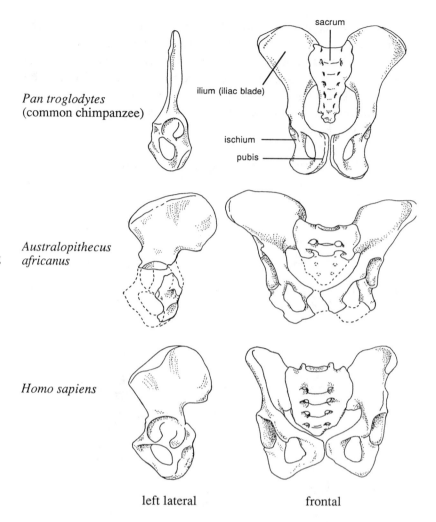

Pan troglodytes (common chimpanzee)

Australopithecus africanus

Homo sapiens

left lateral   frontal

concomitant reduced emphasis on the anterior dentition and greater emphasis on the cheek teeth in mastication, coincident with a reorganization of the temporalis and masseter muscles, which control jaw movement (T. D. White et al. 1981). In this respect, *A. africanus* appears to have been divergent from *A. afarensis* in the direction of *A. robustus* and *A. boisei*.

In spite of cranial and dental differences, postcranially *Australopithecus africanus* was remarkably similar to *A. afarensis* (McHenry 1986a). Perhaps most striking are resemblances between their locomotor skeletons, which differentiate them, in detail, from *Homo sapiens*. There is no doubt that both were capable bipeds, but the differences from *H. sapiens* may mean they were also agile tree climbers (McHenry 1986a). Some of their pelvic distinctions could also reflect the birth of relatively small-brained young.

Estimates of body weight in *Australopithecus africanus* vary widely (Steudel 1980; McHenry 1982, 1988; Jungers 1988), mainly because they must be based on the mathematical relationship between skeletal dimensions and body weight in living primates (including humans). The results will differ depending on which skeletal dimension(s) and which living primates are used. However, the most recent estimates suggest that adult weight probably ranged between 33 and 67 kg (72 and 142 lbs), with a mean perhaps near 46 kg (101 lbs). Average stature was probably around 1.45 m (4' 9") (McHenry 1974). Much of the size variation was probably due to sexual dimorphism, which was perhaps slightly less than that in *A. afarensis.*

Australopithecus robustus and *A. boisei*

Australopithecus robustus and *A. boisei* are commonly lumped as the robust australopithecines. They were broadly contemporaneous, and some authorities regard them as geographic variants of a single species (inhabiting south and east Africa, respectively). However, as already has been indicated, to emphasize their distinction from other australopithecines, some specialists assign them to the genus *Paranthropus*. They shared the largest cranial capacity of all the australopithecines (range 500–530 cc, with a mean of about 520 cc [Holloway 1975, 1983b]), though the difference is insignificant when corrected for their somewhat larger body size. In addition, if the KNM-WT 17000 skull (Fig. 3.28), found at West Turkana in 1985, is included in *A. boisei*, its very small cranial capacity of about 410 cc significantly lowers both the minimum and the average.

The robust australopithecines differ from *Australopithecus afarensis* primarily in the same features as does *A. africanus,* but to a much greater extent. Their incisors and canines were relatively small, while their cheek teeth were greatly expanded, and their premolars (both deciduous and permanent) were almost fully molarized (Figs. 3.17, 3.21). Their long, powerfully built zygomatic arches arose far forward on the maxilla and flared outward, causing the face to appear concave or dished shaped. Their mandibles were very thick and deep (Figs. 3.17, 3.23), with heavy buttressing in the symphyseal region and with tall, broad ascending rami arising much more laterally and inferiorly than those in *A. afarensis.* Anteriorly placed sagittal crests in most, if not all, specimens and marked postorbital constriction reflect even greater emphasis on the anterior fibers of the temporalis muscles than is seen in *A.*

Figure 3.28. Robust-australopithecine skulls from West Turkana (KNM-WT 17000) and Olduvai Gorge (OH5 = "*Zinjan-thropus*"), dated to about 2.5 mya and 1.8 mya, respectively (drawn by K. Cruz-Uribe from casts and photos). The West Turkana skull combines features of *Australopithecus afarensis* with those of the later robust australopithecines, *A. boisei* and *A. robustus*. This clearly strengthens arguments that *A. afarensis* was ancestral to the robust australopithecines. At the same time, the West Turkana skull is perhaps distinct enough to be placed in a separate robust-australopithecine species, for which the name *A. aethiopicus* is available. *A. aethiopicus*, as represented by specimens from West Turkana and the lower Omo River Valley, is a plausible ancestor for both *A. boisei* and *A. robustus*.

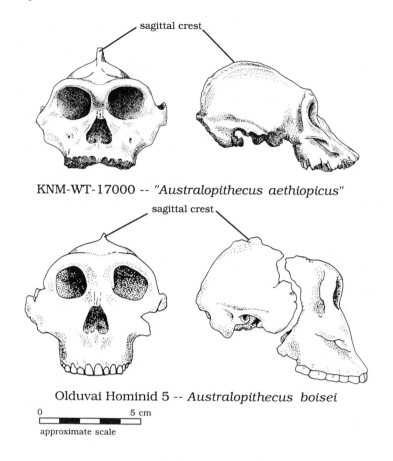

KNM-WT-17000 -- *"Australopithecus aethiopicus"*

Olduvai Hominid 5 -- *Australopithecus boisei*

africanus. Overall, the distinctive craniofacial architecture of *A. robustus* and *A. boisei* may be viewed as a specialization for applying substantial vertical force between the upper and lower cheek-tooth rows during mastication (Rak 1983).

Robinson (1954, 1963) proposed that the powerful masticatory apparatus of *Australopithecus robustus* was adapted for an exclusively vegetarian diet and that the less specialized dentition of *A. africanus* implied a more omnivorous diet. In support of this hypothesis, he suggested that the cheek teeth of *A. robustus* showed more enamel chipping, from soil grit that clung to bulbs or other subterranean plant foods. Subsequent research failed to confirm a difference in the degree of enamel chipping (Tobias 1967a; Wallace 1975), but a dietary difference is still implied by the lower, less pointed molar cusps of *A. robustus*; by the tendency for *A. robustus* molars to wear flat (vs. the tendency for *A. africanus* molars to be buccolingually beveled in advanced wear); and by microscopic differences in occlusal wear between the species. These dental contrasts need not imply that either species ate meat (or more meat than the other), but they do suggest that *A. robustus* ate harder, more fibrous vegetal foods than did *A. africanus* (Grine 1981, 1985b, 1986). The microwear on *A. boisei* molars indicates that fruits, masticated whole, were probably the preferred vegetal foods and that leaves and grass seeds were avoided (Walker 1981a). The molar microwear specifically rules out bone crunching.

Postcranially, *Australopithecus robustus* and *A. boisei* were generally similar to *A. africanus*, though probably somewhat larger, with an mean adult weight probably between 46 and 62 kg (101 and 136 lbs) (Steudel 1980; McHenry 1982, 1988; Jungers 1988) and an average stature of perhaps 1.5–1.6 m (4′ 11″–5′ 4″) (McHenry 1974). The degree of sexual dimorphism was perhaps similar to that in *A. africanus*.

As discussed below, the phylogenetic relationship between the robust australopithecines and earlier hominids is still being debated, but their highly derived craniodental features clearly eliminate them from the ancestry of any subsequent humans. Their distinctiveness is further underlined by a unique dental development and eruption sequence that differentiates them not only from other hominids but also from apes (B. H. Smith 1986).

The Morphology of *Homo habilis*

Homo habilis is difficult to characterize, because specialists disagree on what fossils it includes (Stringer 1986b). In the original definition of L. S. B. Leakey et al. (1964), it incorporated specimens from Olduvai Bed I and Lower Bed II that appeared to have larger cranial capacities and smaller cheek teeth than did known *Australopithecus*. However, later discoveries, especially at Koobi Fora, showed that during the interval including Bed I and Lower Bed II (roughly 2.0–1.6 mya), some individuals (most notably KNM-ER 1470) had relatively large skulls combined with large *Australopithecus*-size teeth (directly observed or inferred from socket size) whereas others (most notably KNM-ER 1813) had small *Australopithecus*-size skulls combined with relatively small, *H. erectus*–size teeth (Fig. 3.29). To many authorities, this variability implies at least two contemporaneous species, either (1) *H. habilis* and a late surviving, east African *A. africanus* or (2) *H. habilis* and an as yet unnamed, small-brained species of *Homo* (Walker and Leakey 1978; Walker 1981b, 1984; Wood 1985, 1987; Bilsborough 1986; Stringer 1986b). In either case, both species coexisted with *A. boisei*, one evolved into *H. erectus*, and the other became extinct about the time *H. erectus* appeared.

Figure 3.29. Reconstructed skulls of *Homo habilis* from Koobi Fora (redrawn after Howell 1978a: Fig. 10.9). Many authorities believe the obvious size difference could reflect sexual dimorphism within a single species (male on the left [KNM-ER 1470], female on the right [KNM-ER 1813]), but a growing number think it reflects the existence of two separate, contemporaneous species of early *Homo* roughly 2 mya.

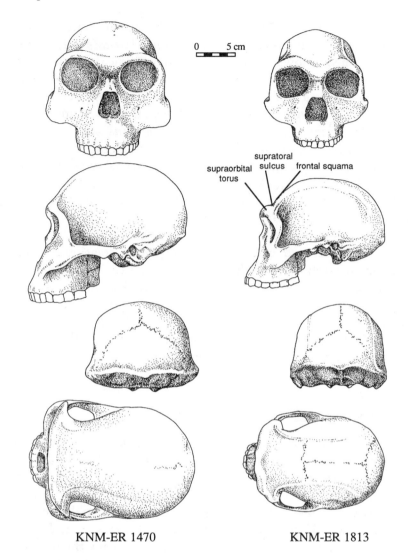

KNM-ER 1470   KNM-ER 1813

The two-species hypothesis is growing in popularity, but at least provisionally, like Howell (1978a) or Johanson et al. (1987), many specialists continue to believe that the diverse specimens behind it come from a single, highly dimorphic species *(Homo habilis.)* If this opinion is accepted, then, in general, *H. habilis* can be distinguished from the australopithecines by larger endocranial volume (range 510–750 cc, with a mean of about 630 cc [Holloway 1983b; Stringer 1986b]), expanded frontal and especially parietal regions, a gutter or sulcus (distinct inflection point) between the supraorbital torus and the frontal squama, a more rounded occipital contour with enlargement of the occipital plane (vs. the nuchal one), a reduction in basicranial pneumatization and ectocranial rugosity (that is, smaller air pockets in the cranial base and less prominent cranial crests), a more parabolic dental arcade, reduced alveolar prognathism (less forwardly projecting jaws), a less robust premaxilla lacking canine juga, smaller jaws, and generally smaller cheek teeth with thinner enamel (T. D. White et al. 1981; Bilsborough 1986). The increase in average endocranial volume is particularly striking, since it was accompanied by little, if any, increase in body size, compared with the australopithecines (McHenry 1982, 1984, 1988). In addition, it may correlate with a restructuring of the brain, producing a distinctly human cortical sulcal pattern as opposed to the apelike pattern that apparently characterized the australopithecines (Falk 1983a, 1987). The implications of this restructuring are debatable, but it could be related to a developing capacity for articulate speech.

The postcranial skeleton of *Homo habilis* is not well known, and some postcranial bones assigned to the species could even derive from a contemporaneous robust australopithecine. This is because they were not directly associated with diagnostic skull or jaw bones and because their species assignment was based mainly on small size or on a priori assumptions about the probable postcranial distinctions between *H. habilis* and the robust australopithecines. Thus, an Olduvai Gorge Bed I partial foot skeleton (OH [= Olduvai Hominid] 8) that implies a completely modern kind of bipedalism (Day 1985) has been attributed to *H. habilis* at least partly because of its modern or near-modern morphology. The attribution would be more secure if the foot could be shown to represent the same individual as does a partial juvenile skull of *H. habilis* (OH 7) found at the same site (FLKNN I).

The least equivocal postcranial bones of *Homo habilis* are (1) hand bones that have been assigned to the same individual as has the partial juvenile skull (OH 7) just mentioned (L. S. B. Leakey 1961) and, more important, (2) portions of the right arm and both legs associated with fragmentary adult cranial bones and teeth (OH 62) at another Bed I locality (DDH) (Johanson et al. 1987). The leg bones confirm bipedalism, but, contrary to prior expectations, they suggest very short stature. The individual was probably only about 1 m (3' 3") tall, perhaps even shorter than the shortest known australopithecine, the famous Lucy *(Australopithecus afarensis)*. Moreover, the arms were remarkably long relative to the legs, perhaps even longer than those of Lucy. Together with the (OH7) hand bones, which imply an apelike ability for underbranch suspension (Susman and Stern 1979, 1982), the long arms suggest that *H. habilis* retained the tree-climbing agility of the australopithecines. This might thus have been lost only with the evolution of *H. erectus* roughly 1.8–1.7 mya. Alternatively, future discoveries may show that some individuals of *H. habilis* possessed distinctly less australopithecine-like postcrania, more closely resembling those of *H. erectus*. This would significantly strengthen the case for dividing the present sample of *H. habilis* into two species, of which only the more derived would be relevant to later human evolution.

The Phylogeny of the Australopithecines and Early *Homo*

The phylogeny of the australopithecines and early *Homo* is controversial, partly because specialists cannot agree on which species and how many species existed at any one time. Thus, most specialists recognize only one species, *Australopithecus afarensis*, existing between 4 mya and 3 mya, but some perceive two, generally distinguished as an early robust australopithecine and an early representative of *A. africanus* or of *Homo* (including *A. africanus* of other authors). Similarly, many specialists regard *A. robustus* and *A. boisei* as closely related geographic variants (perhaps only subspecies) derived from a common robust ancestor between 2.5 mya and 2.0 mya, while others believe they were more distinct, with separate evolutionary histories extending from a nonrobust ancestor that existed at or before 3.0 mya. Perhaps most crucial of all, authorities differ on the relationship between the different australopithecines and earliest *Homo*. None would place a robust australopithecine (*A. boisei* or *A. robustus*) on the line to *Homo*, but there is considerable disagreement about whether *A. africanus* should also be ruled out. An added complication is that authorities also disagree strongly on the taxonomy of very early *Homo*. As already indicated, a growing number believe that the lone, stem species that is commonly recognized—that is, *H. habilis*—actually comprises at least two species. With the problem of *H. habilis* put aside, Figure 3.30 (from Delson 1987) summarizes the main, currently debated alternative phylogenies involving the australopithecines alone.

Those who believe *Australopithecus afarensis* comprises two distinct species generally place them on two phylogenetic branches stemming from an as yet unknown Miocene or early-Pliocene common ancestor (Fig. 3.30C). One branch, which already shows distinct robust-australopithecine traits, leads to the later robust australopithecines, *A. robustus* and *A. boisei*, which can be regarded as two distinct species or simply as geographic variants of a single species. The other branch leads to *Homo* through *A. africanus*, if in fact the earliest representatives are not already *A. africanus*. In this phylogeny, later (South African) *A. africanus* is specifically excluded from the ancestry of *A. robustus* + *A. boisei*, because it lacks basicranial, nasal, and endocranial characters that they share with *A.*

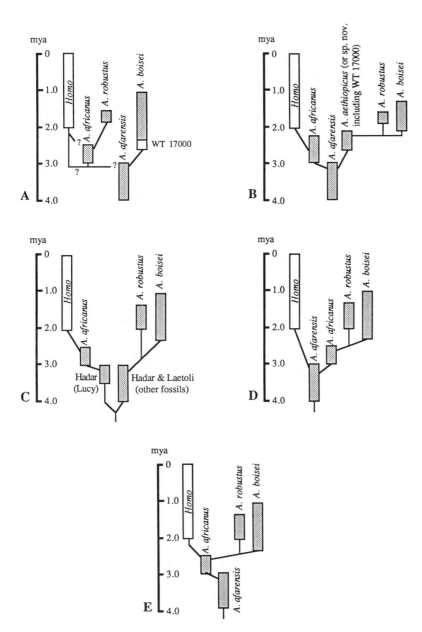

Figure 3.30. *Australopithecus* and *Homo* phylogenetic schemes supported by (A) Walker and Johanson, (B) Delson, Grine, Howell, and Olson, (C) Olson (1981–85) (now abandoned), (D) Johanson and White (1979–85) (now abandoned), and (E) Skelton, McHenry, and Drawhorn (drawing modified after Grine, from Delson 1987). Scheme B is probably the most popular as of this writing.

afarensis—that is, it is derived in another direction (Olson 1981, 1985; Falk and Conroy 1983; Falk 1986b). One great strength of this scheme is that it does not have to be recast to accommodate KNM-WT 17000, the spectacular 2.5-million-year-old robust-australopithecine skull recently found at West Turkana (Fig. 3.28). This skull simply becomes an intermediary on the line leading from the robust segment of *A. afarensis* to the later robust australopithecines (Falk 1986c).

The KNM-WT 17000 skull may even lend support to this scheme, since it possibly provides new evidence for dividing *Australopithecus afarensis* into two species. In important features, including very small endocranial capacity, the absence of a distinct articular eminence, the presence of a compound temporal/nuchal crest, and the relative lack of basicranial flexion, the braincase of WT 17000 strongly resembles that of the *A. afarensis* skull reconstructed by Kimbel et al. (1984). The face, however, in its pronounced dish shape and other features, contrasts sharply with that on the reconstructed *A. afarensis* skull. Since the reconstructed skull is composed of face and braincase parts from different individuals, it has been suggested that the braincase may represent an early robust australopithecine (similar to WT 17000) while the face represents another kind of australopithecine or perhaps early *Homo* broadly defined (Shipman 1986a).

In defending the integrity of *Australopithecus afarensis*, Johanson and White (1979) initially proposed a contrasting phylogeny in which *A. afarensis* was the common ancestor of all later hominids—both later australopithecines and *Homo* (Fig. 3.30D). In their view *A. africanus* represented an entirely predictable intermediate form between the primitive *A. afarensis*, whose craniofacial morphology reflects a relative emphasis on the anterior dentition in feeding and perhaps other activities, and *A. robustus + A. boisei*, whose craniofacial morphology reflects extraordinary emphasis on the cheek teeth in grinding mastication. Structural-functional analyses of the australopithecine dentition (Wallace 1975) and face (Rak 1983, 1985) strongly supported the derivation of *A. robustus* from *A. africanus*.

Following Rak and other authorities, Johanson and White suggested that *Australopithecus boisei* was derived from *A. robustus*, since it exhibits the most extreme features of the robust lineage. However, the discovery of KNM-WT 17000 has led Johanson (1986) to alter his phylogeny so that *A. robustus* and *A. boisei* are now on separate branches leading from *A. afarensis* (Fig. 3.30A). In this revision, the similarities between

A. robustus and *A. boisei* are seen as the result of parallelism rather than of an ancestor-descendant relationship.

In a frequently proposed alternative to the Johanson and White (1979) phylogeny, it has been suggested that *Australopithecus africanus* was ancestral to both *Homo* and the robust australopithecines. Some proponents of this idea, such as Tobias (1980) and Wolpoff (1983), include *A. afarensis* within *A. africanus*, while others, especially McHenry (1985; also McHenry and Skelton 1985), retain *A. afarensis* as the ancestor of *A. africanus* (Fig. 3.30E). McHenry has supported his view with more than fifty derived characters that *A. africanus* and *A. robustus* + *A. boisei* share with *H. habilis* but not with *A. afarensis*. These characters include a prominent articular eminence, the absence of compound temporal-nuchal crests (except in some very large male *A. boisei*), a relatively long occipital plane, increased basicranial flexion, reduced subnasal prognathism, nonprojecting upper canines lacking mesial or distal wear, and a lower third premolar with a round occlusal outline and strong lingual cusp. McHenry's scheme is more parsimonious than Johanson's in providing a known link between *A. afarensis* and *H. habilis*. The alternative possibility is that fossils representing this link have so far eluded field researchers.

However, it is possible that many of the derived traits shared by *Homo habilis* and *Australopithecus africanus* were evolved in parallel, as the lineage leading to *H. habilis* reduced the overall size of its masticatory apparatus and as the *A. africanus*-to-*A. robustus* + *A. boisei* lineage increasingly emphasized the anterior fibers of the temporalis muscle. In addition, Johanson and White have argued that to make *A. africanus* ancestral to *Homo* would require a reversal of evolutionary trends—initial expansion of the postcanine dentition and the development of associated craniofacial specializations in *A. africanus* would have to be followed by significant reduction of the postcanine teeth and the loss of functionally related craniofacial features in *Homo*. McHenry has argued that this is possible, particularly since dental reduction clearly characterized the ongoing evolution of *Homo*, from *H. habilis* to modern *H. sapiens*. McHenry (1984) also notes apparent evolutionary reversals in other oft-cited morphological traits. These include both the thickness of the cranial vault bones (from thin in *Australopithecus* to thick in *H. erectus* back to thin in modern *H. sapiens*) and browridge development (from minimal in *Australopithecus* to substantial in *H. erectus* back to minimal in modern *H. sapiens*).

Like Johanson, to incorporate WT 17000, McHenry could reorganize his phylogeny to place *Australopithecus boisei* on a branch of its own (leading directly from *A. afarensis*), still leaving *A. africanus* as the link between *A. afarensis* on the one hand and *A. robustus* and *Homo habilis* on the other. McHenry's phylogeny may be indirectly weakened, however, by the WT 17000 skull. If the remarkable similarities between *A. robustus* and *A. boisei* could evolve in parallel, then clearly the same could be true for the derived features shared by *A. africanus* and early *Homo*.

Many other phylogenies are possible, particularly if fresh evidence eventually demonstrates that either *Australopithecus afarensis* or *Homo habilis* comprises more than one species. However, at the moment, most specialists would probably favor an alternative in which *A. africanus* was ancestral to *Homo* and in which the population represented by the robust WT 17000 skull was ancestral to later (and very closely related) *A. robustus* and *A. boisei*. Disagreement exists on whether WT 17000 should be allocated to (early) *A. boisei* or to a distinct ancestral robust species. If future discoveries support a distinct ancestral species, it could be called *A. aethiopicus*, based on a name proposed in 1967 (and then largely ignored) for a very robust, 2.5-million-year-old mandible from the lower Omo River Valley (Arambourg and Coppens 1967). In this scheme, *A. afarensis* would represent the common ancestor of both *A. africanus* and the WT 17000 population (Fig. 3.30B).

It is important to emphasize that, despite continuing controversy over australopithecine phylogeny, the known fossil record nonetheless permits reconstruction of the major patterns in early hominid evolution. Thus, the earliest well-documented hominids, dating from between 4 mya and 3 mya at Hadar and Laetoli, still bore the clear stamp of ape ancestry in their skulls and teeth and—to a lesser but still significant extent--in their postcranial bones. They were both proficient bipeds and agile tree climbers. By 3–2.5 mya, at least two distinct hominid lineages had emerged, each characterized by distinctively hominid teeth and postcrania. Bipedalism clearly antedated brain expansion, and in one or more early hominid lineages (the robust australopithecines), now extinct, substantial brain expansion never occurred; instead, their evolution was distinguished mainly by the progressive development of a powerful grinding premolar and molar dentition. In contrast, in the other lineage, leading to later people, significant brain expansion did occur, and it was accompanied by a progressive reduction in the masticatory apparatus, probably related to increasing reliance on tools.

Geologic Antiquity of the Earliest Artifacts

A reader unfamiliar with stone artifacts may wish to consult Appendix 2 (Stone Artifact Technology and Typology) before continuing on. The known or inferred dates for sites with very early artifacts are summarized in Figure 3.6.

The oldest known stone artifacts are perhaps those from Kada Gona (Hadar) which could approach 3.1 million years in age, though a more conservative assessment of the available radiopotassium and fission-track dates would place their age at roughly 2.4–2.5 million years (J. W. K. Harris 1983; Hall et al. 1985). Stone artifacts recently found at Senga in the Lusso (ex-Kaiso) Beds of the Upper Semliki Valley in eastern Zaire are roughly 2.3 million years old, to judge from the associated fauna (J. W. K. Harris et al. 1987), while artifacts dating to about 2.4–2.3 mya are known from the Shungura Formation of the lower Omo River Valley (Howell 1978b; Howell et al. 1987). Somewhat later occurrences, dating between 2.0 mya and 1.6 mya, are well established at Olduvai and Koobi Fora (M. D. Leakey 1971; Isaac and Harris 1978). At least some artifacts from West Turkana (Kalochoro and Natoo Members of the Nachukui Formation) (J. M. Harris et al. 1988), Chemoigut (Chesowanja) (Gowlett et al. 1981), Melka Kunturé (Ethiopia) (Chavaillon et al. 1979). Mwimbi (Chiwondo Beds, Malawi) (Kaufulu and Stern 1987), Swartkrans (Member 1) (Brain 1985a), and Sterkfontein (Member 5) (Stiles and Partridge 1979) are probably contemporaneous with the earliest artifacts from Olduvai and Koobi Fora. In sum, there is good evidence that stone artifacts were being widely made in eastern and southern Africa by 2 mya—and, in eastern Africa, probably much earlier, by 2.3 mya or before. The very oldest stone artifacts may prove difficult to find, since, unlike later artifact makers, the earliest ones may have been too mobile to accumulate archeologically visible clusters of debris. The archeological record would be largely invisible if people had not developed the uniquely human habit of returning to the same site for at least a few days (or nights).

Some controversy surrounds the oldest known bone artifacts. Dart (1957) argued that numerous animal bones from Makapansgat Member 3 (the "grey breccia") were in fact tools of an "osteodontokeratic" (bone-tooth-horn) culture practiced by the australopithecines. Member 3 is now estimated to be 2.5–3 million years old, and Dart's bone tools would thus be the oldest known artifacts of any kind. In reaching his conclusion, Dart was especially impressed by the disproportionate abundance of certain antelope skeletal parts, such as the distal humerus and the mandible, which he felt were chosen by the australopithecines as clubs, saws, or other useful artifacts. However, the unequal pattern of skeletal part representation that Dart observed tends to characterize almost all fossil assemblages, mainly because some skeletal parts are more durable than others and are thus more likely to survive pre- and postdepositional destruction (Brain 1981). The Makapansgat bones reveal no damage that can be specifically attributed to artifact manufacture or use, and it seems increasingly unlikely that they were tools. Instead, they were probably damaged and accumulated almost entirely by hyenas (Maguire et al. 1980).

The next oldest bone artifacts include 125 flaked, battered, or polished pieces from Olduvai Beds I and II (M. D. Leakey 1971) and a series of long-bone fragments with polished tips from Swartkrans Member 1 and Sterkfontein Member 5 (Brain 1985a, 1988). At all three sites, the bone implements certainly or probably date from between 2 mya and 1.5 mya. Microscopic examination supports the artifactual nature of 41 Olduvai pieces (Shipman 1984a, and in press). Of these, 4 were not tools in the narrow sense but apparently served as anvils or platforms on which soft substances such as skin were repeatedly punctured by sharp-ended stone artifacts. The remaining 37 are large, flaked pieces of bone, including (a) 26 with polish of the kind that forms on experimental pieces used to cut or smooth soft materials such as hide and (b) 11 with wear that probably formed from contact with a more abrasive substance such as soil. Experiments show that the polish on the Swartkrans and Sterkfontein pieces could have been produced by digging for subterranean plant foods in rocky soil (Brain 1985a).

The microscopic and experimental results indicate that the flaking, battering, or polishing on the Olduvai and the South African bones is almost certainly not natural and thus that artifactual use of bone began at least 2–1.5 mya. However, it is important to stress that at each site the bones identified as artifacts represent only a tiny fraction of the total number of bones recovered. Even more important, for the most part the bone artifacts were minimally shaped before use, and truly formal bone implements, made to a repetitive pattern in advance of use, appear only much later, in the Eurasian Upper Paleolithic/African Later Stone Age, beginning between 60,000 and 50,000–40,000 years ago. Until that time, people certainly handled bones regularly and used them occasionally, but they did not recognize bone as a material that could be broken, carved, and ground into a variety of functionally useful artifact types.

Form and Function of the Earliest Stone Artifacts

In both eastern and southern Africa, the oldest stone artifact assemblages are generally assigned to the Oldowan Industrial Complex, named for Olduvai Gorge, where some of the largest and best-described assemblages have been found (M. D. Leakey 1971; Isaac 1984). Typically, Oldowan assemblages include rather crude, amorphous artifacts that are difficult to divide among discrete artifact types (Figs. 3.31, 3.32). A basic division is usually possible among (1) *manuports* (= pieces of rock that must have been carried to a locality but that were not artificially modified); (2) *hammerstones* (= rocks that were battered or pitted by striking against other hard objects, probably mainly other rocks from which flakes were struck); (3) *core forms* (= pebbles and rock fragments from which flakes were removed); and (4) *flakes*. Core forms may be further divided into (1) cores that served only as a source of flakes and (2) core tools that were flaked to produce useful edges or a desirable shape.

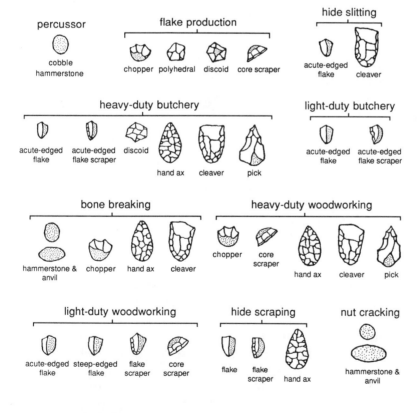

Figure 3.31. The basic types of stone artifacts found at Oldowan and Acheulean sites in Africa (adapted from Toth 1985b: Fig. 7). The Acheulean is usually distinguished from the preceding Oldowan by the presence of hand axes, cleavers, and other large bifacial tools. Large bifacial tools do, however, occur in some "Developed Oldowan" assemblages. The suggested uses are based on feasibility experiments with replicas.

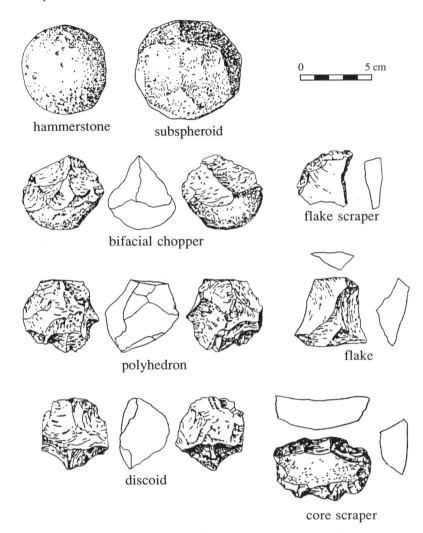

hammerstone   subspheroid

bifacial chopper

flake scraper

polyhedron

flake

discoid

core scraper

Figure 3.32. Range of typical Oldowan stone tools and their conventional typological designations (redrawn after originals by B. Isaac and J. Ogden in Toth 1985b: Fig. 1).

Most specialists use a scheme such as that of M. D. Leakey (1971) to assign core tools and modified (retouched) flakes to specific tool types. The types are differentiated mainly by how they are flaked or retouched, their size, and their shape. Thus, a flake with intentional retouch along an edge is called a *scraper;* a small scraper is *light duty,* a large one *heavy duty.* A core tool on which flaking is restricted to one edge is called a *chopper.* If the flaking is restricted to one surface, the chopper is *unifacial;* if the flaking occurs on two intersecting surfaces, the chopper is *bifacial.* A core tool that has been extensively flaked to resemble a disk is known as a *discoid.* If it is relatively spherical, it is a *spheroid,* and if it resembles a crude, multifacetted cube, it is a *polyhedron.* A *bifacial chopper* on which the flaking tends to extend around the entire periphery is a *proto-biface,* which grades into a true biface (hand ax) on which the flaking generally covers both surfaces as well as the entire periphery. Bifaces are unknown in the Oldowan proper; they appear about 1.5–1.4 mya in later assemblages variously labeled Developed Oldowan or Early Acheulean.

Further types and subtypes have been recognized in addition to these basic ones, but even the basic types may overemphasize the formality of Oldowan assemblages, where variation among artifacts tends to be continuous rather than discrete. Experimental replication, in fact, suggests that much of the variation among Oldowan core tools was controlled by the shape of the initial blank and not by a template in the maker's head (Toth 1985b). This helps explain why core forms tend to intergrade and why archeologists find it difficult to sort them into discrete types.

The crudeness and typological poverty of the Oldowan are related to a third important feature—remarkable uniformity through time and space. Most differences between Oldowan assemblages from different times and places can probably be attributed to available stone raw material. Thus, in the lower Omo River Valley, where small quartz pebbles were the most readily accessible raw material, the range of artifact types is restricted mainly to small sharp-edged quartz splinters produced by smashing (Merrick and Merrick 1976). At Koobi Fora and Olduvai, where large pieces of volcanic rock were more abundant, various core forms are much more common (Isaac 1984; Toth 1985b).

Koobi Fora also shows that the size of available stone blanks was probably an important determinant of interassemblage variability. The Oldowan tool makers found their blanks in stream gravels derived ultimately from volcanic uplands to the east of Lake Turkana. Understandably, the average gravel clast (particle) was smaller further from the uplands, and sites located in areas with smaller clasts tend to contain a smaller range of core forms, since smaller pieces cannot be so extensively flaked (Toth 1985b).

Until recently, archeologists describing and interpreting Oldowan assemblages focused on the modified flakes and on the core-tool category or subcategories. It was assumed that the accompanying unmodified flakes were mainly waste *(débitage)* from core-tool manufacture. This assumption can be tested by microscopically examining unmodified flakes for wear polishes that formed during use (Keeley 1980). Unfortunately, only flakes made in relatively homogeneous, nongrainy rocks are likely to preserve such polishes clearly, and most Oldowan flakes were made in inappropriate, coarse volcanic rock types. However, there are a small number of Oldowan flakes and flake fragments in suitable stone, and microscopic examination of fifty-six unmodified specimens from Koobi Fora isolated nine with unmistakable use wear or polish (Keeley and Toth 1981). Comparison with wear created on experimental tools shows that three of the Koobi Fora pieces were used for scraping or sawing wood, four for cutting meat, and two for cutting grass stems or reeds. Sharp, unretouched flakes probably produced some of the cut marks found on animal bones at Oldowan sites (Bunn 1981; Potts and Shipman 1981), and, in modern experiments, such flakes have proved especially useful for penetrating hides (Toth 1985b). Experimental knapping further suggests that many Oldowan core tools were only incidental by-products of flake production (Toth 1985b; Toth and Schick 1986).

All this is not to say that core tools were unimportant. Modern experiments show that sharp-edged core tools are generally more efficient than average-size flakes for prolonged or heavy-duty butchering, because they are heavier, have longer cutting edges, and are easier to hold (P. Jones 1980, 1981). Blunter core tools were probably ideal for fracturing animal bones to obtain marrow, while spheroids or polyhedrons could have been effective, even lethal, projectiles (Isaac 1984). That core tools were not simply sources of flakes is shown in Olduvai Beds I and II, where core tools tend to be made from lava and flakes tend to be made from quartz (M. D. Leakey 1971). Nonetheless, the developing evidence indicates that Oldowan stone knappers were at least as interested in fresh flakes as in core tools.

Unexpectedly, perhaps, the same replication experiments that emphasize the probable importance of flakes to Oldowan people also suggest they were usually right-handed (Toth 1985a). To produce flakes, a knapper usually holds the hammerstone in the dominant or active hand and the core in the less favored or passive hand. The first flakes that are struck from the core generally bear cortex (weathering rind) whose position tends to reflect which hand held the hammerstone and which hand held the core. Knappers who hold the hammerstone in the right hand produce slightly more flakes with cortex on the right side (when each flake is viewed from the dorsal [= cortical] surface with the butt or striking platform up). Oldowan assemblages from Koobi Fora contain more right-than left-sided cortical flakes, and the disproportion is about the same as in modern assemblages produced by a right-handed person. This implies that the Koobi Fora Oldowans were usually right-handed, like modern people—and unlike other animals, including chimpanzees, who are divided about equally between left- and right-handers. In modern people, the tendency for right-handedness is correlated with pronounced lateralization of the brain and marked functional separation of the cerebral hemispheres, and the Oldowan preference for right hands may indicate that these distinctively human features had already developed by 2–1.5 mya (Toth 1985a). The same inference may be drawn from the typically human, cerebral cortical asymmetries that characterize endocasts of the australopithecines and, more certainly, those of *Homo erectus* (Holloway 1981a; Holloway and de La Coste-Lareymondie 1982). At least incipient human cognitive and communicational abilities are almost certainly implied.

One vexing question that remains unsatisfactorily answered is, who made Oldowan tools? The possible candidates are robust australopithecines and early *Homo* (or the immediate ancestor of early *Homo*), both of which were broadly contemporaneous with the Oldowan. In Bed I at Olduvai Gorge, remains of a robust australopithecine and of *H. habilis* have even been found with Oldowan tools on the same ancient "living floor" (the FLK Zinj site; M. D. Leakey 1971). No one doubts that *H. habilis* was responsible for many of the tools, since it (or one of the constituents into which it may ultimately be split) was ancestral to later tool-making hominids. The issue is whether the robust australopithecines also produced some of the tools.

In favor of robust-australopithecine tool manufacture, there is the repeated, although rudimentary, use and manufacture of tools by chimpanzees, suggesting that a similar proclivity characterized the common ancestor of chimpanzees and hominids and thus all early hominids. Moreover, unlike chimpanzees and earlier australopithecines, at least *Australopithecus robustus* apparently had hands that were well adapted for precision grasping, facilitating tool use and manufacture. In fact, in morphology and potential function, its hands probably did not differ significantly from those of *H. habilis* and later members of the genus *Homo* (Susman 1988). However, if both early *Homo* and the robust australopithecines made tools, we might expect to find two distinct, contemporaneous tool-making traditions. The amorphous nature of Oldowan assemblages might obscure two separate traditions, but this is not true of the more patterned, less amorphous Acheulean assemblages which succeeded Oldowan ones about 1.4 mya. There is broad agreement that the early Acheulean was produced by the *Homo* lineage, since it plainly anticipates the later Acheulean when only this lineage persisted. The robust australopithecines certainly survived after the emergence of the Acheulean, perhaps for more than 500,000 years; yet there is no compelling evidence for a second contemporaneous, divergent artifact tradition. The implication is that the robust australopithecines made relatively few, if any, chipped stone artifacts. Their limited reliance on stone tools (if it existed) may have been correlated with their emphasis on vegetal food and on powerful jaws to process it, as well as with their failure to develop larger brains. Conversely, an increasing dependence on stone tools may be strongly related to the reduced jaws, enlarged brain, and probable greater carnivory of early *Homo*. Very likely, an enlarged brain, reduced jaws, and increased carnivory also promoted greater stone-tool use, which may thus have been both cause and effect in the emergence and ongoing evolution of *Homo*.

Structures and Fire

At site DK in Olduvai Gorge Bed I, Oldowan artifacts and fragmentary animal bones were associated with natural lava blocks, 10–25 cm across, clustered in a circle 4–5 m in diameter (Fig. 3.33) (M. D. Leakey 1971). A partial skull of *Homo habilis* was found at the same level nearby. It has been suggested that the circle is the remnant of a low stone wall that served as a windbreak or as the base of a brush superstructure. However, it is possible that the circle was created when the radiating roots of a tree penetrated and fractured a lava layer that lies directly underneath (Potts 1984). Modern trees are known to do this, and no truly comparable structural remnants have been reported from other Oldowan sites. Concentrations of large natural stones, Oldowan artifacts, and animal bones have been recorded at Melka Kunturé (Chavaillon et al. 1979), but the sedimentary context suggests that stream flow could be responsible.

The evidence for Oldowan use of fire is equally ambiguous. Most compelling would be concentrations of charcoal surrounded by stone artifacts and other cultural debris, but charcoal does not survive long in dry, open-air African sites (Isaac 1984). Attention has therefore been focused on burned or heated sediments, particularly the reddened patches found at Koobi Fora site FxJj 20E (J. W. K. Harris and Isaac 1976) and the

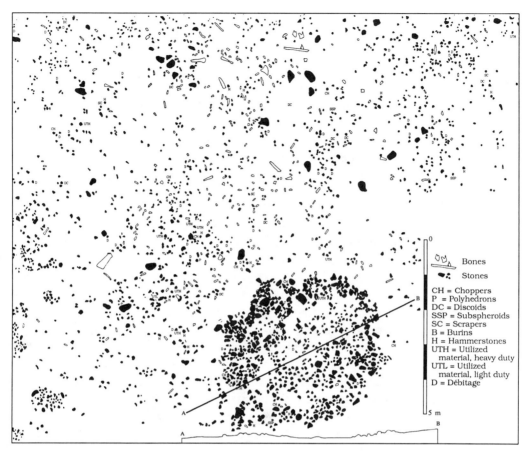

Bones

Stones

CH = Choppers
P = Polyhedrons
DC = Discoids
SSP = Subspheroids
SC = Scrapers
B = Burins
H = Hammerstones
UTH = Utilized
      material, heavy duty
UTL = Utilized
      material, light duty
D = Débitage

5 m

Figure 3.33. A partial floor plan of the excavation of site DK I at Olduvai Gorge (redrawn after M. D. Leakey 1971: Fig. 7). The most striking feature is the large circular concentration of basalt fragments in the right foreground. This may mark the base of the oldest known structure in the world or perhaps only the location of a tree whose radiating roots fractured and forced up pieces of basalt from immediately below the occupation surface.

fragments of burnt clay associated with Oldowan artifacts at Chesowanja (Gowlett et al. 1981). However, in both instances, vegetation smoldering after a brushfire could have caused the burning (Isaac 1982, 1984), and the first appearance of burnt bones at Swartkrans only in Member 3 may indicate that control over fire was an Acheulean (post-Oldowan) achievement (Brain 1988), postdating 1 mya. For the moment, the oldest reasonably secure evidence for human use of fire comes from relatively young sites in midlatitude Eurasia, where fire was probably essential for human survival. The oldest commonly accepted site is Zhoukoudian Cave in north China, putatively dated to about 500,000 years ago.

Subsistence and Behavior

Compared with chimpanzees or other nonhuman primates, most modern hunter-gatherers eat much more meat, and paleoanthropologists have long assumed that increased meat eating characterized even the early phases of human evolution. As proof they have cited the fragmentary animal bones found with Oldowan artifacts at many sites, especially at Olduvai Gorge and Koobi Fora. However, recently, archeologists have realized that a stratigraphic association between artifacts and bones does not demonstrate a functional link. The problem is that nearly all the associations occur at ancient lakeside or streamside sites where artifacts and bones could have been brought together by various events or even by chance. For any site, the a priori possibilities include (1) hunting by people, possibly followed by carnivore scavenging; (2) "natural" deaths from carnivore predation, accidents, disease, etc., followed by human scavenging; (3) human accumulation of bones at a central place, variously known as a living site, occupation site, or home base, perhaps followed by carnivore scavenging; (4) animal accumulation of bones at a den, followed by human scavenging; (5) the coincidental association of artifacts and bones at watering points used by people and animals at separate times; and (6) stream flow concentrating artifacts and bones from different original sites on a sandbar or gravel bar. Stream action or sheet wash could also disturb or smudge a bone/artifact association created another way, impeding interpretation of it.

The hypothesis that Oldowan artifact/bone concentrations represent ancient home bases was particularly popular in the 1970s, owing to a thoughtful exposition by Isaac (1978, 1981, 1984). He pointed out that the repeated use of a "home base" or "base camp" where garbage accumulates is a uniquely human (vs. ape) behavioral trait and that it implies other distinctively human traits, such as food sharing among group members and a division of labor between the sexes. Accepting Oldowan artifact/bone concentrations as home bases therefore indicates that an important constellation of typically human behavior patterns appeared at least 2 mya. The home-base hypothesis remains intriguing, but it has been placed in limbo, at least temporarily, as archeologists struggle to isolate the actual human contribution to Oldowan artifact/bone assemblages.

Separating the human from potential "natural" contributions is difficult, but stream action can generally be ruled out when (1) bones and artifacts appear unabraded (fresh); (2) pieces of different sizes and weights are present and not obviously sorted by size across the surface of a site; and (3) numerous bone or stone fragments in close proximity can be conjoined to reconstruct the larger pieces from which they came. Conjoinable bone fragments and artifacts have proved especially useful in demonstrating that some early Koobi Fora sites were probably not seriously disturbed by flowing water (Bunn et al. 1980; Kroll and Isaac 1984). In addition, of course, the possible or probable effects of flowing water can usually be established from the sedimentologic/geologic context.

Where stream disturbance or transport was unimportant, and where bones were probably concentrated by a biological agent, the problem is to separate the potential role played by people from that of other known bone collectors—carnivores and porcupines. The most useful criteria are the nature of bone damage and the pattern of skeletal part representation. Studies of recent bone assemblages accumulated by porcupines show that they usually leave their distinctive gnaw marks on more than 60% of the bones (Brain 1981). If this criterion is used, porcupines probably did not accumulate any of the bone assemblages associated with Oldowan tools or early-hominid remains in either eastern or southern Africa. In addition, at early east African sites, a porcupine role is ruled out by the sites' location on ancient land surfaces, near streams or lakes; porcupines accumulate bones in abandoned ant-bear holes, caves, and other recesses, not in the open air.

In general, a human role in bone collection is clearly implied by the presence of artifacts and, more directly, by bones with damage marks from stone tools. Similarly, a carnivore role is indicated by the presence of fossilized carnivore feces (coprolites) and by bones with damage from carnivore teeth. Damage from carnivore chewing is common at southern African australopithecine sites, and at those sites where artifacts are totally absent (Makapansgat and Sterkfontein Member 4) carnivores were probably the sole collectors (Maguire et al. 1980; Brain 1981). This is in spite of Dart's (1949) claim that these sites contain australopithecine and baboon skulls fractured by clubs before death. In fact, the skulls were probably damaged after burial, by pressure from hard objects in the ground (Brain 1972, 1981).

Some human role is obviously plausible at those southern African sites with possible Oldowan artifacts (Sterkfontein Member 5 and Swartkrans Member 1), but in each case the tools are relatively rare, and the concreted sediments have precluded excavations to demonstrate the precise nature of bone and artifact associations and to obtain large, unbiased bone and artifact samples. In general, bone damage and the absence or rarity of artifacts imply that the South African australopithecine sites were mainly carnivore lairs, and carnivore feeding could explain why these sites are so poor in australopithecine postcranial bones versus more durable skulls and jaws (Brain 1981). It could also explain why, compared with *Australopithecus robustus*, *A. africanus* is so much better represented by adults (vs. juveniles) (Tobias 1972; Mann 1975). Being somewhat smaller on average, *A. africanus* adults were probably easier for the carnivore bone accumulators to carry. Both kinds of australopithecine are remarkably abundant in the South African sites, and this may mean that live individuals were also relatively common nearby, since no carnivore is likely to have fed so heavily on very rare species. Nonetheless, the South African sites still reflect carnivore more than human behavior, and inferences about early human behavioral evolution must thus depend more on east African evidence.

However, interpretation of the east African sites is far from straightforward, partly because the evidence from bone damage is ambiguous. Large carnivore teeth and stone tools tend to fracture and flake bones in very similar ways, and marks left by stone tools can closely resemble ones made by other agencies, especially carnivore teeth. Some specialists believe that stone-tool marks can be identified with the naked eye or a light microscope (Bunn 1983), while others think that reliable identification requires a scanning electron microscope, with its superb depth of field and high resolution (Shipman and Rose 1983; Shipman 1986b). A further complication is that contact with sharp particles during trampling or other postdepositional disturbance can simulate cut marks on bones (Andrews and Cook 1985; Behrensmeyer et al. 1986). Moreover, at most early archeological sites, even when the sources of bone damage can be reasonably identified, damage or associated objects (artifacts and coprolites) usually implicate both people and carnivores, and the problem is how to estimate their relative contributions. The bone assemblage associated with Oldowan artifacts at the FLK Zinj site in Olduvai Bed I, described in detail by Bunn and Kroll (1986), is an excellent case in point.

The excavations at the FLK Zinj site were conducted mainly by M. D. Leakey (1971), who exposed an area of about 300 square m on an ancient land surface bordering the Bed I Olduvai Lake. A volcanic ash that covers the site has been dated to approximately 1.75 mya. The spatial distribution of bones and stone artifacts demonstrates that they were not significantly affected by moving water (Kroll and Isaac 1984).

Most bones are relatively unweathered, and observable differences in weathering could result from different times of final burial (Bunn and Kroll 1986) or from differences in the extent of shade before burial (Brain 1981). Alternatively, the weathering differences might reflect different times of first arrival, implying that the bone accumulation spanned at least 5–10 years (Potts 1984, 1986). If it took this long, and if people were the prime accumulators, their behavior was peculiar by comparison with that of modern tropical hunter-gatherers, who rarely occupy the same spot for more than a few months and then abandon it for even longer periods. The implication might be that the FLK Zinj people used the site in a unique, nonmodern way, perhaps as a place to cache stones for processing animal bones (Potts 1984).

In total, the FLK Zinj excavations produced about twenty-five hundred classic Oldowan artifacts and sixty thousand bones. The bones include approximately sixteen thousand from very small mammals (microfauna) and about thirty-five hundred that definitely came from large mammals (mainly various antelopes; Fig. 3.34). The remaining specimens are small fragments (mostly less than 20 mm long) that probably also came from large mammals but that cannot be assigned to skeletal part or taxon. In their analysis, Bunn and Kroll focused on skeletal part representation and on the abundance and placement of stone-tool cut marks on the thirty-five hundred indisputable large mammal bones. The sample need represent no more than forty to forty-five individual animals, and it is admittedly very small compared with many later archeological samples. However, it remains the largest and one of the best preserved bone samples from any Oldowan site (Bunn 1986; Bunn and Kroll 1986).

Among the large mammal bones, especially the largest ones, Bunn and Kroll found that crania, vertebrae, ribs, and metapodials were rare compared with mandibles, humeri, radio-ulnae, femora, and tibiae. The rare parts are ones that are relatively bulky, unnutritious, or both and that are thus often left at carcasses by both large predators and human hunters. The most abundant parts at FLK Zinj are meaty or marrow-rich bones that predators and people frequently take away. From this, Bunn and Kroll conclude that FLK Zinj was certainly not a kill or butchery site but rather a place to which bones were carried; equally important is their conclusion that the bone collector had early access to carcasses, either as a primary predator or as an efficient and perhaps high-ranking (dominant) scavenger.

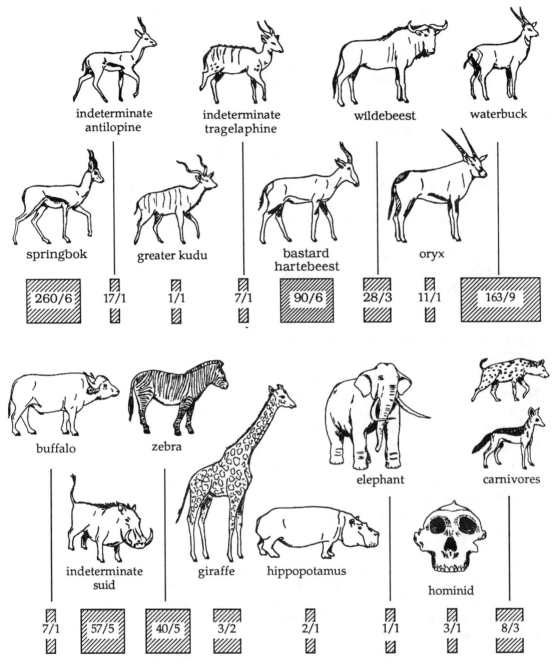

Figure 3.34. The abundance of various large mammals at the FLK Zinj site in Olduvai Gorge Bed I (data after Bunn and Kroll 1986: 433). The bars are proportional to the minimum number of individuals by which each species is represented. The numbers superimposed on the bars are the number of bones assigned to each species over the minimum number of individuals. The sample is small, but it still shows the preponderance of antelopes and other medium-size species which tends to characterize all African Stone Age sites, regardless of age. As discussed in the text, specialists disagree on how the animal bones accumulated at FLK Zinj—whether mainly through human activity and, if so, whether the people were mainly hunting or scavenging.

Since investigators disagree on the identification of cut marks, Bunn and Kroll dealt only with marks they felt were totally convincing both macroscopically and microscopically. These occurred on 172 specimens, mainly limb bones, where about two-thirds of the marks were on midshafts and only one-third were near joints (epiphyses). This is the pattern Bunn and Kroll predicted for a situation in which the people were not simply disarticulating carcasses, but were removing meat from them afterward; that is, it is the pattern they expected for a situation in which there was still substantial meat to remove. From the abundance of cut marks and artifacts, Bunn and Kroll conclude that it was Oldowan people who brought most of the bones to the FLK Zinj site, and, from skeletal part representation and the positioning of cut marks, they argue that the people were probably primary predators or efficient scavengers with early carcass access.

Bunn and Kroll suggest that the people were probably hunters more than scavengers, since Stone Age humans probably could not find fresh carcasses before other scavengers did. In Africa today, early-arriving scavengers, particularly hyenas, often quickly consume or remove meaty parts, leaving little for latecomers. Initially, Bunn and Kroll also suggested that hunting was more likely than scavenging because the FLK Zinj sample was dominated by prime-age adult animals and not by the very young and post-prime-age individuals whose carcasses are most available to scavengers. On reconsideration, however, they concluded that many individuals they originally called prime were actually past prime, which makes the age (mortality) profile consistent with either scavenging or hunting.

The abundance and placement of cut marks clearly provide the strongest support for Bunn and Kroll's hunting or efficient-scavenging hypothesis. However, Behrensmeyer (1986) suggests that postdepositional trampling of juxtaposed artifacts and bones could have produced many of Bunn and Kroll's midshaft cut marks. Perhaps even more crucial, Shipman (1986b) indicates that many of Bunn and Kroll's cut marks do not meet the scanning electron microscope criteria she considers crucial for cut-mark identification, and Potts (1982), using tighter criteria similar to Shipman's, found far fewer cut marks on the same bones.

In addition, Shipman (1984b, 1986b, 1986c) disagrees that early carcass access is indicated by a high proportion of cut marks on midshafts. She thinks that disarticulation implied by hunting would produce relatively more marks near joints, while marks on limb-bone midshafts would be rarer because of thick overlying muscle masses. An abundance of midshaft marks might in fact mean that some other creature had already consumed the muscles (meat). Shipman's argument may be countered by the relative abundance of midshaft marks on bones of domestic animals from a very–Late Stone Age (Pastoral Neolithic) site in Kenya where people clearly had first access to animals (Marshall 1986), but many more comparative observations will be necessary for firm resolution of the issue.

Finally, in her examination of bones from various Bed I Oldowan sites, Shipman (1984b, 1986b) found thirteen bones on which cut marks and carnivore tooth marks overlapped. In eight cases, the tooth marks overlay the cut marks; in five cases the cut marks were on top. The full implications of the overlapping marks are debatable, but at a minimum they indicate that people sometimes did scavenge carcasses on which other animals had already fed, and they suggest that carnivores contributed significantly to some Bed I assemblages, perhaps including FLK Zinj.

Another possible objection to Bunn and Kroll's interpretation is that it implies the FLK Zinj people were remarkably successful at obtaining meat. This seems at odds not only with a priori expectations for this remote period of 1.75 mya but also with inferences drawn from much later archeological bone assemblages, which suggest relatively limited human ability to obtain meat (Klein 1983). Additional objections stem from other FLK Zinj data. Bunn and Kroll found that approximately four hundred of the bones were damaged by carnivore teeth, which could mean that carnivores scavenged bones that people had abandoned, but which could also mean that carnivores had access to the bones before people did. Even if it only reflects carnivores scavenging bones left by people, it still implies that carnivore feeding or removal helped shape the final pattern of skeletal part survival. This is a possibility that Bunn and Kroll do not explicitly consider. They also do not address the possibility that the pattern of skeletal part composition was modified significantly by leaching, profile compaction, and other postdepositional processes that selectively remove softer or more fragile bones or that render them unidentifiable. Selective postdepositional destruction has probably affected skeletal part abundance in most fossil assemblages, and behavioral interpretations that do not take this into account are bound to be flawed (Klein and Cruz-Uribe 1984).

Finally, the abundant microfaunal bones at the FLK Zinj site require special attention. Microfaunal bones are also common at other Bed I Oldowan sites, and almost certainly they were introduced not by people but by raptors or small carnivores such as genets (Andrews 1983b). The implication may be that FLK Zinj and other sites were originally clusters of shade trees or bushes near water that attracted a variety of creatures, some of which brought in bones or found the presence of bones an additional attraction. The trees may have provided people with refuge from predators or other scavengers (Shipman 1986b) or with protected, shady places to cache artifacts for processing scavenged bones (Potts 1984). The artifacts and cut marks show that people were important at FLK Zinj, but they need not have been the principal bone accumulators, since clusters of bones occur under shade trees or bushes in Africa today, in the absence of human hunter-gatherers. With regard to FLK Zinj and other Bed I sites, the shade-tree/artifact-cache hypothesis becomes especially plausible if bone accumulation spanned many years, as Potts (1984, 1986) has suggested.

For other Oldowan sites, the full implications of the animal bones are at least as equivocal as for FLK Zinj, and truly compelling interpretations will probably require many fresh, large, well-preserved samples from new sites. These may permit the controlled interassemblage comparisons that are necessary to separate the roles of people, carnivores, and probable postdepositional destructive factors in shaping the composition of individual assemblages. However, it is possible to overemphasize the difficulties in interpreting Oldowan bone assemblages, and these difficulties should not be allowed to obscure the genuine knowledge that Oldowan people were processing animal parts in a way and to a degree unknown among chimpanzees or any other nonhuman primates (Isaac 1984). This is demonstrated by the cut-marked bones on which all specialists agree and by the stone flakes with polish from meat cutting. Cut-marked bones have even been found at sites where stone artifacts are absent, and some of the bones come from elephants, hippos, and other animals far larger than those on which other primates are known to feed. Whatever the precise meaning of FLK Zinj and other sites, the cut-marked bones and utilized flakes argue that an increased emphasis on animal food was indeed important in early human evolution.

What remains contentious is how the food was gotten—whether mainly by hunting, by scavenging, or by some mix of the two. A priori, it seems likely that there was some scavenging, particularly of carcasses of large animals that would be difficult or dangerous to kill. The potential importance of scavenging can be inferred from living Hadza hunter-gatherers in northern Tanzania, who scavenge perhaps one large mammal carcass for every four they obtain by hunting (O'Connell et al. 1988). Moreover, sedimentary and fossil evidence from

Olduvai, Koobi Fora, and other east African sites indicates that ancient human bones, artifacts, or both often accumulated in relatively well-wooded, water-edge environments where scavenging opportunities may have been particularly abundant (Blumenschine 1986, 1987). In comparable environments today, substantial amounts of scavengeable meat and marrow bone escape hyenas, lions, and other scavengers/predators and are especially available in the drier parts of the year. The amounts may have been even greater 1.8–2.0 mya, when the carnivore guild included saber-toothed cats and perhaps other species whose capacity to clean or crack bones was relatively limited. Scavenging would have been especially productive if early people were even moderately successful at driving off large cats or hyenas, as the Hadza often do today.

However, proof to check or supplement the logic of the hypothesis of early hominid scavenging remains elusive. It is not the studies of Bunn, Potts, Shipman, and others that are at fault but the sheer complexity of the problem and the ambiguity of the surviving evidence. An equally compelling question that is even harder to answer concerns the degree to which Oldowan people relied on animal food. Plant tissues that could represent food debris do not survive in such ancient sites, and, even if they did, it might be difficult to gauge how much food they represent versus the meat represented by bones. Again, we must turn to logic, supplemented in this instance by studies of recent hunter-gatherers. These studies suggest that Oldowan people relied mostly on plants and perhaps on other gathered foods, such as insects. In this light, their day-to-day food quest was probably far less bloodthirsty than popular authors such as Ardrey (1961, 1976) have imagined.

Summary and Conclusion: Natural Selection and Hominid Origins

The time when two species diverged may be estimated directly from the fossil record or indirectly from their biomolecular differences, if it is assumed that such differences accumulate at a constant rate. Together, the known fossil record and the "biomolecular clock" indicate that protopeople probably diverged from protochimpanzees and gorillas between 10 mya and 5 mya, in the late Miocene (Pilbeam 1985, 1986; Sibley and Ahlquist 1987). The split almost certainly occured in Africa, though, so far, the sparse African late-Miocene fossil record refuses to illuminate the event.

During the late Miocene, global climate became cooler and drier, promoting the spread of grasslands and savannas at the expense of forests at lower latitudes throughout the world. One indication of this is that high-crowned, grassland ungulates burgeoned, while forest creatures declined in numbers and diversity. Among the adversely affected animals were various ape species which had prospered in the Middle Miocene, between 17 mya and 10 mya. As the forests shrank in the late Miocene, many ape species became extinct, especially in Eurasia, but in Africa at least one ape species adapted to the changed conditions by spending more time on the ground, perhaps to exploit scattered clumps of trees. Living on the ground presented new challenges and opportunities which selected for those individuals whose morphology and behavior gave them an edge, however slight, over their peers. The known fossil record implies that living on the ground especially favored a new mode of habitual locomotion, bipedal rather than quadrupedal.

The initial advantages of bipedalism may have included (1) the ability to carry meat or other food items to trees or other refuges or to other group members (Hewes 1961, 1964; Lovejoy 1981); (2) a reduction in the amount of skin surface exposed to direct sunlight, thus reducing heat stress during midday activities (Wheeler 1984); (3) the freeing of the hands for tool use (Darwin 1871, Washburn 1960) or for carrying the young long distances (Sinclair et al. 1986); (4) a decrease in the energy required to walk at normal (low) speeds (Rodman and McHenry 1980); and/or (5) the ability to see over tall vegetation during passage from place to place. A link to tool use may seem unlikely, since the fossil record suggests that bipedalism antedates stone-tool manufacture by more than 1 million years, but, like the tools living chimpanzees use to probe for termites, to crack nuts, and so forth, the earliest human tools may have been made of wood or other highly perishable materials. It is also important to recall that the earliest people (broadly defined) probably lacked the typically human habit of occupying a single locale for several days (or nights), which means they may not have left stone tools in archeologically visible clusters.

Whatever the first advantages of bipedalism, it provided the basis for two distinct hominid adaptations to grassland or savanna environments: one in which subsequent change involved mainly an increased emphasis on the cheek teeth for masticating relatively coarse vegetal foods and one in which later change involved dramatic brain expansion, a reliance on tools far exceeding that of living chimpanzees, and an increase in meat eating. Adaptations stressing the grinding of vegetal foods with the cheek teeth may have arisen in two separate bipedal lines, one leading to *Australopithecus boisei* in eastern Africa and the other to *A. robustus* in southern Africa. More probably, these species were actually closely related, geographic variants (possibly even subspecies) of the same basic form. The adaptation involving radical brain expansion, increased tool use, and increased meat eating resulted ultimately in the genus *Homo*. Very possibly, early *Homo* comprised two contemporaneous species, in which case there must have been yet a third adaptation, whose basis remains obscure. The only certain fact is that, if this adaptation existed, it was eventually unsuccessful, like the adaptations of the robust australopithecines.

In both southern and eastern Africa, ongoing evolution in all hominid lineages was probably fostered by a continuing trend toward cooler, drier climates. Fossil pollens, sediments, and, especially, animal remains indicate the drying trend accelerated around 2.5–2 mya, broadly coinciding with a rapid evolutionary spurt in many African mammal lineages, including the hominids (Vrba 1985a, 1985b). The available evidence suggests that the 2.5–2-million-year interval witnessed particularly rapid advances in the lineage leading to large-brained, tool-using, meat-eating *Homo*.

As larger-brained, tool-using people became more carnivorous, they surely reduced the amount of meat available to large carnivores, and the emergence of *Homo* may have been partly or wholly responsible for a decrease in the number of African carnivore species after 2 mya (Walker 1984). The ever-expanding niche of *Homo* may also explain the demise of the robust australopithecines sometime between 1.2 mya and 700,000 years ago. More certainly, the behavioral advances tied to larger brains account for the eventual spread of *Homo* to Eurasia, probably beginning at or shortly before 1 mya. The archeological record postdating 1 mya is actually better known in Eurasia than in Africa, mainly because there have always been more archeologists in Eurasia than in Africa. The unique selection pressures that Eurasian environments presented may help explain some of the major morphological and behavioral advances that occurred after 1 mya (discussed below), but Africa did not become a backwater. To the contrary, evidence is accumulating that it may have remained the main center of human evolutionary change up to and including the emergence of anatomically modern people.

HOMO ERECTUS

4

About 1.8–1.7 million years ago (mya), *Homo habilis* (or one of the species into which it may ultimately be split) evolved into the primitive human species, *H. erectus*. Like *H. habilis* and the australopithecines, early *H. erectus* was apparently confined to Africa, but about 1 mya or shortly before, it dispersed to Eurasia, and the majority of known *H. erectus* fossils come from the Far East (Fig. 4.1). In Africa, *H. erectus* eventually colonized some relatively dry regions that had previously been unoccupied, and in parts of Eurasia, it became the first hominid species to adapt to truly cool-temperate conditions. Its morphological and behavioral advances over earlier hominids probably explain its ability to penetrate new environments, while the selection pressures it encountered in new environments help explain its further evolution.

Nearly all specialists agree that *Homo erectus* was directly ancestral to the modern human species, *H. sapiens* (broadly understood), which appeared in Europe and Africa about 500,000–400,000 years ago. *H. erectus* thus existed for more than 1 million years. In both morphology and behavior, it may have been remarkably conservative, hardly changing over this long interval, and *H. sapiens* may thus have evolved in a rapid spurt of morphological change. However, the alternative of more gradual evolution toward *H. sapiens* cannot yet be ruled out. This question is important not only to paleoanthropologists but also to theorists attempting to determine whether the common pattern in evolution has been relatively constant, gradual change through time or has been long periods of stasis (equilibrium) punctuated by short bursts of rapid change (Gould and Eldredge 1977; Stanley 1981). Unfortunately, with regard to *H. erectus*, this question is difficult to resolve because many key fossils are very difficult to date, even in relative terms. Dating problems and small sample size also hinder a full evaluation of geographic variability within *H. erectus*, including the possibility that populations on different continents followed very different evolutionary trajectories,

Figure 4.1. Approximate locations of the main sites providing fossils here assigned to *Homo erectus.*

perhaps even culminating in separate species. Fortunately, as this chapter shows, many fundamental morphological and behavioral attributes of *H. erectus* can be established despite the deficiencies in the record.

History of Discovery

The first fossils of *Homo erectus* were discovered by the Dutch physician and visionary Eugene Dubois. The story has been clearly summarized by Oakley (1964). Born in 1858, Dubois was a firm follower of Darwin and other evolutionists, and he became eager to find fossils that would demonstrate human evolution. He believed that tropical Asia was a logical place to look, particularly since it still contained apes that might broadly resemble protohumans. In 1887 he secured a medical appointment in the Dutch East Indian Army, which posted him to Sumatra. He excavated in several limestone caves which he knew were particularly favorable places to find fossils, but he found nothing relevant to human evolution. Then, in 1890, he heard about the discovery of an interesting skull at Wajak (Wadjak) in nearby Java. He visited the site and discovered a second, similar skull but was disappointed to find that both skulls were essentially modern. Today, they are widely regarded as fossil representatives of anatomically modern people *(H. sapiens sapiens)*.

Dubois remained in Java and directed excavations at some promising fossil sites in the central part of the island. In 1891, near the village of Trinil on the Solo River, he found a low-vaulted, thick-walled skullcap with large browridges that was clearly far more primitive than the Wajak skulls. On the basis of the animal fossils associated with it, it was also obviously much more ancient. The following year, in what Dubois thought was the same bed at Trinil, he found a femur that was morphologically indistinguishable from a modern human one. He believed the skullcap and femur came from the same species, which he concluded was an erect, apelike transitional form between apes and people. In 1866 the German biologist Ernst Haeckel had suggested the genus *Pithecanthropus* for a hypothetical missing link. In 1894 Dubois appropriated Haeckel's name and called his fossil species *Pithecanthropus erectus* ("erect ape-man").

Ironically, it is now clear that Dubois did not appreciate the stratigraphic complexity of the Trinil locality, and it is possible that the femur came from a much younger horizon than did the skullcap (Bartstra 1982b). In some important respects, it looks much more modern than other, undoubted *Homo erectus* femora (G. E. Kennedy 1983), and sophisticated measurement of the trace elements it contains may ultimately show it is much younger (Day 1984). However, early debate on Dubois's finds did not center on their stratigraphic association but on whether they really represented a single species and, beyond this, on whether the skullcap was from an early human as opposed to an ape. The issue was ultimately resolved, in favor of early-human status, by fresh discoveries, first in China and then again in Java.

The story of the Chinese discoveries has been recounted in detail by Shapiro (1971, 1974). For centuries, Chinese folk doctors collected fossils to pulverize into medicines. In 1899, a European doctor found a probable human tooth among fossils in a Beijing (Peking) drugstore. Paleontologists attracted by the discovery learned that a particularly rich complex of fossiliferous limestone caves and fissures existed about 40 km southwest of Beijing, near the village of Zhoukoudian (formerly spelled Choukoutien). In 1921, the Swedish geologist J. G. Andersson initiated excavations in a collapsed cave at Zhoukoudian that became known as Locality 1, a cave that he thought was particularly promising, because, in addition to fossils, it contained quartz fragments that could only have been introduced by prehistoric people. In 1923, Otto Zdansky, an Austrian paleontologist who was working with Andersson, discovered a human molar among the Locality 1 fossils, and, in 1926, after the excavations had stopped, he found a human premolar among fossils that had been shipped to Sweden.

The teeth came to the attention of Davidson Black, a Canadian anatomist at the Peking Union Medical School. Black convinced the Rockefeller Foundation to sponsor renewed excavations at Locality 1, which were begun in 1927, under the field direction of Birgir Bohlin. Later in the same year, these excavations produced a large human molar with a wrinkled crown, for which Black erected a new species and genus of fossil people, *Sinanthropus pekinensis* ("Peking Chinese Man"). Many specialists felt Black had been too hasty, but, in 1928, excavations at Locality 1 uncovered two partial archaic human mandibles and some skull fragments. In 1929, W. C. Pei, the new field director, found a skullcap that removed any remaining doubts. Black died in 1933 and was succeeded in 1935 by Franz Weidenreich, a distinguished German anatomist who had been working at the University of Chicago. Excavations continued at Zhoukoudian until 1937, eventually producing 5 more or less complete skullcaps, 9 large skull fragments, 6 facial fragments, 14 partial mandibles, 147 isolated teeth, and 11 postcranial bones. These are estimated to represent more than forty *Sinanthropus* individuals, including men, women, and children.

The next discoveries to be made were again in Java, first in 1936 near Perning (= Modjokerto) in the east and then between 1937 and 1941 near Sangiran in the central part, about 65 km west of Trinil. The person who reported the new Javan finds was a German paleontologist, G. H. R. von Koenigswald. The Perning find consisted of a partial immature skull which nonetheless exhibited, in incipient form, the large browridges, flat receding forehead, narrowing (constriction) behind the orbits, and angulated occipital of Dubois's *Pithecanthropus*. The Sangiran fossils included some partial jaws and also several dozen isolated teeth, which are only now being described (Grine 1984). Most important were three partial crania ("*Pithecanthropus* II–IV") that in all essential respects were simliar to the one Dubois had found in 1891. Two of the crania were associated with animal fossils (the "Trinil Fauna") that suggested they were roughly contemporaneous with Dubois's original find. The third cranium was associated with somewhat different fossils (the "Djetis Fauna") that suggested it was somewhat older (G. H. R. von Koenigswald 1962).

In 1939, von Koenigswald traveled to China to compare his fossils with the Zhoukoudian ones that Franz Weidenreich was describing. Von Koenigswald and Weidenreich agreed that the Javan fossils and the Chinese fossils were extremely similar. Weidenreich (1940) even proposed reducing *Pithecanthropus* and *Sinanthropus* to subspecies of the single species *Homo erectus*, though he continued to use the original generic names as labels.

The Japanese Imperial Army occupied north China in 1937, and, in 1941, anticipating intensified hostilities, Weidenreich moved to New York. For safety's sake, the Chinese authorities also decided to ship the *Sinanthropus* fossils to the United States, and they were entrusted to marine guards who were helping to evacuate the American embassy from Beijing. With their marine caretakers, the fossils arrived at the port serving Beijing on 7 December 1941, the day that Imperial Japan attacked Pearl Harbor. The marines were captured and later interned by the Japanese, and the fossils vanished. There has been much speculation on their whereabouts, but they were probably simply discarded by persons who did not realize their value. Fortunately, Weidenreich had prepared an excellent set of plaster casts, which are now housed at the American Museum of Natural History in New York City. Along with his detailed monographic descriptions (Weidenreich 1936, 1937, 1941, 1943), they permit continued analysis of the fossils.

Von Koenigswald's fossils survived the war in Java, and he later took them to Frankfurt. Some remain there, but many important specimens have been returned to Indonesia. Dubois had taken his original finds to the Netherlands, where they are still kept in Leiden.

In 1950, Mayr (1950) emphasized that the differences between *Pithecanthropus erectus* ("Java Man") and *Sinanthropus pekinensis* ("Peking Man") were no greater than those between nonhuman populations that are usually placed in the same species. As Weidenreich had earlier suggested, Mayr also pointed out that the differences from modern people were not sufficient to justify generic separation. In 1955, the prominent British anatomist Le Gros Clark (1955) strongly supported placing *Sinanthropus* within *Pithecanthropus* and, in 1964 (Le Gros Clark 1964), *Pithecanthropus* within *Homo*. Other authorities, such as Howell (1960) and Howells (1966), agreed, and today Java Man, Peking Man, and all similar fossils are known as *H. erectus*.

Additional *Homo erectus* fossils have been found in both Java and China, in Africa, and, arguably, in Europe. The new Javanese specimens were recovered between 1952 and 1975 and were reported by the Indonesian scientists S. Sartono and T. Jacob. They comprise a cranium from the new locality of Sambungmachan between Sangiran and Trinil and at least five isolated teeth, six partial jaws, some skull fragments, and three crania from near Sangiran (Jacob 1975, 1980; Day 1986). One of the Sangiran specimens (Sangiran 17 = "*Pithecanthropus* VIII") is the most complete *H. erectus* skull from Java and one of the most complete in the world (Sartono 1975).

The new Chinese specimens include a partial skull, a fragmentary mandible, six isolated teeth, and two fragmentary limb bones found at Zhoukoudian between 1949 and 1966 (Wu and Dong 1985; Wu and Lin 1985); a mandible found at Chenjiawo (formerly Chenchiawo) in 1963; a skull found at Gongwangling (formerly Kungwangling) in 1964; a partial skull, two skull fragments (from a second individual), a fragmentary mandible, and nine isolated teeth found in Lontandong Cave, Hexian County, in 1980–81; and isolated teeth found at Yuanmou, Jianshi, and six other localities between 1975 and 1982 (Wu 1985; Wu and Dong 1985; Wu and Lin 1985). Chenjiawo and Gongwangling are often known as the Lantian localities. Although only three teeth were found at Jianshi, they are important for providing the best-documented stratigraphic association between a hominid and the extinct ape *Gigantopithecus* (Y. Zhang 1985). Other associations, involving *Homo erectus* teeth or mandibles and *Gigantopithecus* teeth, have been reported from the *Gigantopithecus* Cave at Liucheng in south China (Y. Zhang 1985) and from Tham Khuyen Cave in nearby northern Vietnam (Ciochon 1986). Among the various Chinese sites, the one with the greatest future potential is probably Zhoukoudian, where major excavations initiated at Locality 1 in 1979 are just now reaching the levels that produced most of the so-called *Sinanthropus* fossils in the 1930's (Wu 1985).

In Africa, fossils now recognized as *Homo erectus* were found first at Swartkrans, South Africa, in 1949. Important additional discoveries were later made in Algeria, Morocco, Ethiopia, Kenya, and Tanzania at sites listed in Table 4.1. Especially noteworthy are some remarkably complete and well-dated fossils from Koobi Fora and Nariokotome in the Lake Turkana Basin of northern Kenya. There are also a series of African fossils which have sometimes been assigned to *H. erectus* but which are now more commonly placed in early ("archaic") *H. sapiens* (Howell 1978a; Howells 1980; Rightmire 1980, 1981a, 1983, 1984b, 1985). The sites from which they come are listed in Table 4.2.

There are also several fossils from outside Africa that have been variably assigned to *H. erectus* or early *H. sapiens*.

Table 4.1. African Sites with Fossils of *Homo erectus*

Site	Fossils	Date Found	References
Ternifine (= Tighennif = Palikao), Algeria	Three mandibles and a skull fragment of "*Atlanthropus mauritanicus*"	1954–55	Arambourg 1955; Howell 1960
Sidi Abderrahman (Littorina Cave), Morocco	Mandibular fragments	1954	Arambourg and Biberson 1956; Howell 1960
Thomas Quarries, Morocco	A mandible and cranial fragments	1969, 1972	Howell 1978a; Rightmire 1980; Bräuer 1984b; Hublin 1985
Gomboré II (Melka Kunturé), Ethiopia	Cranial fragment	1973	Chavaillon *et al.* 1974; Howell 1978a
Omo, Shungura Fm Mb K	Parietal and temporal fragments (L. 996-17)	??	Howell 1978a
Koobi Fora (East Turkana), Kenya	Partial skeleton (KNM-ER-1808) and two nearly complete skulls (KNM-ER-3733 & 3883) Parts of three other skulls, nine partial mandibles, and some isolated limb bones	1973–75	R. E. F. Leakey and Walker 1976, 1985b; Walker and Leakey 1978; Walker *et al.* 1982
Nariokotome (West Turkana), Kenya	Nearly complete skeleton (KNM-WT 15000)	1984	F. H. Brown 1985a; R. E. F. Leakey and Walker 1985a
Lainyamok, Kenya	Three maxillary teeth and a femoral shaft fragment	1976, 1984	Shipman *et al.* 1983; Potts *et al.*, 1988
Olduvai Gorge, LLK II, Tanzania	Cranium (Olduvai Hominid (= OH) 9)	1960	L. S. B. Leakey 1961
Olduvai Gorge, VEK IV, Tanzania	Fragmentary cranium (=OH 12)	1962	Rightmire 1979a
Olduvai Gorge, WK IV, Tanzania	Partial pelvis and a femoral shaft (= OH 28)	1970	Day 1971
Swartkrans, South Africa	Various bones from Mbs 1, 2, and 3, including especially two mandibles and the partial skull of "*Telanthropus capensis*" from Mb 2	1949 and later	Clarke *et al.* 1970; Clarke 1977; Brain 1981, 1988; Grine, in press

They include a skullcap found in the Narmada Valley of northern India in 1982 (M. A. de Lumley and Sonakia 1985; Sonakia 1985), fifteen skulls or skull fragments and two tibial fragments recovered at Ngandong (= Solo) in central Java in 1931–33 and 1976 (Weidenreich 1951; Jacob 1978), and all the oldest known fossils of *Homo* from Europe. These include the famous Mauer jaw found near Heidelberg, Germany, in 1907; the Petralona skull found in Greece in 1960; more than fifty specimens (a partial cranium, two mandibles, isolated teeth, and postcranial bones) found at Arago (Tautavel), France, since 1964; the Vértesszöllös skull fragment found in Hungary in

Table 4.2. African Sites with Fossils Variably Assigned to *Homo erectus* or early *H. sapiens*

Site	Fossils	Date Found
Rabat (= Kébibat), Morocco	Mandible	1933
Salé, Morocco	Fragmentary skull	1971
Wadi Dagadlé, Djibouti	Left maxilla	1983
Bodo, Ethiopia	Partial skull and fragment of a second skull	1976, 1981
Garba III (Melka Kunturé), Ethiopia	Cranial fragments	1976
Kapthurin (Baringo), Kenya	Two mandibles and upper-limb bones	1966, 1983
Ndutu, Tanzania	Skull	1973
Broken Hill (= Kabwe), Zambia	Skull	1921
Elandsfontein (= Hopefield = Saldanha), South Africa	Skull and mandible fragment	1953, 1954

Note: Specimens are regarded as *H. sapiens* here. For individual references, see chap. 5.

1965; the Bilzingsleben (Steinrinne Quarry) cranial fragments and teeth found in East Germany between 1972 and 1984; and the approximately ninety fossils (twenty-one cranial fragments, one nearly complete mandible, four partial mandibles, thirty-eight isolated teeth, and roughly twenty postcranial bones) recovered from the Cueva Mayor (Ibeas, Atapuerca), Spain, between 1976 and 1984.) (Howells 1980; Howell 1984, 1986; Stringer 1984; further references in Chapter 5).

Among the disputed specimens, those from Ngandong are particularly problematic, because they resemble classic *Homo erectus* (Java Man) in important respects (Santa Luca 1980; Rightmire 1988), but they appear to be somewhat younger, certainly overlapping in time with indisputable *H. sapiens* from Africa and Europe. In contrast, the controversial African and European fossils variably assigned to *H. erectus* or *H. sapiens* do not closely conform to the morphology of classic *H. erectus*, though at least some may be just as old. This may mean that geographically far-flung human populations were diverging along separate evolutionary paths in the middle Quaternary. Ultimately, checking the validity of this hypothesis is far more important than finding a precise taxonomic assignment for key European, African, and Asian fossils.

Geologic Antiquity

Figure 4.2 summarizes the approximate ages of the principal *Homo erectus* and early *H. sapiens* fossils discussed in this chapter and in Chapter 5. The best-dated specimens of *Homo erectus* are those from east Africa, particularly from Koobi Fora at East Turkana and from Nariokotome at West Turkana. At Koobi Fora, radiopotassium dates on volcanic tuffs indicate

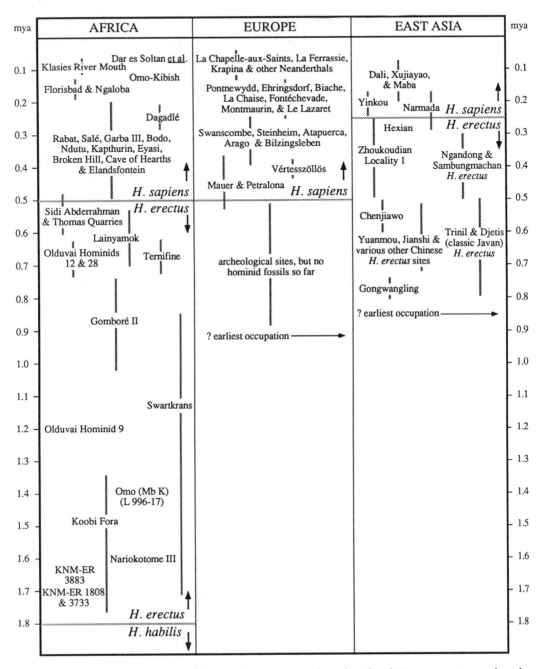

Figure 4.2. Approximate ages of the main sites providing fossils of *Homo erectus* and early *H. sapiens*. The hachured vertical lines indicate time ranges in which fossils may lie.

that a nearly complete *H. erectus* skull (KNM-ER 3733) and a partial *H. erectus* skeleton (KNM-ER 1808) are roughly 1.8–1.7 million years old, while a second nearly complete skull (KNM-ER 3883) is probably only slightly younger. The stratigraphic relationship of the Nariokotome (III) skeleton to a dated tuff indicates an age of about 1.6 million years (F. H. Brown and Feibel 1985). Other, less complete *H. erectus* specimens from Koobi Fora and some cranial fragments from the Shungura Formation (Member K) in the lower Omo River Valley probably date to roughly 1.3–1.4 mya. Together, the specimens from the Lake Turkana Basin are the oldest well-documented *H. erectus* in the world.

There are no firm radiometric dates for *Homo erectus* fossils from Olduvai Gorge, but paleomagnetic readings and average sedimentation rates calculated between dated levels permit reasonable estimates. On this basis, a skullcap (OH [Olduvai Hominid] 9) from Upper Bed II has an estimated age of 1.2 mya, while *H. erectus* fossils from Upper Bed IV (OH 12 and 28) are bracketed between 730,000 and 620,000 years ago (M. D. Leakey and Hay 1982). The lower limit is based on their occurrence above the Bed IV horizon containing the boundary between the Matuyama and Brunhes Paleomagnetic Chrons (Hay 1976). The upper limit is based on extrapolated sedimentation rates and is less secure.

The *Homo erectus* skull fragment from Gomboré II (Melka Kunturé) occurred in sediments that preserve the reversed polarity of the Matuyama Chron and that overlie a tuff that has been radiopotassium dated to 1.1–1.3 mya (Chavaillon 1979, 1982). The fragment is thus between 1.3 million and 730,000 years old, which is consistent with the faunal evidence. The partial maxilla and femoral fragment from Lainyamok came from mudflow deposits bracketed between 730,000 and 380,000 years ago by paleomagnetism and radiopotassium dates. Mineralogical and faunal similarities to a dated horizon at nearby Olorgesailie suggest a narrower age, between 700,000 and 560,000 years (Potts et al. 1988).

The remaining African *Homo erectus* fossils (Table 4.1) can be only broadly dated, mainly by the animal species found with them. Paleomagnetic readings and animal fossils imply that the Ternifine mandibles and skull fragment are broadly coeval with the fossils from Olduvai Upper Bed IV; that is, they are between 730,000 and 600,000 years old (Geraads et al. 1986). The fossils from Sidi Abderrahman and from the Thomas Quarries are somewhat younger (Geraads 1980; Geraads et al. 1980), perhaps on the order of 500,000 years old. Some of the Swartkrans fossils (from Mb 1) are probably older and could

approach the 1.8–1.6-million-year age of the Turkana specimens (Vrba 1985a). However, the best-known Swartkrans specimen, the partial skull (from Mb 2) once assigned to *"Telanthropus capensis,"* is probably between 1 million and 700,000
years old (Brain 1988; see also the discussion of Swartkrans in
Chapter 3). The putative early *H. sapiens* fossils from Salé,
Bodo, Ndutu, Broken Hill, and Elandsfontein (Table 4.2) are
probably all much younger, perhaps in the 500,000–300,000-
year-old range.

Among the East Asian *Homo erectus* fossils, the Chinese
ones are ostensibly better dated, thanks primarily to their better-
documented stratigraphic provenience and to recent paleomagnetic determinations. Within the framework provided by the paleomagnetic determinations, Chinese scientists have attempted
more precise dates by correlating the climatic fluctuations recorded at important sites (especially Zhoukoudian) with the
dated oxygen-isotope stages of the global marine stratigraphy
(Liu 1985; Wu 1985). The correlation procedure is open to many
possible errors, so the results can only be provisional. For the moment, they suggest that (1) the *H. erectus* fossils at Zhoukoudian
Locality 1 accumulated between 500,000 and 240,000 years ago;
(2) the Hexian fossils are roughly 280,000–240,000 years old; (3)
the Gongwangling (Lantian) skull is perhaps 800,000–750,000
years old; (4) the Chenjiawo (Lantian) mandible is approximately
590,000–500,000 years old; and (5) the isolated teeth from Yuanmou and other sites mentioned by Wu (1985) are all younger than
730,000 years old. The age estimate for Zhoukoudian is tentatively supported by uranium-series dates on bone (Chen et al.
1984; Chen and Yuan 1988), but a thorough review of the Zhoukoudian fauna, pollen, and sediments (Aigner 1986) suggests that
most of the sequence, including the human fossils, may date
from a single interglaciation, perhaps closer to 500,000 than to
240,000 years ago.

The Javan specimens of *Homo erectus* remain the most
poorly dated. In the Sangiran-Trinil area of Central Java, they
are conventionally said to come from two rock-stratigraphic
units, each with its own distinctive fauna (G. H. R. von
Koenigswald 1962; Bartstra 1983). The older unit, providing
relatively few *H. erectus* remains, comprises the Pucangan (or
Putjangan) Beds with the Djetis (= Jetis) fauna; the younger
unit, which has provided most of the *H. erectus* fossils,
comprises the Kabuh Beds with the Trinil Fauna. In fact, both
the litho- and biostratigraphy are probably far more complex
(Sondaar 1984), and the precise stratigraphic provenience of
most of the *H. erectus* fossils is uncertain in any case. Fluorine
analysis has been used to narrow the provenience possibilities

(Matsu'ura 1986), but it is still difficult to relate the fossils to paleomagnetic determinations or to radiopotassium and fission-track dates that have been obtained both on volcanic tuffs in the Pucangan Beds and on tuffs, pumices, and tektites in the Kabuh Beds (Semah 1984; Howell 1986). In the Pucangan Beds, the dates range from 2 mya to 570,000 years ago and in the Kabuh Beds from 1.6 mya to 470,000 years ago. The obvious discrepancy is underlined by contradictions between some of the dates and paleomagnetic readings on the same sediments. There are many possible reasons for contradictory dates, including the dating of samples that were redeposited from older sediments. For the moment, the dates are obviously not very helpful for estimating the antiquity of Javan *H. erectus*, though it may be meaningful that the majority are less than 800,000 years.

It is probably also pertinent that there is no firm evidence of people on the east Asian mainland before 1 mya, and it is from Southeast Asia that people must have come to Java, across the Sunda Shelf which was repeatedly exposed during Quaternary glaciations. The amplification of glacial pulses in the later part of the early Quaternary, roughly 800,000 years ago, increased the amount of shelf exposed and also provided the most favorable environmental conditions for crossings by a wide range of species, including open-country forms such as people (Ninkovich et al. 1982; Sondaar et al. 1983). In sum, when all factors are considered, it is reasonable to conclude, following Pope (1983), that "0.5–0.8 MYA seems the most reasonable estimate for the age of the earliest known Indonesian hominids." This estimate is consistent with dates that have been proposed for the fauna(s) associated with Javan *H. erectus*, following fresh research in the Sangiran area (Leinders et al. 1985).

The upper age limit of Javan *Homo erectus* is also highly uncertain. However, if the Ngandong specimens are included, as their morphology argues they should be, then *H. erectus* probably persisted in Java until the late mid-Quaternary, perhaps until 300,000–250,000 years ago. This estimate is based on faunal associations and on a fission-track date from the Notopuro Beds that provided the Ngandong fossils (Jacob 1978; Semah 1984). At that time, *H. erectus* may still have been present in China (at Zhoukoudian and Hexian), but it was gone from Europe and Africa, where most specialists agree that archaic *H. sapiens* had already appeared. Although it is widely accepted that *H. sapiens* evolved from *H. erectus*, this need not have occurred everywhere, and, on present evidence, it is possible that *H. sapiens* emerged, in the middle Quaternary, from a marginal *H. erectus* population experiencing stringent selection under very cold conditions in Europe or very dry conditions in Africa (Delson 1981).

Morphology

Most morphological descriptions of *Homo erectus* depend primarily on the Javan and Chinese samples, since these are the largest. They also comprise the type specimens of *H. erectus*, that is, those to which other specimens must be likened before they can be assigned to the same species. The following description is based primarily on ones by Le Gros Clark (1964), Howell (1978a), Howells (1980), Rightmire (1984a, 1985, 1988), and Hublin (1986). It defines an average, to which not all specimens conform exactly. The anatomical features to which it refers are illustrated in Figures 4.3–4.9.

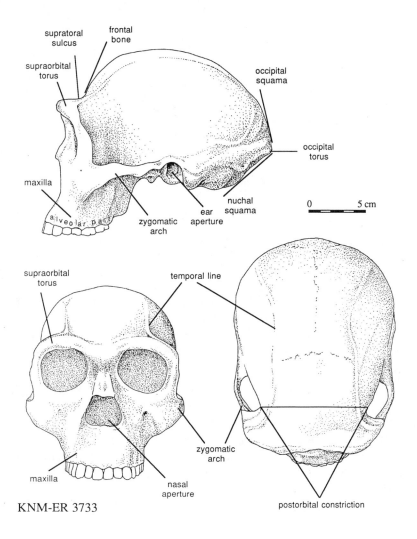

KNM-ER 3733

Figure 4.3. Skull KNM-ER 3733 from Koobi Fora, East Turkana (formerly East Rudolf), northern Kenya (redrawn after Howell 1978a: Fig. 10.10) (KNM-ER = Kenya National Museum–East Rudolf). The skull exhibits several features characteristic of *Homo erectus*, including a large, forwardly projecting supraorbital torus, a supratoral sulcus separating the torus from a low, receding frontal, and a highly angulated occipital bone with a pronounced occipital torus. It is one of several north Kenyan fossils documenting the emergence of *H. erectus* about 1.7–1.6 mya.

Figure 4.4. Franz Weidenreich's restorations of *Homo erectus* skulls from Sangiran in Java and from Zhoukoudian Locality 1 in China (redrawn partly after originals by Janis Cirulis in Howells 1967: 156, 169). Typical *H. erectus* features visible in both restorations include a large forwardly projecting, shelflike supraorbital torus, a distinct supratoral sulcus, a low, receding frontal bone, sagittal keeling, a highly angulated occipital with a very prominent occipital torus, and pronounced alveolar prognathism.

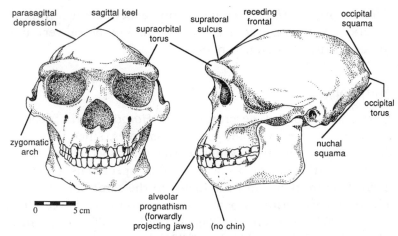

Indonesian *Homo erectus* (Weidenreich restoration)

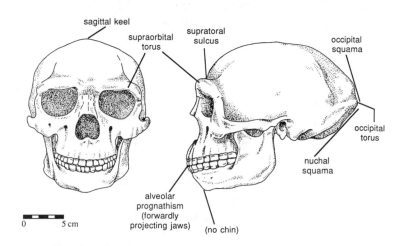

Zhoukoudian *Homo erectus* (Weidenreich restoration)

Braincase

Long, low-vaulted, and thick-walled; average cranial capacity slightly more than 1,000 cc, probably increasing through time, from perhaps 850–900 cc in the earliest *H. erectus* to 1,050–1100 cc or more in the latest (Rightmire 1981b, 1985; largely on the basis of endocranial volume determinations by Weidenreich and Holloway); greatest breadth near the base, often coincident with biauricular breadth (= breadth between the ear apertures); frontal bone low and receding, with a large supraorbital torus (or bar) (browridge) that tends to be straight when viewed from in front or above; variable development of a supratoral sulcus (= an inflection in the frontal profile just behind the torus) and also of sinuses within the torus; pronounced postorbital constriction.

Variable development of a sagittal keel along the midline at the top of the braincase, associated with (parasagittal) depressions on either side of the midline and a thickening of the bone at and near bregma along the coronal suture; occipital bone always sharply angled in profile, with the upper (occipital) plate (= scale or squama) usually smaller than the lower (nuchal) one; at the juncture of the occipital and nuchal plates, a conspicuous mound or bar of bone (the transverse occipital torus), usually projecting farthest near the midline, where it can form a blunt triangular eminence; basicranium moderately flexed or arched between the hard palate and foramen magnum (Laitman 1985).

Face

Short, but massive and relatively wide, with the nasal aperture projecting forward relative to the adjacent maxillary and zygomatic regions; pronounced alveolar prognathism (= forward

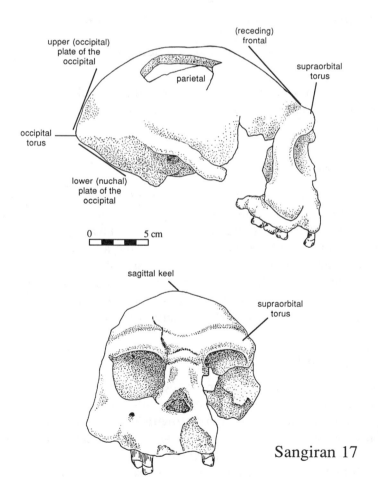

Sangiran 17

Figure 4.5. Skull Sangiran 17 (or Pithecanthropus VIII) from Java, the most complete specimen of Java Man (drawn by K. Cruz-Uribe from photos). Combining a face and braincase in a single specimen, Sangiran 17 broadly confirms conjectural reconstructions of face and skull that were done before it was found (Fig. 4.4). The skull exhibits all the classic features of *Homo erectus,* including a massive supraorbital torus, a low, receding frontal, sagittal keeling, a highly angulated occipital with a pronounced transverse torus, and thick cranial walls.

Figure 4.6.
Mandibles of
Javan *Homo erec-
tus* and a robust
modern person (*H.
sapiens sapiens*),
viewed from the
side and showing
the absence of a
chin, an absence
that distinguishes
H. erectus (and
other fossil homi-
nids) from modern
people (redrawn
after Le Gros
Clark 1964: 94).
In further distinc-
tion, mandibles of
H. erectus tend to
have multiple
mental foramina.

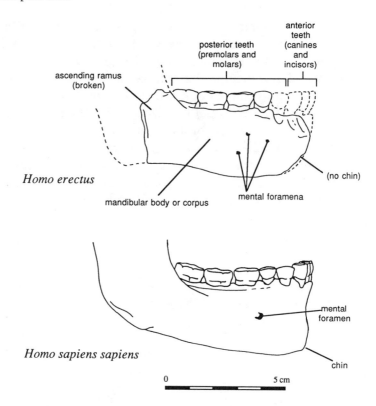

projection of the jaws); mandible robust and backward sloping
below the incisors, resulting in the absence of a chin ("mental
eminence").

Dentition

Cheek teeth large relative to those of modern people, but
generally reduced compared with those of *Homo habilis* or the
australopithecines; sporadic occurrence (in Javan specimens) of
a diastema (gap) between the upper canine and lateral incisor,
associated with a projecting, though spatulate upper canine;
third molar generally smaller than the second, as in *H. sapiens*
but not in the australopithecines; incisors large and often
spatulate or shoveled (curled inward at the lateral edges).

Postcranium

Known mainly from the femur and the pelvis, which are generally similar to those of modern people (Day 1984); however,
pelvis remarkably robust and distinguished especially by a thick
buttress of cortical (outer) bone arising vertically above the
acetabulum (= the socket for the femur); femur equally robust,
with extraordinarily thick external (cortical) bone, a relatively

narrow internal (medullary or marrow) canal, and pronounced muscle markings; femoral shaft differing from that of later people in its greater fore-to-aft compression (greater platymeria, resulting in a more oval, less round shaft circumference), in the absence of a longitudinal bony ridge or pilaster on the rear surface, and in the more distal position of minimal shaft breadth (Weidenreich 1941; G. E. Kennedy 1983, 1984b).

The features that distinguish *Homo erectus* most clearly from *H. habilis* are an increase in the size of the brain, a reduction in the postcanine dentition (and in the robusticity of the associated jaw bones), a vertical shortening of the face, the formation of a pronounced supraorbital torus with supratoral sulcus, the development of an occipital torus, and the forward projection of the nasal aperture. The increase in brain size may be related to the cultural advances reflected in the appearance of the Acheulean Industrial Tradition roughly 1.4–1.5 mya and in the subsequent spread of *H. erectus* out of Africa into southern Asia and perhaps Europe.

The smaller cheek teeth, thick, forwardly projecting supraorbital torus, and powerful occipital torus may form a functional complex reflecting decreased use of the posterior teeth in mastication and increased emphasis on the anterior teeth for biting, gripping, or tearing of food and other objects (Wolpoff 1980, 1985a). Increased use of the anterior teeth could also explain why *Homo erectus* incisors tend to be relatively

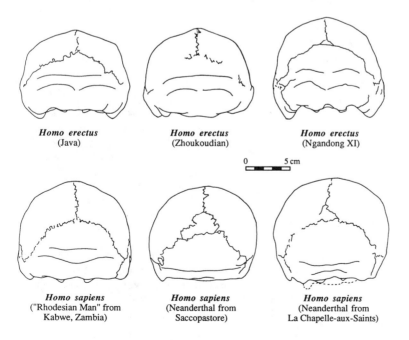

Homo erectus
(Java)

Homo erectus
(Zhoukoudian)

Homo erectus
(Ngandong XI)

0   5 cm

Homo sapiens
("Rhodesian Man" from
Kabwe, Zambia)

Homo sapiens
(Neanderthal from
Saccopastore)

Homo sapiens
(Neanderthal from
La Chapelle-aux-Saints)

Figure 4.7. Skulls of *Homo erectus* and nonmodern *H. sapiens*, viewed from the rear (redrawn after Weidenreich 1951). Note that the maximum breadth of the *H. erectus* skulls is very near the base and that they appear more angular (less rounded) in this view, particularly compared with Neanderthal skulls.

large and shovel shaped, since larger size and shoveling would increase the occlusal area and prolong the life of the teeth. Considered intuitively, the least obvious component in the functional complex may be the supraorbital torus, but M. D. Russell (1985) has presented biomechanical evidence that a thick, forwardly projecting torus would function "to resist bending stresses which concentrate on the frontal bone above the orbit during habitual anterior tooth loading."

The change in the position of the nasal aperture marks the first appearance of the typically human external nose with downwardly facing nostrils (vs. the relatively flat nose, with more forwardly facing nostrils, of the apes and of hominids before *Homo erectus*) (Franciscus and Trinkaus 1988). Since the temperature inside the external nose is usually less than that in the central body, moisture tends to condense in the nose during exhalation. This would have helped *H. erectus* (and later hominids) conserve moisture during periods of heightened activity (Trinkaus 1987a), which would have been

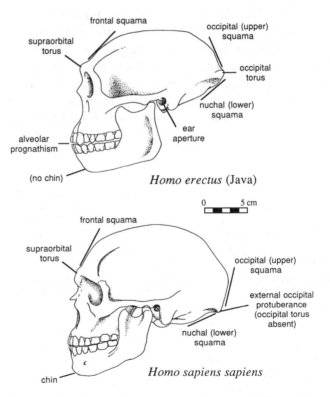

Figure 4.8. Skulls of Javan *Homo erectus* and a robust modern person (*H. sapiens sapiens*), illustrating important differences, including the more prominent supraorbital torus, lower, more receding frontal, more highly angulated occipital, and greater alveolar prognathism of *H. erectus* (redrawn after Le Gros Clark 1964: 98).

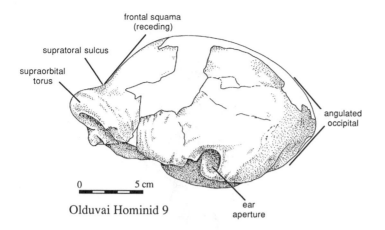

frontal squama
(receding)

supratoral sulcus

supraorbital
torus

angulated
occipital

0   5 cm

Olduvai Hominid 9

ear
aperture

Figure 4.9. Skullcap of Olduvai Hominid 9 from Upper Bed II, Olduvai Gorge (drawn by K. Cruz-Uribe from a cast and slides). Dated to roughly 1.2–1.1 mya, the skullcap exhibits such typical features of *Homo erectus* as a massive, forwardly projecting supraorbital torus, a low, receding frontal bone, and a highly angulated occipital.

especially advantageous in the warm, arid environments in which *H. erectus* initially evolved.

With respect to basicranial flexion (= upward arching between the posterior edge of the palate and the anterior margin of the foramen magnum), *Homo erectus* was apparently intermediate between the australopithecines, in whom flexion was limited (as in extant apes and very young humans), and modern adult humans, in whom flexion is pronounced (Laitman 1985). In extant primates, the degree of flexion is related to the anatomy of the upper respiratory tract, including the position of the larynx, which rests much lower in the neck of modern humans (with pronounced flexion) than in the neck of apes (with limited flexion). Since the low position of the larynx permits people to make crucial vowel sounds found in all languages, the moderate basicranial flexion in *H. erectus* suggests at least an incipient capacity for true speech. Since the basicranium is unknown in unequivocal specimens of *H. habilis*, *H. erectus* is the earliest hominid for which articulate speech can be inferred.

The locomotor skeleton indicates that *Homo erectus* was a habitual biped in fundamentally the same way as *H. sapiens*, but the robusticity of the lower limb bones (only the femur and pelvis are well known) suggests that they were subject to extraordinary stress during extended periods of heightened muscular exertion (Trinkaus 1987a). Markings on the few known upper-limb bones imply exceptional upper-body strength (muscular hypertrophy) by modern standards.

In regard to stature, it has often been assumed that individuals of *Homo erectus* were relatively short and that even the males did not exceed 1.67 m (5′6″). However, the immature (at most 12-yr-old) male represented by the Nariokotome (III) skel-

Figure 4.10.
Skeleton KNM-
WT-15000 from
Nariokotome III,
West Turkana,
northern Kenya,
partially restored
and rearticulated
(drawn from a
photograph in
R. E. F. Leakey
and Walker 1985a)
(KNM-WT =
Kenya National
Museum–West
Turkana). Dated
to roughly 1.6
mya, the skeleton
is the most com-
plete known for
Homo erectus.
The individual
was an immature
(roughly 12-year-
old) male who
stood about
1.63 m (5′4″) tall
and might have
reached 1.83 m
(6′) as an adult.

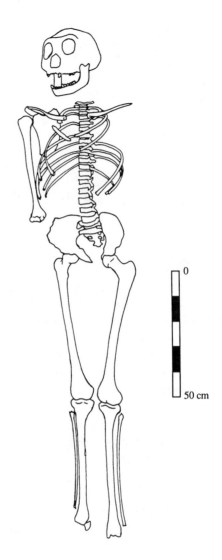

eton (Fig. 4.10) was already about that tall and might have approached 1.83 m (6′) as an adult (F. H. Brown et al. 1985a).

Many important questions concerning the morphology of
Homo erectus remain unresolved, and some specialists have
even questioned the validity of including the African and east
Asian specimens in the same species. The 1.8–1.6-million-
year-old skulls from Koobi Fora (East Turkana) (KNM-ER 3733
and 3883) are particularly problematic because they differ from
classic east Asian *H. erectus* in a few respects. For example,
their cranial bones tend to be somewhat thinner, and their
browridges, though equally projecting, are less thick from top
to bottom (Wood 1984). Since they may be older than all
known east Asian *H. erectus,* the Koobi Fora specimens could
represent an African population that was ancestral to it, but, in

those respects in which the Koobi Fora skulls differ from east Asian *H. erectus*, they tend to be more like *H. sapiens* (Andrews 1984). This raises the possibility that they were also (or uniquely) ancestral to a so far poorly known African (or European) population that was directly ancestral to *H. sapiens* and that east Asian *H. erectus* represents a specialized evolutionary offshoot that became extinct. In this event, African "*H. erectus*" should probably be designated as a separate (new) species.

This leads to the even more basic issue of whether *Homo erectus* is a valid biological species or simply a grade or stage erected by specialists to subsume a variety of medium-sized, long, low, thick-walled fossil human skulls with large brow-ridges, receding foreheads, and angular occiputs. A quick glance at Figures 4.3–4.9 will show that the skulls illustrated there all share these features, but to different degrees and in somewhat different combinations with other features. Conceivably, this means that the fossils assigned to *H. erectus* derive from several different species widely dispersed in time and space, most or all of which have nothing to do with later human evolution. The degree of variability is less than in some living species but much more than in others, and living species are thus not helpful in determining how many species may be represented (Tattersall 1986).

This issue is difficult to address, partly because the available fossils are so few and often so fragmentary, partly because their temporal relationships are so poorly established, and, perhaps most of all, because the functional meaning of the variable features is not well understood. However, for the moment, most specialists continue to lump the Koobi Fora specimens, other African fossils listed in Table 4.1, and the classic east Asian fossils into the single widespread and long-lived species *Homo erectus*. Justification for this can be found in detailed morphological analyses based on the broadest possible range of features and specimens, taking into account variation within regional samples as well as between them. Thus, following a thorough comparison of Javan and east African crania, Rightmire (1984a, 1986, 1988) concluded that, as samples, they overlapped significantly and differed in only minor ways, such as the greater degree of sagittal keeling in the Javan specimens and the tendency for the tympanic plate to be more robust in the east African ones. (The tympanic plate partially surrounds the middle ear and supports the ear drum. It is fused to the temporal bone on the base of the skull.) Similarly, Day (1984) found strong basic resemblances between African and Asian *H. erectus* femora.

If it is assumed that *Homo erectus* conventionally conceived is a single species, a further controversial issue concerns
the extent to which it changed during its duration of 1 million
or more years (between roughly 1.8–1.7 mya and 500,000–
400,000 years ago). Wolpoff (1984) has presented metrical evidence for significant, more or less gradual expansion of the cranial vault over this long interval, combined with progressive
reduction in the posterior dentition. However, Rightmire
(1981b, 1985, 1988) found that cranial capacity increased only
marginally and suggests that other key morphological features
also changed very little from early to late *H. erectus*. The implication is that the much enlarged cranium and other distinctive morphological traits of early (or archaic) *H. sapiens* evolved
very rapidly at the end of the *H. erectus* time span roughly
500,000–400,000 years ago. This controversy will be resolved
only with larger—and, especially, much-better-dated—samples
of *H. erectus* fossils.

Geographic Distribution

Archeological evidence shows that, unlike the australopithecines or even *Homo habilis*, *H. erectus* was distributed
throughout Africa, except for only the extreme deserts of the
north and south and the lowland rain forest of the Zaire Basin.
Archeological sites indicate that, about 1.5 mya, not long after
the emergence of *H. erectus*, people more intensively occupied
the drier peripheries of sedimentary basins on the floor of the
eastern Rift Valley (J. W. K. Harris 1983) and colonized the
Ethiopian high plateau (at 2,300–2,400 m) for the first time
(J. D. Clark and Kurashina 1979). Perhaps by 1 mya, and
certainly before 730,000 years ago, they had extended their
range to the far northern and southern margins of Africa. Range
extension north inevitably led to dispersal out of Africa,
probably mainly around the eastern end of the Mediterranean,
though artifactual ("cultural") similarities between north Africa and southern Europe could imply routes across the Straits
of Gibraltar or even across the central Mediterranean from
Tunisia to Italy (Alimen 1975). The main objection to considering these last as routes is that it would have been necessary
for early people to cross open water, even during glacial
intervals when sea level was lower. In contrast, the Dar-
danelles were often dry during glaciations, facilitating movement from southwest Asia to Europe. The importance of the
east Mediterranean route through southwest Asia is clearly
supported at 'Ubeidiya in the Jordan Valley of Israel (Fig. 4.11)

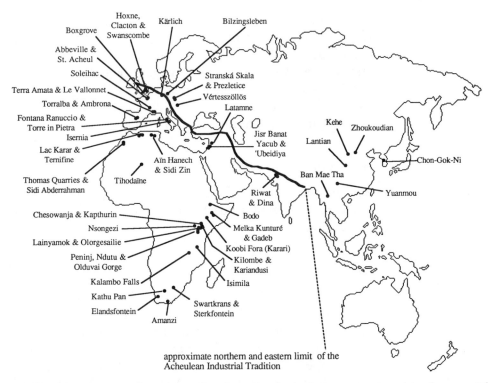

Figure 4.11. Approximate locations of early archeological sites mentioned in the text. The thick line trending southeastward from England to India shows the approximate northern and eastern limits of the Acheulean Industrial Tradition. To the east of the line, hand axes and similar bifacial tools appear to be rare or absent in mid-Quaternary archeological sites, suggesting a basic, but still poorly understood, cultural division between east and west.

(Bar-Yosef 1980; Goren 1981), which contains the oldest secure evidence that people had emigrated from Africa 1 mya or even before (Tchernov 1987).

In Asia, *Homo erectus* was apparently limited to middle and lower latitudes, even during interglaciations, and the site of Zhoukoudian (approximately 39.50° N) still ranks as the northernmost well-established occurrence. Siberian artifacts that might be attributed to *H. erectus* are either not clearly artifactual or are almost certainly too young (Yi and Clark 1983).

As already noted, unequivocal *Homo erectus* fossils have not yet been found in Europe, possibly because few fossiliferous sites of the right age have been extensively sampled or possibly because the species never existed there (Howell 1981, 1986). Still, it is probably significant that European archeological sites dating from the time range of *H. erectus* then extant elsewhere are limited to the warmest regions in the south and west, and even sites of early *H. sapiens* are unknown to the north and east of a line through Bilzingsleben in East Germany and through Vértesszöllös in Hungary (Fig. 4.11). Apparently the biological and behavioral advances that promoted the spread of *H. erectus* out of Africa did not permit the colonization of harsher environments in Eurasia.

Artifacts

Readers unfamiliar with basic stone-artifact technology and typology may find it useful to consult Appendix 2 before proceeding.

East Asia

No artifacts have been reported in direct association with *Homo erectus* fossils in Java, nor are they known from the same stratigraphic units. It has long been assumed that classic *H. erectus* or the succeeding Solo (= Ngandong) people made the choppers, chopping tools, flakes, and hand axes assigned to the Pacitanian (= Patjitanian) Industry in south-central Java, but it has recently been shown that Pacitanian tools in the type area come from alluvial terrace fills probably dating to the late Quaternary (Bartstra 1984). It is therefore likely that the Pacitanian Industry postdates *H. erectus*, and it may be coeval with the typologically simlar end-Pleistocene/early-Holocene Hoabinhian Industry of mainland Southeast Asia. A flake and a chopper from alluvial deposits near Sambungmachan probably also date from the late Quaternary (Bartstra 1985), rather than from the mid-Quaternary as originally suggested by Jacob et al. (1978). At present, the oldest known tools in Java may be some small, relatively amorphous cores and flakes found by von Koenigswald in alluvial sediments near Sangiran in the 1930s (Bartstra 1982a, 1985). These probably date from the earlier part of the late Quaternary, but it is possible they were made by the late-mid-Quaternary population represented at Ngandong.

Artifacts that are demonstrably as old as the oldest *Homo erectus* are unknown on the Southeast Asian mainland, with three possible exceptions. The oldest and potentially the most important case concerns three flaked quartzite cobbles and two quartzite flakes from Riwat, near Rawalpindi in northeast Pakistan (Fig. 4.11) (Dennell et al. 1988a, 1988b). The deposit from which they came has been dated to roughly 2 mya by a combination of paleomagnetism and geologic correlation with a fission-track-dated layer in the same region. Unfortunately, however, the deposit is a consolidated gravel (conglomerate) in which it is difficult to separate flaking produced by natural collisions between cobbles from flaking by human action, and the presumed artifacts have been distinguished from other, apparently naturally produced flakes or flaked cobbles mainly by quantitative criteria, including a somewhat greater number of flake scars (never very great), a smaller amount of remaining cobble cortex, and clearer bulbs of percussion. If the supposed artifacts are genuine, their 2-million-year age has profound implications for the history and nature of human dispersal to Eurasia, but it remains possible that they represent simply one extreme along a continuum of naturally flaked pieces.

The remaining two exceptions are less momentous. The first involves three flaked pebbles from alluvial deposits near Ban Mae Tha, northern Thailand (Fig. 4.11) (Pope et al. 1986). The alluvium is overlain by a paleomagnetically reversed basalt radiopotassium dated to 800,000–300,000 and 600,000–200,000 years ago. Together the paleomagnetic and radiopotassium readings imply an age near the end of the Matuyama Reversed Polarity Chron, approximately 730,000 years ago. If the stratigraphic position of the pebbles has been properly assessed, and if they are genuinely artifactual, they could represent the oldest well-dated artifacts in east Asia. The next oldest, well-dated artifacts are probably Acheulean hand axes and other artifacts from alluvial gravels near Dina, northeast Pakistan, bracketed between 730,000 and 400,000 years ago by paleomagnetism and stratigraphic correlation with radiometrically dated sediments (Rendell and Dennell 1985). In this instance, the artifactual nature of the pieces is not in doubt.

In China, artifacts directly associated with *Homo erectus* have been found at Yuanmou, Gongwangling, Chenjiawo, and Zhoudoudian and also at several sites where geologic or paleontologic context implies that *H. erectus* was the artifact maker, although *H. erectus* fossils are absent (Aigner 1978a, 1978b). Yi and Clark 1983; Jia 1985; S. Zhang 1985; Howell 1986). The oldest unquestionable artifacts in good context are probably those from the Lantian sites (Gongwangling and Chenjiawo), tentatively bracketed between 800,000 and 500,000 years ago, so artifact discoveries do not affect estimates for the antiquity of people in east Asia.

The artifact assemblages related to *Homo erectus* in China share many common features, which are best illustrated in the very large and relatively well-described assemblage from Zhoukoudian Locality 1 (Wu and Lin 1983; Pei and Zhang 1985; S. Zhang 1985). Comprising perhaps one hundred thousand pieces, the Locality 1 assemblage lacks hand axes and other well-made bifacial tools that characterize many contemporaneous assemblages in Africa and Europe. Although often called the Choukoutienian (Zhoukoudianian) chopper/chopping-tool industry, it contains relatively few choppers and chopping tools (= bifacial choppers) and is heavily dominated by flakes, some modified by retouch (Fig. 4.12). In systematic overviews of the east Asian Paleolithic, Movius (1944, 1948, 1949, 1955) emphasized the absence of hand axes in the Choukoutienian and likened this industry to the Pacitanian of Java, the Anyathian of Burma, the Tampanian of Malaysia, and the Soan (or Soanian) of Pakistan, in all of which hand axes are rare or absent. Movius assumed that all these industries were broadly contemporaneous with each other and with industries in Africa and Europe where hand axes abound, and he concluded that there were two great early-Paleolithic culture areas—the hand-ax (Acheulean) area from peninsular India westward across southern Asia into Europe and Africa (Fig. 4.11) and the chopper/chopping-tool area eastward from northern India through eastern and southeastern Asia.

Movius's formulation is questionable today on several counts. First, the east Asian industries assigned to the chopper/chopping-tool complex are not necessarily contemporaneous with each other or with hand-ax industries to the west (Hutterer 1985). Some, like the Pacitanian, are clearly later. Second, some important early-Paleolithic assemblages in the west also lack hand axes. Examples include the large assemblages from Isernia la Pineta (Coltorti et al. 1982, 1983) and Vértesszöllös (Vértes 1965, 1975), two of the oldest Paleolithic sites yet found in Europe, and also assemblages from several somewhat younger European sites such as Clacton (Collins 1969; Singer et al. 1973; Ohel 1977, 1979) and Bilzingsleben (Harmon et al. 1980; Mania and Vlcek 1981; Mania 1986, with references). At the same time, pieces that fit the typological definition of a hand ax or of the related artifact type known as the cleaver have now been recorded at several east Asian early-Paleolithic sites, including especially Lantian and Kehe (K'oho) in China and Chon-Gok-Ni in South Korea (Yi and Clark 1983). The rarity or absence of hand axes and similar bifacial tools at Zhoukoudian and other sites might reflect only the absence of suitable raw material, and it may be that Movius's distinction between east and west was mistaken. However, where hand axes and other bifaces have been found in east Asia, they appear to be much rarer than at many Acheulean sites in southwest Asia, Europe, and Africa, and their true morphological resemblance to Acheulean artifacts is

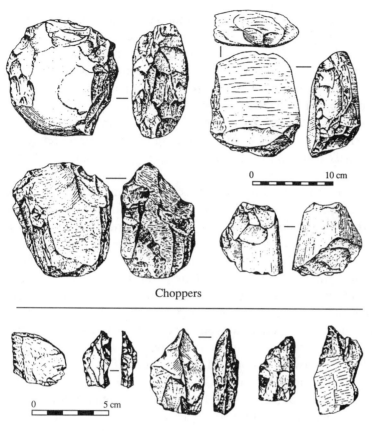

Choppers

Retouched or Utilized Flakes

Figure 4.12. Sandstone and quartz artifacts associated with *Homo erectus* at Zhoukoudian Locality 1 (redrawn after Movius 1949: Figs. 22, 23). The Zhoukoudian assemblage lacks hand axes and other typical Acheulean tools found at many sites in Africa, western Asia, and Europe and probably represents a totally distinct mid-Quaternary artifact tradition widespread in eastern Asia.

not clear. In addition, at least some of the east Asian sites may date from the late or even the very late Quaternary, long after the Acheulean had terminated in the west. This is especially possible for Chon-Gok-Ni, where the dating is based solely on the supposed Acheulean affinities of the artifacts (Ayres and Rhee 1984). In sum, continuing research may still show that the "Movius line" in north India did have broad cultural significance in the mid-Quaternary.

Africa

In Africa, stone artifacts are stratigraphically associated with *Homo erectus* fossils primarily at Ternifine (Balout et al. 1967), Sidi Abderrahman (Biberson 1964; Jaeger 1975), the Thomas Quarries (Geraads et al. 1980), Gomboré II (Melka Kunturé). (Chavaillon 1979), Lainyamok (Shipman et al. 1983; Potts et al. 1988), Olduvai Gorge Beds II and IV (M. D. Leakey 1975, 1977), and Swartkrans (Volman 1984). In each case, the artifacts include hand axes and other bifacial tools (Fig. 4.13) that are the hallmark of the Acheulean Industrial Tradition, named after the site of St. Acheul in northern France, where numerous hand axes were recovered in the last century. Radiopotassium dates from Peninj in northern Tanzania and from East Turkana (the Karari Escarpment) in northern Kenya show that the Acheulean replaced the preceding Oldowan Tradition in east Africa about 1.5–1.4 mya, not long after the emergence of *H. erectus* (Isaac and Curtis 1974; Isaac 1975; Isaac and Harris 1978).

From a typological and technical perspective, Acheulean hand axes and other bifaces are a logical development from preceding Oldowan bifacial choppers, and the Oldowan and Acheulean are commonly lumped together in the Early Stone Age. Oldowan tool types continued on in the Acheulean, where they sometimes dominate assemblages at the expense of hand axes and other bifaces. At Olduvai Gorge and elsewhere in east Africa, such biface-poor assemblages have been assigned to the Developed Oldowan B, which is presumed to be an outgrowth of the Developed Oldowan A, a late facies (variant) of the Oldowan proper (M. D. Leakey 1971, 1975). However, the differences between Developed Oldowan B assemblages and contemporaneous Acheulean ones may simply reflect differences in the activities carried on by the same people at different sites or, in some cases, differences in raw material availability; and most authorities subsume the Developed Oldowan B within the Acheulean Tradition.

In Africa, Acheulean artifacts occur not only at sites with *Homo erectus* but also at sites such as Elandsfontein (Singer and Wymer 1968; Volman 1984), Ndutu (Mturi 1976; M. D. Leakey 1977), and Bodo (Middle Awash) (Kalb et al. 1982a; J. D. Clark et al. 1984; J. D. Clark 1987), where associated human fossils are more commonly assigned to early (archaic) *Homo sapiens*, and there is general agreement that early *H. sapiens* made essentially the same kinds of tools as did preceding *H. erectus*. At some sites, even where human remains are absent, dates earlier than 400,000–500,000 years ago imply that *H. erectus* was the artifact maker. In Ethiopia, such sites include (1) Gadeb 2 and 8 (J. D. Clark and Kurashina 1979; J.D. Clark 1987), dated by radiopotassium and reversed magnetism to between 1.5 mya and 730,000 years ago and (2) several localities at Melka Kunturé (Chavaillon 1979), especially *(a)* the lower levels of Garba XII, radiopotassium dated to approximately 1.1–1.3 mya, and *(b)* Simbirro III, Garba II, and the upper levels at Garba XII, dated by radiopotassium and paleo-

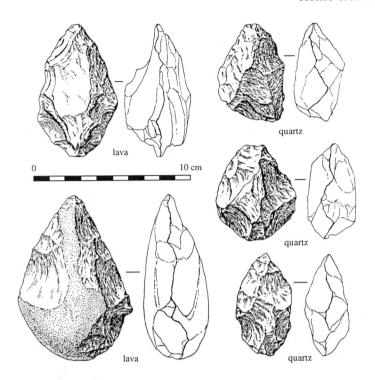

lava

0   10 cm

quartz

quartz

lava

quartz

Figure 4.13.
Bifaces from site
TK in Upper Bed
II, Olduvai Gorge
(redrawn after
M. D. Leakey
1971: 190). Dated
to roughly 1.2–1.1
mya, they are
among the oldest
known artifacts of
the Acheulean
Industrial Tradi-
tion, which
emerged in Africa
roughly 1.4 mya.

magnetism to the later part of the Matuyama Reversed Chron, before 730,000 years ago. Broadly coeval sites in Kenya include Kariandusi, radiopotassium dated to 800,000–900,000 years ago (Evernden and Curtis 1965), Kilombe (Gowlett 1978), where reversed magnetism implies an age greater than 730,000 years, and Olorgesailie, originally radiopotassium dated to less than 500,000 years ago (Isaac 1977) but, more recently, to between 900,000 and 700,000 years ago (Bye et al. 1987). At other sites, the dating is more uncertain, and the hand-ax makers could be either *H. erectus* or *H. sapiens*. In southern Africa, important ambiguous sites include Amanzi Springs (H. J. Deacon 1970) and Kathu Pan (Beaumont et al. 1984; Klein 1988); in east Africa, Kalambo Falls (J. D. Clark, 1969, 1974), Isimila (Howell et al. 1962, 1972), and Nsongezi (Cole 1967); and in north Africa, Tihodaïne (Thomas 1979), Lac Karar (Balout 1955), and Sidi Zin (Gobert 1950; Balout 1955).

The total time span of the Acheulean in Africa remains to be established, but it certainly exceeded 1 million years, from 1.5–1.4 mya to perhaps 200,000 years ago (Volman 1984). Although many crucial sites remain poorly dated within this long interval, it nonetheless appears that Acheulean artifacts changed remarkably little through time. In east Africa, later-Acheulean assemblages may contain a wider variety of artifact types than do earlier ones, and later hand axes perhaps tend be thinner and to possess more trimming scars than do earlier ones (Isaac 1975); but the trends are weak, and it is difficult, if not impossible, to date an Acheulean assemblage on typological or technical grounds alone. There is also little, if any, regional differentiation within the African Acheulean that cannot be explained by differences in raw material availability, and the overall impression is one of remarkable behavioral conservatism through time and space. The almost imperceptible pace of cultural change may be related to the slow rate of morphological change in *Homo erectus,* though, if cultural and biological change were coupled, it seems strange that there was no significant artifactual change when early *H. sapiens* appeared. From the artifactual evidence it could in fact be argued that the transition to *H. sapiens* was very gradual.

Europe and Western Asia

Since no sites in Europe or southwest Asia have provided indisputable fossils of *Homo erectus,* artifacts that *H. erectus* may have made can be identified only by their probable contemporaneity with *H. erectus* elsewhere. Considered on this basis, probably the least equivocal *H. erectus* site in either Europe or southwest Asia is 'Ubeidiya in the Jordan Valley of Israel (Bar-Yosef 1980; Goren 1981). Here, a combination of radiopotassium dates, reversed paleomagnetic readings, and faunal correlations with both Europe and east Africa indicate that (early) Acheulean tool makers were present at least 1 mya, if not before (Tchernov 1987). As already noted, 'Ubeidiya almost certainly contains the oldest evidence for human presence outside of Africa.

In Europe, stones that may be artificially flaked or animal bones that may be humanly broken occur at several sites that are probably 1 million years old or more (Nicolaescu-Plopsor and Nicolaescu-Plopsor [1963] and Fridrich [1976] list some eastern and central European examples, Bordes and Thibault [1977] some French ones). However, none of these sites provides truly compelling evidence for human presence, and the oldest reasonably secure sites are perhaps Le Vallonnet Cave near Nice (H. de Lumley. 1975, 1976) and the Soleihac open-air (lake) site near Le Puy in the Massif Central of southeastern France (Bonifay et al. 1976; Bonifay and Tiercelin 1977). At both sites, horizons with artifacts have been dated by paleomagnetism and faunal associations to the Jaramillo Normal Subchron, between roughly 970,000 and 900,000 years ago (Thouveny and Bonifay 1984). At Le Vallonnet, the artifacts comprise a handful of choppers and associated flakes; at Soleihac, the somewhat larger collection contains several retouched flakes ("scrapers"), choppers, and one "proto-biface." At Soleihac, a 20-m-long line of basalt blocks may represent the oldest structural remnant in Europe, if it is truly of human origin.

Among other sites that may antedate 730,000 years ago, the most convincing are probably Isernia La Pineta in central Italy (Coltorti et al. 1982, 1983), Přezletice near Prague, Czechoslovakia (Fejfar 1976b; Fridrich 1976; Valoch 1976, 1982b, 1986), and Kärlich in the Neuwied Basin of west-central Germany (Brunnacker 1975; Bosinski et al. 1980, 1986; Bosinski et al. 1986; Kulemeyer 1986; Würges 1986). At Isernia, radiopotassium dates and reversed paleomagnetism indicate that a large assemblage of choppers and flakes found in fluvio-lacustrine deposits dates from near the end of the Matuyama Reversed Chron, somewhat before 730,000 years ago. At Přezletice, a combination of paleomagnetism and associated fauna in ancient lake deposits imply a broadly similar late-Matuyama age for an assemblage of choppers, chopping tools, crudely made bifaces, and flakes. They have been assigned to the Prezletician Industry and likened overall to the Developed Oldowan of east Africa. Similar artifacts occur at other Czech sites, most notably in cave and slope sediments at Stránská Skála near Brno (Musil and Valoch 1969; Fridrich 1976; Valoch 1976, 1986), where the fauna and reversed magnetism again imply a late-Matuyama date for the earliest pieces. The Stránská Skála assemblage, however, is much smaller than the Přezletice one and less convincingly of human origin.

At Kärlich, flakes, choppers, and cores occur in river gravels just below and within the part of the section that records the Brunhes/Matuyama boundary. The oldest occurrence could approach or even exceed the 900,000-year-old age of the Soleihac and Le Vallonnet sites. There was significant vulcanism in the Neuwied Basin during the middle and later Quaternary, resulting in tuffs (ash layers) that can be used to correlate separate sites, much the way that earlier (Plio-Pleistocene) tuffs can be used in the Turkana Basin of east Africa. They also permit radiopotassium dating, which, together with thermoluminescence dating on quartz grains, confirms that human occupation at Kärlich began more than 600,000 years ago. The dates are further pertinent to fossil faunas (including microfaunas with stratigraphically significant vole species) and to a relatively detailed local climate stratigraphy. The climate stratigraphy is based mainly on a sequence of loesses (wind-blown silts) that accumulated during glaciations and that are interrupted by weathering horizons (soils) that formed during interglaciations. Taken as a whole, the assembled information from Kärlich and other Neuwied Basin sites promises to provide the most tightly controlled mid-Quaternary human-occupation sequence in the world, and, through faunal correlations, it may ultimately allow more precise dating of many other European mid-Quaternary sites.

The very ancient artifacts from Le Vallonnet, Soleihac, Isernia, Přezletice, Kärlich, and other European sites that probably or possibly antedate 730,000 years ago all lack hand axes and other well-formed bifacial tools typical of the Acheulean Industrial Tradition. In each case, the reason could be the evolution of a local, non-hand-ax cultural tradition, the failure of people to bring hand axes to a particular site because they did not need them there, the local absence of raw material suitable for hand-ax manufacture, or simply small sample size. Whatever the explanation, as in Africa, most later artifact assemblages in Europe that are potentially attributable to *Homo erectus* do contain hand axes and other bifaces that place them firmly in the Acheulean Industrial Tradition (Fig. 4.14). However, once again, there is the problem that early *H. sapiens* also made Acheulean artifacts, as shown especially clearly at Swanscombe, England (Waechter 1973). At many European sites where human remains are absent and where the date could be at or near 500,000–400,000 years ago, the people could thus be either *H. erectus* or *H. sapiens*. Among the problematic sites are Fontana Ranuccio near Rome (Segre and Ascenzi 1984), radiopotassium dated to approximately 450,000 years ago, and such important additional sites as Hoxne and Boxgrove in Britain (Singer and Wymer 1976; Roe 1981; M. Roberts et al. 1986), Abbeville (Porte du Bois) and St. Acheul in northern France (Commont 1908; Breuil 1939; Howell 1966; Tuffreau 1978; Haesaerts and Dupuis 1986), Terra Amata in southern France (H. de Lumley 1969b; Villa 1983), and Torralba and Ambrona in central Spain (Howell 1966; Freeman 1975), all of which probably date from somewhere between 600,000 and 300,000 years ago. It is possible that Torre in Pietra in Italy (Malatesta et al. 1978) should be included in the same group, though Acheulean artifacts here overlie reworked volcanic debris radiopotassium dated to about 430,000 years ago and may be substantially younger than this (Segre and Ascenzi 1984). For the same reasons as in Europe, either *H. sapiens* or *H. erectus* could be the tool maker at some important Acheulean sites in southwest Asia, such as Latamne in Syria (J. D. Clark 1967, 1968b) and Jisr Banat Yacub in Israel (Bar-Yosef 1980).

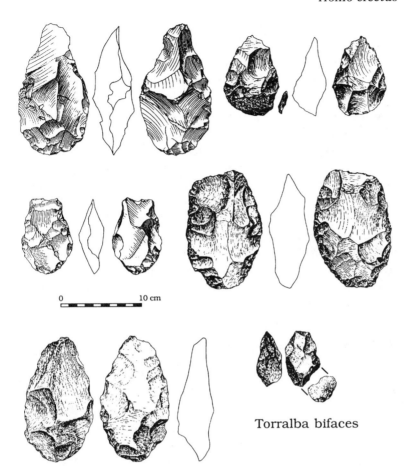

0   10 cm

Torralba bifaces

Figure 4.14. Acheulean bifaces from Torralba (courtesy of F. C. Howell and L. G. Freeman). They probably date from sometime between 600,000 and 300,000 years ago and were stratigraphically associated with bones of elephants, horses, and other large animals. As at most sites in the same time range, the extent to which the bifaces and other tools were used to kill or butcher the animals remains unclear.

The terminal date for the Acheulean in Europe is not well fixed and may vary from place to place. Thus, in northern France, Mousterian (or Middle Paleolithic) Industries lacking hand axes may have fully replaced Acheulean Industries during the Glaciation-before-Last—that is, perhaps 190,000 years ago (Tuffreau 1979, 1982)—whereas in southwest France the Acheulean persisted to the end of this glaciation, 130,000 years ago, or perhaps even into the Last Interglaciation, between 130,000 and 74,000 years ago (Bordes 1968; Laville et al. 1980; Laville 1982). Whenever it ended, the European Acheulean still spanned at least 300,000 years (from before 500,000 to at least 200,000 years ago); yet, as in Africa, there appears to have been little artifactual change through time or cultural differentiation through space. Hand axes do appear to be unusually abundant and well made in some important Acheulean assemblages from northern France, but this probably reflects biased collecting by unskilled quarry workers in the last century (Jelinek 1977; Villa 1983), while most differences among unbiased Acheulean assemblages from different regions could be due to differences in available raw material or to differences in the activities undertaken at different sites (Villa 1983). Either a lack of suitable raw material or the specific activities in which people engaged could also explain why some European sites dating from the Acheulean time interval totally lack hand axes or other bifaces.

Overall, the European artifactual data, like those from Africa and southwest Asia, suggest remarkable behavioral conservatism over long periods. This in turn may reflect limited cognitive and communicational abilities in *Homo erectus* and early *H. sapiens* compared with modern *H. sapiens*. More specifically, the lack of innovation and the limited evidence for differentiation of tool types during the long Acheulean time span may mean that the stone tools were "the product of complex forms of imitative behavior in a pattern no longer to be found among the Hominidae" (Jelinek 1977: 15).

Other Aspects of Behavior

In total, the fossil sample of *Homo erectus* comes from perhaps one hundred individuals, represented mainly by bits and pieces, and the behavior of the species must be inferred from fewer than fifty reasonably well-excavated archeological sites. The skeletal remains and sites are widely scattered in time and space, and the time dimension is poorly contolled, particularly outside Africa. Compounding these problems of small sample size and poor temporal control, it also appears that much of the archeological evidence for behavior is ambiguous at best.

Artifact Function

The stone artifacts made by *Homo erectus* were undoubtedly used for many purposes, including cutting, whittling, scraping, shredding, and butchering. The mode of use and, more often, the material to which an artifact was applied can sometimes be inferred from damage and wear polish on tool edges (Keeley 1977, 1980). Studies of tools from sites occupied by *H. erectus* or early *H. sapiens* suggest use on a wide range of materials, including nearly all those (bone, antler, meat, hide, wood, and nonwoody plant tissue) that can be detected from wear polishes. However, only a small proportion of tools preserve diagnostic-quality use traces, and their identification is very time-consuming. Since there is also no obvious one-to-one relationship between tool form and inferred function, it remains impossible to assess the functional significance of complete assemblages. Flakes and other light-duty tools are much more common than hand axes at some sites where animal bones suggest that butchering was important, which may mean that flakes, rather than hand axes, were the primary butchering tools (J. D. Clark and Haynes 1970; J. D. Clark 1975). However, experiments by P. R. Jones (1980) show that hand axes or other large bifacial cutting tools are more efficient than flakes for butchering large animals, and probably nothing about butchery can be inferred from either the rarity or abundance of hand axes. In truth, it may be that hand axes were used for butchering and for many other purposes, perhaps even as cores to obtain small, sharp flakes (Jelinek 1977). An additional puzzle, which may hold clues to the function of hand axes, is why they were sometimes discarded in vast numbers, as, for example, at Olorgesailie and other Acheulean sites in eastern and southern Africa. One intriguing speculation is that large accumulations served as caches for future artifact use or manufacture (Jelinek 1977).

Raw Material Use

From locally available rock types, *Homo erectus* populations generally selected those with the best flaking properties. However, even high-quality stone could not fill all needs, and it is almost certain that some artifacts were made of highly perishable raw materials such as wood, reeds, and skins. The typological poverty of some east Asian stone artifact assemblages versus contemporaneous Acheulean ones in the west may mean that perishable materials (including bamboo) were more intensively used in east Asia (Pope and Cronin 1984), but this remains speculative. Considered more concretely, it appears that *H. erectus* made remarkably little use of bone, which was widely available and is abundantly preserved at many important sites. Animal bones that have been used as hammers, retouchers, anvils, cutting platforms, etc. do occur, but there are none that were deliberately fashioned into standardized points, awls, borers, etc. In fact, formal bone tools only appear 50,000–40,000 years ago, after the emergence of fully modern people. Like the limited typological differentiation within stone-artifact assemblages and the almost imperceptible pace of artifactual change over long periods, the absence of formal bone tools suggests that *H. erectus* was behaviorally primitive compared with modern people.

Site Modification

Patterned arrangements or concentrations of large rocks that may represent either the foundations of structures or some other cultural feature occur at several certain or putative *Homo erectus* sites, including Soleihac (Bonifay et al. 1976), Terra Amata (H. de Lumley 1969b), Olorgesailie (Isaac 1977), Latamne (J. D. Clark 1967, 1968b), and some of the Melka Kunturé sites (Chavaillon 1976; Chavaillon et al. 1979). However, in each case, it is difficult to rule out stream flow, slope creep, or some other natural process that might have created concentrations or patterns, and the argument for *H. erectus* as builder remains hypothetical. Climatic conditions in midlatitude Europe and Asia probably necessitated shelters of some kind, but most may have been too flimsy to leave unmistakable archeological traces.

Fire

Control of fire for warmth and cooking may have been necessary before *Homo erectus* could colonize Eurasia, but direct archeological evidence is tenuous. The oldest evidence may be patches of baked earth in deposits dated to 1.4–1.5 mya at Koobi Fora and Chesowanja, Kenya, but naturally ignited, smoldering vegetation might have produced the same results (Gowlett et al. 1981; Isaac 1982; J. D. Clark and Harris 1985). Natural fires could also account for evidence of burning at most other early-Paleolithic sites; such evidence includes patches of burnt earth at Olorgesailie (Isaac 1977), burnt bones at Swartkrans (Brain 1988), burnt flints at Terra Amata (H. de Lumley 1969b; Villa 1983), and dispersed charcoal at Přezletice (Fridrich 1976) and at Torralba and Ambrona (Howell 1966).

At present, the oldest, most compelling evidence for human use of fire comes from Zhoukoudian Locality 1, which contains burnt bones and stones, thick ash beds, and thinner lenses of ash, charcoal, and charred bone. Some of the thicker beds may represent naturally ignited organic detritus, and some charring may actually be mineral staining (Binford and Ho 1985), but some of the thinner ash lenses almost certainly represent true fossil hearths (LÜ Zune 1985; Pei and Zhang 1985). Hearths that are only slightly younger or even the same age (perhaps 400,000 years old) may be represented by concentrations of charred bones (but no charred wood) in depressions 50–60 cm across at Vértesszöllös in Hungary (Vértes 1965, 1975).

Subsistence

Like fire, an advance in subsistence ecology could explain how
Homo erectus managed to colonize new regions. However, the
evidence bearing on subsistence is very limited. Both logic and
observations on historic hunter-gatherers suggest that, in general, *H. erectus* depended more on plants than on animals, but
no plant residues to support this have survived. Chemical
analysis of *H. erectus* fossils may someday fill the void, but the
elemental composition of the fossils has been extensively
altered in the ground, and few, if any, may retain an antemortem component that reflects diet (Sillen 1986). So far, the only
fossil of *H. erectus* to provide a hint of diet is a partial skeleton
from Koobi Fora, dated to roughly 1.7–1.6 mya. The long-bone
shafts of this individual (KNM-ER 1808) are covered by a layer
of abnormal, coarse-woven bone, as much as 7 mm thick.
Among all known disorders of living people, the one that could
explain this best is a large excess of vitamin A (= hypervitaminosis A). On the assumption (by analogy with the situation
in modern people) that the most likely source for so much
vitamin A in a hunter-gatherer diet would be carnivore livers,
it has been hypothesized that the individual belonged to a
population that was relatively new to substantial meat eating
and thus unaware of potentially toxic organs (Walker et al.
1982). The carnivores that Koobi Fora *H. erectus* ate may have
been killed during competition for carcasses of other animals.

Except perhaps at Koobi Fora, inferences about the subsistence of *Homo erectus* must be based almost entirely on the
animal bones associated with artifacts at sites such as Torralba
and Ambrona in Spain or Olorgesailie in Kenya. Until the
1970s, most archeologists simply assumed that the artifacts
had been used to kill and butcher the animals. The implication
was that the people were successful big-game hunters, since
the animals included such formidable prey as elephants (abundant at Torralba and Ambrona—Howell 1966; Freeman 1975;
and see Fig. 4.15) and giant gelada baboons (numerous in one
occurrence at Olorgesailie—Isaac 1977; Shipman et al. 1981).

However, in the 1970s, a growing number of archeologists
began to specialize in the analysis of animal bones, and, after
close scrutiny, it was soon realized that a stratigraphic association between bones and artifacts need not imply a functional
relationship. Most key sites where *Homo erectus* was certainly
or probably present were located in the open air near ancient
streams or lakes to which both people and animals would have
been naturally attracted. The bones found at such sites could

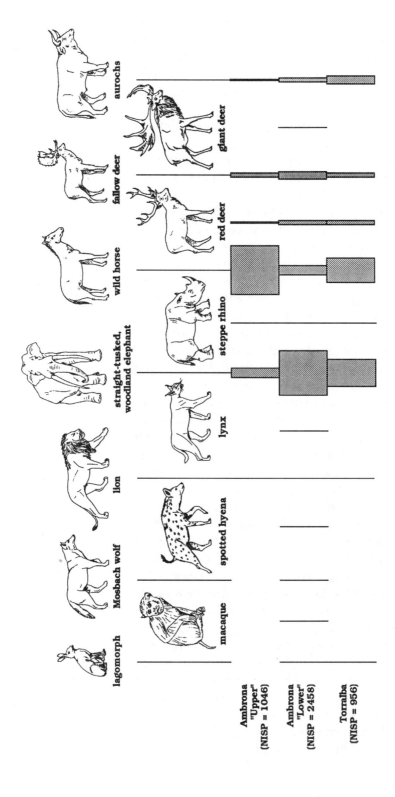

Torralba & Ambrona: taxonomic abundance.

Figure 4.15. Abundance of large mammals at the Acheulean sites of Torralba and Ambrona, north-central Spain. The bars are proportional to the number of identifiable bones (NISP) assigned to each species. Torralba is about the same age as Ambrona "Lower" and has been placed below Ambrona for display purposes only. Like other Acheulean sites, Torralba and Ambrona contain many bones of large mammals, including elephants, but, as at other sites, the bones could represent natural deaths or carnivore kills, and so far it has not been possible to determine the hunting capabilities of Acheulean people.

represent human kills, or they could represent carnivore kills or even natural deaths (from starvation, disease, etc.) that totally escaped human notice or that were subsequently scavenged by people (or carnivores). The famous Torralba and Ambrona "elephant kill sites" provide good cases in point (Klein 1987; Klein and Cruz-Uribe, in press).

At Torralba and Ambrona, as at most other sites, some human role is clearly implied by the presence of stone tools and of occasional stone-tool marks on bones, but the tools are thinly scattered among the more numerous bones, and there are also carnivore coprolites (fossilized feces), bones damaged by carnivore teeth, and numerous bones abraded by flowing water. Among the bones of most species the relative abundance of axial elements (skulls, vertebrae, and pelvises) versus limb bones may indicate that predators/scavengers often removed meatier parts from the site, but either people or large carnivores would create the same pattern. Similarly, people, large carnivores, or, especially, natural mortality could account for the apparent overrepresentation of older adults among the elephants (other species are too poorly represented for the construction of age profiles). In sum, the available data do not allow us to isolate the relative roles of humans, carnivores, and factors such as starvation, accidents, and stream action in creating the bone assemblages. In the present state of our knowledge, Torralba and Ambrona need not have differed significantly from the margins of historic African streams or water holes, where the events that produce carcasses can be complex and need not involve people. Certainly, as presently understood, the sites do not tell us how successful or effective *Homo erectus* was at obtaining meat.

Assessing human ability to obtain animals requires, at a minimum, a site where people were the only—or at least the principal—bone accumulators. In this regard, caves are generally more promising than open-air sites, because the main game animals available to early people do not enter caves voluntarily. In most instances, therefore, it is safe to assume that their bones were introduced by a predator or scavenger. If the cave fill contains numerous artifacts, hearths, etc. and little or no evidence for carnivore activity (corprolites, chewed bones, etc.), then people are clearly implicated as the principal bone accumulators.

Unfortunately, caves themselves have a limited life span, and few survive from the *Homo erectus* era. Zhoukoudian Locality 1 is by far the most prominent exception, and it was literally filled with bones from many species, ranging from small rodents and insectivores through rhinoceroses and elephants (Kahlke 1962; Aigner 1978a; Howell 1986). Two extinct species of deer were especially common, and it has sometimes been said that Peking man was a proficient deer stalker (Wu and Lin 1983). However, this interpretation is complicated by the presence of numerous hyena bones and coprolites and of bones plainly damaged by hyena teeth, indicating that hyenas sometimes occupied the site. They may have introduced many of the animal bones, and their activities, combined with profile compaction and other postdepositional destructive pressures, could also explain why the Zhoukoudian human crania lack faces and basal parts and, more generally, why the human fossils are so fragmentary (Binford and Ho 1985). A less plausible alternative is that the Peking people were cannibals.

There are layers at Zhoukoudian, particularly near the top of the deposit, where evidence for hyenas is rare or absent and evidence for people (artifacts, hearths, etc.) is especially abundant. The surviving bone sample from these layers is very small and was biased during excavation and curation (Binford and Stone 1986), but fresh excavations now underway may provide an unbiased sample from which it will eventually be possible to infer whether *Homo erectus* was truly an accomplished hunter.

Conclusion

Clearly, much remains to be learned about both the morphology and behavior of *Homo erectus*. Both practically and theoretically, perhaps the most important question to be resolved is the nature of the relationship between *H. erectus* and *H. sapiens*. While it is widely agreed that *H. erectus* was ancestral to *H. sapiens*, debate continues about whether the former evolved toward *H. sapiens* gradually or in a burst after a long period of morphological stasis. An even more crucial question is how and why the long, low-vaulted, thick-walled cranium of *H. erectus*, with its sharply angled occiput, changed into the higher, shorter, thinner-walled cranium of *H. sapiens*, with its much more rounded occiput. The issue is particularly vexing, because in some aspects of cranial form *H. sapiens* is actually more like *H. habilis*,—and thus the evolution of *H. sapiens* from *H. erectus* would appear to require an evolutionary reversal. On the basis of cranial morphology, some have even argued that *H. sapiens* was derived directly from *H. habilis* and that *H. erectus* was an evolutionary side branch and dead end (L. S. B. Leakey 1966; Andrews 1984), but, if this is true, it is puzzling that, so far, the only human fossils in the time gap between *H. habilis* and *H. sapiens* come from *H. erectus*.

Perhaps future discoveries will show that *H. erectus* was accompanied by a contemporaneous, more *sapiens*-like species in Africa or Europe, but for the moment it seems more likely that the distinctive cranial features of *H. erectus* were mechanically determined by its brain size (or form) and by the way it used its jaws and that it evolved into *H. sapiens* when the mechanical constraints were altered or relaxed by changes in behavior and brain size.

The outstanding uncertainties concerning *Homo erectus* cannot be ignored, but they should not be allowed to obscure the important information that is available. Thus, *H. erectus* combined an essentially modern, if robust, postcranial skeleton with an expanded but still primitive skull. The postcranial skeleton implies that strenuous physical activity was common, while the skull suggests that the brain was limited by modern standards. In postcranium, dentition, and skull size (if not in skull morphology), *H. erectus* represents a logical, intermediate link between *H. habilis* and *H. sapiens*, and it confirms the mosaic nature of human evolution, in which the locomotor apparatus and the remainder of the postcranium became fully modern before the skull and brain.

In general, *Homo erectus* made more sophisticated artifacts than did earlier people, and significant behavioral advance is also implied by its ability to colonize new environments, particularly cool-temperate ones in Eurasia. Arguably, this colonization reflects both an increased ability to obtain meat and at least incipient control of fire. At the same time, the great skeletal robusticity of *H. erectus* suggests that, compared with later people (particularly anatomically modern people), individuals of *H. erectus* relied more on bodily power and less on artifactual skill to accomplish essential tasks. Equally important, the remarkable uniformity of their artifacts over vast distances and long time intervals suggests that *H. erectus* populations were extraordinarily conservative behaviorally, perhaps because of limitations imposed by their brains.

The wide dispersal of *Homo erectus* enhanced the possibility that far-flung populations would diverge genetically, whether through natural selection or through sheer chance ("gene drift"). Thus, the spread of the species provided the basis for the emergence of geographically and morphologically distinct lineages, which are a striking feature of early *H. sapiens*, as discussed in the next chapter.

5

EARLY *HOMO SAPIENS*

As discussed in the last chapter, most human fossils dating between roughly 1.7 million years ago (mya) and 500,000–400,000 years ago are currently assigned to *Homo erectus*. The main fossils are those from the Pucangan and Kabuh Beds in Java; from Lantian, Zhoukoudian, and possibly Hexian in China; and from the Lake Turkana Basin, Olduvai Gorge Beds II–IV, and Ternifine in Africa. Beyond this core, however, there are many specimens whose assignment to *H. erectus* is disputed or uncertain. In some cases, this is because they are too fragmentary for secure morphological diagnosis and because they could lie outside the time range of classic *H. erectus* elsewhere. However, the largest group of questionable specimens are some relatively complete mid-Quaternary fossils from Africa, Asia, and Europe that share many basic features with *H. erectus* but that also exhibit some important differences. The shared features include large browridges, a low, flattened frontal bone, a relatively broad cranial base, thick cranial walls, and relatively massive, chinless jaws with large teeth; the differences include endocranial volumes generally much larger than the average (of just more than 1,000 cc) for the *H. erectus* core, more rounded occipitals, expanded parietals, and broader frontals with more arched (vs. more shelf-like) browridges. Following widespread practice, the late-middle-Quaternary specimens defined by this mix of features are referred to here as early ("archaic") *H. sapiens,* though, depending on the balance in the mix, some might be better regarded as advanced *H. erectus*. The issue of nomenclature is less important than the evolutionary implications, which are considered below.

Morphologically, the fossils involved are too variable, even within restricted geographic regions, for summary description. For the most part, they are also poorly dated, and some of the variability probably reflects significant differences in age. All probably date to between 500,000 and 130,000 years ago, and most are probably between 500,000 and 200,000 years

Figure 5.1. Approximate locations of the main sites that have provided fossils herein assigned to mid-Quaternary (= early) *Homo sapiens.*

old. Because they are difficult to characterize as a group, they will be treated individually here, according to continent. The approximate locations of the sites from which they come are shown in Figures 5.1, 5.6, and 5.13, while Figures 5.2–5.5 and 5.8–5.15 illustrate some key specimens. Figures 5.2, 5.3, and 5.7 show the specific time intervals in which important African and European specimens probably lie, and Figure 4.2 (in the last chapter) shows their chronological relationships to the *Homo erectus* fossils already discussed. Readers who are less concerned with the nature of the early *H. sapiens* sample than with the conclusions that can be drawn from it may wish only to skim the next three sections, attending mostly to the accompanying illustrations.

Africa

The principal African specimens assigned to early *Homo sapiens* come from Elandsfontein and the Cave of Hearths in South Africa, Broken Hill in Zambia, Lake Ndutu and Eyasi in Tanzania, Kapthurin in Kenya, Bodo and Garba 3 (Melka-

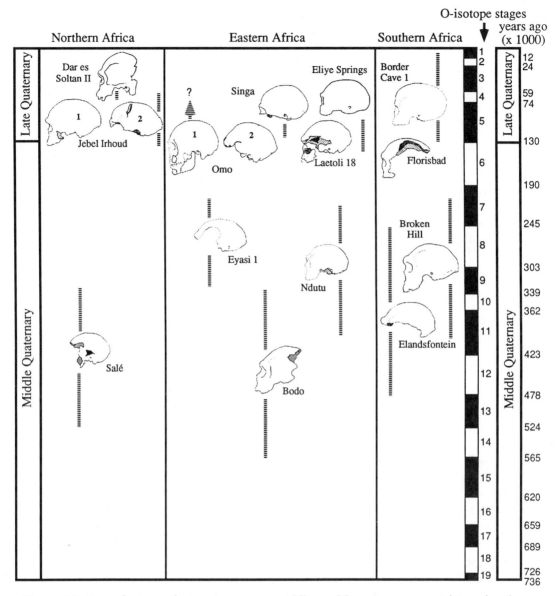

Figure 5.2. Lateral views of some important middle- and late-Quaternary African fossil skulls, as well as the time ranges within which they probably lie (adapted partly from Bräuer 1984a: 148; and Bräuer, pers. comm.). The skulls from Salé, Bodo, Ndutu, Eyasi, Elandsfontein, and Broken Hill represent early or archaic *Homo sapiens* as discussed in this chapter. Those from Dar es Soltan, Jebel Irhoud, Omo, Laetoli, Singa, Eliye Springs, Florisbad, and Border Cave represent later, near-modern, or modern *H. sapiens* as discussed in later chapters. Depending on the site, the dating is based on associated faunal remains, associated artifacts, U-S determinations, or some mix of these. All the dates are subject to revision when and if more precise methods can be applied. The global oxygen-isotope stratigraphy for the middle and late Quaternary is included for reference purposes only. The climatic phases it reflects are difficult or impossible to detect at most African mid-Quaternary sites.

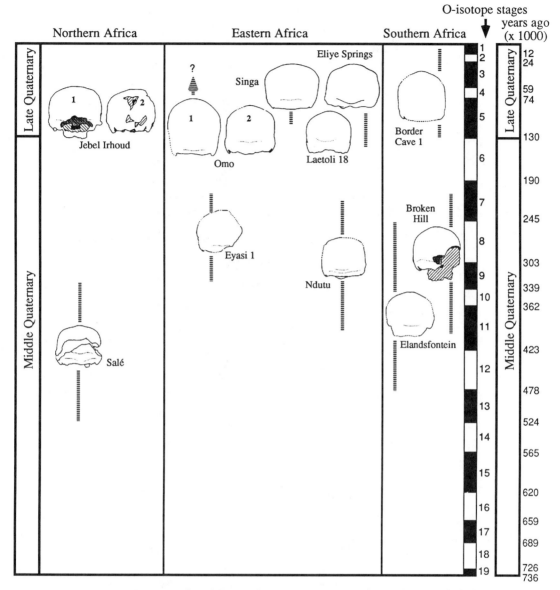

Figure 5.3. Occipital views of middle- and late-Quaternary African hominid skulls, as well as the time ranges within which they probably lie (adapted partly from Bräuer 1984a: 152; and Bräuer, pers. comm.) The skulls from Salé, Eyasi, Elandsfontein, and Broken Hill represent early or archaic *Homo sapiens* as discussed in this chapter. Those from Jebel Irhoud, Omo, Laetoli, Singa, Eliye Springs, and Border Cave represent later, near-modern, or modern *H. sapiens* as discussed in later chapters. Depending on the site, the dating is based on associated faunal remains, associated artifacts, U-S determinations, or some mix of these. All the dates are subject to revision when and if more precise methods can be applied. The global oxygen-isotope stratigraphy for the middle and late Quaternary is included for reference purposes only. The climatic phases it reflects are difficult or impossible to detect at most African mid-Quaternary sites.

Kunturé) in Ethiopia, Wadi Dagadlé in Djibouti, and Kébibat and Salé in Morocco. The Garba 3 fossil, comprising cranial fragments associated with "Late Acheulean" artifacts, will not be discussed further, because no morphological details are available. Figures 5.2 and 5.3 present the probable time relationships of the more complete fossils, both to each other and to some important late-Quaternary fossils that are now commonly assigned to modern or near-modern *H. sapiens*. The descriptions below rely heavily on Howell (1978a), Rightmire (1976, 1981a, 1983, 1984b), and Bräuer (1984a, 1984b).

Elandsfontein (= Saldanha = Hopefield)

A skullcap and mandibular ramus fragment were found in 1953 on the surface of a deflation hollow ("bay") on the farm of Elandsfontein near Hopefield and Saldanha Bay in the Cape Province of South Africa. Since the fossils were found on the surface, their artifactual and faunal associations cannot be directly determined, but the majority of animal fossils at the site, also from deflation hollows, probably date from the later middle Quaternary, between perhaps 500,000 and 200,000 years ago (Klein 1988). Both the human and animal bones are probably broadly contemporaneous with Acheulean hand axes that have also been found in deflation hollows and that were found in place with mid-Quaternary animal bones in the excavation known as Cutting 10 (Singer and Wymer 1968; Klein 1978).

The rameal fragment is robust but otherwise nondiagnostic. The skullcap, with its maximum breadth near the base, its massive browridge, and flat, receding frontal (Fig. 5.4), recalls *Homo erectus*. However, its inferred cranial capacity of 1,200–1,250 cc (Drennan 1953) far exceeds the *H. erectus* average, its side walls tend to rise more vertically than in typical *H. erectus*, its frontal is relatively broader, and its occipital is more rounded.

Cave of Hearths

A portion of the right half of a juvenile mandible with three teeth, found in 1947, was directly associated with Acheulean artifacts in hard, brecciated cave deposits near Potgietersrus in the northern Transvaal Province of South Africa (Tobias 1971). The sparse fauna recovered in association is not very helpful in dating, but the associated artifacts imply a mid-Quaternary age (Mason 1962; Volman 1984). The specimen is robust and was probably chinless, in keeping with an assignment to either *Homo erectus* or early *H. sapiens*.

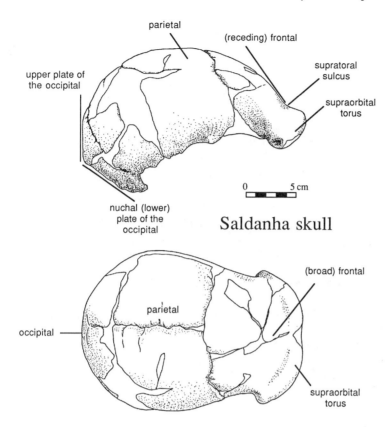

parietal

(receding) frontal

supratoral sulcus

supraorbital torus

upper plate of the occipital

0   5 cm

nuchal (lower) plate of the occipital

Saldanha skull

(broad) frontal

parietal

occipital

supraorbital torus

Figure 5.4. Mid-Quaternary skull-cap from Elands-fontein (= Saldanha = Hope-field), South Africa (drawn by K. Cruz-Uribe from casts and photos). The massive supraorbital torus and low, receding frontal recall those of *Homo erectus,* but the parietals are more expanded, the occipital is more rounded, and the frontal is broader than in typical *H. erectus.* Most specialists therefore consider the skull to be from early or archaic *H. sapiens.*

Broken Hill (= Kabwe = "Rhodesian Man")

A nearly complete cranium, cranial fragments of at least one other individual, and postcranial bones of perhaps three individuals were recovered in 1921 by lead and zinc miners in cave deposits near Kabwe, Zambia (then Broken Hill, Northern Rhodesia). Numerous animal bones and artifacts also occurred in the cave fill, but their stratigraphic relationship to the human remains is unknown (J. D. Clark 1959). The fauna includes extinct forms probably dating from the later mid-Quaternary (Klein 1973a). The faunal evidence and strong similarity to the Elandsfontein skull suggest that the nearly complete Broken Hill skull also dates to the later mid-Quaternary, almost certainly before 130,000 years ago. The other Broken Hill human fossils may or may not be the same age.

The nearly complete skull has a massive face, large browridges, a flat, retreating frontal, and relatively great basal breadth, all reminiscent of *Homo erectus* (Fig. 5.5). However, its departs sharply from *H. erectus* in its large endocranial capacity (about 1,280 cc) and in the morphology of its occipital, on which the upper scale rises nearly vertically from the torus (instead of sloping forward as in typical *H. erectus*). Curiously,

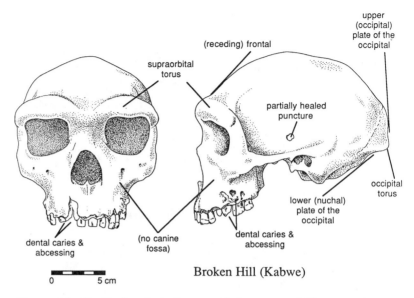

Figure 5.5. Skull of archaic (later-mid-Quaternary) *Homo sapiens* from Broken Hill (Kabwe) in Zambia (drawn by K. Cruz-Uribe from casts and photographs). In its massive face, thick browridges, flat, retreating frontal, and relatively great basal breadth, the skull recalls *H. erectus*. However, it clearly departs from *H. erectus* in braincase size and in its occipital, whose upper scale or plate rises nearly vertically from the torus.

the isolated maxilla of a second individual is less robust and, unlike the maxilla on the nearly complete skull, exhibits a canine fossa (deflation or hollowing of the facial bone above the canine tooth between the nasal aperture and the zygomatic arch). In its overall morphology, the second maxilla resembles that on a nearly complete skull found in the Ngaloba Beds at Laetoli (Tanzania) (Stringer 1986a). The Ngaloba skull is believed to date from near the boundary between the middle and late Quaternary, roughly 130,000 years ago (references in Chapter 6; also see Figs. 5.2, 5.3), and is notably less archaic than the more complete Broken Hill cranium, though still not fully modern.

The Broken Hill limb bones also contain a mix of decidedly archaic and more-modern-looking specimens. A sacrum, a distal humerus, and an innominate are identical to their modern counterparts, but a second innominate exhibits a thick buttress of cortical (outer compact) bone rising vertically above the acetabulum (= the socket for the femur) (Stringer 1986a). This feature is known elsewhere only in innominates usually assigned to *Homo erectus* from Olduvai and Koobi Fora and in one assigned (below) to archaic *H. sapiens* from Arago, France. Moreover, although the Broken Hill femoral fragments and an accompanying tibia are morphologically modern, they are characterized by extraordinarily thick cortical (outer) bone, equaling or exceeding the thickness in *H. erectus* (G. E. Kennedy 1984b). Pending controlled excavation of a similar sample at another site of similar age, it remains unclear whether the overall variability in the Broken Hill sample reflects differences among individuals within a single early *H. sapiens* population or a mixture of individuals from two or more temporally successive populations.

The dentition of the principal Broken Hill skull is taxonomically unremarkable, but most of the teeth are strongly affected by caries (decay). In this sense, the dentition is virtually unique among fossil specimens, which rarely show caries, probably because human diets were generally low in sugar until the origins and spread of agriculture, beginning about 10,000 years ago.

Ndutu

A relatively complete skull, missing mainly parts of the face and frontal, was found in 1973 with Acheulean artifacts and fragmentary animal bones in ancient deposits of seasonal Lake Ndutu near the western end of the Main Gorge at Olduvai, northern Tanzania. A tuff overlying the fossiliferous deposits may be equivalent to one at Olduvai believed to be nearly 400,000 years old, or it may be somewhat younger (M. D. Leakey and Hay 1982); but a later-mid-Quaternary age for the human skull is almost certain.

The skull exhibits a broad mix of typical *Homo erectus* and more-advanced features (Clarke 1976). It is broadly reminiscent of the Elandsfontein and Broken Hill skulls, though it is smaller (endocranial capacity = 1,100 cc)—perhaps because it is female and they are male. Sexual dimorphism could also explain its less pronounced occipital torus. It has large browridges and a low frontal, but the side walls rise relatively steeply from the cranial base, and the parietals are more expanded than in typical *H. erectus*. Equally significant, the upper scale of the occipital is large relative to the lower (nuchal) one, and it rises vertically rather than sloping forward as in typical *H. erectus*. A robust, partial mandible (OH 23) found in 1968 in direct association with Acheulean artifacts in the Masek Beds at Olduvai Gorge may represent the same population.

Eyasi

Cranial fragments from two or three individuals were found on the shore of Lake Eyasi, northern Tanzania, in 1935 and 1938. A recent evaluation of their probable stratigraphic origin suggests they date from the late middle Quaternary, before 130,000 years ago (Mehlman 1984, 1987). At one time they were probably stratigraphically associated with some of the Acheulean artifacts and fragmentary animal bones found on the surface nearby.

Only Eyasi 1, comprising most of the left half of the vault and part of the right, is complete enough for reasonably detailed comparisons. In overall morphology and estimated cranial capacity (1,285 cc), it recalls the Elandsfontein, Broken Hill, and Ndutu skulls and probably samples the same early *Homo sapiens* population.

Kapthurin (Lake Baringo)

A nearly complete mandible and some upper-limb fragments were found in 1966 (Margaret Leakey et al. 1969), and a second more fragmentary mandible was found in 1983 (van Noten 1983) in fluvial deposits near Lake Baringo, Kenya. The normal magnetism of the deposits, together with associated Acheulean artifacts and faunal remains, suggest a mid-Quaternary age, without allowing a more precise determination. The more complete mandible is robust, but less so than other east African mandibles attributed to *Homo erectus*. It could belong to either *H. erectus* or early *H. sapiens*. The second less complete mandible is basically similar to the first (Day 1986).

Bodo

A skull comprising most of the face and the anterior part and central parts of the braincase was found in 1976 (Kalb et al. 1982a), and part of a second braincase was found in 1983 in the Middle Awash region of east-central Ethiopia (Asfaw 1983; J. D. Clark et al. 1984). Associated Acheulean artifacts and animal bones imply a mid-Quaternary date, again without greater precision. In preserved parts, the braincase of the more complete skull is morphologically similar to that of the Broken Hill skull, but the face is much more massive, particularly in the middle part. The occipital region, which could prove critical in making a taxonomic choice, is missing, but, of all the African specimens considered in this chapter, the Bodo skull is perhaps the best candidate for true *Homo erectus*.

Wadi Dagadlé

A left maxilla with the fourth premolar through the third molar, the root of the third premolar, and the incisor and canine sockets was found in sands at the Wadi Dagadlé, southwestern Djibouti, in 1983 (de Bonis et al. 1984, 1988). Tentative thermoluminescence (TL) dates of 250,000 years ago or less for an underlying basalt suggest a late-mid Quaternary age, which is consistent with animal fossils found at the level of the maxilla. The maxilla is robust, with large teeth and pronounced alveolar prognathism. On strictly morphological grounds, it could come from either *Homo erectus* or early *H. sapiens*. If the dating is correct, *H. sapiens* is more likely.

Kébibat (Mifsud-Giudice Quarry, Rabat)

A mandible, left maxilla, and occipital fragments were found in eolianite (dune rock) at Rabat in 1933. No artifacts were directly associated with them, but animal bones from the same basic unit suggest a later-mid-Quaternary age, consistent with a thorium/uranium date of more than 200,000 years ago for marine shell from an overlying bed (Stearns and Thurber 1965). The occipital is relatively well rounded with little trace of a torus (Saban 1977). It could derive from the same archaic *Homo sapiens* population represented by the more complete fossil skull at nearby Salé.

Salé

A braincase, natural endocast, and left maxilla fragment were found in eolianite near Rabat in 1971 (Jaeger 1975; Hublin 1985). Few animal bones and no artifacts were directly associated, but rodent bones from an overlying level imply a later-mid-Quaternary age. The skull has a sagittal keel and very small cranial capacity (930–960 cc), characteristics that recall *Homo erectus*, but it also exhibits parietal expansion that allies it with other skulls assigned to early *H. sapiens*. It also has a well-rounded occipital with a weakly expressed occipital torus, but the occipital shows signs of pathology and its taxonomic significance is thus questionable (Hublin 1985).

Europe

The principal European specimens that have been assigned to early (= mid-Quaternary) *Homo sapiens* are from Swanscombe and Pontnewydd in Great Britain; Montmaurin, Arago, Lazaret, La Chaise, Fontéchevade, and Biache-Saint-Vaast in France; Atapuerca in Spain; Mauer, Steinheim, and Bilzingsleben in Germany; Vértesszöllös in Hungary; and Petralona in Greece. Figure 5.6 shows the locations of the sites, and Figure 5.7 shows the probable time ranges in which the human fossils lie. The descriptions below rely heavily on Cook et al. (1982) and Stringer et al (1984).

Swanscombe

An occipital (found 1935), left parietal (1936), and right parietal (1956) of a single individual were found in the Upper Middle Gravels of the Thames in the Barnfield Pit, Swanscombe, Kent, southeastern England. The associated animal remains and

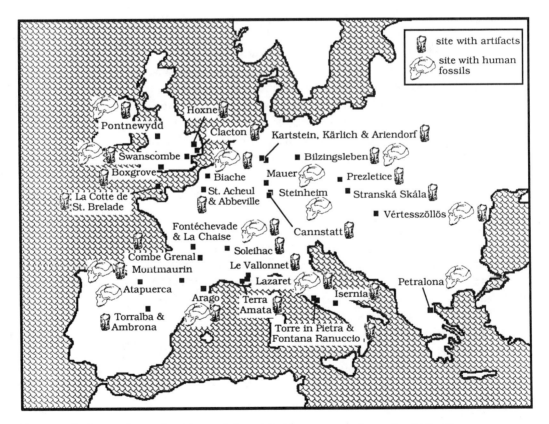

Figure 5.6. Approximate locations of the main European early- and middle-Quaternary sites that have provided artifacts, human fossils, or both.

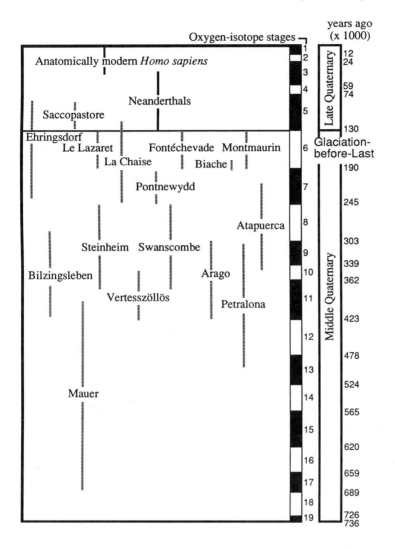

Figure 5.7. Probable time intervals bracketing European fossils of mid-Quaternary *Homo sapiens*. The datings are based on a varying mix of (1) faunal correlations, (2) U-S or TL determinations, and (3) presumed correspondences between glacial/interglacial events recorded at the sites and the global oxygen-isotope stratigraphy. This is shown to the right, with approximate boundary dates for the main stages. "Cold" (even-numbered) stages are in white, and "warm" (odd-numbered) stages are in black. The Glaciation-before-Last or Penultimate Glaciation referred to in the text corresponds to stage 6.

Middle Acheulean artifacts imply a later-middle-Quaternary age, probably between 400,000 and 250,000 years ago. The skull bones are thick as in *Homo erectus*, but the inferred cranial capacity (1,325 cc) significantly exceeds the *H. erectus* average, and the occipital is much less sharply angulated than in typical *H. erectus* (Fig. 5.8). The occipital also bears an elliptical depression just above the center of the moderately developed occipital torus. Commonly called the suprainiac fossa, this depression is a distinctive (derived) feature of Neanderthal skulls (Santa Luca 1980), and Stringer et al. (1984) have noted that, with somewhat greater flattening of the occipital in the area of lambda (Fig. 5.9), the Swanscombe occipital would closely resemble the later one from Biache-Saint-Vaast, which in turn clearly anticipates the occipitals of

Figure 5.8. Skulls of archaic (later mid-Quaternary) *Homo sapiens* from Steinheim in Germany and Swanscombe in England (redrawn partly after originals by Janis Cirulis in Howells 1967: 218). Both skulls are thick walled like those of *H. erectus*, and the Steinheim skull has a large, projecting supraorbital torus, but both are distinguished from skulls of *H. erectus* by expanded parietals and a more rounded occipital.

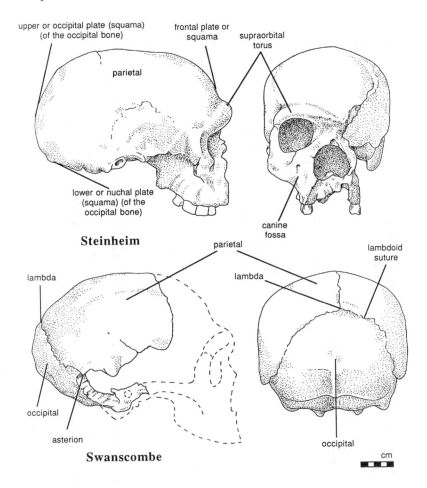

the Neanderthals, who occupied Europe in the earlier part of the late Quaternary, between roughly 130,000 and 50,000–35,000 years ago (as discussed in chapter 6).

Pontnewydd

Three isolated teeth and a right maxilla fragment were found with Upper Acheulean artifacts in the late 1970s and early 1980s in slumped cave deposits at Pontnewydd, north Wales (H. S. Green et al. 1981; H. S. Green 1984). An additional tooth, a mandible fragment, and a vertebra were found in backdirt from earlier excavations. Uranium-series (U-S) and TL dates suggest the human remains could date from within the interglaciation corresponding to oxygen-isotope stage 7, between roughly 245,000 and 190,000 years ago (Aitken et al. 1986). In their root morphology and taurodontism (= fusion of the roots with expansion of the pulp cavity), the teeth recall those of the classic Neanderthals, as discussed in the next chapter.

Montmaurin

A nearly complete mandible was found in 1949 in a limestone fissure deposit at Montmaurin, Haute Garonne, southwestern France (Billy and Vallois 1977). A combination of faunal, palynological, and archeological data suggest a late-mid- Quaternary age, perhaps during the Glaciation-before-Last (=isotope stage 6), between roughly 190,000 and 130,000 years ago. The mandibular bone is massive, but the teeth are relatively small (Fig. 5.10). As on all other *Homo erectus* or early *H. sapiens* mandibles, the symphysis is receding and lacks a chin. An incipient retromolar space (= a gap between the posterior edge

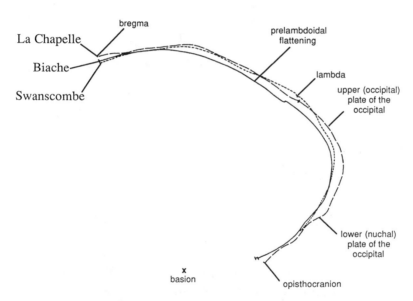

Figure 5.9. Midsagittal sections of the skulls from Swanscombe, Biache, and La Chapelle (redrawn after Vandermeersch 1978: Fig. 2). The Swanscombe skull is older than that from Biache, which in turn is older than that from La Chapelle, a late-Quaternary classic Neanderthal skull. Bregma, lambda, opisthocranion, and basion are craniological landmarks commonly used to describe or orient skulls. Substantial flattening of the skull just before lambda is a characteristic trait of the Neanderthals, anticipated in the Swanscombe and Biache skulls. Together with an incipient suprainiac depression on Swanscombe and a clear occipital bun on Biache, the basic similarity in midsagittal sections can be used to argue that they represent successive populations along an evolutionary continuum leading to the Neanderthals.

Figure 5.10.
Mandible of
archaic (later-mid-
Quaternary)
Homo sapiens
from Montmau-
rin, France
(redrawn after
Billy and Vallois
1977: 280). The
mandible exhibits
several archaic
features, including
large size and the
absence of a chin.
The occurence of
an incipient retro-
molar space sug-
gests links to the
late-Quaternary
Neanderthals.

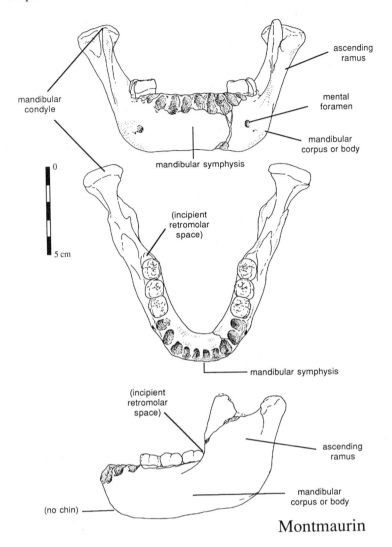

Montmaurin

of the third molar and the anterior margin of the ascending ramus), molar taurodontism, and other features suggest evolutionary links to the Neanderthals.

Arago (Tautavel)

More than fifty human fossils have been recovered since 1964 in cave deposits of La Caune de l'Arago, near Tautavel, southwestern France (H. de Lumley et al. 1979). Depending on the level within the cave, the associated artifacts can be called either Tayacian or Upper Acheulean. (These industries are discussed in the section on artifacts below.) Widely varying ages have been estimated from U-S dates and from analysis of the fauna, but a mid-middle-Quaternary age (?400,000 years ago) seems probable.

Most of the human remains are isolated teeth and fragmentary postcranial bones. From a diagnostic point of view, the most important specimens include a face (Arago 21) and parietal (Arago 47) believed to come from the same individual, a mandible (Arago 2), a half mandible (Arago 13), and a left innominate (Arago 44). The face (Arago 21) has a thick supraorbital torus and receding frontal (Fig. 5.11 top). To judge from the parietal (Arago 47), the maximum breadth was relatively low and the cranial capacity was relatively small (about 1,160 cc). The face is very broad, with marked alveolar prognathism, but without the midfacial projection of the Neanderthals. The parietal is large and resembles the Swanscombe parietals morphologically.

The two mandibles differ strongly, perhaps because of sexual dimorphism. The more complete specimen (Arago 2) is relatively gracile with retromolar spaces, as in the Neanderthals. The other specimen (Arago 13) is much more robust and indistinguishable from specimens elsewhere that have been assigned to *Homo erectus* or early *H. sapiens*.

In its robusticity and in particular morphological features, the innominate (Arago 44) recalls ones commonly assigned to *Homo erectus* (or simply to archaic *Homo*) at Olduvai Gorge and Koobi Fora. However, it also shares its most prominent archaic feature with an innominate assigned to early *H. sapiens* from Broken Hill, Zambia (discussed above).

If it is assumed that the Arago fossils represent a single population, as a group they can be included in early *Homo sapiens*, with possible links to the Neanderthals.

Le Lazaret

A juvenile parietal, a deciduous upper incisor, and an adult lower canine were found between 1953 and 1964 in the cave of Le Lazaret within the city of Nice (H. de Lumley 1969a, 1975). The associated fauna and Acheulean artifacts imply a later-mid-Quaternary (?Penultimate Glacial) age. The teeth are very large but otherwise nondiagnostic. The parietal is difficult to interpret because of a pathological lesion and the young age of the owner, but it is morphologically consistent with either the Neanderthals or the population that was immediately ancestral to them.

La Chaise

Approximately eighty human fossils were recovered in the 1960's and 1970's from the caves of Bourgeois-Delaunay and

Suard at La Chaise, Charente (Debénath 1976, 1977, 1988). U-S and TL dates, together with paleobiological and artifactual evidence, suggest that most of the fossils date from the late middle Quaternary, between perhaps 250,000 and 130,000 years ago (Blackwell et al. 1983). Some may date to the early part of the late Quaternary, between perhaps 130,000 and 80,000 years ago.

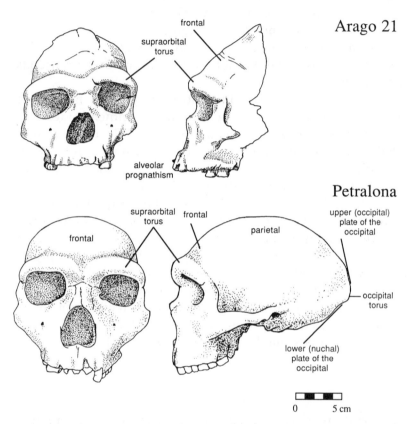

Figure 5.11. *Top:* Face of archaic (later-mid-Quaternary) *Homo sapiens* from Arago, France (drawn by K. Cruz-Uribe from casts and photos). The face was slightly distorted in the ground, but in most observable respects, including the massive supraorbital torus, receding frontal, and degree of alveolar prognathism, it recalls the face of *H. erectus.* However, a parietal fragment possibly from the same individual suggests that the braincase was shaped like those assigned to early *H. sapiens* from other European and African sites. *Bottom:* Mid-Quaternary human skull from Petralona, Greece (drawn by K. Cruz-Uribe from photographs). The skull combines a massive supraorbital torus, receding frontal, and a relatively angulated occipital, all characteristic of *H. erectus,* with parietal expansion, an enlarged braincase, and other advanced features that anticipate later *H. sapiens.* Most specialists today consider it to represent archaic *H. sapiens.*

The fossils are mainly isolated teeth and cranial fragments, with a few fragmentary postcranial bones. The more complete specimens exhibit metrical and morphological features—including, for example, a large retromolar space on the most complete mandible—that anticipate the later Neanderthals.

Fontéchevade

A frontal fragment (Fontéchevade I), a skullcap (Fontéchevade II), and a worn parietal fragment were recovered in 1947 (I and II) and 1957 (parietal) from deposits in the Fontéchevade Cave, Charente (Henri-Martin 1965). The age of the fossils is obscure (Vandermeersch et al. 1976), partly because of uncertainty about their stratigraphic position and associations in the cave and partly because of apparent contradictions between the microfauna and the macrofauna. A best guess now is perhaps the Penultimate Glaciation (between roughly 190,000 and 130,000 years ago), which is consistent with the associated Tayacian artifacts.

The human fossils are difficult to interpret because they are so fragmentary, and the most complete specimen (II) may not be properly reconstructed. It is clearly primitive on the basis of bone thickness and great breadth near the base, and in some metrical characters it foreshadows the Neanderthals.

Biache-Saint-Vaast

The back half of a cranium, a fragmentary maxilla with all six molars, and five isolated teeth were recovered in 1976 from fluvial deposits in a salvage excavation at Biache-Saint-Vaast, Pas-de-Calais, northern France (Tuffreau et al. 1982). TL analysis of burnt flints suggests the skull and an associated flake industry (without hand axes) date between 196,000 and 159,000 years ago (Aitken et al. 1986). This is broadly consistent with the stratigraphic context and associated paleobiological materials (Sommé et al. 1986), which suggest a date early in the Penultimate Glaciation (= oxygen-isotope stage 6), which began roughly 190,000 years ago.

The endocranial capacity of the Biache skull (ca. 1,200 cc) is well below the average for later Neanderthal skulls, but morphologically it resembles them closely in its marked occipital bun (chignon), prelambdoid flattening (Fig. 5.9), and subspherical (oval) profile when viewed from behind, with maximum breadth low on the parietals (Vandermeersch 1978). It can be seen as a morphological link between the presumably earlier Swanscombe and Steinheim skulls and the later classic Neanderthal ones.

Atapuerca (Ibeas)

Nearly ninety fragments, including twenty-one pieces of skull, one nearly complete mandible, four partial mandibles, thirty-eight isolated teeth, and roughly twenty postcranial bones, were recovered from ancient mudflow deposits in the Cueva Mayor (SH site), Ibeas, in the Sierra de Atapuerca near Burgos, northern Spain (Aguirre and de Lumley 1977; Aguirre and Rosas 1985; Rosas 1987). Only three of the pieces were recovered in controlled excavations, but all were apparently associated with a fauna including several mid-Quaternary mammalian species. Especially notable and abundant is *Ursus deningeri,* commonly believed to be the lineal ancestor of the later-Quaternary cave bear, *U. spelaeus.* Although the date is tentative, U-S analysis of one of the in situ human fragments suggests an age between 350,000 and 200,000 years. In their dimensions and morphology, the human fossils are said to exhibit some features (for example, very thick cranial walls and a very robust mandibular body with large molars) that recall *Homo erectus* and other features (for example, incipient retromolar spaces on two of the mandibles) that anticipate the Neanderthals. As a group, they have been likened to the broadly coeval assemblage from Arago.

Mauer (Heidelberg)

A mandible was found by quarry workers in 1907 in fluvial sands at Mauer near Heidelberg (Howell 1960). The sands have not supplied any indisputable artifacts, but on the basis of their normal remanent magnetism (Brunnacker 1975) and vole fossils (W. von Koenigswald 1973), they clearly postdate the Matuyama/Brunhes paleomagnetic boundary at 730,000 years ago. The precise faunal associations of the mandible are unclear, but the fauna in general implies a mid-middle-Quaternary age, perhaps between 700,000 and 400,000 years. Conceivably, the mandible is the most ancient human fossil yet found in Europe.

In its robousticity, the mandible matches mandibles of *Homo erectus,* but the molars are at the small end of the *H. erectus* range and well within the size limits of late-Quaternary *H. sapiens.* Aside from moderate taurodontism, there are no Neanderthal features.

Steinheim

A nearly complete skull was found in 1933 in fluvial deposits in a quarry at Steinheim an der Murr, Württemburg, Germany (Howell 1960; Adam 1985). There were no associated artifacts, but the associated fauna suggests a mid-Quaternary date close to that of the Swanscombe skull. The supraorbital torus is pronounced and the frontal is low, but the occipital is rounded as in the Swanscombe skull, with a relatively weak occipital torus (Fig. 5.8). The relatively small cranial capacity (1,100–1,200 cc) may indicate the skull is female. The face was partially distorted in the ground but, unlike Neanderthal faces, appears to have a canine fossa and a nonprojecting midfacial region.

Bilzingsleben

A nearly complete occipital bone, frontal and parietal fragments, three permanent molars, and a deciduous premolar were found between 1972 and 1984 in fluvio-lacustrine deposits at the Steinrinne Quarry at Bilzingsleben near Erfurt, Germany (Harmon et al. 1980; Mania and Vlcek 1981; Mania 1986). The accompanying artifacts represent a nonhand-ax flake industry. Together with the sediments, the associated fauna and flora reflect an interglaciation within the same portion of the mid-Quaternary represented at Swanscombe and Steinheim. Mutually inconsistent U-S and electron-spin-resonance dates imply an age between perhaps 425,000 and 200,000 years (Cook et al. 1982; Schwarcz et al. 1988). A critical review of all the results suggests the minimum age may lie closer to 280,000 years (Schwarcz et al. 1988).

Except for the deciduous premolar, all the human fossils are believed to come from the same individual. The occipital is broad but sharply flexed (Fig. 5.12), with a continuous transverse torus. One of the frontal fragments indicates a thick, powerful supraorbital torus. On occipital morphology, of all the known European specimens, the Bilzingsleben one is the best candidate for *Homo erectus* (Vlcek 1978), and its morphology is certainly puzzling if it is truly the same age as the Swanscombe and Steinheim skulls.

Vértesszöllös

Lower deciduous teeth and an adult occipital bone were found in 1964–65 in spring deposits in a travertine quarry at Vértess-

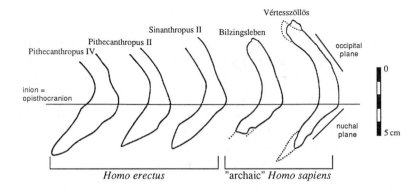

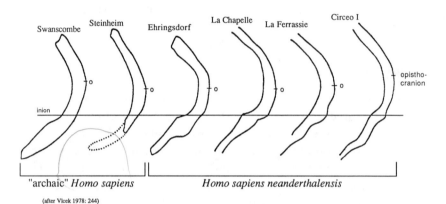

(after Vlcek 1978: 244)

Figure 5.12. Midline (midsagittal) sections through the occipital bones of some key fossils assigned here to *Homo erectus* ("*Pithecanthropus* IV," "*Pithecanthropus* II," and "*Sinanthropus* II"), early *H. sapiens* (Bilzingsleben, Vértesszöllös, Swanscombe, and Steinheim), and *H. s. neanderthalensis* (Ehringsdorf, La Chapelle, La Ferrassie, and Circeo 1) (redrawn after Vlcek 1978: 244). Note that with respect to occipital flexion (angulation between the occipital and nuchal planes), the Vértesszöllös and especially the Bilzingsleben fossils are more like *H. erectus* than they are like the Swanscombe, Steinheim, and Neanderthal fossils.

zöllös near Budapest, Hungary. The associated artifacts comprise a variety of flake and pebble tools (no hand axcs) assigned to the Buda Industry. The fauna includes water voles belonging to an early stage in the *Arvicola* lineage, suggesting that the human remains are perhaps slightly younger than those from Mauer and certainly older than those from Steinheim, Swanscombe, and Bilzingsleben. Among a series of mutually inconsistent U-S dates, the most reliable ones suggest an age between perhaps 210,000 and 160,000 years (Schwarcz and Latham 1984), which is, however, significantly younger than the age implied by the fauna.

The occipital is thick and angulated (Fig. 5.12), with a continuous transverse torus, but its size suggests a skull significantly larger than that of typical *Homo erectus*. The specimen is too fragmentary for a firmer diagnosis.

Petralona

A nearly complete skull embedded in stalagmite (Fig. 5.11 bottom) was found in 1960 in a cave near Petralona, Halkidiki, northeastern Greece (Stringer et al. 1979; Stringer 1983). U-S and electron-spin-resonance dates, together with the normal paleomagnetism of the cave fill, imply an age between 730,000 and 200,000 years (G. J. Hennig et al. 1982; Wintle and Jacobs 1982; Papamarinopoulos et al. 1987). No artifacts or faunal remains were recorded with the skull, but if it was originally associated with early-mid-Quaternary faunal elements known from the cave (Kurtén 1983), it could rival the Mauer mandible as the oldest known human fossil from Europe, with a potential age of perhaps 500,000 years.

The skull has thick walls, a well-developed supraorbital torus, and an angulated occipital reminiscent of *Homo erectus*, combined with parietal expansion, extensive pneumatization of the facial bones and browridge, a relatively large cranial capacity (ca. 1,230 cc), and other features that might imply links to later Neanderthals. In overall morphology it is also similar to the Broken Hill and Bodo skulls, perhaps implying a shared ancestry in the earlier middle Quaternary.

Asia

The principal Asian fossils that have been assigned to early *Homo sapiens* are from Ngandong (= Solo) and Sambung-machan in Java; from Dali, Xujiayao, Maba, and Yinkou in China; and from the Narmada Valley in north-central India. The Chinese specimens have been dated by U-S analysis of associated animal bones, but the reliability of the results (reported below) is questionable, because of the possibility that the bones exchanged uranium with their burial environment (Chen and Yuan 1988). The problem is perhaps least acute with regard to Yinkou. Figure 5.13 shows the approximate locations of the main Chinese and Indonesian sites and compares some of the skulls from them with skulls of anatomically modern (late-Quaternary) *H. sapiens* from Zhoukoudian (Upper Cave), Ziyang, and Liujiang in China; Niah Cave in Borneo; and Wajak in Java.

Figure 5.13. Later-
Quaternary homi-
nid fossil sites in
east Asia (adapted
from Bräuer
1984a: 161; and
Bräuer, pers.
comm.) Sambung-
machan, Solo (=
Ngandong), Maba,
Dali, and Xujiayao
have provided fos-
sils of archaic
Homo sapiens, as
discussed in this
chapter. The
remaining sites
have provided fos-
sils of anatomi-
cally modern *H.
sapiens*, as dis-
cussed in later
chapters. A ques-
tion mark next to
a site name
implies special
uncertainty about
the age of the site.

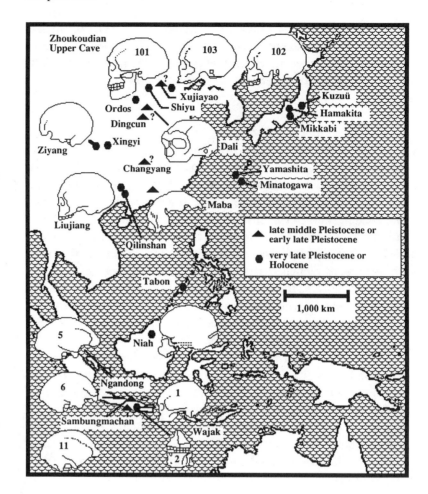

Ngandong (and Sambungmachan)

Fifteen skulls or skull fragments, a nearly complete tibia, and
a tibia fragment were recovered from terrace deposits of the
Solo River (the Notopuro Beds) at Ngandong in central Java in
1931–33 and 1976 (Weidenreich 1951; Le Gros Clark 1964;
Jacob 1978; Santa Luca 1980). A few non-nondescript stone
artifacts and numerous faunal remains were associated. The
fauna is clearly younger than the fauna(s) thought to be
associated with classic *Homo erectus* in the Pucangan and
Kabuh Beds and probably dates from the later mid-Quaternary,
between perhaps 500,000 and 200,000 years ago. A similar
skull found at Sambungmachan (between Trinil and Sangiran
in east-central Java) in 1973 may be the same age. Additional
contemporaries may include most or all of the undisputed *H.
erectus* fossils from Zhoukoudian and Hexian in China.

The Ngandong and Sambungmachan skulls resemble those of *Homo erectus* not only in features that are shared by *H. erectus* and early *H. sapiens* in the West (large browridges, low, receding frontals, prominent occipital tori, and very thick cranial bones) but also in details of occipital and parietal morphology that generally distinguish early *H. sapiens* from *H. erectus* (Fig. 5.14). The similarity is particularly obvious in rear view, where the side walls on the Ngandong vaults slope inward from a broad cranial base. In endocranial capacity (1,150–1,300 cc), the Ngandong skulls do tend to be larger than those of classic *H. erectus*, their browridges are thinner in the central part, and they exhibit less postorbital constriction; but the differences are small compared with the similarities. Although they have sometimes been placed in their own species *(H. soloensis)*, included in the Neanderthals, or referred to as early *H. sapiens*, on strictly morphological grounds they might best be assigned to *H. erectus* (Santa Luca 1980; Rightmire 1988). They are certainly not Neanderthals.

Dali

A nearly complete skull was found in 1978 in fluvial deposits in Dali County, Shaanxi Province, north China (Wu and Wu 1985). Associated stone artifacts included relatively nondescript flake tools. U-S datings on associated animal bones range between 180,000 and 230,000 years (Chen and Yuan 1988). The skull has a massive supraorbital torus, a low, flat frontal, and an angulated occipital with a prominent transverse torus, all features shared with *Homo erectus*. The cranial capacity (1,120 cc) does not significantly exceed the *H. erectus* average, but the parietals are far more expanded than in *H. erectus* and there is significantly less post-orbital constriction. The face is flat with a canine fossa and without the midfacial projection typical of the Neanderthals.

Xujiayao

A parietal, an occipital, jaw fragments, and isolated teeth from several individuals were found in 1976–77 in fluvial deposits near the village of Xujiayao, Shaanxi Province, north China (Wu and Wu 1985). Numerous flake tools and animal bones were directly associated. The animal species suggest a late-middle-Quaternary or early-late-Quaternary date. U-S dates on associated animal bones vary between 125,000 and 100,000 years (Chen and Yuan 1988). The fragmentary parietal is very

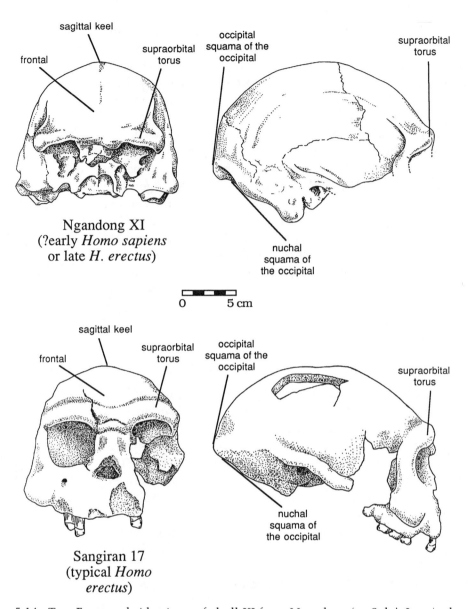

Figure 5.14. *Top:* Front and side views of skull XI from Ngandong (= Solo), Java (redrawn mainly after originals by Janis Cirulis in Howells 1967: 160). *Bottom:* Front and side views of skull 17 from Sangiran, Java (drawn by K. Cruz-Uribe from photos). The Sangiran skull is widely accepted as *Homo erectus* and probably antedates the one from Ngandong by several hundred thousand years, yet they are generally similar in overall morphology, including the shared presence of a sagittal keel, an angulated (flexed) occipital, and the tendency for the skull walls to slope inward from a broad base. The similarity has been used to argue that the Ngandong people were a late variety of *H. erectus*, occupying the Far East after early *H. sapiens* was well established in Africa and Europe. Whatever the proper taxonomic designation for the Ngandong skull, together with others from the same site it suggests that late-mid-Quaternary populations in the Far East were on a different evolutionary trajectory than their European and African contemporaries.

thick but indicates greater parietal expansion than in *Homo erectus*. The occipital is moderately angulated with a pronounced transverse torus.

Maba (Mapa)

A partial human skull was found in 1958 in a limestone cave near the village of Maba in Guangdong Province, south China (Wu and Wu 1985). There were no associated artifacts. The geologic age is imprecisely established, but the associated fauna suggests a late-middle or possibly early-later-Quaternary age. U-S dates on associated animal bones range from 119,000 to 140,000 years (Chen and Yuan 1988). On the basis of its morphology and presumed age, the Maba skull could represent the same distinctive late-middle-Quaternary/early-late-Quaternary population of early *Homo sapiens* also represented at Dali and Xujiayao.

Yinkou (Jingniushan)

A skull and partial skeleton were excavated in 1984 from Jingniushan Cave, Yinkou County, northeast China. A small number of artifacts and a larger number of animal fossils have been recovered from the same deposits. Very tentatively, U-S dates on animal bones associated with the human remains suggest an age of 263,000 ± 30,000 years (Chen and Yuan 1988).

According to Wu (reported in Bunney 1986), the skull has a receding forehead, prominent browridges, and large cheek teeth, all features recalling *Homo erectus*, combined with a relatively rounded occiput, thin walls, and a cranial capacity of 1,390 cc, anticipating modern *H. sapiens*. In overall morphology, it is said to resemble the Dali skull more than it does any other, and it may exemplify the same basic early *H. sapiens* population. However, its U-S date of roughly 263,000 years is significantly earlier than the U-S estimate for Dali and is within the time range that has been suggested for *H. erectus* at Zhoukoudian. This apparent inconsistency highlights both the problems of U-S dating (especially as applied to bone) and the uncertainty surrounding the age of Chinese *H. erectus*.

Narmada

A skullcap was found in cemented alluvial gravels of the Narmada River near the village of Hathnora in Madhya

Pradesh State, north-central India in 1982 (H. de Lumley and Sonakia 1985; Sonakia 1985). Associated animal bones and Upper Acheulean artifacts imply a mid-Quaternary age. As do the other skulls considered in this chapter, the Narmada skullcap shares important features with *Homo erectus*, such as a thick, forwardly projecting supraorbital torus, thick cranial walls, and greatest breadth near the base (Fig. 5.15) (M. de Lumley and Sonakia 1985). However, its estimated endocranial capacity of more than 1,200 cc exceeds that of typical *H. erectus*, from which it is further distinguished by a somewhat steeper (less receding) frontal, a more rounded occipital, and more expanded parietals. It thus deviates from *H. erectus* in broadly the same way as do the other archaic *H. sapiens* skulls considered previously.

Evolutionary Implications

The major conclusion that can be drawn from this brief survey of early *Homo sapiens* is the apparent divergence of evolutionary pathways between East and West. Thus, while later-mid-Quaternary people in Africa and Europe were generally distinguished from *H. erectus* by larger cranial capacities, more expanded parietals, and less angulated occipitals, the later-mid-Quaternary occupants of Java and China remained remarkably similar to classic *H. erectus* in virtually all significant cranial features and proportions. The contrast would be reduced to some extent if further research shows that the Zhoukoudian and Hexian *H. erectus* fossils are older, rather than broadly contemporaneous with those from Steinheim, Swanscombe, etc. However, it is still true that among the east Asian fossils considered here, only those from Dali, Maba, Xujiayao, and Yinkou represent a significant departure from *H. erectus*, and they may date from the very-late middle Quaternary or even from the early late Quaternary, after 130,000 years ago.

In the West, uncertainties in dating, the small number of fossils on hand, and their often fragmentary state make it difficult to draw further inferences. However, the European fossils suggest that an earlier-mid-Quaternary population little differentiated from *Homo erectus* may have evolved into a later-mid-Quaternary one that clearly anticipates the late-Quaternary classic Neanderthals (Stringer 1985; Vandermeersch 1985). In Africa, earlier-mid-Quaternary people broadly similar to their European contemporaries may have evolved in a different direction, leading ultimately to anatomically modern *H. sapiens*.

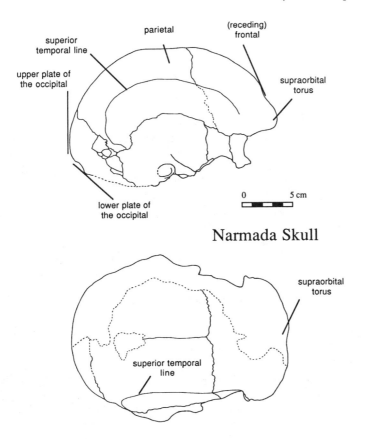

Narmada Skull

Figure 5.15. Skullcap of archaic *Homo sapiens* from the Narmada Valley, north-central India (redrawn after M.-A. de Lumley and Sonakia 1985: 26, 30). The skullcap shares with skulls of *H. erectus* a thick, projecting supraorbital torus, thick walls, and great basal breadth, but it also departs from the *H. erectus* skulls in significant ways, including its expanded parietals and less angulated (flexed) occipital.

Artifacts

From a strictly archeological perspective, there is little to distinguish early *Homo sapiens* from *H. erectus*. Formal artifacts of bone, the only potential raw material besides stone that survives in many sites, are still absent. Stone-artifact assemblages that were possibly or probably made by early *H. sapiens* in China continue to lack hand axes and other well-made bifacial tools. Instead, as are earlier assemblages made by local *H. erectus*, they are dominated by flake tools, accompanied by choppers and chopping tools (= bifacial choppers) (Qiu 1985).

In Africa and Europe, the Acheulean Tradition persisted after the emergence of *Homo sapiens* and is well represented at some of the same sites that contain early *H. sapiens* fossils— for example, at Elandsfontein in South Africa (Fig. 5.16) (Singer and Wymer 1968), at Kapthurin in Kenya (Margaret Leakey et al. 1969), in at least one level at Arago in France (H. de Lumley 1975), and at Swanscombe in England (Fig. 5.17) (Wymer 1964; Roe 1981). In both Africa and Europe, there are numerous additional Acheulean sites, many undated or undatable, where

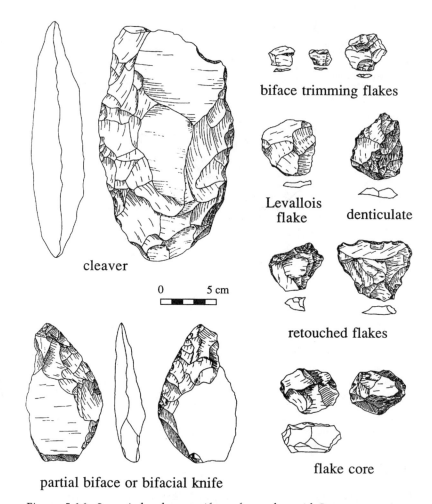

cleaver

biface trimming flakes

Levallois flake

denticulate

retouched flakes

flake core

0   5 cm

partial biface or bifacial knife

Figure 5.16. Late-Acheulean artifacts from the mid-Quaternary site of Elandsfontein (Cutting 10), South Africa (courtesy of T. P. Volman). All are in silcrete, a very fine-grained, locally available siliceous rock. Elandsfontein has furnished numerous distinctively Acheulean large bifacial tools, exemplified here by a cleaver and partial biface or bifacial knife. Also present are small, thin flakes that were probably produced during biface manufacture or trimming; larger, thicker flakes that were struck for use as tools in their own right; and some of the cores from which they came. A radial pattern of scars on the dorsal surfaces of some flakes indicates they were struck by the so-called Levallois technique which allowed a knapper to predetermine flake size and shape. The Levallois technique was probably a late-Acheulean invention. Most of the flakes are unretouched or only lightly retouched, perhaps partly from use. Some were retouched to produce a serrate or denticulated edge, perhaps for sawing or shredding.

hand axes and other artifacts were probably or possibly made by early *H. sapiens*. On average, the hand axes may be somewhat better made than earlier ones and there may be a wider variety of accompanying flake tools. In addition, later-Acheulean sites in both Africa and Europe suggest that early *H. sapiens* invented the Levallois technique for predetermining flake size and shape (see Appendix 2 for further discussion).

In Africa, the Acheulean Tradition is lumped with the preceding Oldowan into the Early Stone Age, while in Europe, where Acheulean people may have been the first inhabitants, the Acheulean is commonly placed in the Lower Paleolithic. In

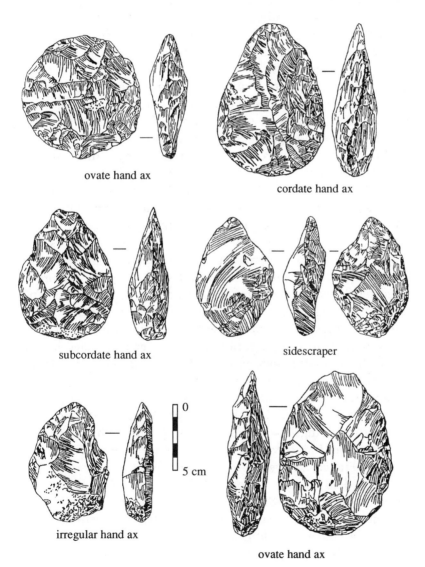

ovate hand ax

cordate hand ax

subcordate hand ax

sidescraper

irregular hand ax

0

5 cm

ovate hand ax

Figure 5.17. Late-Acheulean artifacts from southern England (redrawn after Wymer 1968: 147). Finely crafted hand axes of various shapes and sizes are the hallmark of the late Acheulean, but biased collection probably artificially raised their frequency in most European assemblages obtained in the later nineteenth and early twentieth centuries. Fine hand axes tend to be much less abundant in samples that have been carefully excavated in more recent decades.

Africa, the Middle Stone Age flake industries that replaced the Acheulean (distinguished from it by their lack of hand axes and other bifaces) may have appeared about 200,000 years ago (Volman 1984). In Europe, broadly similar Middle Paleolithic industries possibly replaced the Acheulean just as early in some places—for example, in northern France (Tuffreau 1979, 1982)—but there is much uncertainty on this question, which is due partly to the absence of truly reliable absolute dates in this time interval and partly to the difficulty of defining the Acheulean. Typical Acheulean bifaces may be rare or absent in some assemblages because suitable raw material was unavailable, because the people who made bifacial tools elsewhere did not make or need them everywhere, or even because the excavations simply failed to intersect the part of a site where bifaces lay. The question then arises, Should an assemblage that might lack bifaces for one of these reasons be separated from the Acheulean?

A similar question affects the numerous nonbiface assemblages in Europe that were clearly contemporaneous with biface assemblages elsewhere. Prominent nonbiface sites include Clacton in England (Singer et al. 1973; Ohel 1977, 1979), Bad-Cannstatt and Kartstein in West Germany (Brunnacker et al. 1982; Wagner 1984), Bilzingsleben in East Germany (Weber 1980; Mania and Vlcek 1981; Mania 1986), and Vértesszöllös in Hungary (Vértes 1965). Vértesszöllös and Bilzingsleben are particularly notable because the aritfacts accompany fossils commonly assigned to early *Homo sapiens*. At both sites, the principal artifacts are small retouched flakes that defy neat typological classification (Svoboda 1987). They are accompanied by flaked pebbles, very small ones at Vértesszöllös and both small and large ones at Bilzingsleben. Some of these were probably cores, while others were almost certainly tools in their own right. Interpretation at both sites is clouded by the difficulty of distinguishing artifacts from pieces that may be naturally flaked (Cook et al. 1982), but it is still clear that typical Acheulean hand axes and other bifaces are absent. The Vértesszöllös artifacts have been assigned to the Buda Industry, while the Bilzingsleben ones fit broadly within the concept of the Tayacian Industry as defined in France (Valoch 1976).

In France, the term Tayacian (or proto-Mousterian) has been used to cover a variety of assemblages that are clearly contemporaneous with Acheulean ones but that lack bifaces and are dominated instead by flake tools, often retouched to form sidescrapers. In addition, these assemblages often contain flaked pebbles (choppers), sluglike tools known as limaces, denticulates, notches, and Tayac (or Tayacian) points (flakes on which two denticulate edges converge to a point) (Fig. 5.18).

Artifacts with abrupt, alternate retouch have sometimes been regarded as a hallmark of the Tayacian, but in many cases these were probably produced by trampling or frost heaving (Bourgon 1957), and in fact there is no distinctive artifact type or set of types that clearly characterizes the diverse Tayacian assemblages as a unit. Nonetheless, it is clear that nonbiface (Tayacian) and biface (Acheulean) assemblages coexisted in Europe—even within restricted regions such as southwestern France—during a large part of the middle Quaternary. The meaning of this has been hotly debated, and no resolution is in sight. Some believe that the nonbiface assemblages were made by entirely different people than were the biface ones (Bordes 1968; H. de Lumley 1975), while others feel that the difference may reflect differences in the raw material that was immediately available for artifact manufacture, differences in the activities the same people carried on at different sites, or some combination of these factors (Villa 1983).

Other Aspects of Behavior

Like *Homo erectus*, early *H. sapiens* occupied both caves and open-air sites. Many more cave sites are known for early *H. sapiens*, but caves themselves have a limited life span and many of those occupied by *H. erectus* probably no longer exist. Also, most of the known caves occupied by early *H. sapiens* are in southern France, where *H. erectus* may have existed only briefly, if at all.

At most early *Homo sapiens* sites where preservation conditions are appropriate, there is evidence for fire. Concentrations of burnt bones in depressions 50–60 cm across at Vértesszöllös may be the oldest such evidence in the world, apart from the hearths at Zhoukoudian Locality 1. Fossil hearths have also been identified at Bilzingsleben (Mania 1986) and in several French caves that were probably occupied by early *H. sapiens* (Villa 1976). In addition, some sites contain concentrations of artifacts, bones, and other debris that may mark places where structures once stood. The evidence is more conjectural than compelling, but noteworthy examples include (1) a scatter of artifacts and bones partly surrounded by large quartz and quartzite blocks in the lowermost archeological level at the open-air (loess) site of Ariendorf in the Rhineland in West Germany (Bosinski 1986; E. Turner 1986) and (2) bounded accumulations of cultural debris at Bilzingsleben in

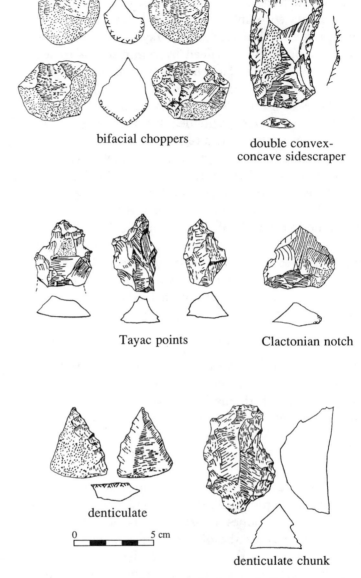

bifacial choppers

double convex-
concave sidescraper

Tayac points

Clactonian notch

denticulate

0   5 cm

denticulate chunk

Figure 5.18. Tayacian artifacts from la Caune de l'Arago, southern France (redrawn after H. de Lumley 1975: Figs. 7, 8). The term *Tayacian* has been applied to a wide range of assemblages that were broadly coeval with Acheulean ones in Europe but that lack hand axes. Among competing explanations for the difference, the most popular are (1) that some mid-Quaternary Europeans simply did not make hand axes and (2) that people who were basically hand ax makers did not leave them at some sites either because they did not need hand axes there or because there was no raw material nearby that was suitable for hand-ax manufacture. Both explanations may be valid, depending on the site or assemblage.

East Germany and in the cave of Le Lazaret in southern France, sites already noted for their human remains.

At Bilzingsleben, the ancient inhabitants camped beside a stream flowing from a nearby spring to a small lake. They also settled on parts of the streambed that were periodically dry. The evidence for structures consists of one circular and two oval concentrations of artifacts, fragmentary animal bones that probably represent food debris, and some large stones and bones that could have been used to build walls. The concentrations are 2–3 m in diameter, and each is immediately adjacent to a spread of charcoal interpreted as a fireplace. Also nearby are clusters of artifactual "waste" that may represent "workshops" (Fig. 5.19).

At Le Lazaret, the presence of a structure is suggested by an 11 × 3.5-m concentration of artifacts and broken animal bones bounded by a series of large rocks on one side and the cave wall on the other (Fig. 5.20) (H. de Lumley 1969a, 1975; H. de Lumley and Boone 1976). The area also contains two hearths, as well as numerous small marine shells and carnivore teeth that could derive from seaweed and skins introduced as bedding. Conceivably, the rocks supported poles over which skins were draped to pitch a tent against the wall of the cave. Like-aged concentrations of artifacts and other cultural debris surrounded or accompanied by natural rocks may represent structure bases in other French caves (especially La Baume Bonne and Ogrnac) (Villa 1976), but the patterning is less compelling.

Although animal bones occur at many sites, it remains unclear what proportion of them was introduced by people, especially at the open-air sites. The hunting prowess of early *Homo sapiens* thus remains unestablished, except perhaps at the cave of La Cotte de Saint-Brelade on the Channel Island of Jersey. Here, Scott (1980, 1986) has shown that the mammoths and woolly rhinoceroses in a late-middle-Quaternary deposit were subadults and prime-age adults whose death is difficult to explain unless they were driven over a headland above the site. Human butchering is implied by associated stone flakes, by damage to the bones (especially to skulls which may have been opened to obtain the brains), and by peculiar patterns of skeletal part representation—mainly skulls in one level and upper-limb bones in another, with virtually no lower-limb bones in either. The evidence is not conclusive, but it certainly suggests butchering, if not the driving of animals over the headland.

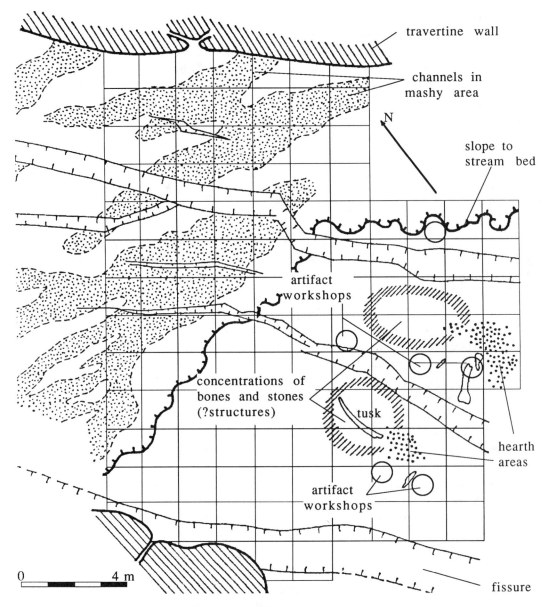

travertine wall

channels in mashy area

slope to stream bed

N

artifact workshops

concentrations of bones and stones (?structures)

tusk

hearth areas

artifact workshops

0   4 m

fissure

Figure 5.19. *Left:* Locations of bone and artifact concentrations at the mid-Quaternary site of Bilzingsleben, East Germany (adapted from Mania 1986: 244). *Right:* Close-up of the oval accumulation of stones and bones whose position is indicated to the left (adapted from Mania 1986: 245). The accumulation may mark the base of a structure in which large stones and bones were used to build walls, though the spatial patterning is less convincing than it is in many late-Quaternary "ruins." The location of a second, similar accumulation is not shown on the plan (left), because it was excavated only after the plan was drawn.

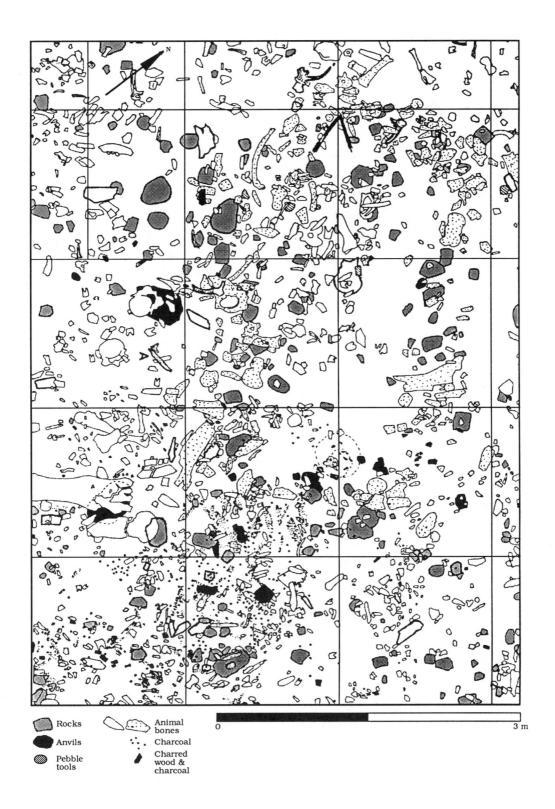

Rocks		Animal bones		
Anvils		Charcoal		
Pebble tools		Charred wood & charcoal		

0   3 m

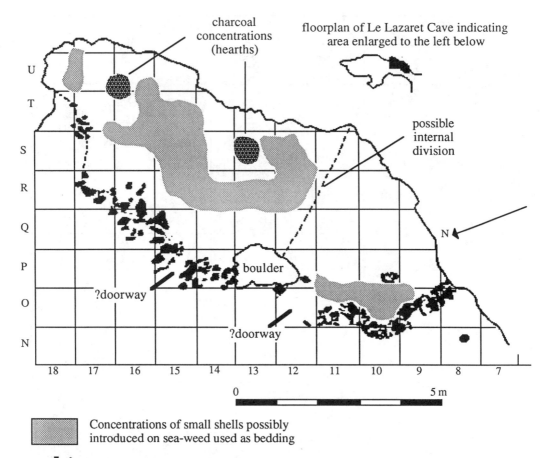

Concentrations of small shells possibly introduced on sea-weed used as bedding

large rocks possibly used as weights to support the poles of a tent pitched against the cave wall

Figure 5.20. Floor plan of an Acheulean (?Penultimate Glacial) layer at Le Lazaret Cave, southern France (adapted from H. de Lumley and Boone 1976: 639). Stone artifacts and fragmentary animal bones were heavily concentrated between the cave wall and a line of large rocks that may have supported the poles of a tent pitched against the wall. Artifacts and bones spilling out from between the rocks at two points might mark former doorways, while concentrations of small seashells could come from seaweed introduced as bedding. Two roughly circular concentrations of charcoal perhaps delineate former fireplaces (hearths).

Finally, interpersonal violence may be implied by the condition or context of some important early *Homo sapiens* fossils (Roper 1969). The Arago skull, for example, was found with the back part broken away amid fragmented animal bones, where it may have been placed after the fleshy parts or brains were eaten (H. de Lumley 1975). The main Broken Hill skull exhibits a partially healed perforation on the left temporal that could have been made by a pointed weapon (Keith 1928), though it is perhaps more consistent with a lesion produced by a particular kind of small benign tumor (Price and Molleson 1974). Alternatively, it may result from a carnivore bite, especially since the skull bears other punctures and striations that can be attributed to carnivore teeth (Tappen 1987). Several of the Ngandong (Solo) skulls bear depressed fractures or other antemortem damage (Coon 1962), and the cranial bases may have been broken away to remove the brains. Finally, the principal Bodo Skull exhibits numerous cut marks that T. D. White (1985, 1986b) convincingly attributes to deliberate defleshing.

Conclusion

Like *Homo erectus*, early *H. sapiens* is difficult to characterize in detail, mainly because there are not very many known sites or human fossils and because dating is generally problematic. Morphologically, early *H. sapiens* was distinguished from classic *H. erectus* in skull size, skull shape, or both—but not always in the same way, and the sparse evidence on hand suggests there may have been major regional differences. Thus, if the Ngandong people are assigned to early *H. sapiens* in the Far East, early *H. sapiens* there was distinguished from classic *H. erectus* mainly by a larger skull. Basic skull form remained the same. Conceivably, depending on the final dating of Zhoukoudian Locality 1 and Hexian, classic *H. erectus* even persisted in China while the Ngandong people lived in Java and after indisputable early *H. sapiens* had emerged in Africa and Europe. Europe and Africa contrast not only with the Far East but with each other. In both places, early *H. sapiens* differed from *H. erectus* not only in larger skull size but also in fundamental skull shape. However, in Europe, shape appears to have changed progressively toward that of the Neanderthals, while, in Africa, where the available fossils are more poorly dated, no trend is detectable. Additional, better-dated fossils may show, however, that African early *H. sapiens* evolved in another direction, toward anatomically modern *H. sapiens*, which, on present evidence, appeared first in Africa, certainly while the Neanderthals were still the sole inhabitants of Europe (see Chapters 6, 7).

Neither the morphological nor the archeological evidence suggests that the emergence of *Homo sapiens* was associated with any dramatic behavioral advances. On average, early *H. sapiens* populations may have made more sophisticated stone artifacts than their predecessors, at least in Africa and Europe, but the difference is subtle. They still did not make formal bone artifacts, and their stone-artifact assemblages exhibit remarkably little variability through time and space, suggesting that innovative ability remained very limited. The archeological evidence for minimal behavioral change may explain why the few known postcranial bones of early *H. sapiens* tend to resemble those of *H. erectus* in their robusticity. Like *H. erectus*, early *H. sapiens* may have required a robust postcranium to accomplish many tasks that anatomically modern *H. sapiens* performs with tools.

In sum, at present, there is no basis for arguing that the evolution of early *Homo sapiens*, as described here, was a particularly important event. Future discoveries may in fact show that it was not an event all and that what we now call early *H. sapiens* is really an amalgam of several distinct species, evolving along separate trajectories in different regions (Tattersall 1986). In this case, the (semi)taxon early *H. sapiens* will have to be discarded, and attention will be focused ever more tightly on the end products of the apparent evolutionary divergence, which are the subject of the next two chapters.

THE NEANDERTHALS AND THEIR CONTEMPORARIES

6

The Neanderthals are the most famous and best understood of all nonmodern fossil people. In their European and west Asian homelands (Fig. 6.1), they were the immediate predecessors of fully modern humans, and they were probably the last truly "primitive" human group. Historically, the term *primitive* has been applied to people whose social organization, technology, economy, and so forth were/are relatively simple, even though the reason was/is their history, not their biology. Whether by force or free will, they have repeatedly demonstrated their ability to participate fully in far more complex societies and cultures.

Many important aspects of Neanderthal behavior remain obscure, but enough is known to show that they were primitive not merely in the sense of simple or unsophisticated. The archeological record indicates that they lacked some funda-

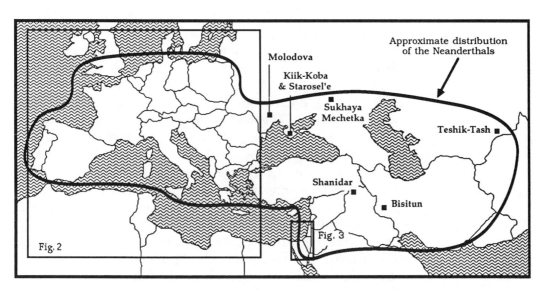

Figure 6.1. European and west Asian realm of the Neanderthals (encircled). The rectangles surround regions shown in greater detail in Figures 6.2 and 6.3.

263

mental behavioral capabilities of living people, probably because their brains were differently organized. The former existence of such truly primitive people is of course totally consistent with the concept of human evolution, but it must also be emphasized that both morphologically and temporally the Neanderthals were far removed from the earliest people, and it is only because they lived so recently and are so abundantly known that their primitiveness is so well documented. The relatively rich record also shows that they resembled living people in many important morphological and behavioral respects and that they were certainly far advanced over earlier peoples.

Because the Neanderthals were morphologically and behaviorally so similar to modern humans, it has sometimes been suggested that they were directly ancestral to living populations. However, at the same time that the Neanderthals occupied Europe and western Asia, other kinds of people lived in the Far East and Africa, and those in Africa were significantly more modern than the Neanderthals. These Africans are thus more plausible ancestors for living humans, and it appears increasingly likely that the Neanderthals were an evolutionary dead end, contributing few if any genes to historic populations. The purpose of this chapter is to summarize the archeological and fossil evidence for both the Neanderthals and their contemporaries, with particular attention to the fate of the Neanderthals and to the origins of anatomically modern humans.

History of Discovery

The discovery of the Neanderthals was important not only to paleoanthropology but to science in general, for they were the first truly fossil, nonmodern people to gain scientific and popular recognition. In essence, they provided the first real evidence for human evolution, and they were found at a time when the concept of evolution itself was still hotly debated.

Strictly considered, the first Neanderthal fossil still on record was a fragmentary child's skull found by P. C. Schmerling at Engis Cave near Liège in Belgium in 1829–30 (Oakley 1964; K. A. R. Kennedy 1975; Grayson 1983; Spencer 1984; Stringer et al. 1984). However, it did not excite great scientific interest, partly because its nonmodern morphology was not demonstrated until more than a century later (Fraipont 1936). The significance of a partial adult Neanderthal skull found in 1848 in a cave in Forbes Quarry on the Rock of Gibraltar was also not recognized for decades. As a result, most authorities trace the discovery of the Neanderthals to 1856, when quarry workers uncovered a human skullcap and some postcranial bones in the Feldhofer Cave in the Neander Valley near Düsseldorf, Germany (Fig. 6.2). In German, valley is *Tal*, then spelled *Thal*; and the kind of people represented at the site therefore came to be known as Neanderthalers—or simply Neanderthals.

The quarry workers may have inadvertently discarded parts of the original Neanderthal skeleton, along with many associated items, possibly including stone tools. Unfortunately, there is almost no record of context and associations.

Figure 6.2. Approximate locations of European Middle Paleolithic sites mentioned in the text.

The quarry owner believed the bones came from a bear, but he turned them over to a local schoolteacher, J. K. Fuhlrott, who realized that they were from an unusual human. The skullcap had large browridges, a low forehead, and bulging sidewalls (vs. the relatively parallel-sided sidewalls of modern skulls). The limb bones were thick and powerfully built. Because Fuhlrott's own expertise was limited, he transferred the bones to the well-known German anatomist, Hermann Schaaffhausen, who decided they belonged to someone from a race that occupied northern Europe before the Germans and the Celts. Although Schaaffhausen was a proponent of organic evolution, he did not explore the potential evolutionary implications of a Neanderthal race.

Darwin knew of the Neanderthal bones when he published *The Origin of Species* in 1859, but he did not mention them, and he all but avoided the touchy issue of human evolution. In 1863, in *The Geological Evidence of the Antiquity of Man*, Charles Lyell, one of the founders of modern geology, stressed the antiquity of Schmerling's Engis fossil, on the basis of the associated animal bones, and he argued, on the basis of its degree of fossilization, that the Feldhofer Neanderthal skull was probably equally old. However, at the time, Lyell was a nonevolutionist who felt that the Engis and Neanderthal fossils had no evolutionary significance. The first person to discuss this possibility at length was probably Thomas Huxley, Darwin's most eminent early supporter. In his *Evidence as to Man's Place in Nature* (1863), Huxley concluded that the Neanderthal skull represented a morphologically primitive person who was nonetheless far removed from the apes and in no sense a missing link. This is close to the opinion that virtually all paleoanthropologists hold today.

In 1864, the Irish anatomist William King suggested that the Neanderthal fossil represented an extinct human species, for which he suggested the name *Homo neanderthalensis*. Most modern specialists follow King to a degree, though they usually place the Neanderthals in an extinct variety or subspecies of *H. sapiens* rather than in a separate species. However, King himself eventually came to agree with the prominent Prussian pathologist Rudolf Virchow, who argued that the Neanderthal skull came from a modern person afflicted by disease and antemortem blows to the head.

Virchow's opinion was widely accepted, partly because it was cogently presented by an expert, partly because many people found it more comfortable than the idea of human evolution, and partly because there were few facts to contradict it. Perhaps most important, there was no evidence that the

Neanderthal skeleton was very ancient. In addition, it was an isolated discovery that could have been idiosyncratic.

In 1866, a robust human mandible, an ulna, and a metacarpal were found in the cave of Trou de la Naulette, Belgium, together with fossils of mammoth, rhinoceros, and reindeer that clearly indicated great antiquity. Unlike modern mandibles, the La Naulette specimen lacked a chin, and we know today it belonged to a Neanderthal. However, this was not obvious at the time, partly because there were no other, nonmodern mandibles to compare it with and partly because Virchow again dismissed it as pathological. He took the same position on a generally similar mandible found in 1880 in Šipka Cave in Moravia (Czechoslovakia). His opinion was first seriously challenged by the discovery of two adult skeletons in a cave near Spy, Belgium, in 1886.

The Spy skulls closely resembled the original Neanderthal one, and it seemed unlikely they shared precisely the same pathological history. Equally important, the Spy skeletons were carefully excavated, at least by the standards of the day, and they were unquestionably associated with stone tools and with the bones of mammoth, rhinoceros, reindeer, and other animals that indicated great antiquity.

The Spy skeletons essentially legitimized the Neanderthals as a kind of fossil people, and the general case for human evolution was strengthened in 1891 when Eugene Dubois found the first "*Pithecanthropus*" specimens in Java. Between 1908 and 1921, any lingering doubts about the Neanderthals were removed by the discovery of a series of relatively complete skeletons in southwestern France. These came from the caves of La Chapelle-aux-Saints, Le Moustier, La Ferrassie, and La Quina, all of which are famous today not only for their Neanderthal fossils but also for the information they contain on Neanderthal behavior.

The French sites were complemented by an equally important discovery at the Krapina Rock-shelter near Zagreb, Yugoslavia, between 1899 and 1905. Relatively systematic excavations here produced roughly eight hundred fragmentary Neanderthal bones now estimated to represent at least fourteen and perhaps many more individuals of both sexes and various ages (Wolpoff 1979; Brace 1982). The human fossils were associated with the same kind of stone artifacts found at Spy and in the French caves and also with faunal remains that demonstrated their great antiquity. The Krapina discovery significantly enlarged both the sample of Neanderthal bones and their known geographic distribution.

The pace of discovery slowed after the 1920s, partly

because many of the more promising sites had already been excavated and partly because archeologists began to adopt slower, more meticulous excavation methods. However, important discoveries continued to be made, and, in the 1930s, the demonstrable range of the Neanderthals was extended to western Asia, first (in 1931) at Tabun Cave in what is now Israel and then (in 1938) at the Teshik Tash Cave in Uzbekistan (Soviet Central Asia) (Fig. 6.1). The west Asian sample was significantly augmented at Shanidar Cave in Iraq between 1953 and 1960 and at Amud Cave (in 1961) and Kebara Cave (in 1965

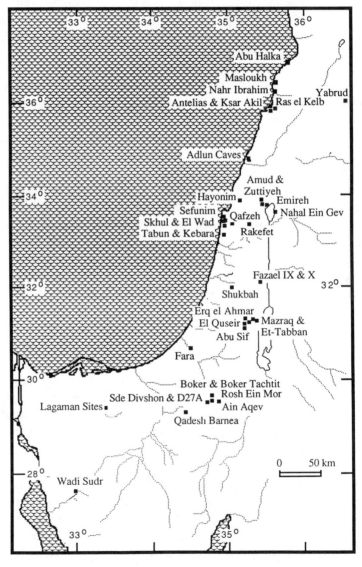

Figure 6.3. Approximate locations of the main Middle and Upper Paleolithic sites in the Levant (adapted from Bar-Yosef 1980: 108).

and 1983) in Israel (Figs. 6.1, 6.3). Among European sites providing Neanderthal fossils after 1920, perhaps the most important are Kiik-Koba ("Wild Cave") in the Crimea (1924), Subalyuk Cave in Hungary (1932), the Ehringsdorf spring site in Germany (1925, also 1908–16), the Saccopastore open-air site (1929 and 1935) and Guattari Cave (Monte Circeo) (1939) in Italy, and a series of French caves, including Régourdou (1957), Hortus (1960–64), and Saint-Césaire (La Roche à Pierrot Rock-shelter) (1979) (Fig. 6.2). Today, more than 275 individual Neanderthals are known from more than seventy sites. Most are represented by fragments, ranging from isolated teeth to partial or nearly complete skulls, but, in sharp contrast to the situation with regard to earlier people, several are represented by complete or nearly complete skeletons, recovered from the world's oldest known intentional graves.

Sometimes the term *Neanderthal* (or *neanderthaloid*) has been extended to include African and east Asian fossils. One problem with this is that the best-known African and east Asian specimens for which the term has been used (the Broken Hill and Ngandong skulls) are almost certainly older than the Neanderthals. More important, the large browridges, low frontal, low position of maximum cranial breadth, and other features that the so-called African and east Asian Neanderthals share with the indisputable European and west Asian ones characterize virtually all nonmodern skulls of the genus *Homo*. At the same time, the African and east Asian skulls generally lack a cluster of traits that tend to be unique to the European and west Asian Neanderthals (Santa Luca 1978; Stringer et al. 1984; Trinkaus 1986.) These traits include the subspheroid form of the skull when viewed from behind, the bunlike form of the occipital bone when viewed from the side, the extraordinary projection of the midfacial region, distinctly double-arched browridges, a suprainiac fossa, a large juxta-(= occipito-)mastoid crest, and other characters that are listed below.

Although much remains to be learned about the African and east Asian contemporaries of the European/west Asian Neanderthals, it is increasingly clear today that they were morphologically different, and calling them Neanderthals only obfuscates their evolutionary significance. They will be discussed here under the heading of "Neanderthal contemporaries."

Geologic Antiquity

In every instance when Neanderthal fossils have been dated by radiocarbon analysis of reliable material, especially charcoal, the dates have been at or clearly beyond the 30,000–40,000-year-ago limit of conventional radiocarbon dating. The same is true for dates on reliable material accompanying the kinds of (Middle Paleolithic = Mousterian) artifacts that Neanderthals are known to have made. It is therefore clear that, as a group, the Neanderthals antedate 30,000 years ago. The youngest known Neanderthal fossil is probably the one from Saint-Césaire, southwestern France (Vandermeersch 1984). This has not been dated radiometrically, but the associated pollens, supported by the associated (Chatelperronian) artifacts, imply it is roughly 34,000–35,000 years old (Arl. Leroi-Gourhan 1984). Some apparent Neanderthal teeth associated with Chatelperronian artifacts at Arcy-sur-Cure (Grotte du Renne), north-central France, are probably about the same age (André Leroi-Gourhan 1959; Leroyer and Leroi-Gourhan 1983). In other regions, especially the Near East (southwestern Asia), the latest Neanderthals may be significantly older perhaps in the vicinity of 50,000 years (Farrand 1979, 1982; Jelinek 1982a; Trinkaus 1983b). It is to be hoped that radiocarbon dating by accelerator-mass spectrometry or thermoluminescence dating of burnt flints soon will permit reliable verification.

The geologic age of the oldest Neanderthals is partly a matter of definition. For example, the partial skull from Biache-Saint-Vaast (northern France), discussed in the last chapter, is relatively small but, in the parts that are preserved, is otherwise not significantly different from typical Neanderthal skulls. The Biache individual could reasonably be included among the Neanderthals but is more commonly regarded as a Neanderthal ancestor. If it were included among the Neanderthals, their antiquity would clearly extend back to the Glaciation-before-Last, to perhaps 190,000 years ago.

Excluding Biache and some other, late-middle Quaternary "ante-Neanderthals," the oldest specimens commonly assigned to the Neanderthals sensu stricto are probably those from Ehringsdorf in East Germany and Saccopastore in Italy. At Ehringsdorf, cranial fragments, mandibles, and some postcranial bones from perhaps nine people occur in a calcareous spring deposit (travertine) with plant and animal remains that imply a Last Interglacial Age (= isotope stage 5e, between roughly 130,000 and 115,000 years ago) (Cook et al. 1982). However, a series of widely divergent and stratigraphically inconsistent uranium-series (U-S) dates on travertine hint at a somewhat older age, perhaps during the Interglaciation-before-Last (= isotope stage 7, between roughly 245,000 and 190,000 years ago) (Blackwell and Schwarcz 1986). If the older date is correct, then Ehringsdorf would join Biache as an ante-Neanderthal site. At Saccopastore, two Neanderthal crania were found in fluvial deposits whose stratigraphic position and floral and faunal contents suggest a Last Interglacial age (Stringer et al. 1984).

The abundant Neanderthal remains from Krapina in Yugoslavia may also belong to the Last Interglaciation, since the associated fauna indicates a relatively mild climate. However, a warmer episode within the early part of the Last Glaciation is also possible (F. H. Smith 1982, 1984). On the basis of stratigraphic position and faunal and floral associations, all other important European Neanderthals are generally assigned to the earlier part of the Last Glaciation, between 74,000 and 50,000–35,000 years ago. However, some may belong to the colder phases of the Last Interglaciation, namely to oxygen-isotope stages 5d and 5b of the global marine record, centering on 109,000 and 92,000 years ago, respectively. These stages probably comprise some of the climatic events commonly attributed to the early part of the Last Glaciation in western Europe (for example, to the "Würm I" in France) (Butzer 1981; Dennell 1983).

The oldest known Neanderthal fossils in western Asia probably date from the earlier part of the Last Glaciation, though the separation of Last Glacial and Last Interglacial deposits is generally more difficult in western Asia than in Europe (Farrand 1979). The best candidates for Last Interglacial Neanderthal fossils in western Asia are a fronto-facial fragment from Zuttiyeh Cave and a femoral shaft from Tabun Cave, both in Israel. The Zuttiyeh fragment exhibits less midfacial prognathism than is typical for the Neanderthals, and its taxonomic assignment is controversial. Vandermeersch (1982) thinks it could represent a population ancestral to robust, early anatomically modern people such as those from Skhul and Qafzeh Caves, also in Israel. However, on the basis of similarities to undoubted Neanderthals from Shanidar Cave in Iraq, Trinkaus (1982, 1983b) believes it comes from an early Neanderthal.

In sum, the Neanderthals date from the earlier part of the late Quaternary, between roughly 130,000 and 50,000–35,000 years ago, the exact terminal date probably depending on the place. It is always important to stress that this relatively limited time span is associated with a relatively limited geographic range, including only Europe and western Asia.

Morphology

Morphologically, the Neanderthals are a remarkably coherent group, and, relative to most earlier human types, they are easy to characterize because they are represented by relatively abundant fossils from virtually all parts of the skeleton. The following description is based on ones by Howell (1951, 1957), Coon (1962), Le Gros Clark (1964), Howells (1973b), Santa Luca (1978), Trinkaus and Howells (1979), Trinkaus (1983a, 1983b, 1984b, 1986), F. H. Smith (1984), and Stringer et al. (1984). It should be read in conjunction with Figures 6.4–6.14, which illustrate some particularly characteristic Neanderthal features.

Braincase

Long and relatively low but not especially thick walled; globular (subspheroid or oval) when viewed from behind, with maximum breadth at the midparietal level; large endocranial capacity, with a range from 1,245 to 1,740 cc and an average around 1,520 cc (Holloway 1981b, 1985) (this compares with an average of about 1,560 cc in the earliest anatomically modern people and of about 1,400 cc in living people); frontal low and receding, with a continuous supraorbital torus (browridge) generally forming a double arch above the orbits, and usually separated from the frontal scale (or squama) by a sulcus or gutter; frontal sinuses generally large and restricted to the torus; occipital squama usually extended backward to form a distinct bun (or chignon), associated with flattening in the region of lambda; prominent, nearly horizontal transverse occipital torus, surmounted by a conspicuous elliptical depression (the suprainiac fossa or depression) generally surrounded by a triangular, uplifted area of bone; mastoid process usually small, with a pronounced mound or bump of bone (the mastoid crest or tuberosity) behind the auditory aperture; ventral to the mastoid process, an equally large or larger mound or ridge of bone (the juxtamastoid crest) bounded by distinct depressions; skull base flatter (less flexed) between the hard palate and the foramen magnum than that in modern people (Laitman et al. 1979).

Face

Long and forwardly protruding (prognathous), especially along the midline; nasal aperture and cavity generally very large; zygomatic arches receding (rather than angled as in modern

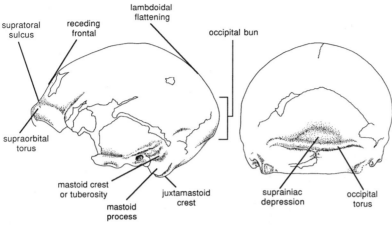

La Ferrassie 1 (Neanderthal)

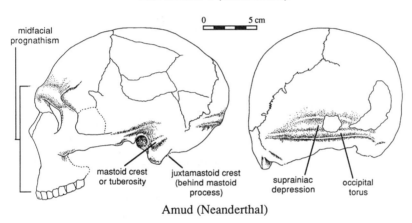

Amud (Neanderthal)

Figure 6.4. Neanderthal skulls from La Ferrassie in France and Amud in Israel, showing some of the key features that characterize Neanderthals as a group (redrawn after Santa Luca 1978: 622, 625). Among the distinctive Neanderthal features illustrated are the extraordinary forward projection of the face along the midline (midfacial prognathism); the well-developed mastoid crest or bump behind the auditory aperture; the large juxtamastoid crest, equaling or exceeding the mastoid process in length; the suprainiac depression or fossa above the occipital torus; and the globular shape of the skull when viewed from behind.

people); maxillary bone inflated above the canine teeth (no canine fossa); orbits large and rounded; chin (= forward protrusion of the mental symphysis) variably developed but usually absent.

Dentition

Cheek teeth smaller than in earlier people and overlapping those of early, robust modern people (*Homo sapiens sapiens*) in size; incisors as large as or larger than those of earlier people and significantly larger than those of modern people, usually shovel shaped (Fig. 6.8), and often exhibiting peculiar, rounded wear on the labial (lip) surface in older individuals (Fig. 6.9); cheek teeth usually less worn than incisors and canines (in contrast to most modern humans, whose anterior and posterior teeth tend to be about equally worn); root fusion with enlargement of the pulp cavity (taurodontism) common in the cheek teeth (Fig. 6.10); a readily discernible gap (retromolar space)

Figure 6.5. One of the Neanderthal skulls from Spy in Belgium, compared with a generally contemporaneous non-Neanderthal skull from Jebel Irhoud, Morocco (redrawn after Santa Luca 1978: 624, 627). The Irhoud skull has sometimes been labeled Neanderthal, but it differs from typical Neanderthal skulls in several key features, including its shorter and flatter face, its more parallel-sided (less globular) braincase, and its lack of a suprainiac fossa or depression. In most of these features, it anticipates anatomically modern people, near whose ancestry it may lie.

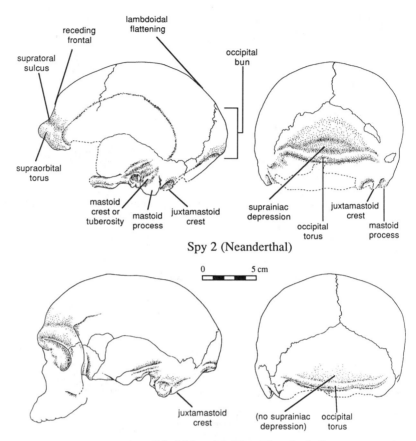

Spy 2 (Neanderthal)

Jebel Irhoud 1 (Non-Neanderthal)

between the posterior wall of the lower third molar and the anterior margin of the ascending ramus, reflecting the forward placement of the jaws; mandibular foramen usually horizontal-oval.

Postcranium

Cervical vertebrae with long, horizontal, robust spines at or beyond the range of modern human variation; ribs extraordinarily thick and curved to encircle a barrel-like chest cavity; muscle- and ligament-attachment areas extremely large and well developed on bones of the arms, legs, hands, and feet; shafts of the femur and radius usually somewhat bowed (Fig. 6.11); distal limb segments (forearm and lower leg) relatively short; scapula relatively broad, commonly with a deep groove or sulcus on the outer edge of the dorsal surface (vs. the shallower one common on the ventral or rib surface in modern people) (Fig. 6.12) (Stewart 1962); distal phalanx of the thumb (pollex) roughly as long as the proximal one (unlike the situation in modern people, in whom the distal phalanx is usually about one-third shorter than the proximal one); tips (apical tufts) of the hand (manual) phalanges large and round (vs. narrower, hemiamygdaloid-shaped tips in modern people) (Fig. 6.13).

Large femoral and tibial epiphyses with robust, cortically thick shafts (diaphyses); femoral shaft round, without the longitudinal bony ridge (pilaster) found on the dorsal surface of modern femoral shafts (Fig 6.11); shafts of the proximal phalanges of the foot expanded mediolaterally; pelvis less massive than in mid-Quaternary hominids and with the same sexual dimorphism seen in the greater sciatic notch of modern humans (Trinkaus 1984a), but with the pubic bone noticeably lengthened and thinned compared with that of modern people (Stewart 1960); average stature, estimated from long bone lengths, about 166 cm (5' 4") (this compares with an average of approximately 178 cm [5' 8"] in the earliest anatomically modern people [Trinkaus 1983a].)

Overall, the Neanderthals were extremely robust, heavily muscled, barrel-chested people with large, long, relatively low, globelike skulls and large, long, prognathic faces. In the first detailed studies, the vertebrate paleontologist Boule (1911–13) and some other prominent investigators concluded that the Neanderthals were apelike in posture, foot structure, and other important features. However, it is now clear that they were indistinguishable from modern people in these characters and, more generally, in the basic structure and function of their limbs and muscles. The postcranial differences between the Neanderthals and modern people relate almost entirely to the Neanderthals' extraordinary robusticity (muscularity). They were in fact only slightly less robust than their mid-Quaternary predecessors.

Morphologically, the Neanderthals can be distinguished from all other people, fossil or living, primarily in the skull and face. The face was particularly striking for the forward projection of the central browridge, the large nose, and the dentition—in short, for its prognathism along the midline, from which both the orbits and cheeks swept backward. Even when the craniofacial differences are considered, however, the Neanderthals differed from anatomically modern people only about as much as do two subspecies in some living mammal species. Consequently, today, the Neanderthals and modern people are commonly separated only at the subspecies level, as

Figure 6.6. Neanderthal skull from La Quina in France, compared with the non-Neanderthal skull from Broken Hill (Kabwe), Zambria (redrawn after Santa Luca 1978: 623, 626). The Broken Hill skull has sometimes been identified as an African Neanderthal, but it lacks such characteristic Neanderthal features as the suprainiac depression and the globular shape in rear view (it is more angular from behind and has its maximum breadth nearer the cranial base). It also antedates the Neanderthals by a substantial interval and is now widely regarded as a representative of mid-Quaternary African *Homo sapiens*, as discussed in Chapter 5.

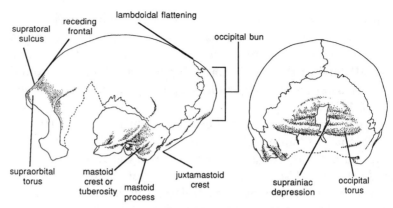

La Quina 5 (Neanderthal)

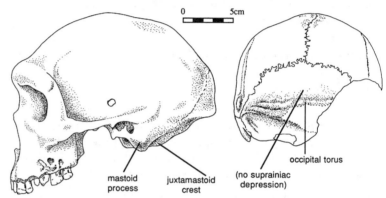

Broken Hill (Kabwe) (Non-Neanderthal)

Homo sapiens neanderthalensis and *H. sapiens sapiens*, respectively.

Trinkaus (1986, 1987a and in press) has succinctly summarized the functional implications of Neanderthal morphology. The large, well-developed muscle and ligament markings on the bones of the limbs and extremities indicate exceptional muscular strength (muscular hypertrophy), which probably accounts for the bowing of the radius and femur. The proportions and morphology of the hand bones imply an extraordinarily powerful grip, especially as exercised by the thumb when opposed to the other fingers. The overall morphology of the scapula reflects the power of the upper-arm muscles that attached to it; hypertrophic development of some of these muscles would have destabilized the arm during throwing or striking if another muscle had not shifted its attachment on the scapula, producing the groove on the outer border of the dorsal face (Trinkaus 1983a). The cortical thickness of the leg bones reflects an ability to endure long periods of intensive use. The mediolaterally expanded shafts of the pedal phalanges were probably an adaptation for prolonged movement over irregular terrain.

The relative shortness of the forearm and lower leg (and of the limbs in general) may have been an adaptation to the cold climates that many Neanderthals faced (Trinkaus 1981, 1983a). This would be consistent with Allen's Rule or generalization that, all other things equal, mammals living in colder climates should have shorter limbs because these reduce heat

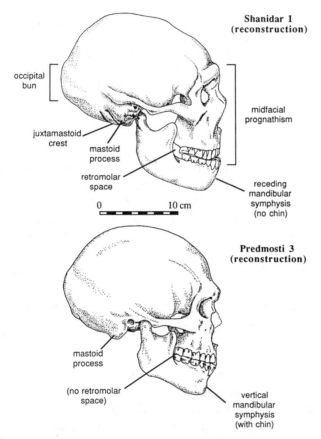

Figure 6.7. Reconstructed skulls of individual 1 from the Mousterian levels of Shanidar Cave, Iraq, and of individual #3 from the early Upper Paleolithic site of Předmostí, Czechoslovakia (drawn by K. Cruz-Uribe from photographs and casts). The Shanidar skull is from a typical Neanderthal, while the Předmostí one comes from a robust, early anatomically modern European. Like other Neanderthal skulls, the one from Shanidar differs from modern skulls in its relatively longer, lower braincase and long, forwardly projecting face, as well as in more detailed features, such as its large juxtamastoid crest. The striking protrusion of the Shanidar face is perhaps most obvious in the forward placement of the nose and front teeth relative to the orbits. The far forward placement of the jaws accounts for the retromolar space.

Krapina tooth set K, lingual view

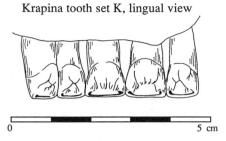

0   5 cm

Figure 6.8. Left upper canine and all four upper incisors of tooth set K from Krapina, Yugoslavia, viewed from the lingual (inside) surface (drawn by K. Cruz-Uribe from a photograph in Wolpoff 1980: 274). The lateral edges of the canine and incisor crowns are curled backward and inward to produce the shovel-shaping that characterizes Neanderthal front teeth in general and the upper front teeth in particular. Shoveling is also common in *Homo erectus* and in some modern populations, especially in some east Asians and Native Americans. It increases the occlusal surface of the front teeth, which may have been particularly significant in the case of the Neanderthals, who used these teeth as tools.

loss from the body core. In modern human populations, there is a clear tendency for the relative lengths of the forearm and lower leg to decrease as mean temperature decreases. (In technical terms, the decrease is in the radius/humerus [= brachial] and the tibia/femur [= crural] ratios or indices.) However, the hypothesis that Neanderthal limb proportions reflect thermal adaptation is problematic, partly because the west Asian Neanderthals who did not experience extreme cold show nearly the same limb proportions as European ones who did, and it is possible that short distal limb segments in Neanderthals relate more to general limb robusticity and muscularity than to climate.

The longer, thinner pubis of the Neanderthal pelvis could indicate that the average diameter of the birth canal (pelvic inlet or aperture) was significantly greater in Neanderthals than in modern people. Among living people, birth-canal size tends to be largest in populations with the largest head size relative to stature, implying that a large Neanderthal birth canal could be simply a structural reflection of their very large heads and very short stature (Rosenberg 1985, 1986; Wolpoff, in press-b). Alternatively, it could indicate that in utero brain growth was faster in Neanderthals than in modern people (Dean et al. 1986) or that the Neanderthal gestation period was longer (Trinkaus 1983a, 1984a, 1984b).

The hypothesis of a longer gestation period is particularly intriguing for its evolutionary implications. It would have meant greater neuromuscular development at birth and a better-developed immune system, but it would also have kept the neonate from exposure to environmental stimuli during an earlier period of rapid brain growth. In addition, it would probably have forced greater spacing between births, reducing the potential for population growth. It might thus have placed the Neanderthals at a selective disadvantage, compared with modern humans. However, the idea of a longer gestation period is controversial, not only because there are alternative explanations for a larger Neanderthal birth canal but also because it is not clear that the birth canal was really larger. The inlet diameter of the most complete Neanderthal pelvis, from Kebara Cave in Israel, is not significantly greater than that in modern people (Fig. 6.14), though the pubis is typically long and thin as in other Neanderthals (Rak and Arensburg 1987). The implication is that the structural differences between Neanderthal and modern pelvises may be due more to slight differences in habitual posture and locomotion than to differences in reproduction.

The long, low shape of the Neanderthal cranium with its typically large occipital bun probably reflects relatively slow postnatal brain growth relative to cranial vault growth (Trinkaus and LeMay 1982). Slower brain growth could have been tied to slower and ultimately more limited intellectual growth and development. The large overall size of the Neanderthal brain is the culmination of a tendency toward increasing brain size throughout the course of human evolution, and

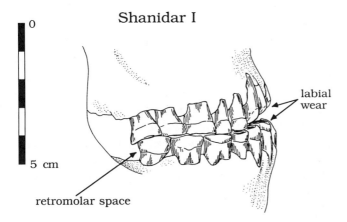

Figure 6.9. Enlarged view of the dentition of Shanidar skull 1, showing the retromolar space and the rounded wear on the labial surface of the incisors that are characteristic features of the Neanderthals (drawn by K. Cruz-Uribe from a photograph). The retromolar space reflects the far forward position of the dental rows, while the wear on the incisors probably resulted from their habitual use for nondietary clamping or gripping.

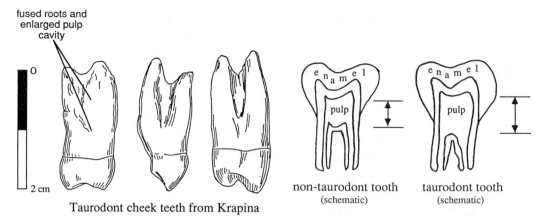

fused roots and
enlarged pulp
cavity

0

2 cm

Taurodont cheek teeth from Krapina

non-taurodont tooth
(schematic)

taurodont tooth
(schematic)

Figure 6.10. *Left:* Upper cheek teeth from Krapina, Yugoslavia, showing the fused roots and enlarged pulp cavity (taurodontism) that is a common feature of the Neanderthals (drawn by K. Cruz-Uribe from a slide). *Right:* schematic cross sections to show the difference between nontaurodont and taurodont teeth in the size of the pulp cavity.

it almost certainly means that the Neanderthals were more intelligent than any of their smaller-brained antecedents. It is more difficult to explain the large average size of the Neanderthal brain relative to modern brains, but this may simply reflect the greater metabolic efficiency of larger brains in colder climates, the larger amount of lean body mass (striated muscle) in Neanderthals, or both (Holloway 1985). Among living people, the largest average brain size, actually about equal to that in Neanderthals, occurs in Eskimos, who live in very cold conditions and who also tend to possess a large quantity of lean body mass.

The structure of the Neanderthal brain cannot be examined directly, but Neanderthal endocranial casts fall generally within the modern range of variation and show the same pattern of asymmetries (petalias) that modern brains do (Holloway 1981b, 1985). Thus, the left occipital lobe tended to be larger than the right, while the right frontal lobe was larger than the left. By analogy with living people, this particular asymmetry implies that the Neanderthals were usually right-handed. Other behavioral inferences are more speculative, and the endocranial casts do not point clearly to behavioral differences, though some average differences in frontal lobe surface morphology and in parietal lobe proportions may be behaviorally significant. One crucial question that is not yet answerable on the basis of the endocranial casts concerns Neanderthal language ability. However, the relatively flat (nonflexed) cranial base suggests that Neanderthals could not make the full range of sounds that modern people can, which possibly limited their ability to communicate orally (Laitman et al. 1979).

The full functional interpretation of Neanderthal facial structure is a matter of ongoing debate (Rak 1986, Trinkaus 1987b), but there are some points of broad agreement. The forward placement of Neanderthal jaws and the large size of the incisors probably reflect habitual use of the anterior dentition as a tool, perhaps mostly as a clamp or vise. Such para- or nonmasticatory use for gripping is implied by the high frequency of enamel chipping and microfractures on Neanderthal incisors (Wolpoff et al. 1981; F. H. Smith 1983; Trinkaus 1983b), by nondietary microscopic striations on incisor crowns (Brace et al. 1981; F. H. Smith 1983), and by the peculiar, rounded wear seen on the incisors of elderly individuals (Fig. 6.9) (Heim 1976). Similar, though less extensive damage occurs on the teeth of Eskimos, who also tend to use their anterior jaws extensively as clamps (Brace et al. 1981).

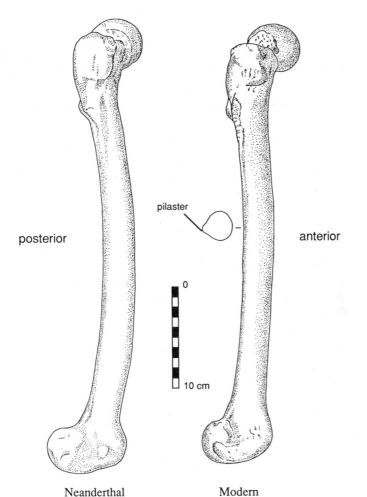

posterior

pilaster

anterior

0

10 cm

Neanderthal

Modern

Figure 6.11. Right femora of a Neanderthal and of a modern person, illustrating the much greater anterior-posterior bowing of the shaft that is characteristic of the Neanderthals (redrawn after Boule and Vallois 1957: 236). The difference probably reflects their extraordinary muscular strength (muscular hypertrophy). Unlike modern femora, Neanderthal ones also have shafts with a rounded cross section, lacking a bony ridge (pilaster) on the posterior surface.

Figure 6.12. Variation in the axillary (lateral) border of the scapula in *Homo sapiens* (redrawn after Trinkaus 1983a: 171). In distinction from modern people, in which a ventral sulcus is the norm, Neanderthals tend to exhibit a dorsal sulcus. The difference probably reflects the greater power of Neanderthal upper-arm muscles. The earliest anatomically modern humans and some living athletes exhibit a composite or bisulcate pattern.

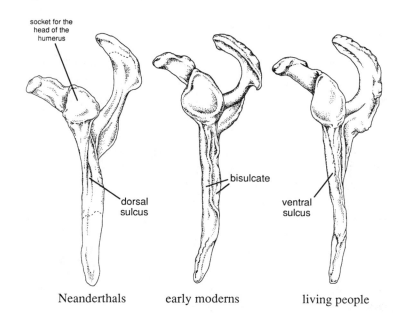

socket for the head of the humerus

dorsal sulcus

bisulcate

ventral sulcus

Neanderthals   early moderns   living people

Biomechanically, the forces exerted by persistent, habitual, nonmasticatory use of the front teeth (= "massive anterior dental loading") could account in whole or in part for such well-known Neanderthal features as the long face, the well-developed supraorbital torus, and even the long, low shape of the cranium (F. H. Smith 1983). Massive anterior dental loading could further explain the unique Neanderthal occipitomastoid region which perhaps provided the insertions for muscles that stabilized the mandible and head during dental clamping (Trinkaus 1986).

Finally, the large Neanderthal nose, located far in front of the brain, may have functioned to warm cold air before it reached the lungs (Coon 1962). However, like relatively short distal limb segments, these large, forwardly placed noses characterized not only European Neanderthals, who were exposed to extreme cold, but also western Asian Neanderthals, who were not. It is in fact possible that large Neanderthal noses served not so much to warm incoming air as to dissipate body heat during frequent periods of heightened activity (Trinkaus 1987a).

The Origin of the Neanderthals

As discussed in the last chapter, it appears likely that the Neanderthals evolved in Europe from local, mid-Quaternary populations of more archaic *Homo sapiens* (Stringer 1985; Vandermeersch 1985). On morphological grounds, the mid-

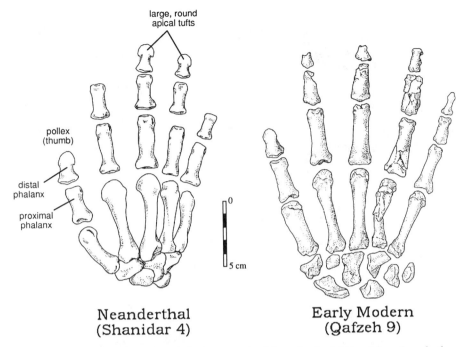

Figure 6.13. Partially restored hand skeletons of a Neanderthal (Shanidar 4) and of a very-early-modern human (Qafzeh 9). Neanderthal hands differed from modern ones in several respects, including larger, rounder apical tufts on the distal (terminal) phalanges and a relatively long distal phalanx on the thumb (Shanidar hand drawn after a photograph in Trinkaus 1983b: 260; Qafzeh hand redrawn after Vandermeersch 1981: 226).

Quaternary *H. sapiens* fossils can be divided into (1) a presumed earlier group comprising the specimens from Petralona, Vertésszöllös, Mauer, Bilzingsleben, Arago, and Atapuerca, all of which tend to lack specific Neanderthal features and to resemble classic *H. erectus* in basic morphology, and (2) a later group from Steinheim, Swanscombe, Montmaurin, La Chaise, and Biache, all of which share one or more unique, derived features with the Neanderthals. The samples are small, but it nonetheless seems reasonable to hypothesize an evolutionary sequence from the earlier group to the later one to the Neanderthals. Perhaps the main difficulty with this hypothesis is the uncertain dating of several crucial mid-Quaternary specimens, above all those from Petralona, Arago, and Bilzingsleben, which may be younger than some of their supposed descendants. Small sample size and dating problems aside, however, some of the European mid-Quaternary fossils clearly anticipate the Neanderthals, while like-aged African and Asian ones do not. Clearly, the implication is that the Neanderthals were an indigenous European development.

It remains uncertain whether western Asia shared in the

284   *Chapter Six*

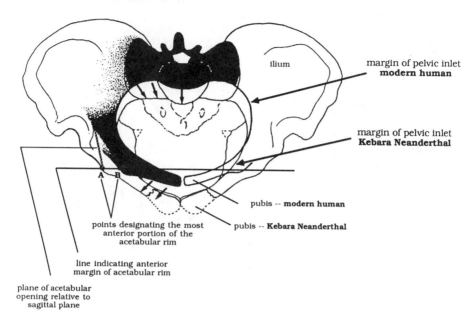

margin of pelvic inlet
modern human

ilium

margin of pelvic inlet
Kebara Neanderthal

pubis -- **modern human**

pubis -- **Kebara Neanderthal**

points designating the most
anterior portion of the
acetabular rim

line indicating anterior
margin of acetabular rim

plane of acetabular
opening relative to
sagittal plane

Figure 6.14. Superior view of the reconstructed Neanderthal pelvis from Kebara Cave, Israel (redrawn after Rak and Arensburg 1987: 230). Like other, more fragmentary Neanderthal examples, the Kebara pelvis shows a distinctive lengthening of the pubis compared with the condition in modern people. However, in spite of this, its pelvic inlet (= birth canal) was about the same size as in a modern person. If it is assumed that other Neanderthal pelvises would have similar-sized inlets if they were complete enough to measure, the most parsimonious explanation of their pubic lengthening is probably minor differences in locomotion and posture between Neanderthals and modern people, rather than differences in gestation period or other obstetrical factors.

evolution of the Neanderthals or whether they spread there from Europe. The Last Interglacial cranial fragment from Zuttiyeh Cave in Israel may bear on this issue, depending on whether it represents an early Neanderthal (Trinkaus 1982, 1983b) or a less specialized form of *Homo sapiens* (Vandermeersch 1982). In the latter case, the Zuttiyeh fossil might imply that the Neanderthals only arrived in western Asia at or near the beginning of the Last Glaciation and displaced a previous, non-Neanderthal population.

The Contemporaries of the Neanderthals

During the earlier part of the late Quaternary (between approximately 130,000 and 50,000–35,000 years ago) when the Neanderthals occupied Europe and western Asia, people had not yet colonized the northeasternmost parts of Europe and northern Asia (Siberia), but they were living nearly throughout Africa and in eastern Asia, from roughly the southern border of the Soviet Union southward. Archeology shows this, especially in

Africa, but so far very few early-late-Quaternary human fossils have been found in either Africa or eastern Asia. Part of the reason is that archeology began relatively late in both places and that even today many fewer archeologists work in either place than in Europe. In addition, Europe is especially rich in limestone caves that are favorable for bone preservation, while many African caves occur in noncalcareous rock types where bones are rapidly destroyed by acid ground waters.

It is also pertinent that the Neanderthals are well known partly because they buried some of their dead in rock-shelters and caves. Under ground, the bodies were protected from destruction by hyenas and other carnivores. During the Last Glaciation in Europe, frost fracturing (alternate daytime thawing and nighttime freezing of moisture trapped in the cracks of cave walls and ceilings) broke off particles that rapidly accumulated as friable deposit on the floors below, making it relatively easy for the Neanderthals to dig graves. We do not know whether their African and east Asian contemporaries also dug graves, but, if they did these were probably often very shallow, because cave-floor deposits were thinner in the absence of frost fracturing. It is thus possible that carnivores found it easier to exhume and eat the bodies, leaving nothing or only a few scraps of human bone.

The east Asian contemporaries of the Neanderthals may be represented by the poorly dated Maba, Dali, and Xujiayao fossils from China (Wu and Wu 1985), discussed in the last chapter. In each case, associated animal fossils suggest a late-middle-Quaternary or early-late-Quaternary age. However, even if these people were contemporaneous with the ante- or pre-Neanderthals of Europe rather than with the Neanderthals proper, they still indicate a different evolutionary trend in east Asia. The most complete specimen, the Dali skull, has large browridges but lacks an occipital bun and has a flat, nonprognathous face with a canine fossa. This suggests that the east Asian contemporaries of the Neanderthals did not develop the latters' peculiar craniofacial specializations, but the contrasting east Asian morphology and its evolutionary implications are difficult to assess, given the small, poorly dated fossil sample.

In Africa (Figs. 6.15, 6.16), human fossils that probably or certainly date from the same (early-late-Quaternary) time interval as do the Neanderthals have been found at Mugharet el 'Aliya (a maxillary fragment and an isolated tooth), Jebel Irhoud Cave (a nearly complete skull, a skullcap, a partial mandible, and an upper-limb bone), Dar es Soltan Cave 2 (a partial adult skull, a child's skull, two partial mandibles, and

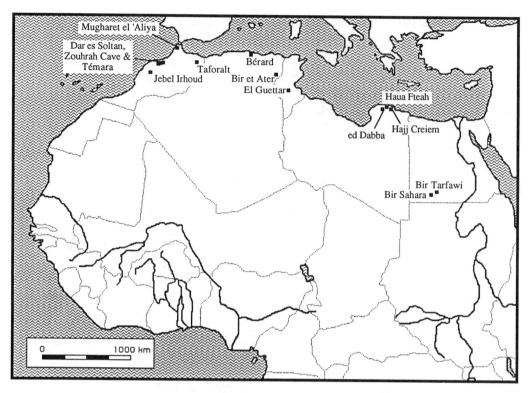

Figure 6.15. Approximate locations of the north African archeological and fossil sites mentioned in the text.

isolated teeth), Zouhrah Cave (a mandible and an isolated canine tooth), and Smugglers' Cave (Témara) (a mandible and an occipito-parietal fragment), all in Morocco (Debénath 1980, Debénath et al. 1982, 1986); the Haua Fteah ("Great Cave") in Libya (two partial mandibles) (McBurney 1967; Tobias 1967b); Singa in the Sudan (a skull) (Stringer 1979); Diré-Dawa (Porc-Épic) (a partial mandible) and Omo-Kibish (two relatively complete skulls and fragments of a third) in Ethiopia (Vallois 1951; Day and Stringer 1982); Eliye Springs, West Turkana, in Kenya (a skull) (Bräuer and Leakey 1986); Laetoli (= Ngaloba) (a skull) and Mumba Sheltcr (isolated teeth) in Tanzania (Day et al. 1980; Bräuer 1984b; Bräuer and Mehlman 1988); and Equus Cave (a partial mandible and isolated teeth), Florisbad (facial, frontal, and parietal fragments of a single skull), Border Cave (an infant's skeleton, an adult skull, two partial adult mandibles, and some postcranial bones), Die Kelders Cave (isolated teeth), and Klasies River Mouth (five partial mandibles, a maxilla, various small cranial fragments, isolated teeth, and postcranial bones) in South Africa (Singer and Wymer 1982; Bräuer 1984b; Rightmire 1984b, 1987; Grine and Klein 1985; H. J. Deacon et al. 1986; H. J. Deacon, in press). It is possible that Kanjera in Kenya (fragments of five skulls) should be added to this list, but it is now known that the Kanjera fossils, which are anatomically modern, are intrusive into middle-Quaternary deposits (M. D. Leakey 1977) and may date from almost any time afterward. Given their highly suspect provenience, they should probably be eliminated from discussions of human evolution, until they can be directly dated.

At the Haua Fteah, Omo-Kibish, Florisbad, Border Cave, and Klasies River Mouth, radiocarbon dates indicate the human fossils are all well beyond the 30,000–40,000-year limit of conventional radiocarbon dating. At Florisbad, the fragmentary

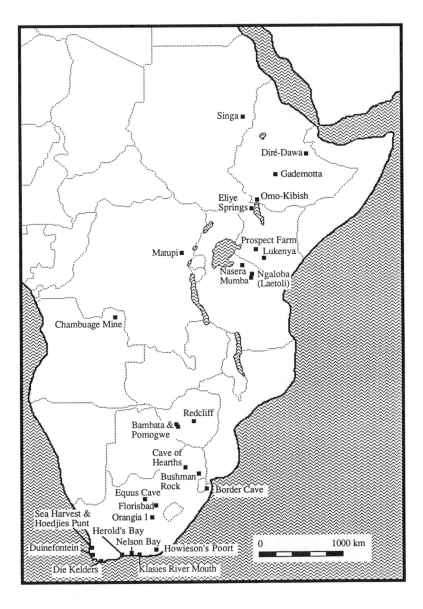

Figure 6.16. Approximate locations of the southern and eastern African archeological and fossil sites mentioned in the text.

skull may actually date from the late middle Quaternary, given the associated fauna and especially the geomorphic position of the spring deposits in which the skull was found (Butzer 1984; Kuman and Clarke 1986). A late-middle-Quaternary age has also been proposed for the Border Cave fossils, on the basis of tentative correlation between the climatic sequence reflected in the Border Cave profile and the dated sequence of the global marine record (Butzer et al. 1978). However, the (Middle Stone Age [MSA]) artifacts associated with the Border Cave fossils closely resemble ones from the Klasies River Mouth that are firmly dated to the Last Interglaciation by a combination of geologic and paleontologic data (Beaumont 1980; Singer and Wymer 1982). At Die Kelders Cave, geologic context and the associated artifacts imply the human teeth belong to the early Last Glaciation (Tankard and Schweitzer 1976). An early–Last Glacial date is also tentatively suggested by the fauna associated with the human fossils from Equus Cave (Grine and Klein 1985).

At Laetoli, mineralogic similarity between a volcanic tuff in the Ngaloba Beds and one in the Lower Ndutu Beds at nearby Olduvai Gorge indicates that the Ngaloba (Laetoli 18) skull is about 120,000 ± 30,000 years old (M. D. Leakey and Hay 1982; Magori and Day 1983). This estimate is supported by U-S dates and is consistent with the associated fauna and artifacts. U-S dates suggest very similar (ca. 130,000-year-old) ages for the Mumba Shelter teeth (Bräuer 1984b; Bräuer and Mehlman 1988) and the principal Omo-Kibish skulls (Butzer et al. 1969), again in keeping with the associated artifacts and fauna. For the Singa skull an inexact, earlier-late-Quaternary age is implied by the associated fauna (Bate 1951), and for the poorly preserved Diré Dawa mandible this age is implied by the associated MSA artifacts (J. D. Clark 1982). The Eliye Springs skull lacks context and associations, and it is only its morphology that suggests it belongs to the same earlier-late-Quaternary interval as the other fossils considered here.

The context in which the more complete Jebel Irhoud skull was found is unclear, but the less complete one and the mandible were associated with (Mousterian) artifacts that imply an earlier-late-Quaternary age (Ennouchi 1968, 1969). The human fossils from el 'Aliya, Dar es Soltan 2, Zouhrah Cave, and Smugglers' Cave were all associated with (Aterian) artifacts that are certainly beyond the limit of conventional radiocarbon dating (Camps 1975) and that could in fact date at least partly from the Last Interglaciation.

The more complete African skulls and jaws range from clearly archaic (especially Jebel Irhoud [Fig. 6.5], Omo-Kibish 2,

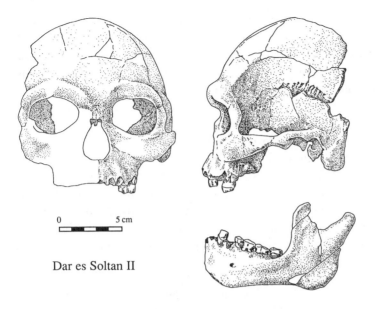

Dar es Soltan II

0   5 cm

Figure 6.17. Modern or near-modern human skull and mandible from the cave of Dar es Soltan 2, Morocco (redrawn after Debénath et al. 1986: 237). The braincase is higher (and probably shorter) than in Neanderthals, and the face is distinctly shorter and less protruding, especially along the midline. Except for the large projecting browridge, the skull exhibits no features that distinguish it significantly from most modern human skulls, yet the population it represents inhabited Morocco at the same time that Neanderthals occupied Europe.

Eliye Springs, Haua Fteah, Témara, and Florisbad) to only marginally archaic (Singa and Laetoli 18) to essentially modern (Zouhrah Cave, Dar es Soltan [Fig. 6.17], Omo-Kibish 1, Border Cave, and Klasies River Mouth). The stark morphological contrast between Omo 1 and Omo 2 may mean that one (or both) were intrusive into the stratigraphic unit from which they derive, and Omo 1 (modern) conceivably is much more recent. Similarly, the very modern Border Cave fossils may derive from relatively recent graves dug into much older deposits. This possibility is especially likely for the adult skull and one of the mandibles, which were found during unsystematic excavations for guano (fertilizer).

However, even when Omo 1 and the Border Cave specimens are not considered, there are no African fossils with indisputably Neanderthal features. Some of the mandibles are large and rugged, but, where the appropriate parts are preserved, they lack retromolar spaces and usually have distinct chins (Fig. 6.18). Together with other facial bones, the mandibles indicate that early-late-Quaternary Africans tended to have significantly shorter and flatter faces than did the Neanderthals. Similarly, some of the skulls (Florisbad, Jebel Irhoud, Omo 2, Singa, and Laetoli 18) are ruggedly built, with large browridges and, in some cases (Jebel Irhoud, Omo 2, and Laetoli 18), relatively prominent transverse occipital tori, as well as pronounced bony crests or mounds in the occipito-mastoid region. (See Fig. 6.5 for an illustration of the Jebel Irhoud skull, Fig. 5.2 and 5.3 [in the last chapter] for schematic illustrations of others.) However, in general, the African skulls tend to be shorter and higher than classic Neanderthal skulls, and some approach or equal modern skulls in basic vault shape. Where endocranial capacity can be reasonably estimated (for Laetoli 18, Omo 1 and 2, Singa, Eliye Springs, Border Cave 1, and Jebel Irhoud 1 and 2), the African skulls range between roughly 1,370 cc (Laetoli 18) and 1,510 cc (Border Cave 1) (Bräuer 1984b), comfortably within the range of both the Neanderthals and anatomically modern people.

Both individually and as a group, the African skulls contrast strongly with Neanderthal skulls, and it would be interesting to know whether postcranial differences were equally marked. Postcranial bones are unfortunately rare in the African fossil sample, but the single upper-limb bone that has been described so far, from Jebel Irhoud, has a hyperrobust

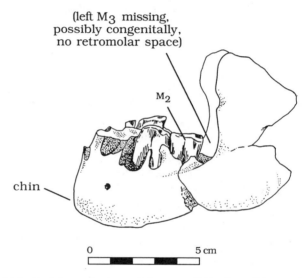

(left M$_3$ missing, possibly congenitally, no retromolar space)

M$_2$

chin

0   5 cm

Figure 6.18. Left buccal view of the mandible from Klasies River Mouth Cave 1B—level 10 (specimen 41815) (drawn by K. Cruz-Uribe from a slide and a photograph in Singer and Wymer 1982: Fig. 68). The specimen probably dates from the Last Interglaciation sensu lato (= isotope stage 5), between 130,000 and 75,000 years ago. The right P$_2$ and M$_1$ and the left M$_1$ and M$_2$ are in place. The remaining teeth were not recovered, but the sockets are present for all except left M$_3$, which probably never developed. The teeth are heavily worn, indicating advanced age, and there are signs of dental disease, including abscesses at the tips of the M$_1$ roots. Except only for the large size of the teeth, the mandible is remarkably modern, with a distinct chin and no retromolar space. The owner probably had a relatively short, broad, flat face, far more like that of modern humans than like that of the Neanderthals. Overall, together with other human fossils from Klasies River Mouth and from other Last Interglacial or early Last Glacial sites elsewhere in Africa, the mandible indicates that the African contemporaries of the Neanderthals had much more modern skulls.

(hypertrophic) shaft recalling that of the Neanderthals or other nonmodern humans (Trinkaus, in press [citing Hublin, in press]). The implication may be that craniofacial change toward modern humanity preceded postcranial change—that is, that the African contemporaries of the Neanderthals reduced their reliance on their jaws as tools while maintaining their need for extraordinarily robust bodies. Many new and better-dated fossils will be necessary to test this hypothesis and to determine when the modern reduction in postcranial robusticity occurred in Africa.

In sum, the African fossil sample is small and dominated by fragments. It is less homogeneous than the Neanderthal sample, perhaps because it represents a larger time range and geographic area, perhaps because it represents populations undergoing more rapid change, or perhaps because it (erroneously) includes some specimens that actually date from the very late Quaternary (the end of the Last Glaciation or even the Holocene). Still, it is clear that, in age, most of the African fossils are similar to the Neanderthals and that none of them exhibit typical Neanderthal morphology. Instead, they possess craniofacial features that are near modern to modern, and as a group they strongly imply that anatomically modern people were developing in Africa at the same time that the Neanderthals occupying Europe remained largely unchanged. Some resemblances between the Florisbad and Omo 2 skulls on the one hand and the mid-Quaternary Broken Hill and Elandsfontein skulls on the other (Rightmire 1984b, 1987) hint that one day it may be possible to trace, from very archaic *Homo sapiens* or even from *H. erectus*, the continuous evolution of anatomically modern people in Africa.

Artifact Industries

The artifacts that the Neanderthals made in Europe and western Asia are almost universally assigned to the Mousterian Industrial Complex, named for the rock-shelters at Le Moustier (southwestern France) where, in 1863, the pioneer prehistorians, Edouard Lartet and Henry Christy, initiated a long series of important excavations. In Europe and western Asia, "Middle Paleolithic" is often used as a synonym for Mousterian, though it has also been used more loosely for any artifact assemblages that are supposedly coeval with Mousterian ones, regardless of their typology. It is in this relatively loose time sense that it has been applied in eastern Asia, where, in general, the artifact assemblages to which it refers are still poorly known and poorly dated (Qiu 1985; Olsen 1987).

In Africa, the contemporaries of the Neanderthals produced artifacts that are very similar to Mousterian ones, and the term *Mousterian* has been applied directly to some north African assemblages, above all to those in the Nile Valley (Marks 1968b), but also in the eastern Sahara (Wendorf and Schild 1980), in Cyrenaica (northern Libya) (McBurney 1967), and in the Maghreb (northwest Africa) (Balout 1955; Camps 1974). Many other north African assemblages have been assigned to the Aterian Industry, named after the site of Bir el Ater in northeastern Algeria. The Aterian is distinguished from the Mousterian primarily by the presence of stemmed or tanged pieces (Ferring 1975), but this difference is no greater than the difference between European industries assigned to different facies (variants) of the Mousterian, and the separation of the Aterian from the Mousterian owes less to its typology than to the now-abandoned idea that the Aterian postdated the European Mousterian. In fact, like the Mousterian, the Aterian is now known to date from the earlier part of the late Quaternary, at or beyond the 30,000–40,000-year limit of conventional radiocarbon dating (Camps 1974, 1975).

In sub-Saharan Africa, the complex of industries that are contemporaneous with the Mousterian are conventionally assigned to the Middle Stone Age or MSA. Like the Aterian, the MSA was once thought to postdate the Mousterian, but numerous radiocarbon dates, obtained mainly since 1970, show it was broadly coeval with the Mousterian in the early part of the late Quaternary, before 30,000–40,000 years ago (Vogel and Beaumont 1972; Volman 1984). Also like the Aterian, on strictly typological grounds the various MSA industries could be regarded simply as facies of the Mousterian. Scholarly tradition and geographic distance are the principal reasons for the distinction.

The time when the Mousterian/MSA began is not firmly established, partly because it lies in the late-middle-/ early-late-Quaternary interval that is currently difficult to date radiometrically. There is also the problem that in both Africa and Europe the Mousterian/MSA differs from the preceding Acheulean mainly in the absence of large bifacial tools (hand axes and cleavers). However, people who made large bifaces need not have left them at every site they visited, and large bifaces do not occur at several African and European sites that are clearly contemporaneous with Acheulean sites in the same regions. In addition, at some sites where large bifaces do occur, they are rare, suggesting that chance (sampling error) could explain their absence elsewhere. Still, although the difficulty of distinguishing the MSA from the Acheulean remains, radio-potassium dates on volcanic ash that overlies probable MSA assemblages at Gademotta in Ethiopia (Wendorf et al. 1975), as well as the stratigraphic or paleontologic context of probable MSA artifacts at Duinefontein and other sites in South Africa (Klein 1983; Volman 1984), suggest the MSA began in the late middle Quaternary, roughly 200,000 years ago.

The situation in Europe and western Asia may be more complex, since Mousterian industries probably replaced Acheulean ones in some places, such as northern France and northwestern Germany, during the Glaciation-before-Last, per-haps as much as 200,000 years ago (Tuffreau 1979, 1982; Bosinski 1982, 1986), while Acheulean industries were still being made in southern France and the Near East during the Last Interglaciation or even during the early part of the Last Glaciation, after 130,000 years ago (Bordes 1968; Laville et al. 1980; Jelinek 1982a).

The various Mousterian/MSA industrial sequences al-most certainly ended at different times, depending on the place. In Africa and the Near East, they were clearly replaced before 35,000 years ago and probably before 40,000 years ago (Solecki 1963; Hole and Flannery 1967; McBurney 1967; Beau-mont 1980; Marks 1981a), but they were replaced only after 35,000 years ago in western Europe (Klein 1973b; Bricker 1976). In central and eastern Europe, the replacement was probably between 40,000 and 35,000 years ago (Klein 1973b; F. H. Smith 1982; Hoffecker 1986, 1987).

Although it is heuristically useful to equate the Neander-thals and the Mousterian, it is important to stress that, strictly considered, this is incorrect. The people who made Mousterian/MSA artifacts in Africa were clearly not Neanderthals, while at Saint-Césaire and Arcy-sur-Cure in France the Neanderthal fos-sils are associated with (Chatelperronian) artifacts that are com-monly assigned to the succeeding Upper Paleolithic complex. Perhaps most important, at the Skhul and Qafzeh Caves in Israel, Mousterian artifacts are associated with fossils of early anatom-ically modern people. The significance of these departures from the Neanderthal = Mousterian formula will be considered in the section below on the fate of the Neanderthals.

Mousterian/MSA Interassemblage Variability

Nearly all Mousterian/MSA assemblages are dominated by flakes, including the retouched pieces or "tools" that archeol-ogists emphasize in their reports. However, the damaged edges

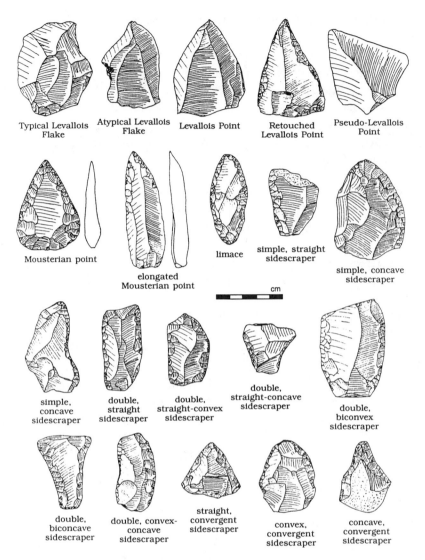

Figure 6.19. Basic Mousterian and MSA stone-tool types, as defined by Bordes (1961b). Most assemblages are dominated by scrapers, points, and denticulates. The distinctions among the types are strictly formal rather than functional, and use-wear studies show that there is no strong relationship between type and function. Thus, pieces assigned to the same type often seem to have been used for different purposes, while different types often appear to have served broadly the same purpose. Moreover, to some extent, different types may represent simply different stages in the progressive refreshing or "reduction" of working tools (Dibble 1987, 1988). For example, many double sidescrapers could reflect the preparation of a second edge on a simple sidescraper whose working edge had become dull or ragged, while many convergent sidescrapers could be the end products of continued refreshing of both edges on double sidescrapers. Similarly, many denticulates may represent "refreshed" notches. An important implication of this is that the abundance of different kinds of sidescrapers or of notches versus denticulates in an assemblage may reflect simply the degree of refreshing or reduction. However, this is a potentially important datum in itself, and most specialists continue to record notches, denticulates, and different kinds of sidescrapers basically as Bordes defined them.

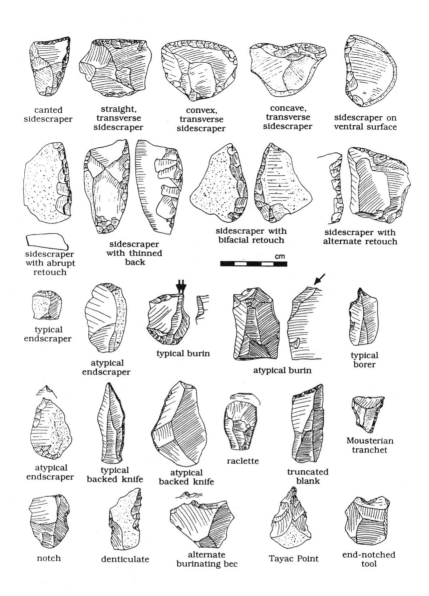

canted
sidescraper

straight,
transverse
sidescraper

convex,
transverse
sidescraper

concave,
transverse
sidescraper

sidescraper on
ventral surface

sidescraper
with abrupt
retouch

sidescraper
with thinned
back

sidescraper with
bifacial retouch

sidescraper with
alternate retouch

cm

typical
endscraper

atypical
endscraper

typical burin

atypical burin

typical
borer

atypical
endscraper

typical
backed knife

atypical
backed knife

raclette

truncated
blank

Mousterian
tranchet

notch

denticulate

alternate
burinating bec

Tayac Point

end-notched
tool

295

of many unretouched flakes show that they too were "tools," at least in the sense that they were used.

The principal retouched tool types in Mousterian/MSA assemblages are sidescrapers, points, and denticulates (Fig. 6.19; see Appendix 2 for background on these and other stone artifact categories). Hand axes are generally absent, but small, usually triangular or cordiform (heart-shaped) ones are a characteristic component of some Mousterian assemblages, mainly in France, and small, pointed, bifacially retouched pieces that fit the technical definition of hand axes occur sporadically elsewhere, especially in central Europe. Endscrapers, burins, borers, and backed pieces (flakes or blades with one edge intentionally dulled)—all typical of succeeding Upper Paleolithic/Later Stone Age (LSA) assemblages—tend to be rare and casually made in Mousterian/MSA assemblages, but endscrapers and burins are relatively common in some assemblages, particularly in the Near East, and well-made backed pieces characterize localized Mousterian/MSA variants in both Africa and Europe.

As a whole, the Mousterian/MSA is remarkably uniform though time and space, and much superficial variability between assemblages from different regions or time intervals can probably be ascribed to differences in the size or flaking quality of available stone raw materials. Flint of variable quality was available throughout much of Europe and the Near East but was generally absent in Africa, where quartzite and even volcanic rock types were widely used. Among the few tool types whose localized distribution cannot be explained by differences in raw material are the triangular and cordiform hand axes mentioned above (largely restricted to France, with extensions to Britain, Belgium, and Germany); small cleavers on flakes ("cleaver-flakes") found mainly in northern Spain; Bockstein "knives" (small, pointed, hand ax–like objects) found mainly in Germany and adjacent parts of central Europe; bifacially flaked, leaf-shaped points (Blattspitzen) restricted mostly to central Europe; backed "knives," common in one of the Mousterian variants of southern France and, independently, in an MSA variant in South Africa; and stemmed or tanged pieces (points, sidescrapers, etc.) restricted essentially to the western two-thirds of North Africa. Except for these types and some others that are less strictly localized, most variability within the Mousterian/MSA is quantitative; that is, it consists of differences in the percentage representation of the same widespread types of sidescrapers, points, and denticulates.

Interassemblage Variability in Europe

Typological variability among Mousterian assemblages has been studied most thoroughly in Europe, above all in France, thanks to the descriptive artifact typology and the analytic methodology developed by the great French prehistorian François Bordes. Working first with data from such crucial French caves as Le Moustier, La Ferrassie, La Quina, Combe-Capelle, and Pech de l'Azé and later with material from his own meticulous, 13-year-long excavations at Combe-Grenal, Bordes (1953, 1961a, 1968, 1972) recognized four basic Mousterian variants or facies:

1. *Mousterian of Acheulean Tradition (MAT).* Characterized by numerous triangular or cordiform hand axes in addition to the sidescrapers, denticulates, and points that are ubiquitous in the Mousterian. In an earlier phase (MAT Type A), backed knives occur but are relatively rare. In a later phase (MAT Type B), they are much more numerous, essentially replacing small hand axes as the type "fossil" of the MAT.
2. *Typical Mousterian.* Characterized mainly by sidescrapers, with some denticulates and points. Hand axes and backed knives are rare or absent.
3. *Denticulate Mousterian.* Characterized by the dominance of denticulates and notches, with much smaller numbers of sidescrapers, points, etc. Hand axes and backed knives are absent.
4. *Quina-Ferrassie Mousterian (or Charentian).* Characterized by a high proportion of sidescrapers; distinguished from the Typical Mousterian by abundant sidescrapers with distinctive steep, "scalar" retouch in which successive ranks of flake scars overlap like scales on a fish. It is also distinguished by the relative abundance of limaces—slug-shaped pieces that could be described as double convergent sidescrapers.

Within each variant, Bordes further distinguished between assemblages with many Levallois flakes and ones with few. He assigned Levallois-rich assemblages to the appropriate Levallois Facies (for example, Typical Mousterian of Levallois Facies), except within the Quina-Ferrassie variant, where he assigned them to the Ferrassie subvariant, as opposed to the Quina subvariant, in which Levallois flakes are rare.

Apart from the Mousterian of Acheulean Tradition B, which was clearly later than Type A, Bordes argued that there

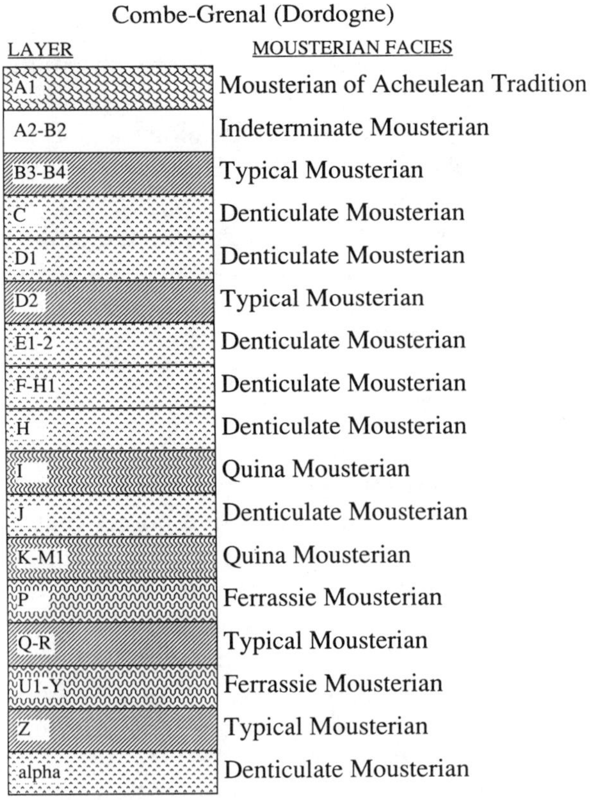

Figure 6.20.
Schematic section
of Combe-Grenal
Cave, southwest-
ern France, show-
ing the partially
random interstrat-
ification of Mous-
terian facies (data
from Bordes
1961a). The appar-
ently random pat-
tern has been
used to argue that
the facies were
produced by eth-
nically distinct
Mousterian
groups who occu-
pied France side-
by-side for thou-
sands of years.

Combe-Grenal (Dordogne)

LAYER	MOUSTERIAN FACIES
A1	Mousterian of Acheulean Tradition
A2-B2	Indeterminate Mousterian
B3-B4	Typical Mousterian
C	Denticulate Mousterian
D1	Denticulate Mousterian
D2	Typical Mousterian
E1-2	Denticulate Mousterian
F-H1	Denticulate Mousterian
H	Denticulate Mousterian
I	Quina Mousterian
J	Denticulate Mousterian
K-M1	Quina Mousterian
P	Ferrassie Mousterian
Q-R	Typical Mousterian
U1-Y	Ferrassie Mousterian
Z	Typical Mousterian
alpha	Denticulate Mousterian

was no chronological order to the facies and that any one of them could overlay any other within a site (Fig. 6.20). He thought this was because the facies were produced by separate Mousterian tribes who moved from site to site, randomly replacing each other.

In Bordes' view, the separate tribes cohabited France for tens of thousands of years, until one or perhaps two evolved into succeeding Upper Paleolithic tribes. He recognized that such prolonged social separation might produce discrete phys-ical types, but he was never able to demonstrate this. Diagnos-tic human remains are still unknown from the Mousterian of Acheulean Tradition and from the Denticulate Mousterian, while fossils with the Typical Mousterian (at Le Moustier) and the Quina-Ferrassie Mousterian (at La Quina, La Chapelle-aux-Saints, La Ferrassie, Le Régourdou, Spy, and other sites) represent typical Neanderthals.

Perhaps the most serious problem with Bordes's tribal hypothesis is to imagine the social or cultural mechanisms that kept the tribes separate for tens of thousands of years. Another difficulty is that Bordes may have underestimated the amount of typological variability that is linked to time. Thus, when some questionably excavated or analyzed occurrences are ignored, it can be argued that there is a consistent sequence from Ferrassie Mousterian to Quina Mousterian to Mousterian of Acheulean Tradition within key French caves (Mellars 1965, 1970, 1986, and in press). The most serious objection to this chronological succession has been the sedimentologic/climatologic correlation of the sequences from Le Moustier (lower shelter) and Combe-Grenal, from which it appeared that the Mousterian of Acheulean Tradition at Le Moustier was as old as or older than the Ferrassie and Quina Mousterian at Combe-Grenal. However, thermoluminescence dating of burnt flints from Le Moustier (Valladas et al. 1986), combined with climatic correlation of the Combe-Grenal sequence with the global oxygen-isotope stratigraphy (Laville et al. 1986), now suggests that the Mousterian sequence at Combe-Grenal largely antedates that at Le Moustier (Fig. 6.21), and the Ferrassie to Quina to Mousterian of Acheulean Tradition succession is thus supported (Mellars 1986). Moreover, some Mousterian assemblages excavated after Bordes first defined the facies clearly fall between them, suggesting that the facies variation is partly continuous rather than discrete (Freeman 1980). Partly in response to this problem, Bordes (1981) modified and loosened the facies definitions.

Still, no one doubts that there is significant quantitative variability among broadly contemporaneous Mousterian assemblages, not just in France but elsewhere in Europe where Bordes's typological methods have been applied (for example, in Spain by Freeman [1966] or in European Russia by Klein [1969a]). Unlike Bordes and many French archeologists, however, most Anglo-American investigators believe the variation reflects different tasks carried out by the same people (or their descendants) at different sites or at the same site at different times, perhaps at different seasons (L. R. Binford and Binford 1966; S. R. Binford and Binford 1969; L. R. Binford 1973). Thus, denticulate-rich assemblages might indicate an emphasis on woodworking (bark stripping, whittling, or shaping), while sidescraper-rich ones might reflect a focus on food preparation or hide processing (cutting and scraping).

The "activity-variant" hypothesis would clearly be strengthened if it could be shown that the principal tools that characterize each facies had a distinctive function. However, so far, studies of the wear left by use on the tools suggest just the opposite (Beyries 1986, 1988; Anderson-Gerfaud, in press). In all the facies, regardless of tool type (denticulate or sidescraper), the majority of tools on which use wear can be observed appear to have been employed for woodworking, while relatively few seem to have been used for butchering, for hide working, or for processing nonwoody plant materials. For reasons that may

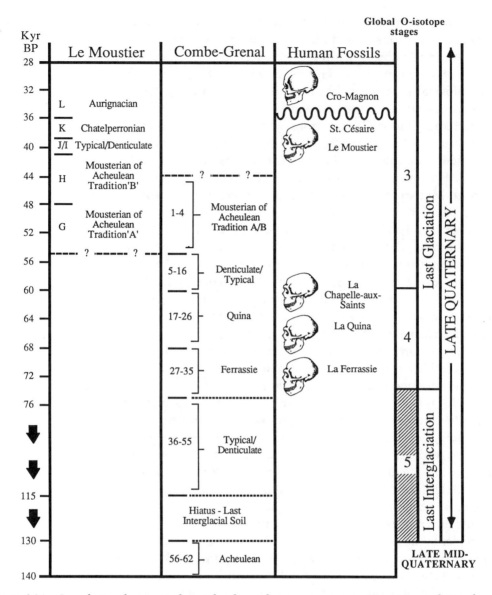

Figure 6.21. Correlation between the archeological sequences at Le Moustier and Combe-Grenal, southwestern France, based on thermoluminescence dates for Le Moustier and climatic correlation of the Combe-Grenal sequence with the global marine stratigraphy (modified after Mellars 1986: 411). The sequence of Ferrassie and Quina Mousterian at Combe Grenal is interrupted by a single level of Denticulate Mousterian in layer 20 and by three levels of either Typical or "attenuated" Ferrassie Mousterian in layers 28–30, but the correlated sequences nonetheless support the idea that Ferrassie Mousterian, Quina Mousterian, and Mousterian of the Acheulean are temporally successive facies. If it is assumed that this succession is valid and has been properly dated at Combe-Grenal, it permits some important southwestern French human fossils to be roughly fixed in time. It would also imply that much of the variability in the French Mousterian reflects temporal change within a single tradition rather than the coexistence of several separate traditions.

have to do with the geographic locations of the sites from which the tools come, this contrasts with the results of use-wear studies on (succeeding) Upper Paleolithic tools, the majority of which appear to have been used for hide working. However, it does not elucidate Mousterian facies variability. It is interesting that a few Mousterian tools show wear from possible friction with a wooden haft or handle, but there is no indication yet that hafting was more common in one facies than in another. Perhaps most important, there is no evidence for a close relationship between Mousterian tool type and tool function. Since there is also no compelling evidence that different tool types or facies tend to associate with different kinds of bones or pollen, in the final analysis, the strongest argument for the activity-variant model remains its plausibility.

Interassemblage Variability in the Near East

The Near East (southwestern Asia) rivals western Europe as a focus of research on the Mousterian, thanks to a multitude of rich sites and to the efforts of many dedicated archeologists for more than half a century. The extraordinary potential of the region was first revealed in the 1930s, when Dorothy Garrod excavated rich Mousterian levels at the caves of Tabun, Skhul, and el Wad in the Wadi el-Mughara ("Valley of the Caves") on the slopes of the Biblical Mount Carmel (Garrod and Bate 1937). Today, the most informative sites occur in two principal areas. The richer area, with more than fifty excavated sites, including the classic Mt. Carmel caves, is the Levant, a relatively narrow strip of land between the Mediterranean coast and the Syro-Arabian deserts (Fig. 6.3). In modern political terms, it includes Lebanon, Israel, and the adjacent parts of Syria and Jordan. The second, poorer area is the Zagros foothills of northeastern Iraq and northwestern Iran, with perhaps six excavated sites, of which Shanidar Cave is by far the most important (Fig. 6.1).

The Near Eastern Mousterian assemblages can be described using Bordes's typology, and they exhibit the same kind of quantitative interassemblage variability seen in Europe. However, typological change linked to time is more obvious in the Near East. The sequence that has been established in the deeply stratified deposits of Tabun seems to characterize most of the Levant (Jelinek 1981, 1982a, 1982b). The Tabun deposits lie entirely beyond the range of conventional radiocarbon dating but have been tentatively dated by correlation between the climatic events they reflect and climatic events recorded in

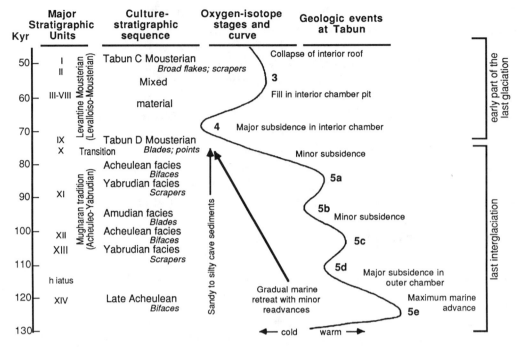

Figure 6.22. Hypothetical correlation between geologic and culture-stratigraphic units at Tabun Cave, Israel (adapted from Jelinek 1982b: Fig. 3). The diagnostic artifacts for each culture-stratigraphic unit are shown in italics. If the proposed correlation is correct, the Acheulean survived into the Last Interglaciation in the Levant, and the Mousterian in the narrow sense (Levantine Mousterian) only appeared at the beginning of the Last Glaciation.

the global marine record (Fig. 6.22). Near the base of the Tabun sequence, there is a late-Acheulean industry, which is believed to date from the early part of the Last Interglaciation. It grades typologically and technically into succeeding "Acheuleo-Yabrudian" assemblages dating to the later part of the Last Interglaciation. Among these assemblages are some that are relatively rich in small hand axes and others that are much richer in sidescrapers, but, in the sidescraper component, all are broadly similar to the Quina-Ferrassie Mousterian of France.

In the midst of the Acheuleo-Yabrudian sequence at Tabun, there is an assemblage that is relatively richer in blades (= flakes that are at least twice as long as wide) and in burins, endscrapers, and backed knives, alongside more typical Acheuleo-Yabrudian sidescrapers. A similar assemblage occurs in basically the same stratigraphic position at the Zumoffen Shelter (Adlun) in Lebanon, Yabrud Shelter I in Syria, and the Haua Fteah in northern Libya (McBurney 1975). At Tabun, it is usually called the Amudian, but elsewhere it is commonly known as the "Pre-Aurignacian," since blades, burins, endscrapers, and backed knives are typical of Upper Paleolithic industries (like the Aurignacian) that succeed the Mousterian in the Near East and Europe. However, the blades and other Upper Paleolithic elements in the Amudian/Pre-Aurignacian tend to be much more casually made than their true Upper Paleolithic counterparts, and careful study of the Amudian at Tabun suggests it was just a facies within a continuum of Acheuleo-Yabrudian variation that also includes a facies very rich in sidescrapers and another relatively rich in small hand axes. All three facies and their intermediates are now assigned to the Mugharan Industrial Tradition.

At Tabun, at a time that probably corresponds to the onset of the Last Glaciation roughly 74,000 years ago, the Mugharan grades typologically and technically into the true Mousterian that succeeds it. Almost everywhere in the Levant, including Tabun, this Mousterian tends to be rich in Levallois flakes, and it is often called Levalloiso-Mousterian. It closely resembles the French Typical Mousterian of Levallois Facies, though it tends to contain a higher proportion of blades and flake blades (elongated flakes that are not quite long enough to qualify as blades). In comparison with earlier Levalloiso-Mousterian assemblages, later ones are usually poorer in blades and Levallois points, and they tend to contain shorter, broader, and thinner Levallois flakes. The very latest Levalloiso-Mousterian assemblages sometimes contain Levallois points on which the butt has been bifacially thinned, perhaps to facilitate hafting. These are known as "Emireh points," after Emireh Cave in Israel, and assemblages in which they occur have sometimes been assigned to a separate Emiran phase or industry (Marks 1983).

The sequence in the Zagros foothills is much less well documented than the one in the Levant, but infinite radiocarbon dates, together with climatic inferences drawn from the sediments, suggest that the Zagros Mousterian dates primarily from the earlier part of the Last Glaciation (Solecki 1963). It is therefore broadly contemporaneous with the Levalloiso-Mousterian of the Levant. It is characterized by variable numbers of sidescrapers and points like those that typify the Mousterian everywhere, but, unlike the Levantine Mousterian, it is relatively poor in Levallois flakes, perhaps because the flint blanks available for flaking tend to be much smaller in the Zagros (Solecki 1963).

In sharp contrast to Europe, in the Near East the Mousterian is clearly associated with both Neanderthals and anatomically modern people. The principal Neanderthal sites are Tabun (a partial skeleton with skull, a mandible from a second individual, and some isolated postcranial bones) (McCown and Keith 1939), Kebara Cave (partial skeletons of an infant and an adult) (P. Smith and Arensburg 1977; Arensburg et al. 1985; Bar-Yosef et al. 1986), Amud Cave (a partial skeleton and the cranial fragments of three other individuals) (Suzuki and Takai 1970), and Shanidar Cave (nine partial skeletons) (Trinkaus 1983b). Mousterian artifacts accompany the remains of robust but fully modern people at Skhul Cave (seven partial skeletons and the isolated bones of three other individuals) (McCown and Keith 1939) and Qafzeh Cave (five partial skeletons and the cranial or postcranial fragments of as many as ten additional individuals) (Vandermeersch 1981). Conceivably, a cranial fragment from Zuttiyeh Cave was in a Mousterian layer, but more likely it was associated with the hand-ax-rich (Acheulean) facies of the Mugharan Tradition (Gisis and Bar-Yosef 1974). It is too incomplete for absolutely firm diagnosis and could represent either an early Neanderthal population (Trinkaus 1982, 1983b) or, perhaps more likely, a population broadly ancestral to the robust early-modern people found at Qafzeh (Vandermeersch 1982).

It is certain that the early-modern people at Skhul and Qafzeh are as old as or older than many European Neanderthals, but their chronological relationship to the Near Eastern Neanderthals remains problematic. The width/thickness ratios of Mousterian flakes associated with the various human remains suggest that the Neanderthals at Tabun antedate the modern people of Skhul and Qafzeh (Jelinek 1981, 1982a, 1982b). At Tabun, the width/thickness ratio changes progressively upward through the sequence, reflecting a progressive decline in average flake thickness relative to width, and flake samples from both Qafzeh and Skhul place habitation of these sites near the end of the Mousterian sequence, later than the Tabun Neanderthals. However, there are archaic rodent species at Qafzeh that do not occur at Tabun and a more modern form at Tabun that is absent at Qafzeh (Bar-Yosef and Vandermeersch 1981; Bar-Yosef, in press). This suggests that Qafzeh may be older than Tabun, which can also be inferred from geologic/sedimentologic analyses (Farrand 1979) and especially from thermoluminescence dates on burnt flint artifacts that place the Qafzeh moderns at roughly 92,000 years ago (Valladas et al. 1988) and the Kebara Neanderthals at only about 60,000 years ago (Valladas et al. 1987). If additional thermoluminescence or other absolute-age determinations sustain this age relationship, the implications for the evolutionary relationship between Neanderthals and modern humans are profound, as discussed in the conclusion to this chapter.

A further issue that remains unsettled is the relationship between the appearance of truly modern people in the Near East and the subsequent appearance of the Upper Paleolithic. At Tabun, an acceleration in the rate of change in flake thickness in the latest Mousterian layers may anticipate the more radical artifactual change that followed (Jelinek 1982b). Artifact assemblages that are supposedly transitional between the Mousterian and the Upper Paleolithic have been reported from several sites in the Levant (Marks 1983), but in most cases their transitional nature is either not truly obvious or could reflect the admixture, either naturally or during excavation, of Mousterian and Upper Paleolithic layers. Probably the best case for a transition comes from the alluvial site of Boker Tachtit in the Negev Desert, Israel. Here, in a sequence of levels that are tentatively bracketed between 47,000 and 38,000 years ago by radiocarbon and U-S dates, a Levallois point technology progressively gives way to a true blade technology, with a concomitant increase in Upper Paleolithic tool types, especially endscrapers (Marks 1981a, 1983).

Interassemblage Variability in North Africa

In north Africa, the Mousterian in the narrow sense is best known in Nubia, straddling the border between Egypt and the Sudan along the Nile (Marks 1968a, 1968b; Wendorf and Schild 1976; Wendorf et al. 1979). There are no long stratified sequences here, and it is difficult to discern valid time trends. Several different kinds of assemblages have been described, including ones that resemble the European Typical Mousterian, others that are more similar to the Denticulate Mousterian, and yet others that are relatively unique, particularly those with numerous burins that were once assigned to a separate "Khormusan" industry. Levallois flakes tend to be common in all Nubian Mousterian facies. Broadly comparable Mousterian assemblages occur in the Egyptian Sahara, where they are often associated with now-defunct springs or shallow lakes (Wendorf and Schild 1980; Wendorf et al. 1987). These indicate relatively moist conditions, probably occurring partly in the Last Interglaciation and partly in the early part of the Last Glaciation.

In the western part of north Africa, the Mousterian narrowly defined is represented at no more than ten to twelve sites, but the Aterian Industry or facies, with its characteristic stemmed pieces (Fig. 6.23), is abundant (Camps 1974; Ferring 1975). Except for the stems, the tool types involved are primarily the same kinds (sidescrapers, points, denticulates, etc.) that characterize Mousterian assemblages elsewhere, and most Aterian assemblages contain numerous Levallois flakes. At Taforalt and el 'Aliya Caves in Morocco and in the Bir Sahara-Bir Tarfawi lacustrine deposits in the Egyptian Sahara, the Aterian appears to postdate the local Mousterian, but this may not be true everywhere. Geographically, the Aterian was concentrated in the Mediterranean borderlands of northwest Africa (the Maghreb) from eastern Morocco to Cap Blanc in Tunisia, with extensions into the Sahara as far east as the Bir Sahara-Bir Tarfawi area in Egypt. It did not reach the Nile Valley.

Like Mousterian assemblages in north Africa, Aterian ones often occur in a sedimentologic/paleontologic context indicating relatively moist conditions, either during the Last Interglaciation or the early part of the Last Glaciation. At

Figure 6.23. Aterian artifacts from Bir el Ater, Algeria (redrawn after Vaufrey 1955: Fig. 44). The tanged or stemmed pieces are the principal artifacts that distinguish the Aterian from the Mousterian.

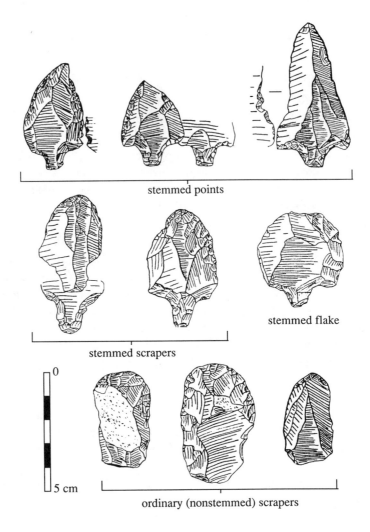

stemmed points

stemmed flake

stemmed scrapers

0

5 cm

ordinary (nonstemmed) scrapers

stratified caves such as Taforalt and Dar es Soltan 2 in Morocco, Aterian layers are separated from overlying Upper (or Epi-)Paleolithic ones by a long occupation gap, from 40,000 years ago or before to 20,000 years ago or later. There is little or no evidence for human presence anywhere in north Africa during this interval, probably because the entire region suffered from extreme aridity in the middle part of the Last Glaciation (Guillien and Laplace 1978).

As indicated above, the relatively sparse human remains associated with Mousterian/Aterian artifacts in north Africa came from people who were clearly distinct from the Neanderthals and whose appearance approached that of modern people in important craniofacial features.

Interassemblage Variability in Sub-Saharan Africa

MSA artifact assemblages have been recovered in east Africa (Anthony 1972; Wendorf and Schild 1974; Phillipson 1976; Mehlman 1977, 1979; J. D. Clark and Williamson 1979) and west Africa (Allsworth-Jones 1986a), but they are far better known in southern Africa, where the MSA was first defined (Goodwin 1928, 1929). Here, the overall nature and extent of interassemblage variability has been established from a series of stratified sequences, including especially those at Pomongwe, Bambata, and Redcliff Caves in Zimbabwe and at the Cave of Hearths, Bushman Rock-shelter, Border Cave, the Klasies River Mouth Caves, Nelson Bay Cave, and Die Kelders Cave in South Africa (Sampson 1974; Volman 1981, 1984).

In general, by comparison with Mousterian assemblages in Europe, western Asia, and north Africa, southern African MSA assemblages are poor in retouched pieces. However, the same basic retouched types—scrapers, points, and denticulates—prevail, and their relative importance varies among MSA assemblages just as it does among Mousterian ones. Denticulates are the most common retouched type in some assemblages, while either scrapers or both scrapers and points dominate others. Most specialists in southern Africa have not counted Levallois flakes separately, but these flakes are clearly more abundant in the interior than along the southern coast. At least in part, this reflects differences in the rock types available for artifact manufacture. The abundance of blades also varies among southern African MSA assemblages, and both the number and size of blades may increase with time.

There is little other variability that is obviously time linked, except for the dramatic increase in well-made backed pieces, mainly segments and trapezoids, in the later part of

Figure 6.24. Howieson's Poort artifacts from Nelson Bay Cave, South Africa (drawings by J. Deacon). The Howieson's Poort Industry is distinguished from other MSA industries mainly by the presence of well-made backed tools, including the segments (or "crescents") pictured here.

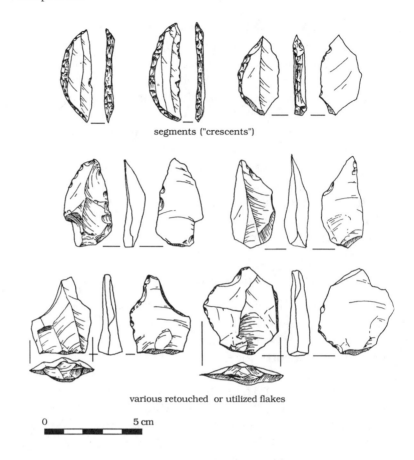

segments ("crescents")

various retouched or utilized flakes

0   5 cm

MSA sequences at numerous sites south of the Limpopo River. The assemblages with backed pieces have sometimes been assigned to the Howieson's Poort Industry (Fig. 6.24), named for the Howieson's Poort Shelter in the eastern Cape Province of South Africa, and they were once thought to represent an intermediate stage between the MSA and LSA. However, it is now clear that they are both overlain and underlain by typical MSA assemblages, and they may be as old as the Last Interglaciation. Today, they are commonly assigned to the Howieson's Poort variant of the MSA. Apart from their large size, Howieson's Poort backed pieces are similar to backed pieces that local LSA people mounted on shafts or handles by using vegetal mastic. If the backing in the Howieson's Poort was to facilitate hafting, Howieson's Poort assemblages may present some of the oldest known evidence for composite tools anywhere in the world.

In southern Africa, stratified cave sites such as Montagu Cave, Nelson Bay Cave, Die Kelders Cave 1, and the Klasies River Mouth Caves often exhibit major occupation gaps be-

tween the latest MSA, antedating 30,000–40,000 years ago, and
succeeding LSA occupations, commonly dating from the very
end of the Last Glaciation or even from the Holocene. As in
north Africa, the occupation hiatus probably reflects a reduction in human population density due to extreme aridity in the
middle part of the Last Glaciation. Although few relevant sites
have been excavated in east Africa, discoveries at Lukenya Hill
in Kenya (Miller 1979), Nasera (= Apis) Shelter (Mehlman
1977) and Mumba Shelter (Mehlman 1979) in Tanzania, and
Matupi Shelter in Zaire (van Noten 1982) suggest greater
occupational continuity there, perhaps because of more favorable climatic conditions throughout the Last Glaciation.

Like their north African contemporaries, the people who
made MSA artifacts in southern and eastern Africa were
near-modern-to-modern people, as detailed above.

Nonstone Artifacts

The Neanderthals and their contemporaries undoubtedly manufactured artifacts of wood and other perishable materials, and
wooden artifacts have survived at a handful of sites. Examples
include a remarkable 2.4-m-long wooden spear found among
the ribs of a straight-tusked elephant at the Mousterian site of
Lehringen in Germany (Movius 1950) and fragments of possible throwing sticks discovered at the MSA sites of Chambuage
Mine in Angola (J. D. Clark 1968a) and Florisbad in South
Africa (J. D. Clark 1955). The tip of the Lehringen spear may
have been deliberately hardened by exposure to fire while it
was still green.

Curiously, although bones are often abundant and well
preserved at Mousterian/MSA sites, deliberately shaped, formal bone tools are almost unknown. Bones or bone fragments
that appear to have been casually used as hammers, scrapers,
anvils, etc. are more common, but even many of these may
have been shaped or damaged by carnivore gnawing or crunching rather than by human use (L. R. Binford 1982). Formal bone
artifacts are so rare in Mousterian/MSA contexts that, where
they do occur, they could easily represent undetected—perhaps
undetectable—intrusions from higher levels. Certainly, it is
reasonable to conclude that few if any Mousterian/MSA people
recognized bone as a raw material that could be cut, carved,
and polished into points, borers, awls, etc. In this respect, they
were similar to their forebears but very different from their
successors.

Also like earlier peoples and unlike later ones, Mousteri-
an/MSA peoples left little or no evidence for art or ornamen-

tation. The list of possible art objects from Mousterian/MSA sites is very brief (Marshack 1976; Chernysh 1982; Chase and Dibble 1987): a reindeer phalange and a fox canine, each punctured or perforated by a hole (?for hanging) from La Quina in France; some grooved bear teeth from Scalyn, Belgium; occasional bones with lines that may have been deliberately engraved or incised, from La Quina and La Ferrassie in France, Bacho Kiro Cave in Bulgaria, Molodova I in the Ukraine, and a handful of other European sites; and a fragment of mammoth molar plate that may have been deliberately carved and polished to an oval shape, from Tata in Hungary. On some of the supposed art objects, the modification may not be artificial, while on many it is not compellingly artistic. The phalange "pendant" from La Quina, for example, could have been punctured by a carnivore's bite, while a bone with parallel "engraved" lines from La Ferrassie could simply represent a "cutting board" on which skin or some other soft material was repeatedly sliced (Chase and Dibble 1987). Perhaps most important, like formal bone artifacts in Mousterian/MSA contexts, "art objects" are so rare that even if they are genuine, the possibility must be considered that they are intrusive from overlying levels.

Fragments of natural red or black pigment (iron oxide and manganese dioxide) that Mousterian/MSA peoples brought to their sites suggest they may have decorated perishable materials, perhaps including their own skins (Bordes 1968). However, unlike their successors, Mousterian/MSA people did not concentrate pigments in graves (Harrold 1980), nor did they intentionally burn (oxidize or reduce) them to obtain a wider range of colors (Perlés 1976). Conceivably, the pigments were used in strictly utilitarian activities such as hide tanning. However, even if the pigments imply some form of art, Mousterian/MSA peoples still differed strikingly from later (Upper Paleolithic/LSA) peoples who left bone, ivory, antler, or shell-art objects or ornaments almost everywhere they lived.

An Overview of Mousterian/MSA Artifacts

The Mousterian/MSA was perhaps characterized by more variability through time and space than were earlier (Lower Paleolithic/Early Stone Age) industries, but it was still remarkably uniform over vast areas and time spans, compared with the succeeding Upper Paleolithic/LSA. Part of the reason for this is that, overall, Mousterian/MSA peoples made a much smaller variety of readily definable artifact types than did their successors. Together, the relative homogeneity of the Mousterian/MSA through time and space and the relatively small number of distinguishable MSA/Mousterian artifact types suggest that the behavior of Mousterian/MSA people differed qualitatively from that of their Upper Paleolithic/LSA successors.

It is further noteworthy that Mousterian people rarely if ever transported raw materials more than a few kilometers, whereas Upper Paleolithic people sometimes transported or imported them over scores of kilometers (Klein 1969a; Mellars 1973; Schild 1984; Gamble 1986). Some of the items that Upper Paleolithic people moved were nonutilitarian goods, such as marine shells and amber, that may not have interested Mousterian people, but some Upper Paleolithic sites contain high-quality stone raw material that was brought dozens or scores of kilometers. In sum, it is clear that, relative to the Mousterians, at least some Upper Paleolithic people either occupied far larger territories or participated in far larger social networks.

The rarity or absence of formal bone artifacts and art objects in the Mousterian/MSA only adds to the contrast. The most general implication is that Mousterian/MSA people were behaviorally more conservative than their successors, with a limited ability to innovate even in the face of significant environmental variability through time and space. At least tentatively, it seems reasonable to propose that the behavioral limitations implied by Mousterian/MSA artifacts were linked to biological distinctions versus fully modern people, distinctions that are clearest in the Neanderthals but that probably also characterized most other Mousterian/MSA peoples.

Site Distribution

The overall distribution of Mousterian/MSA sites closely resembles the distribution of earlier (Lower Paleolithic/Early Stone Age) sites, except that Mousterian sites occur in the European part of the USSR where earlier sites are so far unknown (Klein 1973b). Since the commercial and archeological activities that promote site discovery have been as intense in the European USSR as in parts of central and western Europe where earlier sites are well known, it seems increasingly likely that earlier sites are absent in the European USSR because earlier people were absent. The most probable reason is that they could not cope with the especially cold winters of the European USSR, whether during glacial or interglacial periods.

At the same time, it is important to stress that even Mousterian sites are restricted to the southern and westernmost parts of the European USSR, and no sites have been discovered in the most continental—central and eastern—parts, in spite of significant commercial and archeological activity there. This activity has revealed numerous rich Upper Paleolithic sites, and it seems increasingly likely that Upper Paleolithic people were the first to occupy these areas, whose climate must have been especially intimidating during the Last Glaciation. Upper Paleolithic people were also apparently the first to inhabit the equally harsh or harsher environments of northern Asia (Siberia), where, in spite of dedicated efforts, no convincing Mousterian (or earlier) sites have so far been found.

Site Types

Most known Mousterian/MSA sites are in rock-shelters or the mouths of caves, but this does not mean that Mousterian/MSA peoples always preferred caves to open-air sites, even where caves were plentiful. Cave sites are better known today because they constitute obvious places to excavate for artifacts and skeletal remains, and Mousterian/MSA peoples lived so recently that most of their caves are still visible. In addition, compared with open-air sites, caves are more likely to retain artifacts, bones, and other human refuse, and they are abundant in areas such as southwestern France, where serious prehistoric archeology has been underway for many decades. Most open-air sites were probably long ago destroyed by erosion, and those that remain are harder to locate than caves. Nonetheless, important open-air Mousterian sites have been found even in southwestern France (Guichard 1976), and they obviously provide most of the Mousterian/MSA record in those parts of Europe, western Asia, and Africa where caves are rare or absent.

With rare exceptions, open-air sites occur near active or once active springs, lakes, or streams, partly because these were favorable places for camping or obtaining food and partly because they were places where sites were likely to be preserved (because there was sediment accumulation vs. erosion). Prominent open-air sites in Europe include Ehringsdorf, Salzgitter-Lebenstedt, Königsaue, and Rheindahlen in Germany (Tode et al. 1953; Behm-Blancke 1960; Bosinski 1967; Mania and Toepfer 1973; Thieme 1983; Thissen 1986), Tata and Érd in Hungary (Vertés 1964; Gábori-Czánk 1968), and Molodova I, Molodova V, and Sukhaya Mechetka (Volgograd) in the European part of the USSR (Klein 1969b). Important examples in Africa include el Guettar in Tunisia (Gruet 1954, 1958), Hajj el Sidi Creiem (Wadi Derna) in Libya (McBurney and Hey 1955), Prospect Farm in Kenya (Anthony 1972), and

Florisbad, Orangia 1, and Duinefontein 2 in South Africa (Sampson 1974; Klein 1976; Kuman and Clarke 1986). The most important examples in western Asia are perhaps Rosh Ein Mor and Nahal Aqev in the central Negev Desert of Israel (Marks 1977; 1981a).

Most Mousterian/MSA caves and rock-shelters were probably living places or camps rather than places where people killed or butchered animals. This is indicated by their very nature and by the fossil fireplaces or "hearths" that are a prominent feature in virtually every well-excavated cave where preservation conditions are appropriate. The hearths are generally simple lenses of ash and charcoal 50 cm–1 m across. Some are surrounded or underlain by rocks (Perlés 1976), but none are as elaborate as some Upper Paleolithic hearths which were fitted with stone liners, air-intake ditches, or other features to control airflow and heat dissipation.

In contrast to caves and rock-shelters, most Mousterian/MSA open-air sites are more difficult to interpret. Some, for example those in the Negev, are located near sources of desirable stone raw material, and the abundance of flaking debris implies they were stone-tool workshops. Most open-air sites, however, are scatters of artifacts or of artifacts and fragmentary animal bones near water sources where people might have camped, killed/butchered animals, or both. Distinguishing camp sites from kill/butchery sites is difficult because few sites preserve distinctive features, such as partial animal skeletons, which might indicate butchering, or traces of possible structures, which would imply a camp. Further, at sites such as Duinefontein 2 where partial skeletons do occur, there is usually the problem of determining who was responsible for skeletal disarticulation—people or other predators such as hyenas or lions. Virtually the only exception to this problem is Lehringen, where a wooden spear was actually found among the ribs of an elephant.

Aside from hearths, indisputable structural traces are very uncommon in Mousterian/MSA sites. Postdepositional smudging or destruction cannot be the entire reason, since relatively fragile hearths are preserved at many sites. More likely, Mousterian/MSA people rarely built structures that were substantial enough to leave clear traces. It is possible that structure bases are marked by distinct concentrations of artifacts and other cultural debris found at many sites, but more compelling structural traces have rarely been detected. The most notable exceptions include possibly artificial depressions containing artifacts and other cultural materials at the open-air sites of Ariendorf ("find-layer II") (Fig. 6.25) and Rheindahlen

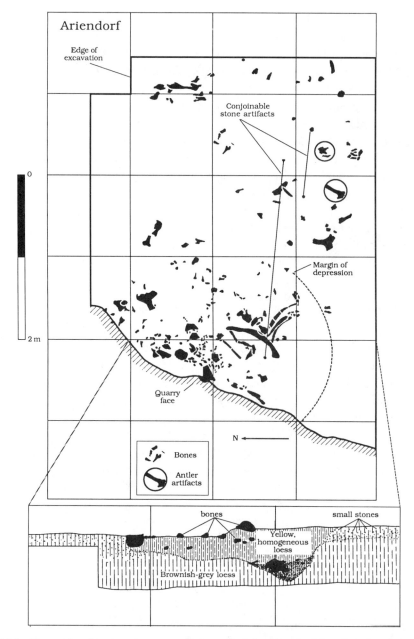

Figure 6.25. Floor plan (*top*) and section (*bottom*) through "find-level II" at the Ariendorf open-air site, West Germany (redrawn after Bosinski et al. 1983: 163, 164). The occurrence of bones and artifacts was revealed by quarrying through wind-blown silts (loess). The quarrying unfortunately destroyed part of the site, but careful excavation showed that elephant ribs, other large bones, and stone artifacts were concentrated in and near an ancient depression 2–3 m across. The depression may have been dug by early Middle Paleolithic (Mousterian) people to level the floor of a hut whose frame was made partly of elephant ribs. Alternatively, it could be a natural feature, perhaps created when a large tree was uprooted. Less equivocal structural traces are remarkably rare in Middle Paleolithic and earlier sites, suggesting that the people rarely built substantial houses.

in West Germany (Bosinski et al. 1983; Thieme 1983; Thissen 1986: E. Turner 1986) and, perhaps more convincingly, the apparent structural features at Cueva Morín in Spain (Freeman 1983), at the caves of La Ferrassie, Pech de I'Azé I, and Combe Grenal in France (Bordes 1972; H. de Lumley and Boone 1976), and at the open-air sites of Molodova I and V in the European USSR (Klein 1969b; Chernysh 1982). Equally unequivocal structural traces from the MSA site of Orangia 1 in South Africa (Sampson 1974) have been ignored here, because the excavator now believes they postdate the MSA artifacts at the site (C. G. Sampson, personal communication).

Cueva Morín contained a dense accumulation of cultural debris bounded by a line of stone piles that may represent the remnant of a low stone wall. La Ferrassie contained a 5 × 3-m spread of limestone fragments possibly marking the base of a tent built within the cave. Pech de l'Azé 1 preserved a small part of a low dry-stone wall, and Combe-Grenal contained an apparent posthole.

The Molodova sites contain large rings or partial rings of large (mainly mammoth) bones surrounding dense concentrations of artifacts, fragmentary bones, and ash spreads ("hearths"). The bones are thought to represent weights that held down skins stretched over a wooden framework that disintegrated long ago. Although the bone rings appear patterned, the structural reconstruction is problematic because of the large areas they enclose. In the case of the most convincing rings (in Molodova I level 4) (Fig. 6.26), these are ovals roughly 8 m long by 5 m across, which would have required considerable architectural skill to cover. The full meaning of the Molodova features remains unclear, and the possibility exists that slope wash or some other natural process is partly responsible for the patterning.

In sum, Mousterian/MSA caves and open-air sites contain limited evidence for structural modification. This is particularly striking in Europe, where many Mousterian sites have now been carefully excavated and where the contrast with subsequent Upper Paleolithic sites is particularly sharp (Klein 1973b; Mellars 1973). Well-excavated Upper Paleolithic sites almost always contain unambiguous and often spectacular evidence of structures, in the form of artificially excavated depressions and pits, patterned arrangements of large bones or stones, postholes, or some combination of these. Even Upper Paleolithic caves commonly preserve structural traces such as stone walls, artificial pavements, and pits, and, to the annoyance of archeologists, Upper Paleolithic cave dwellers sometimes dug out preexisting deposits, perhaps to enlarge the

Molodova I level 4 -- floor plan

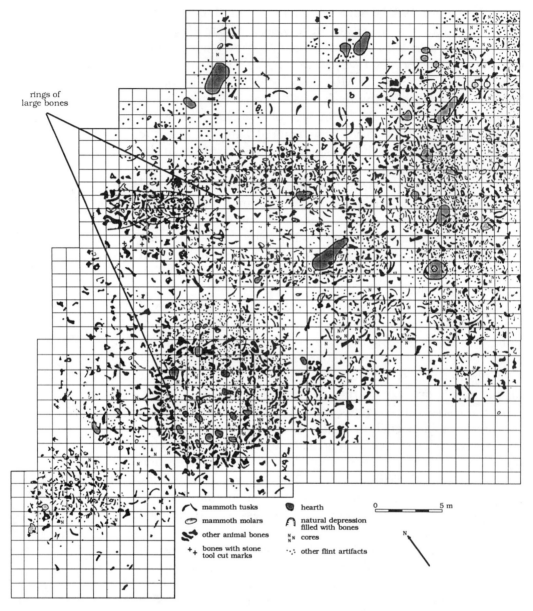

rings of
large bones

mammoth tusks   hearth

mammoth molars   natural depression
                     filled with bones

other animal bones   N N cores
                     N

+ bones with stone   ·.·: other flint artifacts
+ tool marks

0   5 m

N

Figure 6.26. Plan of the excavations in Molodova I, level 4, Ukrainian SSR (redrawn
after Chernysh 1982: Fig. 8). The two large rings of large bones may represent the foundations of structures built by the Mousterian occupants of the site. Alternatively, they may
have been formed partly by a natural process such as slope wash.

living area or to level out a floor. As in many other aspects of culture, in site modification Mousterian/MSA people seem to have been quantitatively, if not qualitatively, different from their successors. At least in part, their limited constructional ability may explain why they were unable to occupy the most continental parts of Eurasia.

Settlement Systems

Mousterian/MSA peoples were certainly nomadic to some extent, occupying different sites for different purposes or at different seasons to take advantage of seasonal differences in resource availability. However, in most regions the distribution of known sites probably does not closely mirror the distribution of utilized sites. More likely, it reflects the distribution of caves and other places that favor preservation—and the distribution of modern settlements and roads used by archeologists. Since it is also impossible to determine whether different sites were occupied by essentially the same people, in most instances it is essentially impossible to reconstruct Mousterian/MSA settlement systems.

However, systematic surveys in the Avdat/Aqev area of the central Negev Desert in Israel have suggested a contrast between Mousterian and Upper Paleolithic settlement patterns that may also pertain to other areas (Marks and Freidel 1977). In the Avdat/Aqev area, Mousterian sites appear to comprise (1) semipermanent base camps near permanent water and (2) outlying, more temporary sites near probable sources of food and stone raw material. Upper Paleolithic sites do not include any semipermanent base camps, but only "ephemerally occupied multipurpose camps and even more ephemeral loci of unknown function" (Marks and Freidel 1977: 141).

The Mousterian pattern suggests a "radiating" system, in which the people moved back and forth between the central base camp and the peripheral resource sites, while the Upper Paleolithic pattern suggests a "circulating" system in which the people simply moved from multipurpose camp to multipurpose camp. The shift from a radiating to a circulating pattern may have been an adaptive response to contemporaneous environmental deterioration (increasing aridity) that has been documented from geomorphic and palynologic evidence in the central Negev (Marks 1977).

The adoption of a circulating system may explain why Upper Paleolithic people abandoned the flake technology of the Mousterians (Marks and Freidel 1977), since the blade technology they adopted reduced the need to deviate from a circulating pattern to renew stone raw-material reserves at quarry sites. This is because, by comparison with the Mousterian flake technology, the Upper Paleolithic blade technology produced more usable blanks per core, that is, more usable blanks per quarry visit.

Subsistence

Mousterian/MSA people undoubtedly used plant foods, particularly in areas nearer the equator where suitable plants probably remained important even during glacial intervals. However, plant tissues are not very durable, and, except for nondietary charcoal and pollen, plant fossils are extremely rare in Mousterian/MSA sites. In contrast, bones that reflect the meat component of Mousterian/MSA diet have been found at many sites.

The principal animals in Mousterian/MSA sites are the medium and large ungulates that were probably most common near the sites. In Eurasia, depending on the time and place, these animal species include red deer, fallow deer, bison, wild oxen (aurochs), wild sheep and goats, gazelles, and horses (including asses and onagers), and in Africa these animal species include various antelopes, zebras, and wild pigs. The largest available ungulates—elephants and rhinoceroses, present in both Africa and Eurasia—tend to be rare, and in sites such as those at Molodova where they do abound, their bones were probably used in construction. Thus, they do not necessarily represent animals that people ate.

Carnivores, particularly large ones such as lions, hyenas, bears, and wolves, also tend to be rare in Mousterian/MSA sites, probably because they avoided people and vice versa. A Neanderthal "bear cult" has sometimes been inferred from apparently patterned arrangements of cave-bear bones in European caves such as Drachenloch (Switzerland) and Petershöhle (southern Germany) (Bergounioux 1958). In these caves, complete bear bones, especially skulls, tend to occur near the walls or near large limestone slabs that have been imaginatively attributed to stone chests built by the Neanderthals. However, there are no stone artifacts or cut-marked bones to demonstrate human activity, and bear trampling that displaced or destroyed whole bones in readily accessible areas could easily explain why complete bones tend to occur near cave walls or large fallen stone slabs. Almost certainly, the bones accumulated naturally from hibernating bears that occasionally died in the caves (Kurtén 1976).

In general, it is difficult to estimate how successful the occupants of any particular Mousterian/MSA site were at obtaining animals. At sites where artifacts, humanly damaged bones, or other clear evidence of human presence is sparse, it is even difficult to tell what proportion of the animals were obtained by people, and it is possible that most were killed by carnivores or died naturally. The problem tends to be particularly acute at open-air sites, where fossilized feces (coprolites), chewed bones, or other evidence of carnivore activity may be as abundant as cultural debris. Even at a site where context and associations indicate that people were the principal bone accumulators, it is generally impossible to establish whether the relative abundance of various species reflects human practices or preferences, the natural abundance of the species near the site, or some combination of these factors.

Separating the relative roles of human behavior and environment is only possible when species abundance can be compared between two or more sites. In this event, it may be possible to control for differences in environment by using palynologic, sedimentologic, or geochemical observations and to control for differences in behavior by using artifacts or other cultural debris. Thus, if pollen and sediment analyses indicate that two sites shared a similar environment, human behavior becomes a likely cause for differences between them in species abundance. Conversely, environment is implicated if artifacts or other cultural remains indicate that the occupants of two sites were behaving very similarly.

In most instances where controlled comparisons are possible, differences in species abundance among Mousterian/MSA sites or between Mousterian/MSA sites and earlier or later ones appear to reflect differences in site environment rather than differences in occupant behavior. This, in France, fluctuations in the relative abundance of reindeer versus red deer, traced from the Acheulean of the late middle Quaternary through the Mousterian of the early late Quaternary, correlate closely with climatic fluctuations indicated by geomorphic and palynologic evidence (Bordes and Prat 1965). Reindeer peaks are closely associated with cold intervals, and red deer peaks are associated with warm ones. Similarly, in the European part of the USSR, where climatic differences through time were perhaps less important than differences through space, in both Mousterian and Upper Paleolithic sites bison tend to be more common in the south and deer and horses tend to be more common in the west (Klein 1969b, 1973b).

In Africa too, most faunal differences or changes among Mousterian/MSA sites relate more clearly to climate than to human behavior. The most dramatic example comes from the Sahara, where episodes of nonoccupation alternated with intervals when Mousterian or Aterian people occurred together with typical African grassland or savanna ungulates (Wendorf et al. 1977, 1987; Wendorf and Schild 1980). Associated deposits from now defunct springs or lakes show clearly that climatic change (not human behavior) accounts for the alternation. More subtle climatic change controlled the abundance of grazing versus browsing species within MSA and LSA archeological sequences in the southern Cape Province at the extreme southern tip of Africa (Klein 1980). Here, independent of associated artifacts, deposits that suggest relatively cool, dry ("glacial") conditions are dominated by grazers, while deposits suggesting relatively warm, wet ("interglacial") climate are dominated by browsers. The same pattern characterizes deposits containing bones that were collected by carnivores, supporting a climatic—versus a human-behavioral (cultural)—explanation for the species differences.

Among the comparatively rare instances of species differences that are probably due to Mousterian/MSA behavior (rather than to environment), perhaps the best examples are the change from gazelle abundance to fallow-deer abundance within the Mousterian sequence at Tabun Cave in Israel and the low ratios of fish + birds to mammals and of wild pigs to eland within the MSA deposits of Klasies River Mouth Cave 1 in South Africa. Fallow deer prefer moister conditions than gazelle, and the sharp increase in deer late in the Tabun Mousterian sequence was originally thought to reflect a regional increase in moisture. However, local and regional sedimentologic and palynologic data do not indicate a climatic change at the same time, though they do suggest an earlier change toward drier (not wetter) conditions. In fact, analysis of the Tabun sedimentary sequence now suggests that fallow deer increased because of a change in the way people used the cave (Jelinek 1982b). In the earlier Mousterian, it was probably a camp to which gazelles were brought from the nearby coastal plain. Later, after a chimney had opened through the roof, it was unsuitable for habitation and became a trap into which deer were driven from the wooded slopes above.

The MSA deposits at Klasies River Mouth have provided one of the richest and most detailed records of Stone Age subsistence anywhere in the world (Singer and Wymer 1982). Together with Herolds Bay Cave (Brink and Deacon 1982) and the Sea Harvest and Hoedjies Punt MSA middens (Volman 1978), also in South Africa; the Haua Fteah (McBurney 1967), Smugglers' Cave (Témara) (Roche and Texier 1976), Zouhrah

Cave (Debénath and Sbihi-Alaoui 1979), el 'Aliya Cave (Howe 1967), and the Bérard open air-site (Roubet 1969), all in north Africa; and Devil's Tower and Gorham's Cave on the Rock of Gibraltar (Garrod et al. 1928; Waechter 1964), the Klasies deposits contain the oldest known evidence for systematic human use of coastal resources, dating from the Last Interglaciation and perhaps the early part of the Last Glaciation.

At most of these sites, the evidence consists primarily of shells of intertidal mollusks. However, at Klasies there are also abundant bones of fur seals and penguins. Curiously, the Klasies deposits contain relatively few bones of flying seabirds (cormorants, gulls, etc.) and, especially, of fish, both of which were certainly common nearby during the Last Interglaciation, just as they were historically. Fish bones and bird bones are extremely abundant in local sites dating to the Present Interglaciation (Holocene), when the coastline and other environmental parameters closely resembled those of the Last Interglaciation, and it seems reasonable to conclude that, unlike LSA people, the MSA inhabitants of Klasies had not yet mastered fishing and fowling. In support of this, unlike LSA sites, MSA sites contain no artifacts that are clearly interpretable as fishing or fowling gear. LSA examples include grooved stones that were probably net or line sinkers and deliberately fashioned, toothpick-size, double-pointed bone splinters that could have been tied to a line and baited to catch either fish or marine birds.

In contrast to Klasies and other pertinent southern African MSA and LSA sites that were located near the coast, most relevant Mousterian and Upper Paleolithic sites in Europe were located near rivers. This may explain why exploitation of water resources is never as evident in European sites as it is at Klasies and other southern African sites. However, the limited European evidence for fishing and fowling also suggests that Mousterian people were significantly less proficient than their Upper Paleolithic successors. The best data are perhaps from southwest France and northern Spain, where advances in fishing and fowling may not have occurred until relatively late in the Upper Paleolithic (Mellars 1973; Straus 1983, 1985). It will be difficult to determine when African LSA people first actively engaged in fishing and fowling, partly because early LSA sites are very rare and partly because the most relevant sites, dating from the middle or end of the Last Glaciation, may now all be submerged on the continental shelf.

Besides implying that MSA people differed from LSA people in their ability to fish and fowl, the Klasies marine fauna also suggests that MSA people knew less about seasonal differences in resources. The evidence for this is a contrast between the age composition of the fur-seal samples from the Last Interglacial, MSA layers at Klasies and the age composition of fur-seal samples from the Present Interglacial, LSA layers at sites such as Elands Bay Cave, Nelson Bay Cave, and Die Kelders Cave. The LSA samples comprise mainly seals near the age when they were probably weaned (at about 9 months), while the Klasies MSA sample contains a much wider range of individuals, including significantly more full adults (Fig. 6.27). The most likely reason for the age clustering in the LSA sites is that people timed their visits to coincide with the weaning season, when newly weaned individuals often become exhausted at sea and come ashore, where they may be easily killed or scavenged. The age distribution of the Klasies seals may mean that MSA people were unaware of the seasonally increased availability of seals and that they simply killed or scavenged occasional individuals they encountered during less seasonally focused visits.

The rich terrestrial fauna from the Klasies MSA deposits is as informative as the marine fauna. It contains thirty-eight large mammal species, including all those that lived nearby historically. However, the relative abundance of different species at Klasies differs dramatically from their historic abundance, or from their abundance in local LSA sites dating from the Present Interglaciation. This seems strange, because geomorphic and geochemical evidence indicates that Last Interglacial environmental conditions near Klasies closely approximated Present Interglacial ones.

Particularly notable at Klasies is the abundance of eland, which outnumbers all other ungulates in the site, though, by historic analogy, it was probably the least abundant ungulate on the ground. At the same time, bushpig, which was very abundant historically, is all but absent at Klasies (Fig. 6.28). The most parsimonious explanation is probably that, among all the species represented at Klasies, eland was the least dangerous to hunt and bushpig was the most. The greater abundance of bushpig in LSA sites, and the general tendency for species in LSA sites to be represented in roughly their historic proportions, probably reflect LSA advances in weaponry, particularly the development of the bow and arrow. Its use by LSA people, at least after 20,000 years ago, is suggested by tiny backed and nonbacked stone bits (microliths) like those that tipped some local arrows historically and especially by blunt-ended bone rods that closely resemble the bone linkshafts or foreshafts of some historic arrows (J. Deacon 1984). There is nothing to suggest that MSA people at Klasies or

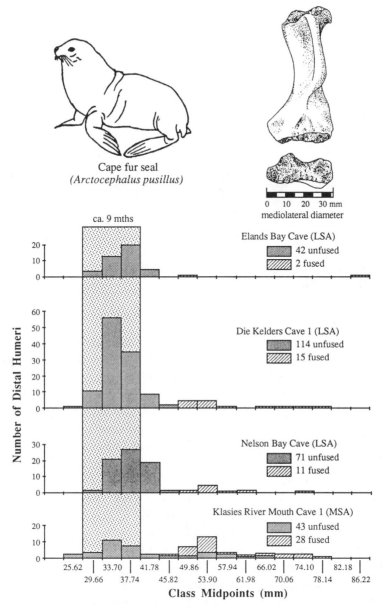

Figure 6.27. Breadths (mediolateral diameters) of Cape fur-seal distal humeri in the LSA layers of Elands Bay Cave, Die Kelders Cave 1, and Nelson Bay Cave and in the MSA layers of Klasies River Mouth Cave 1. The LSA samples all date from the Present Interglaciation (the last 12,000 years), while the MSA sample dates from the Last Interglaciation (mainly between 130,000 and 115,000 years ago). The LSA samples differ from the MSA one in two related ways: they contain significantly fewer shafts with fused epiphyses, and they show a more distinct peak in unfused shafts from individuals that were probably recently weaned—that is, at about 9 months old, given the similarity in size between their humeri and those of modern 9-month-old fur seals obtained by Graham Avery of the South African Museum. As discussed in the text, the paucity of newly weaned individuals in the MSA sample suggests that, unlike their LSA successors, MSA people did not know seals are particularly easy to catch at the weaning season. The relatively small differences among the LSA samples may reflect slightly different seasons of site occupation.

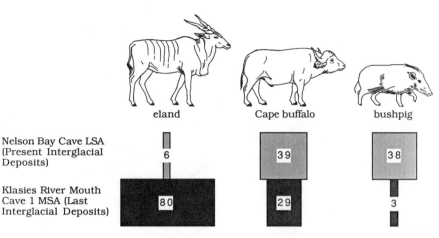

eland   Cape buffalo   bushpig

Nelson Bay Cave LSA
(Present Interglacial
Deposits)   6   39   38

Klasies River Mouth
Cave 1 MSA (Last
Interglacial Deposits)   80   29   3

Figure 6.28. Minimum numbers of individuals by which eland, Cape buffalo, and bushpig are represented in samples from the Last Interglacial deposits of Klasies River Mouth Cave 1 and from the Present Interglacial deposits of nearby Nelson Bay Cave, South Africa. The relatively greater abundance of buffalo and bushpig at Nelson Bay probably reflects the technological superiority of local LSA hunters over their MSA predecessors.

anywhere else had the bow and arrow, which means that, relative to LSA hunters, the Klasies people probably had to approach game very closely to make a kill. As a result, they probably approached very dangerous game less often.

Thus, the species-frequency data suggest that the Klasies people were less successful hunters than their LSA successors. L. R. Binford (1984) has argued that they did not hunt large mammals at all but simply scavenged carcasses they found in the veld. This could explain the pattern of large-ungulate skeletal part representation at Klasies, where skull and foot bones dominate and limb bones are relatively scarce. Skull and foot bones have less nutritional value than limb bones and thus tend to be left at large carcasses by nonhuman predators or scavengers. However, large-ungulate skull and foot bones are comparatively numerous not only at Klasies but at most prehistoric sites throughout the world, including, for example, African Iron Age sites (Voigt 1983), where the large ungulates were mainly domestic cattle that were almost certainly not scavenged. It is not totally clear why the pattern is so widespread, but relative bone durability may be largely responsible. The particular skull and foot bones involved are among the densest parts of the skeleton, and compared with limb bones, they were probably subjected to less intensive butchering or breakage during food preparation. They were thus more likely to be buried intact, and, together with their initial density, this probably helped them to remain identifiable even in the face of relatively intense postdepositional leaching and profile compaction. Thus, large-ungulate limb bones may be relatively rare in the Klasies MSA bone assemblage because they were destroyed or rendered unidentifiable by butchering, profile compaction, etc., not because the people did not obtain them.

At Klasies, the issue of scavenging versus hunting may also be addressed by analysis of the ages of large ungulates at time of death (Klein 1983). Most of the ungulates, including, for example, the buffalos, are characterized by age profiles dominated by very young animals and relatively old ones (Fig. 6.29). Prime-age adults are very rare, particularly compared with their abundance in live herds. Paleobiologists call age profiles that are poor in prime-age adults "attritional," because they could result from normal everyday mortality factors—such as endemic disease, accidents, and carnivore predation—that tend to bypass prime-age individuals and affect mainly the very young and the old. Conceivably, the Klasies people only scavenged the species represented by attritional profiles, though it seems unlikely they could have obtained so many very young individuals this way. This is because the people almost certainly could not have located very young carcasses before hyenas and other scavengers did. Modern observations indicate that these scavengers consume young carcasses quickly and completely, leaving nothing for people arriving even a little while later.

Whatever means the Klasies people used to obtain buffalo and other species characterized by attritional profiles, they clearly obtained eland very differently. This is shown by the eland age profile (Fig. 6.29), in which, relative to the very young and the old, prime-age adults are well represented, roughly in proportion to their abundance in live herds. Paleobiologists call the kind of age profile represented by the eland "catastrophic," because it could be fixed in the ground only by a great flood, volcanic eruption, or other catastrophe that kills individuals in rough proportion to their live abundance, regardless of their age. With regard to the Klasies eland, the most likely catastrophe was human driving of whole groups into traps or over cliffs such as those that occur immediately above the Klasies sites. Modern observations show that among all the species represented at Klasies, eland are the most amenable to driving, and it would appear that the Klasies people had discovered this special vulnerability.

However, the Klasies people could not have driven eland very often, or the repeated removal of numerous prime adults would have sapped the reproductive vitality of the species; and there is no evidence that eland numbers declined during or after the occupation of Klasies. Historically in Africa, eland

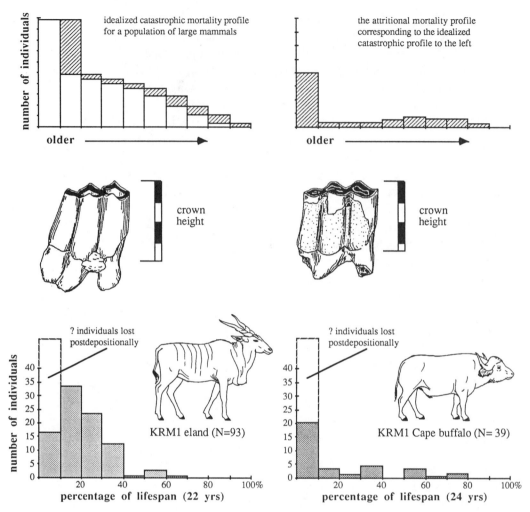

Figure 6.29. *Top left:* Schematic catastrophic-age (mortality) profile for a population of large mammals that is basically stable in size and age structure. The blank bars represent the number of individuals that survive in each successive age cohort, the hatched bars the number that die between successive cohorts. *Top right:* Separate plot of the hatched bars, showing the corresponding schematic attritional age profile. The basic form of corresponding catastrophic and attritional profiles is the same for all large mammals, but the precise form will differ from population to population, depending on species biology and specific mortality factors. *Middle:* Eland and buffalo lower third molars (M$_3$'s) showing the crown height dimension from which individual age at death may be estimated. *Bottom:* Mortality profiles based on crown heights for eland and Cape buffalo from the MSA layers of Klasies River Mouth Cave 1 (redrawn after Klein 1983). It is probable that postdepositional leaching, profile compaction, and other destructive factors have selectively destroyed teeth of the youngest eland and buffalo. When this consideration is taken into account, the eland profile is clearly catastrophic and the buffalo profile is attritional. As discussed in the text, this suggests that the Klasies people obtained eland by driving entire social groups over cliffs or into other traps, situations in which differences in individual vulnerability due to age are rendered meaningless. In contrast, the Klasies people must have obtained buffalo by using a method(s) to which prime-age adult buffalo were relatively invulnerable.

were extremely widespread but nowhere very numerous, and eland herds tended to be widely dispersed and difficult to locate. This means that the Klasies people probably rarely found eland in a position suitable for driving—and thus that they probably killed only a small fraction of the available animals. If eland were rare in the environment and if the Klasies people did not obtain them very often, it follows that the people must have been even less successful at obtaining other ungulates, such as buffalo, which were more common in the environment but are rarer in the site. In short, overall the Klasies people probably obtained very few ungulates, whether by hunting or by scavenging.

Theoretically, it might be possible to evaluate MSA hunting success at open-air sites such as Duinefontein 2, where MSA artifacts are associated with partial ungulate skeletons at probable death sites. The difficulty is that most such sites also contain carnivore coprolites or bones damaged by carnivore teeth, and it is impossible to determine the extent to which people, rather than carnivores or even accidents, were responsible for the deaths of the animals—or even the extent to which people, rather than carnivores, fed on the carcasses. In fact, open-air "kill sites" such as Duinefontein 2 are less suitable for studying Stone Age hunting or meat acquisition than are "camp sites" such as the Klasies River Mouth caves, in which the context and associations of the animal bones indicate that they were overwhelmingly accumulated by people.

Burials

One of the reasons that the Neanderthals are so well known is that they buried their dead, at least on occasion. The skeletons found at Spy Cave, Belgium, probably occurred in graves, as did more certainly those from La Chapelle-aux-Saints, La Ferrassie, Le Moustier, and other important sites in southwestern France (Bouyssonie 1954; Vandermeersch 1976). Neanderthal graves have also been uncovered at Kiik-Koba in the Crimea (USSR) and at Tabun, Amud, and Kebara Caves in Israel, at Shanidar Cave in Iraq, and at Teshik-Tash Cave in Soviet Uzbekistan (S. R. Binford 1968; Harrold 1980). La Ferrassie was a veritable cemetery of eight graves, while Shanidar may have contained five, though it remains unclear whether some skeletons were in graves or under natural rockfalls.

The skeletons of the anatomically modern, Mousterian people at Skhul and Qafzeh caves in Israel were also found in graves. So far, there is no evidence that the African contemporaries of the Neanderthals buried their dead, but the site sample is relatively small, and, as discussed above, in general, the conditions for grave preservation were not as good as in Europe and the Near East.

The Neanderthals and their contemporaries may have been the first people to bury the dead, but earlier burials may be missing because there are so few sites, particularly caves, where burials are most likely to be preserved. Even at most sites occupied by the Neanderthals and their contemporaries, isolated, fragmentary human remains, scattered among artifacts and animal bones, are far more common than intentional burials. These fragmentary bones may indicate cannibalism, which has been suggested particularly for the large quantity of Neanderthal bone fragments found at Krapina Cave in Yugoslavia (Malez 1970) and at Hortus Cave in southern France (M. A. de Lumley 1972). Alternatively, at many sites, the human bones may have become fragmented and dispersed when carnivores consumed human bodies exhumed from shallow graves or left on the surface. Partly empty graves such as those at Teshik-Tash and Kiik-Koba provide circumstantial evidence for carnivore disturbance. The spotted hyena is known to exhume human bodies in Africa today, and spotted hyenas were widespread throughout both Africa and Eurasia in the Neanderthal time range. Spotted hyenas apparently occupied Krapina Cave, at least occasionally, and tooth marks of hyenas or other carnivores occur on some of the Krapina Neanderthal bones (M. D. Russell 1987a, 1987b).

Carnivore damage has also been reported on fossil human bones from other sites, including the partial skull from Florisbad in South Africa (Clarke 1985; Tappen 1987) and the limb bones of the Neanderthal child from Teshik-Tash (Movius 1953). At the same time, there are few Neanderthal bones that were unequivocally damaged by human activity. For example, none of the breakage on the approximately eight hundred Neanderthal fragments from Krapina Cave need be attributed to people. It probably resulted mainly from rockfalls and postdepositional crushing, compounded by relatively careless excavation (Trinkaus 1985a; M. D. Russell 1987b). Arguably, some of the Krapina bones do bear scratches from stone tools, but the form and anatomical disposition of the marks suggest they were produced by the defleshing of partially decomposed bodies before burial rather than by butchery (M. D. Russell 1987a).

Neanderthal graves represent the best evidence for Neanderthal spirituality or religion (Bergounioux 1958), but, more prosaically, they may have been dug simply to remove corpses from habitation areas. In sixteen of twenty well-documented Mousterian graves in Europe and western Asia, the bodies were tightly flexed (in near-fetal position) (Harrold 1980), which could imply a burial ritual or simply a desire to dig the smallest possible burial trench. Ritual has been inferred from well-made artifacts or once-meaty animal bones found in at least fourteen of thirty-three Mousterian graves for which information is available (Harrold 1980), but there are no Mousterian burials in which the "grave goods" differ significantly from the artifacts and bones in the surrounding deposit, and in virtually all cases, accidental incorporation in the grave fill is thus a distinct possibility. In their lack of truly unusual or distinctive items, Mousterian graves contrast sharply with many later, Upper Paleolithic burials (Harrold 1980; Chase and Dibble 1987).

Perhaps the best case for ceremony being associated with Neanderthal bones comes from Monte Circeo, Italy, where construction work in 1939 exposed a cave that had been sealed by rock debris for perhaps 50,000 years (Blanc 1958; Stringer 1986c; Chase and Dibble 1987). Inside, on the cave floor, a small circle of rocks reportedly surrounded a Neanderthal skull, whose base had been broken away, perhaps to extract the brains. Unfortunately, the original position of the skull inside the circle is open to question, since the skull was moved and replaced before it was first seen by scientists. The limited additional evidence for Neanderthal ritual includes the scratched bones from Krapina, if it is assumed that the scratches were produced by methodical defleshing before burial, and the items associated with Neanderthal burials at Teshik-Tash (Movius 1953) and Shanidar Cave (Solecki 1975). At Teshik-Tash, the skull of an 8–9-year-old boy in a shallow grave was surrounded by five or six pairs of mountain goat (ibex) horns. However, goat horns were common throughout the Teshik-Tash deposit, and no plot of their overall distribution has ever been published to demonstrate the special character of the horn circle. At Shanidar, the grave fill associated with skeleton number 4 contained numerous clumps of flower pollen. However, the fill was heavily disturbed by rodent burrows, and it is possible the pollen is intrusive (Chase and Dibble 1987). The Shanidar "flower burial" will probably remain problematic as long as it is unique.

In sum, the Neanderthals and possibly their contemporaries clearly buried their dead, at least sometimes; but it does not follow that the motivation was religious, and the graves tended to be far simpler than those of their anatomically modern successors.

Population Numbers

There are no practical or theoretical grounds for estimating the absolute population densities of the Neanderthals or their contemporaries, though there is good evidence for population fluctuation through time. This is especially true in northern and southern Africa, where site paucity suggests a population crash in the later Mousterian (Aterian)/MSA, probably because of extremely arid conditions during the middle part of the Last Glaciation. Early–LSA/Upper Paleolithic sites are also rare, probably for the same reason.

Population fluctuations attributable to climatic change are less obvious in the Near East and especially in Europe, but they may well have occurred. Together with an obvious preservation bias against older sites, the possible effects of climatic change must be considered before using site numbers or densities to draw inferences about the numbers of Mousterian/MSA or later people. Still, when only sites that are about equally rich in occupational debris and that were probably occupied about the same length of time under broadly similar climatic conditions are considered, it appears that per unit time, Mousterian sites were much less abundant in Europe than were Upper Paleolithic ones. In southwestern France and neighboring northwest Spain, there is probably less than one Mousterian cave for every five Upper Paleolithic ones (Mellars 1973, 1982; Straus 1977; G. A. Clark and Straus 1983). The implication is that the Mousterians were less numerous than their successors, probably because they exploited the available animal and plant resources less efficiently. In addition, the bodily robusticity of the Neanderthals, which was probably linked to their relatively unsophisticated technology, meant that they required more calories per individual than their successors, which in turn meant that they could support fewer individuals with a given number of calories. Thus, even if Neanderthals extracted as much energy from nature as their successors, their population would have been smaller.

Smaller site numbers could also be used to infer smaller Mousterian/MSA populations in Africa, relative to Upper Paleolithic/LSA ones, but the data are more problematic because of a smaller overall site sample and because of the known complication introduced by climatic effects. However, in southern Africa, smaller MSA populations are probably implied by the relatively large size of limpets and tortoises in MSA sites, relative to those in LSA sites occupied under broadly comparable climatic conditions (Figs. 6.30, 6.31) (Klein 1979; Klein and Cruz-Uribe 1983). Both limpets and tortoises

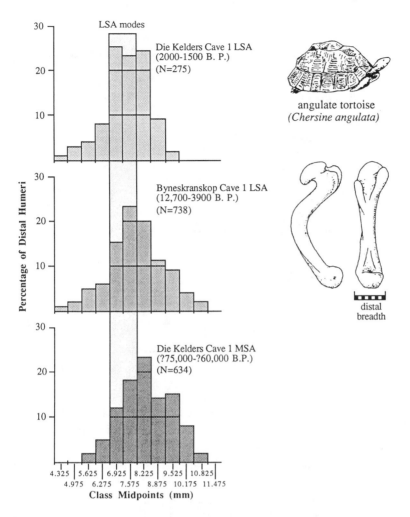

Percentage of Distal Humeri

LSA modes

Die Kelders Cave 1 LSA
(2000-1500 B. P.)
(N=275)

angulate tortoise
(Chersine angulata)

Byneskranskop Cave 1 LSA
(12,700-3900 B. P.)
(N=738)

distal
breadth

Die Kelders Cave 1 MSA
(?75,000-?60,000 B.P.)
(N=634)

Class Midpoints (mm)

Figure 6.30. Mediolateral diameters (breadths) of angulate tortoise distal humeri from the MSA and LSA deposits of Die Kelders Cave 1 and the LSA deposits of nearby Byneskranskop Cave 1, South Africa. The histograms lump humeri from long time periods, and subdivision of the samples by layer shows that there was size variation within these periods, particularly at Byneskranskop. However, the layer-by-layer samples reveal the same broad pattern as the histograms: on average the MSA humeri are significantly larger than the LSA ones. The implication is that LSA people collected tortoises more intensively, perhaps because LSA people were more numerous. (For additional discussion, see Klein and Cruz-Uribe 1983.)

grow more or less continuously through life, and larger average size in MSA sites implies limited human predation pressure, probably because MSA populations themselves were relatively small.

Demography and Disease

The Neanderthals and their contemporaries are represented by both sexes and by both children and adults. However, it is impossible to estimate most Neanderthal demographic characteristics, partly because the total fossil sample is relatively small and is a composite of many subsamples from diverse times and places and partly because the record is certainly biased against younger individuals, whose bones are much less durable than those of adults and therefore far more likely to have been destroyed by profile compaction, leaching, and other

Figure 6.31. Maximum diameter of limpet (*Patella granatina*) shells in modern samples, LSA samples from the Paternoster Midden and Elands Bay Cave, and the MSA sample from the Sea Harvest Midden site, South Africa. In each case, the vertical line indicates the mean, the horizontal line indicates one standard deviation from the mean, and the figure in parentheses after the sample name is the number of measured specimens. The modern samples were collected by students, in 10-minute intervals, from intertidal rocks that are not being exploited today. The data suggest that LSA people exploited limpets more intensively than did their MSA predecessors, perhaps because the LSA people were more numerous. (The modern and LSA data are from Buchanan et al. 1978; the Sea Harvest data are from J. E. Parkington, personal communication).

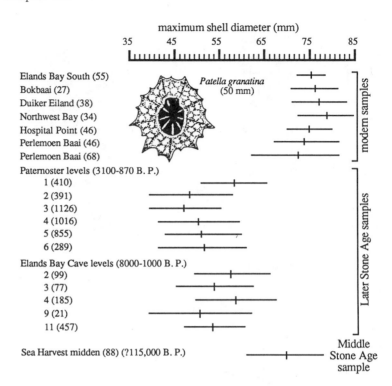

postdepositional destructive pressures. The only Neanderthal demographic statistic that may be reasonably calculated from the available sample is maximum life expectancy.

If it is assumed that Neanderthals and living people shared the same basic pattern of skeletal development, the ages of adult Neanderthals at death can be estimated from macroscopic features such as the morphology of the pubic symphysis and the sacroiliac joint, the degree of cranial suture obliteration, and the extent of dental wear. Among these, dental wear is the least reliable in absolute terms, because, on average, the Neanderthals plainly wore their teeth more rapidly than most living people do. Ultimately, the most accurate age estimates for Neanderthal adults may come from microscopic examination of fossilized bone cells or osteons in long-bone shafts (Thompson and Trinkaus 1981). At the moment, macroscopic and osteon aging of the oldest Neanderthals suggests they were only in their late thirties to mid-forties (Trinkaus 1986; Trinkaus and Thompson 1987). They may have been even younger, if the rate of aging in Neanderthal adults matched the relatively rapid rate of development that can be inferred from the skulls of Neanderthal children (Dean et al. 1986). By comparison, as discussed in the next chapter, the early modern successors of the Neanderthals had a maximum life expectancy exceeding 50 years. One important implication is that early modern populations probably contained far more individuals beyond reproductive age. They probably constituted an economic burden on younger people, but this would have been more than offset by the knowledge and experience they could provide, especially in times of crisis.

The skeletons of elderly Neanderthals usually exhibit pathologies or injuries that must have made life difficult and that in some cases were probably the cause of death. The most famous case is certainly the "old man" of La Chapelle-aux-Saints, who at age 40–45 years suffered both from severe periodontal disease that caused substantial antemortem tooth loss and from degenerative joint disease (osteoarthritis) that is particularly obvious in the articulation of the mandible to the skull and in the spinal column, hip, and foot (Trinkaus 1985b). Other Neanderthals with obvious pathologies or injuries include Shanidar individuals 1 and 3–5, La Ferrassie 1, La Quina 5, the original (Feldhofer) Neanderthal from Germany, one of the individuals from Krapina Cave, and Šala 1 (Czechoslovakia) (Trinkaus 1978, 1983b). On Shanidar 1, the left orbit was crushed from the side (Fig. 6.32), the right arm was withered, and the right ankle was afflicted by extensive arthritic degen-

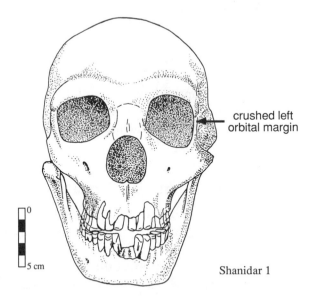

crushed left
orbital margin

0

5 cm

Shanidar 1

Figure 6.32. Face of Shanidar 1, showing the crushed outer margin of the left orbit (drawn by K. Cruz-Uribe from a photograph). The crushing was not fatal and the orbit healed, but associated brain damage may have partially paralyzed the individual's right side, accounting for a withered right arm. Like other injured or aged Neanderthals, he survived only with the help of other members of his group.

eration. The blow that damaged the left orbit perhaps caused brain damage that partially paralyzed the right side, inducing the arm and ankle pathologies.

Shanidar 3 suffered from debilitating arthritis of both the right ankle and adjacent foot joints and probably died of a stab wound that pierced the lung, leaving an ugly scar on one of the ribs. Shanidar 4 had a healed rib fracture (also seen in the individual from La Chapelle-aux-Saints), and Shanidar 5 had a large scar, caused by a sharp blow to the head, on the left frontal. La Ferrassie 1 had an injured right femur and, like other aged Neanderthals, suffered from periodontal disease. La Quina 5 had a withered left arm. The original Neanderthal individual and one of the Krapina Neanderthals had damaged ulnae that deformed the forearm. On the Šala 1 skull, the right supraorbital torus exhibits a healed lesion.

Antemortem trauma has also been observed in the skeletons of the earliest fully modern people, but much less frequently (Trinkaus, in press). The implication is probably that Neanderthal technology (or culture in general) was relatively ineffective at reducing wear and tear on Neanderthal bodies. However, the same skeletal pathologies and injuries that show that the Neanderthals lived risky lives and aged early also reveal a strikingly "human" feature of their social life. The La Chapelle-aux-Saints and Shanidar 1 individuals, for example, must have been severely incapacitated and would have died even earlier without substantial help and care from their comrades. The implicit group concern for the old and sick may have permitted Neanderthals to live longer than any of their predecessors, and it is the most recognizably human, nonmaterial aspect of their behavior that can be directly inferred from the archeological record.

Conclusion: The Fate of the Neanderthals

It is not difficult to understand why the Neanderthals failed to survive after behaviorally modern humans appeared. The archeological record shows that in virtually every detectable aspect—artifacts, site modification, ability to adapt to extreme environments, subsistence, and so forth—the Neanderthals were behaviorally inferior to their modern successors, and, to judge from their distinctive morphology, this behavioral inferiority may well have been rooted in their biological makeup.

A far more difficult question to answer is how the Neanderthals succumbed—were they physically replaced by anatomically modern intruders, or did they evolve into modern people? Increasingly, the answer seems to be that they were physically usurped, but the issue remains debatable. It is best addressed by considering the evidence from various regions.

Western Europe

Physical displacement seems almost certain for France and adjacent parts of western Europe, now that the Saint-Césaire skeleton and typically Neanderthal (taurodont) teeth from Arcy-sur-Cure show that Neanderthals survived in France until at least 35,000 years ago. The geologic age of the oldest anatomically modern fossils in France is not well fixed, but a date of at least 30,000 years ago is probable. Most notably, this can be inferred for the famous modern fossils found at the Cro-Magnon shelter, on the basis of their presumed (Aurignacian) artifact associations (Movius 1969a). If the oldest known French and Spanish Aurignacian artifacts indicate modern human presence even in the absence of human fossils, modern humans appeared in western Europe at least 33,000–34,000 years ago.

The Saint-Césaire and Arcy artifacts might be used to argue for continuity between Neanderthals and later people, since these artifacts clearly belong to the Chatelperronian Industry. This industry is commonly regarded as the earliest Upper Paleolithic manifestation in the limited area of northern Spain and western and central France (west of the Rhône River) where it occurs (Harrold 1983; Lévêque and Miskovsky 1983), and the Upper Paleolithic, in turn, is usually equated with anatomically modern people. However, in terms of stone artifacts, the Chatelperronian resembles the Mousterian of Acheulean Tradition type B (with numerous backed knives), and the possibility that its distinctive Upper Paleolithic traits reflect the diffusion of Upper Paleolithic elements into a local Mousterian context must be seriously considered (Harrold 1983, and in press; Klein 1973b). These elements include well-made endscrapers and burins, as well as formal bone artifacts and pierced animal teeth, especially those from the Grotte du Renne at Arcy-sur-Cure (Fig. 6.33) (André Leroi-Gourhan 1965a; Movius 1969b).

At the Grotte du Renne, the Chatelperronians also modified their living area to an extent that is common only in the Upper Paleolithic. The Grotte du Renne Chatelperronian layers contain traces of several "hut emplacements," of which the best preserved is a rough circle of eleven postholes, enclosing an area 3–4 m across that was partially paved with limestone plaques (Fig. 6.34). Pollen analysis indicates that wood was rare nearby, and the postholes probably supported mammoth tusks,

Figure 6.33. Stone and bone artifacts from the Chatelperronian levels of the Grotte du Renne, Arcy-sur-Cure, north-central France (redrawn after Movius 1969b: Figs. 3–8). Numerous well-made burins, bone artifacts, and items of personal adornment justify assigning the Chatelperronian to the Upper Paleolithic, but the morphology of the backed knives suggests links to an immediately preceding variant of the Mousterian (Middle Paleolithic), and the possibility exists that the Chatelperronian resulted from the diffusion of Upper Paleolithic traits into a basically Mousterian context. Its makers, insofar as they are known, were Neanderthals.

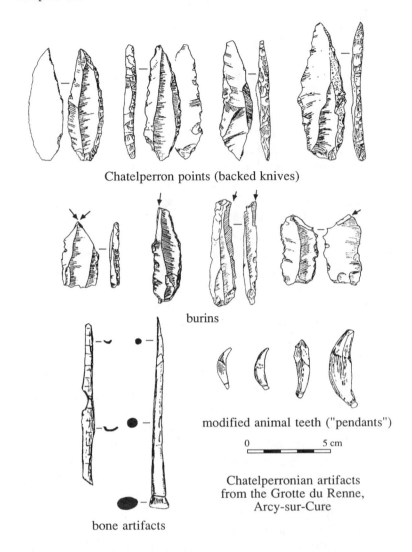

Chatelperron points (backed knives)

burins

modified animal teeth ("pendants")

0   5 cm

Chatelperronian artifacts
from the Grotte du Renne,
Arcy-sur-Cure

bone artifacts

which are more abundant in the Grotte du Renne than in any other known Paleolithic cave.

The most probable diffusionary source for the Chatelperronian was the Upper Paleolithic Aurignacian Industry, which clearly intruded into western Europe. The interstratification of Chatelperronian and early Aurignacian layers at the Roc du Combe and Le Piage shelters (southwestern France) and at el Pendo Cave (northern Spain) plainly demonstrates chronological overlap, probably beginning around 35,000 years ago. Intersite correlations based on paleoclimatic inferences from pollen and sediments imply that Aurignacian people appeared first in the south of France and then spread progressively northward, replacing the last Chatelperronians (in north-central France) around 32,500 years ago (Leroyer and Leroi-Gourhan 1983).

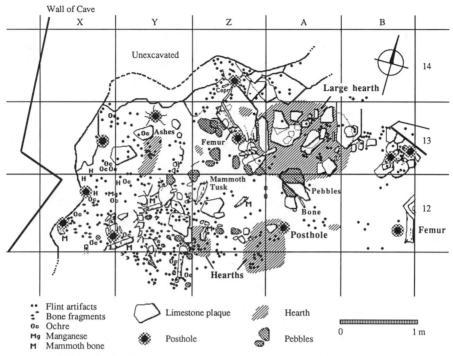

Grotte du Renne, Arcy-sur-Cure, Chatelperronian hut emplacement

Figure 6.34. Plan of the Chatelperronian hut emplacement in level XI of the Grotte du Renne, Arcy-sur-Cure, north-central France (redrawn after Movius 1969b: 119). Eleven postholes delimit the area of the hut, partially paved with limestone plaques in the north and west sectors. Each cross indicates a fragment of bone, while each dot indicates a flint tool, each "M" indicates a mammoth-bone fragment, each "Mg" indicates a fragment of manganese pigment, and each "Oc" indicates a fragment of ochreous (iron oxide) pigment.

Central Europe

In central Europe, the skeletal evidence bearing on the relationship between Neanderthals and early modern people is more ambiguous, partly because the Neanderthal sample consists almost entirely of fragments rather than of complete or nearly complete skulls and skeletons. On the basis of geological context and artifact or faunal associations, F. H. Smith (1982, 1984) has divided the central European Neanderthals into an early group (from Krapina in Yugoslavia, Gánovce and Ochoz in Czechoslovakia, and Subalyuk Cave in Hungary), which perhaps dates from the Last Interglaciation and the earliest part of the Last Glaciation, and a later group (from Vindija Cave in Yugoslavia and Kulna Cave, Šipka Cave, and perhaps Šala in Czechoslovakia), which may date from the middle of the Last Glaciation. The majority of specimens come from Krapina (about eight hundred pieces) and Vindija (about thirty-five pieces). Smith argues that, compared with earlier central European Neanderthals, the later ones had smaller, thinner, and less projecting browridges, foreheads that were perhaps less receding, smaller and somewhat less prognathous faces, mandibles with a greater tendency for chin development, and perhaps smaller anterior teeth. They may thus have been evolving toward early-modern central Europeans, such as those from the Mladeč (Lautsch) Caves and from Předmostí in Czechoslovakia, who perhaps approached the late Neanderthals in browridge size and general cranial ruggedness.

However, Smith's argument is problematic, not only because the Neanderthal fossils tend to be so fragmentary but also because the sample of truly diagnostic specimens is relatively small, especially with regard to the supposed later Neanderthals. Additionally, in general, the specimens are poorly dated and their context and associations are often poorly established or specified. Finally, the trends that Smith has postulated plainly involve reductions in craniofacial size or ruggedness more than they do changes in morphology (Howells 1982; Stringer 1982). The early modern (Aurignacian and Pavlovian) inhabitants of central Europe, especially the males, certainly had rugged skulls, often with large browridges, prominent muscle markings, and occipitals that exhibit some posterior projection (a "hemi-bun") and extensive nuchal planes. However, in overall morphological pattern, both cranially and postcranially they are unmistakably modern, with no true Neanderthal features (Fig. 6.7).

Parallel to the skeletal remains, central European artifact assemblages may imply local continuity between the Mousterian and the Upper Paleolithic, but the evidence is not compelling. Like the Chatelperronian Industry to the west, the central European Szeletian Industry is often said to be an early Upper Paleolithic manifestation with roots in the local Mousterian. However, the Szeletian has not been clearly and consistently defined by central European archeologists (Valoch 1969, 1972). It includes diverse assemblages whose principal shared feature are bifacially worked pieces, mainly (but not always) leaf-shaped (foliate) points. Most Szeletian assemblages are dominated by Mousterian sidescrapers, denticulates, and so forth, but some are relatively rich in endscrapers and burins, and it is these assemblages that suggest continuity between the local Mousterian and the Upper Paleolithic. However, it is possible that Szeletian assemblages with well-made endscrapers and burins reflect the inadvertent mixture of Mousterian and Upper Paleolithic assemblages during excavation. It is further possible that if an Upper Paleolithic Szeletian truly exists, then, like the Chatelperronian, it reflects the diffusion of Aurignacian traits into a Mousterian context, rather than a local origin of the Upper Paleolithic (Valoch 1969, 1972, 1982a; Allsworth-Jones 1986b).

As in Western Europe, so in central Europe, the Aurignacian represents the earliest unequivocal Upper Paleolithic, and it was almost certainly intrusive (Valoch 1969, 1972). It is remarkably similar to the west European Aurignacian but probably appeared in central Europe at least 1,000 years earlier, certainly by 36,000 years ago (F. H. Smith 1982, 1984; Valoch 1982a; Gamble 1986) and perhaps before 40,000 years ago (Kozlowski 1982).

Eastern Europe

In Eastern Europe, except for the skeleton of an 18–19-month-old child from the Mousterian deposits of Starosel'e Cave in the Crimea, there is very little skeletal evidence bearing directly on the fate of the Neanderthals. The Starosel'e child is anatomically modern and could imply that the earliest modern people in eastern Europe made Mousterian artifacts, just as they did in the Near East. However, the excavator of Starosel'e could not detect any stratigraphy in the 4-m-thick profile, and chemical analysis of the Starosel'e child's bones suggests that they are considerably younger than the animal bones from the same deposits (Klein 1969b). It is therefore possible, perhaps even likely, that the child was buried from a much more recent level.

There is no convincing evidence for continuity between the Mousterian and the Upper Paleolithic in eastern Europe, but the Upper Paleolithic was certainly established there by 36,000 years ago (Hoffecker 1986), undoubtedly earlier than in western Europe. The earliest Upper Paleolithic industries of eastern Europe are still poorly known or described, but there is no trace of the Aurignacian, at least east of the Carpathian Mountains, and, from its very inception, the east European Upper Paleolithic appears to have followed a distinct course.

Western Asia

The Near East perhaps presents the best evidence for a local evolution of Neanderthals into modern people, namely, from Neanderthals like those represented at Tabun, Amud, and Shanidar Caves into early modern people like those represented at Skhul and Qafzeh Caves (Fig. 6.35). In both their cranial and postcranial morphology, the Skhul and Qafzeh people are unquestionably modern; but they were extremely robust, and the Skhul people in particular are noticeably variable in features such as the degree of chin or forehead development. As a result of their variability and robusticity, when the Skhul skeletons were first monographically described (McCown and Keith 1939), they were actually lumped with the Neanderthal fossils from nearby Tabun. Subsequently, the Tabun and Skhul people together were sometimes called

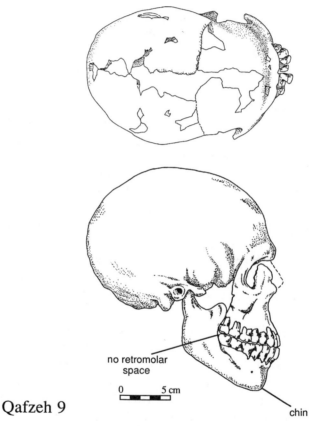

Qafzeh 9

Figure 6.35. *Top:* Top view of the skull of Qafzeh 9, partially reconstructed. *Bottom:* Lateral view of the same skull, more fully reconstructed (adapted from Vandermeersch 1981: Figs. 9, 10, 43). The human fossils from Qafzeh Cave (Israel) are associated with Mousterian artifacts, but in all important respects they are anatomically modern. In contrast to the Neanderthals, the Qafzeh people had relatively high, short braincases that overlapped the face below. Retraction of the face beneath the braincase is reflected in the absence of a retromolar space and in the presence of a chin. Thermoluminescence readings suggest that Qafzeh fossils date from near the end of the Last Interglaciation, when Neanderthals were the sole inhabitants of Europe. The population they represent may have been displaced from southwest Asia by Neanderthals spreading from Europe at the beginning of the Last Glaciation.

"Progressive Neanderthals," as opposed to "Classic Neanderthals" such as those from the caves of southwestern France.

One obvious difficulty with postulating continuity between the Near Eastern Neanderthals and their early modern successors is the strong possibility that the early moderns partly or wholly antedate the local Neanderthals. As discussed earlier, this is suggested by rodent biostratigraphy, by sedimentologic/geomorphic data, and especially by thermoluminescence dates placing the Qafzeh moderns at about 92,000 years ago and the Kebara Neanderthals at about 60,000 years ago. If this dating is even broadly correct, it would rule out an evolutionary link between the local Neanderthals and modern humans (Stringer 1988). It would also raise some fresh questions, such as how the two groups could have shared the Near East for tens of thousands of years and what kept the early moderns of Qafzeh or their descendants from spreading to Europe for perhaps 50,000 years.

With regard to the problem of prolonged coresidence, the answer may be that it did not actually occur. The early moderns of Qafzeh (and Skhul) could represent the descendants of modern or near-modern Africans who spread to the Levant under the relatively mild and moist conditions of the Last Interglaciation. Alternatively, they could be simply the northeasternmost result of a process of natural selection and gene flow that produced modern or near-modern people at the same time, if not earlier, in nearby Africa. In contrast, the Near Eastern Neanderthals could represent migrants from Europe who displaced early moderns in the Levant when climatic conditions deteriorated at the beginning of the Last Glaciation (Howell 1957; Vandermeersch 1981, 1982; Bar-Yosef 1987). Neanderthal physiques may have been better adapted to relatively cool conditions, and there is nothing in the cultural debris of the Qafzeh/Skhul people (or of their putative modern or near-modern African ancestors and contemporaries) to suggest they had a special cultural (behavioral) advantage over the Neanderthals. In fact, from a strictly archeological (behavioral) perspective, there is nothing to differentiate the Qafzeh/Skhul people (or their African contemporaries) from the Neanderthals in either the Near East or Europe.

The hypothesis that Neanderthals displaced very early moderns in the Near East can be checked by fresh fossil and archeological discoveries and especially by additional dates. However, whatever these show, they will not explain why it took so long for early moderns to develop fully modern behavior. It was almost surely this behavior—or, more precisely, the modern capacity for culture—that allowed later "early moderns" to supplant the Neanderthals and other nonmodern people throughout the world. One possible explanation is that the Qafzeh/Skhul people (and their African modern or near-modern contemporaries) were not really as modern as their skeletal remains suggest. Perhaps their brains lacked some crucial feature that is not detectable in skeletal remains. Conceivably, this appeared only relatively late in modern human evolution, perhaps as an adaptive response to the especially arid conditions that stressed early "modern" populations during the Last Glaciation over much of Africa. Unfortunately, this idea will be very difficult to test.

In keeping with the proximity of the Near East to a putative African center of modern human evolution, the archeological record indicates that people who were behaviorally modern appeared in the Near East relatively early. The Upper Paleolithic was locally established before 35,000 years ago, probably before 40,000 years ago, and Boker Tachtit in Israel may record the transition from the Mousterian to the Upper Paleolithic broadly understood. The Aurignacian may have originated in the Near East, though it was probably not the earliest Upper Paleolithic industry there (Gilead 1981; Marks 1981b).

Africa

Among all the places from which skeletal evidence is available, Africa appears to present the best case for a local or regional evolution of anatomically modern people, certainly during the period while Neanderthals still occupied western Europe and before they had disappeared from the Near East. An essentially African origin for early modern Europeans could explain why they had relatively long distal limb segments (forearms and lower legs) compared with those of the Neanderthals, if it is assumed that distal limb length in both the Neanderthals and early modern people was mainly a genetic response to climate. It is also consistent with studies of modern human genetic diversity, discussed further in the next chapter, which suggest that modern Europeans and Asians are descended from a common African founder population (J. S. Jones, and Rouhani 1986; Wainscoat et al. 1986; Cann et al. 1987b). Genetic-distance analyses do not allow an unequivocal estimate of when Eurasians diverged from their African ancestral population, but this divergence was almost certainly after the distinctive Neanderthal morphology was already established in Europe. The implication is that Neanderthals played little or no role in the evolution of modern Europeans.

The archeological record in Africa lends further support to the notion that modern people originated there. The Upper Paleolithic/LSA was almost certainly underway at least as early in Africa as anywhere else—by 38,000–40,000 years ago, if not before. The earliest known Upper Paleolithic industry in north Africa, from ed Dabba Cave and the Haua Fteah in Libya, is broadly similar to the earliest known Upper Paleolithic industries in the Near East and Europe in the prevalence of blades and of well-made endscrapers and burins, but the resemblances do not suggest any direct connections. The earliest LSA industries south of the Sahara are still poorly known, partly because they appeared during a long dry interval when human populations were dramatically depressed in many regions. Consequently, early LSA occupation sites are rare; though, on present evidence, they appear to be more common in east Africa than in southern Africa. East Africa is probably the best place not only to date the origins of the LSA but also to seek human fossils that may conclusively demonstrate the African origin of fully modern people.

Overview

In sum, both the question of what happened to the Neanderthals and the closely related question of where and when modern people originated remain inconclusively resolved. However, on present evidence, it is certainly reasonable to hypothesize that modern people appeared first in Africa. They may have spread early on to the Near East, if in fact the Near East was not essentially part of the basic African area in which they first evolved. Initially, their behavioral capabilities apparently differed little from those of the Neanderthals, but eventually, perhaps because of a neurological change that is not detectable in the fossil record, they developed a capacity for culture that gave them a clear adaptive advantage over the Neanderthals and all other nonmodern people. The result was that they spread throughout the world, physically replacing all nonmoderns, of whom the last to succumb were perhaps the Neanderthals of western Europe. This hypothesis is discussed further in the next chapter, devoted specifically to the earliest fully modern humans.

7 ANATOMICALLY MODERN HUMANS

A combination of fossil and genetic evidence indicates that modern humans evolved between 200,000 and 50,000 years ago, probably in Africa. A more conclusive, more precise statement will require a much denser fossil record and either new dating methods or significant refinements to existing ones that cover the 200,000–50,000-years-ago range. However, even if the time and place are not yet fully fixed, the significance of modern human origins cannot be overstated. Prior to the emergence of modern people, the human form and human behavior evolved together slowly, hand in hand. Afterward, fundamental evolutionary change in body form ceased, while behavioral (cultural) evolution accelerated dramatically. The implication is that the modern human form—or, more precisely, the modern human brain—permitted the full development of culture in the modern sense and that culture then became the primary means by which people responded to natural selective pressures. As an adaptive mechanism, culture is not only far more malleable than the body, but cultural innovations can accumulate far more rapidly than genetic ones; and the result is that in a remarkably short time the human species has transformed itself from a relatively rare, even insignificant large mammal to the dominant life form on the planet. This chapter summarizes what is known about modern human origins, emphasizing especially the very significant behavioral differences between even very early modern people and their nonmodern predecessors.

History of Discovery

Until the mid-nineteenth century, human origins were a subject mainly for theologians, not scientists (C. C. Gillespie 1951; Eiseley 1961; Grayson 1983). Medieval clerics summed the ages of post-Adamite generations in the Bible and concluded that the present world was created about 4,000 B. C. This estimate became gospel, and even most eighteenth- and early-nineteenth-century geologists and paleontologists accepted it. To explain extinct species they postulated a series of earlier, imperfect creations, each terminated by a great flood or other global catastrophe. This notion, commonly termed "creationism" or "catastrophism," was widely questioned only after 1859, when Darwin's *Origin of Species* showed how living species could have evolved from earlier ones through the process of natural selection.

Creationism clearly implied that people had not coexisted with long-extinct species. However, during the first half of the nineteenth century, fossil hunters searching in European caves repeatedly found bones of anatomically modern humans alongside those of extinct animals (Oakley 1964; Grayson 1983). Excavation methods were crude, and in some cases the associations were probably erroneous, created, for example, when excavators failed to recognize a relatively recent grave dug into much more ancient deposits. In other cases, however, the associations were undoubtedly valid and implied that modern people had lived in Europe long before popular theology allowed. Since the theology was largely unquestioned, the associations were generally discounted, though some have been vindicated in the present century. Perhaps the most famous example was from Goat's Hole (Cave) at Paviland, South Wales, where the Rev. William Buckland, Professor of Geology at Oxford, excavated a skeleton in 1822–23 (Molleson 1976). It was covered by a layer of red ochre and was accompanied by numerous mammoth-ivory artifacts, but Buckland concluded it belonged to a Welsh woman of the Roman era whose kinfolk made artifacts from tusks they found in the cave. In fact, direct radiocarbon dating now shows the skeleton is about 18,500 years old and thus represents a person (actually a young male) who was a contemporary of the mammoth (Oakley 1980).

Probably the best-known discovery after Paviland occurred in 1852, when a road repairman pulled a human bone from a rabbit hole in a hillside near Aurignac, southern France (Oakley 1964). He dug a trench into the hillside and found a cave whose mouth was blocked by a collapsed limestone slab. Behind the slab lay the skeletons of seventeen people, while backdirt from the trench contained bones from extinct animals, some of which were engraved. The skeletons were reburied in a local Christian cemetery, but the site attracted the attention of the pioneer French prehistorian, Edouard Lartet, who excavated the cave floor systematically in 1860. He found some isolated human bones apparently associated with those of extinct mammals, but the association was never conclusively established. It is now thought the skeletons were of Neolithic (Holocene) age, postdating the extinct animals.

The first widely accepted discovery of clearly very ancient but anatomically modern human remains occurred only in 1868, when railway workers exposed deposits with human bones in the Cro-Magnon rock-shelter near the town of Les Eyzies in the Dordogne region of southwestern France. An excavation by Edouard Lartet's son, Louis, showed that the bones were stratified in a layer that also contained bones of mammoth, lion, and reindeer, along with numerous artifacts (Lartet 1868). These latter included both stone tools (of the kind now called Evolved Aurignacian), as well as artificially perforated seashells and animal teeth. The human bones represented at least five people, including a middle-aged male (subsequently called the "Old Man of Cro-Magnon"), two younger adult males, a young adult female, and a very young infant (Oakley et al. 1971). From their well-established associations, it was clear that they were very ancient, and radiocarbon dates associated with similar artifacts excavated in the 1950s at the nearby Abri Pataud now suggest an age of about 30,000 years (Movius 1969a). Curiously, for a brief period, the Cro-Magnon skeletons could be cited against the concept of human evolution, for it could be argued that the Cro-Magnon people were in Europe as early as or earlier than nonmodern kinds of people, particularly the Neanderthals, who were discovered at broadly the same time. However, even before the turn of the century, it became apparent that, while the Cro-Magnons were indeed very ancient, they still postdated the Neanderthals.

Not long after the discovery at the Cro-Magnon shelter, several other European sites provided modern human remains clearly associated with animal bones or artifacts indicating great antiquity. Some of the most important early discoveries were made at Lautsch (Mladeč) (1881–82, 1903–4), Brno (Francouzská Street) (1891), and Předmostí (1894), all in Moravia (Czechoslovakia) (F. H. Smith 1982, 1984); at the Chancelade (Raymonden) Shelter (1888) and Combe-Capelle Cave (1909) in France; and at the Grimaldi Caves in Italy (1874–1901) (Oakley et al. 1971; Stringer et al. 1984) (Fig. 7.1). Together, the finds made at these and many other, more recently excavated sites show that anatomically modern people have occupied Europe for at least the past 35,000 years. The exact period may vary from place to place, as discussed below.

Remains of ancient, anatomically modern people have also been found in other parts of the world, though in smaller numbers than in Europe. The first were the Wajak skulls found

Figure 7.1. Approximate locations of the European Upper Paleolithic sites mentioned in the text.

in central Java in 1890 (Dubois 1922). Among the best known are the anatomically modern skeletons found in the "Upper Cave" at Zhoukoudian in north China in 1933–34 (Jia 1980), but for unraveling modern human origins, the most important finds outside Europe have been made in the Near East, in Australia, and, most recently, in Africa. Colloquially, all early modern people are sometimes called Cro-Magnons after the early and historically significant French discovery. However, technically, only people who closely resembled the original Cro-Magnons should be known by this term, and here all early, anatomically modern people will be referred to simply as early

Figure 7.2. Skull of an anatomically modern adult male buried more than 25,000 years ago at the Upper Paleolithic site of Kostenki XIV (layer 3) on the Don River in European Russia (redrawn after Debets 1955: 46). The skull exhibits slightly more alveolar prognathism (forward protrusion of the jaws) than do most Upper Paleolithic skulls but is otherwise typical of early modern Europeans. Its distinctively modern (as opposed to Neanderthal) features include the relatively high, short braincase with a nearly vertical frontal (forehead), the relatively short face with a distinct hollowing (canine fossa) between the nasal cavity and the anterior root of the zygomatic arch, the pronounced chin (vertical mandibular symphysis), and the absence of a retromolar space.

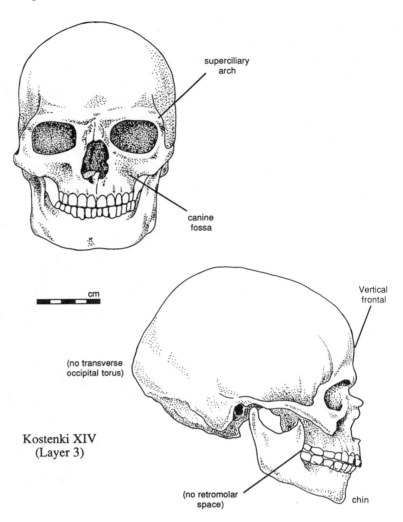

moderns, meaning fossil people whose skeletons are not meaningful distinguished from those of living people. Together with living people, early moderns are commonly assigned to the subspecies *Homo sapiens sapiens.*

Morphology

Any osteological diagnosis of *Homo sapiens sapiens* must encompass a far greater range of variation than is known for any earlier hominid taxon, each of which is represented by far fewer specimens. A succinct diagnosis is thus almost bound to fail, since marginal exceptions will always exist. Nonetheless, the following is a reasonably accurate description of the subspecies as it is distinguished osteologically from other hominids:

Cranium (Fig. 7.2)

Average endocranial capacity variable from population to population, but generally greater than 1,350 cc; frontal bone (forehead) relatively vertical; vault (braincase) relatively high, more or less parallel sided, usually with some outward bulging (bossing) in the parietal region; occipital contour relatively rounded and lacking a prominent transverse torus; browridge development generally greater in males than in females and variable among populations, rarely forming a continuous bar (supraorbital torus) across the top of the orbits but instead usually consisting of two parts—a variably bulging lateral (superciliary) arch at the upper outer corner of each orbit, separated by a (supraorbital) notch or groove from an elongated (supraorbital) swelling along the upper inner margin (Fig. 7.3.) (these swellings meet in a V between the orbits to form the so-called supraorbital trigone); face relatively flat and tucked in beneath the anterior portion of the braincase; distinct hollowing of the bone (canine fossa) below each orbit, between the nasal cavity and the cheek bone (zygomatic arch); mandible variably robust, partly in keeping with significant interpopulational variation in tooth size, but almost always with a distinct chin; usually no gap (retromolar space) between the third molar and the ascending ramus when viewed from the side, reflecting the retraction of the face under the skull; substantial variability in the expression of many features (as discussed, for example, by Howells 1973a, 1973b), but never sufficient to incorporate earlier forms of people.

Postcranium

Limb bones sometimes very robust, with pronounced muscle markings, particularly in the earliest modern people, but still significantly less robust than in earlier kinds of people; distinctions from the Neanderthals, thanks to the large available sample of Neanderthal postcrania (Trinkaus 1983a), are especially clear, and, besides decreased overall robusticity, include axillary margin of the scapula sometimes bisulcate, most commonly unisculate, with the sulcus or groove located on the ventral surface, rather than on the dorsal surface as in Neanderthals; distal phalange of the thumb usually about two-thirds the length of the proximal one, rather than being nearly equal in length as in the Neanderthals; apical tufts or tuberosities on the terminal phalanges of the hand relatively small and elongated, versus large and round in Neanderthals; cortical bone of the femur and tibia much thinner than in the Nean-

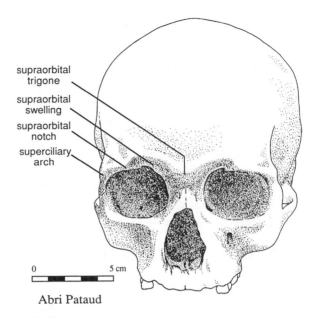

supraorbital
trigone

supraorbital
swelling

supraorbital
notch

superciliary
arch

0   5 cm

Abri Pataud

Figure 7.3. Skull of an anatomically modern, 15–18 year-old woman buried roughly 22,000 years ago in the Pataud Rock-shelter, southwestern France (drawn by K. Cruz-Uribe from a slide). The drawing has been deliberately oriented and shaded to emphasize the characteristically modern, two-part structure of the browridge. The two distinct parts are the supraorbital swelling and superciliary arch, separated from each other by the supraorbital notch.

derthals; distal limb segments (lower arm and lower leg) usually longer relative to the entire limb than in the Neanderthals; and pubis significantly shorter and thicker than in the Neanderthals.

The probable significance of these features was considered in the last chapter. In brief, the relatively flat, retracted face, together with some aspects of skull shape, probably reflect decreased use of the anterior teeth as tools, at least by comparison with the Neanderthals. The distinctive shape of the skull may also partly mirror underlying structural changes in the brain that permit fully modern human behavior, including the distinctive innovative capability that Neanderthals and other nonmodern people apparently lacked. The decline in overall postcranial robusticity and muscularity, coupled with the cited morphological changes in the scapula, hand, femur, and tibia, probably signal a shift toward less reliance on bodily strength and more on culture (especially technology) in the performance of everyday tasks (Trinkaus 1983a, 1987a). The selective advantage of reduced robusticity was that it reduced individual food requirements and permitted a given quantity of food to support more people. At least in Europe, where skeletal data are most abundant, during the 20,000 years after modern people appeared, bodily dimensions and robusticity continued to decline, probably in relation to ongoing cultural advances (Frayer 1984). Relatively long distal limb segments may reflect an ancestral adaptation to relatively warm climates and thus an African origin for all modern people, as discussed below. The shorter, thicker pubis might reflect a smaller average birth canal (pelvic inlet), perhaps because cultural advances enabled a shorter gestation period. As a result, infants would have been exposed to critical environmental stimuli when they were neurologically especially responsive. A shorter gestation period would also allow a reduction in birth spacing, increasing the potential for population growth. However, as discussed in the last chapter, it is perhaps more probable that the differences between Neanderthal and modern human pelvises are due more to slight, if consistent, differences in habitual posture and locomotion than to differences in reproductive physiology.

Much has been written on the racial affinities of early modern people, and it has sometimes been said that "racial types" occurred in areas where they were absent historically, as for example, black Africans in Europe (Grimaldi in northern Italy and Kostenki XIV in Russia), Eskimos in Europe (Chancelade in France), and Melanesians and Eskimos in north China (Zhoukoudian Upper Cave). However, insofar as racial attributes can be established, early modern people everywhere tend to be most like the historic inhabitants of the same region (Howells 1973b). This is clear above all for Europe, where the variability in early modern (Upper Paleolithic) cranial form is completely encompassed by the variability in living Europeans and where early modern people are set off only by a tendency toward greater robusticity (Howells 1973a, 1973b).

Modern Human Origins

Much of the evidence concerning modern human origins was discussed in the last chapter in the section on "The Fate of the Neanderthals," and only a summary will be presented here. In essence, recent genetic studies suggest that all living humans are derived from a common ancestor who lived in Africa within the past 200,000 years (Wainscoat et al. 1986; J. S. Jones and Rouhani 1986; Cann et al. 1987a, 1987b; Wainscoat 1987; summary in Stringer and Andrews 1988). The most influential study so far has been the one by Cann et al. (1987b) employing mitochondrial or cytoplasmic (nonnuclear) DNA from 147 different people characterized as (sub-Saharan) Africans (20), Asians (34), Caucasians (Europeans, North Africans, and Near Easterners) (46), aboriginal Australians (21), and New Guineans

(26). The 147 subjects possessed 133 different types of mito-chondrial DNA, all assumed to originate ultimately from a single type through the process of mutation—or, more pre-cisely, through a series of mutations. Assuming that the smallest number of possible mutations is closest to the actual number that created the observed DNA diversity, Cann and her colleagues computed a genealogical diagram or tree linking the observed DNA types by their degree of evolutionary relation-ship. The tree turned out to have two main branches—one comprised exclusively of Africans and the other of some Africans and everyone else. The most parsimonious root link-ing the two main branches is in Africa, indicating that Africa was the source of the original mitochondrial DNA type from which the observed modern types originated.

This conclusion is further supported by the degree of diversity in African mitochondrial DNA, which equals or exceeds that among non-African populations, suggesting that the mutations producing the diversity have been underway longest in Africa. To estimate the time when the single, ancestral type of mitochondrial DNA existed in Africa, Cann and her colleagues used a mutation rate of 2%–4% per 1 million years, the rate necessary to account for the mitochon-drial DNA diversity specific to New Guinea, Australia, and the Americas, if it is assumed they were first colonized 30,000, 40,000, and 12,000 years ago, respectively. Applied to the wider range of DNA data bearing on modern human origins, this rate gives a date of between 290,000 and 140,000 years ago for the common African ancestor. It may also be used to estimate that modern humans first left Africa between 180,000 and 90,000 years ago (= the calculated time of divergence between the two main branches of the mitochondrial DNA tree).

None of the genetic studies bearing on modern human origins are conclusive, and the one by Cann and her colleagues can be criticized from various points of view. One important criticism concerns their African sample, which in fact con-sisted mainly of American blacks (eighteen of twenty individ-uals). This raises the possibility that much of the diversity in "African" mitochondrial DNA was created by admixture with other population groups rather than by mutation. Also, a case can be made for a mutation rate much slower than 2%–4%, which would place the last common African ancestor for living people at roughly 850,000 years ago, at or perhaps only shortly after the time when *Homo erectus* first dispersed from Africa (Wolpoff, in press-a).

Nonetheless, genetic studies indicating a more recent African origin for modern humans are directly supported by the discovery of modern or near-modern human fossils in African sites that were certainly or probably occupied between 130,000 and 50,000–40,000 years ago, when the Neanderthals were the sole occupants of Europe. Among the crucial African sites, which were listed in the last chapter, two in South Africa are cited particularly often. These are Border Cave (Beaumont et al. 1978; Rightmire 1979b, 1984b; Beaumont 1980); and the Klasies River Mouth Caves (Singer and Wymer 1982; Rightmire 1984b, 1987; H. J. Deacon et al. 1986; H. J. Deacon, in press).

Border Cave has provided an infant's skeleton, an adult skull, two partial adult mandibles, and some postcranial bones whose assignment to *Homo sapiens sapiens* is undisputed. The deposits containing the fossils are clearly older than the 50,000–40,000-years-ago range of conventional radiocarbon dating and contain artifacts resembling those which are thought to date from the Last Interglaciation at Klasies River Mouth, that is, sometime between 130,000 and 74,000 years ago (Fig. 7.4). There is the complication, however, that none of the Border Cave fossils were found during tightly controlled excavations, and it is thus possible that some or all came from graves intruding into more ancient deposits. This possibility is strengthened by the fact that, as a group, the Border Cave human bones are remarkably untouched by the leaching and profile compaction that have severely damaged the animal bones in the same horizons. The Border Cave evidence for very early modern people should probably be held in abeyance until it is confirmed by fresh discoveries from well-controlled excavations.

The Klasies River Mouth Caves have provided five partial human mandibles, a maxilla, about a dozen small cranial fragments, a handful of isolated teeth, and four postcranial bones. The containing deposits are again demonstrably beyond the range of conventional radiocarbon dating, and paleoclimatic interpretation of the sediments and fauna, together with uranium disequilibrium and electron-spin-resonance determinations, indicate that most of the fossils probably date from the latter part of the Last Interglaciation, between perhaps 115,000 and 74,000 years ago (H. J. Deacon et al. 1986; Goede and Hitchman 1987; H. J. Deacon, in press). A smaller number probably date from the earlier part of the Last Glaciation, between roughly 74,000 and 60,000 years ago. The stratigraphic origin of the fossils is not contested, and the estimated dates, if imprecise, are secure approximations. Two pieces—a relatively complete mandible with a strongly developed chin (Fig. 6.17 in the last chapter) and a fronto-nasal

Figure 7.4. Later-Quaternary climatic and cultural stratigraphy. The interval referred to in the text as "late Pleistocene" is the later part of the Last Glaciation, between 40,000–35,000 and 10,000 years ago. This interval corresponds to the time span of the European Upper Paleolithic.

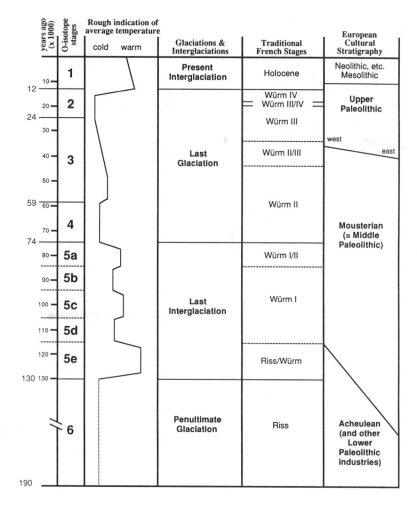

fragment lacking any sign of a continuous supraorbital torus—exhibit modern morphology especially clearly. Other specimens are less diagnostic, but none suggest the presence of nonmodern people.

A larger number of more complete specimens would obviously be desirable, but, together with mostly somewhat later modern or near-modern human fossils from other African sites, the Klasies fossils certainly suggest that modern people had appeared in Africa while the Neanderthals were at their apogee in Europe. From a fossil perspective, perhaps the major obstacles to proving that Africa was the principal, if not the sole, cradle of modern humanity are, first, the possibility that modern people were present just as early at Qafzeh Cave and other sites in the Levant (Near East) (Bar-Yosef and Vandermeersch 1981; Vandermeersch 1982; Valladas et al. 1988; Bar-Yosef, in press) and, second, the murkiness (some would say the contrariness) of the fossil record in the Far East. As discussed in the last chapter, the Qafzeh evidence need not contradict the African case, since the proximity of Qafzeh to Africa raises the possibility that the Qafzeh people were simply a part of the broader African modernization process or were the descendants of early modern African immigrants.

The Far Eastern fossil record is another matter, and it has been repeatedly used to support a model of modern human origins that is different from the one promoted here. Known as the "regional continuity" or "multiregional" model, this alternative posits that, following the initial dispersal of *Homo erectus*, this species diversified into morphologically distinct regional populations, each of which then evolved progressively toward modern *H. sapiens*. The principal recent proponent of this theory, Wolpoff (1985b and press-a; also Wolpoff et al. 1984), argues that natural selection and gene drift created and maintained the diversity and that selection and gene flow promoted the universal evolutionary trend toward modern humanity. In support of the theory, Wolpoff has especially emphasized morphological continuities between Javan *H. erectus* and some early anatomically modern Australian fossils and between Chinese *H. erectus* and the oldest known anatomically modern Chinese fossils.

However, the case for links between Javan *Homo erectus* and the earliest known modern Australians is complicated by the remarkable morphological variability of the Australian fossils, only some of which recall archaic Javan *Homo* in any meaningful sense. This variability is discussed briefly below and is a puzzle that no available theory of modern human origins parsimoniously accommodates. There is also the problem that some of the features that some early modern Australians share with archaic Javan *Homo* are also shared with archaic *Homo* elsewhere, including Africa (Stringer and Andrews 1988). They therefore do not demonstrate a unique local linkage. Perhaps most important, the multiregional model as Wolpoff presents it predicts that different regional populations progressed toward modern *H. sapiens* at about the same pace; yet, as discussed in Chapters 4 and 5, the fossil record suggests that Far Eastern populations may have lagged behind African and European ones by 250,000 years or more. Finally, the multiregional model ultimately requires the discovery of unequivocal transitional fossils between archaic and modern forms of *Homo*; but so far these are as conspicuously lacking in the Far East, as they are in Europe, where the case against regional continuity is especially strong. The lack is particularly glaring in China, where fossils that could conceivably link Chinese *H. erectus* to local anatomically modern *H. sapiens* are too few, too weakly dated, and too poorly described to make a convincing case.

The multiregional model cannot be dismissed, but at the moment the bulk of the genetic and fossil evidence more strongly favors the alternative promoted here, namely, that modern *Homo sapiens* originated in Africa and subsequently dispersed to other parts of the globe, largely or entirely supplanting local nonmodern populations. Further checking of this hypothesis will require a much larger number of well-dated, relatively complete human fossils from Africa, Eurasia, and Australia. Fresh discoveries of very early anatomically modern people may also resolve a major objection that Wolpoff has raised against the hypothesis. This objection is that, in his analysis, contrary to what the hypothesis predicts, the geologically oldest anatomically modern people so far found in Europe, the Far East, and Australia tend to look more like the historic inhabitants of these regions than they look like their putative common African ancestor.

The Relationship between Biological and Cultural Change

In Europe, there is a strong correlation between Neanderthals and Mousterian (= Middle Paleolithic) artifacts, on the one hand, and between anatomically modern people and Upper Paleolithic artifacts, on the other. The principal exception is the association between indisputable Neanderthal skeletal remains and early Upper Paleolithic artifacts at La Roche à Pierrot Rockshelter, Saint-Césaire, southern France. As discussed in the last chapter, the artifacts involved belong to the Chatelperronian Industry, which closely resembles the Mousterian of Acheulean Type B, and it is possible that the Chatelperronian reflects the diffusion of Upper Paleolithic elements into a local Mousterian context (Klein 1973b; Harrold 1983, and in press). In this event, the equation between modern people and Upper Paleolithic cultural traits would remain intact.

The Upper Paleolithic contrasts with the Mousterian in many ways, of which the most often-cited is the widespread Upper Paleolithic emphasis on stone flakes whose length was at least twice their width. Archaeologists distinguish such elongated flakes as "blades." Mousterian people produced blades, but usually in very low frequencies and unsystematically. In contrast, Upper Paleolithic people developed sophisticated techniques to produce blades regularly and consistently.

In general, compared with more basic flake technology, blade production provides more cutting edge from a given stone core (Bordaz 1970), and among the very earliest Upper Paleolithic people, it may have helped to conserve scarce raw material. However, most Upper Paleolithic people probably produced blades for purely historical reasons, that is, as a part of their cultural heritage.

Besides emphasizing blades, most Upper Paleolithic people regularly manufactured stone-tool types such as endscrapers and burins which are generally rare and crudely made ("atypical") in Mousterian assemblages. Further, unlike Mousterians, they commonly cut, carved, polished, or otherwise shaped bone, ivory, and antler into a wide variety of formal artifact types. These not only include pieces that were probably projectile points, awls, punches, needles, and so forth but nonutilitarian items that are clearly interpretable as art objects or items of personal adornment. In the last chapter, it was noted that art and decorative items are essentially unknown in a Mousterian context.

In general, Upper Paleolithic people made a much wider variety of readily distinguishable artifact types than did their predecessors, and Upper Paleolithic industries or "cultures" varied far more in time and space. Finally, as detailed below, in virtually every conceivable category of recoverable items—graves, house ruins, fireplaces,etc.—Upper Paleolithic examples are commonly far more elaborate than Mousterian ones. In short, in the long-term perspective of culture history, the Upper Paleolithic represents a quantum change from the Mousterian.

It has sometimes been suggested that an "early Upper Paleolithic" antedating 25,000–20,000 years ago should be distinguished from a "late Upper Paleolithic" afterward and that the early Upper Paleolithic was significantly less developed, resembling the Mousterian in some important respects. The case is perhaps clearest for Cantabrian Spain (Straus 1977), where there was a dramatic increase in the number of sites after about 20,000 years ago, accompanied by an artistic florescence and by important changes in the location of settlements and in hunting patterns. However, if northern Spain and perhaps other parts of western Europe were relatively quiescent before 20,000 years ago, parts of central and eastern Europe were not, and the cultural elaboration indicated by sites such as Dolní Vestonice and Předmostí in Czechoslovakia or Sungir' in Russia (references below), all antedating 20,000 or even 25,000 years ago, rivals any later developments in Spain or France. Moreover, it could be argued that the "late" Upper Paleolithic of central

Europe began with a cultural decline, since much of the region was apparently abandoned about 20,000 years ago and was reoccupied only many millennia later (Hahn 1976; Kozlowski and Kozlowski 1979).

In large part, the shifting locus of especially abundant, rich, or elaborate Upper Paleolithic sites probably reflects the vicissitudes of Last Glacial climatic change, which sometimes favored one area, sometimes another (Guillien and Laplace 1978). Significantly, the time at or around 20,000 years ago was a major climatic inflection point, corresponding to the maximum development of the Last Glacial ice sheets. Paradoxically, from a human perspective, the most dramatic climatic impact was probably in Africa, where people were able to reoccupy areas they had largely abandoned from before 30,000 or 40,000 years ago, both in the north (Camps 1974; Wendorf et al. 1979) and in the south (Klein 1983; H. J. Deacon and Thackeray 1984). The reason was a significant increase in regional precipitation. Together with temperature variation, similar, if less dramatic, long-term moisture fluctuations in Last Glacial Europe probably partly explain local long-term population and cultural variations.

This is not to say that all the known features of the Upper Paleolithic were present from its very beginning and that all subsequent elaboration (or decline) was due directly to climate. Some of the specific cultural innovations discussed below were undoubtedly developed after the Upper Paleolithic began, and they diffused more or less widely, depending on geographic constraints, their local utility, and so forth. Undoubtedly, some did promote local or regional population increases or cultural florescences, but none were as fundamental as those that distinguish the Upper Paleolithic from everything that went before. In fact, to the extent that an "early" Upper Paleolithic can be distinguished from a "late," the apparent differences are less than those between many historic hunter-gatherer cultures, and nowhere is the early Upper Paleolithic truly a link or evolutionary transition between the Mousterian and the late Upper Paleolithic.

From the characteristics that have been listed and that will be discussed further below, it can be argued that the Upper Paleolithic signals the most fundamental change in human behavior that the archeological record may ever reveal, barring only the primeval development of those human traits that made archeology possible. The strong correlation between Upper Paleolithic artifacts and modern human remains further suggests that it was the modern human physical type that made the Upper Paleolithic (and all subsequent cultural developments) possible. The question then arises whether there is a detectable link between the evolution of modern people and the development of those behavioral traits that mark the Upper Paleolithic.

The answer is, not clearly. In the last chapter, it was noted that the earliest known Upper Paleolithic artifacts come from north Africa, the Near East, and southeastern Europe, where they were being made between 40,000 and 36,000 years ago, as much as 5,000 years earlier than the earliest Upper Paleolithic artifacts in western Europe. The apparent spread of the Upper Paleolithic from east to west across Europe can in fact be used to support the argument that the European Neanderthals were physically displaced by modern people who originated else-where. It is equally clear, however, that the earliest known modern people in the Near East—those from Skhul and Qafzeh Caves in Israel—made Mousterian artifacts that differ in no essential respect from Mousterian artifacts made by Neander-thals in either Europe or the Near East. The Israeli site of Boker Tachtit, discussed in the last chapter, may show that the initial transition from Mousterian to Upper Paleolithic technology occurred in the Near East, but the Skhul and Qafzeh sites nonetheless demonstrate that the appearance of modern people antedates the transition, perhaps by a substantial interval.

Similarly, the early modern or near-modern people who occupied sites such as Klasies River Mouth in sub-Saharan Africa made Middle Stone Age (MSA) artifacts that are distin-guished from Mousterian artifacts in name only. MSA people employed basically the same knapping technology as the Mousterians, and they produced basically the same tool types. Like the Mousterians, they failed to make formal bone artifacts or art objects, and their cultures varied relatively little through time and space. In these respects and others, they differed from their Later Stone Age (LSA) successors exactly as the Mouste-rians differed from Upper Paleolithic people. The earliest LSA is very poorly known, in part because many sites were aban-doned in the 60,000–30,000-years-ago interval during which it appeared, probably reflecting widespread hyperaridity in Af-rica. However, the available evidence is sufficient to show that the early modern or near-modern people from Klasies River Mouth and other sites substantially antedate the earliest LSA industry.

In sum, anatomical and behavioral modernity may have appeared simultaneously in Europe, but in both the Near East and Africa, anatomical modernity antedates behavioral moder-nity, at least as it is detectable in the archeological record. This observation is difficult to explain. Perhaps as suggested in the last chapter, the earliest anatomically modern humans of Africa and the Near East were not as modern as their skeletons suggest. Neurologically, they may have lacked the fully modern capacity for culture. This may have appeared only as recently as 50,000–40,000 years ago, when it allowed then fully modern humans to spread rapidly throughout the world. The behavioral gulf that separated fully modern humans from archaic populations may have all but precluded interbreeding, which could explain why the fossil record provides so little clear evidence for it (F. H. Smith 1982).

Cultural Variability

Prior to 40,000–35,000 years ago, before the Upper Paleolithic and comparable cultural manifestations had completely supplanted earlier ones, vast areas were characterized by remarkably uniform artifact assemblages that differed from one another mainly in the relative abundance of the same basic artifact types. In addition, artifactual change through time was painfully slow: basic assemblage types lasted tens or even hundreds of thousands of years. After 40,000–35,000 years ago, however, the general pattern changed radically. Like-aged artifact assemblages from neighboring regions often differed qualitatively, and, within single regions, the pace of artifactual change accelerated dramatically. Both spatial and temporal variability are illustrated especially clearly by the numerous Upper Paleolithic sites of the east European plain, many of which have provided artifact assemblages that are unique and that cannot be assigned to an industry or culture represented by other assemblages from the same region (Klein 1969a, 1973b; Soffer 1985; Hoffecker 1986).

The dramatic acceleration in change through time is further illustrated by the classic Upper Paleolithic sequence of southwestern France, established long ago by meticulous excavations in caves such as La Ferrassie and Laugerie-Haute (de Sonneville-Bordes 1963, 1973). Here, the interval between 34,000–33,000 and 11,000 years ago witnessed a remarkable succession of Upper Paleolithic industries, known to archeologists as (from older to younger) the Aurignacian, Gravettian (= Perigordian), Solutrean, and Magdalenian. Each industry (or culture) was characterized by specific artifact types that are rare or unknown in the others. Thus, the Aurignacian, which probably intruded France from the east about 33,000–34,000 years ago and was present until roughly 27,000 years ago, was distinguished by large, laterally retouched ("Aurignacian") blades, "beaked" burins, nosed and keeled (carinate) endscrap-

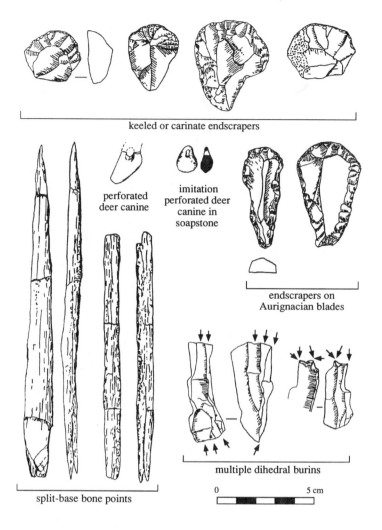

keeled or carinate endscrapers

perforated deer canine

imitation perforated deer canine in soapstone

endscrapers on Aurignacian blades

multiple dihedral burins

split-base bone points

0   5 cm

Figure 7.5. Typical Aurignacian split-base bone points, "pendants," and chipped stone artifacts. The split-base points (redrawn after Bernaldo de Quiros 1982: 98) come from the cave of el Castillo, northern Spain. The remaining artifacts (redrawn after González Echegaray 1980: 36, 39, 153) come from the nearby cave of el Pendo.

ers, and special kinds of bone points, the most famous of which are those with split bases (Fig. 7.5). The Gravettian, spanning the interval between about 27,000 and 21,000 years ago and extending eastward to central Europe and southward to Italy and Spain, was marked especially by numerous small, narrow, parallel-edged, often pointed, steeply backed blades (Fig. 7.6). Aurignacian-type bone points were absent, and the principal bone artifacts were "awls," "punches," and other presumably domestic implements, accompanied by well-made bone art objects and items of personal adornment.

The Solutrean, present between about 21,000 and 16,500 years ago and essentially confined to France and Spain, was characterized above all by finely made foliate (leaf-shaped) stone points of various shapes and sizes (Fig. 7.7). Finally, the Magdalenian, between about 16,500 and 11,000 years ago, restricted initially to France and found later also in northern

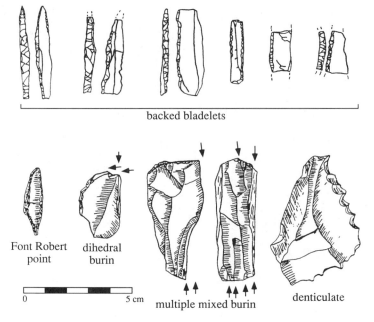

backed bladelets

Font Robert point   dihedral burin

multiple mixed burin   denticulate

0   5 cm

Figure 7.6. Range of Gravettian (= Perigordian) stone artifacts. Backed bladelets are especially characteristic. The ones shown here (redrawn after Bernaldo de Quiros Guidotti 1982: 145) come from the Gravettian deposits of Cueva Morín, northern Spain. The remaining pieces (redrawn after González Echegaray 1980: 113) come from Gravettian levels in the nearby cave of el Pendo.

Figure 7.7. Solutrean artifacts from La Riera, Cave, northern Spain (redrawn after Straus and Clark 1986: 99, 103, 107). The Solutrean is distinguished especially by various kinds of well-made unifacial and bifacial points.

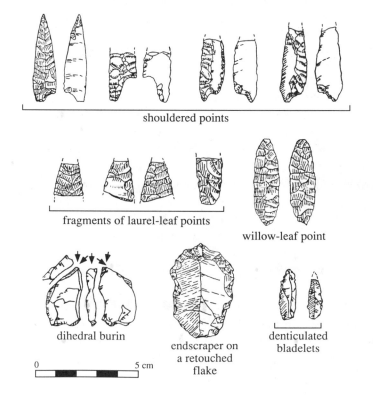

shouldered points

fragments of laurel-leaf points

willow-leaf point

dihedral burin   endscraper on a retouched flake   denticulated bladelets

0   5 cm

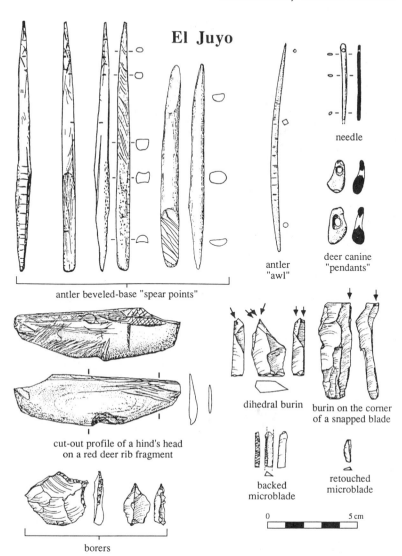

El Juyo

antler beveled-base "spear points"

antler "awl"

needle

deer canine "pendants"

cut-out profile of a hind's head on a red deer rib fragment

dihedral burin

burin on the corner of a snapped blade

backed microblade

retouched microblade

0   5 cm

borers

Figure 7.8. Magdalenian bone and stone artifacts from the cave of el Juyo, northern Spain. The Magdalenian is distinguished above all by a wide variety of well-made bone and antler artifacts, including many decorated or artistic pieces.

Spain, Switzerland, Germany, Belgium, and southern Britain, was distinguished primarily by a sophisticated bone and antler technology that produced points, harpoons, and other implements and weapons (Fig. 7.8), sometimes elaborately incised or decorated. Not only did each major industry replace its predecessor far more quickly than pre–Upper Paleolithic industries did, but artifactual change within each major Upper Paleolithic unit was also far more conspicuous. Thus, archeologists can readily recognize distinctive subdivisions within the Aurignacian, Gravettian, Solutrean, and Magdalenian. The number and content of the subdivisions varies from region to region, thereby complicating formal definition (Straus 1987), but this only underlines the remarkable internal diversity of the Upper Paleolithic.

Some of the extensive spatial and temporal variability that characterized artifact assemblages after 40,000–35,000 years ago was undoubtedly functional, reflecting the fact that a particular people began to manufacture new or distinctive artifacts because they had a new or distinctive purpose for them. However, much of the variability was probably stylistic, reflecting culturally different ways of doing the same thing. While it may seem peculiar to us that material items should suggest so little cultural differentiation before 40,000–35,000 years ago, the amount that characterizes the succeeding interval is reminiscent of more-recent history. Th extensive cultural variability of the past 40,000–35,000 years almost certainly required the existence of modern people, with their seemingly infinite capacity for innovation.

Late-Pleistocene Economies

In this section and those that follow, my purpose is to describe various aspects of culture in the period between 40,000–35,000 and 12,000–10,000 years ago, by which period early anatomically modern people had completely replaced their predecessors. This interval corresponds to the time span of the European Upper Paleolithic, as it is conventionally defined, and encompasses the later part of the Last Glaciation (Fig. 7.4)—or, more generally, the very late Pleistocene. For simplicity's sake, the people who lived in this interval will be referred to here as "late Pleistocene" to include both Upper Paleolithic people and their early modern contemporaries elsewhere in the world, particularly the contemporaneous LSA people of Africa.

Although the emphasis here is on the differences between late-Pleistocene (early modern) people and their predecessors, there was one major respect in which they were certainly similar—they made their living entirely by hunting and gathering wild resources. Only in the transition from the Pleistocene to the Holocene, between roughly 11,000 and 9000 years ago, is there sound evidence for a significant change, when some people, particularly in the Near East, began to domesticate animals, plants, or both. Even these people, however, probably continued to depend upon wild resources for centuries, if not millennia.

Ethnographic observations on historic hunter-gatherers show that the gathered, mostly vegetal component of the diet commonly outweighs the hunted component. Undoubtedly, late-Pleistocene people also relied heavily on plants, but plant residues are rarely preserved in Paleolithic sites. The use of water, sometimes chemically charged, to "float" off small, light objects from sediment samples has sometimes revealed large numbers of ancient seeds, for example in the 22,000–10,000-year-old (and later) levels of Franchthi Cave in Greece (Hansen and Renfrew 1978) and in the 14,000–13,000-year-old layers of El Juyo Cave in Spain (Freeman et al. 1988). At Franchthi, the seeds from deposits older than 13,000 years come from species whose cultural utility is unclear, and they may in fact have been introduced by birds or rodents. However, the seeds in deposits younger than 13,000 years come mainly from wild lentils, vetches, pistachios, and almonds that were probably eaten by people, and many of the El Juyo seeds also come from possible food plants. Still, Franchthi and El Juyo remain exceptional. In this light, it is understandable that archeologists have probably overstressed the importance of hunting in Paleolithic economies. The overemphasis is probably most misleading for low-latitude sites where gatherable plant foods were probably always abundant relative to game. It is less misleading for middle- and upper-latitude sites, where, relatively speaking, game animals were much more numerous, particularly during glacial intervals.

Game was especially abundant at middle latitudes in late-Pleistocene Eurasia, because glacial climate favored the formation of grasslands over vast areas where forests prevailed in interglaciations, including the Present or Holocene Interglaciation. The principal species were gregarious ungulates such as woolly mammoth, reindeer, bison, horse, and saiga antelope, which could never have prospered in forested environments. Reindeer reached the far south of France, and some even penetrated the Pyrenees to northern Spain. In France they were probably the most common large herbivores during the closing phases of the Last Glaciation, between roughly 20,000 and 11,000 years ago, and their bones dominate many sites of this period, including such well-known ones as Pincevent, Laugerie-Haute, La Madeleine, and Isturitz (Bouchud 1959, 1975; Delpech 1975, 1983; Bahn 1983; Audouze 1987). Because of regional environmental differences, other species prevail in contemporaneous sites elsewhere—for example, red deer at La Riera, El Juyo, Tito Bustillo, and other sites in northern Spain (Altuna 1972; G. A. Clark and Straus 1983; Straus and Clark 1986) and bison at Amvrosievka, Bol'shaya Akkarzha, Zolotovka I, and other sites on the south Russian plain (Klein 1973b; Hoffecker 1986)—but everywhere there was a common emphasis on large gregarious herbivores.

In contrast to large herbivores, large carnivores such as lions and hyenas rarely occur in late-Pleistocene archeological sites, though they ranged nearly everywhere in Eurasia and

Africa that people did and though their bones are usually present in contemporaneous nonarcheological bone assemblages, even relatively small ones. Their rarity in archeological samples probably reflects a long-standing mutual avoidance relationship with people, based on the limited potential gain /substantial risk attendant on interaction.

Large herbivores were not only a vital source of food, but they also provided critical raw materials, including hides, sinews, and, most obviously, bone, antler, or ivory. Upper Paleolithic people not only used bone, antler, and ivory to fashion a wide variety of implements and art objects, but they also used larger pieces as weights, supports, and other structural elements in their dwellings. Patterned arrangements of large bones constitute the main evidence for dwellings at many important Upper Paleolithic sites in central and eastern Europe (Klima 1963; Klein 1969a, 1973b; Kozlowski and Kubiak 1972; Kozlowski 1983; Gladkih et al. 1984; Soffer 1985; Hoffecker 1986). In parts of central and eastern Europe where trees were especially scarce, the people even used fresh bone for fuel to judge by the large amount of bone ash and charred bone fragments in their fireplaces. Like some historic Indians on the American Great Plains, they probably also burned the dried dung of large herbivores.

Although it is probable that late-Pleistocene people exploited local resources more effectively than did earlier people, firm evidence remains relatively limited. In western Europe, perhaps the best indication is that, per unit time, Upper Paleolithic sites are much more numerous than Mousterian ones (Mellars 1973, 1982; Straus 1977; G. A. Clark and Straus 1983), implying that Upper Paleolithic populations were larger and denser. The principal alternative—that Upper Paleolithic people simply moved camp more often—seems unlikely, since Upper Paleolithic sites tend, if anything, to be richer and more extensive than Mousterian ones. Since Upper Paleolithic and Mousterian people lived under broadly the same conditions, Upper Paleolithic people could have been more numerous only if they used local resources more efficiently. Theoretically, this should be reflected in contrasts between Upper Paleolithic and Mousterian food refuse, but studies to check this are only being undertaken now (Chase 1986). For the moment, the most obvious difference is that bird and fish bones are more common in Upper Paleolithic sites, and it may be that active fishing and fowling were unique to the Upper Paleolithic. Increased reliance on fish may especially account for Upper Paleolithic florescence in parts of northern Spain, southwest France, and south Russia, where annual salmon runs probably provided knowledgeable hunter-gatherers with an unusually rich and reliable resource.

It has also been suggested that some Upper Paleolithic people were unique or advanced in their tendency to specialize on just one or two herbivorous species, such as reindeer in southwestern France or red deer in northern Spain (Fig. 7.9) (Straus 1977). However, Mousterian and Acheulean levels in southwestern France are sometimes dominated by a single species (for example, reindeer at Combe Grenal [Bordes and Prat 1965; Chase 1986]), and single-species dominance is a striking characteristic of some Mousterian sites elsewhere, such as Starosel'e in the Crimea (wild ass) or Sukhaya Mechetka and Il'skaya on the south Russian plain (bison) (Klein 1969b). More important, in virtually all cases where bones of a single species predominate at an Upper Paleolithic or earlier site, the species might also have dominated the ancient environs of the site, and the bones therefore need not demonstrate human hunting specialization or preference. Finally, it is not even necessarily true that people hunted or even ate the species whose bones are most common at a site. This is most obvious with respect to the woolly mammoth, whose bones predominate in many Mousterian and Upper Paleolithic sites in central and eastern Europe. In many cases mammoth bones appear to have been used extensively as building material, fuel, or as raw material for artifact manufacture, and they may simply have been scavenged from long-dead animals. This possibility is directly implied at Mezin in the Ukraine, where chemical analysis shows that the mammoth bones comprising a "ruin" came from individuals that probably lived and died decades apart (Pidoplichko 1969). Differences in superficial bone weathering may indicate the same thing at other sites, though these might also occur because some bones remained exposed longer than others after the sites were abandoned.

As discussed in the last chapter, the extreme southern tip of Africa has provided perhaps the best evidence for a late-Pleistocene advance in resource exploitation (Klein 1983). In brief summary, unlike their MSA predecessors, local LSA people living under similar environmental conditions actively fished and fowled, and they killed dangerous game such as buffalo and wild pigs much more often. In addition, the significantly smaller size of shellfish and tortoises in LSA sites probably reflects larger, denser LSA populations. LSA advances in resource exploitation were probably due mainly to technological innovations, including the development of fishing and fowling gear and also of snares or weapons that reduced the hunters' exposure to risk. The contrasts are stark, but unfor-

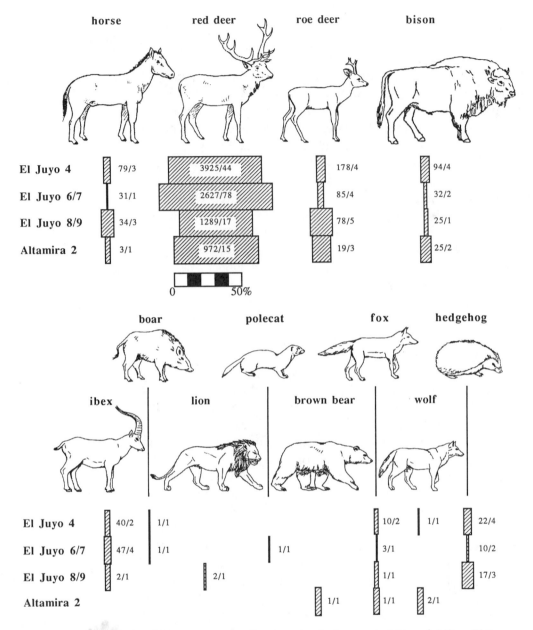

Figure 7.9. Abundance of various mammalian species in layers 4, 6/7, and 8/9 at El Juyo Cave and in layer 2 at nearby Altamira Cave, northern Spain. The associated artifacts belong to the local "Lower" Magdalenian, bracketed, at both sites, between roughly 15,000 and 13,000 years ago. The bars represent the percentages of each species in each layer, as measured by the minimum number of individuals (MNI) necessary to account for the bones of each species. The numbers attached to the bars are the numbers of specimens (NISP) assigned to each species, divided by MNI. The chart illustrates the abundance of red deer and the rarity of large carnivores, which are characteristic aspects of most Magdalenian sites in northern Spain.

tunately it is not yet clear that they characterize the very
earliest LSA people, whose sites are locally rare, probably
because they date from a time (between 60,000 and 30,000
years ago) when hyperaridity had greatly reduced human
numbers.

Late-Pleistocene Technology

Late-Pleistocene people were far more inventive than their
predecessors and made technological innovations at an unprecedented pace. It is these innovations that I particularly want to
stress here. Many remain imprecisely dated, and even when
dates are available, it seems unlikely that the earliest known
occurrences were actually the first. For this reason, and because specific dates are not crucial to the main point, the
discussion will treat the entire 40,000–10,000-years-ago late-
Pleistocene interval as a single unit. The basic information for
this summary is drawn from syntheses by J. G. D. Clark
(1967), Bordes (1968), Coles and Higgs (1969), Bordaz (1970),
and de Sonneville-Bordes (1973), as well as from more specialized references cited below.

In general, late-Pleistocene artifact assemblages contain a
much wider range of recognizable artifact types than do earlier
ones, suggesting that late-Pleistocene people were engaged in a
wider range of activities. These clearly included the shaping of
formal bone, ivory, and antler artifacts and probably also
included the manufacture of more tools for creation of other
tools rather than for immediate use as hide scrapers, projectile
points, etc. To judge by the small size or the shape of many
late-Pleistocene stone artifacts and by the form of many bone
pieces, the people probably also manufactured many more
composite tools, that is, implements combining separate
pieces of stone, bone, or other materials. Unfortunately, because the composite tools were held together mainly by perishable glues, leather thongs, and so forth, few have survived
to the present.

Although Middle Paleolithic and even earlier people had
adapted to glacial climates in central and western Europe, late-
Pleistocene (Upper Paleolithic) people were the first to inhabit
easternmost Europe and northern Asia (Siberia) (Fig. 7.10),
where the winters were exceptionally long and cold even during
interglaciations. Upper Paleolithic innovations for dealing with
intense cold probably included both better clothing and better
housing. Winter clothing almost certainly incorporated fur, and
Russian Upper Paleolithic sites, including, for example, Mezin,
Mezhirich, Eliseevichi I, Avdeevo, and Kostenki XIV have pro-

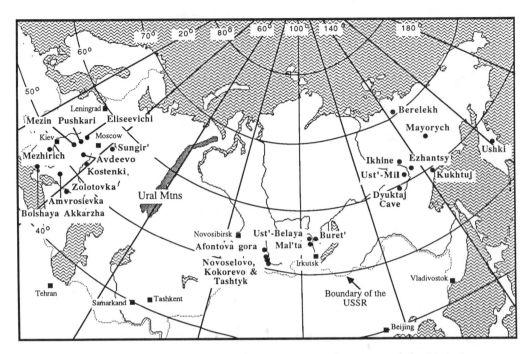

Figure 7.10. The Soviet Union, showing the approximate locations of the Upper Paleolithic sites mentioned in the text. The Ural Mountains divide the European part of the Soviet Union from the north Asian part (Siberia). Upper Paleolithic people were probably the first to inhabit most of the European part and the entire north Asian part.

vided the oldest known evidence that fur-bearing animals were caught for their skins (Klein 1971, 1973b; Soffer 1985; Hoffecker 1986). The remains of wolves or arctic foxes are extraordinarily abundant at these sites and tend to occur either as whole or nearly whole skeletons lacking the paws or as articulated paw skeletons, occurring separately. The implication is that the people removed the feet with the skins, as modern trappers often do, and then discarded the skinned carcasses. The "awls," "punches," and other pointed bone objects that appear in even the earliest Upper Paleolithic sites could have been used to sew skins together, and eyed bone needles that would have greatly facilitated the process were certainly in use by 19,000–18,000 years ago (Stordeur-Yedid 1979). The existence of sophisticated, well-tailored clothing is directly documented in some Upper Paleolithic burials, especially those found at the site of Sungir', 210 km northeast of Moscow (Bader 1978). Here, the pattern of discolored soil and of strings of beads surrounding, girdling, and paralleling the skeletons of three people buried at least 22,000 years ago even suggest the details of fur or leather dress, comprising a cap, a shirt, a jacket, trousers, and moccasins. The beads and other objects found with the skeletons were apparently sewn on the clothing as decorations or fasteners.

Like their predecessors, late-Pleistocene people often occupied rock-shelters or cave mouths in areas, such as southwestern France and northern Spain, where these were available. Meticulous modern excavations such as those at Cueva Morín (Freeman and González Echegaray 1970) and El Juyo (Barandiarán et al. 1985; Freeman et al. 1988) in northern Spain show that these people sometimes built walls or otherwise modified natural shelters to make them more habitable. Over much of their range, however, late-Pleistocene people did not have access to caves, and in such situations they commonly constructed dwellings that were far more substantial than any known or inferred for earlier people. The superstructures were made mainly of wooden poles, hides, and other materials that long ago vanished, but the foundations have been exposed in careful excavations. The most spectacular examples come from the harsh open plains of central and eastern Europe, where they variously comprise large, artificial depressions in the ground, regular arrangements of postholes, patterned concentrations of large bones or stone blocks (serving as constructional material), sharply defined concentrations of cultural debris, or a combination of these features (Figs. 7.11–7.13) (Klein 1969a, 1973b; Soffer 1985; Hoffecker 1986). The "ruins" usually border, encircle, or cover patches of ash and charcoal

0   5 m

Mezin Complex 1

concentration of
large bones

Figure 7.11. *Top:* Roughly circular concentration of large bones believed to mark the base of a ruined hut at the Upper Paleolithic site of Mezin (complex 1) in the Ukraine. *Below:* Hypothetical reconstruction of the hut, showing the bones used as weights to hold down skins stretched over a wooden framework (redrawn after Boriskovskij 1958: Fig. 1).

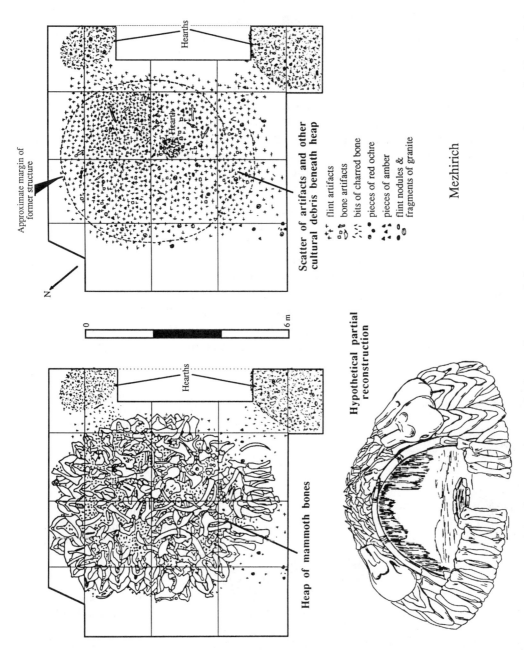

Approximate margin of former structure

Hearths

N

0   6 m

Hearths

Scatter of artifacts and other cultural debris beneath heap

⊹⊹ flint artifacts

ᵃₒ bone artifacts

ʹʹʹ bits of charred bone

● pieces of red ochre

▲▲ pieces of amber

⊘ flint nodules & fragments of granite

Hypothetical partial reconstruction

Heap of mammoth bones

Mezhirich

Figure 7.12. *Top left:* Plan view of a circular heap of mammoth bones used to construct a hut at the Upper Paleolithic site of Mezhirich in the Ukraine. *Top right:* Distribution of artifacts, fragmentary animal bones, and other debris beneath the bone heap. *Bottom right:* Conjectural reconstruction of the hut (Adapted from Gladkih et al. 1984: 165).

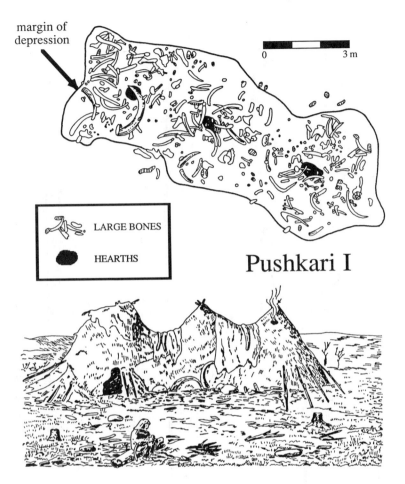

margin of
depression

0   3 m

LARGE BONES

HEARTHS

Pushkari I

Figure 7.13. *Top:*
Plan of a roughly
rectangular, 30-
cm-deep depres-
sion dug by the
Upper Paleolithic
inhabitants of
Pushkari 1 in the
Ukraine, showing
the internal distri-
bution of hearths
and large bones.
Below: Recon-
struction of a
hypothetical
three-part struc-
ture that may
have covered the
depression
(redrawn after
Boriskovskij 1958:
Fig. 3).

that mark ancient fireplaces for heating and cooking. Some of
the fireplaces are more complex than any earlier ones, with
intentionally corrugated floors or small ditches leading out
from the central ash accumulation. Modern experiments show
that these modifications increase oxygen flow and thus produce a hotter flame.

For the most part, we do not know precisely what
late-Pleistocene people did with individual artifacts they produced, but it is safe to assume that many were used to obtain
or process foods and raw materials. Bone shaping and incising,
for example, almost certainly involved stone burins, which are
named for the modern metal-engraving tools that they broadly
resemble. Hide processing was probably often accomplished by
using stone endscrapers to remove hair and fat and then using
spatulate bone "burnishers" to smooth or spread softening
agents or pigment. Enigmatic bone objects found at many sites
may have been trips or other parts of compound traps for
snaring foxes, hares, and other valuable fur-bearing animals.

Figure 7.14. Grooved antler artifacts from the Siberian Upper Paleolithic site of Kokorevo I, dated to approximately 13,000–14,000 years ago (redrawn after Abramova 1982: Fig. 1). The grooves were probably designed to receive microblades, some of which were still present in one piece (*left center*). Most of the artifacts were probably projectile points, and the broken piece in the upper left-hand corner was found stuck in a bison shoulder blade. The piece on the far right is less pointed than the others and may have been a knife handle. The grooved-antler technology and the associated microblade technology are well documented in Siberia only after 18,000 years ago, but may have been present earlier.

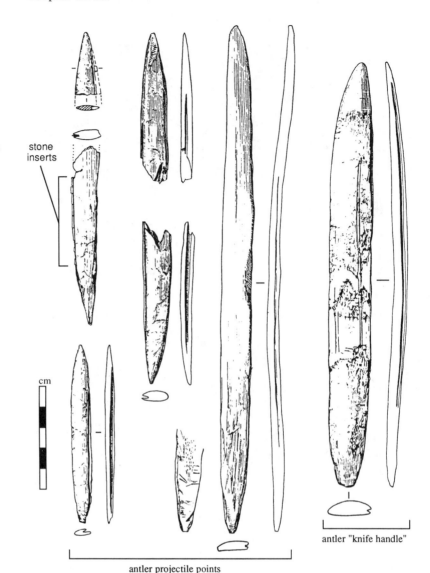

stone inserts

cm

antler projectile points

antler "knife handle"

More certainly, many pointed stone and bone artifacts were certainly used to tip spears or arrows whose perishable wooden shafts have long since disappeared. Proof can be found in points still stuck in animal bones—for example, the flint point in a wolf skull at the "East Gravettian" (or Pavlovian) site of Dolní Vestonice in Czechoslovakia (Klíma 1963), another in a reindeer vertebra at the terminal Pleistocene ("Hamburgian") site of Stellmoor in north Germany (Schild 1984), and the bone point in a bison scapula at the Siberian late-Pleistocene site of Kokorevo I (Abramova 1964).

Like other formal bone artifacts, bone points were essentially a late-Pleistocene innovation, and their variety constitutes a further indication of late-Pleistocene inventiveness. Some, including the very earliest examples from Europe, have split or beveled bases (Fig. 7.5), probably to facilitate hafting. Others that are especially common in Siberia bear longitudinal grooves or slots into which sharp stone bits were probably inserted to produce a more ragged wound (Fig. 7.14). Points with the inserts still in place have been found at several sites, including Kokorevo I mentioned above. On some points the grooves were too broad and shallow to accept inserts, and they may have been runnels to promote bleeding in a wounded animal. Finally, among all the known point types, among the most striking are those with backward-pointing barbs. Almost certainly these were harpoon heads used for spearing fish or perhaps reindeer or other mammals crossing a stream. They were present in various parts of Eurasia by 14,000 years ago or a little after.

Bone points are only one of many late-Pleistocene novelties that promoted hunting efficiency. Others that were at least as significant include the spearthrower and the bow and arrow. The spearthrower is a bone or wooden rod hooked at one end to accommodate the dimpled or notched nonpointed end of a spear shaft (Fig. 7.15). With the shaft resting against the rod, the rod can then be used to extend a person's arm, so that the spear can be thrown harder and farther. Bone spearthrowers were in use by at least 14,000 years ago.

The antiquity of the bow and arrow is more difficult to establish because the most diagnostic parts were made of perishable materials. However, small sharp stone bits, well-fashioned stone points, or small backed bladelets very similar to ones that tipped arrows later on occur from at least 20,000 years ago in various parts of Eurasia and Africa. Once the bow and arrow were invented, they would obviously have diffused very rapidly, and a sharp increase in the abundance of tiny backed bladelets in both Africa and Eurasia about 21,000–20,000 years ago may signal their spread. More concretely, blunt-ended bone rods strikingly similar to historic or proto-historic linkshafts or foreshafts suggest their presence in southern Africa by 20,000 years ago or a little later (J. Deacon 1984). However, the oldest conclusive evidence, comprising fragmentary wooden bows or arrows, comes only from much later sites, dating between 12,000–10,000 years ago in France and north Germany (Tyldesley and Bahn 1983).

Late-Pleistocene sites in Europe have also provided the oldest known fishing hooks, dated to roughly 14,000 years ago, while objects believed to be "fish gorges"—shaped bone slivers resembling double-pointed toothpicks (Fig. 7.16)—occur in

Figure 7.15. *Top:*
Diagrammatic
indication of how
a spearthrower
"lengthens" the
arm, permitting a
spear to be
thrown harder and
farther (adapted
from Hahn et al.
1985: 102). *Below:*
Decorated ("the
fawn and the
birds") spear-
thrower from the
Magdalenian
deposits of Mas
d'Azil, southern
France (redrawn
after Sonneville-
Bordes 1973: 55).

Use of the spear-thrower

South African sites that are only slightly younger. Fishing with
spears, traps, etc. had probably been underway for some time
before 14,000 years ago, to judge by fish bones found in earlier
sites.

In sum, late-Pleistocene people were obviously very cre-
ative, and it seems likely that by 12,000–10,000 years ago they
had devised the entire range of technology observed among
historic hunter-gatherers. The Upper Paleolithic people who
occupied the Czech site of Dolní Vestonice 28,000–27,000
years ago even discovered that soft clay, properly mixed with
other materials (temper) and heated to a high temperature,
hardens into a much more durable material. The site contains
both the kiln they used for firing and numerous fire-hardened
clay objects, especially fragmentary animal and human figures.
Roughly 15,000 years later, about 13,000–12,000 years ago,
some very late-Pleistocene occupants of Japan independently
rediscovered fired clay technology, which they used to manufacture the world's oldest known ceramic vessels (Reynolds
and Barnes 1984; Teruya 1986).

Late-Pleistocene Social Organization

The archeological record provides little direct indication of
late-Pleistocene social organization, except perhaps for greater

contact or interchange between groups than ever before. In Europe and northern Asia, "luxury" items such as amber and seashells occur at Upper Paleolithic sites that are scores or even hundreds of kilometers from where the items originated. Even the stone used to make tools was sometimes transported over great distances. Perhaps the most spectacular examples come from very late Upper Paleolithic (terminal Pleistocene) sites on the great plain of north central Europe, which demonstrate that particularly desirable types of flint were routinely transported 100–200 km and even more (Schild 1984). However, there are also earlier examples, such as those from the complex of Upper Paleolithic sites near Kostenki-on-the-Don

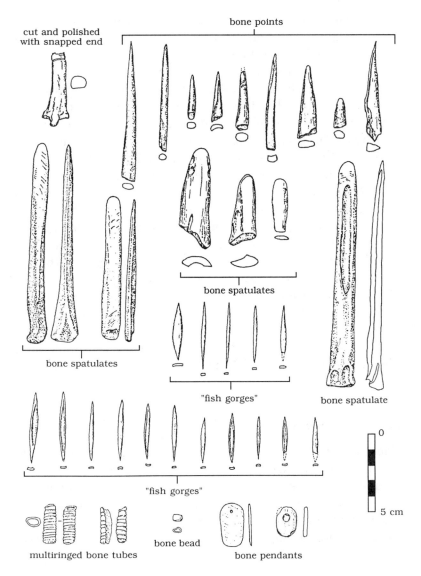

cut and polished with snapped end

bone points

bone spatulates

bone spatulates

bone spatulate

"fish gorges"

"fish gorges"

bone bead

multiringed bone tubes

bone pendants

0

5 cm

Figure 7.16. Range of formal bone artifacts from the LSA layers of Nelson Bay Cave, South Africa (after J. Deacon 1984: 176). Formal bone artifacts are rare or absent in MSA sites, and where they occur they could easily represent undetected intrusions from LSA levels. By ethnographic analogy, the Nelson Bay LSA "fish gorges" were probably baited and attached to lines to catch many of the fish represented in the same layers. In preceding MSA sites, objects interpretable as fishing gear are absent and fish bones are correspondingly rare.

in the USSR, to which large quantities of high-quality flint were probably brought from at least 130 km away (Klein 1969a). There is no evidence that either "luxury" or "basic" goods were moved comparable distances before the late Pleistocene. The wider intergroup contacts implied for late-Pleistocene people may have been both cause and effect of the enhanced cognitive and communicational abilities that are probably implied by their art.

Direct evidence aside, the physical and material cultural similarities of late-Pleistocene people to many historic hunter-gatherers suggest that they were similarly organized or, perhaps more precisely, that they enjoyed broadly the same range of social structures. Some late-Pleistocene people occupying more marginal environments in which relatively limited resources supported only sparse populations probably lived in small egalitarian bands of related families, like many of the historic hunter-gatherers of Australia and of the dry interiors of western North America and southern Africa.

At the other extreme, some late-Pleistocene people inhabiting very rich settings that supported much denser populations may have lived in complex, "ranked" societies like those of the historic hunter-gatherers of the American Pacific Northwest. In this instance, a cadre of hereditary chiefs may have coordinated many activities, including food acquisition and distribution, rituals and ceremonies, trade, and even warfare. Relatively complex social organization has been posited particularly for the very-late-Pleistocene (ca. 15,000–11,000-years-ago) Magdalenian people of southwestern France and northern Spain, whose sites are especially numerous, rich, and closely packed. It may also be reflected in some of the extremely rich sites of central and eastern Europe, with their elaborate structural "ruins" (Soffer 1985). While the simpler societies of the late Pleistocene may have differed little in basic organization from Middle Paleolithic and even earlier ones, the more complex societies that characterized some late-Pleistocene people probably had no earlier counterparts.

Late-Pleistocene "Ideology": Art and Graves

The thoughts, ideas, beliefs, and values of late-Pleistocene people are not preserved in the archeological record, but their art and their graves provide the first clear evidence for ideological systems like those of historic people. The art has been summarized or analyzed many times (for example, by Breuil 1952; Graziosi 1960; André Leroi-Gourhan 1965b; Abramova

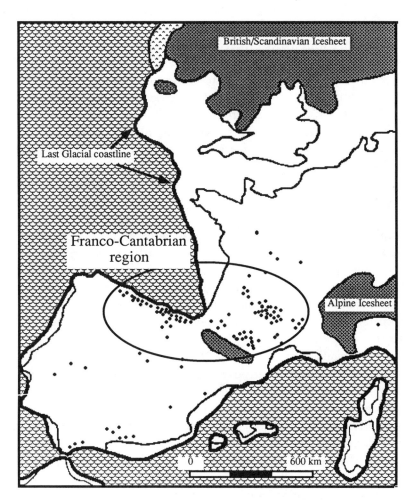

Figure 7.17. Approximate distribution of Upper Paleolithic decorated caves west of Italy, showing the dense concentration in southwestern France and northern Spain, which together comprise the so-called Franco-Cantabrian region (modified after Jochim 1983: Fig. 19.1).

1967; Ucko and Rosenfeld 1967; Sieveking 1979; Conkey 1981, 1983, 1987; R. White 1986; Freeman et al. 1987) and may be divided between two basic categories—wall art, comprising paintings and engravings on rock surfaces, and portable or home art, comprising items that occur alongside other artifacts in the ground.

Paintings and engravings weather off rock surfaces that are exposed to the elements, and late-Pleistocene wall art is therefore confined almost entirely to caves. The first examples were discovered by Marcelino Sanz de Sautuola in Altamira Cave in the Cantabrian region of northern Spain in 1879, but for many years their great antiquity and authenticity were disputed. Full acceptance came only in the early 1900s, after important additional examples were found nearby in southwestern France. More than 150 caves with late-Pleistocene paintings or engravings have now been identified in Franco-Cantabria (Fig. 7.17), making it by far the richest region in the world. In other regions with apparently suitable caves, late-Pleistocene wall art is either rare or absent, suggesting it was not an aspect of local culture. However, it is also possible that, like diverse historic or late-prehistoric hunter-gatherers throughout the world, many late-Pleistocene peoples produced wall art on exposed rock surfaces where it no longer survives. It is both puzzling and fortunate that, almost uniquely, the late-Pleistocene artists of Franco-Cantabria often chose cave walls as a basic medium.

In most cases, the Franco-Cantabrian art cannot be dated precisely, and it is the depiction of mammoth, bison, reindeer, wild horse, and other locally or wholly extinct animals that implies a Pleistocene age. Stylistic comparisons to animal figures carved from or engraved in bone, antler, or ivory suggest that the final Pleistocene (15,000–11,000-years-ago) Magdalenians painted most, if not all, of the striking, naturalistic animals at Altamira and famous French caves such as Lascaux, Font-de-Gaume, and Niaux. They may in fact have produced all the wall art, but earlier Upper Paleolithic people could also have produced some.

The meaning or purpose of the wall art remains obscure, though almost certainly, like the art of historic hunter-gatherers, it was not done for its own sake. Instead, it was probably deeply embedded in other aspects of culture and perhaps functioned variously to enhance hunting success, to ensure the bounty of nature, to illustrate sacred beliefs and traditions (perhaps on ritual occasions), or to mark the territorial boundaries of an identity-conscious group. Conceivably, much of it symbolizes or encodes the social structure or worldview of its makers, and some could record the experiences of shamans or medicine men in the trance state, as Lewis-Williams (1981, 1982; also Lewis-Williams and Loubser 1986; Lewis-Williams and Dowson 1988) has proposed for the much more recent rock art of southern Africa. The deeply cultural (vs. strictly artistic) meaning of much Franco-Cantabrian art is probably reflected in its location, not only in caves but sometimes deep within them, in chambers or passages that were difficult to reach. To penetrate the darkness, the artists hollowed out pieces of rock in which they burnt animal fat or oil. These have been found in several French Magdalenian sites and broadly recall the animal-oil lamps used historically by the Eskimo.

By its mode of occurrence, portable or home art, including items of personal adornment, is much easier to date. In Europe, perforated animal teeth that were probably pendants or beads, carefully shaped ivory or soft stone beads, and other carved,

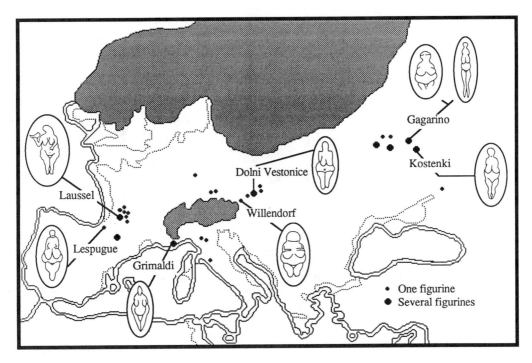

Figure 7.18. Approximate locations of the European Upper Paleolithic sites that have provided female figurines or engravings (redrawn after Champion et al. 1984: Fig. 3.19). At most sites, the figurines or engravings were certainly or probably associated with the "Gravettian" culture complex, dated to between roughly 27,000 and 20,000 years ago. Dotted lines mark present coastlines, double lines mark Last Glacial coastlines, and shaded areas mark major Last Glacial ice sheets.

incised, or engraved bone objects date from the very dawn of the Upper Paleolithic (Movius 1969b; de Sonneville-Bordes 1973; Hahn 1977; Kozlowski 1982; Gamble 1986; Hoffecker 1986; R. White, in press), while in Africa ostrich eggshell beads remarkably similar to those of the historic aborigines occur in even the earliest LSA, dating to at least 38,000 years ago (Beaumont et al. 1978; Beaumont 1980). Africa has also provided what may be the oldest known paintings—animal figures on rock slabs from deposits, dated to at least 19,000 and perhaps as much as 27,500 years ago, at Apollo 11 Rock-shelter in Namibia (Wendt 1976).

Like the stone artifacts that accompany them, art objects and personal ornaments vary significantly in form through time and space. For example, in Europe, well-produced naturalistic engravings of animals are concentrated in Magdalenian (15,000–11,000-years-old) sites, while human figurines occur most commonly in Gravettian (27,000–20,000-years-old) levels (Fig. 7.18). Like the wall art, the portable art is impossible to interpret precisely, but little of it probably was done for artistic

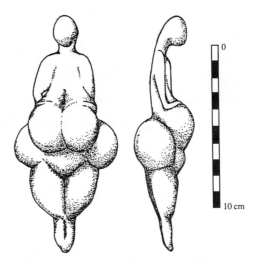

Figure 7.19. Famed "Venus of Lespugue," from a probable Gravettian layer at the site of Lespugue, southwestern France (drawn by K. Cruz-Uribe from a cast).

purposes alone. Some engraved or incised objects that are otherwise enigmatic may have been gaming pieces, while others were perhaps counting or recording devices, even lunar calendars (Marshack 1972a, 1972b). Many animal figurines could be the totemic symbols of kinship groups, while the human figurines could obviously represent deities or spirits. Most are highly stylized, lacking facial features or details of the hands and feet. Many, known popularly as "Venus figurines" (Figs. 7.18, 7.19), have exaggerated buttocks and breasts, leading to speculation that they were fertility symbols or depictions of earth-mother goddesses. Whatever the case, with the remainder of the art, they clearly imply that late-Pleistocene people were not only physically identical to their living descendants but possessed basically the same cognitive and communicational abilities, almost certainly including languages as complex as any historic ones. Enhanced cognition and communication were surely crucial to many late-Pleistocene activities, particularly to ones that depended upon within- and between-group cooperation, and the art therefore provides a vital clue as to why other aspects of late-Pleistocene culture appear so advanced.

Graves are of course known from Mousterian sites, and late-Pleistocene people were thus not the first to bury their dead. However, late-Pleistocene sites are the earliest to contain undoubted multiple burials. The famous Aurignacian Cro-

Magnon skeletons (Lartet 1868) probably came from a communal grave, and some truly spectacular examples have been found at Pavlovian (= "Eastern Gravettian") open-air sites in Czechoslovakia, radiocarbon dated to 27,000–26,000 years ago. These Pavlovian cases include a triple burial (of a young woman flanked by two young men) found recently at Dolní Vestonice (Klíma 1987) and, most notably, the veritable graveyard found at Předmostí near the end of the last century (Absolon and Klíma 1978; F. H. Smith 1982, 1984). Here, a large (4 × 2.5-m) oval pit covered by limestone slabs and mammoth bones contained the skeletons of eighteen individuals of various ages and both sexes. Even richer cemeteries, containing dozens of individuals, have been found at terminal Pleistocene (ca. 15,000–10,000-years-old) sites such as Taforalt and Afalou-Bou-Rhummel in northwest Africa (Fig. 7.1), where they are associated with artifacts of the Upper Paleolithic Iberomaurusian Industry (Camps 1974).

Equally important, it will be recalled from the last chapter that Mousterian graves tend to be very simple, with no clear indication for a burial ritual or for the inclusion of valued items or "grave goods." Some Upper Paleolithic graves are also relatively simple, but many are much more elaborate, and individuals were often buried with special bone or stone artifacts (Fig. 7.20) (Harrold 1980). These suggest a burial ritual and perhaps notions of an afterlife similar to those that exist among historic hunter-gatherers. In contrast to Mousterian graves, some Upper Paleolithic ones, such as that at Předmostí, were covered by large rocks or bones, perhaps to conclude a ritual or simply to prevent wolves or hyenas from exhuming the body. As in earlier sites, exhumation by carnivores may account for the isolated and fragmentary human bones that occur at many late-Pleistocene sites.

Isolated human bones might also reflect human activity, and some French Upper Paleolithic sites have provided the oldest known examples of human bones that were intentionally shaped or perforated, possibly as trophies or heirlooms (de Sonneville-Bordes 1973). Conceivably, the bones come from people who were cannibalized, and cannibalism might also be inferred from stone-tool marks on the modern-appearing fronto-nasal fragment from the much more ancient MSA deposit at Klasies River Mouth, South Africa (T. D. White 1987). Some of the Klasies human bones were also burnt, just like animal bones in the same deposit. However, the burning could reflect incomplete cremation or even accidental charring of partially buried bones under hearths, and the cut marks could come from ritual defleshing. Even if cannibalism is implied at Klasies, it seems unlikely it was widespread or important among early modern people. Until the end of the Pleistocene, they were all hunter-gatherers, living mainly in relatively small groups which could not afford the kind of risk-for-limited-return involved in hunting their neighbors. Insofar as cannibalism was practiced historically, it was largely restricted to agricultural peoples, and compelling archeological evidence in the form of numerous broken, cut, or burnt human bones is also limited to post-Pleistocene agriculturist sites

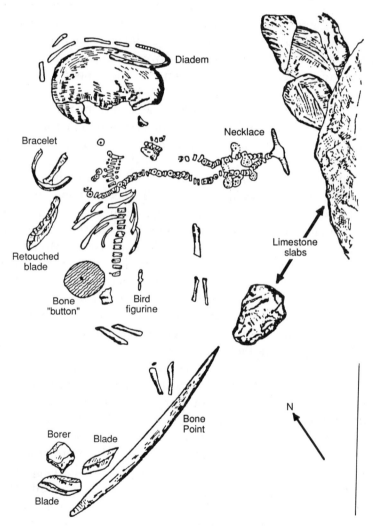

Figure 7.20. Skeleton of a child buried roughly 15,000 years ago at the Siberian Upper Paleolithic site of Mal'ta (redrawn after Gerasimov 1935: Fig. 36). Like many other late-Pleistocene graves, the one at Mal'ta contained special artifacts that may represent funeral offerings, the deceased's personal belongings, or both.

such as Fontbrégoua Cave, a Neolithic site in southeastern France dated to about 5,000 years ago (Villa et al. 1986).

Mortality and Disease

The vital statistics of late-Pleistocene people can be only crudely estimated, because of the relatively small number of skeletons whose owners' age and sex can be established. However, a composite sample of 76 Eurasian Upper Paleolithic skeletons from various times and places, supported by a remarkable series of 163 skeletons from the terminal Pleistocene Iberomaurusian levels of Taforalt in Morocco suggest that the common mortality pattern resembled that of most later prehistoric and historic hunter-gatherers (Vallois 1961). Child mortality was high, and women apparently had a lower life expectancy than did men, probably because of the risks associated with childbearing. Women probably rarely reached 40 years of age, and men probably rarely reached 60 or even 50 years of age; but, significantly, maximum life expectancy probably exceeded that of the Neanderthals, perhaps by as much as 20%. As a consequence, late-Pleistocene human groups probably contained more older people, whose accumulated knowledge could promote group survival, particularly in times of crisis.

Unlike Neanderthal skeletons, late-Pleistocene ones rarely show evidence of serious accidents or disease, suggesting that late-Pleistocene culture provided a far more effective shield against environmentally induced trauma. Skeletal anomalies that may reveal cause of death are particularly rare but include conspicuous lesions, perhaps caused by a severe fungal infection (Dastugue 1982), on the skull, mandible, pelvis, and femur of the famous Old Man of Cro-Magnon (actually a person in his late forties) and dental abscessing that may have produced a fatal septicemia (blood infection) in a 15–18-year-old woman buried about 22,000 years ago at the Abri Pataud, very near Cro-Magnon (Legoux 1975; Dastugue and de Lumley 1976). Her dental infection was probably related to partial destruction of her normal right upper molars caused by the eruption of aberrant, supernumerary teeth alongside. This abnormality has not been observed in any other Upper Paleolithic people, most of whom had relatively healthy teeth, probably because their diets included few foods that encouraged caries or plaque formation.

Additional late-Pleistocene skeletal anomalies that probably reflect cause of death have been reported from the cave sites of Rochereil in France and Romito in Italy. At Rochereil, a child in a Magdalenian grave had a bulging forehead and other features that suggest hydrocephaly (a normally fatal excess of cerebrospinal fluid in the skull) (Vallois 1971; Dastugue and de Lumley 1976). An artificial perforation that was probably intended to relieve the condition may have been the immediate cause of death. At Romito, an adolescent male in a late "Epigravettian" or "Romanellian" grave apparently suffered from a kind of genetic dwarfism (acromesomelic dysplasia) that certainly reduced life expectancy under Paleolithic conditions (Frayer et al. 1988). Dated to 12,000–11,000 years ago, the Romito dwarf antedates the next oldest by at least 5,000 years and is the only case of dwarfism yet recorded in a prehistoric Stone Age context.

Other known late-Pleistocene skeletal abnormalities, reported mainly from Czech and French sites, were variably debilitating but probably not fatal. Like the ones already cited, none indicate epidemic diseases, which were probably rare until the greater population densities permitted by the development of food production, beginning 12,000–10,000 years ago. The Czech examples include bone deformation of the left temporomandibular joint, suggesting partial facial paralysis, in one woman buried at Dolní Vestonice (Klíma 1962, 1963) and a shortened, deformed right leg, accompanied by pronounced spinal curvature (scoliosis) to the left, in a second (Klíma 1987). The French cases include fused cervical vertebrae (cervicoarthrosis) in skeletons from Cro-Magnon, Chancelade, and Combe-Capelle; a healed skull fracture, bone lesions/degeneration implying a permanently dislocated left shoulder, and a laterally deviated right big toe (*hallux valgus*) in the skeleton from Chancelade; and an asymmetric sacrum, reflecting lateral curvature of the spine (scoliosis) in the one skeleton from Combe-Capelle (Dastugue and de Lumley 1976). By modern analogy, the occurrence of cervical fusion may mean that some older Upper Paleolithic people were relatively sedentary, literally remaining seated much of the time. Similarly, if modern people are guides, the laterally deviated big toe of the Chancelade skeleton may reflect poorly fitting footwear, though other explanations are possible.

Skeletal evidence for deliberate injury is also rare (Roper 1969), probably because, like most ethnographically recorded hunter-gatherers, late-Pleistocene ones rarely engaged in warfare or interpersonal violence. In some instances, such as the healed fracture on the skull of the Chancelade man, the cause could clearly have been accidental (Dastugue and de Lumley 1976), and in many others bone fracturing or crushing probably occurred after death, in the ground. Prominent examples of damage that was once believed to be antemortem but that was probably postdepositional include the fractured female skull (individual 2) from the Cro-Magnon site (Dastugue 1982) and the four fractured or crushed skulls from the Upper Cave at Zhoukoudian (Pei 1939). However, although evidence for violence is rare, it does exist—for example, at the Grimaldi Caves in northern Italy, where a (?Aurignacian) child was buried with a projectile point embedded in its spinal column (Dastugue and de Lumley 1976); at Wadi Kubbaniya near Aswan in Egypt, where a young adult male, buried perhaps 25,000–20,000 years ago, had a healed parry fracture on the right ulna, a stone chip embedded in the left humerus, and two blades (?projectile armatures) in the abdominal cavity (Wendorf and Schild 1986); and, above all, in an extraordinary terminal Pleistocene (ca. 14,000–12,000 years-old) cemetery near Jebel Sahaba in Sudanese Nubia (Anderson 1968; Wendorf 1968). Nearly half the fifty-nine individuals exhumed here either had unhealed antemortem skeletal injuries or had stone artifacts lodged in or near their bones. They provide a remarkably graphic exception to the stated rule that there was limited violence among hunter-gatherers.

Both the Old Man of Cro-Magnon and the man buried at Chancelade were probably too disabled to fend for themselves, and their survival shows that Upper Paleolithic people, like Neanderthals before them and historic people later, cared for their old and sick. Such care need not have been entirely philanthropic or unselfish, since older people in hunter-gatherer societies commonly possess vital knowledge and experience. However, care in a more emotional, abstract sense not known for the Neanderthals may be indicated for the Dolní Vestonice woman with the deformed temporomandibular joint. Both the face engraved on an ivory fragment and the face of a sculpted clay head found nearby droop on the left side, just as hers probably did. It is arguable that they represent the oldest known human portraits.

Late-Pleistocene Population Expansion

In previous sections, it was noted that in Europe and southern Africa late-Pleistocene peoples were probably much more abundant than their predecessors. At least equally important, late-Pleistocene people greatly extended the geographic range of humankind by colonizing easternmost Europe, Siberia, the Americas, and Australia.

Easternmost Europe

Mousterian and earlier sites are unknown in the easternmost parts of Europe (within the USSR today), in spite of extensive archeological reconnaissance and the kind of intensive commercial activity that leads to site discovery. Therefore, as each year passes, it seems increasingly likely that Mousterian and earlier people simply could not live in easternmost Europe because of the harsh continental climate that prevailed even during interglaciations. Upper Paleolithic people obviously did not find the climate an insuperable problem, and their sites have been found in the extreme northeast, virtually on the Arctic Circle at the latitude of the Ural Mountains.

Siberia

Climatic conditions over most of Siberia are even harsher than in easternmost Europe. Thus, in spite of more limited archeological reconnaissance and commercial activity, it is probably significant that the oldest firm evidence for people in Siberia postdates 35,000 years ago. The earliest sites are perhaps Ezhantsy, Ikhine I and II, and Ust'-Mil' II in the Lena Basin (Fig. 7.10), where artifact assemblages from alluvial deposits have been dated either directly by radiocarbon or indirectly by stratigraphic correlation, to between 35,000 and 20,000 years ago (McBurney 1976; Dolitsky 1985; Morlan 1987, with references to original Russian sources). The dating is controversial (Hopkins 1985; Yi and Clark 1985), partly because the artifact samples tend to be very small and could conceivably have been displaced from higher levels, partly because some of the radiocarbon-dated wood fragments could have been reworked from older sediments (this could explain some stratigraphic inversions in the dates), and partly because there are inconsistencies in the published stratigraphic descriptions. On the other hand, human penetration of Siberia by 35,000–30,000 years ago is perhaps implied by the occupation of Japan at this date, if not before (Reynolds and Barnes 1984; Reynolds 1985), if it is assumed that the initial colonization of Japan occurred across a dry land bridge that linked the main Japanese islands to southeastern Siberia during the Last Glaciation. Whatever the case, human occupation of Siberia in the 20,000–10,000-years-ago interval is well established, for example, at Afontova Gora, Novoselovo, Kokorevo, Tashtyk, Mal'ta, Ust'-Belaya, Buret', Verkhne-Troitskaya, Nizhne-Troitskaya, Dyuktaj Cave, Kukhtuj, Berelekh, Mayorych, and Ushki (Fig. 7.10) (Klein 1971; Dolitsky 1985, with references to Russian sources).

The cultural materials from Siberian late-Pleistocene sites postdating 20,000 years ago are commonly assigned to the "Siberian Upper Paleolithic," which differs in detail from the European Upper Paleolithic but shares with it the extensive manufacture of bone, ivory, and antler artifacts; the presence of readily identifiable art objects and decorative items; the construction of substantial dwellings; relatively elaborate burial of the dead; significant stylistic variation through time and space; and so forth. By and large, Siberian Upper Paleolithic people seem to have lived very much as did their European contemporaries, subsisting largely on gregarious herbivores that had become especially numerous and widespread under glacial climatic conditions.

The Americas

The growth of glaciers requires moisture as well as cold, and during the late Pleistocene most of Siberia was too dry for large glaciers to form. However, the huge ice sheets of Europe and especially North America locked up so much water that sea level fell by up to 140 m, exposing large areas of land at the margins of the continents. A dry land bridge up to 1,000 km wide formed across the Bering Straits between northeastern Siberia and Alaska (Fig. 7.21), and Alaska and the adjacent ice-free areas of northwest Canada became an extension of Siberia, largely separated from the rest of North America by the vast ice sheets that covered most of Canada. The blood and especially the teeth of all Native Americans point unambiguously to northeast Asian roots (C. G. Turner 1985, 1987; Greenberg et al. 1986; Zegura 1987), and the first occupants of North America were almost certainly Siberian Upper Paleolithic people who, like the saiga antelope, the yak, and other typical north Asian species, naturally expanded westward across the Bering land bridge. The oldest unequivocal sites in Alaska and adjacent ice-free Canada all postdate 12,000 years ago (Dumond 1980; Hoffecker 1982), but much of the region has not been prospected archeologically, and older sites may exist. The Bluefish Caves in the Yukon Territory have already provided artifacts that could approach 20,000 years in age (Morlan 1987).

The antiquity of human occupation south of Alaska has been hotly debated for decades (Bray 1988). Many authorities see little or no compelling evidence for human presence before

12,000–11,000 years ago, while others point to sites where
stone artifacts or other humanly modified objects may be
much older. However, most such sites are highly problematic,
and the claimed antiquity variously depends on absolute dates
that are inconsistent with each other or with other strati-

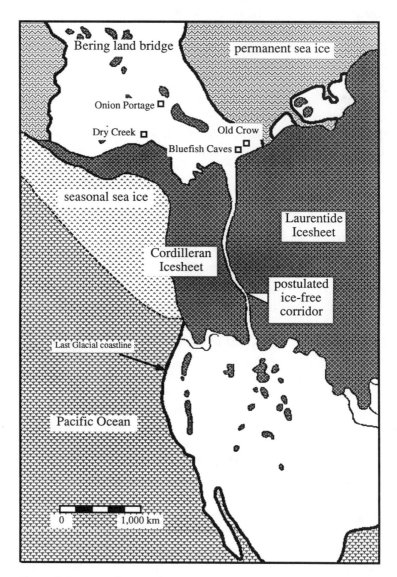

Figure 7.21. Northeast Siberia and western North America, showing the extent of the Bering land bridge in relation to the modern
land configuration, the maximum extent of the Last Glacial ice
sheets, and the ice-free corridor that existed between the major
Canadian ice sheets before and after the glacial maximum. Some
important archeological sites that may bear on the initial colonization of the Americas are also shown. The oldest are perhaps the
Bluefish Caves, with artifacts that may approach 20,000 years in
age.

graphic evidence; on the crude nature of the artifacts; on artifacts whose artifactual quality is often arguable or whose stratigraphic context is not really clear; on charred wood, earth, or bones which could have been burnt naturally; or on other data that can be readily challenged (Dincauze 1984; Owen 1984). However, fresh claims continue to surface, including important, recent ones from the rockshelter of Boqueirão do Sitio da Pedra Furada in northeastern Brazil (Guidon and Delibrias 1986) and the streamside site of Monte Verde in south-central Chile (Dillehay 1987; Dillehay and Collins 1988).

At Pedra Furada, charcoal from hearths associated with numerous coarse flakes and crudely flaked pebbles has provided a series of stratigraphically consistent radiocarbon dates extending beyond 10,000 years ago to approximately 32,000 years ago. Several layers within the sequence contain painted rock fragments exfoliated from the shelter wall, which still bears paintings. At Monte Verde, eight battered or crudely flaked stone artifacts, three naturally fractured pebbles that show traces of use, and fifteen naturally fractured pebbles that were apparently carried to the locality but not necessarily used, were found deeply buried in riverine sands. Charcoal from the same level nearby has been radiocarbon dated to about 33,000 years ago. Basically similar, but more numerous, naturally fractured or crudely flaked artifacts also occur at a much higher level, dated to about 13,000 years ago, where they are associated with mastodon bones, parts of edible or medicinal plants, and logs and branches preserved by dense, boggy deposits (Dillehay et al. 1982; Dillehay 1984). The spatial arrangement of the logs and branches suggests they could have anchored pole-frame huts. Even the 13,000-years-ago occupation is as old as or older than any site elsewhere in the Americas that is widely accepted as proving human habitation, and if both this date and the claims for yet older occupations at Monte Verde and Pedra Furada are sustained, their practical and theoretical implications are profound. Scholars will be hard pressed to explain either (a) why, in contrast to contemporaneous Eurasians and Africans, Native Americans seem to have been so rare in the millennia preceding 12,000 years or conversely, (b) why, unlike the earliest Americans, their Eurasian and African contemporaries left hundreds of rich, unmistakable sites with well-made artifacts and an abundance of other cultural debris.

There is also the problem that Last Glacial migrants from Siberia to Alaska would have found it difficult or impossible to spread farther south in North America. This is because Canada was almost completely covered by two great ice sheets, the Cordilleran on the west and the Laurentide on the east. If people arrived in Alaska before 25,000 years ago, they could have moved south only through a relatively narrow, inhospitable ice-free corridor in western Canada. Alternatively, if they arrived only between 25,000 and 14,000 years ago, during the peak of Last Glacial cold, dispersal southward would have been totally blocked by continuous ice (Rutter 1980). Southward movement would have become practical only after 14,000 years ago, when the ice sheets began to melt. This could readily explain why the oldest firm and universally accepted archeological sites south of the Canadian/American border date from only about 12,000–11,000 years ago (Haynes 1980, 1984). The ecological shock of human arrival, perhaps combined with dramatic climatic change in the transition to the Present Interglaciation, may further explain why North America lost thirty-three large mammal genera, more than 70% of its total, between perhaps 12,000 and 10,000 years ago (Kurtén and Anderson 1980; P. S. Martin 1984). An even larger number apparently disappeared from South America at about the same time (P. S. Martin 1984). The vanished "megafauna" included mammoths, horses, and native camels whose brief association with the earliest well-documented Americans, called Paleoindians, has been established at several very-late-Pleistocene sites located chiefly in the western United States (Fig. 7.22).

The possibility that the Paleoindians caused or contributed to large mammal extinctions is a potent reminder of the level of hunting-gathering competence that late-Pleistocene peoples may have achieved. Similar, though less extensive, extinctions occurred at or near the end of the Pleistocene in Eurasia and Africa (Klein 1984; Vereshchagin and Baryshnikov 1984), and once again it seems likely that people were involved, perhaps delivering the coup de grâce to species whose numbers and distribution had already been reduced by environmental change. Environmental change alone is an inadequate explanation, since the extinct species had survived the similar change that occurred at the end of the Glaciation-before-Last, roughly 130,000 years ago. What differentiated the end of the Last Glaciation most clearly was the presence of more advanced hunter-gatherers, whose behavioral innovations and capabilities have been emphasized here.

Australia

Unlike the Americas, Australia has not been connected to another continent since the late Cretaceous, roughly 70 million years ago. Lower sea levels dramatically enlarged the Malay Peninsula, fusing it with Sumatra, Java, Borneo, Bali, and smaller Southeast Asian islands to form a subcontinent paleogeographers call "Sunda Land," and Tasmania and New Guinea were similarly joined to Australia, to produce a super-continent called "Sahul Land"; but Sunda and Sahul remained separate (Fig. 7.23). Travelers between the two could have island hopped, but some open-sea travel remained unavoidable, including several voyages of roughly 30 km and at least one of 90 km (Birdsell 1977). Such distances required the invention of boats that could maintain buoyancy for several days, and this

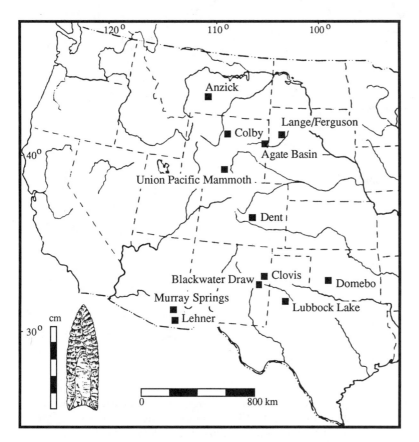

Figure 7.22. Main in situ occurrences of Clovis Paleoindian arti-facts in the western United States (adapted from Bonnichsen et al. 1987; point redrawn after Wormington 1964: Fig. 68). The most dis-tinctive Clovis artifacts are finely crafted, bifacial, concave-based projectile points with one or more basal flutes (elongated flake scars), proceeding from the base, on both faces. Bracketed by radio-carbon dating to between 12,000 and 11,000 years ago, the Clovis tradition comprises the oldest universally accepted evidence for human presence in the region. At Clovis sites where animal bones are preserved, some usually come from extinct species, including mammoth, camel, and horse.

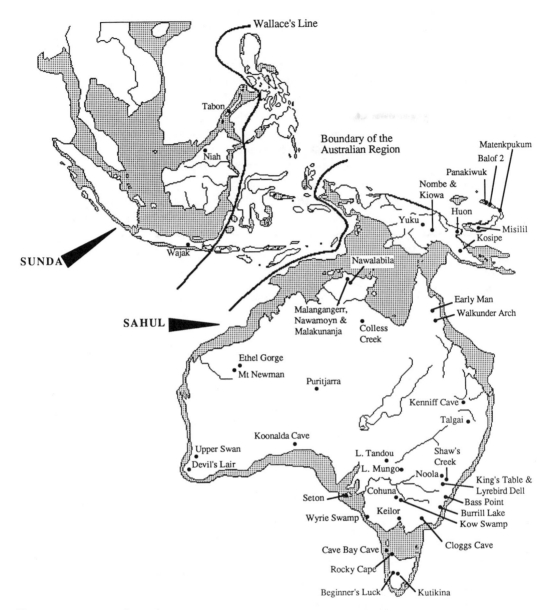

Figure 7.23. Map of Sunda and Sahul, showing major zoogeographic boundaries and some important late-Pleistocene sites (adapted from J. P. White and O'Connell 1979: Fig. 1). Shaded areas indicate continental shelf that would be exposed by a 200-m drop in sea level. Even with a drop of this magnitude, substantial stretches of open sea would separate Sahul from Sunda, indicating that the earliest human inhabitants of Sahul arrived by boat.

probably explains why people failed to reach Sahul until the late Pleistocene. The boats themselves probably perished long ago, and in any case the sites where remnants might persist are now inaccessible on the drowned continental shelves of Sunda and Sahul.

Until the mid-1960s, it could be argued that Sahul Land was not colonized until the early Holocene, but it is now clear that people were present by 33,000 years ago and probably from 40,000 years ago (R. Jones 1979, and in press; Thorne 1980; J. P. White and O'Connell 1979, 1982; J. P. White and Habgood 1985; Lourandos 1987). By 30,000 years ago they had even reached the oceanic island of New Ireland to the east of New Guinea, presumably by crossing the 30-km-wide strait between New Guinea and the island of New Britain and then the equally wide strait between New Britain and New Ireland (Allen et al. 1988; R. Jones, in press). The earliest inhabitants of Sahul probably entered from the northwest, where coastal environments resembled those in Sunda Land. At first they may have spread mainly along the coasts (Bowdler 1977, and in press), but they had occupied much of the Australian interior by 25,000–20,000 years ago. Their stone and bone artifacts, their hunting-gathering way of life, and, on occasion, even their rock art are now well documented at more than fifty sites, dating between 33,000 and 10,000 years ago, in various parts of New Guinea, Australia, and Tasmania (R. Jones 1979, and in press; J. P. White and O'Connell 1982; J. P. White and Habgood 1985). Even the boomerang now has a known antiquity of more than 10,000 years, thanks to discoveries at Wyrie Swamp in South Australia.

Among the oldest and certainly most informative Australian sites are those at Lake Mungo in the Willandra Lakes district of western New South Wales (Bowler et al. 1970, 1972; Bowler and Thorne 1976). Here, parts of three anatomically modern human skeletons labeled Mungo 1–3 have been dated directly or indirectly by radiocarbon. Mungo 1, a 20–25-year-old female dated to about 26,000 years ago, had been partially cremated before her bones were intentionally fragmented and placed in a small, shallow pit. Mungo 2, found with Mungo 1, was too fragmentary and too poorly represented for analysis. Mungo 3, an older adult male dated to about 30,000 years ago, had been laid out in a shallow grave and liberally sprinkled with red ochre before burial. Artifacts and faunal remains found nearby show that the Mungo people belonged to groups who exploited shellfish, fish, emus, marsupials, and probably plants around the Willandra Lakes from roughly 33,000 until 15,000 years ago, when climatic change caused the lakes to shrink and eventually disappear.

Curiously, compared with the historic Australian aborigines, the Lake Mungo people, together with broadly contemporaneous or somewhat younger ones from Keilor (Victoria) and Lake Tandou (New South Wales), possessed relatively high-vaulted, thin-walled, smooth-browed, spherical skulls with relatively flat faces, while the people who lived at Kow Swamp (northern Victoria) between about 14,000 and 9,000 years ago and at the roughly contemporaneous sites of Cohuna (Victoria) and Talgai (Queensland) had exceptionally rugged skulls with relatively low vaults, thick walls, flat and receding foreheads, strong browridges, and projecting faces. The range of variation is extraordinary and may indicate that Australia was colonized more than once, by very different people (Thorne 1977, 1980). A very late incursion, perhaps as recent as 3,000–4,000 years ago, is indicated by the introduction of the dingo, a semidomesticated dog widely associated with the historic aborigines (R. Jones, in press).

The Lake Mungo people may derive from a population represented by broadly contemporaneous skeletal remains from Wajak on Java, Niah Cave on Borneo, Tabon on Palawan Island (Philippines), and, further afield, from Zhoukoudian (Upper Cave), Liujiang, and Ziyang in China. The origin of the Kow Swamp people is much less clear, and it has been suggested they inherited their rugged skulls more or less directly from Southeast Asian *Homo erectus* (Thorne and Wolpoff 1981; Wolpoff et al. 1984; Habgood 1985, and in press; Wolpoff 1985b). However, it is at least as likely that they represent an indigenous Australian development whose receding foreheads and perhaps other of their "archaic" cranial features are due wholly or partly to artificial cranial deformation (P. Brown 1981). Taking possible deformation into account, sophisticated morphometric analysis employing several key cranial, facial, and dental measurements does not in fact differentiate the Kow Swamp people strongly from the Lake Mungo people (P. Brown 1987). Moreover, their postcranial anatomy is decidedly nonarchaic, and their femora in particular lack the relatively thick cortical bone and distinctive shaft shape of archaic *Homo*. Instead, their femora closely resemble those of recent Australian aborigines (G. E. Kennedy 1984a).

Like the peopling of the Americas, the peopling of Australia may be linked to a wave of extinctions, involving the disappearance of about fifty species of large vertebrates, mostly herbivorous marsupials, from Australia between roughly

40,000 and 15,000 years ago (Horton 1984; Murray 1984). Unlike the American extinctions, the Australian ones cannot be attributed to terminal Pleistocene climatic change, which they clearly antedate, and a human role may be even more strongly implied. There were remarkably few predator species in Australia before human arrival, and the indigenous herbivores may have been particularly vulnerable to the sudden appearance of an unusually potent one. However, as in the Americas, the case for human involvement in Australia remains open. Minimally, it will require both more precise estimates of when the extinctions occurred and firmer evidence that the early Australians hunted or otherwise interacted with the extinct species.

Conclusion

Together, the fossil and archeological records suggest that the modern physical form evolved before the modern capacity for culture. From a behavioral (archeological) perspective, the earliest anatomically modern people were not significantly different from their nonmodern predecessors and contemporaries, and this probably explains why they were geographically restricted for thousands or even tens of thousands of years. It was only sometime between 60,000 and 40,000 years ago, when anatomically modern people developed the fully modern capacity for culture, that they were able to spread more widely. The importance of their unique behavioral (cultural) capabilities is underlined by the apparent rapidity of their spread, as well as by their subsequent evolution. While the basic human form did not change significantly in the succeeding 40,000–35,000 years, cultural evolution accelerated dramatically. Plainly, it was culture and not body form that propelled the human species from a relatively rare and insignificant large mammal 35,000 years ago to a geologic force today, impinging as a natural selective agent on all other species.

However, if the evolutionary significance of modern human behavior is clear, many other important questions about modern human origins still remain unanswered. Did anatomically modern people truly originate in Africa within the past 200,000 years, as the accumulating fossil and genetic evidence implies? Why did behavioral modernity appear so much later than anatomical modernity? Did behavioral modernity also appear first in Africa? Under what circumstances did it arise? Did it perhaps depend on a neurological change that will be difficult or impossible to detect in the fossil record? Did the behavioral gulf between modern humans and the archaic populations they encountered largely preclude interbreeding, leading to complete replacement of archaic populations, or did archaic populations contribute genes to at least some modern groups? These questions will not be answered quickly, but the relative recency of modern human origins and the relative richness of the record make the long-term prospects for answers far greater than is the case for any other important event in human evolution.

SYNOPSIS: A PARTLY CONJECTURAL OUTLINE OF HUMAN EVOLUTION

8

Throughout this book, I have tried to strike a balance between what we know about human evolution and what we do not know about it but would like to. In this final chapter, my aim is to present a similarly balanced summary, stressing what we know but also highlighting what remains conjectural and thus subject to future change or refinement. Figure 8.1 summarizes some of the key points diagrammatically.

Hominid Origins

Almost certainly, hominids separated from apes in tropical or subtropical Africa during the late Miocene, sometime between 10 million years ago (mya) and 6 mya. Africa is indicated partly by its possession of humanity's closest living relatives, the chimpanzee and the gorilla, and, much more directly, by its unique human fossil record. This shows not only that people existed in Africa at least 2.5 million years earlier than in Eurasia, the continent with the second oldest record; it also suggests an African origin for the first Eurasians. The exact time when hominids diverged from apes has yet to be fixed in the fossil record, mostly because late-Miocene fossil sites are rare in Africa and some of the most promising ones are politically inaccessible. A time between 10 mya and 6 mya is indicated mainly by the bimolecular or genetic differences between living people and other primates, coupled with the best available estimates for the rate at which the differences have accrued.

In the absence of direct fossil evidence, the physical appearance and behavior of the earliest hominids must be inferred from their successors. Among fossil forms, the most relevant is surely the oldest known hominid species, *Australopithecus afarensis*, which is now well documented at east African sites dated to between 4 mya and 3 mya. Extrapolation backward from *A. afarensis* suggests that the earliest hominid was very apelike in its skull, teeth, and upper-limb morphol-

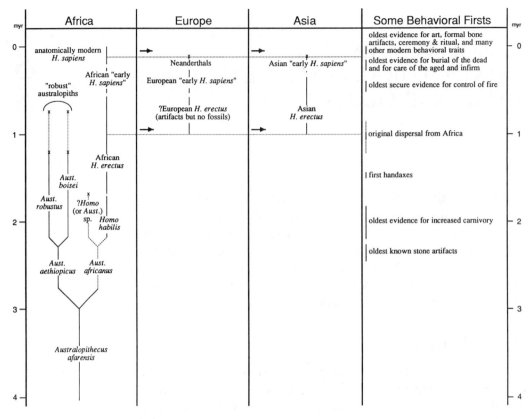

Figure 8.1. Conjectural phylogeny of the Hominidae. Branches or lines that are particularly uncertain or controversial are dotted. An arrow indicates dispersal, and an "x" indicates certain or possible extinction (termination). Two dispersal events from Africa to Europe and Asia are hypothesized, the first involving *Homo erectus* about 1 mya or somewhat before and the second involving fully modern *H. sapiens* probably between 60,000 and 40,000 years ago. The diagram implies that fully modern *H. sapiens* spreading from Africa extinguished nonmodern populations in Europe and Asia. If this is confirmed by fresh finds, the extinct nonmodern populations could be assigned to separate species of *Homo*. The available fossils already suggest that these populations were the end products of regionally distinct evolutionary trajectories.

ogy. It differed from contemporary apes primarily in its lower-limb anatomy, which became increasingly specialized for bipedalism. In a broad sense, bipedalism was probably an adaptive response to pressure for a more terrestrial (vs. arboreal) life-style in the savanna and light woodland that progressively replaced forest in the late Miocene. However, the precise adaptive advantage of bipedalism in a savanna setting remains speculative. The most plausible suggestions are that it reduced the amount of energy required to walk long distances, that it freed the hands for carrying or for tool and weapon use, or both. Tool use has not been and may never be directly documented, but it can be inferred from its rudimentary occurrence among chimpanzees. Observations on chimpanzees also suggest that the earliest hominids possessed some propensity to eat meat, and the potential importance of meat is undoubtedly greater in savanna settings than in the more forested surroundings chimpanzees prefer. Greater reliance on meat probably required greater reliance on tools and perhaps an enhanced ability to walk long distances, whether to hunt or to scavenge.

The Australopithecines

Whatever the initial adaptive value of bipedalism, *Australopithecus afarensis* shows it was successfully established by 4 mya. Equally important, *A. afarensis* demonstrates the fundamentally mosaic nature of human evolution, in which changes in the teeth and skull lagged behind changes in the locomotor anatomy. *A. afarensis* retained many extraordinarily apelike dental and craniofacial features, including relatively large, sexually dimorphic canines, an extremely prognathic face, and a remarkably small braincase. Its upper-limb skeleton also bore the clear mark of ape ancestry and suggests a residual apelike ability to climb trees, perhaps mainly to escape large, terrestrial predators. Tool use and meat eating by *A. afarensis* have not been documented directly but seem probable, for reasons already cited with respect to its still hypothetical ancestor.

Future research may show that *Australopithecus afarensis* was not the only hominid species that existed between 4 mya and 3 mya or that the fossils assigned to it must be divided into two species. However, at the moment, most specialists believe that the fossils represent a single, if highly dimorphic species that is a plausible ancestor for all later hominids. If this assessment is correct, *A. afarensis* gave rise to at least two distinct savanna-dwelling, hominid lineages at or shortly after 3 mya. Both differed from *A. afarensis* in the progressive development of distinctly less apelike skulls with less prognathic faces and significantly smaller front teeth. However, subsequent evolution in the first lineage centered on the grinding potential of the cheek teeth (premolars and molars), as reflected in their enormous size and in the impressive development of those craniofacial structures to which the chewing muscles attached. In contrast, later evolution in the second lineage involved a reduction in the size and power of the cheek teeth and in the functionally related bony structures, accompanied by progressive expansion of the brain, a dramatically increased dependence on the manufacture and use of tools, and a significantly greater emphasis on meat as a dietary staple.

The earliest known form of the lineage stressing the grinding power of the cheek teeth dates from 2.6–2.5 mya in east Africa. In its craniofacial morphology, it was intermediate between *Australopithecus afarensis* and the later "robust" australopithecines, *A. boisei* in east Africa and *A. robustus* in southern Africa. Its unique combination of primitive (apelike) and advanced (stereotypic robust) features may justify assignment to a new species, *A. aethiopicus*, which, on morphological and geographical grounds, could be directly ancestral to *A. boisei*. Morphologically, it is also a plausible ancestor for *A. robustus*, especially if some authorities are correct in proposing that *A. robustus* and *A. boisei* were no more than unusually distinct geographic variants of a single widespread species. However, it is possible that *A. robustus* was the end product of a second, separate natural experiment combining bipedalism with massive jaws and cheek teeth. In this case, *A. afarensis* gave rise to three (vs. just two) separate lineages.

In their respective geographic areas, *Australopithecus boisei* and *A. robustus* are both represented by relatively abundant fossils dating from 2 mya or a little before. Their craniofacial morphology, together with the structure and wear of their cheek teeth, strongly suggest they were specialized for masticating coarse vegetal foods. By emphasizing a vegetarian diet, they probably minimized competition with the second, contemporaneous hominid lineage, which was almost certainly more omnivorous. For reasons that are unclear, the robust australopithecines became extinct in both eastern and southern Africa sometime between 1.2 mya and 700,000 years ago. Among possible causes, perhaps the most plausible is that the second hominid lineage subsumed their resource base as it progressively expanded its ecological niche.

At present, the origins of the second lineage are unclear. There is widespread agreement that it emerged from *Australopithecus afarensis* around 3 mya and culminated in the appearance of the genus *Homo* between 2.5 mya and 2 mya, but the nature of the linkage is controversial. This is mainly because east Africa has provided few pertinent hominid fossils dating between 3 mya and 2 mya, while the more abundant fossils from southern Africa are ambiguous in their implications. They come from the "gracile" australopithecine, *A. africanus*, whose evolutionary relationships can be variously interpreted. In its enlarged cheek teeth and some aspects of its craniofacial structure, *A. africanus* appears to anticipate *A. robustus*, but in other aspects, including overall braincase form, it can also reasonably be considered an ancestor for the earliest known species of *Homo*, *H. habilis*. It may even have been ancestral to both *A. robustus* and *H. habilis*, and a conclusive assessment will probably require significant enlargement of the 2–3 million-year-old fossil sample from east Africa.

Homo habilis

Homo habilis occurs at eastern and, less certainly, at southern African sites that date from roughly 2.3 mya until perhaps 1.7 mya. It was remarkably variable in skull and tooth size, and fresh finds may confirm a growing suspicion that it is a mix of at least two species, *H. habilis* proper and a second, unnamed species of *Homo*. Whatever the case, the available fossils show that *H. habilis* (or one of its constituents) had a much larger braincase and smaller cheek teeth than the australopithecines. Its braincase was also differently shaped, anticipating later human skulls in having more expanded frontal and parietal regions, a more rounded occipital contour, and diminished basal pneumatization. Its reduced dentition and enlarged brain suggest that it differed behaviorally from the australopithecines, and almost certainly *H. habilis* (broadly understood) or its immediate precursor produced most or all of the stone artifacts that appear at east African sites beginning roughly 2.4–2.5 mya. These artifacts are important not only because they provide the oldest firm evidence for tool use but also because they occur in concentrations that signal the development of a uniquely human behavioral trait—the repeated occupation of a single location or site where members of a group accumulate durable refuse. Without this habit the archeological record would be largely invisible, and stone artifacts that were made before it developed will be very hard to find.

The oldest known stone artifacts and all those made until roughly 1.5–1.4 mya are commonly grouped in the Oldowan Industrial Tradition. They consist mainly of coarse flakes and flaked pebbles that are crudely fashioned and hard to classify into discrete types but that nonetheless imply a commitment to tool making far beyond that of chimpanzees. Both the flakes and flaked pebbles were probably critical in the food quest, perhaps above all in supporting another developing human trait—an increasing emphasis on carnivory. Plants were undoubtedly the primary staple of Oldowan people, but an increased interest in meat is implied by the fragmentary animal bones that almost always accompany Oldowan artifacts at sites where preservation conditions are appropriate. Most Oldowan sites are located near ancient streams or lakes where a variable mix of natural deaths, carnivore kills, and human activities could account for the association of bones and artifacts, and even if people did accumulate most of the bones, it is arguable whether they obtained them by hunting or by some form of scavenging. Nonetheless, both bones damaged by stone tools and the tools polished by contact with meat imply an involvement with carnivory far exceeding that of chimpanzees. Increasing dependence on tools and meat may have been both cause and effect of the increase in brain size and the reduction in cheek-tooth size that characterize *Homo habilis.*

Homo erectus

A growing emphasis on carnivory and tool use may help explain the emergence of *Homo erectus* from *H. habilis* (or one of its constituents) in Africa, roughly 1.8–1.7 mya. In its skull, *H. erectus* was distinguished from *H. habilis* by a still larger brain and smaller cheek teeth and by several morphological features, including a vertically shortened face, a massive brow-ridge, an occipital torus or bar, and forward projection of the nasal aperture. The functional significance of these and other characteristics is not totally clear, but the browridge and occipital torus were perhaps part of a structural complex reflecting reduced emphasis on the cheek teeth and increased use of the front teeth for biting, gripping, or tearing food or other objects. The forward projection of the nasal aperture marks the development of the typically human external nose with its downwardly facing nostrils (vs. the relatively flat nose with more forwardly facing nostrils of the apes and of homi-nids before *H. erectus*). The initial selective advantage of the external nose may have been its contribution to conserving body moisture during bouts of heightened activity. Together with the remarkably robust locomotor skeleton that also characterizes *H. erectus*, the external nose may announce an inclination to periods of intense muscular exertion, perhaps in increasingly active hunting/scavenging.

To begin with, like *Homo habilis* and the australopithe-cines, *H. erectus* was confined to Africa, but about 1 mya or shortly before it dispersed to Eurasia. In Africa, it eventually colonized some relatively dry regions that had previously been unoccupied, and in mid-latitude Eurasia it became the first hominid to adapt to truly cool-temperate conditions. Its adapt-ability may have been largely due to an enhanced ability to acquire meat by scavenging, hunting, or both, but direct archeological evidence to confirm this is still lacking. A significant behavioral advance over *H. habilis* is indicated most firmly by the appearance of artifacts that required more foresight and effort to prepare. These include the hand axes and other large bifacial tools of the Acheulean Industrial Tradition, which emerged in Africa roughly 1.5–1.4 mya. *H. erectus* was probably also the first hominid to control fire, though it is arguable that this occurred only near the end of its tenure, roughly 500,000 years ago.

However, in keeping with its distinctly primitive cranial morphology, *Homo erectus* was still behaviorally primitive by modern standards. It was unable to penetrate truly cold environments in Eurasia, and everywhere its numbers were probably very small. Its great skeletal robusticity suggests that, compared with much later people, it relied far more on bodily strength and endurance and far less on artifactual skill to accomplish essential tasks. The artifacts themselves were still relatively undifferentiated into obviously discrete functional types, and, perhaps most telling of all, they changed remarkably little over vast distances and long time intervals. This implies extraordinary behavioral conservatism that may have been neurologically imposed.

As presently conceived, *Homo erectus* was the sole species of *Homo* between 1.7 mya and at least 500,000 years ago. However, the fossil sample is still heavily dominated by the "type" specimens of *H. erectus* from Java and China. Future discoveries may show that, despite obvious morphological overlap, African *H. erectus* differed in some significant ways from the classic Far Eastern population. Fresh finds may also show that the earliest Europeans were distinctive in their morphology. So far, no European site older than 500,000 years has provided any diagnostic human fossils, and the physical appearance of the earliest Europeans is unknown. Some geographic divergence in morphology before 500,000 years ago is perhaps expectable, given the great distances separating populations and the significant geographic differences that are known from the immediately succeeding period. The question is whether regional morphological differentiation before 500,000 years ago was great enough to suggest divergent evolutionary pathways, perhaps even culminating in distinct, geographically separate species. In the latter case, only the Far Eastern population would be clearly entitled to the name *H. erectus*. Other populations would require new species names, and, more important, only one could be ancestral to living people. The others would be evolutionary dead ends.

A final decision on whether *Homo erectus* as conventionally defined was simply a grade of human evolution comprising more than one species or a valid species in its own right will require a greatly expanded fossil sample, particularly in Europe and Africa. If it is assumed, as most specialists do, that it was a valid species, a much enlarged and also much-better-dated sample will also be necessary to determine how it changed through time. The crucial question is whether it evolved gradually toward *H. sapiens* or was essentially static, changing rapidly and abruptly only near the end.

Early ("Archaic") Homo sapiens

Whatever the course of evolution within *Homo erectus*, the current consensus is that more-advanced people had appeared in Africa and Europe by about 500,000 years ago. They were distinguished from *H. erectus* mainly by a larger braincase with expanded parietals and a more rounded occiput, but they maintained large, projecting browridges, a relatively low, flattened frontal, and other features that clearly recall *H. erectus*. To reflect this mixed and still submodern morphology, they are commonly lumped together as "early" or "archaic" *Homo sapiens*. However, this designation obscures a great deal of diversity and a tendency toward increasing morphological differentiation along geographic lines. Thus, between roughly 500,000 and 130,000 years ago, early *H. sapiens* in Europe progressively approached the morphological condition of the Neanderthals. In Africa, the trend was clearly different, perhaps toward the morphology of modern people, though additional fossils are necessary for confirmation. In the Far East, the people remained morphologically similar or even identical to classic *H. erectus*. All this raises the question of whether "early *H. sapiens*" is a meaningful concept. The alternative is that there were several geographically distinct species of *Homo* after 500,000 years ago, if not before. In this view, still far from widely accepted, the African species would be the most likely ancestor of living ("anatomically modern") *H. sapiens*.

In all detectable aspects of behavior, early *Homo sapiens* seems to have been generally similar to *H. erectus*. It was still unable to penetrate truly harsh environments in Eurasia, and there is no evidence for a significant advance in the ability to obtain food, particularly animals. On average, the stone artifacts were more carefully made, but they still comprised few readily distinguishable functional or stylistic types, and artifact assemblages remained remarkably uniform over vast distances and long time spans.

Further understanding of early *Homo sapiens* is hampered by the same problem that besets the study of *H. erectus*—a relatively sparse and poorly dated fossil record. Among populations of nonmodern *H. sapiens* only one, the Neanderthals, is relatively well understood.

The Neanderthals

The Neanderthals were a morphologically homogeneous group of people who inhabited western, central, and southeastern Europe beginning 130,000 years ago or somewhat before. They apparently evolved in place from yet earlier nonmodern *Homo sapiens*. It is possible that western Asia (the Near East) shared in their early evolution, but it is at least equally likely that they spread to western Asia, fully formed, only at the beginning of the Last Glaciation, about 75,000 years ago. They disappeared from both Europe and western Asia between 50,000 and 35,000 years ago, the exact time probably depending on the place.

Morphologically, the Neanderthals were distinguished from all other people, fossil or living, mainly in the skull and face. In average size, the braincase equaled or exceeded that of living people, but in shape it was generally much lower, longer, and more globular. The face was impressive for its great length and for its extreme forward projection along the midline, from which both the orbits and the cheeks swept backward. The morphology and wear of the front teeth indicate that the front of the mouth routinely functioned as a clamp or vise, and the structure and position of the face were probably related to this behavior.

Like earlier people, the Neanderthals had extremely robust postcranial skeletons, suggesting both extraordinary muscular strength and remarkable endurance. Their forearms and lower legs were relatively short, perhaps as a functional correlate of general limb robusticity or perhaps as part of a physical adaptation to the generally cool climatic conditions in which they evolved.

Behaviorally, the Neanderthals were strikingly modern in their apparent care for people who were handicapped or incapacitated long before death. They are also the earliest people for whom intentional burial of the dead has been recorded. However, in most other detectable aspects of behavior, they were still very primitive. Their graves were extremely simple, lacking any unequivocal evidence for ritual or ceremony. No religious or ideological motivation need be implied, and the aim of burial may have been simply to remove bodies from sight. The artifacts the Neanderthals produced are assigned to the Mousterian Industrial Tradition, which, in general, can be distinguished from earlier traditions by the scarcity or lack of large bifacial tools, by a concomitantly greater emphasis on flake tools, and, arguably, by greater manufacturing refinement and a wider range of readily distinguishable tool types. However, like earlier assemblages, Mousterian ones still varied remarkably little through time and space, and they indicate that the Neanderthals rarely if ever carved, polished, or otherwise shaped bone, antler, ivory, and shell into recognizable formal artifacts. Perhaps partly for this reason, like earlier people, they left us no firm evidence for art. To judge from relative site abundance per unit time, Neanderthal populations were relatively small, and they were unable to colonize the harshest, most continental parts of Eurasia, probably at least in part because they did not construct substantial, well-heated dwellings. In this and most other archeologically observable respects, they remained similar to their predecessors and very unlike their anatomically modern successors.

The Contemporaries of the Neanderthals

The contemporaries of the Neanderthals in the Far East and Africa are less well known physically. The sparse and poorly dated Far Eastern fossils are not Neanderthal-like, though they are equally nonmodern. In contrast, the available African fossils, together with some from the immediately adjacent part of southwest Asia (the Levant), suggest that anatomically modern humans had appeared in Africa before 80,000 years ago, while nonmodern people were still the sole occupants of Europe and the Far East. The fossil evidence for an African origin of modern humans is strongly supported by genetic evidence implying that all living people share a common African ancestor probably within the past 200,000–100,000 years.

The archeology of the Far Eastern contemporaries of the Neanderthals is no better known than their bones, but the archeology of the contemporaneous, modern or near modern Africans has been well studied. Their artifact assemblages are commonly lumped in the Middle Stone Age (succeeding the Early Stone Age, which comprises the Oldowan and Acheulean Traditions). However, the assemblages could as well be called Mousterian. They include the same basic artifact types, and they exhibit the same limited degree of change through time and space. They also lack formal bone artifacts and art objects. Moreover, the modern or near-modern people who occupied the South African coast during the Last Interglaciation, between roughly 130,000 and 75,000 years ago, have provided some of the clearest evidence for a distinctly nonmodern subsistence economy. This can be inferred from a sharp contrast between the animal remains they left in their sites and those left by the next people to occupy the region under similar environmental conditions, during the Present Interglaciation or past 12,000 years.

The Present Interglacial people were physically similar or identical to the historic hunter-gatherers of southern Africa, to whom they were certainly ancestral, and they made essentially the same kind of (Later Stone Age) artifacts, including numerous art objects and formal bone tools and weapons. Their behavior thus provides a fully modern standard for judging the behavior of their Last Interglacial counterparts. In contrast to the Last Interglacial people, they exploited fish and seabirds extensively and obtained truly dangerous terrestrial animals, such as wild pigs and buffalo, much more often. They also seem to have been much more numerous, that is, their population density was significantly greater. In large part, the reason for the contrasts is probably technological. To judge from the accompanying artifacts, it seems likely that only the Present Interglacial people possessed a fishing-fowling technology, along with the bow and arrow and perhaps other weapons or techniques that reduced personal risk in hunting. In sum, the combined economic and artifactual evidence indicates that however modern or near-modern Last Interglacial southern Africans were in their anatomy, they were far from modern in their behavior. Unfortunately, both the timing and the nature of the shift to behavioral modernity in Africa remain obscure, owing mainly to a shortage of sites dating from the 60,000–40,000-years-ago interval when it probably occurred.

Modern Human Origins: Some Unresolved Questions

If anatomically modern people were present in Africa and adjacent southwest Asia before 80,000 years ago, it may be asked why they took so long to displace the Neanderthals, who continued to occupy southeastern Europe until at least 50,000 years ago and western Europe until 35,000 years ago. It is even possible that Neanderthals spreading from Europe displaced early moderns in southwest Asia at the beginning of the Last Glaciation, about 75,000 years ago. The answer to the puzzle is probably that the earliest anatomically modern people were not behaviorally modern and that it was only with the evolution of modern behavior—or, perhaps more precisely, the modern capacity for culture—that they were able to supplant the Neanderthals and contemporaneous, archaic populations that probably existed farther east in Eurasia. The question then becomes, Why did the evolution of behavior lag behind the evolution of form? Perhaps the answer is that body form was only superficially modern and that some further neurological change was still necessary for full modernity.

Beyond this issue, which may prove very difficult to address on the basis of the fossil record, there are many other interesting—and potentially more tractable—unanswered questions concerning modern human origins. When and where did the modern human behavioral syndrome first appear? Did all its subsequent, archeologically visible features (art; the tendency to manufacture various formal artifacts in bone, shell, etc.; a significant increase in the variety of readily distinguishable stone artifact types; greatly increased spatial and temporal vaiability in artifact assemblages; more complex burials, implying ritual or ceremony; significant advances in subsistence practices, etc.) appear at more or less the same time?

Wherever modern behavior evolved, were there particular environmental conditions (natural selection pressures) that might help explain its appearance? Why do the earliest known Europeans and Australians tend to look more like their historic successors than like their presumed African ancestors? Were the Far Eastern contemporaries of the Neanderthals fully replaced, as seems increasingly likely for the Neanderthals, or did they perhaps contribute significantly to the gene pools of local historic populations? These and many subsidiary questions will not be answered quickly, but the recency of modern human origins means that the prospects for answers in this matter are probably greater than they are for any other important event in human evolution.

APPENDIX 1: CLASSIFICATION AND NOMENCLATURE

This appendix summarizes the basic principles behind the modern systems of biological classification and nomenclature to support their use in the text. It is based largely on the classic books of A. J. Cain (1960) and G. G. Simpson (1961), which contain much more comprehensive treatments.

Classification

The modern system of biological classification was devised in the seventeenth and eighteenth centuries and achieved essentially its present form in the tenth edition of Carolus Linnaeus's *Systema Naturae*, published in 1758. Its most basic unit is the species, usually defined today as a population of organisms that look more or less alike and that can interbreed and produce fertile offspring. On the basis of their (presumed) degree of evolutionary relationship, species are then classified into progressively higher categories, minimally including (from bottom to top) genus, family, order, class, phylum, and kingdom. Thus, species that are presumed to share a very recent common ancestor are generally placed in the same genus; species that are more distantly related are placed in different *genera* (the plural of *genus*); genera that share a relatively recent common ancestor are placed in a common family; more distantly related genera are placed in separate families; and so forth, up to the level of the kingdom.

Since Linnaeus's time, many new levels have been inserted among the seven principal ones, mainly to accommodate the great proliferation of known species. Depending on the species being classified, twenty or more levels may be recognized today; twenty-one levels are illustrated in Table A1.1, which presents a classification of *Homo sapiens* according to the Linnaean system. Whatever number of levels are used, the principle remains the same. A category at any given level contains a group of species whose overall degree of

Table A1.1. A classification of living people involving twenty-one potential levels in the Linnaean hierarchy

---

*KINDGOM: Animalia

---

  *PHYLUM: Chordata
   SUBPHYLUM: Vertebrata
    SUPERCLASS: Tetrapoda
    *CLASS: Mammalia
     SUBCLASS: Theria
      INFRACLASS: Eutheria
       COHORT: Unguiculata
        SUPERORDER: _____
         *ORDER: Primates
          SUBORDER: Anthropoidea
           INFRAORDER: Catarrhini
            SUPERFAMILY: Hominoidea
            *FAMILY: Hominidae
             SUBFAMILY: Homininae
              TRIBE: Hominini
               SUBTRIBE: _____
                *GENUS: *Homo*
                 SUBGENUS: (*Homo*)
                 *SPECIES: *sapiens*
                  SUBSPECIES: *sapiens*

Note: A blank follows a level for which no taxon is in common use. Asterisks designate the seven obligatory and most basic levels in the Linnaean system.

relationship is reflected by the level at which they are grouped in the hierarchy. Thus, although *H. sapiens* is the only surviving human species, as discussed in the text, it had at least two very close extinct relatives (*H. habilis* and *H. erectus*) which are therefore included in the same genus. Other extinct species that are more distantly related and that are human only in the broad sense are usually placed in the separate genus, *Australopithecus* and are united with species of *Homo* only at the family level, in the Hominidae. The Hominidae in turn are usually joined with the apes (several families living and extinct) in a common superfamily, the Hominoidea; the Hominoidea with the Old World Monkeys (constituting a single superfamily, the Cercopithecoidea) in the infraorder Catarrhini; the Catarrhini with the New World monkeys (Platyrrhini) in a common suborder, the Anthropoidea (higher primates); and, finally, the Anthropoidea with the lower primates (Prosimii) in the order Primates. The details of this particular hierarchy are subject to change as new information on evolutionary relationships is developed, but the basic outline is firm.

From what has been said, it follows that each category above the species comprises a group of related species (except in those rare instances where a species has no close relatives living or extinct, in which case a higher category may include only one species). For the sake of convenience, each species in the Linnaean hierarchy and each group of related species at any level is called a *taxon* (plural *taxa*). Thus, the species *Homo sapiens* is a taxon, as are the genus *Homo*, the family Hominidae, the superfamily Hominoidea, the infraorder Catarrhini, the suborder Anthropoidea, the order Primates, and even the kingdom Animalia. Species and genera are commonly referred to as "lower taxa" as opposed to categories above the genus, which are known as "higher taxa." Etymologically based on the words *taxon* and *taxa*, the term *taxonomy* is often used as a synonym for classification, though it more properly refers to the system of rules for constructing a classification.

Although evolutionary relationships are the basis for classification, they cannot be observed directly and must be inferred from the degree of similarity among taxa. In general, the greater the similarity, the closer the assumed relationship. This explains how the modern classification system could develop before evolution became popular and also how it can be used today even by antievolutionists. More important, the unavoidable reliance on degree of resemblance can distort evolutionary classifications, since common descent is not the only cause of similarities among taxa. Among others, undoubtedly the most important is similar adaptation to shared environmental conditions. Resemblances due to similar adaptations are often called "analogies" (or "convergences") in distinction to "homologies," which are similarities due to common descent. A very conspicuous and oft-cited analogy is the streamlined, finned body form shared by fish and whales, which, despite this morphological similarity, are not very closely related. A less famous but equally clear analogy is the independent, parallel development in apes and some New World monkeys of an upper-limb structure that facilitates hanging or swinging below branches. In contrast, the numerous obvious, detailed similarities in head and body form between people and chimpanzees exemplify homologies, inherited from a relatively recent common ancestor.

In many instances (the fish and the whales, for example), careful scrutiny of multiple characters allows the unambiguous separation of homologies from analogies. In other cases, the distinction can be difficult, particularly in fossil taxa, in which the number of assessable characters is limited. In addition, even when homologies have been isolated, they are not in themselves sufficient to establish the degree of evolutionary relationship among taxa. A further distinction must be made between homologies that are shared widely and ones that have a narrower distribution within a taxonomic group. In general, widely shared characters have only limited taxonomic value, even if they are prominent and numerous. Characters with a limited distribution are more likely to reveal the basic evolutionary links among taxa in the group. The realization that different characters must be assigned different weights in evolutionary studies is central to the increasingly popular perspective on classification known as *cladistics* (Eldredge and Cracraft 1980; Wilcy 1981, with further references). Following W. Hennig (1966), cladists usually distinguish between two fundamental kinds of homologous characters:

1. Primitive (or generalized) characters (plesiomorphies or symplesiomorphies), which arose early in the evolutionary history of a taxonomic group. These will be very widespread and will therefore not help in dividing the group into lower-level taxa, that is, in determining their genealogical relationships.
2. Derived (or advanced) characters (apomorphies), which arose relatively late in members of a group and which will differ among them. By definition, in contrast to primitive characters, derived characters are useful in assessing genealogical links among taxa. They can be further subdivided into two basic types: (1) shared, derived characters (synapomorphies), which demonstrate a special evolutionary tie among taxa that have them, and (2) unique, derived characters (autapomorphies) or novelties, which distinguish a taxon from all others. Unique, derived characters are not useful for inferring evolutionary connections, though they may eliminate one taxon from the ancestry of another that lacks them.

The application of cladistics to a group of related taxa results in a *cladogram* or tree diagram which organizes taxa according to the number of derived features they have in common. The greater the number of derived features that two taxa share, the more likely it is that they will reside on branches that connect to each other before connecting to other branches farther down the tree. In form, cladograms resemble traditional evolutionary phylogenies ("family trees"), but, unlike phylogenies, which place taxa at different points or branching nodes within a tree, cladograms range them at the ends of terminal branches (Fig A1.1). Also, unlike phylogenies, cladograms do not take time relationships into account, and they generally do not include a time scale. The essential difference is that cladograms illustrate perceived degrees of derived similarity among taxa, not ancestor-descendant relationships.

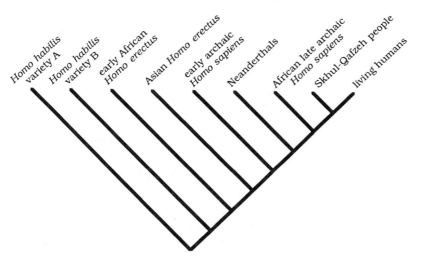

Figure A1.1. Cladogram linking fossil and living members of the
genus *Homo* according to their apparent degree of derived similarity
in eleven key features (cranial robusticity, postcranial robusticity,
supraorbital torus morphology, cranial flattening and elongation,
occipital angulation, midfacial projection, the ratio of nasal height
to biorbital breadth, the extent to which the vault overlies the face,
the size of the occipital plane relative to the nuchal plane on the
occipital bone, endocranial volume, and dental size) (after Stringer
1987: 143). The cladogram indicates that living people and the fossil people designated "Skhul-Qafzeh" share a greater number of
derived (advanced) characters or character states than either does
with African late archaic *Homo sapiens*. In turn, African late
archaic *Homo sapiens*, the Skhul-Qafzeh people, and living humans
share more derived features with each other than any one of them
does with the Neanderthals, and so forth. The cladogram illustrates
only the perceived degree of derived similarity, not ancestor-
descendant relationships. However, it could be used to support a
variety of phylogenies, including ones in which the Skhul-Qafzeh
people and living humans were derived from African late archaic
Homo sapiens, but in which the Neanderthals (and possibly other
groups, such as Asian *Homo erectus*) were evolutionary dead ends,
without living descendants. These possibilities (and others) are discussed in the main chapters of the text.

In their exclusive focus on degree of similarity or difference, cladograms are less abstract than phylogenies, which
must be more conjectural or hypothetical. However, if the
principles behind cladistics are straightforward, the practice is
often problematic. Cladistic analysis may stumble if shared,
derived features that are actually analogies (or parallelisms) are
mistaken for homologies. In addition, it is not always easy to
determine whether a character is primitive or derived within a
group. In fact, it can be both, since character reversals are an
occasional feature of the evolutionary process. Skull bone

thickness, for example, changed from relatively thin in the earliest hominids (the australopithecines and *Homo habilis*) to relatively thick later on (in *H. erectus* and early *H. sapiens*) back to thin (in later *H. sapiens*, including living people.) In a situation such as this, functional understanding of a character or character state would obviously be useful for determining its cladistic value. A functional understanding is also crucial for determining whether two (or more) shared, derived characters are truly independent. If not, they may comprise only one character, and their implications for an especially close taxonomic relationship are diminished. Some of these problems, together with the substantial fruits of cladistic analysis, are illustrated in the text, though the emphasis there is on potential phylogenies and on broad evolutionary trends, independent of taxonomy or phylogeny.

Nomenclature

In keeping with the practice of Linnaeus, taxa are always given Latin names, or at least names whose form has been Latinized. The Latin name of a taxon may be intended as a substantive characterization (*Homo sapiens*, for example, means "wise man"), but, in general, a name should be regarded simply as a label, not as a definition. The name of a species always consists of two words—the genus (generic) name followed by the species (specific) designation in the narrow sense. Grammatically, the genus name is a Latin noun and the species designation is a Latin modifier (either an adjective or a noun in the genitive singular) or another Latin noun in apposition. The name of a genus is always capitalized and italicized (or underlined, in typescript), whether it stands alone or is modified by a species designation. The second part of the species name (that is, the species designation narrowly understood) is italicized but not capitalized. If a genus has already been cited, a closely following citation of a species in the same genus may abbreviate the genus name to its first letter and a period, for example, *H. sapiens* or *H. erectus* closely following the citation of *Homo sapiens*.

In those relatively rare instances in which a subgenus name is used, it is capitalized, italicized, and placed in parentheses between the genus and the species terms, for example, *Australopithecus (Paranthropus) robustus*. If a subspecies name is used, it is italicized but not capitalized and is appended to the full species name, for example, *Homo sapiens sapiens*. Subspecies are commonly defined as morphologically and geographically distinct populations of a species, but, strictly considered, they have no place in the Linnaean hierarchy, except in those instances in which there is evidence that such populations are in the process of becoming separate species (that is, are undergoing progressive genetic divergence because of differing natural selective pressures in different environments). There is no evidence that any populations of living *H. sapiens* are such "species in the making," but the case can be made for some extinct populations, for example, the Neanderthals, who are often placed in the subspecies *H. sapiens neanderthalensis.*

The names of categories above the genus level are capitalized but not italicized. Higher taxa, up to the level of the superfamily, always derive their names from one of the genera they include. By convention, they also have endings that designate their level: (in vertebrates) "-ini" for tribe, "-inae" for subfamily, "-idae" for family, and "-oidea" for superfamily. Above the superfamily level, the only rule is that the name must be a Latin (or Latinized) noun. The Latin names are usually anglicized by dropping the Latin ending (for example, hominid is used instead of Hominidae). In their anglicized form, they are generally not capitalized and can be used as either adjectives or nouns.

Technically, the full name of a taxon at any level includes the name of its inventor and the date of its invention (for example, *Homo sapiens* Linnaeus, 1758). In practice, this requirement is frequently ignored, particularly when, as in the present book, taxonomy itself is not a primary concern.

Ideally, all specialists would refer to the same taxon by the same name, but problems arise when one taxon has been given two or more names and when there is disagreement about which has priority (that is, which was suggested or legitimized first). Even if one name clearly has priority, many specialists may retain a second name that has a long history of use. However, the most important nomenclatural disagreements do not involve only names but are concerned with more basic differences of opinion about the evolutionary relationships among taxa. Thus, many specialists believe that the relationship between the gorilla and the chimpanzee is distant enough to place them in the separate genera *Gorilla* and *Pan,* while others believe they are much more closely related and should be lumped into the single genus *Pan* (in this instance, *Gorilla* would be "sunk" into *Pan,* because the name *Pan* has priority). Nomenclatural disagreements that stem from taxonomic (classificatory) disputes are particularly common among paleontologists, as illustrated in this book.

APPENDIX 2: FLAKED STONE ARTIFACT TECHNOLOGY AND TYPOLOGY

This appendix provides vocabulary and additional background for the text's discussions of stone artifacts. The information has been drawn from many sources, of which the most important are Bordes (1947, 1961b), de Sonneville-Bordes and Perrot (1954–56), and Oakley (1959).

Assemblages, Industries, and Cultures

The stone artifacts from a single excavation unit, such as a layer within a site, are usually referred to as an *assemblage*. Generally similar assemblages from the same region and time interval are lumped into an *industry*, and groups of related industries are placed in the same *industrial complex* or *tradition*. Sometimes, *culture* and *cultural* are used instead of *industry* and *industrial*, although, even where artifacts are abundant and diverse, they clearly reflect only a small part of culture in its anthropological sense.

Types of Stone Suitable for Artifact Manufacture

Nearly all types of rock can be used for artifact manufacture, but the most desirable ones are relatively hard, fracture easily when struck, and have a smooth, homogeneous internal consistency. Among widespread rock types, the ones that meet these criteria best are very-fine-grained siliceous varieties such as flint and chert. Flint is common throughout Europe, where it was used so often that the local Stone Age could almost be called the "flint age." In Africa, where large nodules of flint and related rocks do not occur in many regions, Stone Age people were compelled to use other materials, mainly quartzites or volcanic rocks. Some fine-grained quartzites approach flint in quality, but among volcanic rocks, only one—obsidian (volcanic glass)—is roughly comparable. It was extensively exploited in those limited areas (of east Africa) where it occurs. Other, more widespread volcanic rocks, such as basalt, are generally more difficult to work, and they therefore result in relatively crude-looking artifacts. Even the very earliest stone-tool makers preferentially selected the most desirable rock types at their disposal.

Techniques of Stone Knapping

The process of flaking stone is called *knapping*. Three fundamental techniques exist: (1) *direct percussion*, (2) *indirect percussion*, and (3) *pressure flaking*.

Direct percussion can take two basic forms. In the most common variant, the knapper uses a *hammerstone* to strike a *flake* from a *core*. For best results, the hammerstone should be softer than the core, so that the core bites into it and slippage between the two pieces is minimized. If the core is flint, quartzite and certain kinds of volcanic rock generally make good hammerstones. Limestone is usually too soft. A wooden or bone rod (billet, or "soft hammer") may be substituted for the hammerstone if the goal is to detach relatively long, thin flakes—for example, in the final shaping of a hand ax (defined below). Wooden or bone rods were almost certainly used to finish some finely made late-Acheulean hand axes from Europe, dating from between about 400,000 and 200,000 years ago.

In the second basic, but less common, variant of direct percussion, the core is mobile and the hammerstone is stationary. The knapper strikes the hammerstone with the core to remove a flake. The hammerstone in this instance is called an *anvil*.

In indirect percussion, a third object, such as a wooden or antler rod, is interposed between the core and the hammerstone. This gives the knapper fine control over the point where the hammer blow enters the core. Indirect percussion was invented later than direct percussion, and it was probably rarely practiced before the emergence of Upper Paleolithic and related "cultures" about 50,000–40,000 years ago.

In pressure flaking, the knapper removes a flake by pressing a pointed antler rod or other hard object against the edge of a core. Alternatively, the object to be flaked can be forced against a stationary compressor. Like indirect percussion, pressure flaking was practiced mainly by Upper Paleolithic and later people, who used it mostly for modifying (retouching) the edges and surface of a flake rather than for primary flake production. Some Upper Paleolithic knappers discovered that pressure can remove longer, thinner flakes from flint pieces that had been previously heated to a high temperature and then allowed to cool. The heated pieces acquire a distinctive, permanent greasy or soapy luster.

The Manufacture and Description of Flakes

Flakes consist of three principal parts—the *striking platform* or *butt*, the *ventral surface*, and the *dorsal surface* (Fig. A2.1,1). The striking platform is the part of the flake that was struck by the hammerstone when the flake was detached from the core. Part of it remains on the core where it forms the striking platform of the core. A given core can have many striking platforms, but a flake will have only one (or, very rarely, two—formed when two blows hit a core at the same time; this can happen when a struck core bounces against another hard object). By convention, unless otherwise noted, flakes are

Figure A2.1. *1:* Flake viewed from the ventral surface; *2:* direct percussion and pressure retouch; *3–9:* various kinds of sidescrapers, defined by the number, shape, and position of the retouched edges (simple = one-edged, double = two-edged; convergent = with two edges converging to a point) (redrawn after Bordes 1961b).

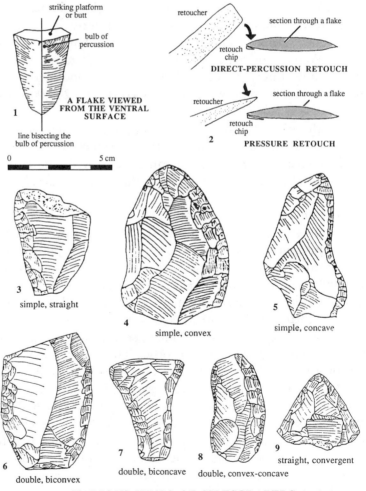

illustrated with the striking platform down. The ventral surface is the one that was originally inside the core; the dorsal surface is the one that was outside the core. The ventral surface is usually smooth, though it always has a variably pronounced bulge or *bulb of percussion* immediately adjacent to the striking platform. This results from the rapid dissipation of the hammer blow through the interior of a core. Unlike the ventral surface, the dorsal one always exhibits either the weathering rind (*cortex*) of the unflaked core, hollows and ridges (*scars*) from previous flake removals, or both.

After a flake has been removed from a core, the negative scar (or facet) left on the core can be used as the striking platform for a second flake, and the process can be repeated until the core becomes too small to produce additional flakes. A core that has been reduced to this extent is said to be exhausted.

Modern replication experiments show that prehistoric knappers often reshaped a core or modified its striking platform to predetermine the size or shape of flakes. Platform modification was commonly done to remove irregularities that would diffuse or misdirect the force of the hammer blow. It results in flakes that have prepared or *faceted* striking platforms (or butts), as opposed to ones with unprepared or *smooth* platforms (or butts). A core that was extensively preshaped to produce one or more flakes with a predetermined shape is called a *Levallois core* (Fig. A2.2 *top*), after a site in the Levallois suburb of Paris where Paleolithic examples have been known since the last century. The corresponding flakes are called *Levallois flakes*. They usually have faceted platforms, but this is not a defining characteristic. Well-made Levallois flakes and cores appear in some later-Acheulean assemblages, dating between perhaps 400,000 and 200,000 years ago, but they are especially common in some succeeding European and Near Eastern Mousterian industries.

For purposes of measurement, the maximum length of a flake is usually measured along a line bisecting the bulb of percussion (or, if necessary, along a line parallel to this one). Maximum width is measured at right angles to this line. Flakes that are longer than they are wide are sometimes called *flake-blades*, while ones that are at least twice as long as wide are called *blades*. Any extensive knapping session will produce some blades, but to produce them consistently a knapper needs special expertise in core preparation. Long, carefully produced blades with nearly parallel edges especially characterize most European and Near Eastern Upper Paleolithic industries. They came from cores that were preshaped so that they resembled prisms (Fig. A2.2, *bottom*), and the blades are therefore known as *prismatic blades.* Most prismatic blades were probably produced by indirect percussion, in which a pointed antler or hardwood rod was interposed between the hammerstone and the core. Modern knappers call the rod a *punch,* and the blades that result are called *punched blades.* The terms *prismatic* and

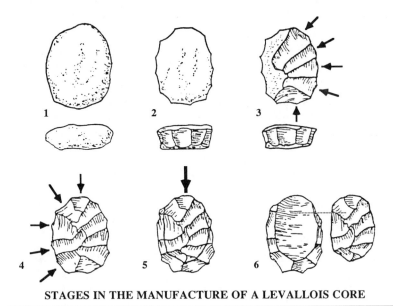

STAGES IN THE MANUFACTURE OF A LEVALLOIS CORE

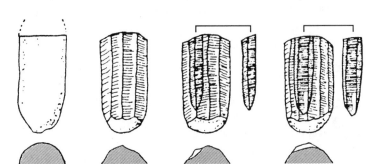

STAGES IN THE MANUFACTURE OF A PRISMATIC BLADE CORE

Figure A2.2. *Top:* Stages in the manufacture of a Levallois core. *1:* Raw nodule; *2:* nodule with flakes struck off around the periphery; *3:* nodule with flakes struck radially inward on one surface, by using the peripheral scars as striking platforms; *4:* radial preparation completed; *5:* final hammer blow (indicated by the arrow) struck on the prepared core; *6:* final Levallois core and flake. *Bottom:* Stages in the manufacture of a prismatic core and blades. *1:* Elongated raw nodule with one end struck off to provide a striking platform; *2:* early stage in the removal of blades around the periphery of the nodule; *3, 4:* later stages in the removal of blades, showing blades with single and double dorsal ridges. (Top redrawn after Bordes 1961a: Fig. 4; bottom redrawn after Bordes 1947: Fig. 4).

punched are sometimes used as synonyms, though, strictly considered, they are not.

Core Tool Types

In many cases, prehistoric knappers were interested in cores primarily as sources of flakes, but in others they were also interested in shaping some cores into tools. The earliest archeological sites, assigned to the Oldowan Industrial Tradition, beginning at least 2.3 million years ago (mya), often contain pebbles or other rock fragments from which a few flakes were struck to produce a sharp edge. These simple tools are called *choppers* and come in two fundamental varieties: *unifacial* ones, in which the edge was created by flaking on one surface only, and *bifacial* ones, in which the edge was created by convergent flaking from two surfaces (Fig. A2.3, *top*). Beginning about 1.4 mya, bifacial flaking was often extended to the entire periphery of a pebble or rock fragment. The resulting tools are known as *bifaces*. By convention, choppers and

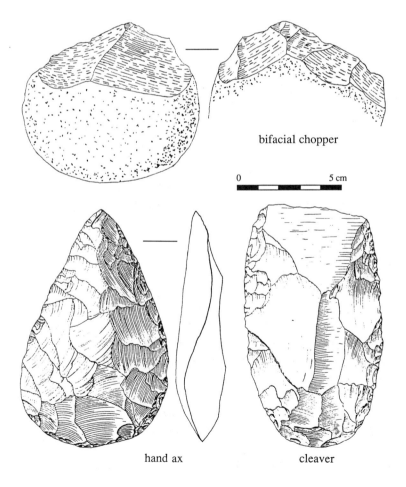

bifacial chopper

0   5 cm

hand ax   cleaver

Figure A2.3. Bifacial chopper, hand ax, and cleaver (redrawn after Bordes 1961b: Pls. 46, 61, 78). Together, hand axes and cleavers are commonly known as bifaces.

bifaces are called *core tools,* to distinguish them from *flake tools.* However, choppers and especially bifaces can be made on large flakes, and the core-tool/flake-tool distinction is thus partly a matter of size.

Bifaces come in two main types: *hand axes* and *cleavers* (Fig. A2.3, *bottom*). The main difference is that hand axes are more or less pointed at one end, while cleavers have a guillotine-like edge in place of the point. In general, cleavers are less abundant than hand axes, especially outside Africa. Hand axes can be divided into many different kinds, depending on plan shape (oval, triangular, heartlike, etc.), overall size, the quality of flaking, and so forth. The quality of biface manufacture was heavily dependent on raw-material availability, and many African examples, made of dense volcanic rock, appear crude next to like-aged European ones made of high-quality flint. Bifaces are the defining characteristic of the Acheulean Industrial Tradition, dated to between about 1.4 mya and 200,000–130,000 years ago, though they were sometimes made afterward, usually in small numbers.

Retouch and Flake Tool Types

After a flake or blade was struck from a core, prehistoric knappers sometimes altered or *retouched* it by striking small flakes or chips from one or more of its edges (Fig. A2.1, 2). In most cases, the ventral surface served as the striking platform for retouch, and the chip scars appear on the dorsal surface. In general, retouching dulls rather than sharpens a fresh edge, so retouch was usually done to modify its shape, to give it greater stability, or to resharpen it after it had been dulled by use.

The position and quality of retouch are the principal criteria for defining different types of flake tools. Thus, a simple flake on which one or more edges bear smooth, continuous retouch is often referred to as a *sidescraper.* Different kinds of sidescrapers can be defined by how many edges are retouched, by their shape (convex, concave, or straight) or combination of shapes, by their position with respect to the line bisecting the bulb of percussion, by the steepness of the retouch, and so forth (Fig. A2.1, 3–9). If the retouch is very steep or abrupt, so that the retouch scars are nearly perpendicular to the ventral surface, a flake (or flake edge) is said to be *backed.* A flake on which two continuously retouched, nonabrupt edges converge to a point is variously regarded as a kind of sidescraper (if the flake is thick) (Fig. A2.1, 9) or as a *point* (if the flake is thin) (Fig. A2.4, 1, 2). A flake on which retouch has been used to produce a deep indentation or several adjacent

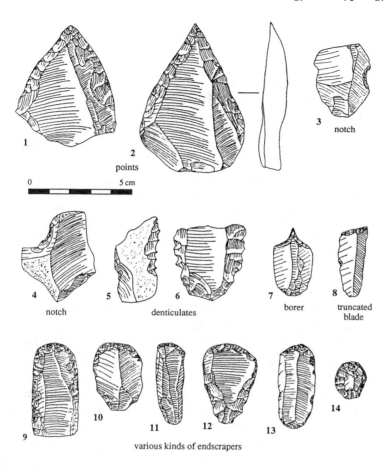

Figure A2.4.
Points, notches,
denticulates,
borer, truncated
blade, and end-
scrapers (1–6
redrawn after Bor-
des 1961b: 7–14
redrawn after de
Sonneville-Bordes
and Perrot 1954–
56).

deep indentations is called a *notch* (Fig. A2.4, *3, 4*). If the
adjacent indentations are relatively shallow, so that the edge
appears ragged or serrate, the flake is a *denticulate* (Fig. A2.4,
5, 6). If one or more barbs between indentations are the flake's
most conspicuous aspect, it is a *borer* (Fig. A2.4, *7*).

Analysis of the size and morphology of different kinds of
sidescrapers in some Paleolithic assemblages suggests that
some types may be mainly stages in the freshening or "reduction" of others (Dibble 1987, 1988). Thus, the second edge on
many double-edged pieces may have been prepared only after
the first edge became dull or ragged, and sidescrapers on which
two edges converge to a point could result from the continued
refreshing of both retouched edges. Similarly, the need to
refresh notches may have produced many denticulates. An
important implication of this is that differences among assemblages in the abundance of different kinds of sidescrapers or of
notches versus denticulates may reflect simply the degree of
refreshing or reduction. However, this is a potentially important datum in itself, and most specialists continue to record

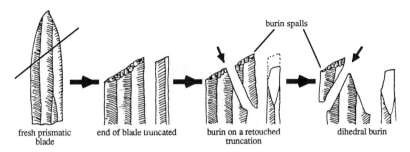

Figure A2.5. Stages in the manufacture of a burin. *1:* Fresh prismatic blade; *2:* striking platform prepared by truncating retouch on
the end of the blade; *3:* initial burin blow, producing a "burin on a
retouched truncation," *4:* second burin blow, struck from the scar
left by the first, producing a "dihedral burin" (redrawn after Howell
et al. 1965).

notches, denticulates, and different kinds of sidescrapers basically as they are described here.

For the most part, the same tool types that occur on flakes
also occur on blades, but some types are restricted to blades by
nature or by definition. For example, an ordinary flake on
which the edge opposite the bulb bears smooth, continuous
retouch is simply a kind of sidescraper, while a blade (or
flake-blade) with retouch in the same position is an *endscraper.*
Different kinds of endscrapers can be defined by the shape and
abruptness of the retouched edge and by the extent to which
retouch occurs elsewhere on the piece (Fig. A2.4, *9–14*). A
blade on which the end has been dulled so that the retouch
scars are nearly perpendicular to the ventral surface is said to
be *truncated* (Fig. A2.4, *8*) rather than backed. The lateral
edge(s) of a blade can be backed, and truncation and backing
can even occur on the same piece, as can various combinations
of other features. In fact, many different feature combinations
are possible on both blades and flakes, allowing many additional kinds of stone tools to be defined.

One additional type of flake or blade tool that requires
special mention is the *burin.* This is a piece from which a
second, smaller flake or blade (a *burin spall*) has been struck
along one edge, leaving a scar at an abrupt angle to the ventral
surface of the parent (Fig. A2.5). As a result, a corner of the
parent becomes chisel-like. Stone burins are named for the
modern metal-engraving tools they resemble, and they were
probably often used for engraving bone, antler, or ivory. They
tend to be rare and casually made until the appearance of
Upper Paleolithic industries, which were also the first to

contain large numbers of carefully crafted, formal bone implements. Many different kinds of burins can be defined, depending on (a) whether the burin spall was struck from a truncation
or a fracture surface, (b) the location of the spall scar, (c) how
many spalls were struck, (d) whether there is retouch elsewhere on the piece, and so forth.

Functions of Stone Tools

The names assigned to stone-artifact types often suggest that
their functions are known, but in general this is not the case.
The types are defined on morphological grounds, and their
functions are speculative, based on resemblances to historic
tools of known function or on feasibility experiments with
modern replicas. Even a widely employed distinction between
tools and manufacturing *waste (débitage)* is strictly morphological. Thus, by convention, only retouched pieces have been
classified as tools, even though feasibility experiments show
that many unretouched pieces could have been used effectively
as knives, scrapers, and so forth. Additionally, many unretouched pieces have macroscopic edge damage or microscopic
wear polishes that could only have formed during use.

   Polishes and other microscopic wear traces on both
retouched and unretouched artifacts can show not only that an
artifact was used but also how it was used (to cut, scrape, saw,
etc.) and on what substance (wood, bone, hide, etc.) (Semenov
1964; Keeley 1977, 1980). Ancient use is inferred from similarities to wear patterns developed on modern replicas used in
known ways. Microwear analysis has revealed the functions of
many individual prehistoric stone tools, but it has some
important limitations: it can only be applied to certain very-
fine-grained rock types, it is very time consuming, and it is
only moderately accurate (Moss 1987). It has not led to a
reformulation of artifact typology along functional (vs. morphological) lines, nor is it likely to. This is partly because of its
inherent practical and technical limitations and partly because
of the loose relationship between form and function. Thus, the
functions inferred for a few examples cannot be assumed to
characterize all examples of a given artifact type. In fact,
functional variability within a single morphological type is the
established norm, particularly for industries that antedate the
Upper Paleolithic and its temporal correlates. Limited understanding of the way(s) in which many ancient stone artifacts
were used remains a major obstacle to a fuller understanding of
ancient human behavior.

REFERENCES

Abramova, Z. A. 1964. On the question of hunting in the Upper Paleolithic (in Russian). *Sovetskaya Arkheologiya* 4:177–180.

———. 1967. Palaeolithic art in the USSR. *Arctic Anthropology* 4(2): 1–179.

———. 1982. Zur Jagd im Jungpaläolithikum. *Archäologisches Korrespondenzblatt* 12:1–9.

Absolon, K., and B. Klíma. 1978. *Předmostí: ein Mammutjägerplatz in Mähren.* Brno: Archeologicky Ustav CSAV v Brne.

Adam, K. D. 1985. The chronological and systematic position of the Steinheim skull. In E. Delson, ed. *Ancestors: the hard evidence,* 272–276. New York: Alan R. Liss.

Aguirre, E., and M. de Lumley. 1977. Fossil men from Atapuerca, Spain: their bearing on human evolution in the Middle Pleistocene. *Journal of Human Evolution* 6:681–738.

Aguirre, E., and A. Rosas. 1985. Fossil man from Cueva Mayor, Ibeas, Spain: new findings and taxonomic discussion. In P. V. Tobias, ed. *Hominid evolution: past, present and future,* 319–328. New York: Alan R. Liss.

Aiello, L. C. 1986. The relationships of the Tarsiiformes: a review of the case for the Haplorhini. In B. Wood, L. Martin, and P. Andrews, eds. *Major topics in primate and human evolution,* 47–65. Cambridge: University of Cambridge Press.

Aigner, J. S. 1978a. Important archaeological remains from North China. In F. Ikawa-Smith, ed. *Early Paleolithic in south and east Asia,* 163–232. The Hague: Mouton.

———. 1978b. Pleistocene faunal and cultural stations in south China. In F. Ikawa-Smith, ed. *Early Paleolithic in south and east Asia,* 129–160. The Hague: Mouton.

———. 1986. The age of Zhoukoudian Locality 1: the newly proposed O^{18} correspondences. *Anthropos* (Brno) 23:157–173.

Aitken, M. J. 1985. *Thermoluminescence dating.* New York: Academic Press.

Aitken, M. J., J. Huxtable, and N. C. Debenham. 1986. Thermoluminescence dating in the Palaeolithic: burned flint, stalagmitic calcite and sediment. In A. Tuffreau, and J. Sommé, eds. *Chronostratigraphie et faciés culturels du Paléolothique inférieur et moyen dans l'Europe du Nord-Ouest,* 7–14. Paris: Supplément au Bullétin de l'Association Française pour l'Étude du Quaternaire.

Alimen, H. M. 1975. Les "isthmes" Hispano-Marocain et Siculo-Tunisien aux temps acheuléens. *L'Anthropologie* 79:399–436.

Allen, J., C. Gosden, R. Jones, and J. P. White. 1988. Pleistocene dates for the human occupation of New Ireland, northern Melanesia. *Nature* 331:707–709.

Allsworth-Jones, P. 1986a. Middle Stone Age and Middle Palaeolithic: the evidence from Nigeria and Cameroun. In G. N. Bailey and P. Callow, Eds., *Stone Age prehistory: studies in memory of Charles McBurney*, 153–168. Cambridge: Cambridge University Press.

———. 1986b. *The Szeletian and the transition from the Middle to Upper Palaeolithic in central Europe*. Oxford: Oxford University Press.

Altuna, J. 1972. Fauna de mamíferos de los yacimientos prehistóricos de Guipúzcoa. *Munibe* 24:1–464.

Anderson, J. E. 1968. Late Paleolithic skeletal remains from Nubia. In F. Wendorf, ed. *The prehistory of Nubia*, vol. 2, 996–1040. Dallas: Southern Methodist University Press.

Anderson-Gerfaud, P. In press. Aspects of behavior in the middle Paleolithic: functional analysis of stone tools from southwest France. In P. Mellars, and C. Stringer, eds. *The human revolution: behavioural and biological perspectives on the origins of modern humans*. Edinburgh: Edinburgh University Press.

Andrews, P. 1980. Ecological adaptations of the smaller fossil apes. *Zeitschrift für Morphologie und Anthropologie* 71:164–173.

———. 1981a. Hominoid habitats of the Miocene. *Nature* 289:749.

———. 1981b. A short history of Miocene field palaeontology in western Kenya. *Journal of Human Evolution* 10:3–9.

———. 1981c. Species diversity and diet in monkeys and apes during the Miocene. In C. B. Stringer, ed. *Aspects of human evolution*, 25–61. London: Taylor and Francis.

———. 1983a. The natural history of *Sivapithecus*. In R. L. Ciochon and R. S. Corruccini, eds. *New interpretations of ape and human ancestry*, 441–463. New York: Plenum.

———. 1983b. Small mammal faunal diversity at Olduvai Gorge, Tanzania. *British Archaeological Reports* 163:77–85.

———. 1984. On the characters that define *Homo erectus*. *Courier Forschungsinstitut Senckenberg* 69:167–178.

———. 1985a. Family group systematics and evolution among Catarrhine Primates. In E. Delson, ed. *Ancestors: the hard evidence*, 14–22. New York: Alan R. Liss.

———. 1985b. Improved timing of hominoid evolution with a DNA clock. *Nature* 314:498–499.

———. 1986a. Aspects of hominoid phylogeny. In C. Patterson, ed. *Molecules and morphology in evolution: conflict or compromise*, 21–53. Cambridge: Cambridge University Press.

———. 1986b. Fossil evidence on human origins and dispersal. *Cold Spring Harbor Symposia on Quantitative Biology* 51:419–428.

Andrews, P., and J. Cook. 1985. Natural modification to bones in a temperate setting. *Man* (n.s.) 20:675–691.

Andrews, P., and J. E. Cronin. 1982. The relationships of *Sivapithecus* and *Ramapithecus* and the evolution of the orang-utan. *Nature* 297:545–546.

Andrews, P., and L. Martin. 1987a. Cladistic relationships of extant and fossil hominoids. *Journal of Human Evolution* 16:101–118.

_____. 1987b. The plyletic position of the Ad Dabtiyah hominoid. *Bulletin of the British Museum of Natural History (Geology)* 41:383–393.

Andrews, P., L. Martin, and P. Whybrow. 1987. Earliest known member of the great ape and human clade. *American Journal of Physical Anthropology* 72:174–175.

Andrews, P., and I. Tekkaya. 1980. A revision of the Turkish Miocene hominoid *Sivapithecus meteai. Palaeontology* 23(1): 85–95.

Andrews, P., and J. A. H. van Couvering. 1975. Palacoenvironments in the East African Miocene. *Contributions to Primatology* 5:62–103.

Anthony, B. W. 1972. The Still Bay question. In H. J. Hugot, ed. *Actes du VIe Congrès Panafricain de Préhistoire, Dakar, 1967*, 80–82. Chambéry: Les Imprimeries Réunies de Chambéry.

Arambourg, C. 1955. A recent discovery in human paleontology: *Atlanthropus* of Ternifine (Algeria). *American Journal of Physical Anthropology* 13:191–202.

Arambourg, C., and P. Biberson. 1956. The fossil human remains from the Paleolithic site of Sidi Abderrahman (Morocco). *American Journal of Physical Anthropology* 14:467–490.

Arambourg, C., and Y. Coppens. 1967. Sur la découverte, dans le Pléistocène inférieur de la vallée de l'Omo (Éthiopie), d'une mandibule d'Australopithécien. *Comptes Rendus des Séances de l'Académie des Sciences (Paris)*, Série D, 265:589–590.

Ardrey, R. 1961. *African genesis.* New York: Dell.

_____. 1976. *The hunting hypothesis.* London: Collins.

Arensburg, B., O. Bar Yosef, M. Chech, P. Goldberg, H. Laville, L. Meignen, Y. Rak, E. Tchernov, A. M. Tillier, and B. Vandermeersch. 1985. Une sépulture néanderthalien dans la grotte de Kebara (Israel). *Comptes Rendus des Séances de l'Académie des Sciences (Paris)*, Série II, 300:227–230.

Asfaw, B. 1983. A new hominid parietal from Bodo, Middle Awash Valley, Ethiopia. *American Journal of Physical Anthropology* 61:367–371.

_____. 1987. The Belohdelie frontal: new evidence of early hominid cranial morphology from the Afar of Ethiopia. *Journal of Human Evolution* 16:611–624.

Audouze, F. 1987. The Paris Basin in Magdalenian times. In O. Soffer, ed. *The Pleistocene Old World: regional perspectives*, 183–200. New York: Plenum.

Ayres, W. S., and S. N. Rhee. 1984. The Acheulean in Asia? a review of research on Korean Palaeolithic culture. *Proceedings of the Prehistoric Society* 50:35–48.

Azzaroli, A. 1985. Historical, chronological and paleoenvironmental background to the study of *Oreopithecus bambolii. American Journal of Physical Anthropology* 65:142.

Azzaroli, A., M. Boccaletti, E. Delson, G. Moratti, and D. Torre. 1986. Chronological and paleogeographical background to the study of *Oreopithecus bambolii. Journal of Human Evolution* 15:533–540.

Baba, M., L. Darga, and M. Goodman. 1980. Biochemical evidence on the phylogeny of Anthropoidea. In R. L. Ciochon and A. B. Chiarelli, eds. *Evolutionary biology of the New World monkeys and continental drift*, 423–443. New York: Plenum.

Bada, J. L. 1985. Amino acid racemization dating of fossil bones. *Annual Review of Earth and Planetary Science* 13:241–268.

Bader, O. N. 1978. *The Sungir' Upper Paleolithic site* (in Russian). Moscow: Nauka.

Bahn, P. 1983. Late Pleistocene economies of the French Pyrenees. In G. Bailey, ed. *Hunter-gatherer economy in prehistory,* 168–186. Cambridge: Cambridge University Press.

Balout, L. 1955. *Préhistoire de l'Afrique du Nord.* Paris: Arts et Métiers Graphiques.

Balout, L., P. Biberson, and J. Tixier. 1967. L'Acheuléen de Ternifine (Algérie): gisement de l'Atlanthrope. *L'Anthropologie* 71:217–238.

Ba Maw, R. L. Ciochon, and D. E. Savage. 1979. Late Eocene of Burma yields earliest anthropoid primate, *Pondaungia cotteri. Nature* 282:65–67.

Bar-Yosef, O. 1980. The prehistory of the Levant. *Annual Review of Anthropology* 9:101–133.

———. 1987. Pleistocene connexions between Africa and Southwest Asia: an archaeological perspective. *The African Archaeological Review* 5:29–38.

———. In press. Upper Pleistocene human adaptations in southwest Asia. In E. Trinkaus, ed. *Corridors, cul de sacs and coalescence: the biocultural foundations of modern people.* Santa Fe: School of American Research.

Bar-Yosef, O., and B. Vandermeersch. 1981. Notes concerning the possible age of the Mousterian layers in Qafzeh Cave. In J. Cauvin and P. Sanlaville, eds. *Préhistoire du Levant,* 281–285. Paris: Centre National de la Recherche Scientifique.

Bar-Yosef, O., B. Vandermeersch, B. Arensburg, P. Goldberg, H. Laville, L. Meignen, Y. Rak, E. Tchernov, and A.-M. Tillier. 1986. New data on the origin of modern man in the Levant. *Current Anthropology* 27:63–64.

Barandiarán, I., L. G. Freeman, J. González Echegaray, and R. G. Klein. 1985. Excavaciones en la cueva del Juyo. *Monografias del Centro. de Investigacion y Museo de Altamira* 14:1–224.

Barry, J. C. 1986. A review of the chronology of the Siwalik hominoids. In P. G. Else and P. C. Lee, eds. *Primate evolution,* 93–106. Cambridge: Cambridge University Press.

Barry, J. C., L. L. Jacobs, and J. Kelley. 1986. An early Middle Miocene catarrhine from Pakistan with comments on the dispersal of catarrhines into Eurasia. *Journal of Human Evolution* 15:501–508.

Barry, J. C., E. H. Lindsay, and L. L. Jacobs. 1982. A biostratigraphic zonation of the middle and upper Siwaliks of the Potwar Plateau of north Pakistan. *Paleogeography, Paleoclimatology and Paleoecology* 37:95–130.

Bartstra, G.-J. 1982a. *Homo erectus erectus:* the search for his artifacts. *Current Anthropology* 23:318–320.

———. 1982b. The river-laid strata near Trinil, site of *Homo erectus erectus,* Java, Indonesia. *Modern Quaternary Research in Southeast Asia* 7:97–130.

———. 1983. The fauna from Trinil, type locality of *Homo erectus:* a reinterpretation. *Geologie en Mijnbouw* 62:329–336.

———. 1984. Dating the Pacitanian: some thoughts. *Courier Forschungsinstitut Senckenberg* 69:253–258.

_____. 1985. Sangiran, the stone implements of Ngebung and the Paleolithic of Java. *Modern Quaternary Research in Southeast Asia* 9:99–113.

Bate, D. M. A. 1951. The mammals from Singa and Abu Hugar. In A. J. Arkell, D. M. A. Bate, L. H. Wells, and A. D. Lacaille. The Pleistocene fauna of two Blue Nile Sites. *Fossil Mammals of Africa* 2:1–28.

Beard, K. C., M. Dagosto, D. L. Gebo, and M. Godinot. 1988. Interrelationships among primate higher taxa. *Nature* 331:712–714.

Beaumont, P. B. 1980. On the age of Border Cave hominids 1–5. *Palaeontologia africana* 23:21–33.

Beaumont, P. B., H. de Villiers, and J. C. Vogel. 1978. Modern man in sub-Saharan Africa prior to 49,000 B.P.: a review and evaluation with particular reference to Border Cave. *South African Journal of Science* 74:409–419.

Beaumont, P. B., E. M. van Zinderen Bakker, and J. C. Vogel. 1984. Environmental changes since 32 KYRS B.P. at Kathu Pan, Northern Cape, South Africa. In J. C. Vogel, ed. *Late Cenozoic palaeoclimates of the Southern Hemisphere*, 324–338. Rotterdam: A. A. Balkema.

Beden, M. 1979. Données récentes sur l'évolution des Proboscidiens pendant le Plio-Pléistocène en Afrique Orientale. *Bulletin de la Société Géologique de France (Paris)* 21(3): 271–276.

Behm-Blancke, G. 1960. Altsteinzeitliche Rastplätze in Travertingebeit von Taubach, Weimar, Ehringsdorf. *Alt Thüringen* 4:1–246.

Behrensmeyer, A. K. 1976. Lothagam Hill, Kanapoi, and Ekora: a general summary of stratigraphy and faunas. In Y. Coppens, F. C. Howell, G. Ll. Isaac, and R. E. F. Leakey, eds. *Earliest man and environments in the Lake Rudolf Basin*, 163–170. Chicago: University of Chicago Press.

_____. 1986. Comment on "Systematic butchery by Plio/Pleistocene hominids at Olduvai Gorge, Tanzania" by H. T. Bunn and E. Kroll. *Current Anthropology* 5:443–444.

Behrensmeyer, A. K., K. D. Gordon, and G. T. Yanagi. 1986. Trampling as a cause of bone surface damage and pseudo cut marks. *Nature* 319:768–771.

Benefit, B. R., and M. Pickford. 1986. Miocene fossil cercopithecoids from Kenya. *American Journal of Physical Anthropology* 69:441–464.

Berger, R. 1979. Radiocarbon dating with accelerators. *Journal of Archaeological Science* 6:101–104.

Bergounioux, F. M. 1958. "Spiritualité" de l'homme de Néandertal. In G. H. R. Koenigswald, ed. *Hundert Jahre Neanderthaler*, 151–166. Utrecht: Kemink en Zoon N. V.

Bernaldo de Quiros Guidotti, F. 1982. Los inicios del Paleolitico Superior Cantabrico. *Centro de Investigacion y Museo de Altamira, Monografias* 8:1–347.

Beynon, A. D., and B. A. Wood. 1987. Patterns and rates of enamel growth in the molar teeth of early hominids. *Nature* 326:493–496.

Beyries, S. 1986. Approche fonctionnelle de l'outillage provenant d'un site Paléolithique moyen du Nord de la France. In A. Tuffreau, and J. Sommé, eds. *Chronostratigraphie et faciés culturels du Paléolithique inférieur et moyen dans l'Europe du Nord-Ouest,*

219–224. Paris: Supplément au Bullétin de l'Association Française pour l'Étude du Quaternaire.

———. 1988. Functional variability of lithic sets in the middle Paleolithic. In H. Dibble and A. Montet-White, eds. *Upper Pleistocene prehistory of western Eurasia*, 213–223. Philadelphia: University of Pennsylvania Museum.

Biberson, P. 1964. La place des hommes du paléolithique marocain dans la chronologie du Pléistocène atlantique. *L'Anthropologie* 68:475–526.

Billy, G., and H. V. Vallois, 1977. La mandibule pré-Rissienne de Montmaurin. *L'Anthropologie* 81:273–312.

Bilsborough, A. 1986. Diversity, evolution and adaptation in early hominids. In G. N. Bailey, and P. Callow, eds. *Stone Age prehistory: studies in memory of Charles McBurney*, 197–220. Cambridge: Cambridge University Press.

Binford, L. R. 1973. Interassemblage variability—the Mousterian and the 'functional' argument. In C. Renfrew, ed. *The explanation of culture change*, 227–254. Pittsburgh: University of Pittsburgh Press.

———. 1982. Comment on R. White, "Rethinking the Middle/Upper Paleolithic transition." *Current Anthropology* 23:177–181.

———. 1984. *Faunal remains from Klasies River Mouth*. Orlando, Fla.: Academic Press.

Binford, L. R., and S. R. Binford. 1966. A preliminary analysis of functional variability in the Mousterian of Levallois facies. *American Anthropologist* 68(2,2): 238–295.

Binford, L. R., and C. K. Ho. 1985. Taphonomy at a distance: Zhoukoudian, "the cave home of Beijing Man"? *Current Anthropology* 26:413–442.

Binford, L. R., and N. M. Stone. 1986. Zhoukoudian: a closer look. *Current Anthropology* 27:453–475.

Binford, S. R. 1968. A structural comparison of disposal of the dead in the Mousterian and Upper Paleolithic. *Southwestern Journal of Anthropology* 24:139–151.

Binford, S. R., and L. R. Binford. 1969. Stone tools and human behavior. *Scientific American* 220(4): 70–84.

Birdsell, J. B. 1977. The recalibration of a paradigm for the first peopling of Greater Australia. In J. Allen, J. Golson, and R. Jones, eds. *Sunda and Sahul: prehistoric studies in southeast Asia, Melanesia, and Australia*, 113–167. London: Academic Press.

Bishop, M. J., and A. E. Friday. 1986. Molecular sequences and hominoid phylogeny. In B. Wood, L. Martin, and P. Andrews, eds. *Major topics in primate and human evolution*, 150–156. Cambridge: University of Cambridge Press.

Bishop, W. W. 1971. The late Cenozoic history of East Africa in relation to hominoid evolution. In K. K. Turekian, ed. *Late Cenozoic glacial ages*, 493–527. New Haven, Conn.: Yale University Press.

———. 1978. The Lake Baringo Basin, Kenya. In W. W. Bishop, ed. *Geological background to fossil man*, 207–373. Toronto: University of Toronto Press.

Bishop, W. W., G. R. Chapman, A. Hill, and J. A. Miller. 1971. Succession of Cainozoic vertebrate assemblages from the northern Kenya Rift Valley. *Nature* 233:389–394.

Bishop, W. W., A. Hill, and M. Pickford. 1978. Chesowanja: a revised geological interpretation. In W. W. Bishop, ed. *Geological background to fossil man*, 309–336. Toronto: University of Toronto Press.

Bishop, W. W., M. Pickford, and A. Hill. 1975. New evidence regarding the Quaternary geology, archeology and hominids of Chesowanja, Kenya. *Nature* 258:204–208.

Blackwell, B., and H. Schwarcz. 1986. U-series analyses of the lower travertine at Ehringsdorf, DDR. *Quaternary Research* 25:215–222.

Blackwell, B., H. P. Schwarcz, and A. Debénath. 1983. Absolute dating of hominids and Palaeolithic artifacts of the cave of La Chaise-de-Vouthon (Charente), France. *Journal of Archaeological Science* 10:493–513.

Blanc, A. C. 1958. Torre in Pietra, Saccopastore, Monte Circeo: on the position of the Mousterian in the Pleistocene sequence of the Rome area. In G. H. R. Von Koenigswald, ed. *Hundert Jahre Neanderthaler*, 167–174. Utrecht: Kemink en Zoon N. V.

Blumenschine, R. J. 1986. Early hominid scavenging opportunities: implications of carcass availability in the Serengeti and Ngorongoro ecosystems. *British Archaeological Reports International Series* 283:1–163.

_____. 1987. Characteristics of an early hominid scavenging niche. *Current Anthropology* 28:383–407.

Bonifay, E., M.-F. Bonifay, R. Panattoni, and J.-J. Tiercelin. 1976. Soleihac (Blanzac, Haute-Loire): nouveau site préhistorique du début du Pléistocène moyen. *Bulletin de la Société Préhistorique Française* 73:293–304.

Bonifay, E., and J.-J. Tiercelin. 1977. Existence d'une activité volcanique et tectonique au début du Pléistocène moyen dans le bassin du Puy (Haute-Loire). *Comptes Rendus des Séances de l'Académie des Sciences (Paris)*, Série D, 284:2455–2457.

Bonis, L. de, G. Bouvrain, G. Koufos, and J. Melentis. 1986. Succession and dating of the late Miocene primates of Macedonia. In J. G. Else, and P. C. Lee, eds. *Primate evolution*, 107–114. Cambridge: Cambridge University Press.

Bonis, L. de, D. Geraads, G. Guérin, A. Haga, J.-J. Jaeger, and S. Sen. 1984. Découverte d'un Hominidé fossile dans le Pléistocène de la République de Djibouti. *Comptes Rendus des Séances de l'Académie des Sciences (Paris)*, Série D, 299:1097–1100.

Bonis, L. de, D. Geraads, J.-J. Jaeger, and S. Sen. 1988. Vertébrés du Plèistocène de Djibouti. *Bulletin de la Société Géologique de France* 4(8): 323–334.

Bonis, L. de, and J. Melentis. 1984. La position phylétique d'*Ouranopithecus*. *Courier Forschungsinstitut Senckenberg* 69:13–23.

Bonnichsen, R., D. Stanford, and J. L. Fastook. 1987. Environmental change and developmental history of human adaptive patterns: the Paleoindian case. In W. F. Ruddiman and H. E. Wright, Jr. eds. *The geology of North America*, vol. K-3, 403–424. Boulder, Colo.: Geological Society of America.

Bordaz, J. 1970. *Tools of the Old and New Stone Age*. New York: Natural History Press.

Bordes, F. H. 1947. Étude comparative des différentes techniques de taille du silex et des roches dures. *L'Anthropologie* 51:1–29.

_____. 1953. Essai de classification des industries moustériennes. *Bulletin de la Société Préhistorique Française* 50:457–466.

_____. 1961a. Mousterian cultures in France. *Science* 134:803–810.

_____. 1961b. Typologie du Paléolithique ancien et moyen. *Institut de Préhistoire de l'Université de Bordeaux Memoire* 1:1–86.

_____. 1968. *The Old Stone Age.* New York: McGraw-Hill.

_____. 1972. *A tale of two caves.* New York: Harper and Row.

_____. 1981. Vingt-cinq ans après: le complexe moustérien révisité. *Bulletin de la Socièté Préhistorique Française* 78:77–87.

Bordes, F. H., and F. Prat. 1965. Observations sur les faunes du Riss et du Würm I en Dordogne. *L'Anthropologie* 69:31–45.

Bordes, F. H., and C. Thibault. 1977. Thoughts on the initial adaptation of hominids to European glacial climates. *Quaternary Research* 8:115–127.

Boriskovskij, P. I. 1958. The study of Paleolithic dwellings in the USSR (in Russian). *Sovetskaya arkheologiya* (1): 3–19.

Bosinski, G. 1967. *Die Mittelpaläolithischen Funde im westlichen Mitteleuropa.* Köln: Fundamenta Reihe A/4.

_____. 1982. The transition Lower/Middle Palaeolithic in northwestern Germany. *British Archaeological Reports International Series* 151:165–175.

_____. 1986. Chronostratigraphie du Paléolithique inférieur et moyen en Rhénanie. In A. Tuffreau and J. Sommé, eds. *Chronostratigraphie et faciés culturels du Paléolithique inférieur et moyen dans l'Europe du Nord-Ouest,* 15–34. Paris: Supplément au Bullétin de l'Association Française pour l'Étude du Quaternaire.

Bosinski, G., K. Brunnacker, K. P. Lanser, S. Stephan, B. Urban, and K. Würges. 1980. Altpaläolithische Funde von Kärlich, Kr. Mayen-Koblenz (Neuwieder Becken). *Archäologisches Korrespondenzblatt* 10:295–314.

Bosinski, G., K. Brunnacker, and E. Turner. 1983. Ein Siedlungsbefund des frühen Mittelpaläolithikums von Ariendorf, Kr. Neuwied. *Archäologisches Korrespondenzblatt* 13:157–169.

Bosinski, G., K. Kroger, J. Schäfer, and E. Turner. 1986. Altsteinzeitliche Siedlungsplatze auf den Osteifel-Vulkanen. *Jahrbuch der Römische-Germanischer Zentral-Muzeums* (Mainz) 33(1): 97–130.

Bouchud, J. 1959. *Essai sur le renne et la climatologie du Paléolithique moyen et supérieur.* Doctoral thesis, Université de Paris.

_____. 1975. Étude de la faune de l'Abri Pataud. *Bulletin of the American School of Prehistoric Research* 39:69–153.

Boule, M. 1911–13. L'homme fossile de La Chapelle-aux-Saints. *Annales de Paléontologie* 6:11–172; 7:21–56, 85–192; 8:1–70.

Boule, M., and H. V. Vallois. 1957. *Fossil men.* New York: Dryden.

Bourgon, M. 1957. Les industries moustériennes et prémoustériennes du Périgord. *Archives de l'Institut de Paléontologie Humaine Mémoire* 27. Paris: Masson et Cie.

Bouyssonie, J. 1954. Les sépultures moustériennes. *Quaternaria* 1:107–115.

Bowdler, S. 1977. The coastal colonization of Australia. In J. Allen, J. Golson, and R. Jones, eds. *Sunda and Sahul: prehistoric studies in southeast Asia, Melanesia, and Australia,* 205–246. London: Academic Press.

———. In press. Ecological models for the human colonisation of Australia: the "coastal colonisation" hypothesis re-examined. In P. Mellars and C. Stringer, eds. *The human revolution: behavioural and biological perspectives on the origins of modern humans*. Edinburgh: Edinburgh University Press.

Bowler, J. M., R. Jones, H. Allen, and A. G. Thorne. 1970. Pleistocene human remains from Australia: a living site and human cremation from Lake Mungo, western New South Wales. *World Archaeology* 2:39–60.

Bowler, J. M., and A. G. Thorne. 1976. Human remains from Lake Mungo: discovery and excavation of Lake Mungo III. In R. L. Kirk and A. G. Thorne, eds. *The origin of the Australians*, 95–112. Canberra: Australian Institute of Aboriginal Studies.

Bowler, J. M., A. G. Thorne, and H. A. Pollach. 1972. Pleistocene man in Australia: age and significance of the Mungo skeleton. *Nature* 240:48–50.

Bown, T. M., M. J. Kraus, S. L. Wing, J. G. Fleagle, B. H. Tiffney, E. L. Simons, and C. F. Vondra. 1982. The Fayum primate forest revisited. *Journal of Human Evolution* 11:603–632.

Brace, C. L. 1982. Comment on "Upper Pleistocene hominid evolution in South-Central Europe: a review of the evidence and analysis of trends." *Current Anthropology* 23:687–688.

Brace, C. L., A. S. Ryan, and B. D. Smith. 1981. Comment on "Tooth wear in La Ferrassie man". *Current Anthropology* 22:426–430.

Brain, C. K. 1972. An attempt to reconstruct the behaviour of australopithecines: the evidence for interpersonal violence. *Zoologica Africana* 7:379–401.

———. 1976. A reinterpretation of the Swartkrans site and its remains. *South African Journal of Science* 72:141–146.

———. 1981. *The hunters or the hunted? an introduction to African cave taphonomy*. Chicago: University of Chicago Press.

———. 1982. The Swartkrans site: stratigraphy of the fossil hominids and a reconstruction of the environment of early *Homo*. In M. A. de Lumley, ed. *L'Homo erectus et la place de l'homme de Tautavel parmi les hominidés fossiles*, 676–706. Nice: ler Congrès International de Paléontologie Humaine.

———. 1984. The Terminal Miocene Event: a critical environmental and evolutionary episode. In J. C. Vogel, ed. *Late Cainozoic palaeoclimates of the Southern Hemisphere*, 491–498. Rotterdam: A. A. Balkema.

———. 1985a. Cultural and taphonomic comparisons of hominids from Swartkrans and Sterkfontein. In E. Delson, ed. *Ancestors: the hard evidence*, 72–75. New York: Alan R. Liss.

———. 1985b. Interpreting early hominid death assemblages: the rise of taphonomy since 1925. In P. V. Tobias, ed. *Hominid evolution: past, present and future*, 41–46. New York: Alan R. Liss.

———. 1988. New information from the Swartkrans cave of relevance to "robust" australopithecines. In F. E. Grine, ed. *The evolutionary history of the robust australopithecines*, 311–316. New York: Aldine de Gruyter.

Bräuer, G. 1984a. The "Afro-European *sapiens* hypothesis," and hominid evolution in East Asia during the Middle and Upper Pleistocene. *Courier Forschungsinstitut Senckenberg* 69:145–165.

———. 1984b. A craniological approach to the origin of anatomically modern *Homo sapiens* in Africa and implications for the appearance of modern Europeans. In F. H. Smith and F. Spencer, eds. *The origins of modern humans: a world survey of the fossil evidence*, 327–410. New York: Alan R. Liss.

Bräuer, G., and R. E. Leakey. 1986. The ES-1693 cranium from Eliye Springs, West Turkana, Kenya. *Journal of Human Evolution* 15:289–312.

Bräuer, G., and M. J. Mehlman. 1988. Hominid molars from a Middle Stone Age level at the Mumba Rock Shelter, Tanzania. *American Journal of Physical Anthropology* 75:69–76.

Bray, W. 1988. The Palaeoindian debate. *Nature* 332:107.

Breuil, H. 1939. Le vrai niveau de l'industrie abbevillienne de la Porte du Bois (Abbeville). *L'Anthropologie* 41:13–34.

———. 1952. *Four hundred centuries of cave art*. Montignac: Centre des Études et de Documentation Préhistorique.

Bricker, H. M. 1976. Upper Palaeolithic archaeology. *Annual Review of Anthropology* 5:133–148.

Brink, J. S., and H. J. Deacon. 1982. A study of a last interglacial shell midden and bone accumulation at Herolds Bay, Cape Province, South Africa. *Palaeoecology of Africa* 15:31–40.

Brock, A., P. L. McFadden, and T. C. Partridge. 1977. Preliminary palaeomagnetic results from Makapansgat and Swartkrans. *Nature* 266:249–250.

Bromage, T. G. 1987. The biological and chronological maturation of early hominids. *Journal of Human Evolution* 16:257–272.

Bromage, T. G., and M. C. Dean. 1985. Re-evaluation of the age at death of immature fossil hominids. *Nature* 317:525–527.

Broom, R., and G. W. H. Schepers. 1946. The South African fossil ape-men: the Australopithecinae. *Transvaal Museum Memoir* 2:1–272.

Brown, F. H., and C. S. Feibel. 1985. Stratigraphical notes on the Okote Tuff Complex at Koobi Fora, Kenya. *Nature* 316:794–797.

———. 1986. Revision of lithostratigraphic nomenclature in the Koobi Fora region, Kenya. *Journal of the Geological Society, London* 143:297–310.

Brown, F. H., J. Harris, R. Leakey, and A. Walker. 1985a. Early *Homo erectus* skeleton from west Lake Turkana, Kenya. *Nature* 316:788–792.

Brown, F. H., F. C. Howell, and G. G. Eck. 1978. Observations on problems of correlation of late Cenozoic hominid-bearing formations in the North Lake Turkana Basin. In W. W. Bishop, ed. *Geological background to fossil man*, 473–498. Toronto: University of Toronto Press.

Brown, F. H., I. McDougall, T. Davies, and R. Maier. 1985b. An integrated chronology for the Turkana Basin. In E. Delson, ed. *Ancestors: the hard evidence*, 82–90. New York: Alan R. Liss.

Brown, P. 1981. Artificial cranial deformation: a component in the variation in Pleistocene Australian aboriginal crania. *Archaeology in Oceania* 16:156–167.

———. 1987. Pleistocene homogeneity and Holocene size reduction: the Australian human skeletal evidence. *Archaeology in Oceania* 22:41–67.

Brunnacker, K. 1975. The mid-Pleistocene of the Rhine Basin. In K. W. Butzer, and G. Ll. Isaac, eds. *After the australopithecines*, 189–224. The Hague: Mouton.

Brunnacker, K., G. J. Hennig, E. Juvigne, H. Lehr, B. Urban, and R. Zeese. 1982. Der Kartstein-Travertin in der nödlichen Westeifel. *Decheniana* 135:179–204.

Buchanan, W. F., S. L. Hall, J. Henderson, A. Olivier, J. M. Pettigrew, J. E. Parkington, and P. T. Robertshaw. 1978. Coastal shell middens in the Paternoster area, southwestern Cape. *South African Archaeological Bulletin* 33:89–93.

Bunn, H. T. 1981. Archaeological evidence for meat-eating by Plio-Pleistocene hominids from Koobi Fora and Olduvai Gorge. *Nature* 291:574–577.

———. 1983. Evidence on the diet and subsistence patterns of Plio-Pleistocene hominids at Koobi Fora, Kenya and at Olduvai Gorge, Tanzania. *British Archaeological Reports* 163:21–30.

———. 1986. Patterns of skeletal representation and hominid subsistence activities at Olduvai Gorge, Tanzania and Koobi Fora, Kenya. *Journal of Human Evolution* 15:673–690.

Bunn, H. T., J. W. K. Harris, G. Isaac, Z. Kaufulu, E. Kroll, K. Schick, N. Toth, and A. K. Behrensmeyer. 1980. FxJj 50: an early Pleistocene site in northern Kenya. *World Archaeology* 12:109–136.

Bunn, H. T., and E. M. Kroll. 1986. Systematic butchery by Plio/Pleistocene hominids at Olduvai Gorge, Tanzania. *Current Anthropology* 5:431–452.

Bunney, S. 1986. Chinese fossil could alter the course of evolution in Asia. *New Scientist* 111 (1525): 25.

Burney, D. A., and R. D. E. MacPhee. 1988. Mysterious island: what killed Madagascar's large native animals. *Natural History* 97(7): 46–55.

Butler, P. M. 1986. Problems of dental evolution in the higher primates. In B. Wood, L. Martin, and P. Andrews, eds. *Major topics in primate and human evolution*, 90–106. Cambridge: University of Cambridge Press.

Butzer, K. W. 1974. Paleoecology of South African australopithecines: Taung revisited. *Current Anthropology* 15:367–382.

———. 1976a. Lithostratigraphy of the Swartkrans Formation. *South African Journal of Science* 72:136–141.

———. 1976b. The Mursi, Nkalabong and Kibish Formations, lower Omo Basin, Ethiopia. In Y. Coppens, F. C. Howell, G. Ll. Isaac, and R. E. F. Leakey, eds. *Earliest man and environments in the Lake Rudolf Basin: stratigraphy, paleoecology, and evolution*, 12–23. Chicago: University of Chicago Press.

———. 1978. Climate patterns in an un-glaciated continent. *The Geographical Journal* 51(3): 201–208.

———. 1980. The Taung australopithecine: contextual evidence. *Palaeontologia Africana* 23:59–60.

———. 1981. Cave sediments, Upper Pleistocene stratigraphy and Mousterian facies in Cantabrian Spain. *Journal of Archaeological Science* 8:133–183.

———. 1984. Archeogeology and Quaternary environment in the interior of southern Africa. In R. G. Klein, ed. *Southern African prehistory and paleoenvironments*, 1–64. Rotterdam: A. A. Balkema.

_____. 1986. Paleolithic adaptations and settlement in Cantabrian Spain. *Advances in World Archaeology* 5:201–252.

Butzer, K. W., P. B. Beaumont, and J. C. Vogel. 1978. Lithostratigraphy of Border Cave, KwaZulu, South Africa: a Middle Stone Age sequence beginning c. 195,000 B.P. *Journal of Archaeological Science* 5:317–341.

Butzer, K. W., F. H. Brown, and D. L. Thurber. 1969. Horizontal sediments of the lower Omo Valley: Kibish Formation. *Quaternaria* 11:15–29.

Bye, B. A., F. H. Brown, T. E. Cerling, and I. McDougall. 1987. Increased age estimate for the Lower Paleolithic hominid site at Olorgesailie, Kenya. *Nature* 329:237–239.

Cain, A. J. 1960. *Animal species and their evolution.* New York: Harper and Brothers.

Campbell, B. 1966. *Human evolution.* Chicago: Aldine.

Camps, G. 1974. *Les civilisations préhistoriques de l'Afrique du Nord et du Sahara.* Paris: Doin.

_____. 1975. The prehistoric cultures of North Africa: radiocarbon chronology. In F. Wendorf and A. E. Marks, eds. *Problems in prehistory: North Africa and the Levant,* 181–92. Dallas: Southern Methodist University Press.

Cann, R. L., M. Stoneking, and A. C. Wilson. 1987a. Disputed African origin of human populations. *Nature* 329:111–112.

_____. 1987b. Mitochondrial DNA and human evolution. *Nature* 325:31–36.

Carney, J., A. Hill, J. A. Miller, and A. Walker. 1971. Late australopithecine from Baringo District, Kenya. *Nature* 230:509–514.

Cartmill, M. 1974. Rethinking primate origins. *Science* 184:436–443.

_____. 1975. *Primate origins.* Minneapolis: Burgess.

_____. 1982. Basic primatology and prosimian evolution. In F. Spencer, ed. *A history of American physical anthropology, 1930–1980,* 147–186. New York: Academic Press.

Chaline, J. 1976. Les Rongeurs. In H. de Lumley, ed. *La Préhistoire Française,* vol. 1(1), 420–424. Paris: Centre National de la Recherche Scientifique.

Chaline, J., and J. Laurin. 1986. Phyletic gradualism in a European Plio-Pleistocene *Mimomys* lineage (Arvicolidae, Rodentia). *Paleobiology* 12:203–216.

Champion, T., C. Gamble, C. Shennan, and A. Whittle. 1984. *Prehistoric Europe.* London: Academic Press.

Chase, P. G. 1986. The hunters of Combe Grenal: approaches to Middle Paleolithic subsistence in Europe. *British Archaeological Reports* 286:1–224.

Chase, P. G., and H. L. Dibble. 1987. Middle Paleolithic symbolism: a review of current evidence and interpretations. *Journal of Anthropological Archaeology* 6:263–296.

Chavaillon, J. 1976. Mission archéologique Franco-Éthiopienne de Melka-Kunturé: rapport préliminaire 1972–1975. *L'Éthiopie avant Histoire* 1:1–11.

_____. 1979. Stratigraphie du site archéologique de Melka-Kunturé (Ethiopie). *Bulletin de la Société Géologique de la France* 21:227–232.

_____. 1982. Position chronologique des hominidés fossils d'Éthiopie. In M. A. de Lumley, ed. *L'Homo erectus et la place de l'homme de Tautavel parmi les hominidés fossiles*, 766–797. Nice: ler Congrés International de Paléontologie Humaine.

Chavaillon, J., C. Brahimi, and Y. Coppens. 1974. Première découverte d'hominidé dans l'un des sites acheuléens de Melka-Kunturé (Ethiopie). *Comptes Rendus des Séances de l'Académie des Sciences (Paris)*, Série D, 278:3299–3302.

Chavaillon, J., N. Chavaillon, F. Hours, and M. Piperno. 1979. From the Oldowan to the Middle Stone Age at Melka Kunturé (Ethiopia): understanding cultural changes. *Quaternaria* 21:87–114.

Chen, T., and S. Yuan. 1988. Uranium-series dating of bones and teeth from Chinese Palaeolithic sites. *Archaeometry* 30:59–76.

Chen, T., S. Yuan, and S. Gao. 1984. The study of uranium-series dating of fossil bones and an absolute age sequence for the main paleolithic sites of North China. *Acta Anthropologica Sinica* 3:268–269.

Chernysh, A. P., ed. 1982. *Molodova I: a unique Mousterian settlement on the Middle Dnestr* (in Russian). Moscow: Nauka.

Ciochon, R. L. 1983. Hominoid cladistics and the ancestry of modern apes and humans: a summary statement. In R. L. Ciochon and R. S. Corruccini, eds. *New interpretations of ape and human ancestry*, 783–843. New York: Plenum.

––––––. 1985. Fossil ancestors of Burma. *Natural History* 94(10): 26–37.

––––––. 1986. Paleoanthropological and archaeological research in the Socialist Republic of Vietnam. *Journal of Human Evolution* 15:623–633.

Ciochon, R. L., and A. B. Chiarelli. 1980. Paleobiogeographic perspectives on the origin of the Platyrrhini. In R. L. Ciochon and A. B. Chiarelli, eds. *Evolutionary biology of the New World monkeys and continental drift*, 459–493. New York: Plenum.

Ciochon, R. L., D. E. Savage, Thaw Tint, and Ba Maw. 1985. Anthropoid origins in Asia? new discovery of *Amphipithecus* from the Eocene of Burma. *Science* 229:756–759.

Clark, G. A., and L. G. Straus. 1983. Late Pleistocene hunter-gatherer adaptations in Cantabrian Spain. In G. Bailey, ed. *Hunter-gatherer economy in prehistory: a European perspective*, 131–148. Cambridge: Cambridge University Press.

Clark, J. D. 1955. A note on a wooden implement from the level of Peat 1 at Florisbad, Orange Free State. *Navorsinge van die Nasionale Museum* (Bloemfontein) 1:135–140.

––––––. 1959. Further excavations at Broken Hill, Northern Rhodesia. *Journal of the Royal Anthropological Institute* 89:201–231.

––––––. 1967. The Middle Acheulian occupation site at Latamne, Northern Syria, I. *Quaternaria* 9:1–68.

––––––. 1968a. *Further palaeo-anthropological studies in northern Lunda*. Publicaçoes culturais no. 78. Diamang, Angola: Museu do Dundo.

––––––. 1968b. The Middle Acheulian occupation site at Latamne, northern Syria, II. Further excavations (1965): general results, definition, and interpretation. *Quaternaria* 10:1–71.

––––––. 1969. *Kalambo Falls prehistoric site volume I*. Cambridge: Cambridge University Press.

––––––. 1974. *Kalambo Falls prehistoric site volume II*. Cambridge: Cambridge University Press.

————. 1975. A comparison of the Late Acheulian industries of Africa and the Middle East. In K. W. Butzer and G. Ll. Isaac, eds. *After the australopithecines*, 605–659. The Hague: Mouton.

————. 1982. The cultures of the Middle Palaeolithic/Middle Stone Age. In J. D. Clark, ed. *The Cambridge history of Africa*, vol. 1, 248–341. Cambridge: Cambridge University Press.

————. 1987. Transitions: *Homo erectus* and the Acheulian: the Ethiopian sites of Gadeb and the Middle Awash. *Journal of Human Evolution* 16:809–826.

Clark, J. D., B. Asfaw, G. Assefa, J. W. K. Harris, H. Kurashina, R. C. Walter, T. D. White, and M. A. J. Williams. 1984. Palaeoanthropological discoveries in the Middle Awash Valley, Ethiopia. *Nature* 307:423–428.

Clark, J. D., and J. W. K. Harris. 1985. Fire and its roles in early hominid lifeways. *The African Archaeological Review* 3:3–27.

Clark, J. D., and C. V. Haynes. 1970. An elephant butchery site at Mwanganda's village, Karonga, Malawi and its relevance for Palaeolithic archaeology. *World Archaeology* 1:390–411.

Clark, J. D., and H. Kurashina. 1979. Hominid occupation of the east-central highlands of Ethiopia in the Plio-Pleistocene. *Nature* 282:33–39.

Clark, J. D., and K. R. Williamson. 1979. A Middle Stone Age occupation site at Porc Épic Cave, Diré Dawa (east-central Ethiopia). Paper presented at Southern African Association of Archaeologists workshop: Towards a Better Understanding of the Upper Pleistocene in Sub-Saharan Africa, Stellenbosch (South Africa), 27–29 June 1979.

Clark, J. G. D. 1967. *The Stone Age hunters.* New York: McGraw-Hill.

Clarke, R. J. 1976. New cranium of *Homo erectus* from Lake Ndutu, Tanzania. *Nature* 262:485–487.

————. 1977. A juvenile cranium and some adult teeth of early *Homo* from Swartkrans, Transvaal. *South African Journal of Science* 73:46–49.

————. 1985. A new reconstruction of the Florisbad cranium, with notes on the site. In E. Delson, ed. *Ancestors: the hard evidence*, 301–305. New York: Alan R. Liss.

————. 1988. Habiline handaxes and Paranthropine pedigree at Sterkfontein. *World Archaeology* 20:1–12.

Clarke, R. J., F. C. Howell, and C. K. Brain. 1970. More evidence of an advanced hominid at Swartkrans. *Nature* 225:1219–1222.

Cole, G. H. 1967. The later Acheulian and Sangoan of southern Uganda. In W. W. Bishop, and J. D. Clark, eds. *Background to evolution in Africa*, 481–528. Chicago: University of Chicago Press.

Coles, J. M., and E. S. Higgs. 1969. *The archaeology of early man.* New York: Praeger.

Collins, D. 1969. Culture traditions and environment of early man. *Current Anthropology* 10:267–316.

Coltorti, M., M. Cremaschi, M. C. Delitala, D. Esu, M. Fornasari, A. McPherron, M. Nicoletti, R. van Otterloo, C. Peretto, B. Sala, V. Schmidt, and J. Sevink. 1982. Reversed magnetic polarity at an early Lower Paleolithic site in Central Italy. *Nature* 300:173–176.

Coltorti, M., R. van Otterloo, J. Sevink, M. Cremaschi, D. Esu, M. C. Delitala, M. Fornasari, M. Nicoletti, A. McPherron, V. Schmidt,

B. Sala, C. Peretto, G. Giusberti, A. Guerreschi, A. Bubellini, G. Lombardini, P. Russo, and G. Martinelli. 1983. *Isernia la Pineta: un accampamento più antico di 700.000 anni.* Bologna: Calderini Editore.

Commont, V. 1908. Les industries de l'ancien Saint-Acheul. *L'Anthropologie* 19:527–572.

Conkey, M. W. 1981. A century of Palaeolithic cave art. *Archaeology* 34(4): 11–28.

———. 1983. On the origins of Paleolithic art: a review and some critical thoughts. *British Archaeological Reports International Series* 164:201–227.

———. 1987. New appraoches in the search for meaning? a review of research in "Paleolithic Art." *Journal of Field Archaeology* 14:413–430.

Conroy, G. C., C. J. Jolly, D. Cramer, and J. E. Kalb. 1978. Newly discovered fossil hominid skull from the Afar depression, Ethiopia. *Nature* 275:67–70.

Conroy, G. C., and M. W. Vannier. 1987. Dental development of the Taung skull from computerized tomography. *Nature* 329:625–627.

Cook, J., C. B. Stringer, A. P. Currant, H. P. Schwarcz, and A. G. Wintle. 1982. A review of the chronology of the European Middle Pleistocene hominid record. *Yearbook of Physical Anthropology* 25:19–65.

Cooke, H. B. S. 1978. Africa: the physical setting. In V. J. Maglio, and H. B. S. Cooke, eds. *Evolution of African mammals,* 17–45. Cambridge, Mass.: Harvard University Press.

———. 1984. Horses, elephants and pigs as clues in the African later Cenozoic. In J. C. Vogel, ed. *Late Cainozoic palaeoclimates of the southern hemisphere,* 473–482. Rotterdam: A. A. Balkema.

Cooke, H. B. S., and A. F. Wilkinson. 1978. Suidae and Tayassuidae. In V. J. Maglio, and H. B. S. Cooke, eds. *Evolution of African mammals,* 435–482. Cambridge, Mass.: Harvard University Press.

Coon, C. S. 1962. *The origin of races.* New York: Knopf.

Corvinus, G. 1975. Palaeolithic remains at the Hadar in the Afar region. *Nature* 256:468–471.

———. 1976. Prehistoric exploration at Hadar, Ethiopia. *Nature* 261:571–572.

Covert, H. H. 1986. Biology of the early Cenozoic Primates. In D. R. Swindler and J. Erwin, eds. *Comparative Primate biology,* vol. 1, 335–359. New York: Alan R. Liss.

Cox, A. 1969. Geomagnetic reversals. *Science* 163:217–245.

———. 1972. Geomagnetic reversals—their frequency, their origin and some problems of correlation. In W. W. Bishop and J. A. Miller, eds. *Calibration of hominoid evolution,* 93–105. Edinburgh: Scottish University Press.

Cronin, J. E., V. M. Sarich, and O. Ryder. 1984. Molecular evolution and speciation in the lesser apes. In D. J. Chivers, H. Preuschoft, W. Y. Brockelman, and N. Creel, eds. *The lesser apes,* 467–485. Edinburgh: Edinburgh University Press.

Dalrymple, G. B., and M. A. Lanphere. 1969. *Potassium-argon dating: principles, techniques, and applications to geochronology.* San Francisco: W. H. Freeman.

Dart, R. A. 1925. *Australopithecus africanus:* the man-ape of South Africa. *Nature* 115:195–199.

———. 1949. The predatory implemental technique of *Australopithecus*. *American Journal of Physical Anthropology* 7:1–38.

———. 1957. The osteodontokeratic culture of *Australopithecus africanus. Memoirs of the Transvaal Museum* 10:1–105.

Dart, R. A., and D. Craig. 1959. *Adventures with the missing link.* New York: Viking.

Darwin, C. 1871. *The descent of man and selection in relation to sex.* London: John Murray and Sons.

Dastugue, J. 1982. Les maladies des nos ancêtres. *La Recherche* 13:980–988.

Dastugue, J., and M.-A. de Lumley. 1976. Les maladies des hommes préhistoriques du Paléolithique et du Mésolithique. In H. de Lumley, ed. *La préhistoire française,* vol. 1, 612–622. Paris: Centre National de la Recherche Scientifique.

Day, M. H. 1971. Postcranial remains of *Homo erectus* from Bed IV, Olduvai Gorge, Tanzania. *Nature* 232:383–387.

———. 1984. The postcranial remains of *Homo erectus* from Africa, Asia, and possibly Europe. *Courier Forschungsinstitut Senckenberg* 69:113–121.

———. 1985. Hominid locomotion—from Taung to the Laetoli footprints. In P. V. Tobias, ed. *Hominid evolution: past, present and future,* 115–127. New York: Alan R. Liss.

———. 1986. *Guide to fossil man.* 4th ed. Chicago: University of Chicago Press.

Day, M. H., M. D. Leakey, and C. Magori. 1980. A new hominid fossil skull (L. H. 18) from the Ngaloba Beds, Laetoli, northern Tanzania. *Nature* 284:55–56.

Day, M. H., and C. B. Stringer. 1982. A reconsideration of the Omo Kibish remains and the *erectus-sapiens* transition. In M. A. de Lumley, ed. *L'Homo erectus et la place de l'homme de Tautavel parmi les hominidés fossiles,* 814–846. Nice: Centre National de la Recherche Scientifique.

Deacon, H. J. 1970. The Acheulian occupation at Amanzi Springs, Uitenhage District, Cape Province. *Annals of the Cape Provincial Museums (Natural History)* 8:89–189.

———. In press. Late Pleistocene palaeoecology and archaeology in the southern Cape, South Africa. In P. Mellars, and C. Stringer, eds. *The human revolution: behavioural and biological pespectives on the origins of modern humans.* Edinburgh: Edinburgh University Press.

Deacon, H. J., V. B. Geleijnse, A. I. Thackeray, J. F. Thackeray, and M. L. Tusenius. 1986. Late Pleistocene cave deposits in the southern Cape: current research at Klasies River Mouth. *Palaeoecology of Africa* 17:31–37.

Deacon, H. J., and J. F. Thackeray. 1984. Late Pleistocene environmental changes and implications for the archaeological record in southern Africa. In J. C. Vogel, ed. *Late Cainozoic palaeoclimates of the Southern Hemisphere,* 375–390. Rotterdam: A. A. Balkema.

Deacon, J. 1984. Later Stone Age people and their descendants in southern Africa. In R. G. Klein, ed. *Southern African prehistory and paleoenvironments,* 221–328. Rotterdam: A. A. Balkema.

Dean, M. C., C. B. Stringer, and T. G. Bromage. 1986. Age at death of the Neanderthal child from Devil's Tower, Gibraltar and the implications for studies of general growth and development in Neanderthals. *American Journal of Physical Anthropology* 70:301–310.

Debénath, A. 1976. Les civilisations du Paléolithqiue inférieur en Charente. In H. de Lumley, ed. *La préhistoire française* 1(2), 929–935. Paris: Centre National de la Recherche Scientifique.

———. 1977. The latest finds of antc-Würmian human remains in Charente (France). *Journal of Human Evolution* 6:297–302.

———. 1980. Nouveaux restes humains atériens du Maroc. *Comptes Rendus des Séances de l'Académie des Sciences (Paris)*, Série D, 290:851–852.

———. 1988. Recent thoughts on the Riss and early Würm assemblages of la Chaise de Vouthon (Charente, France). In H. Dibble and A. Montet-White, eds. *Upper Pleistocene prehistory of western Eurasia*, 85–93. Philadelphia: University of Pennsylvania Museum.

Debénath, A., J.-P. Raynal, J. Roche, J.-P. Texier, and D. Ferembach. 1986. Stratigraphie, habitat, typologie et devenir de l'Atérien Marocain: données récentes. *L'Anthropologie* 90:233–246.

Debénath, A., J.-P. Raynal, and J.-P. Texier. 1982. Position stratigraphique des restes humains paléolithiques marocains sur la base des travaux récents. *Comptes Rendus des Séances de l'Académie des Sciences (Paris)*, Série D, 294:972–976.

Debénath, A., and F. Sbihi-Alaoui. 1979. Découverte de deux nouveaux gisements préhistoriques près de Rabat (Maroc). *Bulletin de la Sociètè Préhistorique Française* 76:11–12.

Debets, G. F. 1955. Paleoanthropological finds at Kostenki (in Russian). *Sovetskaya etnografiya* (1): 43–53.

Delpech, F. 1975. *Les faunes du Paléolithique Supérieur dans le Sud-Ouest de la France.* Doctoral thesis, Université de Bordeaux.

———. 1983. *Les faunes du Paléolithique Supérieur dans le Sud-Ouest de la France.* Paris: Centre National de la Recherche Scientifique.

Delson, E. 1979. *Prohylobates* (Primates) from the early Miocene of Libya: a new species and its implications for cercopithecid origins. *Geobios* 12:725–733.

———. 1981. Paleoanthropology: Pliocene and Pleistocene human evolution. *Paleobiology* 7:298–305.

———. 1984. Cercopithecid biochronology of the African Plio-Pleistocene: correlation among eastern and southern hominid-bearing localities. *Courier Forschungsinstitut Senckenberg* 69:199–218.

———. 1985. Catarrhine evolution. In E. Delson, ed. *Ancestors: the hard evidence*, 9–13. New York: Alan R. Liss.

———. 1987. Evolution and paleobiology of robust *Australopithecus*. *Nature* 327:654–655.

Delson, E., and P. Andrews. 1975. Evolution and interrelationships of the Catarrhine Primates. In W. P. Luckett, and F. S. Szalay, eds. *Phylogeny of the Primates*, 405–446. New York: Plenum.

Delson, E., and A. L. Rosenberger. 1980. Phyletic perspectives on platyrrhine origins and anthropoid relationships. In R. L. Ciochon, and A. B. Chiarelli, eds. *Evolutionary biology of the New World monkeys and continental drift*, 445–458. New York: Plenum.

Dennell, R. W. 1983. A new chronology for the Mousterian. *Nature* 301:199–200.

Dennell, R. W., H. Rendell, and E. Hailwood. 1988a. Early tool-making in Asia: two-million-year-old artefacts in Pakistan. *Antiquity* 62:98–106.

_____. 1988b. Late Pliocene artefacts from Northern Pakistan. *Current Anthropology* 29:495–498.

Dewar, R. E. 1984. Extinctions in Madagascar. In P. S. Martin and R. G. Klein, eds. *Quaternary extinctions: a prehistoric revolution*, 574–593. Tucson: University of Arizona Press.

Dibble, H. L. 1987. The interpretation of Middle Paleolithic scraper morphology. *American Antiquity* 52:109–117.

_____. 1988. Typological aspects of reduction and intensity of utlization of lithic resources in the French Mousterian. In H. L. Dibble and A. Montet-White, eds. *Upper Pleistocene prehistory of western Eurasia*, 181–197. Philadelphia: University of Pennsylvania Museum.

Dillehay, T. 1984. A late ice-age settlement in southern Chile. *Scientific American* 251(4): 106–117.

_____. 1987. By the banks of the Chinchilhuapi. *Natural History* 96(4): 8–12.

Dillehay, T., and M. B. Collins. 1988. Early cultural evidence from Monte Verde in Chile. *Nature* 332:150–152.

Dillehay, T., M. Pino, S. Valastro, A. G. Varela, and R. Casamiquela. 1982. Monte Verde: radiocarbon dates from an early-man site in south-central Chile. *Journal of Field Archaeology* 9:547–550.

Dincauze, D. F. 1984. An archaeo-logical evaluation of the case for pre-Clovis occupations. *Advances in World Archaeology* 3:275–323.

Dolitsky, A. B. 1985. Siberian Paleolithic archaeology: approaches and analytic methods. *Current Anthropology* 26:361–378.

Drake, R., and G. H. Curtis. 1987. K-Ar geochronology of the Laetoli fossil localities. In M. D. Leakey and J. M. Harris, eds. *Laetoli: a Pliocene site in northern Tanzania*, 48–51. Oxford: Clarendon.

Drennan, M. R. 1953. A preliminary note on the Saldanha Skull. *South African Journal of Science* 50:7–11.

Dubois, E. 1922. The proto-Australian fossil man of Wadjak. *Koninklijke Akademie van Wetenschappen te Amsterdam*, Series B, 23:1013–1051.

Dumond, D. E. 1980. The archaeology of Alaska and the peopling of America. *Science* 209:984–991.

Eiseley, L. 1961. *Darwin's century: evolution and the men who discovered it*. New York: Doubleday.

Eldredge, N., and J. Cracraft. 1980. *Phylogenetic patterns and the evolutionary process*. New York: Columbia University Press.

Emiliani, C. 1955. Pleistocene temperatures. *Journal of Geology* 63:538–578.

_____. 1969. The significance of deep-sea cores. In D. Brothwell and E. Higgs, eds. *Science in archeology*, 109–117. London: Thames and Hudson.

Ennouchi, E. 1968. Le deuxième crâne de l'homme d'Irhoud. *Annales de Paléontologie* 54:117–128.

_____. 1969. Présence d'un enfant néanderthalien au Jebel Irhoud (Maroc). *Annales de Paléontologie* 55:251–265.

Evernden, J. F., and G. H. Curtis. 1965. The potassium-argon dating of Late Cenozoic rocks in east Africa and Italy. *Current Anthropology* 6:343–385.

Falk, D. 1983a. Cerebral cortices of East African early hominids. *Science* 221:1072–1074.

_____. 1983b. A reconsideration of the endocast of *Proconsul africanus:* implications for primate brain evolution. In R. L. Ciochon and R. S. Corruccini, eds. *New interpretations of ape and human ancestry,* 239–248. New York: Plenum.

_____. 1985. Hadar AL-162-28 endocast as evidence that brain enlargement preceded cortical reorganization in hominid evolution. *Nature* 313:45–47.

_____. 1986a. Endocast morphology of Hadar hominid AL 162-28. *Nature* 321:536–537.

_____. 1986b. Evolution of cranial blood drainage in hominids: enlarged occipital/marginal sinuses and emissary foramina. *American Journal of Physical Anthropology* 70:311–324.

_____. 1986c. Hominid evolution (letter to the editor). *Science* 234:11.

_____. 1987. Hominid paleoneurology. *Annual Review of Anthropology* 16:13–30.

Falk, D., and G. C. Conroy. 1983. The cranial venous sinus system in *Australopithecus afarensis. Nature* 306:779–781.

Farrand, W. R. 1979. Chronology and palaeoenvironment of Levantine prehistoric sites as seen from sediment studies. *Journal of Archaeological Science* 6:369–392.

_____. 1982. Environmental conditions during the Lower/Middle Paleolithic transition in the Near East and the Balkans. *British Archaeological Reports International Series* 151:105–112.

Fejfar, O. 1976a. Plio-Pleistocene mammal sequences. In D. J. Easterbook and V. Sibrava, eds. *Quaternary glaciations in the Northern Hemisphere report no. 3.* project 73/1/24, 351–366. Bellingham, Wash.–Prague: IGCP.

_____. 1976b. Recent research at Prezletice. *Current Anthropology* 17:343–344.

Ferring, C. R. 1975. The Aterian in North African prehistory. In F. Wendorf and A. E. Marks, eds. *Problems in prehistory: North Africa and the Levant,* 113–126. Dallas: Southern Methodist University Press.

Fleagle, J. G. 1978. Size distributions of living and fossil primate faunas. *Paleobiology* 4:67–76.

_____. 1983. Locomotor adaptations of Oligocene and Miocene hominoids and their phyletic implications. In R. L. Ciochon and R. S. Corruccini, eds. *New interpretations of ape and human ancestry,* 301–324. New York: Plenum.

_____. 1984. Are there any fossil gibbons? In H. Preuschoft, D. J. Chivers, W. Y. Brockleman, and N. Creel, eds. *The lesser apes,* 432–447. Edinburgh: Edinburgh University Press.

_____. 1986a. Early anthropoid evolution in Africa and South America. In P. G. Else and P. C. Lee, eds. *Primate evolution*, 133–142. Cambridge: Cambridge University Press.

_____. 1986b. The fossil record of early catarrhine evolution. In B. Wood, L. Martin, and P. Andrews, eds. *Major topics in primate and human evolution*, 130–149. Cambridge: University of Cambridge Press.

Fleagle, J. G., T. M. Bown, J. D. Obradovich, and E. L. Simons. 1986a. Age of the earliest African anthropoids. *Science* 234:1247–1249.

_____. 1986b. How old are the Fayum Primates? In P. G. Else and P. C. Lee, eds. *Primate evolution*, 3–17. Cambridge: Cambridge University Press.

Fleagle, J. G., and W. L. Jungers. 1982. Fifty years of higher primate phylogeny. In F. Spencer, ed. *A history of American physical anthropology, 1930–1980*, 187–230. New York: Academic Press.

Fleagle, J. G., and R. F. Kay. 1983. New interpretations of the phyletic position of Oligocene hominoids. In R. L. Ciochon and R. S. Corruccini, eds. *New interpretations of ape and human ancestry*, 181–210. New York: Plenum.

_____. 1985. The paleobiology of catarrhines. In E. Delson, ed. *Ancestors: the hard evidence*, 23–36. New York: Alan R. Liss.

_____. 1987. The phyletic position of the Parapithecidae. *Journal of Human Evolution* 16:483–532.

Fleagle, J. G., and E. L. Simons. 1978. *Micropithecus clarki*, a small ape from the Miocene of Uganda. *American Journal of Physical Anthropology* 49:427–440.

Fleischer, R. L., L. S. B. Leakey, P. B. Price, and R. M. Walker. 1965. Fission track dating of Bed I, Olduvai Gorge. *Science* 148:72–74.

Fleischer, R. L., P. B. Price, and R. M. Walker. 1969. Quaternary dating by the fission-track technique. In D. Brothwell and E. Higgs, eds. *Science in archaeology*, 58–61. London: Thames and Hudson.

Fraipont, C. 1936. Les hommes fossiles d'Engis. *Archives de l'Institut de Paléontologie Humaine* 16:1–52.

Franciscus, R. G., and E. Trinkaus. 1988. Nasal morphology and the emergence of *Homo erectus*. *American Journal of Physical Anthropology* 75:517–527.

Frayer, D. W. 1984. Biological and cultural change in the European late Pleistocene and early Holocene. In F. H. Smith, and F. Spencer, eds. *The origin of modern humans: a world survey of the fossil evidence*, 211–250. New York: Alan R. Liss.

Frayer, D. W., R. Macchiarelli, and M. Mussi. 1988. A case of chondrodystrophic dwarfism in the Italian late Upper Paleolithic. *American Journal of Physical Anthropology* 75:549–565.

Freeman, L. G. 1966. The nature of Mousterian facies in Cantabrian Spain. *American Anthropologist* 68(2,2): 230–237.

_____. 1975. Acheulean sites and stratigraphy in Iberia and the Maghreb. In K. W. Butzer and G. Ll. Isaac, eds. *After the australopithecines*, 661–743. The Hague: Mouton.

_____. 1980. Ocupaciones musterienses. In J. González Echegaray, ed. *El yacimiento de la Cueva de "El Pendo" (Excavaciones 1953–57)*, 29–74. Madrid: Consejo Superior de Investigaciones Cientificas.

_____. 1983. More on the Mousterian: flaked bone from Cueva Morín. *Current Anthropology* 24:366–372.

Freeman, L. G., and J. González Echegaray. 1970. Aurignacian structural features and burials at Cueva Morín (Santander, Spain). *Nature* 226:722–726.

Freeman, L. G., J. González Echegaray, F. Bernaldo de Quiros, and J. Ogden. 1987. *Altamira revisited and other essays on early art.* Santander, Spain: Instituto de Investigaciones Prehistoricas.

Freeman, L. G., J. González Echegaray, R. G. Klein, and W. T. Crowe. 1988. Dimensions of research at El Juyo, an earlier Magdalenian site in Cantabrian Spain. In H. L. Dibble and A. Montet-White, eds. *Upper Pleistocene prehistory of western Eurasia,* 3–39. Philadelphia: University of Pennsylvania Museum.

Fridrich, J. 1976. The first industries from Eastern and South-Eastern Central Europe. In K. Valoch, ed. *Les premières industries de l'Europe* (Colloque VIII), 8–23. Nice: Union International des Sciences Préhistoriques et Protohistoriques.

Gábori-Czánk, V. 1968. *La station du Paléolithique moyen d'Érd—Hongrie.* Budapest: Akadémiai Kiadó.

Gamble, C. 1986. *The Palaeolithic settlement of Europe.* Cambridge: Cambridge University Press.

Garrod, D. A. E., and D. M. Bate. 1937. *The Stone Age of Mount Carmel,* vol. 1. Oxford: Oxford University Press.

Garrod, D. A. E., L. H. D. Buxton, G. E. Smith, and D. M. A. Bate. 1928. Excavation of a Mousterian Rock-shelter at Devil's Tower, Gibraltar. *Journal of the Royal Anthropological Institute of Great Britain and Ireland* 58:33–113.

Gebo, D. L., and E. L. Simons. 1987. Morphology and locomotor adaptations of the foot in early Oligocene anthropoids. *American Journal of Physical Anthropology* 74:83–101.

Gentner, W., and H. J. Lippolt. 1969. The potassium-argon dating of Upper Tertiary and Pleistocene deposits. In D. Brothwell and E. Higgs, eds. *Science in archaeology,* 88–100. London: Thames and Hudson.

Geraads, D. 1980. La faune des sites à "*Homo erectus*" des carrières Thomas (Casablanca, Maroc). *Quaternaria* 22:65–94.

Geraads, D., P. Beriro, and H. Roche. 1980. La faune et l'industrie des sites à *Homo erectus* des carrières Thomas (Maroc): précisions sur l'age de ces hominidés. *Comptes Rendus des Séances de l'Academie des Sciences (Paris),* Série D, 291:195–198.

Geraads, D., J.-J. Hublin, J.-J. Jaeger, H. Tong, S. Sen, and P. Tourbeau. 1986. The Pleistocene hominid site of Ternifine, Algeria: new results on the environment, age, and human industries. *Quaternary Research* 25:380–386.

Gerasimov, M. M. 1935. Excavations of the paleolithic site in the village of Mal'ta (preliminary report on the 1928–32 work) (in Russian). *Izvestiya Gosudarsvennoj Akademii Istorii material-'noj Kul'tury* 118:78–124.

Gilead, I. 1981. Upper Palaeolithic tool assemblages from the Negev and Sinai. In J. Cauvin and P. Sanlaville, eds. *Préhistoire du Levant,* 331–342. Paris: Centre National de la Recherche Scientifique.

Gillespie, C. C. 1951. *Genesis and geology.* New York: Harper and Brothers.

Gillespie, R., R. E. M. Hedges, and J. O. Wand. 1984. Radiocarbon dating of bone by accelerator mass spectrometry. *Journal of Archaeological Science* 11:165–170.

Gingerich, P. D. 1973. First record of the Palaeocene primate *Chiromyoides* from North America. *Nature* 244:517–518.

————. 1977. Radiation of Eocene Adapidae in Europe. *Géobios, Mémoire Spéciale* 1:165–182.

————. 1980. Eocene Adapidae, paleobiogeography, and the origin of South American Platyrrhini. In R. L. Ciochon and A. B. Chiarelli, eds. *Evolutionary biology of the New World monkeys and continental drift*, 123–138. New York: Plenum.

————. 1984a. Paleobiology of tarsiiform primates. In C. Niemitz, ed. *Biology of tarsiers*, 34–44. Stuttgart: Gustav Fischer.

————. 1984b. Primate evolution. In T. W. Broadhead, ed. *Mammals: notes for a short course. University of Tennessee Studies in Geology* 8:167–184.

————. 1984c. Primate evolution: evidence from the fossil record, comparative morphology, and molecular biology. *Yearbook of Physical Anthropology* 27:57–72.

————. 1986a. Early Eocene *Cantius torresi*—oldest primate of modern aspect from North America. *Nature* 319: 319–321.

————. 1986b. *Plesiadapis* and the delineation of the order Primates. In B. Wood, L. Martin, and P. Andrews, eds. *Major topics in primate and human evolution*, 32–46. Cambridge: University of Cambridge Press.

————. 1986c. Temporal scaling of molecular evolution in primates and other mammals. *Molecular Biology and Evolution* 3:205–221.

Gingerich, P. D., and A. Sahni. 1984. Dentition of *Sivaladapis nagrii* (Adapidae) from the late Miocene of India. *International Journal of Primatology* 5:63–79.

Gingerich, P. D., and M. Schoeninger. 1977. The fossil record and primate phylogeny. *Journal of Human Evolution* 6:483–505.

Ginsburg, L. 1986. Chronology of the European pliopithecids. In J. G. Else and P. C. Lee, eds. *Primate evolution*, 46–57. Cambridge: Cambridge University Press.

Gisis, I., and O. Bar-Yosef. 1974. New excavations in Zuttiyeh Cave. *Paléorient* 2:175–180.

Gladkih, M. I., N. L. Kornietz, and O. Soffer. 1984. Mammoth bone dwellings on the Russian Plain. *Scientific American* 251(5): 164–175.

Gleadow, A. J. W. 1980. Fission track age of the KBS Tuff and associated hominids in northern Kenya. *Nature* 284:225–230.

Gobert, E. G. 1950. Le gisement paléolithique de Sidi Zin, avec une notice sur la faune de Sidi Zin de R. Vaufrey. *Karthago* 1:1–64.

Goede, A., and M. A. Hitchman. 1987. Electron spin resonance analysis of marine gastropods from coastal archaeological sites in southern Africa. *Archaeometry* 29:163–174.

González Echegaray, J. 1980. El yacimiento de la Cueva de "el Pendo" (Excavaciones 1953–57). *Bibliotheca Praehistorica Hispana* 17:1–270.

Goodwin, A. J. H. 1928. An introduction to the Middle Stone Age in South Africa. *South African Journal of Science* 25:410–418.

———. 1929. The Middle Stone Age. *Annals of the South African Museum* 29:95–145.

Goren, N. 1981. *The lithic assemblages of the site of Ubeidiya, Jordan Valley.* Ph.D. thesis, Hebrew University of Jerusalem.

Gould, S. J., and N. Eldredge. 1977. Punctuated equilibria: tempo and mode of evolution reconsidered. *Paleobiology* 3:115–151.

Gowlett, J. A. J. 1978. Kilombe—an Acheulian site complex in Kenya. In W. W. Bishop, ed. *Geological background to fossil man,* 337–360. Edinburgh: Scottish Acadmic Press.

Gowlett, J. A. J., J. W. K. Harris, D. A. Walton, B. A. Wood. 1981. Early archaeological sites, further hominid remains and traces of fire from Chesowanja, Kenya. *Nature* 294:125–129.

Grayson, D. K. 1983. *The establishment of human antiquity.* New York: Academic Press.

Graziosi, P. 1960. *Paleolithic art.* New York: McGraw-Hill.

Green, H. S. 1984. *Pontnewydd Cave: a Lower Palaeolithic hominid site in Wales: the first report.* Cardiff: National Museum of Wales.

Green, H. S., C. B. Stringer, S. N. Collcutt, A. P. Currant, J. Huxtable, H. P. Schwarcz, N. Debenham, C. Embleton, P. Bull, T. I. Molleson, and R. E. Bevins. 1981. Pontnewydd Cave in Wales—a new Middle Pleistocene hominid site. *Nature* 294:707–713.

Green, P. 1979. Tracking down the past. *New Scientist* 84:624–626.

Greenberg, J. H., C. G. Turner, and S. L. Zegura. 1986. The settlement of the Americas: a comparison of the linguistic, dental and genetic evidence. *Current Anthropology* 27:477–497.

Gregory, W. K., and M. Hellman. 1939. The dentition of the extinct South African man-ape *Australopithecus (Plesianthropus) transvaalensis* Broom: a comparative and phylogenetic study. *Annals of the Transvaal Museum* 19:339–373.

Gribbin, J. 1979. Making a date with radiocarbon. *New Scientist* 82:532–534.

Grine, F. E. 1981. Trophic differences between "gracile" and "robust" australopithecines: a scanning electron miscroscope analysis of occlusal events. *South African Journal of Science* 77:203–230.

———. 1982. A new juvenile hominid (Mammalia, Primates) from Member 3, Kromdraai Formation, Transvaal, South Africa. *Annals of the Transvaal Museum* 33:165–239.

———. 1984. Comparison of the deciduous dentitions of African and Asian hominids. *Courier Forschungsinstitut Senckenberg* 69:69–82.

———. 1985a. Dental morphology and the systematic affinities of the Taung fossil hominid. In P. V. Tobias, ed. *Hominid evolution: past, present and future,* 247–253. New York: Alan R. Liss.

———. 1985b. Was interspecific competition a motive force in early hominid evolution? *Transvaal Museum Memoir* 4:143–152.

———. 1986. Dental evidence for dietary differences in *Australopithecus* and *Paranthropus:* a quantitative analysis of permanent molar microwear. *Journal of Human Evolution* 15:783–822.

———. In press. New hominid fossils from the Swartkrans Formation (1979–1986 excavations): craniodental specimens. *American Journal of Physical Anthropology.*

Grine, F. E., and R. G. Klein. 1985. Pleistocene and Holocene human remains from Equus Cave, South Africa. *Anthropology* 8:55–98.

Groves, C. P. 1986. Systematics of the great apes. In D. R. Swindler and J. Erwin, eds. *Comparative primate biology*, vol. 1, 187–217. New York: Alan R. Liss.

Gruet, M. 1954. Le gisement moustérien d'El-Guettar. *Karthago* 5:1–79.

———. 1958. Le gisement d'El-Guettar et sa flore. *Libyca* 6–7:79–126.

Guichard, J. 1976. Les civilisations du Paléolithique moyen en Périgord. In H. de Lumley, ed. *La préhistoire française*, vol. 2, 1053–1069. Paris: Centre National de la Recherche Scientifique.

Guidon, N., and G. Delibrias. 1986. Carbon-14 dates point to man in the Americas 32,000 years ago. *Nature* 321:769–771.

Guillien, Y., and G. Laplace. 1978. Les climates et les hommes en Europe et en Afrique septentrionale de 28000 B.P. à 10000 B.P. *Bulletin de l'Association Française pour l'Étude du Quaternaire* 4:187–193.

Habgood, P. J. 1985. The origin of the Australian aborigines: an alternative approach and view. In P. V. Tobias, ed. *Hominid evolution: past, present and future*. New York: Alan R. Liss.

———. In press. The evolution of modern humans: evidence from Australasia seen in a global context. In P. Mellars and C. Stringer, eds. *The human revolution: behavioural and biological perspectives on the origins of modern humans*. Edinburgh: Edinburgh University Press.

Haesaerts, P., and C. Dupuis. 1986. Contribution à la stratigraphie des nappes alluviales de la Somme et de l'Avre dans la région d'Amiens. In A. Tuffreau and J. Sommé, eds.*Chronostratigraphie et faciés culturels du Paléolithique inférieur et moyen dans l'Europe du Nord-Ouest*, 171–186. Paris: Supplément au Bullétin de l'Association Française pour l'Étude du Quaternaire.

Hahn, J. 1976. Das Gravettien in Westlichen Mitteleuropa. In B. Klíma, ed. *Périgordien et Gravettien en Europe* (Colloque XV), 100–120. Nice: IXe Congrès de l'Union Internationale des Sciences Préhistoriques et Protohistoriques.

———. 1977. Aurignacien—das altëre Jungpaläolithikum in Mittel- und Osteuropa. *Fundamenta* (Köln) A9:1–355.

Hahn, J., H. Müller-Beck, and W. Taute. 1985. *Eiszeithöhlen im Lonetal*. Stuttgart: Konrad Theiss.

Hall, C. M., R. C. Walter, and D. York. 1985. Tuff above "Lucy" is over 3 ma old. *Eos* 66:257.

Hall, C. M., and D. York. 1984. The applicability of $^{40}Ar/^{39}Ar$ dating to young volcanics. In W. C. Mahaney, ed. *Quaternary dating methods*, 67–74. Amsterdam: Elsevier.

Hansen, J., and J. Renfrew. 1978. Palaeolithic-Neolithic seed remains at Franchthi Cave, Greece. *Nature* 271:349–352.

Hare, P. E. 1980. Organic geochemistry of bone and its relation to the survival of bone in the natural environment. In A. Behrensmeyer and P. Hill, eds. *Fossils in the making*, 208–219. Chicago: University of Chicago Press.

Harland, W. B., A. V. Cox, P. G. Llewellyn, C. A. G. Pickton, A. G. Smith, and R. Walters. 1982. *A geologic time scale*. Cambridge: Cambridge University Press.

Harmon, R. S., J. Glazek, and K. Nowak. 1980. 230Th/234U dating of travertine from the Bilzingsleben archaeological site. *Nature* 284:132–135.

Harmon, R. S., L. S. Land, R. M. Mitterer, P. Garrett, H. P. Schwarcz, and G. J. Larson. 1981. Bermuda sea level during the last interglacial. *Nature* 239:481–483.

Harris, J. M. 1985. Age and paleoecology of the Upper Laetolil Beds, Laetoli, Tanzania. In E. Delson, ed. *Ancestors: the hard evidence*, 76–81. New York: Alan R. Liss.

Harris, J. M., F. H. Brown, M. G. Leakey, A. C. Walker, and R. E. Leakey. 1988. Pliocene and Pleistocene hominid-bearing sites from west of Lake Turkana, Kenya. *Science* 239:27–33.

Harris, J. M., and T. D. White. 1979. Evolution of the Plio-Pleistocene African Suidae. *Transactions of the American Philosophical Society* 69(2): 1–128.

Harris, J. W. K. 1983. Cultural beginnings: Plio-Pleistocene archaeological occurrences from the Afar, Ethiopia. *The African Archaeological Review* 1:3–31.

Harris, J. W. K., J. A. J. Gowlett, R. J. Blumenschine, and J. E. Maiers. In press-a. Chesowanja—a summary of the early Pleistocene archaeology. In *Proceedings of the 9th Panafrican Congress of Prehistory and Quaternary Studies (Jos, Nigeria)*.

Harris, J. W. K., and K. Harris. 1981. A note on the archaeology at Laetoli. *Nyame Akuma* 18:18–21.

Harris, J. W. K., and G. Ll. Isaac. 1976. The Karari Industry: early Pleistocene archaeological evidence from the terrain east of Lake Turkana, Kenya. *Nature* 262:102–107.

Harris, J. W. K., D. C. Johanson, and M. Taieb. In press-b. Results of further archaeological studies at Hadar, Ethiopia. In *Proceedings of the 9th Panafrican Congress of Prehistory and Quaternary Studies (Jos, Nigeria)*.

Harris, J. W. K., P. G. Williamson, J. Verniers, M. J. Tappen, K. Stewart, D. Helgren, J. de Heinzelin, N. T. Boaz, and R. V. Bellomo. 1987. Late Pliocene hominid occupation of the Senga 5A site, Zaire. *Journal of Human Evolution* 16:701–728.

Harrison, T. 1986a. New fossil anthropoids from the Middle Miocene of east Africa and their bearing on the origin of the Oreopithecidae. *American Journal of Physical Anthropology* 71:265–284.

———. 1986b. A reassessment of the phylogenetic relationships of *Oreopithecus bambolii* Gervais. *Journal of Human Evolution* 15:541–583.

———. 1987. The phylogenetic relationships of the early catarrhine primates: a review of the current evidence. *Journal of Human Evolution* 16:41–80.

Harrold, F. B. 1980. A comparative analysis of Eurasian Paleolithic burials. *World Archaeology* 12:195–211.

———. 1983. The Chatelperronian and the Middle-Upper Paleolithic transition. *British Archaeological Reports International Series* 164:123–140.

———. In press. Mousterian, Chatelperronian, and early Aurignacian: continuity and discontinuity. In P. Mellars and C. Stringer, eds. *The human revolution: behavioural and biological perspectives on the origins of modern humans*. Edinburgh: Edinburgh University Press.

Hay, R. L. 1976. *Geology of the Olduvai Gorge: a study of sedimentation in a semiarid basin*. Berkeley: University of California Press.

_____. 1987. Geology of the Laetoli area. In M. D. Leakey and J. M. Harris, eds. *Laetoli: a Pliocene site in northern Tanzania*, 23–47. Oxford: Clarendon Press.

Hay, R. L., and M. D. Leakey. 1982. The fossil footprints of Laetoli. *Scientific American* 246(2): 50–57.

Haynes, C. V. 1980. The Clovis culture. *Canadian Journal of Anthropology* 1:115–121.

_____. 1984. Stratigraphy and late Pleistocene extinction in the United States. In P. S. Martin and R. G. Klein, eds. *Quaternary extinctions: a prehistoric revolution*, 345–353. Tucson: University of Arizona Press.

Hays, J. D., J. Imbrie, and N. J. Schackleton. 1976. Variations in the earth's orbit: pacemaker of the ice ages. *Science* 194:1121–1132.

Hedberg, H. D. 1976. *International stratigraphic guide*. New York: John Wiley and Sons.

Hedges, R. E. M. 1981. Radiocarbon dating with an accelerator: review and preview. *Archaeometry* 23:3–18.

Heim, J.-L. 1976. Les hommes fossiles de la Ferrassie I. *Archives de l'Institut de Paléontologie Humaine* 35:1–331.

Heinrich, W.-D. 1982. Zur Evolution und Biostratigraphie von *Arvicola* (Rodentia, Mammalia) im Pleistozän Europas. *Zeitschrift für geologische Wissenschaften* 10:683–735.

_____. 1987. Neue Ergebnisse zur Evolution und Biostratigraphie von *Arvicola* (Rodentia, Mammalia) im Quartär Europas. *Zeitschrift für geologische Wissenschaften* 15:389–406.

Heinz, E., M. Brunet, and B. Battail. 1981. A cercopithecoid primate from the late Miocene of Moloyan, Afghanistan, with remarks on *Mesopithecus. International Journal of Primatology* 2:273–284.

Hendey, Q. B. 1981. Palaeoecology of the Late Tertiary fossil occurrences in 'E' Quarry, Langebaanweg, South Africa, and a reinterpretation of their geological context. *Annals of the South African Museum* 84:1–104.

_____. 1984. Southern African late Tertiary vertebrates. In R. G. Klein, ed. *Southern African prehistory and paleoenvironments*, 81–106. Rotterdam: A. A. Balkema.

Hennig, G. J., and R. Grün. 1983. ESR dating in Quaternary geology. *Quaternary Science Reviews* 2:157–238.

Hennig, G. J., R. Grün, and K. Brunnacker. 1983. Speleothems, travertines, and paleoclimates. *Quaternary Research* 20:1–29.

Hennig, G. J., W. Herr, E. Weber, and N. L. Xirotiris. 1982. Petralona cave dating controversy. *Nature* 299:281–282.

Hennig, W. 1966. *Phylogenetic systematics*. Urbana: University of Illinois Press.

Henri-Martin, G. 1965. La grotte de Fontéchevade. *Bulletin de l'Association Française pour l'Étude du Quaternaire* 3–4:211–216.

Hester, J. J. 1987. The significance of accelerator dating in archaeological method and theory. *Journal of Field Archaeology* 14:445–451.

Hewes, G. W. 1961. Food transport and the origin of hominid bipedalism. *American Anthropologist* 63:687–710.

_____. 1964. Hominid bipedalism: independent evidence for the food-carrying theory. *Science* 146:416–418.

Hill, A. 1985. Early hominid from Baringo District, Kenya. *Nature* 315:222–224.

Hill, A., R. Drake, L. Tauxe, M. Monaghan, J. C. Barry, A. K. Behrens-meyer, G. Curtis, B. F. Jacobs, L. Jacobs, N. Johnson, and D. Pilbeam. 1985. Neogene palaeontology and geochronology of the Baringo Basin, Kenya. *Journal of Human Evolution* 14:759–773.

Hoffecker, J. F. 1982. The Moose Creek Site: an early man occupation in central Alaska. Report to the National Park Service and the National Geographic Society.

————. 1986. *Upper Paleolithic settlement on the Russian Plain.* Ph.D. dissertation, University of Chicago.

————. 1987. Upper Pleistocene loess stratigraphy and Paleolithic site chronology on the Russian Plain. *Geoarchaeology* 2:259–284.

Hoffstetter, R. 1969. Un Primate de l'Oligocène inférieur sud-américain: *Branisella boliviana* gen. et sp. nov. *Comptes Rendus des Séances de l'Académie des Sciences, Paris,* Séries D, 269:434–437.

————. 1974. Phylogeny and geographical deployment of the primates. *Journal of Human Evolution* 3:327–350.

————. 1980. Origin and deployment of New World monkeys emphasizing the southern continents route. In R. L. Ciochon and A. B. Chiarelli, eds. *Evolutionary biology of the New World monkeys and continental drift,* 103–122. New York: Plenum.

Hole, F., and K. V. Flannery. 1967. The prehistory of southwestern Iran: a preliminary report. *Proceedings of the Prehistoric Society* 33:147–206.

Holloway, R. L. 1970. Australopithecine endocast (Taung specimen, 1924): a new volume determination. *Science* 168:966–968.

————. 1975. Early hominid endocasts: volumes, morphology, and significance for hominid evolution. In R. H. Tuttle, ed. *Primate functional morphology and evolution,* 393–415. The Hague: Mouton.

————. 1981a. The Indonesian *Homo erectus* brain endocasts revisited. *American Journal of Physical Anthropology* 55:43–58.

————. 1981b. Volumetric and asymmetry determinations on recent hominid endocasts: Spy I and II, Djebel Irhoud I, and the Salé *Homo erectus* specimens, with some notes on Neanderthal brain size. *American Journal of Physical Anthropology* 55:385–393.

————. 1983a. Cerebral brain endocast pattern of *Australopithecus afarensis* hominid. *Nature* 303:420–422.

————. 1983b. Human brain evolution: a search for units, models and synthesis. *Canadian Journal of Anthropology* 3:215–230.

————. 1985. The poor brain of *Homo sapiens neanderthalensis:* see what you please. . . . In E. Delson, ed. *Ancestors: the hard evidence,* 319–324. New York: Alan R. Liss.

Holloway, R. L., and M. C. de la Coste-Lareymondie. 1982. Brain endocast asymmetry in pongids and hominids: some preliminary findings on the paleontology of cerebral dominance. *American Journal of Physical Anthropology* 58:101–110.

Holloway, R. L., and W. H. Kimbel. 1986. Endocast morphology of Hadar hominid AL 162-28. *Nature* 321:536–537.

Hooker, P. J., and J. A. Miller. 1979. K-Ar dating of the Pleistocene fossil hominid site at Chesowanja, North Kenya. *Nature* 282:710–712.

Hopkins, D. M. 1985. Comment on Dolitsky (1985). *Current Anthropology* 26:371–372.

Horton, D. R. 1984. Red kangaroos: last of the Australian megafauna. In P. S. Martin and R. G. Klein, eds. *Quaternary extinctions: a prehistoric revolution*, 639–680. Tucson: University of Arizona Press.

Howe, B. 1967. The Palaeolithic of Tangier, Morocco: excavations at Cape Ashakar, 1939–1947. *Bulletin of the American School of Prehistoric Research* 22:1–200.

Howell, F. C. 1951. The place of Neanderthal man in human evolution. *American Journal of Physical Anthropology* 9:379–416.

———. 1957. The evolutionary significance of variation and varieties of "Neanderthal" man. *The Quarterly Review of Biology* 32:330–347.

———. 1960. European and northwest African Middle Pleistocene hominids. *Current Anthropology* 1:195–232.

———. 1966. Observations on the earlier phases of the European Lower Paleolithic. *American Anthropologist* 68(2/2): 88–201.

———. 1978a. Hominidae. In V. J. Maglio and H. B. S. Cooke, eds. *Evolution in African mammals*, 154–248. Cambridge, Mass.: Harvard University Press.

———. 1978b. Overview of the Pliocene and earlier Pleistocene of the lower Omo basin, southern Ethiopia. In C. Jolly, ed. *Early hominids of Africa*, 85–130. London: Duckworth.

———. 1981. Some views of *Homo erectus* with special reference to its occurence in Europe. In B. A. Sigmon and S. Cybulski, eds. *Homo erectus—papers in honor of Davidson Black*, 153–157. Toronto: University of Toronto Press.

———. 1984. Introduction. In F. H. Smith and F. Spencer, eds. *The origins of modern humans*, xiii–xxii. New York: Alan R. Liss.

———. 1986. Variabilité chez *Homo erectus*, et problème de la présence de cette espèce en Europe. *L'Anthropologie* 90:447–481.

Howell, F. C., G. H. Cole, and M. R. Kleindienst. 1962. Isimila, an Acheulian occupation site in the Iringa Highlands. *Actes du IVe Congrès Panafricain de Préhistoire et de l'Étude du Quaternaire*, 43–80. Tervuren, Belgium: Musée Royal de l'Afrique Centrale.

Howell, F. C., G. H. Cole, M. R. Kleindienst, B. J. Szabo, and K. P. Oakley. 1972. Uranium series dating of bone from the Isimila prehistoric site, Tanzania. *Nature* 237:51–52.

Howell, F. C., and the editors of Time-Life. 1965. *Early man.* New York: Time.

Howell, F. C., P. Haesaerts, and J. de Heinzelin. 1987. Depositional environments, archeological occurrences and hominids from Members E and F of the Shungura Formation (Omo Basin, Ethiopia). *Journal of Human Evolution* 16:665–700.

Howells, W. W. 1966. *Homo erectus. Scientific American* 215(5): 46–53.

———. 1967. *Mankind in the making.* New York: Doubleday.

———. 1973a. Cranial variation in man: a study by multivariate analysis. *Peabody Museum Papers* 67:1–259.

———. 1973b. *The evolution of the genus Homo.* Reading, Mass.: Addison-Wesley.

_____. 1980. *Homo erectus*—who, when, and where: a survey. *Yearbook of Physical Anthropology* 23:1–23.

_____. 1982. Comment on "Upper Pleistocene hominid evolution in south-Central Europe: a review of the evidence and analysis of trends." *Current Anthropology* 23:688–689.

Hublin, J. J. 1985. Human fossils from the North African Middle Pleistocene and the origins of *Homo sapiens.* In E. Delson, ed. *Ancestors: the hard evidence,* 282–288. New York: Alan R. Liss.

_____. 1986. Some comments on the diagnosic features of *Homo erectus. Anthropos* (Brno) 23:175–187.

Hurford, A. J., A. J. W. Gleadow, and C. W. Naeser. 1976. Fission-track dating of pumice from the KBS tuffs. *Nature* 263:738–740.

Hutterer, K. L. 1985. The Pleistocene archaeology of Southeast Asia in regional context. *Modern Quaternary Research in Southeast Asia* 9:1–23.

Huxley, T. H. 1863. *Zoological evidences as to man's place in nature.* London: Williams and Norgate.

Imbrie, J., J. D. Hays, D. G. Martinson, A. McIntyre, A. C. Mix, J. J. Morley, N. G. Pisias, W. L. Prell, and N. J. Shackleton. 1984. The orbital theory of Pleistocene climate: support from a revised chronology of the marine delta 18O record. In A. L. Berger, et al., eds. *Milankovitch and climate: understanding the response to astronomical forcing,* Part 1, 169–305. Boston: Reidel.

Imbrie, J., and K. P. Imbrie. 1979. *Ice ages: solving the mystery.* New York: MacMillan.

Isaac, G. Ll. 1967. The stratigraphy of the Peninj Group—early Middle Pleistocene formations west of Lake Natron, Tanzania. In W. W. Bishop and J. D. Clark, eds. *Background to evolution in Africa,* 229–257. Chicago: University of Chicago Press.

_____. 1975. Stratigraphy and cultural patterns in East Africa during the middle ranges of Pleistocene time. In K. W. Butzer and G. Ll. Isaac, eds. *After the australopithecines,* 543–569. The Hague: Mouton.

_____. 1977. *Olorgesailie.* Chicago: University of Chicago Press.

_____. 1978. The food sharing behavior of proto-human hominids. *Scientific American* 238(4): 90–108.

_____. 1981. Archaeological tests of alternative models of early human behavior: excavation and experiments. *Philosophical Transactions of the Royal Society* (London) B 292:177–188.

_____. 1982. Early hominids and fire at Chesowanja, Kenya. *Nature* 296.870.

_____. 1984. The archaeology of human origins: studies of the Lower Pleistocene in East Africa: 1971–1981. In F. Wendorf and A. E. Close, eds. *Advances in world archaeology,* vol. 3, 1–87. New York: Academic Press.

_____. 1986. Foundation stones: early artifacts as indicators of activities and abilities. In G. N. Bailey, and P. Callow, eds. *Stone Age Prehistory,* 221–242. Cambridge: Cambridge University Press.

Isaac, G. Ll., and G. H. Curtis. 1974. The age of early Acheulian industries in East Africa—new evidence from the Peninj Group, Tanzania. *Nature* 249:624–627.

Isaac, G. Ll., and J. W. K. Harris. 1978. Archaeology. In M. G. Leakey and R. E. F. Leakey, eds. *Koobi Fora research project*, vol. 1, 64–85. Oxford: Clarendon.

Ishida, H., M. Pickford, H. Nakaya, and Y. Nakano. 1984. Fossil anthropoids from Nachola and Samburu Hills, Samburu District, Kenya. *African Studies Monographs (Kyoto), Supplementary Issue* 2:73–85.

Jacob, T. 1975. Morphology and paleoecology of early man in Java. In R. H. Tuttle, ed. *Paleoanthropology, morphology and paleoecology*, 311–325. The Hague: Mouton.

_____. 1978. The puzzle of Solo Man. *Modern Quaternary Research in Southeast Asia* 4:31–40.

_____. 1980. The Pithecanthropus of Indonesia: phenotype, genetics and ecology. In L.-K. Königsson, ed. *Current argument on early man: report from a Nobel Symposium*, 170–179. Oxford: Pergamon.

Jacob, T., R. P. Soejono, L. G. Freeman, and F. H. Brown. 1978. Stone tools from mid-Pleistocene sediments in Java. *Science* 202:885–887.

Jaeger, J.-J. 1975. The mammalian faunas and hominid fossils of the Middle Pleistocene in the Maghreb. In K. W. Butzer and G. Ll. Isaac, eds. *After the australopithecines*, 399–410. The Hague: Mouton.

Jánossy, D. 1975. Mid-Pleistocene microfaunas of Continental Europe and adjoining areas. In K. W. Butzer, and G. Ll. Isaac, eds. *After the australopithecines*, 375–397. The Hague: Mouton.

Jelinek, A. J. 1977. The Lower Paleolithic: current evidence and interpretations. *Annual Review of Anthropology* 6:11–32.

_____. 1981. The Middle Paleolithic in the southern Levant from the perspective of the Tabun Cave. In J. Cauvin and P. Sanlaville, eds. *Préhistoire du Levant*, 265–280. Paris: Centre National de la Recherche Scientifique.

_____. 1982a. The Middle Palaeolithic in the southern Levant, with comments on the appearance of modern *Homo sapiens*. *British Archaeological Reports International Series* 151:57–104.

_____. 1982b. The Tabun Cave and Paleolithic man in the Levant. *Science* 216:1369–1375.

Jia, L. 1980. *Early man in China*. Beijing: Foreign Languages Press.

_____. 1985. China's earliest Paleolithic assemblages. In R. Wu and J. W. Olsen, eds. *Palaeoanthropology and Palaeolithic archaeology in the People's Republic of China*, 135–145. Orlando, Fla.: Academic Press.

Jochim, M. A. 1983. Palaeolithic cave art in ecological perspective. In G. Bailey, ed. *Hunter-gatherer economy in prehistory*, 212–219. Cambridge: Cambridge University Press.

Johanson, D. C. 1986. Thoughts on the "Black Skull" from Kenya. *Institute of Human Origins Newsletter* 4(1): 5.

Johanson, D. C., and M. A. Edey. 1981. *Lucy: the beginnings of humankind*. New York: Simon and Schuster.

Johanson, D. C., F. T. Masao, G. G. Eck, T. D. White, R. C. Walter, W. H. Kimbel, B. Asfaw, P. Manega, P. Ndessokia, and G. Suwa. 1987. New partial skeleton of *Homo habilis* from Olduvai Gorge, Tanzania. *Nature* 327:205–209.

Johanson, D. C., M. Taieb, and Y. Coppens. 1982. Pliocene hominids from the Hadar Formation, Ethiopia (1973–1977): stratigraphic, chronologic, and paleoenvironmental contexts, with notes on hominid morphology and systematics. *American Journal of Physical Anthropology* 57:373–402.

Johanson, D. C., and T. D. White. 1979. A systematic assessment of early African hominids. *Science* 202:321–330.

Johanson, D. C., T. D. White, and Y. Coppens. 1978. A new species of the genus *Australopithecus* (Primates: Hominidae) from the Pliocene of eastern Africa. *Kirtlandia* 28:1–14.

Jones, D. L., A. Brock, and P. L. McFadden. 1986. Palaeomagnetic results from the Kromdraai and Sterkfontein hominid sites. *South African Journal of Science* 82:160–163.

Jones, J. S., and S. Rouhani. 1986. How small was the bottleneck? *Nature* 319:449–450.

Jones, P. R. 1980. Experimental butchery with modern stone tools and its relevance for Palaeolithic archaeology. *World Archaeology* 12:153–175.

———. 1981. Experimental implement manufacture and use: a case study from Olduvai Gorge. *Philosophical Transactions of the Royal Society* (London) B 292:189–195.

Jones, R. 1979. The fifth continent: problems concerning the human colonization of Australia. *Annual Review of Anthropology* 8:445–466.

———. In press. East of Wallace's Line: issues and problems in the colonisation of the Australian continent. In P. Mellars and C. Stringer, eds. *The human revolution: behavioural and biological perspectives on the origins of modern humans.* Edinburgh: Edinburgh University Press.

Jungers, W. L. 1988. New estimates of body size in australopithecines. In F. E. Grine, ed., *The evolutionary history of the robust australopithecines,* 115–116. New York: Aldine de Gruyter.

Kahlke, H. D. 1962. Zur relativen Chronologie ostasiatischer Mittelpleistozän-Faunen und Hominoidea-Funde. In G. Kurth, ed. *Evolution und Hominisation,* 84–107. Stuttgart: Gustav Fischer.

Kalb, J. E., C. Jolly, A. Mebrate, S. Tebedge, C. Smart, E. B. Oswald, D. Cramer, P. Whitehead, C. B. Wood, G. C. Conroy, T. Adefris, L. Sperling, and B. Kana. 1982a. Fossil mammals and artifacts from the Awash Group, Middle Awash Valley, Afar, Ethiopia. *Nature* 298:25–29.

Kalb, J. E., E. B. Oswald, S. Tebedge, A. Mebrate, E. Tola, and D. Peak. 1982b. Geology and stratigraphy of Neogene deposits, Middle Awash Valley, Ethiopia. *Nature* 298:17–25.

Kashiwaya, K., A. Yamamoto, and K. Fukuyama. 1988. Statistical analysis of grain size distribution in Pleistocene sediments from Lake Biwa, Japan. *Quaternary Research* 30:12–18.

Kaufulu, Z. M., and N. Stern. 1987. The first stone artefacts found *in situ* within the Plio-Pleistocene Chiwondo Beds in northern Malawi. *Journal of Human Evolution* 16:729–740.

Kay, R. F. 1981. The nut-crackers: a new theory of the adaptation of the Ramapithecinae. *American Journal of Physical Anthropology* 55:141–151.

Kay, R. F., J. C. Fleagle, and E. L. Simons. 1981. A revision of the Oligocene apes of the Fayum Province, Egypt. *American Journal of Physical Anthropology* 55:293–322.

Kay, R. F., R. H. Madden, J. M. Plavcan, R. L. Cifelli, and J. G. Diaz. 1987. *Stirtonia victoriae,* a new species of Miocene Columbian primate. *Journal of Human Evolution* 16:173–196.

Kay, R. F., and E. L. Simons. 1980. The ecology of Oligocene African Anthropoidea. *International Journal of Primatology* 1:21–37.

_____. 1983. Dental formulae and dental eruption patterns in Parapithecidae (Primates, Anthropoidea). *American Journal of Physical Anthropology* 62:363–375.

Keeley, L. H. 1977. The functions of paleolithic flint tools. *Scientific American* 237(5): 108–126.

_____. 1980. *Experimental determination of stone tool use: a microwear analysis.* Chicago: University of Chicago Press.

Keeley, L. H., and N. Toth. 1981. Microwear polishes on early stone tools from Koobi Fora, Kenya. *Nature* 293:464–465.

Keith, A. 1928. *The antiquity of man.* Philadelphia: Lippincott.

Kelley, J. 1986. Species recognition and sexual dimorphism in *Proconsul* and *Rangwapithecus. Journal of Human Evolution* 15:461–495.

Kelley, J., and D. Pilbeam. 1986. The dryopithecines: taxonomy, comparative anatomy, and phylogeny of Miocene large hominoids. In D. R. Swindler and J. Erwin, eds. *Comparative primate biology,* vol. 1, 361–411. New York: Alan R. Liss.

Kennedy, G. E. 1983. Some aspects of femoral morphology in *Homo erectus. Journal of Human Evolution* 12:587–616.

_____. 1984a. Are the Kow Swamp hominids 'archaic'? *American Journal of Physical Anthropology* 65:163–168.

_____. 1984b. The emergence of *Homo sapiens:* the post-cranial evidence. *Man* 19:94–110.

Kennedy, K. A. R. 1975. *Neanderthal man.* Minneapolis: Burgess.

Kimbel, W. H., T. D. White, and D. C. Johanson. 1984. Cranial morphology of *Australopithecus afarensis:* a comparative study based on a composite reconstruction of the adult skull. *American Journal of Physical Anthropology* 64:337–388.

Kimbel, W. H., T. D. White, and D. C. Johanson. 1985. Craniodental morphology of the hominids from Hadar and Laetoli: evidence of *"Paranthropus"* and *Homo* in the mid-Pliocene of Eastern Africa? In E. Delson, ed. *Ancestors: the hard evidence,* 120–137. New York: Alan R. Liss.

Klein, R. G. 1969a. *Man and culture in the late Pleistocene: a case study.* San Francisco: Chandler.

_____. 1969b. The Mousterian of European Russia. *Proceedings of the Prehistoric Society* 35:77–111.

_____. 1971. The Pleistocene prehistory of Siberia. *Quaternary Research* 1:133–161.

_____. 1973a. Geological antiquity of Rhodesian Man. *Nature* 244:311–312.

_____. 1973b. *Ice-Age hunters of the Ukraine.* Chicago: University of Chicago Press.

———. 1976. A preliminary report on the Duinefontein 2 "Middle Stone Age" open-air site (Melkbosstrand, South-Western Cape Province, South Africa). *South African Archaeological Bulletin* 31:12–20.

———. 1978. The fauna and overall interpretation of the "Cutting 10" Acheulean site at Elandsfontein (Hopefield), Southwestern Cape Province, South Africa. *Quaternary Research* 10:69–83.

———. 1979. Stone age exploitation of animals in southern Africa. *American Scientist* 67:151–160.

———. 1980. Environmental and ecological implications of large mammals from Upper Pleistocene and Holocene sites in southern Africa. *Annals of the South African Museum* 81:223–283.

———. 1983. The stone age prehistory of southern Africa. *Annual Review of Anthropology* 12:25–48.

———. 1984. Mammalian extinctions and Stone Age people in Africa. In P. S. Matrin and R. G. Klein, eds. *Quaternary extinctions: a prehistoric revolution*, 553–573. Tucson: University of Arizona Press.

———. 1987. Problems and prospects in understanding how early people exploited animals. In M. H. Nitecki and D. V. Nitecki, eds. *The evolution of human hunting*, 11–45. New York: Plenum.

———. 1988. The archaeological significance of animal bones from Acheulean sites in southern Africa. *The African Archaeological Review* 6:3–26.

Klein, R. G., and K. Cruz-Uribe. 1983. Stone age population numbers and average tortoise size at Byneskranskop Cave 1 and Die Kelders Cave 1, southern Cape Province, South Africa. *South African Archaeolgical Bulletin* 38:26–30.

———. 1984. *The analysis of animal bones from archaeological sites.* Chicago: University of Chicago Press.

———. In press. An overview of the Torralba fauna. In L. G. Freeman and F. C. Howell, eds. *Torralba: an Acheulean butchering site on the Spanish Meseta.* Tübingen: Tübingen Monograph Series.

Klíma, B. 1962. The first ground-plan of an Upper Paleolithic loess settlement in Middle Europe and its meaning. In R. J. Braidwood and G. B. Willey, eds. *Courses towards urban life*, 193–210. Chicago: Aldine.

———. 1963. *Dolní Vestonice.* Prague: Ceskosolvenská Akademie Ved.

———. 1987. A triple burial from the Upper Paleolithic of Dolní Vestonice. *Journal of Human Evolution* 16:831–835.

Kozlowskı, J. K. 1982. *Excavation in the Bacho Kiro Cave (Bulgaria): final report.* Warsaw: Panstwowe Wydanicstwo Naukowe.

———. 1983. Le Paléolithique supérieur en Pologne. *L'Anthropologie* 87:49–82.

Kozlowski, J. K., and S. K. Kozlowski. 1979. *Upper Paleolithic and Mesolithic in Europe: taxonomy and paleohistory.* Warsaw: Polska Akademia Nauk.

Kozlowski, J. K., and H. Kubiak. 1972. Late Palaeolithic dwellings made of mammoth bones in south Poland. *Nature* 237:463–464.

Kroll, E., and G. Ll. Isaac. 1984. Configurations of artifacts and bones at early Pleistocene sites in East Africa. In H. Hietala, ed.

Intrasite spatial analysis in archaeology, 4–31. Cambridge: Cambridge University Press.

Ku, T.-L. 1976. The uranium-series methods of age detemination. *Annual Review of Earth and Planetary Sciences* 4:347–379.

Kukla, G. J. 1975. Loess stratigraphy of central Europe. In K. W. Butzer and G. Ll. Isaac, eds. *After the australopithecines*, 99–188. The Hague: Mouton.

———. 1987. Loess stratigraphy in central China. *Quaternary Science Reviews* 6:191–219.

Kulemeyer, J. 1986. Kärlich, un site du Paléolithique inférieur dans le bassin de Neuwied. In A. Tuffreau and J. Sommé, eds. *Chronostratigraphie et faciés culturels du Paléolithique inférieur et moyen dans l'Europe du Nord-Ouest*, 43–48. Paris: Supplément au Bullétin de l'Association Française pour l'Étude du Quaternaire.

Kuman, K., and R. J. Clarke, 1986. Florisbad—new investigations at a Middle Stone Age hominid site in South Africa. *Geoarchaeology* 1:103–125.

Kurtén, B. 1976. *The cave bear story: life and death of a vanished animal*. New York: Columbia University Press.

———. 1983. Faunal sequence from Petralona Cave. *Anthropos* (Greece) 10:53–59.

Kurtén, B., and E. Anderson. 1980. *Pleistocene mammals of North America*. New York: Columbia University Press.

Laitman, J. T. 1985. Evolution of the hominid upper respiratory tract: the fossil evidence. In P. V. Tobias, ed. *Hominid evolution: past, present and future*, 281–286. New York: Alan R. Liss.

Laitman, J. T., and R. C. Heimbuch. 1982. The basicranium of Plio-Pleistocene hominids as an indicator of their upper respiratory systems. *American Journal of Physical Anthropology* 59:323–344.

Laitman, J. T., R. C. Heimbuch, and C. S. Crelin. 1979. The basicranium of fossil hominids as an indicator of their upper respiratory systems. *American Journal of Physical Anthropology* 51:15–34.

Lamothe, M., A. Dreimanis, M. Morency, and A. Raukas. 1984. Thermoluminescence dating of Quaternary sediments. In W. C. Mahaney, ed. *Quaternary dating methods*, 153–170. Amsterdam: Elsevier.

Laporte, L. F., and A. L. Zihlman. 1983. Plates, climate and hominoid evolution. *South African Journal of Science* 79:96–110.

Lartet, L. 1868. Une sépulture des troglodytes du Périgord (crânes des Eyzies). *Bulletin de la Société d'Anthropologie de Paris* 3:335–349.

Latimer, B., J. C. Ohman, and C. O. Lovejoy. 1987. Talocrural joint in African hominoids: implications for *Australopithecus afarensis*. *American Journal of Physical Anthropology* 74:155–175.

Laville, H. 1982. On the transition from "Lower" to "Middle" Palaeolithic in southwest France. *British Archaeological Reports International Series* 151:131–135.

Laville, H., J.-P. Raynal, and J.-P. Texier. 1986. Le dernier interglaciaire et le cycle climatique wurmien dans le sud-ouest et le Massif

Central français. *Bulletin de l'Association française pour l'-Etude du Quaternaire* 23:35–46.

Laville, H., J. -Ph. Rigaud, and J. Sackett. 1980. *Rock shelters of the Perigord.* New York: Academic Press.

Leakey, L.S.B. 1961. New finds at Olduvai Gorge. *Nature* 189: 649-650.

———. 1966. *Homo habilis, Homo erectus* and the australopithecines. *Nature* 209: 1279-1281.

Leakey, L.S.B., J.F. Evernden, and G.H. Curtis. 1961. Age of Bed I, Olduvai Gorge, Tanganyika. *Nature* 191: 478.

Leakey, L. S. B., P. V. Tobias, and J. R. Napier. 1964. A new species of the genus *Homo* from Olduvai Gorge, Tanzania. *Nature* 202:308–312.

Leakey, M. D. 1971. *Olduvai Gorge: excavations in Beds I and II, 1960–1963.* Cambridge: Cambridge University Press.

———. 1975. Cultural patterns in the Olduvai sequence. In K. W. Butzer and G. Ll. Isaac, eds. *After the australopithecines,* 476–493. The Hague: Mouton.

———. 1977. The archaeology of the early hominids. In T. H. Wilson, ed. *A survey of the prehistory of eastern Africa,* 61–79. Nairobi: VIII Panafrican Congress of Prehistory and Quaternary Studies.

———. 1978. Olduvai fossil hominids: their stratigraphic positions and associations. In C. Jolly, ed. *Early hominids of Africa,* 3–16. London: Duckworth.

———. 1980. Early man, environment and tools. In L. K. Königsson, ed. *Current argument on early man: report of a Nobel symposium,* 114–133. Oxford: Pergamon.

———. 1987a. Introduction. In M. D. Leakey and J. M. Harris, eds. *Laetoli: a Pliocene site in northern Tanzania,* 1–22. Oxford: Clarendon.

———. 1987b. Introduction (to the hominid footprints). In M. D. Leakey and J. M. Harris, eds. *Laetoli: a Pliocene site in northern Tanzania,* 490–496. Oxford: Clarendon.

———. 1987c. The Laetoli hominid remains. In M. D. Leakey and J. M. Harris, eds. *Laetoli: a Pliocene site in northern Tanzania,* 108–117. Oxford: Clarendon.

Leakey, M. D., and R. L. Hay. 1979. Pliocene footprints in the Laetolil Beds at Laetoli, northern Tanzania. *Nature* 278:317–323.

———. 1982. The chronological position of the fossil hominids of Tanzania. In M. A. de Lumley, ed. *L'Homo erectus et la place de l'homme de Tautavel parmi les hominidés fossiles,* 753–765. Nice: Ier Congrès International de Paléontologie Humaine.

Leakey, M. D., R. L. Hay, G. H. Curtis, R. E. Drake, M. K. Jackes, and T. D. White. 1976. Fossil hominids from the Laetolil Beds, Tanzania. *Nature* 262:460–465.

Leakey, Margaret, P. V. Tobias, J. E. Martyn, and R. E. Leakey. 1969. An Acheulian industry with prepared core technique and the discovery of a contemporary hominid at Lake Baringo, Kenya. *Proceedings of the Prehistoric Society* 25:48–76.

Leakey, R. E. F., and M. G. Leakey. 1986a. A new Miocene hominoid from Kenya. *Nature* 324:143–146.

———. 1986b. A second new Miocene hominoid from Kenya. *Nature* 324:146–148.

———. 1987. A new Miocene small-bodied ape from Kenya. *Journal of Human Evolution* 16:369–387.

Leakey, R. E. F., and A. Walker. 1976. *Australopithecus, Homo erectus,* and the single species hypothesis. *Nature* 261:572–574.

———. 1983. New higher primates from the early Miocene of Buluk, Kenya. *Nature* 318:173–175.

———. 1985a. A fossil skeleton 1,600,000 years old: *Homo erectus* unearthed. *National Geographic* 168:625–629.

———. 1985b. Further hominids from the Plio-Pleistocene of Koobi Fora, Kenya. *American Journal of Physical Anthropology* 67:135–163.

———. 1988. New *Australopithecus boisei* specimens from East and West Lake Turkana, Kenya. *American Journal of Physical Anthropology* 76:1–24.

Legoux, P. 1975. Présentation des dents des restes humains de l'Abri Pataud. *American School of Prehistoric Research Bulletin* 30:262–305.

Le Gros Clark, W. E. 1955. *The fossil evidence for human evolution,* 1st ed. Chicago: University of Chicago Press.

———. 1960. *The antecedents of man.* Chicago: Quadrangle.

———. 1964. *The fossil evidence for human evolution,* 2d ed. Chicago: University of Chicago Press.

———. 1967. *Man-apes or ape-men?* New York: Holt, Rinehart and Winston.

Leinders, J. J. M., F. Aziz, P. Y. Sondaar, and J. de Vos. 1985. The age of the hominid-bearing deposits of Java: state of the art. *Geologie en Mijnbouw* 64:167–173.

Leroi-Gourhan, André. 1959. Étude des restes humains fossiles provenant des Grottes d'Arcy-sur-Cure. *Annales de Paléontologie* 44:87–148.

———. 1965a. Le Châtelperronien: problème ethnologique. In E. Ripoll Perello, ed. *Miscelanea en homenaje al Abate Henri Breuil,* vol. 2, 75–81. Barcelona: Diputacion Provincial de Barcelona, Instituto de Prehistória y Arqueológia.

———. 1965b. *Treasures of prehistoric art.* New York: Abrams.

Leroi-Gourhan, Arl. 1984. La place du Néandertalien de St-Césaire dans la chronologie Würmienne. *Bulletin de la Société Préhistorique Française* 81:196–198.

Leroyer, C., and Arl. Leroi-Gourhan. 1983. Problèmes de chronologie: le castelperronien et l'aurignacien. *Bulletin de la Société Préhistorique Française* 80:41–44.

Lévêque, F., and J. -C. Miskovsky. 1983. Le Castelperronien dans son environnement géologique. *L'Anthropologie* 87:369–391.

Lewin, R. 1988. Molecular clocks turn a quarter century. *Science* 239:561–563.

Lewis-Williams, J. D. 1981. *Believing and seeing: symbolic meanings in southern San rock art.* London: Academic Press.

———. 1982. The economic and social context of southern San rock art. *Current Anthropology* 23:429–449.

Lewis-Williams, J. D., and T. A. Dowson. 1988. The signs of all times: entoptic phenomena in Upper Palaeolithic art. *Current Anthropology* 29:201–245.

Lewis-Williams, J. D., and J. H. N. Loubser. 1986. Deceptive appearances: a critique of southern African rock art studies. *Advances in World Archaeology* 5:253–289.

Libby, W. F. 1955. *Radiocarbon dating.* Chicago: University of Chicago Press.

Liu, ZeChun. 1985. Sequence of sediments at Locality 1 in Zhou-koudian and correlation with loess stratigraphy in northern China and with the chronology of deep sea cores. *Quaternary Research* 23:139–153.

Lourandos, H. 1987. Pleistocene Australia: peopling of a continent. In O. Soffer, ed. *The Pleistocene Old World: regional perspectives*, 147–165. New York: Plenum.

Lovejoy, C. O. 1979. A reconstruction of the pelvis of Al-288 (Hadar Formation, Ethiopia) (abstract). *American Journal of Physical Anthropology* 50:460.

———. 1981. The origin of man. *Science* 211:341–350.

Lowe, J. J., and M. J. C. Walker. 1984. *Reconstructing Quaternary environments*. New York and London: Longman.

Lowenstein, J. M., T. Molleson, and S. L. Washburn. 1982. Piltdown jaw confirmed as orang. *Nature* 299:294.

Lumley, H. de 1969a. Une cabane acheuléene dans la grotte du Lazaret. *Mémoires de la Société Préhistorique Française* 7:1–234.

———. 1969b. A Paleolithic camp at Nice. *Scientific American* 220(5): 42–50.

———. 1975. Cultural evolution in France in its paleoecological setting during the Middle Pleistocene. In K. W. Butzer and G. Ll. Isaac, eds. *After the australopithecines*, 745–808. The Hague: Mouton.

———. 1976a. Les premières industries humains en Provence. In H. de Lumley, ed. *La préhistoire française*, vol. 1, no. 2, 765–794. Paris: Centre National de la Recherche Scientifique.

Lumley, H. de, and Y. Boone. 1976. Les structures d'habitat au Paléolithique inférieur. In H. de Lumley, ed. *La préhistoire française*, vol. 1, 625–643. Paris: Centre National de la Recher-che Scientifique.

Lumley, H. de, and A. Sonakia. 1985. Contexte stratigraphique et archéologique de l'homme de la Narmada, Hathnora, Madhya Pradesh, Inde. *L'Anthropologie* 89:3–12.

Lumley, H. de, ed. 1979. L'Homme de Tautavel. *Dossiers de l'Archéo-logie* 36.

Lumley, M. A. de. 1972. Les Néandertaliens de la grotte de l'Hortus (Valflaunès, Hérault). In H. de Lumley, ed. *La Grotte de l'Hortus*, 375–385. Marseille: Université de Provence.

Lumley, M. -A. de, and A. Sonakia. 1985. Première découverte d'un *Homo erectus* sur le Continent indien, à Hathnora, dans le Moyenne Vallée de la Narmada. *L'Anthropologie* 89(1): 13–61.

LÜ Zune. 1985. Reply to Binford and Ho. 1985. *Current Anthropology* 26:432–433.

McBurney, C. B. M. 1967. *The Haua Fteah (Cyrenaica) and the Stone Age of the South-East Mediterranean*. Cambridge: Cambridge University Press.

———. 1975. Current status of the Lower and Middle Paleolithic in the entire region from the Levant through North Africa. In F. Wendorf and A. E. Marks, ed. *Problems in prehistory: North Africa and the Levant*, 411–426. Dallas: Southern Methodist University Press.

———. 1976. *Early man in the Soviet Union*. Oxford: Oxford University Press.

McBurney, C. B. M., and R. W. Hey. 1955. *Prehistory and Pleistocene geology in Cyrenaican Libya*. Cambridge: Cambridge University Press.

McCown, T. D., and A. Keith. 1939. *The Stone Age of Mount Carmel*, vol. 2. Oxford: Clarendon.

MacFadden, B. J. 1985. Drifting continents, mammals, and time scales: current developments in South America. *Journal of Vertebrate Paleontology* 5:169–174.

MacFadden, B. J., K. E. Campbell, Jr., R. L. Cifelli, O. Siles, N. Johnson, C. W. Naeser, and P. K. Zeitler. 1985. Magnetic polarity stratigraphy and mammalian biostratigraphy of the Desedean (Late Oligocene–Early Miocene) Salla Beds of northern Bolivia. *Journal of Geology* 93:223–250.

McFadden, P. L. 1980. An overview of palaeomagnetic chronology with special reference to the South African hominid sites. *Palaeontologia africana* 23:35–40.

McFadden, P. L., and A. Brock. 1984. Magnetostratigraphy at Makapansgat. *South African Journal of Science* 80:482–483.

McHenry, H. M. 1974. How large were the Australopithecines? *American Journal of Physical Anthropology* 40:329–340.

———. 1982. The pattern of human evolution: studies on bipedalism, mastication, and encephalization. *Annual Review of Anthropology* 11:151–173.

———. 1984. Relative cheek tooth size in *Australopithecus*. *American Journal of Physical Anthropology* 64:297–306.

———. 1985. Implications of postcanine megadontia for the origin of *Homo*. In E. Delson, ed. *Ancestors: the hard evidence*, 178–183. New York: Alan R. Liss.

———. 1986a. The first bipeds: a comparison of the *A. afarensis* and *A. africanus* postcranium and implications for the evolution of bipedalism. *Journal of Human Evolution* 15:177–191.

———. 1986b. Size variation in the postcranium of *Australopithecus afarensis* and extant species of Hominoidea. *Human Evolution* 1:149–156.

———. 1988. New estimates of body weight in early hominids and their significance to encephalization and megadontia in "robust" australopithecines. In F. E. Grine, ed. *The evolutionary history of the robust australopithecines*, 133–146. New York: Aldine de Gruyter.

McHenry, H. M., and R. S. Corruccini. 1983. The wrist of *Proconsul africanus* and the origin of hominoid postcranial adaptations. In R. L. Ciochon and R. S. Corruccini, eds. *New interpretations of ape and human ancestry*, 353–367. New York: Plenum.

McHenry, H. M., and R. R. Skelton. 1985. Is *Australopithecus africanus* ancestral to *Homo?* In P. V. Tobias, ed. *Hominid evolution: past, present and future*, 221–226. New York: Alan R. Liss.

McKenna, M. C. 1980. Early history and biogeography of South America's extinct land mammals. In R. L. Ciochon and A. B. Chiarelli, eds. *Evolutionary biology of the New World monkeys and continental drift*, 43–77. New York: Plenum.

MacPhee, R. D. E., M. Cartmill, and P. D. Gingerich. 1983. New Palaeogene primate basicrania and the definition of the order Primates. *Nature* 301:509–511.

Maglio, V. J. 1973. Origin and evolution of the Elephantidae. *Transactions of the American Philosophical Society* 63(3): 1–149.

Magori, C. C., and M. H. Day. 1983. Laetoli Hominid 18: an early *Homo sapiens* skull. *Journal of Human Evolution* 12:747–753.

Maguire, J. M. 1985. Recent geological, stratigraphic and palaeontological studies at Makapansgat Limeworks. In P. V. Tobias, ed. *Hominid evolution: past, present and future*, 151–164. New York: Alan R. Liss.

Maguire, J. M., D. Pemberton, and M. H. Collett. 1980. The Makapansgat Limeworks Grey Breccia: Hominids, Hyaenas, Hystricids, or Hillwash? *Palaeontologia Africana* 23:75–98.

Malatesta, A., A. Jaccabacci, G. Nappi, V. Conato, V. Molinari Paganelli, A. van der Werff, S. Durante, F. Settepassi, I. Biddittu. 1978. Torre in Pietra, Roma. *Quaternaria* 20:205–577.

Malez, M. 1970. A new look at the stratigraphy of the Krapina site. In *Krapina: 1899–1969*, 40–44. Zagreb: Yugoslavenska Akademija Znanosti i Umjetnosti.

Mania, D. 1986. Die Forschungsgrabung bei Bilzingsleben. *Jahresschrift für Mitteldeutsche Vorgeschichte* 69:235–255.

Mania, D., and V. Toepfer. 1973. Königsaue: Gliederung. Ökologie und mittelpaläolithische Funde der letzen Eiszeit. *Veröffentlichungen des Landes museums für Vorgeschichte in Halle* 26:1–164. Verlag der Wissenschaften.

Mania, D., and E. Vlcek. 1981. *Homo erectus* in middle Europe: the discovery from Bilzingsleben. In B. A. Sigmon and S. Cybulski, eds. *Homo erectus—papers in honor of Davidson Black*, 133–151. Toronto: University of Toronto Press.

Mankinen, E. A., and G. B. Dalrymple. 1979. Revised geomagnetic polarity time scale for the interval 0–5 m.y. B. P. *Journal of Geophysical Research* 84:615–626.

Mann, A. E. 1975. Paleodemographic aspects of the South African australopithecines. *University of Pennsylvania Publications in Anthropology* 1:1–171.

Marks, A. E. 1968a. The Khormusan: an Upper Pleistocene industry in Sudanese Nubia. In F. Wendorf, ed. *The prehistory of Nubia*, vol. 1, 315–391. Dallas: Southern Methodist University Press.

———. 1968b. The Mousterian industries of Nubia. In F. Wendorf, ed. *The prehistory of Nubia*, vol. 1, 194–314. Dallas: Southern Methodist University Press.

———. 1977. Introduction: a preliminary overview of Central Negev prehistory. In A. E. Marks, ed. *Prehistory and Paleoenvironments in the central Negev, Israel*, vol. 2, 3–34. Dallas: Department of Anthropology, Southern Methodist University.

———. 1981a. The Middle Palaeolithic of the Negev, Israel. In J. Cauvin and P. Sanlaville, eds. *Préhistoire du Levant*, 287–298. Paris: Centre National de la Recherche Scientifique.

———. 1981b. The Upper Paleolithic of the Negev. In J. Cauvin and P. Sanlaville, eds. *Préhistoire du Levant*, 343–352. Paris: Centre National de la Recherche Scientifique.

———. 1983. The Middle to Upper Paleolithic transition in the Levant. *Advances in World Archaeology* 2:51–98.

Marks, A. E., and D. A. Freidel. 1977. Prehistoric settlement patterns in the Avdat/Aqev area. In A. E. Marks, ed. *Prehistory and Paleoenvironments in the Central Negev, Israel*, vol. 2, 131–

158. Dallas: Department of Anthropology, Southern Methodist University.

Marshack, A. 1972a. *The roots of civilization.* New York: McGraw-Hill.

Marshack, A. 1972b. Upper Paleolithic notation and symbol. *Science* 178:817–828.

———. 1976. Implications of the Paleolithic symbolic evidence for the origin of language. *American Scientist* 64:136–145.

Marshall, F. 1986. Implications of bone modification in a Neolithic faunal assemblage for the study of early hominid butchery and subsistence practices. *Journal of Human Evolution* 15:661–672.

Martin, L. 1985. Significance of enamel thickness in hominoid evolution. *Nature* 314:260–263.

Martin, L., and P. Andrews. 1982. New ideas on the relationships of the Miocene hominoids. *Primate Eye* 18:4–7.

Martin, P. S. 1984. Prehistoric overkill: the global model. In P. S. Martin and R. G. Klein, eds. *Quaternary extinctions: a prehistoric revolution,* 354–403. Tucson: University of Arizona Press.

Martin, R. D. 1986. Primates: a definition. In B. Wood, L. Martin, and P. Andrews, eds. *Major topics in primate and human evolution,* 1–31. Cambridge: University of Cambridge Press.

———. 1988. Several steps forward for Eocene primates. *Nature* 331:660–661.

Martinson, D. G., N. G. Pisias, J. D. Hays, J. Imbrie, T. C. Moore, Jr., and N. J. Shackleton. 1987. Age dating and the orbital theory of the ice ages: development of a high-resolution 300,000 year chronostratigraphy. *Quaternary Research* 27:1–29.

Mason, R. J. 1962. *Prehistory of the Transvaal.* Johannesburg: University of the Witwatersrand Press.

Matsuda, T., M. Torii, T. Koyaguchi, T. Makinouchi, H. Mitsushio, and S. Ishida. 1986. Geochronology of Miocene hominids east of the Kenya Rift Valley. In J. G. Else and P. C. Lee, eds. *Primate evolution,* 35–45. Cambridge: Cambridge University Press.

Matsu'ura, S. 1986. Age of the early Javanese hominids: a review. In J. G. Else and P. C. Lee, eds. *Primate-evolution,* 115–121. Cambridge: Cambridge University Press.

Mayr, E. 1950. Taxonomic categories in fossil hominids. *Cold Spring Harbor Symposia on Quantitative Biology* 15:109–118.

Mehlman, M. J. 1977. Excavations at Nasera Rock, Tanzania. *Azania* 12:111–118.

———. 1979. Mumba-Höhle revisited: the relevance of a forgotten excavation to some current issues in East African prehistory. *World Archaeology* 11:80–94.

———. 1984. Archaic *Homo sapiens* at Lake Eyasi, Tanzania: recent misinterpretations. *Journal of Human Evolution* 13:487–501.

———. 1987. Provenience, age, and associations of archaic *Homo sapiens* crania from Lake Eyasi, Tanzania. *Journal of Archaeological Science* 14:133–162.

Mellars, P. A. 1965. Sequence and development of Mousterian traditions in South-western France. *Nature* 205:626–627.

———. 1970. The chronology of Mousterian industries in the Périgord region of South-West France. *Proceedings of the Prehistoric Society* 35:134–171.

———. 1973. The character of the Middle-Upper Palaeolithic transition in south-west France. In C. Renfrew, ed. *The explanation of culture change*, 255–276. Pittsburgh: University of Pittsburgh Press.

———. 1982. On the Middle/Upper Palaeolithic transition: a reply to White. *Current Anthropology* 23:238–240.

———. 1986. A new chronology for the Mousterian period. *Nature* 322:410–411.

———. In press. Chronological structure in the French Mousterian: a review of the current evidence. In P. Mellars and C. Stringer, eds. *The human revolution: behavioural and biological perspectives on the origins of modern humans.* Edinburgh: Edinburgh University Press.

Mercer, J. H. 1983. Cenozoic glaciation in the southern hemisphere. *Annual Review of Earth and Planetary Sciences* 11:99–132.

Merrick, H. V., and J. P. S. Merrick. 1976. Archaeological occurrences of earlier Pleistocene age from the Shungura Formation. In Y. Coppens, F. C. Howell, G. Ll. Isaac, and R. E. F. Leakey, eds. *Earliest man and environments in the Lake Rudolf Basin*, 574–584. Chicago: University of Chicago Press.

Miller, K. G., and R. G. Fairbanks. 1985. Cainozoic $\partial^{18}O$ record of climate and sea level. *South African Journal of Science* 81:248–249.

Miller, S. 1979. Lukenya Hill, GvJm 46, excavation report. *Nyame Akuma* 14:31–34.

Molleson, T. I. 1976. Remains of Pleistocene man in Paviland and Pontnewydd Caves, Wales. *Transactions of the British Cave Research Association* 3:112–116.

Morbeck, M. E. 1983. Miocene hominoid discoveries from Rudabánya: implications from the postcranial skeleton. In R. L. Ciochon and R. S. Corruccini, eds. *New interpretations of ape and human ancestry*, 369–404. New York: Plenum.

Morlan, R. E. 1987. The Pleistocene archaeology of Beringia. In M. H. Nitecki and D. V. Nitecki, eds. *The evolution of human hunting*, 267–307. New York: Plenum.

Moss, E. 1987. A review of "Investigating microwear polishes with blind tests." *Journal of Archaeological Science* 14:473–482.

Movius, H. L. 1944. Early man and Pleistocene stratigraphy in southern and eastern Asia. *Papers of the Peabody Museum* 19(3): 1–125.

———. 1948. The Lower Palaeolithic cultures of southern and eastern Asia. *Transactions of the American Philosophical Society* 38(4): 329–420.

———. 1949. Lower Paleolithic archaeology in southern and eastern Asia. *Studies in Physical Anthropology* 1:17–81.

———. 1950. A wooden spear of third interglacial age from lower Saxony. *Southwestern Journal of Anthropology* 6:139–142.

———. 1953. Palaeolithic and Mesolithic sites in Soviet Central Asia. *Proceedings of the American Philosophical Society* 97: 383–421.

———. 1955. Palaeolithic archaeology in southern and eastern Asia, exclusive of India. *Cahiers d'Histoire Mondiale* 2(2): 257–282.

———. 1969a. The Abri de Cro-Magnon, Les Eyzies (Dordogne), and the probable age of the contained burials on the basis of the nearby Abri Pataud. *Anuario de Estudios Atlanticos* 15:323–344.

_____. 1969b. The Châtelperronian in French archaeology: the evidence of Arcy-sur-Cure. *Antiquity* 43:111–123.

Mturi, A. A. 1976. New hominid from Lake Ndutu, Tanzania. *Nature* 262:484–485.

Murray, P. 1984. Extinctions Downunder: a bestiary of extinct Australian late Pleistocene monotremes and marsupials. In P. S. Martin and R. G. Klein, eds. *Quaternary extinctions: a prehistoric revolution*, 600–628. Tuscon: University of Arizona Press.

Musil, R., and K. Valoch. 1969. Stránská Skála: its meaning for Pleistocene studies. *Current Anthropology* 9:534–539.

Naeser, N. D., and C. W. Naeser. 1984. Fission-track dating. In W. C. Mahaney, ed. *Quaternary dating methods*, 87–100. Amsterdam: Elsevier, Nagatoshi, K. 1987. Miocene hominoid environments of Europe and Turkey. *Palaeogeography, Palaeoclimatology, Palaeoecology* 61:145–154.

Napier, J. R., and P. H. Napier. 1967. *A handbook of living Primates.* New York: Academic Press.

Nicolaeşçu-Plopsor, L. S., and D. Nicolaeşçu-Plopsor. 1963. The possible existence of Proto-Hominids in Romania's Villafranchian. *Dacia* 7 (n. s.): 9–25.

Ninkovich, D., L. H. Burckle, and N. D. Opdyke. 1982. Palaeogeographic and geologic setting for early man in Java. In R. A. Scrutton and M. Talwani, eds. *The ocean floor*, 221–225. New York: Wiley and Sons.

Oakley, K. P. 1959. *Man the tool-maker.* Chicago: University of Chicago Press.

_____. 1964. The Problem of man's antiquity: an historical survey. *Bulletin of the British Museum (Natural History) Geology* 9(5):86–155.

_____. 1969. Analytical methods of dating bones. In D. Brothwell and E. Higgs, eds. *Science in archaeology*, 35–45. London: Thames and Hudson.

_____. 1980. Relative dating of the fossil hominids of Europe. *Bulletin of the British Museum (Natural History) (Geology)* 34:1–63.

Oakley, K. P., B. G. Campbell, and T. I. Molleson. 1971. *Catalogue of fossil hominids. Part II: Europe.* London: The British Museum (Natural History).

O'Connell, J. F., K. Hawkes, and K. Blurton Jones. 1988. Hadza scavenging: implications for Plio/Pleistocene hominid subsistence. *Current Anthropology* 29:356–363.

Ohel, M. Y. 1977. The Clactonian: reexamined, redefined, and reinterpreted. *Current Anthropology* 18:329–331.

_____. 1979. The Clactonian: an independent complex or an integral part of the Acheulian. *Current Anthropology* 20: 685–726.

Olsen, J. W. 1987. Recent developments in the Upper Pleistocene prehistory of China. In O. Soffer, ed. *The Pleistocene Old World: regional perspectives*, 135–146. New York: Plenum.

Olson, S. L., and D. T. Rasmussen. 1986. Paleoenvironment of the earliest hominids: new evidence from the Oligocene avifauna of Egypt. *Science* 233:1202–1204.

Olson, T. R. 1981. Basicranial morphology of the extant hominoids and Pliocene hominids: the new material from the Hadar Formation, Ethiopia, and its significance in early human evolution and taxonomy. In C. B. Stringer, ed. *Aspects of human evolution*, 99–128. London: Taylor and Francis.

———. 1985. Cranial morphology and systematics of the Hadar Formation hominids and *"Australopithecus" africanus*. In E. Delson, ed. *Ancestors: the hard evidence*, 102–119. New York: Alan R. Liss.

Owen, R. C. 1984. The Americas: the case against an ice-age human population. In F. H. Smith and F. Spencer, eds. *The origins of modern humans: a world survey of the fossil evidence*, 517–563. New York: Alan R. Liss.

Papamarinopoulos, S., P. W. Readman, Y. Maniatis, and A. Simopoulos. 1987. Palaeomagnetic and mineral magnetic studies of sediments from Petralona Cave, Greece. *Archaeometry* 29:50–59.

Partridge, T. C. 1973. Geomorphological dating of cave opening at Makapansgat, Sterkfontein, Swartkrans, and Taung. *Nature* 246:75–79.

———. 1978. Re-appraisal of lithostratigraphy of Sterkfontein hominid site. *Nature* 275:282–287.

———. 1979. Re-appraisal of lithostratigraphy of Makapansgat Limeworks hominid site. *Nature* 279:484–488.

———. 1982a. The chronological positions of the fossil hominids of southern Africa. In M. A. de Lumley, ed. *L'Homo erectus et la place de l'homme de Tautavel parmi les hominidés fossiles*, 617–675. Nice: Ier Congrès International de Paléontologie Humaine.

———. 1982b. Some preliminary observations on the stratigraphy and sedimentology of the Kromdraai B hominid site. *Palaeoecology of Africa* 15:3–12.

———. 1985. Spring flow and tufa accretion at Taung. In P. V. Tobias, ed. *Hominid evolution: past, present and future*, 171–187. New York: Alan R. Liss.

———. 1986. Palaeoecology of the Pliocene and Lower Pleistocene hominids of Southern Africa: how good is the chronological and palaeoenvironmental evidence? *South African Journal of Science* 82:80–83.

Peabody, F. E. 1954. Travertines and cave deposits of the Kaap Escarpment of South Africa and the type locality of *Australopithecus africanus* Dart. *Bulletin of the Geological Society of America* 65:671–706.

Pei, W. C. 1939. The Upper Cave industry of Choukoutien. *Palaeontologica Sinica* 9 (n.s. D), 1–41.

Pei, W., and S. Zhang. 1985. A study on lithic artifacts of *Sinanthropus Palaeontologia Sinica* 168(n.s.): 1–277 (English summary, pp. 259–277).

Penck, A., and E. Bruckner. 1909. *Die Alpen im Eiszeitalter*. Leipzig: Tachnitz.

Perlés, C. 1976. Le feu. In H. de Lumley, ed. *La Préhistoire française*, vol. 1, 679–683. Paris: Centre National de la Recherche Scientifique.

Phillipson, D. W. 1976. *The prehistory of eastern Zambia*. Nairobi: British Institute in Eastern Africa.

Pickford, M. 1983. Sequence and environments of the Lower and Middle Miocene hominoids of Western Kenya. In R. L. Ciochon and R. S. Corruccini, eds. *New interpretations of ape and human ancestry*, 421–439. New York: Plenum.

_____. 1985. *Kenyapithecus:* a review of its status based on newly discovered fossils from Kenya. In P. V. Tobias, ed. *Hominid evolution: past,* present and future, 107–112. New York: Alan R. Liss.

_____. 1986a. The geochronology of Miocene higher primate faunas of East Africa. In J. G. Else and P. C. Lee, eds. *Primate evolution,* 19–33. Cambridge: Cambridge University Press.

_____. 1986b. A reappraisal of *Kenyapithecus.* In J. G. Else and P. C. Lee, eds. *Primate evolution,* 163–171. Cambridge: Cambridge University Press.

Pickford, M., D. C. Johanson, C. O. Lovejoy, T. D. White, and J. L. Aronson. 1983. A hominoid humeral fragment from the Pliocene of Kenya. *American Journal of Physical Anthropology* 60:337–346.

Pidoplichko, I. G. 1969. *Upper Paleolithic mammoth bone dwellings in the Ukraine* (in Russian). Kiev: Naukova Dumka.

Pilbeam, D. R. 1983. New hominoid skull material from the Miocene of Pakistan. *Nature* 295:232–234.

_____. 1985. Patterns of hominoid evolution. In E. Delson, ed. *Ancestors: the hard evidence,* 51–59. New York: Alan R. Liss.

_____. 1986. Hominoid evolution and hominoid origins. *American Anthropologist* 88:295–312.

Pope, G. G. 1983. Evidence on the age of the Asian hominidae. *Proceedings of the National Academy of Sciences* 80:4988–4992.

_____. 1985. Taxonomy, dating and paleoenvironment: the paleo-ecology of the early Far Eastern hominids. *Modern Quaternary Research in Southeast Asia* 9:65–80.

Pope, G. G., S. Barr, A. Macdonald, and S. Nakabanlang. 1986. Earliest radiometrically dated artifacts from Southeast Asia. *Current Anthropology* 27:275–279.

Pope, G. G., and J. E. Cronin. 1984. The Asian Hominidae. *Journal of Human Evolution* 13:377–396.

Potts, R. B. 1982. *Lower Pleistocene site formation and hominid activities at Olduvai Gorge, Tanzania.* Unpublished Ph.D. dissertation, Harvard University.

_____. 1984. Home bases and early hominids. *American Scientist* 72:338–347.

_____. 1986. Temporal span of bone accumulations at Olduvai Gorge and implications for early hominid foraging behavior. *Paleobiology* 12:25–31.

Potts, R. B., and P. Shipman. 1981. Cutmarks made by stone tools on bones from Olduvai Gorge, Tanzania. *Nature* 291:577–580.

Potts, R. B., P. Shipman, and E. Ingsall. 1988. Taphonomy, paleoecology, and hominids at Lainyamok, Kenya. *Journal of Human Evolution* 17:597–614.

Prell, W. L., J. V. Gardner, et al. 1982. Oxygen and carbon isotope stratigraphy for the Quaternary of Hole 502B: evidence for two modes of isotopic variability. *Initial Reports of the Deep Sea Drilling Project* 68:455–464.

Price, J. L., and T. I. Molleson. 1974. A radiographic examination of the left temporal bone of Kabwe Man, Broken Hill Mine, Zambia. *Journal of Archeological Science* 1:285–289.

Qiu, Zhonglang. 1985. The Middle Palaeolithic of China. In R. Wu and J. Olsen, eds. *Palaeoanthropology and Palaeolithic archaeology in the People's Republic of China,* 187–210. Orlando, Fla.: Academic Press.

Radinsky, L. B. 1975. Primate brain evolution. *American Scientist* 63:656–663.

———. 1977. Early primate brains: facts and fiction. *Journal of Human Evolution* 6:79–86.

Rak, Y. 1983. *The australopithecine face.* New York: Academic Press.

———. 1985. Systematic and functional implications of the facial morphology of *Australopithecus* and early *Homo.* In E. Delson, ed. *Ancestors: the hard evidence,* 168–170. New York: Alan R. Liss.

———. 1986. The Neanderthal: a new look at an old face. *Journal of Human Evolution* 15:151–164.

Rak, Y., and B. Arensburg. 1987. Kebara 2 Neanderthal pelvis: first look at a complete inlet. *American Journal of Physical Anthropology* 73:227–231.

Rasmussen, D. T. 1986. Anthropoid origins: a possible solution to the Adapidae-Omomyidae paradox. *Journal of Human Evolution* 15:1–12.

Raza, S. M., J. C. Barry, D. Pilbeam, M. D. Rose, S. M. Ibrahim Shah, and S. Ward. 1983. New hominoid primates from the middle Miocene Chinji Formation, Potwar Plateau, Pakistan. *Nature* 306:52–54.

Rendell, H., and R. W. Dennell. 1985. Dated Lower Palaeolithic artefacts from northern Pakistan. *Current Anthropology* 26:393.

Repenning, C. A. 1980. Faunal exchanges between Siberia and North America. *Canadian Journal of Anthropology* 1:37–44.

Reynolds, T. E. G. 1985. The early Palaeolithic of Japan. *Antiquity* 59:93–96.

Reynolds, T. E. G., and G. L. Barnes. 1984. The Japanese Palaeolithic: a review. *Proceedings of the Prehistoric Society* 50:49–62.

Richard, A. F. 1985. *Primates in nature.* New York: W. H. Freeman.

Rightmire, G. P. 1976. Relationships of Middle and Upper Pleistocene hominids from sub-Saharan Africa. *Nature* 260:238–240.

———. 1979a. Cranial remains of *Homo erectus* from Beds II and IV, Olduvai Gorge, Tanzania. *American Journal of Physical Anthropology* 51:99–115.

———. 1979b. Implications of the Border Cave skeletal remains for later Pleistocene human evolution. *Current Anthropology* 20:23–35.

———. 1980. *Homo erectus* and human evolution in the African Middle Pleistocene. In L.-K. Königsson, ed. *Current argument on early man,* 70–85. Oxford, Pergamon.

———. 1981a. Late Pleistocene hominids of Eastern and Southern Africa. *Anthropologie* (Brno) 19:15–26.

———. 1981b. Patterns in the evolution of *Homo erectus. Paleobiology* 7:241–246.

—— . 1983. The Lake Ndutu cranium and early *Homo sapiens* in Africa. *American Journal of Physical Anthropology* 61:245–254.

—— . 1984a. Comparisons of *Homo erectus* from Africa and Southeast Asia. *Courier Forschungsinstitut Senckenberg* 69:83–98.

—— . 1984b. *Homo sapiens* in Sub-Saharan Africa. In F. H. Smith and F. Spencer, eds. *The origin of modern humans: a world survey of the fossil evidence*, 295–325. New York: Alan R. Liss.

—— . 1985. The tempo of change in the evolution of mid-Pleistocene *Homo*. In E. Delson, ed. *Ancestors: the hard evidence*, 255–264. New York: Alan R. Liss.

—— . 1986. Species recognition and *Homo erectus*. *Journal of Human Evolution* 15:823–826.

—— . 1987. Africa and the origin of modern humans. In R. Singer and J. K. Lundy, eds. *Variation, culture and evolution in African populations: papers in honour of Dr. Hertha de Villiers*, 209–220. Johannesburg: Witwatersrand University Press.

—— . 1988. *Homo erectus* and later middle Pleistocene humans. *Annual Review of Anthropology* 17:239–259.

Roberts, M. B., M. R. Bates, C. Bergman, A. Currant, J. R. Haynes, R. Macphail, A. McConnell, R. Scaife, R. Unger-Hamilton, and R. C. Whatley. 1986. Excavation of the Lower Palaeolithic site at Amey's Eartham Pit, Boxgrove, West Sussex: a preliminary report. *Proceedings of the Prehistoric Society* 52:215–245.

Roberts, N. 1984. Pleistocene environments in time and space. In R. Foley, ed. *Hominid evolution and community ecology*, 25–53. London: Academic Press.

Robinson, J. T. 1954. Prehominid dentition and hominid evolution. *Evolution* 8:324–334.

—— . 1963. Adaptive radiation in the australopithecines and the origin of man. In F. C. Howell and F. Bourlière, eds. *African ecology and human evolution*, 385–416. Chicago: Aldine.

Roche, J., and J. -P. Texier. 1976. Découverte des restes humains dans un niveau atérien supérieur de la grotte des Contrabandiers, à Témara (Maroc). *Comptes Rendus des Séances de l'Académie des Sciences (Paris)*, Série D, 282:45–47.

Rodman, P. S., and H. M. McHenry. 1980. Energetics and the origin of hominid bipedalism. *American Journal of Physical Anthropology:* 52:103–106.

Roe, D. A. 1981. *The Lower and Middle Palaeolithic periods in Britain*. London: Routledge and Kegan Paul.

Roper, M. K. 1969. A survey of the evidence for intrahuman killing in the Pleistocene. *Current Anthropology* 10:427–459.

Rosas, A. 1987. Two new mandibular fragments from Atapuerca/Ibeas (SH site): a reassessment of the affinities of the Ibeas mandibles. *Journal of Human Evolution* 16:417–429.

Rose, K. D., and J. G. Fleagle. 1981. The fossil history of non-human primates in the Americas. In A. F. Coimbra-Filho and R. A. Mittermeier, eds. *Ecology and behavior of neotropical Primates*, vol. 1, 111–167. Rio de Janeiro: Academia Brasileira de Ciencias.

Rose, K. D., and A. C. Walker. 1985. The skeleton of early Eocene *Cantius*, oldest lemuriform primate. *American Journal of Physical Anthropology* 66:73–89.

Rose, M. D. 1983. Miocene hominoid postcranial morphology: monkey-like, ape-like, neither or both? In R. L. Ciochon and

R. S. Corruccini, eds. *New interpretations of ape and human ancestry*, 405–417. New York: Plenum.

———. 1984. Hominoid postcranial specimens from the Middle Miocene Chinji Formation, Pakistan. *Journal of Human Evolution* 13:503–516.

———. 1986. Further hominoid postcranial specimens from the late Miocene Nagri Formation of Pakistan. *Journal of Human Evolution* 15:333–367.

Rosenberg, K. R. 1985. Neanderthal birth canals (abstract). *American Journal of Physical Anthropology* 66:222.

———. 1986. *The functional significance of Neandertal pubic morphology.* Ph. D. dissertation, University of Michigan.

Rosenberger, A. L. 1986. Platyrrhines, catarrhines and the anthropoid transition. In B. Wood, L. Martin, and P. Andrews, eds. *Major topics in primate and human evolution,* 66–88. Cambridge: University of Cambridge Press.

Rosenberger, A. L., and E. Delson. 1985. The dentition of *Oreopithecus bambolii:* systematic and paleobiological implications. *American Journal of Physical Anthropology* 66:222–223.

Rosenberger, A. L., and F. S. Szalay. 1980. On the Tarsiiform origins of Anthropoidea. In R. L. Ciochon and A. B. Chiarelli, eds. *Evolutionary biology of the New World monkeys and continental drift,* 139–157. New York: Plenum.

Roubet, F. -E. 1969. Le niveau atérien dans la stratigraphie côtière à l'Ouest d'Alger. *Palaeoecology of Africa* 4:124–129.

Rucklidge, J. C. 1984. Radioisotope detection and dating with particle accelerators. In W. C. Mahaney, ed. *Quaternary dating methods,* 17–32. Amsterdam: Elsevier.

Russell, D. E., and P. D. Gingerich. 1987. Nouveaux Primates de l'Éocene du Pakistan. *Comptes Rendus de l'Académie des Sciences (Paris),* Série D, 304:209–214.

Russell, M. D. 1985. The supraorbital torus: "a most remarkable peculiarity." *Current Anthropology* 26:337–360.

———. 1987a. Bone breakage in the Krapina hominid collection. *American Journal of Physical Anthropology* 72:373–380.

———. 1987b. Mortuary practices at the Krapina Neandertal site. *American Journal of Physical Anthropology* 72:381–398.

Rutter, N. W. 1980. Late Pleistocene history of the Western Canadian ice-free corridor. *Canadian Journal of Anthropology* 1:1–8.

Saban, R. 1977. The place of Rabat Man (Kébibat, Morocco) in human evolution. *Current Anthropology* 18:518–524.

Sampson, C. G. 1974. *The Stone Age archaeology of southern Africa.* New York: Academic Press.

Santa Luca, A. P. 1978. A re-examination of presumed Neanderthal fossils. *Journal of Human Evolution* 7:619–636.

———. 1980. The Ngandong fossil hominids. *Yale University Publications in Anthropology* 78:1–175.

Sarich, V. M. 1971. A molecular approach to the question of human origins. In P. Dolhinow and V. M. Sarich, eds. *Background for man,* 60–81. Boston: Little, Brown.

———. 1983. Retrospective on hominoid macromolecular systematics. In R. L. Ciochon and R. S. Corruccini, eds. *New interpretations of ape and human ancestry,* 137–150. New York: Plenum.

Sarich, V. M., and J. E. Cronin. 1980. South American mammal molecular systematics, evolutionary clocks, and continental drift. In R. L. Ciochon and A. B. Chiarelli, eds. *Evolutionary biology of the New World monkeys and continental drift*, 399–421. New York: Plenum.

Sarich, V. M., and A. C. Wilson. 1967. Immunological time scale for hominid evolution. *Science* 158:1200–1203.

Sarna-Wojcicki, A. M., C. E. Meyer, P. H. Roth, and F. H. Brown. 1985. Ages of tuff beds at East African early hominid sites and sediments in the Gulf of Aden. *Nature* 313:306–308.

Sartono, S. 1975. Implications arising from *Pithecanthropus* VIII. In R. H. Tuttle, ed. *Paleoanthropology, morphology and paleoecology*, 327–360. The Hague: Mouton.

Savage, D. E., and D. E. Russell. 1983. *Mammalian paleofaunas of the world*. Reading, Mass.: Addison-Wesley.

Schild, R. 1984. Terminal Paleolithic of the north European plain: a review of lost chances, potential and hopes. *Advances in World Archaeology* 3:193–274.

Schmitt, T. J., and A. E. M. Nairn. 1984. Interpretations of the magnetostratigraphy of the Hadar hominid site, Ethiopia. *Nature* 309:704–706.

Schultz, A. H. 1969. *The life of Primates*. New York: Universe.

Schwarcz, H. P. 1980. Absolute age determination of archaeological sites by uranium series dating of travertines. *Archaeometry* 22:3–24.

Schwarcz, H. P., and M. Gascoyne. 1984. Uranium-series dating of Quaternary sediments. In W. C. Mahaney, ed. *Quaternary dating methods*, 33–51. Amsterdam: Elsevier.

Schwarcz, H. P., R. Grün, A. G. Latham, D. Mania, and K. Brunnacker. 1988. The Bilzingsleben archaeological site: new dating evidence. *Archaeometry* 30:5–17.

Schwarcz, H. P., and A. G. Latham. 1984. Uranium-series age determination of travertines from the site of Vértesszöllös, Hungary. *Journal of Archaeological Science* 11:327–336.

Schwartz, J. H., and I. Tattersall. 1987. Tarsiers, adapids, and the integrity of Strepsirhini. *Journal of Human Evolution* 16:23–40.

Scott, K. 1980. Two hunting episodes of Middle Palaeolithic Age at La Cotte de Saint-Brelade, Jersey (Channel Islands). *World Archaeology* 12:137–152.

———. 1986. The large mammal fauna. In P. Callow and J. M. Cornford, eds. *La Cotte de Saint Brelade 1961–1978: excavations by C. B. M. McBurney*, 109–138. Norwich, United Kingdom: Geo.

Segre, A., and A. Ascenzi. 1984. Fontana Ranuccio: Italy's earliest Middle Pleistocene hominid site. *Current Anthropology* 25:230–233.

Semah, F. 1984. The Sangiran Dome in the Javanese Plio-Pleistocene chronology. *Courier Forschungsinstitut Senckenberg* 69:245–252.

Semenov, S. A. 1964. *Prehistoric technology* (translated from Russian by M. W. Thompson). New York: Barnes and Noble.

Senut, B., and C. Tardieu. 1985. Functional aspects of Plio-Pleistocene hominid limb bones: implications for taxonomy and phylogeny. In E. Delson, ed. *Ancestors: the hard evidence*, 193–201. New York: Alan R. Liss.

Seuss, H. E. 1986. Secular variations of cosmogenic ^{14}C on earth: their discovery and interpretation. *Radiocarbon* 28:259–265.

Shackleton, N. J. 1967. Oxygen isotope analyses and Pleistocene temperatures re-assessed. *Nature* 215:15–17.

———. 1975. The stratigraphic record of deep-sea cores and its implications for the assessment of glacials, interglacials, stadials, and interstadials in the Mid-Pleistocene. In K. W. Butzer and G. Ll. Isaac, eds. *After the australopithecines*, 1–24. The Hague: Mouton.

———. 1986. Paleogene stable isotope events. *Palaeogeography, Palaeoclimatology, Palaeoecology* 57:91–102.

———. 1987. Oxygen isotopes, ice volume, and sea level. *Quaternary Science Reviews* 6:183–190.

Shackleton, N. J., J. Backman, H. Zimmerman, D. V. Kent, M. A. Hall, D. G. Roberts, D. Schnitker, J. G. Baldauf, A. Desprairies, R. Homrighausen, P. Huddlestun, J. B. Keene, J. Kaltenback, K. A. O. Krumsiek, A. C. Morton, J. W. Murray, and J. Westberg-Smith, 1984. Oxygen isotope calibration of the onset of ice-rafting and history of glaciation in the North Atlantic region. *Nature* 307:620–623.

Shackleton, N. J., and J. P. Kennett. 1975. Paleotemperature history of the Cenozoic and the initiation of Antarctic glaciation: oxygen and carbon isotope analysis in DSDP sites 277, 279, and 281. *Initial Reports of the Deep Sea Drilling Project* 29:743–755.

Shackleton, N. J., and N. Opdyke. 1973. Oxygen isotope and palaeomagnetic stratigraphy of equatorial Pacific core V28-238. *Quaternary Research* 3:39–55.

———. 1976. Oxygen-isotope and palaeomagnetic stratigraphy of Pacific core V28-239: late Pliocene to latest Pleistocene. *Geological Society of American Bulletin* 145:449–464.

———. 1977. Oxygen isotope and palaeomagnetic evidence for early Northern Hemisphere glaciation. *Nature* 270:216–219.

Shapiro, H. L. 1971. The strange, unfinished saga of Peking Man. *Natural History* 80(9): 8–18, 74, 76–77.

———. 1974. *Peking man.* New York: Simon and Schuster.

Shipman, P. 1984a. The earliest tools: re-assessing the evidence from Olduvai Gorge. *Anthroquest* 29:9–10.

———. 1984b. Scavenger hunt. *Natural History* 93(4): 20–27.

———. 1986a. Baffling limb on the family tree. *Discover* 7(9): 87–93 and 7(11): 116.

———. 1986b. Scavenging or hunting in early hominids: theoretical framework and tests. *American Anthropologist* 88:27–43.

———. 1986c. Studies of hominid-faunal interactions at Olduvai Gorge. *Journal of Human Evolution* 15:691–706.

———. In press. Altered bones from Olduvai Gorge, Tanzania: techniques, problems, and implications of their recognition. In M. Sorg, ed. *Bone modification.* Orono, Me.: Center for the Study of Early Man.

Shipman, P., W. Bosler, and K. L. Davis. 1981. Butchering of giant geladas at an Acheulian site. *Current Anthropology* 22:257–268.

Shipman, P., R. Potts, and M. Pickford. 1983. Lainyamok, a new middle Pleistocene hominid site. *Nature* 306:365–368.

Shipman, P., and J. Rose. 1983. Early hominid hunting, butchering, and carcass-processing behaviors: approaches to the fossil record. *Journal of Anthropological Archaeology* 2:57–98.

Sibley, C. G., and J. E. Ahlquist. 1984. The phylogeny of the hominoid primates, as indicated by DNA-DNA hybridization. *Journal of Molecular Evolution* 20:2–15.

———. 1987. DNA hybridization evidence of hominoid phylogeny: results from an expanded data set. *Journal of Molecular Evolution* 26:99–121.

Sieveking, A. 1979. *The cave artists.* London: Thames and Hudson.

Sillen, A. 1986. Biogenic and diagenetic Sr/Ca in Plio-Pleistocene fossils in the Omo Shungura Formation. *Paleobiology* 12:311–323.

Simons, E. L. 1967. The earliest apes. *Scientific American* 217(65): 28–35.

———. 1972. *Primate evolution: an introduction to man's place in nature.* New York: Macmillan.

———. 1981. Man's immediate forerunners. *Philosophical Transactions of the Royal Society (London)* B 292:21–41.

———. 1984. Dawn ape of the Fayum. *Natural History* 93(5): 18–20.

———. 1985. Origins and characteristics of the first hominoids. In E. Delson, ed. *Ancestors: the hard evidence,* 37–41. New York: Alan R. Liss.

———. 1986. *Parapithecus grangeri* of the African Oligocene: an archaic catarrhine without lower incisors. *Journal of Human Evolution* 15:205–213.

———. 1987. New faces of *Aegyptopithecus* from the Oligocene of Egypt. *Journal of Human Evolution* 16:273–289.

Simons, E. L., T. M. Bown, and D. T. Rasmussen. 1986. Discovery of two additional prosimian primate families (Omomyidae, Lorisidae) in the African Oligocene. *Journal of Human Evolution* 15:431–437.

Simons, E. L., D. T. Rasmussen, and D. L. Gebo. 1987. A new species of *Propliopithecus* from the Fayum, Egypt. *American Journal of Physical Anthropology* 73:139–148.

Simpson, G. G. 1955. The Phenacolemuridae, a new family of early Primates. *Bulletin of the American Museum of Natural History* 85:1–350.

———. 1961. *Principles of animal taxonomy.* New York: Columbia University Press.

Sinclair, A. R. E., M. D. Leakey, and M. Norton-Griffiths. 1986. Migration and hominid bipedalism. *Nature* 324:307–308.

Singer, R., and J. J. Wymer. 1968. Archaeological investigations at the Saldanha skull site in South Africa. *South African Archaeological Bulletin* 25:63–74.

———. 1976. The sequence of Acheulian industries at Hoxne, Suffolk. In J. Combier, ed. *L'Évolution de l'Acheuléen en Europe,* 14–30. Nice: Union International des Sciences Préhistoriques et Protohistoriques (Colloque X).

———. 1982. *The Middle Stone Age at Klasies River Mouth in South Africa.* Chicago: University of Chicago Press.

Singer, R., J. J. Wymer, B. G. Gladfelter, and R. G. Wolff. 1973. Excavation of the Clactonian Industry at the golf course, Clacton-on-Sea, Essex. *Proceedings of the Prehistoric Society* 39:6–74.

Smith, B. H. 1986. Dental development in *Australopithecus* and early *Homo. Nature* 323:327–330.

Smith, F. H. 1982. Upper Pleistocene hominid evolution in south-central Europe: a review of the evidence and analysis of trends. *Current Anthropology* 23:667–703.

———. 1983. Behavioral interpretation of changes in craniofacial morphology across the archaic/modern *Homo sapiens* transition. *British Archaeological Reports International Series* 164:141–163.

———. 1984. Fossil hominids from the Upper Pleistocene of central Europe and the origin of modern Europeans. In F. H. Smith and F. Spencer, eds. *The origins of modern humans: a world survey of the fossil evidence,* 137–209. New York: Alan R. Liss.

Smith, P., and B. Arensburg. 1977. A Mousterian skeleton from Kebara Cave. *Eretz Israel* 13:164–176.

Soffer, O. 1985. *The Upper Paleolithic of the central Russian plain.* Orlando, Fla.: Academic Press.

Solecki, R. S. 1963. Prehistory in Shanidar valley, northern Iraq. *Science* 139: 179–193.

———. 1975. Shanidar IV, a Neanderthal flower burial in northern Iraq. *Science* 190:880–881.

Sommé, J., A. V. Munaut, J. J. Puisségur, and N. Cunat. 1986. Stratigraphie et signification climatique du gisement paléolithique de Biache-Saint-Vaast (Pas-de-Calais, France). In A. Tuffreau and J. Sommé, eds. *Chronostratigraphie et faciés culturels du Paléolithique inférieur et moyen dans l'Europe du Nord-Ouest,* 187–195. Paris: Supplément au Bullétin de l'Association Française pour l'Étude du Quaternaire.

Sonakia, A. 1985. Early *Homo* from Narmada Valley, India. In E. Delson, ed. *Ancestors: the hard evidence,* 334–338. New York: Alan R. Liss.

Sondaar, P. Y. 1984. Faunal evolution and the mammalian biostratigraphy of Java. *Courier Forschungsinstitut Senckenberg* 69:219–235.

Sondaar, P. Y., J. de Vos, and J. J. M. Leinders. 1983. Facts and fiction around the fossil mammals of Java (Reply to Bartstra). *Geologie en Mijnbouw* 62:339–343.

Sonneville-Bordes, D. de. 1963. Upper Paleolithic cultures in western Europe. *Science* 142:347–355.

———. 1973. The Upper Paleolithic: c. 33,000–10,000 B.C. In S. Piggott, G. Daniel, and C. McBurney, eds. *France before the Romans,* 30–60. London: Thames and Hudson.

Sonneville-Bordes, D. de, and J. Perrot. 1954–56. Lexique typologique du Paléolithique supérieur. *Bulletin de la Société Préhistorique Française* 51:327–335; 52:76–79; 53:408–412; and 53:547–549.

Spencer, F. 1984. The Neandertals and their evolutionary significance: a brief historical survey. In F. H. Smith and F. Spencer, eds. *The origins of modern humans: a world survey of the fossil evidence,* 1–49. New York: Alan R. Liss.

Stanley, S. M. 1981. *The new evolutionary timetable.* New York: Basic Books.

Stearns, C. E. 1984. Uranium-series dating and the history of sea level. In W. C. Mahaney, ed. *Quaternary dating methods,* 53–65. Amsterdam: Elsevier.

Stearns, C. E., and D. L. Thurber. 1965. Th^{230}/U^{234} dates of late Pleistocene marine fossils from the Mediterranean and Moroccan littorals. *Quaternaria* 7:29–42.

Stern, J. T., and R. L. Susman. 1983. The locomotor anatomy of *Australopithecus afarenis. American Journal of Physical Anthroplogy* 60:279–317.

Steudel, K. 1980. New estimates of early hominid body size. *American Journal of Physical Anthropology* 52:63–70.

Stewart, T. D. 1960. Form of the pubic bone in Neanderthal man. *Science* 131:1437–1438.

_____. 1962. Neanderthal scapulae with special attention to the Shanidar Neanderthals from Iraq. *Anthropos* 57:781–800.

Stiles, D. N., and T. C. Partridge. 1979. Results of recent archaeological and palaeoenvironmental studies of the Sterkfontein Extension Site. *South African Journal of Science* 75:346–352.

Stordeur-Yedid, D. 1979. *Les aiguilles à chas au Paléolithique.* Paris: Centre National de la Recherche Scientifique (XIIIe supplément à *Gallia Préhistoire.*)

Strasser, E., and E. Delson. 1987. Cladistic analysis of cercopithecid relationships. *Journal of Human Evolution* 16:81–99.

Straus, L. G. 1977. Of deerslayers and mountain men: Paleolithic faunal exploitation in Cantabrian Spain. In L. R. Binford, ed. *For theory building in archaeology,* 41–76. New York: Academic Press.

_____. 1983. From Mousterian to Magdalenian: cultural evolution viewed from Vasco-Cantabrian Spain and Pyrenean France. *British Archaeological Reports International Series* 164:73–111.

_____. 1985. Stone Age prehistory of Northern Spain. *Science* 230:501–507.

_____. 1987. Paradigm lost: a personal view of the current state of Upper Paleolithic research. *Helinium* 27:157–171.

Straus, L. G., and G. Clark. 1986. La Riera Cave: stone age hunter-gatherer adaptations in northern Spain. *Arizona State University Anthropological Research Papers* 36:1–497.

Street, F. A. 1980. Ice Age environments. In A. Sherratt, ed. *The Cambridge encyclopaedia of archaeology,* 52–56. Cambridge: Cambridge University Press.

Stringer, C. B. 1979. A re-evaluation of the fossil human calvaria from Singa, Sudan. *Bulletin of the British Museum of Natural History (Geology)* 32:77–83.

_____. 1982. Comment on "Upper Pleistocene hominid evolution in south-central Europe: a review of the evidence and analysis of trends." *Current Anthropology* 23:690–691.

_____. 1983. Some further notes on the morphology and dating of the Petralona hominid. *Journal of Human Evolution* 12:731–742.

_____. 1984. The definition of *Homo erectus* and the existence of the species in Africa and Europe. *Courier Forschungsinstitut Senckenberg* 69:131–144.

_____. 1985. Middle Pleistocene hominid variability and the origin of late Pleistocene humans. In E. Delson, ed. *Ancestors: the hard evidence,* 289–295. New York: Alan R. Liss.

_____. 1986a. An archaic character in the Broken Hill innominate E. 719. *American Journal of Physical Anthropology* 71:115–120.

_____. 1986b. The credibility of *Homo habilis.* In B. Wood, L. Martin, and P. Andrews, eds. *Major topics in Primate and human evolution,* 266–294. Cambridge: Cambridge University Press.

———. 1986c. Ice Age relation. *The Geographical Magazine* 58:652–656.

———. 1987. A numerical cladistic analysis for the genus *Homo*. *Journal of Human Evolution* 16:135–146.

———. 1988. The dates of Eden. *Nature* 331:565–566.

Stringer, C. B., and P. Andrews. 1988. Genetic and fossil evidence for the origin of modern humans. *Science* 239:1263–1268.

Stringer, C. B., F. C. Howell, and J. K. Melentis. 1979. The significance of the fossil hominid skull from Petralona, Greece. *Journal of Archaeological Science* 6:235–253.

Stringer, C. B., J. J. Hublin, and B. Vandermeersch. 1984. The origin of anatomically modern humans in Western Europe. In F. H. Smith and F. Spencer, eds. *The origin of modern humans: a world survey of the fossil evidence*, 51–135. New York: Alan R. Liss.

Stuart, A. J. 1982. *Pleistocene vertebrates in the British Isles.* London: Longman.

Susman, R. L. 1988. Hand of *Paranthropus robustus* from Member 1, Swartkrans: fossil evidence for tool behavior. *Science* 240:781–784.

Susman, R. L., and J. T. Stern. 1979. Telemetered electromyography of flexor digitorum profundus and flexor digitorum superficialis in *Pan troglodytes* and implications for interpretation of the O. H. 7 hand. *American Journal of Physical Anthropology* 50:565–574.

———. 1982. Functional morphology of *Homo habilis. Science* 217:931–934.

Susman, R. L., J. T. Stern, and W. L. Jungers. 1985. Locomotor adaptations in the Hadar hominids. In E. Delson, ed. *Ancestors: the hard evidence*, 184–192. New York: Alan R. Liss.

Suzuki, H., and F. Takai, eds. 1970. *The Amud Man and his cave site.* Tokyo: The University of Tokyo.

Svoboda, J. 1987. Lithic industries of the Arago, Bilzingsleben, and Vértesszöllös hominids: comparison and evolutionary interpretation. *Current Anthropology* 28:219–227.

Syvanen, M., 1987. Molecular clocks and evolutionary relationships: possible distortions due to horizontal gene flow. *Journal of Molecular Evolution* 26:16–23.

Szalay, F. S. 1972. Paleobiology of the earliest Primates. In R. H. Tuttle, ed. *The functional biology of Primates*, 3–35. Chicago: Aldine-Atherton.

Szalay, F. S., and E. Delson. 1979. *Evolutionary history of the Primates.* New York: Academic Press.

Szalay, F. S., and C. K. Li. 1986. Middle Paleocene Euprimate from southern China and the distribution of Primates in the Paleogene. *Journal of Human Evolution* 15:387–397.

Szalay, F. S., I. Tattersall, and R. L. Decker. 1975. Phylogenetic relationships of *Plesiadapis*—postcranial evidence. *Contributions to Primatology* 5:136–166.

Tague, R. G., and C. O. Lovejoy. 1986. The obstetric pelvis of A. L. 288-1 (Lucy). *Journal of Human Evolution* 15:237–255.

Tallon, P. W. J. 1978. Geological setting of the hominid fossils and Acheulean artifacts from the Kapthurin Formation, Baringo District, Kenya. In W. W. Bishop, ed. *Geological background to fossil man*, 361–373. Toronto: University of Toronto Press.

Tankard, A. J., and F. R. Schweitzer. 1976. Textural analysis of cave sediments: Die Kelders, Cape Province, South Africa. In D. A. Davidson and M. L. Shackley, eds. *Geoarchaeology,* 289–316. London: Duckworth.

Tappen, N. C. 1987. Circum-mortem damage to some ancient African hominid crania: a taphonomic and evolutionary essay. *The African Archaeological Review* 5:39–47.

Tattersall, I. 1986. Species recognition in human paleontology. *Journal of Human Evolution* 15:165–175.

Tauber, H. 1970. The Scandinavian varve chronology and C14 dating. In I. U. Olsson, ed. *Radiocarbon variations and absolute chronology,* 173–195. New York: Wiley.

Tauxe, L., N. D. Opdyke, G. Pasini, and C. Elmi. 1983. Age of the Pliocene-Pleistocene boundary in the Vrica section, southern Italy. *Nature* 304:125–129.

Taylor, R. E., D. J. Donahue, T. H. Zabel, P. E. Damon, and J. T. Jull. 1984. Radiocarbon dating by particle accelerators: an archaeological perspective. *Advances in Chemistry Series* 205:333–356.

Tchernov, E. 1987. The age of the 'Ubeidiya Formation, an early Pleistocene hominid site in the Jordan Valley, Israel. *Israel Journal of Earth Science* 36:3–30.

Teaford, M. F., and A. Walker. 1984. Quantitative differences in dental microwear between primate species with different diets and a comment on the presumed diet of *Sivapithecus. American Journal of Physical Anthropology* 64:191–200.

Temerin, L. A., and J. G. H. Cant. 1983. The evolutionary divergence of Old World monkeys and apes. *The American Naturalist* 122:335–351.

Terasmae, J. 1984. Radiocarbon dating: some problems and potential developments. In W. C. Mahaney, ed. *Quaternary dating methods,* 1–15. Amsterdam: Elsevier.

Teruya, E. 1986. The origins and characteristics of Jomon Ceramic Culture: a brief introduction. In R. J. Pearson, G. L. Barnes, and K. L. Hutterer, eds. *Windows on the Japanese past: studies in archaeology and prehistory,* 223–228. Ann Arbor: Center for Japanese Studies, University of Michigan.

Thieme, H. 1983. Mittelpaläolithische Siedlungsstrukturen in Rheindahlen (BRD). *Ethnographisch-Archäologische Zeitschrift* 24:362–374.

Thissen, J. 1986. Ein weiterer Fundplatz der Westwandfundschicht (B1) von Rheindahlen. *Archäologisches Korrespondenzblatt* 16:111–121.

Thomas, H. 1979. Géologie et paléontologie du gisement acheuléen de l'erg Tihodaïne. *Mémoires du Centre de Recherches Anthropologiques, Préhistoriques et Ethnographiques* 27:1–122.

Thompson, D. D., and E. Trinkaus. 1981. Age determination for the Shanidar 3 Neanderthal. *Science* 212:575–577.

Thorne, A. G. 1977. Separation or reconciliation? biological clues to the development of Australian society. In J. Allen, J. Golson, and R. Jones, eds. *Sunda and Sahul: prehistoric studies in southeast Asia, Melanesia, and Australia,* 197–204. London: Academic Press.

———. 1980. The arrival of man in Australia. In A. Sherratt, ed. *The Cambridge encyclopaedia of archaeology,* 96–100. Cambridge: Cambridge University Press.

Thorne, A. G., and M. H. Wolpoff. 1981. Regional continuity in Australasian Pleistocene hominid evolution. *American Journal of Physical Anthropology* 55:337–349.

Thouveny, N., and E. Bonifay. 1984. New chronological data on European Plio-Pleistocene faunas and hominid occupation sites. *Nature* 308:355–358.

Tobias, P. V. 1967a. *The cranium and maxillary dentition of Australopithecus (Zinjanthropus) boisei. Olduvai Gorge,* vol. 2. Cambridge: Cambridge University Press.

———. 1967b. The hominid skeletal remains of Haua Fteah. In C. B. M. McBurney, ed. *The Haua Fteah (Cyrenaica) and the Stone Age of the south-east Mediterranean,* 338–352. Cambridge: Cambridge University Press.

———. 1971. Human skeletal remains from the Cave of Hearths, Makapansgat, Northern Transvaal. *American Journal of Physical Anthropology* 34:335–368.

———. 1972. Progress and problems in the study of early man in sub-Saharan Africa. In R. H. Tuttle, ed. *The functional and evolutionary biology of Primates,* 63–93. Chicago: Aldine.

———. 1978. The earliest Transvaal members of the genus *Homo* with another look at some problems of hominid taxonomy and systematics. *Zeitschrift für Morphologie und Anthropologie* 69:225–265.

———. 1980. "*Australopithecus afarensis*" and *A. africanus:* critique and an alternative hypothesis. *Palaeontologia Africana* 23:1–71.

———. 1984. *Dart, Taung and the Missing Link.* Johannesburg: Witwatersrand University Press.

———. 1985. The former Taung Cave system in light of contemporary reports and its bearing on the skull's provenance: early deterrents to the acceptance of *Australopithecus.* In *Hominid evolution: past, present and future,* 25–40. New York: Alan R. Liss.

Tode, A., F. Preul, A. Richter, and A. Kleinschmidt. 1953. Die Untersuchung der paläolithischen Freilandstation von Salzgitter-Lebenstedt. *Eiszeitalter und Gegenwart* 3:144–220.

Toth, N. 1985a. Archeological evidence for preferential right-handedness in the lower and middle Pleistocene, and its possible implications. *Journal of Human Evolution* 14:607–614.

———. 1985b. The Oldowan reassessed: a close look at early stone artifacts. *Journal of Archaeological Science* 12:101–120.

Toth, N., and K. Schick. 1986. The first million years: the archaeology of protohuman culture. *Advances in Archaeological Method and Theory* 9:1–96.

Trinkaus, E. 1978. Hard times among the Neanderthals. *Natural History* 87(10): 58–63.

———. 1981. Neanderthal limb proportions and cold adaptation. In C. B. Stringer, ed. *Aspects of human evolution,* 187–224. London: Taylor and Francis.

———. 1982. Evolutionary continuity among archaic *Homo sapiens. British Archaeological Reports International Series* 151:301–319.

———. 1983a. Neandertal postcrania and the adaptive shift to modern humans. *British Archaeological Reports International Series* 164:165–200.

_____ . 1983b. *The Shanidar Neandertals*. New York: Academic Press.

_____ . 1984a. Neanderthal pubic morphology and gestation length. *Current Anthropology* 25:508–514.

_____ . 1984b. Western Asia. In F. H. Smith and F. Spencer, eds. *The origin of modern humans: a world survey of the fossil evidence:* 251–293. New York: Alan R. Liss.

_____ . 1985a. Cannibalism and burial at Krapina. *Journal of Human Evolution* 14:203–216.

_____ . 1985b. Pathology and posture of the La Chapelle-aux-Saints Neandertal. *American Journal of Physical Anthropology* 67:19–41.

_____ . 1986. The Neanderthals and modern human origins. *Annual Review of Anthropology* 15:193–218.

_____ . 1987a. Bodies, brawn, brains and noses: human ancestors and human predation. In M. Nitecki and D. V. Nitecki, eds. *The evolution of human hunting*, 107–145. New York: Plenum.

_____ . 1987b. The Neandertal face: evolutionary and functional perspectives on a recent hominid face. *Journal of Human Evolution* 16:429–443.

_____ . In press. The Upper Pleistocene transition: biocultural patterns and processes. In *Corridors, cul-de-Sacs and coalescence: the biocultural foundations of modern people*. Santa Fe: School of American Research.

Trinkaus, E., and W. W. Howells. 1979. The Neanderthals. *Scientific American* 241(6): 118–133.

Trinkaus, E., and M. LeMay. 1982. Occipital bunning among later Pleistocene hominids. *American Journal of Physical Anthropology* 57:127–135.

Trinkaus, E., and D. D. Thompson. 1987. Femoral diaphyseal histomorphometric age determinations for the Shanidar 3, 4, 5 and 6 Neandertals and Neandertal longevity. *American Journal of Physical Anthropology* 72:123–129.

Tuffreau, A. 1978. Les industries acheuléenes de Cagny-la-Garenne (Somme). *L'Anthropololgie* 82:37–60.

_____ . 1979. Les débuts du Paléolithique moyen dans la France septentrionale. *Bulletin de la Société Préhistorique Française* 76:140–142.

_____ . 1982. On the transition Lower/Middle Palaeolithic in Northern France. *British Archaeological Reports International Series* 151:137–149.

Tuffreau, A., A. V. Munaut, J. J. Puisségur, and J. Sommé. 1982. Stratigraphie et environment de la séquence archéologique de Biache-Saint-Vaast (Pas-de-Calais). *Bulletin de l'Association Française pour l'Étude du Quaternaire* 19:57–62.

Turner, C. G. 1985. The dental search for native American origins. In R. Kirk and E. Szathmary, eds. *Out of Asia: peopling of the Americas and the Pacific*, 31–78. Canberra: Australia National University.

_____ . 1987. Telltale teeth. *Natural History* 96(1): 6–10.

Turner, E. 1986. The 1981–83 excavations in the Karl Schneider Quarry, Ariendorf, West Germany. In A. Tuffreau and J. Sommé, eds. *Chronostratigraphie et faciés culturels du Paléolithique inférieur et moyen dans l'Europe du Nord-Ouest*, 35–42. Paris: Supplément au Bullétin de l'Association Francaise pour l'Étude du Quaternaire.

Tuttle, R. H. 1981. Evolution of hominid bipedalism and prehensile capabilities. *Philosophical Transactions of the Royal Society (London)* B 292:89–94.

———. 1985. Ape footprints and Laetoli impressions: a response to the SUNY claims. *Hominid evolution: past, present and future*, 129–130. New York: Alan R. Liss.

———. 1986. *Apes of the world: their social behavior, communication, mentality and ecology*. Park Ridge, N.J.: Noyes.

———. 1987. Kinesiological inferences and evolutionary implications from Laetoli bipedal trails G-1, G-2/3, and A. In M. D. Leakey, and J. M. Harris, eds. *Laetoli: a Pliocene site in northern Tanzania*, 503–523. Oxford: Clarendon.

Tyldesley, J. A., and P. Bahn. 1983. Use of plants in the European Palaeolithic: a review of the evidence. *Quaternary Science Reviews* 2:53–81.

Ucko, P., and A. Rosenfeld. 1967. *Paleolithic cave art*. New York: McGraw-Hill.

Valladas, H., J. M. Geneste, J. L. Joron, and J. P. Chadelle. 1986. Thermoluminescence dating of Le Moustier (Dordogne, France). *Nature* 322:452–454.

Valladas, H., J. L. Joron, G. Valladas, B. Arensburg, O. Bar-Yosef, A. Belfer-Cohen, P. Goldberg, H. Laville, L. Meignen, Y. Rak, E. Tchernov, A. M. Tillier, and B. Vandermeersch. 1987. Thermoluminescence dates for the Neanderthal burial site at Kebara in Israel. *Nature* 330:159–160.

Valladas, H., J. L. Reyss, J. L. Joron, G. Valladas, O. Bar-Yosef, and B. Vandermeersch. 1988. Thermoluminescence dating of Mousterian "Proto-Cro-Magnon" remains from Israel and the origin of modern man. *Nature* 331:614–616.

Valladas, H., and G. Valladas. 1987. Thermoluminescence dating of burnt flints and quartz: comparative results. *Archaeometry*, 29:214–220.

Vallois, H. V. 1951. La mandibule humaine fossile de la grotte du Porc Épic près Diré Daoua (Abyssinie). *L'Anthropologie* 55:231–238.

———. 1961. The social life of early man: the evidence of skeletons. In S. L. Washburn, ed. *The social life of early man*, 214–235. Chicago: Aldine.

———. 1971. Le crâne trépané magdalénien de Rochereil. *Bulletin de la Société Préhistorique Française* 68:485–495.

Valoch, K. 1969. The beginning of the Upper Paleolithic in central Europe (in Russian). *Bulletin of the Commission for the Study of the Quaternary Period* (Academy of Sciences of the USSR) 36:63–74.

———. 1972. Rapports entre le Paléolithique moyen et le Paléolithique supérieur en Europe Centrale. In F. Bordes, ed. *The origin of Homo sapiens*, 161–171. Paris: UNESCO.

———. 1976. Aperçu des premières industries en Europe. In K. Valoch, ed. *Les Premières Industries de l'Europe*, 178–183. Nice: Union International des Sciences Préhistoriques et Protohistoriques (Colloque VIII).

———. 1982a. Comment on "Upper Pleistocene hominid evolution in south-central Europe: a review of the evidence and analysis of trends." *Current Anthropology* 23:692.

_____ . 1982b. The Lower/Middle Palaeolithic transition in Czecho-slovakia. *British Archaeological Reports International Series* 151:193–201.

_____ . 1986. The central European early Palaeolithic. *Anthropos* (Brno) 23:189–206.

Van Couvering, J. H., and J. A. Van Couvering. 1976. Early Miocene mammal fossils from East Africa. In G. L. Isaac and E. R. McCown, eds. *Human origins: Louis Leakey and the East African evidence*, 155–207. Menlo Park, Calif.: W. A. Benjamin.

Van der Hammen, T. 1974. The Pleistocene changes of vegetation and climate in tropical South America. *Journal of Biogeography* 1:3–26.

Van der Hammen, T., T. A. Wijmstra, and W. H. Zagwijn. 1971. The floral record of the late Cenozoic of Europe. In K. K. Turekian, ed. *Late Cenozoic glacial ages*, 391–424. New Haven, Conn.: Yale University Press.

Vandermeersch, B. 1976. Les sépultures néandertaliennes. In H. de Lumley, ed. *La Préhistoire Française*, vol. 1, 725–727. Paris: Centre National de la Recherche Scientifique.

_____ . 1978. Étude préliminaire du crâne human du gisement paléolithique de Biache-Saint-Vaast (Pas-de-Calais). *Bulletin de l'Association Française pour l'Étude du Quaternaire* 15:65–67.

_____ . 1981. *Les hommes fossiles de Qafzeh (Israel)*. Paris: Centre National de la Recherche Scientifique.

_____ . 1982. The first *Homo sapiens sapiens* in the Near East. *British Archaeological Reports International Series* 151:297–299.

_____ . 1984. A propos de la découverte du squelette néandertalien de Saint-Césaire. *Bulletin et Mémoires de la Société d'Anthropologie de Paris*, Série XIV, 1:191–196.

_____ . 1985. The origin of the Neanderthals. In E. Delson, ed. *Ancestors: the hard evidence*, 306–309. New York: Alan R. Liss.

Vandermeersch, B., A. M. Tillier, and S. Krukoff. 1976. Position chronologique des restes humains de Fontéchevade. In A. Thoma, ed. *Le peuplement anténéandertalien de l'Europe*, 19–26. Nice: Union Internationale des Sciences Préhistoriques et Protohistoriques.

van Donk, J. 1976. 0^{18} record of the Atlantic Ocean for the entire Pleistocene epoch. *Geological Society of America Memoir* 145:147–163.

van Noten, F. 1982. *The archaeology of Central Africa*. Graz: Akademische Druck-u. Verlagsanstalt.

_____ . 1983. News from Kenya. *Antiquity* 57:139–140.

Van Valen, L., and R. E. Sloan. 1965. The earlies Primates. *Science* 150:743–745.

Vaufrey, R. 1955. *Préhistoire de l'Afrique*, vol. 1, *Maghreb*. Paris: Masson.

Vereshchagin, N. K., and G. G. Baryshnikov. 1984. Quaternary mammalian extinctions in northern Eurasia. In P. S. Martin, and R. G. Klein, eds. *Quaternary extinctions: a prehistoric revolution*, 483–516. Tucson: University of Arizona Press.

Vértes, L. 1964. *Tata: Eine Mittelpaläolitische Travertin Seidlung in Ungarn*. Budapest: Akadémiai Kiadó.

_____ . 1965. Typology of the Buda industry: a pebble-tool industry from the Hungarian Lower Paleolithic. *Quaternaria* 7:185–195.

———. 1975. The Lower Palaeolithic site of Vértesszöllös, Hungary. In R. Bruce-Mitford, ed. *Recent archaeological excavations in Europe*, 287–301. London: Routledge and Kegan Paul.

Villa, P. 1976. Sols et niveaux d'habitat du Paléolithique inférieur en Europe et au Proche Orient. *Quaternaria* 19:107–134.

———. 1983. Terra Amata and the Middle Pleistocene archaeological record of southern France. *University of California Publications in Anthropology* 13:1–303.

Villa, P., C. Bouville, J. Courtin, D. Helmer, E. Mahieu, P. Shipman, G. Belluomini, and M. Branca. 1986. Cannibalism in the Neolithic. *Science* 233:431–437.

Vlcek, E. 1978. A new discovery of *Homo erectus* in central Europe. *Journal of Human Evolution* 7:239–251.

Vogel, J. C. 1985. Further attempts at dating the Taung tufas. In P. V. Tobias, ed. *Hominid evolution: past, present and future*, 189–194. New York: Alan R. Liss.

Vogel, J. C. and P. B. Beaumont. 1972. Revised radiocarbon chronology for the Stone Age in South Africa. *Nature* 237:50–51.

Vogel, J. C., and T. Partridge. 1984. Preliminary radiometric ages of the Taung tufas. In J. C. Vogel, ed. *Late Cainozoic Palaeoclimates of the Southern Hemisphere*, 507–514. Rotterdam: A. A. Balkema.

Voigt, E. A. 1983. Mapungubwe: an archaeozoological interpretation of an Iron Age community. *Transvaal Museum Monograph* 11:1–203.

Volman, T. P. 1978. Early archaeological evidence for shellfish collecting. *Science* 201:911–913.

———. 1981. The Middle Stone Age in the southern Cape. Unpublished Ph.D. dissertation, University of Chicago.

———. 1984. Early prehistory of southern Africa. In R. G. Klein, ed. *Southern African prehistory and paleoenvironments*, 169–220. Rotterdam: A. A. Balkema.

Vondra, C. F., and B. E. Bowen, 1976. Plio-Pleistocene deposits and environments, East Rudolf, Kenya. In Y. Coppens, F. C. Howell, G. Ll. Isaac, and R. E. F. Leakey, eds. *Earliest man and environments in the Lake Rudolf Basin*, 79–93. Chicago: University of Chicago Press.

Von Koenigswald, G. H. R. 1962. *The evolution of man.* Ann Arbor: University of Michigan Press.

Von Koenigswald, W. 1973. Veränderungen in der Kleinsäugerfauna von Mitteleuropa zwischen Cromer und Eem (Pleistozän). *Eiszeitalter und Gegenwart* 23–24:159–167.

Vrba, E. S. 1981. The Kromdraai Australopithecine Site revisited in 1980: recent investigations and results. *Annals of the Transvaal Museum* 33(3): 18–60.

———. 1982. Biostratigraphy and chronology, based particularly on Bovidae, of southern hominid-associated assemblages: Makapansgat, Sterkfontein, Taung, Kromdraai, Swartkrans; also Elandsfontein (Saldanha), Broken Hill (now Kabwe) and Cave of Hearths. In M. A. de Lumley, ed. *L'Homo erectus et la place de l'homme de Tautavel parmi les hominidés fossiles*, 707–752. Nice: ler Congrès International de Paléontologie Humaine.

———. 1985a. Early hominids in southern Africa: updated observations on chronological and ecological background. In P. V. Tobias, ed. *Hominid evolution: past, present and future,* 195–200. New York: Alan R. Liss.

———. 1985b. Ecological and adaptive changes associated with early hominid evolution. In E. Delson, ed. *Ancestors: the hard evidence,* 63–71. New York: Alan R. Liss.

Vrba, E. S., and D. C. Panagos. 1982. New perspectives on taphonomy, palaeoecology and chronology of the Kromdraai apeman. *Palaeoecology of Africa* 15:13–26.

Waechter, J. D'A. 1964. The excavation of Gorham's Cave, Gibraltar, 1951–54. *Bulletin of the Institute of Archaeology* 4:189–213.

———. 1973. The late Middle Acheulian industries of the Swanscombe area. In D. E. Strong, ed. *Archaeological theory and practice,* 67–86. New York: Seminar.

Wagner, E. 1984. Ein Jagdplatz des *Homo erectus* im mittelpleistozänen Travertin in Stuttgart-Bad Cannstatt. *Germania* 62:229–267.

Wainscoat, J. 1987. Out of the garden of Eden. *Nature* 325:13.

Wainscoat, J., A. V. S. Hill, A. L. Boyce, J. Flint, M. Hernandez, S. L. Thein, J. M. Old, J. R. Lynch, A. G. Falusi, D. J. Weatherall, and J. B. Clegg. 1986. Evolutionary relationships of human populationsfrom an analysis of nuclear DNA polymorphism. *Nature* 319:491–493.

Walker, A. C. 1978. Prosimian primates. In V. J. Maglio and H. B. S. Cooke, eds. *Evolution of African mammals,* 90–99. Cambridge, Mass.: Harvard University Press.

Walker, A. C. 1981a. Dietary hypotheses and human evolution. *Philosophical Transactions of the Royal Society (London)* B 292:57–64.

———. 1981b. The Koobi Fora hominids and their bearing on the origins of the genus *Homo.* In B. A. Sigmon and J. S. Cybulski, eds. *Homo erectus—papers in honor of Davidson Black,* 193–215. Toronto: University of Toronto Press.

———. 1984. Extinction in hominid evolution. In M. H. Nitecki, ed. *Extinctions,* 119–152. Chicago: University of Chicago Press.

Walker, A. C., D. Falk, R. Smith, and M. Pickford. 1983. The skull of *Proconsul africanus:* reconstruction and cranial capacity. *Nature* 305:525–527.

Walker, A. C., and R. E. F. Leakey. 1978. The hominids of East Turkana. *Scientific American* 239(2): 54–66.

Walker, A. C., R. E. F. Leakey, J. M. Harris, and F. H. Brown. 1986a. 2.5-Myr *Australopithecus boisei* from west of Lake Turkana, Kenya. *Nature* 322:517–522.

Walker, A. C., and M. Pickford. 1983. New postcranial fossils of *Proconsul africanus* and *Proconsul nyanzae.* In R. L. Ciochon and R. S. Corruccini, eds. *New interpretations of ape and human ancestry,* 325–351. New York: Plenum.

Walker, A. C., M. F. Teaford, and R. E. Leakey. 1986b. New information concerning the R114 *Proconsul* site, Rusinga Island, Kenya. In J. G. Else and P. C. Lee, eds. *Primate evolution,* 144–149. Cambridge: Cambridge University Press.

Walker, A. C., M. R. Zimmerman, and R. E. F. Leakey. 1982. A possible case of hypervitaminosis A in *Homo erectus. Nature* 296:248–250.

Wallace, J. A. 1975. Dietary adaptations of *Australopithecus* and early

Homo. In R. H. Tuttle, ed. *Paleoanthropology, morphology and paleoecology,* 203–223. The Hague: Mouton.

Walter, R. C., and J. L. Aronson. 1982. Revisions of K/Ar ages for the Hadar hominid site, Ethiopia. *Nature* 295:140–142.

Ward, S. C., and B. Brown. 1986. The facial skeleton of *Sivapithecus indicus.* In D. R. Swindler and J. Erwin, eds. *Comparative Primate biology,* vol. 1, 413–452. New York: Alan R. Liss.

Ward, S. C., and A. Hill. 1987. Pliocene hominid partial mandible from Tabarin, Baringo, Kenya. *American Journal of Physical Anthropology* 72:21–37.

Ward, S. C., and D. R. Pilbeam. 1983. Maxillofacial morphology of Miocene hominoids from Africa and Indo-Pakistan. In R. L. Ciochon and R. S. Corruccini, eds. *New interpretations of ape and human ancestry,* 211–238. New York: Plenum.

Washburn, S. L. 1960. Tools and human evolution. *Scientific American* 203(9): 63–75.

———. 1985. Human evolution after Raymond Dart. In P. V. Tobias, ed. *Hominid evolution: past, present and future,* 3–18. New York: Alan R. Liss.

Weber, T. 1980. Analytische Untersuchungen und Entwicklungstendenzen der Technologie altpaläolithischer Inventare von Wallendorf, Bilzingsleben und Markleeberg. *Ethnographische-Archäologische Zeitschrift* 21:53–71.

Weidenreich, F. 1936. The mandibles of *Sinanthropus pekinensis:* a comparative study. *Palaeontologia Sinica,* Series D, 7(3): 1–162.

———. 1937. The dentition of *Sinanthropus pekinensis:* a comparative odontography of the hominids. *Palaeontologia Sinica,* New Series D, 1:1–180.

———. 1940. Some problems dealing with ancient man. *American Anthropologist* 42:375–383.

———. 1941. The extremity bones of *Sinanthropus pekinensis. Palaeontologia Sinica,* New Series D, 5:1–150.

———. 1943. The skull of *Sinanthropus pekinensis:* a comparative study on a primitive hominid skull. *Palaeontologia Sinica,* New Series D, 10:1–485.

———. 1951. Morphology of Solo Man. *Anthropological papers of the American Museum of Natural History* 43:205–290.

Weiner, J. S. 1955. *The Piltdown forgery.* London: Oxford University Press.

Weiner, J. S., K. P. Oakley, and W. E. Le Gros Clark, 1953. The solution of the Piltdown problem. *Bulletin of the British Museum (Natural History), Geology* 2(3).139–146.

Wendorf, F. 1968. Site 117: a Nubian Final Paleolithic graveyard near Jebel Sahaba, Sudan. In F. Wendorf, ed. *The prehistory of Nubia,* vol. 2, 954–995. Dallas: Southern Methodist University Press.

Wendorf, F., A. E. Close, and R. Schild. 1987. Recent work on the Middle Palaeolithic of the eastern Sahara. *The African Archaeological Review* 5:49–63.

Wendorf, F., and members of the Combined Prehistoric Expedition. 1977. Late Pleistocene and recent climatic changes in the Egyptian Sahara. *Geographical Journal* 143:211–234.

Wendorf, F., E. L. Laury, C. C. Albritton, R. Schild, C. V. Haynes, P. E. Damon, M. Shafiqullah, and R. Scarborough. 1975. Dates for the Middle Stone Age of East Africa. *Science* 187:740–742.

Wendorf, F., and R. Schild. 1974. *A Middle Stone Age sequence from the Central Rift Valley, Ethiopia*. Warsaw: Polish Academy of Sciences.

———. 1976. *Prehistory of the Nile Valley*. New York: Academic Press.

———. 1980. *Prehistory of the eastern Sahara*. New York: Academic Press.

———. 1986. *The Wadi Kubbaniya skeleton: a late Paleolithic burial from southern Egypt*. Dallas: Southern Methodist University Press.

Wendorf, F., R. Schild, and H. Haas. 1979. A new radiocarbon chronology for prehistoric sites in Nubia. *Journal of Field Archaeology* 6:219–223.

Wendt, W. E. 1976. "Art mobilier" from Apollo 11 Cave, South West Africa: Africa's oldest dated works of art. *South African Archaeological Bulletin* 31:5–11.

Wheeler, P. 1984. The evolution of bipedality and the loss of functional body hair in hominids. *Journal of Human Evolution* 13:91–98.

White, J. P., and P. J. Habgood. 1985. La préhistoire de l'Australie. *La Recherche* 16:730–737.

White, J. P., and J. F. O'Connell. 1979. Australian prehistory: new aspects of antiquity. *Science* 203:21–28.

———. 1982. *A prehistory of Australia, New Guinea and Sahul*. New York: Academic Press.

White, R. 1986. *Dark caves, bright visions: life in Ice Age Europe*. New York: W. W. Norton.

———. In press. Production complexity and standardization in early Aurignacian bead and pendant manufacture: evolutionary implications. In P. Mellars and C. Stringer, eds. *The human revolution: behavioural and biological perspectives on the origins of modern humans*. Edinburgh: Edinburgh University Press.

White, T. D. 1980. Evolutionary implications of Pliocene hominid footprints. *Science* 208:175–176.

———. 1981. Primitive hominid canine from Tanzania. *Science* 213:348–349.

———. 1982. Les Australopithèques. *La Recherche* 13:1258–1270.

———. 1984. Pliocene hominids from the Middle Awash, Ethiopia. *Courier Forschungsinstitut Senckenberg* 69:57–68.

———. 1985. *Acheulian man in Ethiopia's middle Awash Valley: the implications of cut marks on the Bodo cranium*. Amsterdam: Nederlands Museum voor Anthropologie en Praehistorie.

———. 1986a. *Australopithecus afarensis* and the Lothagam mandible. *Anthropos* 23:79–90.

———. 1986b. Cut marks on the Bodo cranium: a case of prehistoric defleshing. *American Journal of Physical Anthropology* 69:503–509.

———. 1987. Cannibals at Klasies? *Sagittarius* 2(1): 6–9.

White, T. D., D. C. Johanson, and W. H. Kimbel. 1981. *Australopithecus africanus*: its phyletic position reconsidered. *South African Journal of Science* 77:445–470.

White, T. D., R. V. Moore, and G. Suwa. 1984. Hadar biostratigraphy and hominid evolution. *Journal of Vertebrate Paleontology* 4:575–583.

Wible, J. R., and H. H. Covert. 1987. Primates: cladistic diagnosis and relationships. *Journal of Human Evolution* 16:1–22.

Wijmstra, T. A., and T. A. van der Hammen. 1974. The Last Interglacial–Glacial cycle: state of affairs of correlation between data obtained from the land and from the ocean. *Geologie en Mijnbouw* 53:386–392.

Wiley, E. O. 1981. *Phylogenetics: the theory and practice of phylogenetic systematics.* New York: John Wiley.

Wilkinson, M. J. 1983. Geomorphic perspectives on the Sterkfontein australopithecine breccias. *Journal of Archaeological Science* 10:515–529.

Wintle, A. G. 1980. Thermoluminescence dating: a review of recent applications to non-pottery materials. *Archaeometry* 22:113–122.

Wintle, A. G., and D. J. Huntley. 1982. Thermoluminescence dating of sediments. *Quaternary Science Reviews* 1:31–53.

Wintle, A. G., and J. A. Jacobs. 1982. A critical review of the dating evidence for Petralona Cave. *Journal of Archaeological Science* 9:39–47.

Woillard, G. M. 1978. Grand Pile peat bog: a continuous pollen record for the past 140,000 years. *Quaternary Research* 9:1–21.

Woillard, G. M., and W. G. Mook. 1982. Carbon-14 dates at Grande Pile: correlation of land and sea chronologies. *Science* 215:159–161.

Wolff, R. 1984. New specimens of the primate *Branisella boliviana. Journal of Vertebrate Paleontology* 4:570–574.

Wolpoff, M. H. 1979. The Krapina dental remains. *American Journal of Physical Anthropology* 50:67–114.

———. 1980. *Paleoanthropology.* New York: Knopf.

———. 1983. Australopithecines: the unwanted ancestors. In K. J. Reichs, ed. *Human origins,* 109–126. Washington, D.C.: University Press of America.

———. 1984. Evolution in *Homo erectus:* the question of stasis. *Paleobiology* 10:389–406.

———. 1985a. On explaining the supraorbital torus. *Current Anthropology* 26:522.

———. 1985b. Human evolution at the peripheries: the pattern at the eastern edge. In P. V. Tobias, ed. *Hominid evolution: past, present and future,* 355–365. New York: Alan R. Liss.

———. In press-a. Multiregional evolution: the fossil alternative to Eden. In P. Mellars and C. Stringer, eds. *The human revolution: behavioural and biological perspectives on the origins of modern humans.* Edinburgh: Edinburgh University Press.

———. In press-b. The place of the Neanderthals in human evolution. In E. Trinkaus, ed. *Corridors, cul-de-sacs and coalescence: the biocultural foundations of modern people.* Santa Fe: School of American Research.

Wolpoff, M. H., F. H. Smith, M. Malez, J. Radovcic, and D. Rukavina. 1981. Upper Pleistocene hominid remains from Vindija Cave, Croatia, Yugoslavia. *American Journal of Physical Anthropology* 54:499–545.

Wolpoff, M. H., Wu Xin Zhi, and A. G. Thorne. 1984. Modern *Homo sapiens* origins: a general theory of hominid evolution involving the fossil evidence from East Asia. In F. H. Smith, and

F. Spencer, eds. *The origins of modern humans: a world survey of the fossil evidence*, 411–483. New York: Alan R. Liss.

Wood, B. A. 1984. The origins of *Homo erectus*. *Courier Forschungsinstitut Senckenberg* 69:99–112.

———. 1985. Early *Homo* in Kenya, and its systematic relationships. In E. Delson, ed. *Ancestors: the hard evidence*, 206–214. New York: Alan R. Liss.

———. 1987. Who is the 'real' *Homo habilis?* *Nature* 327:187–188.

Wood, B. A., and F. van Noten. 1986. Preliminary observations on the BK 8518 mandible from Baringo, Kenya. *American Journal of Physical Anthropology* 69:117–127.

Wormington, H. M. 1964. *Ancient man in North America*. Denver: Denver Museum of Natural History.

Wu, R. 1985. New Chinese *Homo erectus* and recent work at Zhoukoudian. In E. Delson, ed. *Ancestors: the hard evidence*, 245–248. New York: Alan R. Liss.

Wu, R., and X. Dong. 1985. *Homo erectus* in China. In R. Wu and J. W. Olsen, eds. *Paleoanthropology and Palaeolithic archaeology in the People's Republic of China*, 79–89. Orlando, Fla.: Academic Press.

Wu, R., and S. Lin. 1983. Peking Man. *Scientific American* 248(6): 86–95.

———. 1985. Chinese palaeoanthropology: retrospect and prospect. In R. Wu and J. W. Olsen, eds. *Palaeoanthropology and Palaeolithic archaeology in the People's Republic of China*, 1–27. Orlando, Fla.: Academic Press.

Wu, X., and M. Wu. 1985. Early *Homo sapiens* in China. In R. Wu and J. W. Olsen, eds. *Palaeoanthropology and Palaeolithic archaeology in the People's Republic of China*, 91–106. Orlando, Fla.: Academic Press.

Würges, K. 1986. Artefakte aus den ältesten Quartärsedimenten (Schichten A-C) der Tongrube Kärlich, Kreis Mayen-Koblenz/Neuwieder Becken. *Archäologisches Korrespondenzblatt* 16:1–6.

Wymer, J. J. 1964. Excavations at Barnfield Pit, 1955–1960. In C. D. Ovey, ed. *The Swanscombe skull*, 19–61. London: Royal Anthropological Institute.

———. 1968. *Lower Paleolithic archaeology in Britain*. London: John Baker.

Yi, S., and G. A. Clark. 1983. Observations on the Lower Paleolithic of Northeast Asia. *Current Anthropology* 24:181–202.

———. 1985. The "Dyuktai Culture" and New World origins. *Current Anthropology* 26:1–20.

Zapfe, H. 1960. Die Primatenfunde aus der miozänen Spaltenfüllung von Neudorf an der March (Devínská Nová Ves), Tschecoslowakei. *Schweizerische Palaeontologische Abhandlungen* 78:4–293.

Zegura, S. L. 1987. Blood test. *Natural History* 96(7): 8–11.

Zhang, S. 1985. The Early Palaeolithic of China. In R. Wu and J. W. Olsen, eds. *Palaeoanthropology and Palaeolithic archaeology in the People's Republic of China*, 147–186. Orlando, Fla.: Academic Press.

Zhang, Y. 1985. *Gigantopithecus* and *"Australopithecus"* in China. In R. Wu and J. W. Olsen, eds. *Palaeoanthropology and Palaeolithic archaeology in the People's Republic of China*, 69–78. Orlando, Fla.: Academic Press.

Zihlman, A. L. 1982. *The human evolution coloring book*. New York: Barnes and Noble.

_____ . 1985. *Australopithecus afarensis:* two sexes or two species. In P. V. Tobias, ed. *Hominid evolution: past, present and future*, 213–220. New York: Alan R. Liss.

AUTHOR INDEX

SUBJECT INDEX

Acheulean Industrial Tradition: antiquity and time span, 199, 210–11, 215, 253–54, 405; associated with *Homo erectus*, 209–10, 404–5; associated with *Homo sapiens*, 210, 214, 251–52; defined, 210, 424; distinguished from the Tayacian Industry, 254–55; form and function of the main artifact types, 165; geographic distribution, 205, 208, 251; hunting ability of makers, 219–22; internal variability, 211–12, 215–16, 253–54

Acheuleo-Yabrudian (*see also* Mousterian: variants in the Near East), 302–3

Adapis, 97

Adapoidea (*see also* Adapoids), 43, 65–66

Adapoids (*see also* Adapoidea), 58, 68

Adaptive radiations, in primates, 95–98

Aegyptopithecus, 69–75, 78, 97

Aeolopithecus, 69

Afropithecus, 78–79, 83–84

AL-199, 147

AL-200, 146–47

AL-288 (*see also* Lucy), 135

AL-333 (*see also* First Family), 135, 144–45, 147

AL-400, 149

Allen's Rule, 277–78

Allophaiomys, 8

Alouatta, 52

Alpine glacial sequence, 32

American Indians. *See* Native American origins

Amino-acid dating, 24–25

Amphipithecus, 66–68, 97

Amud Neanderthal, 273, 304

Amudian Industry, 302–3

Analogy (in evolution), 36, 413

Anatomically modern *Homo sapiens*. *See Homo sapiens* (modern)

Ante-Neanderthals, 270

Anterior (anatomical term defined), 40

Anterior dental loading, 282

Anthropoidea (*see also* Ceboidea; Cercopithecoidea; Hominoidea; Parapithecoidea; Propliopithecoidea), 43, 45–52, 68, 412

Antidorcas, 111

Anvil (defined), 419

Anyathian Industry, 208

Aotus, 52

Apatemyidae, 60

Apes. *See* Hominoidea; Hylobatidae; Pongidae

Apidium, 69–71, 94, 97

Apomorphy, 414

Arago human fossils, 189, 231, 238–40, 260

Archaic *Homo sapiens*. *See Homo sapiens* (archaic)

Archeological record, initial development of (*see also* Stone Artifacts; Tool making), 163, 172–73, 403

Ariendorf Mousterian structure, 313–14

509

Dental enamel: dietary
significance, 90–91;
taxonomic significance, 92
Denticulate artifact (defined),
425
Denticulate Mousterian,
297–98, 300
Dentition: of
Australopithecus afarensis,
140–41, 146–47, 149; of *A.
africanus*, 146–47, 149,
151; of *A. boisei* and *A.
robustus*, 142, 146–47, 153;
general description, 37–39;
hominid vs pongid, 46–47,
146–47, 149; of *Homo
erectus*, 198; of *H. habilis*,
157; of Miocene Primates,
85, 87–88, 90–92, 94; of
Neanderthals, 273–74; of
Oligocene Primates, 71–72
Derived character (in
evolution), 36, 414
Dermoptera, 97
Developed Oldowan Industry
(*see also* Acheulean
Industrial Tradition;
Oldowan Industrial
Complex), 167, 210
Diastema (defined), 47, 146
Dicrostonyx, 7–8
Die Kelders human fossils,
286
Diet. *See* Fishing; Fowling;
Hunting; Meat eating;
Scavenging
Dingo, 396
Dinosaurs, 56, 59
Dionysopithecus, 90
Direct percussion, 419
Diré-Dawa mandible, 286
Discoid (defined), 166
Disease: in archaic *H.
sapiens*, 231, 233; in early
modern *H. sapiens*, 290,
385–87; in *Homo erectus*,
219; in Neanderthals,
333–34
Distal (anatomical term
defined), 39–40
Division of labor, 172
Djetis Fauna, 186, 193
DK I, 170
DNA hybridization, 28–29,
79

Domestication of plants and
animals, 364
Donrusselia, 97
Dryopithecus, 78, 86–88
Dwarfism, 386

Early Stone Age (*see also*
Acheulean Industrial
Tradition; Oldowan
Industrial Complex), 210,
253, 408
East Gravettian Industry, 375,
382
Ectotympanic bone, 60
Eem Interglaciation, 9
Ehringsdorf skulls, 244,
270–71
Elandsfontein: artifacts, 252;
skull, 226–29, 291
Elephant biostratigraphy, 11
Elephas, 10–11
Eliye Springs skull, 226–27,
286, 289
Elster Glaciation, 9
Emiran Industry, 303
Emireh point, 303
Endocast (defined), 101
Endocranial capacity (*see
also* Brain: expansion): in
African archaic *H. sapiens*,
228–29, 231–33; in African
contemporaries of the
Neanderthals, 290; in
Asian archaic *H. sapiens*,
247, 249–50; in
Australopithecus afarensis,
140; in *A. africanus*, 148;
in *A. robustus* and *A.
boisei*, 153; in European
archaic *H. sapiens*, 235,
239, 241, 243, 245; in
Homo habilis, 156; in *H.
erectus*, 196; in modern *H.
sapiens*, 272, 349; in
Neanderthals, 272
Endscraper (defined), 426
Entotympanic bone, 60
Eocene Epoch: dates, 3;
geography, 57; primates,
63–68
Equid biostratigraphy, 11–12
Equus Cave human fossils,
286
Equus, 11, 13, 111, 131
Erythrocebus, 50